MAPPING
MODERN
THEOLOGY

MAPPING MODERN THEOLOGY

• • •

A Thematic and Historical Introduction

EDITED BY
KELLY M. KAPIC
AND BRUCE L. MCCORMACK

Baker Academic
a division of Baker Publishing Group
Grand Rapids, Michigan

© 2012 by Kelly M. Kapic and Bruce L. McCormack

Published by Baker Academic
a division of Baker Publishing Group
P.O. Box 6287, Grand Rapids, MI 49516-6287
www.bakeracademic.com

Printed and bound by CPI Group (UK) Ltd, Croydon, CR0 4YY

Library of Congress Cataloging-in-Publication Data
Mapping modern theology : a thematic and historical introduction / edited by Kelly M. Kapic and Bruce L. McCormack.
  p. cm.
Includes bibliographical references and index.
ISBN 978-0-8010-3535-7 (pbk.)
  1. Theology, Doctrinal. I. Kapic, Kelly M., 1972– II. McCormack, Bruce L.
BT28.M275 2012
230—dc23   2011045092

Unless otherwise indicated, Scripture quotations are from The Holy Bible, English Standard Version® (ESV®), copyright © 2001 by Crossway, a publishing ministry of Good News Publishers. Used by permission. All rights reserved. ESV Text Edition: 2007

Scripture quotations labeled KJV are from the King James Version of the Bible.

The internet addresses, email addresses, and phone numbers in this book are accurate at the time of publication. They are provided as a resource. Baker Publishing Group does not endorse them or vouch for their content or permanence.

12   13   14   15   16   17   18   7   6   5   4   3   2   1

To our students, past and present—
you are a great gift to us.
Kelly M. Kapic
and
Bruce L. McCormack

CONTENTS

ACKNOWLEDGMENTS

One of the strongest motivators many of us have for writing and editing books comes from teaching. When, after consistently teaching a course, we determine that there is a hole in the literature that leaves our students less than ideally prepared, we are moved to act. Teaching on modern theology over the past decade, I noticed such a need. There are strong books covering modern theology, but they are primarily arranged chronologically and/or around particular theologians or movements. There was no study covering this period that was also arranged around the classic theological loci. One could read books on systematic theology, or on modern theology. But synthesizing the two was a burden often borne by the student. Consequently, I found that students (and even teachers) could tell you about a theologian or movement, but rarely could they adequately trace particular loci through the tumultuous period of the past 150–200 years. They had a larger sense of the story of modern theology, but when it came down to specific theological themes, they too often lacked the tools necessary to fully understand the key issues, reactions, and developments that took place. Out of this need *Mapping Modern Theology* was born. While there is no question that more topics and chapters could be added, we hope that these fifteen chapters will serve students—of all sorts—who have felt the vacuum we sought to fill.

While preparing this volume for publication, one step we added was to test the majority of the material on a set of my students taking an upper division course on modern theology. They read earlier versions of many of the chapters and offered helpful feedback: our hope is that the extra time this took in the production process makes the volume stronger. Special thanks in particular go to former students Matthew Baddorf, Justin Borger, Cameron Moran, and Grady Dickinson who provided even more detailed assistance and feedback. Thanks also to the assistance of librarians John Holberg, Tom Horner, and Tad Mindeman, each providing different forms of support for this project.

We would like to thank the various contributors to this volume. Each was willing to take time out of their demanding schedules to add their voice and skill to this work, showing great grace as they listened to various forms of editorial feedback (including student feedback). Each contributor has shown admirable patience, ability, and insight in the contributions they have made; clearly they are the heart of this volume.

Bob Hosack and the team at Baker Academic deserve special mention. Over countless meals and conversations Bob has proven to be both a conscientious editor and a delightful friend, for which I am deeply grateful. Additionally, the editorial team at Baker has been unfailingly accommodating and productive, helping carry much of the heavy load associated with such a large and complex manuscript.

And what can I say about Bruce? I am so thankful. Through various circumstances, Bruce was a compassionate and timely voice in my life when my mentor Colin Gunton died; for such kindnesses I remain deeply in his debt. In terms of this project, from early on Bruce was a great supporter helping to see this project through. That is saying something given the astonishing scholarly demands that have been on him over these years of preparation. Yet not only did Bruce lend his scholarly skills to this venture, but his friendship proved just as meaningful, especially as my family has faced various health challenges during this period. Thank you, Bruce, for your grace, encouragement, and prayers through these years.

As usual, it was my wife, Tabitha, and children Jonathan and Margot who provided laughter, love, and perspective during the season in which this book was completed. When the waves of challenge and discouragement come, your smiling faces and warm embraces inevitably provide needed hope and rest. You three are so beautiful.

Finally, Bruce and I would like to dedicate this volume to our students, both past and present. They are a living bibliography: their questions, struggles, zeal, and genuine love of the things of God always humble us even as they stir us to press on. Let there be no doubt, they are great gifts to us, and so as a small token of our appreciation we dedicate this volume to them. Thank you for putting up with us, for offering words of encouragement, and for allowing us to be a small voice in your lives.

Kelly M. Kapic

1

• • •

INTRODUCTION

On "Modernity" as a Theological Concept

BRUCE L. McCORMACK

The present work intends a new approach to organizing the study of the Christian theology of the last two hundred years or so. There are a number of very fine histories of doctrinal development that set forth the pivotal moments in which Christian theology in the West is understood *as a whole*.[1] There are also works that take as their focus leading theologians and/or spheres of influence.[2] Our idea is to organize modern theology along the lines of classical doctrinal topics or themes so that more complete coverage of significant developments in each area of doctrinal construction might be achieved. In this way, students might be introduced to the problems that

---

1. E.g., Claude Welch, *Protestant Thought in the Nineteenth Century*, 2 vols. (1972; repr., New Haven: Yale University Press, 1985); Hendrikus Berkhof, *Two Hundred Years of Theology: Report of a Personal Journey* (Grand Rapids: Eerdmans, 1989); Helmut Thielicke, *Modern Faith and Thought* (Grand Rapids: Eerdmans, 1990).

2. Where a leading-theologians approach is concerned, see H. R. Mackintosh, *Types of Modern Theology* (London: Nisbet, 1937); Karl Barth, *Protestant Theology in the Nineteenth Century: Its Background and History*, trans. Brian Cozens and John Bowden (Grand Rapids: Eerdmans, 2002). The two strategies are combined in David Ford, ed., *The Modern Theologians: An Introduction to Christian Theology in the Twentieth Century*, 2nd ed. (Oxford: Blackwell, 1997).

1

have been basic to reflection on all the major doctrines treated by modern theologians.

The purpose of this introduction is to address the basic question of the meaning of a term central to this project, namely, "modernity." To do so will help to establish a rationale not only for the temporal limits of our inquiry but also for what it includes and excludes. Not everything that has happened in the last two hundred years is "modern." There have always been some who are quite willing to defend "premodern" trains of thought more or less unchanged (though the ways in which they have gone about this often say more about their historical location—within modernity—than they would care to admit). And the last fifteen years or so have seen the emergence of trends of thought that can only be described as "anti-modern" ("paleo-orthodoxy" is the new neo-orthodoxy). And yet, establishing what it means to be "modern" in the realm of theology is no easy task. The theologies rightly covered by the term are diverse, and what unites them is not easily captured. No definitive definition can be offered here—that would be the proper subject of a book-length treatment. What I can do is simply point out certain defining moments in which those commitments emerge that will help us in identifying "modern" theologies.[3]

The Meaning of "Modernity"

To ask after the meaning of "modernity" as a strictly *theological* concept is already to distinguish its use among theologians and historians of Christian doctrines from its use by, say, sociologists, political scientists, natural scientists, or even philosophers. Sociologists typically point to the shift in the West from largely agrarian economies to capitalism, industrialization, and secularization. Political scientists discuss the importance of political theorists going back to Machiavelli and of epochal events like the French Revolution. Natural scientists speak of the destruction of the biblical-Aristotelian cosmology that took place between Copernicus and Newton. Philosophers quite rightly begin their story with Cartesian rationalism and the internal development of their discipline through great thinkers like Leibniz, Hume, and Kant. "Modernity" as a cultural concept is all of these things. As a theological concept, however, the meaning of "modernity" is not finally reducible to any of these elements (though some have more to do with our subject than others).

The origins of what historians of theology refer to as "modern" theology are to be found in Germany—a country to which industrialization came quite

---

3. It should be noted that because this is a textbook, written for students rather than academics, the criterion for selecting secondary literature relevant to the interpretation of the figures and themes treated below will be accessibility in the first instance, rather than what might be considered "best" in the view of specialists. This will, in some cases, mean pointing to older works.

late in comparison with England especially; a country in which secularization of the kind that took place in France was resisted with a measure of success; a country which only became a democracy in 1918 (and even then, in a tragically flawed form).[4] The truth is that these social and political developments took root only after the advent of modern theology; they conditioned its further development but not its creation. We come closer to the truth when we look for the preconditions that helped pave the way for modern German theology in the scientific revolution, in the growth in knowledge of non-European cultures and their histories as a consequence of the voyages of discovery, in Hume's devastating critique of natural religion and Kant's limitation of knowledge to the realm of phenomenal appearances—in other words, in the intellectual rather than the material conditions of life.[5] These are, however, preconditions only; they are not yet the thing itself.

"Modern" theology emerged, in my view, at the point at which (on the one hand) church-based theologians ceased trying to defend and protect the received orthodoxies of the past against erosion and took up the more fundamental challenge of asking how the theological values resident in those orthodoxies might be given an altogether new expression, dressed out in new categories for reflection. It was the transition, then, from a strategy of "accommodation" to the task of "mediation" that was fundamental in the ecclesial sphere.[6] In philosophy, as it relates to the theological enterprise (on the other hand), the defining moment that effected a transition entailed a shift from a cosmologically based to an anthropologically based metaphysics of divine being.

The transitions I have in mind, insofar as they registered a decisive impact on Christian theology, were effected by means of a few very basic decisions in particular. Every period in the history of theology has had its basic questions and concerns that shaped the formulation of doctrines in all areas of reflection. In the early church, it was Trinity and Christology that captured the attention of the greatest minds. In the transition to the early Middle Ages, Augustinian anthropology played a large role—which would eventually effect a shift in attention from theories of redemption to the need to understand how God is reconciled with sinful human beings. The high Middle Ages were

---

4. For more on the significance of Germany in modern theology, see John E. Wilson, *Introduction to Modern Theology: Trajectories in the German Tradition* (Louisville: Westminster John Knox, 2007).

5. For an admirably clear and convincing portrayal of the role played by the scientific revolution and the expansion of knowledge in the fields of geography and world history to the rise of biblical criticism, see Klaus Scholder, *The Birth of Modern Critical Theology: Origins and Problems of Biblical Criticism in the Seventeenth Century* (London: SCM/Philadelphia: Trinity, 1990), 46–87. More extensive discussion of theological engagement with the natural sciences can be found in John Dillenberger, *Protestant Thought and Natural Science: A Historical Interpretation* (Westport, CT: Greenwood, 1977).

6. The meaning of these terms will be made clear in the following section.

the heyday of sacramental development, in which definitions of sacraments were worked out with great care, the number of sacraments established, and so on. The Reformation period found its center of gravity in the doctrine of justification. In the modern period, the question of questions became *the nature of God and his relation to the world*. Basic decisions were thus made in the areas of creation, the being of God and his relation to the world, and revelation, which were to become foundational for further development in other areas of doctrinal concern. It is to a consideration of these basic decisions that we must now turn in our efforts to understand what it means to be "modern" in Christian theology.

The Doctrine of Creation: From Accommodation to Mediation

Rumors of the ideas set forth in Copernicus's *De revolutionibus orbium caelestium* were in circulation for some years before its publication in 1543. That is why Martin Luther was able to adopt a tentative position as early as 1539. He did not see how it could possibly be that the earth moves through the heavens since Joshua had commanded the sun to stand still, not the earth (Josh. 10:12–14).[7] And, in any case, the "fit" between what could be known of the physical universe with the help of Aristotle and the biblical cosmology set forth in the early chapters of Genesis especially would continue to make the synthesis of the two compelling to theologians for a good while yet. In the interim, it fell to Andreas Osiander to create the conditions that made possible a certain peaceful coexistence between the churchly theology and free scientific inquiry. In an unsigned preface attached to Copernicus's great work, Osiander asserted that astronomers cannot discover the true causes of the movements of heavenly bodies. That being the case, their observations help only in understanding how such movements have appeared to one firmly planted on the earth, and they lay the foundations for calculating how they must appear in the future. Their work is "hypothetical" only; it does not correspond to the way things truly are.[8]

As unhappy as these claims made later astronomers like Kepler (since they believed their hypotheses to be true and not merely an exercise in artistic construction), Osiander had done natural science a favor of sorts. Until Galileo laid claim to having seen the movements described by Copernicus and Kepler with his own eyes (with the aid of a telescope), church officials in both of the great communions (Catholic and Protestant) were content to regard the work of astronomers as merely "hypothetical" and, therefore, as posing no threat to received orthodoxies. The consequence was that scientists could pursue their investigations in relative freedom, unhindered by the churches.

7. Scholder, *Modern Critical Theology*, 47.
8. Dillenberger, *Protestant Thought and Natural Science*, 42. (It should be noted that a large excerpt from Osiander's preface appears here.)

Kepler unintentionally returned the favor. He was not happy to have his work characterized as "hypothetical," so he pointed to a rather different basis for a negotiated peace between the churches and natural science, a basis lying in the nature of revelation itself. A one-time member of the famous Tübingen *Stift*, Kepler was well trained in theology. He understood that the worry among theologians was that we make the Holy Spirit, the ultimate author of Holy Scripture, to be a liar if we say that the earth moves around the sun. Kepler solved the problem this way: "the Holy Scriptures already speak with men of ordinary things (about which it is not their intention to teach them) in a human way so that they may be understood by men; they use what is indubitable among them in order to communicate higher and divine things."[9] The Holy Spirit did not intend to teach us how things really are with regard to the movements of bodies in space when he inspired Joshua to command the sun to stand still; he was accommodating revelation to the level of what could be comprehended at the time. Since it was not his intention to teach Joshua anything where natural science is concerned, the Holy Spirit made himself guilty of no falsehood.

Now the idea of "accommodation" is a rather old one, as Kepler was undoubtedly aware. Both Augustine and Calvin had made use of the notion in interpreting the six days of creation in Gen. 1—with strikingly different results![10] In fact, Calvin made it central to his understanding of divine revelation.[11] Kepler's use of it was not intended, however, simply to resolve "difficulties" in biblical texts; it was intended to purchase the space needed for free scientific inquiry. But he unintentionally had also shown conservative exegetes how to avoid conflicts with the natural sciences once the results of specific inquiries had been rendered indisputable. One simply took the truth of science for granted and insisted that no passage of Scripture could possibly bear a meaning that conflicted with such truth. Given that the sun is the center of the solar system, the real problem posed by Josh. 10 has to do (now) with the movement of the

9. Scholder, *Modern Critical Theology*, 55, here citing from Kepler's introduction to his *Astronomia nova*.

10. Augustine held that an omnipotent God did not need six days to create, that God created all things simultaneously (in a single moment), and that the revelation of God's creative activity in terms of "six days" was an accommodation to human understanding designed to convey certain logical or causal relationships among the creatures. See Augustine, *The Literal Meaning of Genesis*, vol. 1, trans. John Hammond Taylor, SJ (New York: Newman Press, 1982), 36–37, 154. Cf. Augustine, *City of God*, trans. Henry Bettenson (Harmondsworth, UK: Penguin Books, 1980), 435–36. Calvin disagreed, maintaining that divine accommodation does not always have to do with what God says but sometimes with what God *does*. That God took six (literal) days to complete his work was itself the divine pedagogy. See John Calvin, *Commentaries on the First Book of Moses Called Genesis* (Edinburgh: Calvin Translation Society, 1847), 78.

11. Edward A. Dowey Jr. makes the idea of divine accommodation to be one of the defining characteristics of Calvin's understanding of the knowledge of God and demonstrates its pervasiveness throughout his writings. See Dowey, *The Knowledge of God in Calvin's Theology*, 3rd ed. (Grand Rapids: Eerdmans, 1994), 3–17.

earth, not the sun (as a literal reading might imply). Thus, the passage itself is "accommodated" to what is known from another source—which means that exegesis is controlled to a greater or lesser degree by science.[12] This is not yet modern theology, but it is a significant concession to the intellectual conditions that finally gave birth to modern theology.

The biblical-Aristotelian cosmology was finally laid to rest by Newton's demonstration that phenomena throughout the universe can be explained by a single law, that is, gravity. In the century that followed the publication of Newton's *Philosophiae Naturalis Principia Mathematica* in 1687, no great step forward in theological engagement of the natural sciences took place. Theologians sought to find "gaps" in scientific explanation, places in which God might be thought necessary if a more complete explanation was to be had. But this was hardly an adequate engagement, and the "gaps" were steadily being reduced in number.

What finally moved things forward was Kant's work in the field of philosophical epistemology. For Kant, there can be no knowledge in the strict sense without empirical data. It is the senses that provide the content of our knowledge; the human mind provides its forms. What then are we to make of Gen. 1, a passage that bears witness to things for which there was no observer, no one to receive sense data? That fact alone was sufficient to call into question the scientific value of this narrative for many. But if Gen. 1 was lacking in scientific value, it might still have theological value in a doctrine of creation—if seen in the right light. For churchly minded Christian theologians like Friedrich Schleiermacher, to see Gen. 1 in the right light meant this: to interpret it with the help of a tool that was devised not in order to address this specific problem (which must surely seem an arbitrary proceeding) but in order to aid the theologian in thinking through the content of all Christian doctrines. Such a "material principle" (if use of later terminology may be permitted) must itself belong to that movement of mind and heart that Christians understand as the experience of redemption; it is not an a priori principle from which the contents of other doctrines are deduced, but rather is an a posteriori description of how all doctrines (including redemption) ought to be generated and organized. Schleiermacher himself found this principle in "the feeling of

12. Gleason Archer says, for example, "It has been objected that if in fact the earth was stopped in its rotation for a period of twenty-four hours, inconceivable catastrophe would have befallen the entire planet and everything on its surface." See Gleason L. Archer, *Encyclopedia of Biblical Difficulties* (Grand Rapids: Zondervan, 1982), 161. Archer seeks to solve the problem he thinks this passage poses by means of the suggestion that the rotation of the earth was merely slowed, not stopped. What is interesting about this is that Archer shows no awareness that even to understand the problem posed in this way is to allow the natural sciences a degree of influence on exegesis. Critics will say: "not nearly enough influence!" But my point here is that Archer is a long way from Luther in making the rotation of the earth to be the "difficulty" in the text—and a long way from understanding how Joshua and his readers would have understood the implications of the command that the sun should stand still.

absolute dependence" as modified by the redemption accomplished in and by Jesus of Nazareth.[13]

We touch here upon something that is basic to at least one major strand of "modern" theology, namely, the use of a material norm as both a heuristic device and a critical principle. As heuristic device, this norm functioned to give the theologian access to the material treated in a particular doctrine that is disciplined and consistent with his/her approach to other doctrines. As critical principle, it functioned to bracket off speculation, to establish the limits of what properly belongs to dogmatics. Taken together, these two functions contributed to a "mediation" of traditional teaching under the conditions of modernity.

It is the step from "accommodation" to "mediation," I want to suggest, that helps us to catch sight of the emergence of a fully "modern" theology. That it happened first in the area of creation theology is an accident of history. But once it happened, it became basic to the construction of Christian dogmatics. Even Karl Barth, who frequently protested against the use of a "material principle" in Christian theology, made use of a material norm in the sense I have just described—and in doing so, testified to the fact that he is rightly viewed as belonging (loosely at the very least) to the mediating tradition in Christian theology. In the first phase of his dogmatic activity, his critical norm was to be found in his concept of revelation. And so his guiding question in elaborating his doctrine of creation was, What must creation be if revelation is as I have described it? Expressed another way, Given that in revelation God both is and is not given to us objectively in a medium of revelation (let us say, the flesh of Jesus), that he is able to make himself objective without ceasing to be the divine Subject he is, what light does this shed on the question of God's relation to the world in creating?[14] After his revision of his doctrine of election, Barth's critical norm was to be found in a largely "historicized" Christology (which signals the emergence of the "christocentrism" with which he is frequently associated). But throughout his dogmatic activity, he did what Schleiermacher had done before him. He made use of a heuristic and critical (a posteriori) principle.

At the dawn of the modern period in theology, Schleiermacher was concerned that the day might come when the natural scientists would be in a position to provide a complete explanation not only of the movements of heavenly bodies but even of the origins of the physical universe. He writes,

> I can only anticipate that we must learn to do without what many are still accustomed to regard as inseparably bound to the essence of Christianity. I am

13. To put it this way is to suggest that Schleiermacher's "material principle" was a function of his definition of the essence of Christianity in §11 of his dogmatics. See Friedrich Schleiermacher, *The Christian Faith*, trans. H. R. Mackintosh and J. S. Stewart (Philadelphia: Fortress, 1976), 52.

14. This train of thought is clearly presented in Karl Barth, *"Unterricht in der christlichen Religion." Zweiter Band: Die Lehre von Gott / Die Lehre vom Menschen, 1924/1925*, ed. Hinrich Stoevesandt (Zürich: TVZ, 1990), 213–20.

not referring to the six-day creation, but to the concept of creation itself, as it is usually understood, apart from any reference to the Mosaic chronology and despite all those rather precarious rationalizations that interpreters have devised. How long will the concept of creation hold out against the power of a world view constructed from undeniable scientific conclusions that no one can avoid?[15]

By means of his heuristic and critical norm, he found a way to limit a theology of creation so as to obviate a conflict with the exact sciences[16] but also to make a reasoned use of the creation story found in Gen. 1.

This is not the place for a comprehensive exposition of Schleiermacher's doctrine of creation. It will suffice here to allow Schleiermacher to describe his approach in his own words and to briefly sketch its results. "The doctrine of creation is to be elucidated preeminently with a view to the exclusion of every alien element, lest from the way in which the question of Origin is answered elsewhere anything steal into our province which stands in contradiction to the pure expression of the feeling of absolute dependence."[17] Since everything that exists must be absolutely dependent upon God, a Christian doctrine of creation must oppose "every representation of the origin of the world which excludes anything whatever from origination by God," and it must oppose all conceptions of the origin of the world that would place "God under those conditions and antitheses which have arisen in and through the world."[18] From this state of affairs, Schleiermacher draws the following conclusions, all of which are supported by exegesis of Gen. 1: (1) God does not work with preexisting materials in creating. For if God found material ready to hand that he himself had not created, such material would be independent of him and the feeling of absolute dependence would have been destroyed. So the idea of a Divine Architect is ruled out of court. (2) If it is the case that the Christian doctrine of creation excludes anything that would place God "under those conditions and antitheses which have arisen in and through the world," then God could not possibly be seen as having deliberated before acting. To be sure, creation

15. Friedrich D. E. Schleiermacher, *On the Glaubenslehre: Two Letters to Dr. Lücke*, trans. James Duke and Francis Fiorenza (Atlanta: Scholars Press, 1981), 60–61.
16. See ibid., 64:
   Unless the Reformation from which our church first emerged endeavors to establish an eternal covenant between the living Christian faith and completely free, independent scientific inquiry, so that faith does not hinder science and science does not exclude faith, it fails to meet adequately the needs of our time and we need another one, no matter what it takes to establish it. Yet it is my firm conviction that the basis for such a covenant was already established in the Reformation. . . . Since I am so firmly convinced of it, I thought I should show as best I could that every dogma that truly represents an element in our Christian consciousness can be so formulated that it remains free from entanglements with science. I set this task for myself especially in my treatment of the doctrines of creation and preservation.
17. Schleiermacher, *Christian Faith*, 148.
18. Ibid., 149–50.

is a "free" act of God, but divine "freedom" is wrongly construed where it is seen to entail "a prior deliberation followed by choice" or as meaning that "God might equally well have not created the world." To define "freedom" in God in this way is to play it off against "necessity"—which is to bring God under an antithesis that is proper to the conditions of life in the world God creates. God's freedom consists in his "otherness" and in his capacity to be who and what he is in all of his activities. It does not consist in a choice among options over which he must first brood before deciding upon the one he thinks "best" (as Leibniz had it). And in any case, as Spinoza put it (in a passage Schleiermacher would have approved), "because in God, essence and will are one, then the claim that God might possibly have willed a different world would be the same as saying that he could have been Another"—that is, a different God.[19] (3) God cannot be conceived as having begun to create. Now this might seem to make creation "eternal," but Schleiermacher resists this formulation of the relation. The reason is that if we say that creation is "eternal," we seem to make it independent of God, which would destroy the feeling of absolute dependence. So Schleiermacher wants to uphold two values: (a) that God has never been without the world, and (b) that the world has always been absolutely dependent upon the divine activity for its existence. His conclusion is that God alone is "eternal" (in the sense of transcending time); the fact that the world does not transcend time but is structured by it is sufficient, in his view, to preserve a proper distinction between Creator and creature. But how then to speak of a creation that has no beginning without resorting to the term "eternal"? Alexander Schweizer would later use the word *Sempiternität* (from the Latin *sempiternitas*—meaning "everlasting" or "perpetual") to describe the existence of a world that knows of no beginning. Such a world is "everlasting," but God alone is "eternal."[20] I should add, perhaps, that this is not a linguistic trick but a real distinction, rooted in the differing kinds of being that God and the world are (God as a being transcending time and the world as a being structured by it). (4) Schleiermacher is willing to use the phrase *creatio ex nihilo* ("creation out of nothing") so long as its meaning is restricted to the understanding that God used no instrument or means in creating. That, he believes, is the force of the New Testament phrasing according to which God created "by His Word" alone. Such a phrase is to be taken in a critical sense, rather than as a positive explanation of how God works.

Now there was another way to address the problems created for the Christian doctrine of creation by the lack of a human observer to God's creative activity, namely, the way of speculation pursued in philosophy by the great

19. Spinoza, *Ethics* I, prop. 33; cited by David Friedrich Strauss, *Die christliche Glaubenslehre in ihrer geschichtlichen Entwicklung und im Kampfe mit der modernen Wissenschaft* (Tübingen: C. F. Osiander/Stuttgart: F. H. Köhler, 1840), 1:636.

20. Alexander Schweizer, *Die christliche Glaubenslehre nach protestantischen Grundsätzen*, 2nd ed. (Leipzig: S. Hirzel, 1877), 1:266.

German idealists. This strategy, however, entailed the subordination of creation to a thoroughly revised understanding of the being of God in relation to the world. So it is to the second of our themes that we must turn.

The Being of God in Relation to the World: The Speculative Theologies

The turn to the "modern" in the realm of philosophical (meaning strictly academic rather than ecclesial) theology presupposes the challenge posed to the knowledge of God by Immanuel Kant's epistemology. Though a wide range of theologians today are inclined to downplay the significance of Kant's achievement, they will not find support from many philosophers in doing so.

For Kant, what is rightly called "knowledge" comes about through the application of what he called "the categories of the understanding" to data received through the senses. The "categories" are like hermeneutical rules that govern the construction of the "objects" of our knowledge from the raw material provided by the senses.[21] Kant believed that the categories were a priori in nature and fixed in number. In fact, he simply read them off of Aristotle's "table of logic" (e.g., quantity, quality, and relation).[22] The net effect of this view was momentous. It meant that the human subject knows only how things appear to her, once they have been processed by the categories of the understanding; she does not know "things in themselves," how things truly are. The result is, therefore, a noetic "split" (an unbridgeable chasm) between a human knower and objects as they truly are.

Now it has to be said that even if Kant was wrong to think that the forms of human knowledge (the so-called categories) are exclusively a priori and fixed in number, he was on to something important in his belief that the human mind contributes something to what we think of as knowledge. The process of knowing has a *constructive* element. We construct toward the objects of our knowledge. A completely "objective" knowledge lies beyond our grasp.

In establishing the limits of human reason in this way, Kant brought an end to Enlightenment confidence in the existence of a "ready-made world"[23]—that is, the idea that the order of the cosmos was simply "out there," waiting to be discovered. The objective ground of the unity of the cosmos ("God") could not be known, for one thing, since we have no sense data in his case with which to work. He could be postulated—and must be, in Kant's view, for the sake of moral living—but he cannot be known. And if God cannot be known, then the very idea of a "world" (as a totalizing concept) must finally be a construct

21. A good brief introduction to Kant for theologians may be found in Diogenes Allen, *Philosophy for Understanding Theology* (Atlanta: John Knox, 1985), 203–19.
22. A. C. Ewing, *A Short Commentary on Kant's "Critique of Pure Reason"* (Chicago: University of Chicago Press, 1938), 136.
23. Hilary Putnam, "Why There Isn't a Ready-Made World," in *Realism and Reason: Philosophical Papers* (Cambridge: Cambridge University Press, 1983), 3:205–28.

of the human imagination. In coming to this conclusion, Kant had put in place the conditions necessary to effect a shift from a cosmologically based metaphysics to an anthropologically based metaphysics. From this point on, metaphysics could survive only to the extent that it took human consciousness (its nature and its history) as its starting point.[24]

After Kant, the great German idealists sought to overcome the split between the epistemological subject and her objects by positing the existence of an unconditioned ground out of which both emerge, an originating point of identity, in other words. For Hegel, the history of the world is explicable as a history of divine Self-knowing. In order to come to full Self-consciousness, God must "go out" from himself, positing a mode of being in himself that is "other" than himself.[25] This act of Self-positing results initially in "alienation," in a differentiation that as yet knows of no higher reconciliation. If reconciliation is to occur, the belonging-together of the Infinite Subject and the finite world (their original identity) must be comprehended. For this to happen, human beings need to have the originating identity revealed to them. The implicit unity of divine and human must be made explicit (revealed). For Hegel, the Self-revelation of God takes place in Jesus of Nazareth. In him, the turn takes place from alienation to reconciliation. In that the originating unity of divine and human is made known in time, it becomes possible for human beings to know God, to overcome their fear of him through a recognition of the Self-love that sets the entire process in motion, a Self-love in which they can now participate.

The key to this entire "system" of thought lies in the basic claim that God comes to full knowledge of himself in and through human knowledge of him. There is a deep-lying ontological connection of God with human beings and, indeed, with the world. In that what takes place in human consciousness is made the vehicle for God's own Self-realization in time, the being of God is made concrete. It is not merely an Idea but the fullness of reality. As a consequence, the ordering of the world is no longer conceived as simply "out there"; it is a historical ordering whose end has been disclosed but which has not yet come.

As for the concept of God that anchors this "system," what Hegel did was to substitute an infinite Subject for Spinoza's infinite substance.[26] In taking this step, the being of God is no longer located in an unchanging "essence" lying in back of or beneath his activities. God is what he does. Hegel could agree with Aquinas that in God, essence and existence are one. But now, it is God's *lived* existence that defines essence rather than the other way around.

24. Even the process philosophies and theologies of the twentieth century, which often give the appearance of being cosmologically driven, tend to understand the God-world relation in personalistic terms—thus testifying to the significance of anthropology to these projects.
25. The synopsis that follows is based upon G. W. F. Hegel, *Lectures on the Philosophy of Religion*, one-vol. ed., *The Lectures of 1827*, ed. Peter C. Hodgson (Oxford: Clarendon, 2006).
26. Frederick Beiser, *Hegel* (New York: Routledge, 2005), 67, 71.

That the God-world relation implied in this conception tends in the direction of pantheism is clear. But it also has to be said that what most people think of as "pantheism" rests on a deduction drawn from the Spinozan formula *Deus sive natura* ("God or nature") rather than anything Spinoza actually said about the God-world relation. Already in Spinoza, the infinite substance is distinguished ontologically from all particulars as that which *alone* is "in itself, and is conceived through itself."[27] All other things are through Another; they are "modes" of this one substance.[28] In the case of Hegel, "pantheism" certainly did not mean that God is identifiable with any and every particular. It meant rather that God is the power at work in all things.[29] And the fact that the meaning of the word "pantheism" could also be extended even further by Schleiermacher to embrace a radical Creator-creature distinction (even to the point of affirming the critical value resident in the notion of a *creatio ex nihilo*) shows just how far most casual definitions of the term are from its actual usage.

Hegel's attractiveness to Christian theologians to this day is due, above all, to three considerations. First, Hegel overcame the agnosticism of Kant. Hegel's God could be known by human reason. Second, in positing the existence of an ultimate ground to natural and historical processes, Hegel had found a way to subordinate the natural sciences to philosophy. The apologetic value of this way of thinking was immense. Hegel's philosophical theology has been called "speculative"—which refers to the fact that the knowledge of the ultimate ground of reality is to be found solely in itself, in its Self-giving. One cannot reason from the order one thinks herself to perceive in the world back to a First Cause; she must begin with God, thinking consistently "from above," or she will not end with the God who is. But it would be a mistake to think that taking God as the starting point for thought requires an irrational leap. The reasonableness of this procedure is guaranteed by the explanatory value of the starting point adopted in this way—its power to explain all else that exists. That is why Hegel was so tempting to theologians with apologetic concerns. Those theologians would always tend to see the "independence of religion" purchased by Schleiermacher's rooting of religion in "feeling" as a

27. Ibid., 59.

28. Michael Della Rocca, *Spinoza* (New York: Routledge, 2008), 58–69.

29. See on this point Peter C. Hodgson's editorial introduction to Hegel, *Lectures on the Philosophy of Religion*, 28–29. Hodgson makes the important remark that "the tendency of Spinoza's philosophy is toward acosmism [denial of the reality of the universe] rather than atheism, since above all it is the actuality of God that is affirmed by this philosophy rather than the actuality of the world." Spinoza's "acosmism" finds an interesting echo in Karl Barth: "Presupposing the certain knowledge of God in His Word, it is actually the case that the existence and being of the world are rendered far more problematical by the existence and being of God than *vice versa*" (*Church Dogmatics* III/1, ed. G. W. Bromiley and T. F. Torrance [New York: T&T Clark, 2004]), 6. Barth's point is that it is easier to believe in God than it is to believe in the world. With that much Spinoza would have agreed.

step toward irrationality. Third, Hegel's "system" provided a basis for a robust theodicy. Hegel's "sublation" (*Aufhebung*) of the finite in the Infinite reaches its goal in God's act of taking the most extreme limit of finitude—death—up into his own being in order to conquer it there. The meaning of Christ's cross and resurrection is that God, not death, is our future. That this provides a powerful solution to the problem of evil is clear where it is realized that God does not merely empathize with us but takes the threat to our being and meaning in this world in hand and overcomes it in himself. God does not remain at a distance but enters fully into our situation, transforming it from within.

Hegel's concept of God marked a large step beyond Schleiermacher in one crucial respect. Schleiermacher could still affirm with classical theism an utter simplicity (or "lack of composition") in God as well as the impassibility (or "nonaffectivity") of God. Not so with Hegel. After Hegel, modern theologians have typically bid farewell to classical theism. From that point on, even Schleiermacher was regarded as something of a transitional figure from whom one had much to learn, but who had been surpassed by Hegel. It was Hegel who, more than anyone else, defined what it meant to be "modern" in this area of doctrine.

The Concept of Revelation: From Information Transfer to Self-Revelation

Wolfhart Pannenberg, whose talents as a historian of doctrine exceed even those of Karl Barth, has noted that two significant changes occurred in the concept of revelation at the dawn of the modern period in theology. The first was the introduction of a distinction between "an outer revelation" consisting in the manifestation of God in and through historical events, and "inspiration as the effect and interpretation of these events in the subjectivity of the biblical witnesses."[30] In making this distinction, Pannenberg "naturalized" the word "inspiration" to a significant degree. Inspiration is, in part at least, the effect of revelatory events on human interpreters of them. This need not exclude the more traditional understanding that the Holy Spirit is the agent of "inspiration," but it does tie the Spirit's work to historical events that are themselves witnessed. And in the process, the older view, of revelation consisting in revealed information about events to which there were no witnesses, is quietly set aside. To the extent that the subjective experience of "inspiration" remains unrelated to historical events, its result will tend to be understood either as the poetic expression of that experience or as an imaginative reflection based on material (theological) considerations. It is the relating of biblical witnesses to historical events that has the more secure foundation. At this stage, historical criticism was still in its infancy and its more radical possibilities were not

---

30. Wolfhart Pannenberg, *Systematic Theology* (Grand Rapids: Eerdmans, 1991), 1:221.

foreseen.[31] Still, the distinction between the objective and the subjective helped to create space for it and opened the door eventually for more critical scholars like David Friedrich Strauss.[32]

The second and arguably more significant development sketched by Pannenberg had to do with the linking of "a historical revelation that is distinct from inspiration" with "the notion that revelation has God not merely as its subject but also as its exclusive content and theme."[33] God does not, in other words, reveal information about this and that; he reveals *himself*. The concept of a divine *Self*-revelation can be found in John 1:1 and Heb. 1:1. But the phrase itself is first employed by the German idealists "in the sense of the strict identity of subject and content."[34] To say that God is both the subject and the content of revelation is to say God is the One who acts in revelation *and is himself the act*. God's being is a being *in the act of revelation*.

There is more than one way to explain the significance of this claim. It could mean that the being of God is *constituted* in and through the historical process of Self-differentiation and reconciliation. Hegel, for example, understood the "becoming" of God in his Self-revelation in time to be "necessary" to him in the sense that his becoming is the result of a "determination" that is intrinsic to the being of God as such. God cannot be God in any other way than through this becoming. But the claim could also be understood as the consequence of an eternal (in the sense of pretemporal) act of *Self*-determination that constitutes God's being as a being for revelation in time. This is the view of Karl Barth. And the difference between his view and that of Hegel is that Barth understands the immanent Trinity to be fully realized in the pretemporal eternity (i.e., before creating the world), whereas Hegel understood it as a strictly eschatological reality. For Barth, God's being is grounded in an *Urentscheidung* (i.e., a "primordial decision") in which he gives to himself his own being as God.[35] That decision is election—which is another point of difference from Hegel, since the latter has no concept of election.

In any event, to understand revelation in the first instance as the Self-revelation of God is to understand the Bible as witness to revelation, as revelation in a secondary and derivative sense. In some ways, this move had been well prepared for in the Christian tradition prior to modern times. From the earliest centuries,

---

31. Pannenberg finds an early instantiation of the distinction here treated in an 1805 essay by Carl Ludwig Nitzsch on the nature of revelation. See ibid., 200–221.

32. Criticism became more negative—even self-consciously destructive—with the 1835 publication of Strauss's study of the life of Jesus. See Strauss, *The Life of Jesus Critically Examined* (Philadelphia: Fortress, 1972).

33. Pannenberg, *Systematic Theology*, 1:222.

34. Ibid., 222–23.

35. Barth, *Church Dogmatics* II/1, 50, 168. Cf. Eberhard Jüngel, *God's Being Is in Becoming: The Trinitarian Being of God in the Theology of Karl Barth*, trans. John Webster (Grand Rapids: Eerdmans, 2001), 86: "we have to understand God's primal decision as an *event* in the being of God which *differentiates* the modes of God's being."

Christians had taken for granted a distinction between the results of the eternal generation of the Son by the Father and the inspiration of the prophets and apostles, though they rarely thought through the consequences of it. The concept of an eternal generation of the Son secures for the Son a participation in the being of the Father; all that the Father has (in the way of being and attributes), he gives to the Son so that the Son is "fully God." On this basis, it also became possible to speak of the hypostatic union of human and divine natures—so that of Jesus Christ alone it could be said (as the Creed puts it) that he is *homoousios* ("of one substance") with the Father as regards his divinity and *homoousios* ("of one substance") with us as regards his humanity. Neither of these things can be said of the writers of Scripture. They are not hypostatically united to the Holy Spirit who indwells and inspires them, and they do not share in the being of God. What is added to this (in itself quite fundamental) distinction in modern theology is the negation of the thought of a divine "instrumentalization" of the writers of Scripture that had, from time to time, tempted premodern theologians to downplay the human contribution to the composition of the Bible.[36]

The net result of this development was, initially, the same as the first. Space was created for a more critical approach to the study of the Bible. In the long run, however, it drew greater attention to Christology as the arena of basic decisions in Christian dogmatics. Pannenberg believes that Karl Barth went too far in linking the idea of Self-revelation with uniqueness, so that Christ alone was seen as the only source of revelation and the knowledge of God.[37] Personally, I think the roots of this linkage were already present in Hegel, so that Barth's move is not entirely unprecedented.[38] Be that as it may, Barth's "christological concentration" had a decisive impact on the theology of the late twentieth century, finding an echo even in the official teaching of the Roman Catholic Church.[39]

36. A rather extreme example of the kind of "instrumentalization" I am referring to may be found in Athenagorus, *Embassy for the Christians [and] The Resurrection of the Dead*, ed. Joseph Hugh Crehan, SJ (Westminster, MD: Newman, 1956), 39: "I expect that you who are so learned and eager for truth are not without some introduction to Moses, Isaias, Jeremias, and the rest of the prophets, who, when the Divine Spirit moved them, spoke out what they were in travail with, their own reasoning falling into abeyance and the Spirit making use of them as a flautist might play upon his flute."

37. Pannenberg, *Systematic Theology*, 1:223.

38. For Hegel, as we have seen, the teleology that is essential to the Idea by means of which the world process is generated is a teleology in which the Infinite takes up the finite into itself and overcomes its limitations. For this to be achieved, the Infinite had itself to "become" finite; the Infinite had to "experience" the furthest extreme of finitude, which consists in death. Now death is something that is experienced concretely in an individual. It is something that, in the nature of the case, God could only "experience" by means of complete identification with an individual. Christians believe this individual to have been Jesus. It is precisely here that Hegel's "principle of concretion" attains coherence and viability.

39. Vatican II—which embraced the concept of Self-revelation and gave it authoritative standing in the Roman Catholic Church—posited the existence of two streams by means of which

In Place of a Definition: Defining Moments

We set out to uncover the "defining moments" that gave birth to "modern" theology. Our efforts have not resulted in a comprehensive definition, but they were not intended to. This much can be said with all due tentativeness. First, "modern" theologians will share a commitment either to mediation or to speculation—if they do not tend simply to bracket off the problems created for Christian theology by the natural sciences altogether. "Mediation" as I have employed the word here has a broader significance than one might think if one knew only the "school" to which that name was applied in the nineteenth century. The originating form of "mediation" found in that school was driven by apologetic concerns and usually consisted in the attempt to "mediate" between Schleiermacher and Hegel.[40] That meant there was a strong element of speculation in their theologies (in Isaak Dorner, for example), which was anathema to the "antimetaphysical" thinking of an Albrecht Ritschl. But Ritschl, like Barth after him, tried to think out of a center in God's Self-revelation in Christ. That this "concentration" opened out in his case into a series of material "viewpoints" that linked the elements of his thought together (i.e., vocation, justification, and reconciliation) shows that he was engaged in reconstructing Christian doctrines with the help of a few, carefully chosen "principles." That means that Ritschl too was engaged in a form of mediation as I am defining it (loosely) here.

Second, "modern" theologians will have left classical theism behind, however much they may continue to respect it. They will see the relation of God to the world that is made concrete in Jesus of Nazareth to be the result of "Self-determination." Whether "Self-determination" is then thought of simply as belonging to God "essentially" or in terms of a "primal decision" (as Barth would have it) is a secondary consideration. In neither case will the divine "freedom" be understood voluntaristically (as a choice among options).

Third, divine Self-revelation will be understood to be "revelation" as such. The Bible will be understood in terms of the category of witness to the event of God's Self-revelation. Critical engagement with the Bible will be affirmed in principle, though "modern" theologians may have serious reservations with respect to how the various kinds of criticism are carried out by biblical scholars. It goes without saying that they may also find the results of critical

---

revelation comes to us. "Sacred Tradition and sacred Scripture . . . are bound closely together, and communicate one with the other. For both of them, flowing out of the same divine well-spring, move towards the same goal. Sacred Scripture is the speech of God as it is put down in writing under the breath of the Holy Spirit. And Tradition transmits in its entirety the Word of God which has been entrusted to the apostles by Christ the Lord and the Holy Spirit." See Walter M. Abbott, SJ, ed., *The Documents of Vatican II* (New York: America Press, 1966), 117.

40. On "mediating theology" as a technical term descriptive of a "school" of apologetically oriented German theologians in the mid- to late nineteenth century, see Welch, *Protestant Thought*, 1:269–73.

engagement with the Bible to be unacceptable, but such judgments are often passed by biblical scholars on the work of other members of their guild as well.

While much more could be said, we must content ourselves with the observation that the defining moments we have considered here created a style of doing Christian theology and launched a new period. Other approaches to Christian theology that do not take seriously the need to take steps like these will be found in the "modern" period, but they will not themselves be "modern." They will show themselves to belong to this period only insofar as they engage directly or indirectly theologies that are "modern" and the cultural conditions that gave rise to the latter.

Conclusion

The story we have told here has focused on the early stages of "modern" theology, at a point when theologians were much more self-conscious of living in a time of change, of crisis even. To understand those changes and to adapt to them was a theological challenge of the highest order. It fell largely to German-speaking Protestants to undertake this challenge in the first instance.[41] The basic decisions we have surveyed were made by them. In its further development, "modern" theology became an international story (albeit, one confined largely to the West). The modulations that "modern" theology experienced in being transported to other lands is an interesting story in its own right, in part because the resistance to modernizing tendencies was greater in the United States and even in Great Britain. And even those who thought themselves "modern" were capable of reacting against what they perceived as the excesses of German Protestant theologians. But that story too is one of adaptation and assimilation.

41. In his posthumously published Croall Lectures on modern theology, H. R. Mackintosh anticipated an objection that I as a teacher often hear as well: "To a patriotic Briton there may appear to be some humiliation in the fact that throughout a study like the present nothing, or next to nothing, is said regarding our native contribution to doctrinal history, or even regarding Anglo-Saxon thought in the wider sense. As in the neighbouring field of philosophy, most of the time is spent in recording movements of opinion on the Continent. The air is mostly filled with German names" (H. R. Mackintosh, *Types of Modern Theology* [London: Nisbet, 1937], 2–3). Mackintosh went on to explain the preeminence of the Germans in nineteenth-century theology in terms of differences in local conditions. He named three. First, German theological faculties were larger than British faculties. The combined efforts of so many talented people were bound to produce significant results. Second, church-state relations in Germany actually served to protect the academic freedom of German theologians, who, on the whole, were less vulnerable to ecclesial examination. And third, there was "the love of thorough and exact knowledge characteristic of the German mind—what we may call its *Gründlichkeit*." Mackintosh consoled himself, however, with the thought that although "the Anglo-Saxon mind on average has considerably less learning," it is still the case that it has quite often exhibited "a much sounder judgment" (Mackintosh, *Types of Modern Theology*, 4).

As time went on, theologians became less and less aware of the degree to which their theologizing reflected the cultural conditions of the historical period they were living in. Modern theologians began to take modernity for granted; the excitement bred by the sense of doing something new and unprecedented receded. As a consequence, many of the theologians treated in this volume—those found in the twentieth century especially—will scarcely give a thought to the question of whether their theologies are modern or not. It has only been since the advent of so-called postmodernity that the question of the meaning of "modernity" as a theological concept is once again a pertinent one to raise.

It remains only to say a few words about the contributors to this volume. Each of them has taken a specialized interest in the doctrine about which he or she writes. Each of them is, broadly speaking, "evangelical." Not all teach in evangelical institutions, though some do; others belong to "mainline" denominations and work in the seminaries of those denominations or in universities.

The contributors were invited to choose their own approach, be it typological, thematic, or more nearly historical. They were given a fair amount of latitude in deciding what should be included and what might reasonably be left out. The discerning reader will also notice that some contributors are inclined to think that the problems dealt with by modern theologians are of largely their own contrivance, that it remains possible to return to more classical trains of thought. Others (I include myself) think that the problems dealt with by modern theologians are problems inherent in classical trains of thought, which must always remain unaddressed where a simple return is attempted. But no attempt was made by the editors to compel contributors to choose one way or the other on this very basic issue. Each contributor was given freedom to describe the lay of the land as he or she sees it. The result is, quite naturally, that the differences of opinion that surround the study of many of the figures and problems treated in this volume are reflections of the contributors. We have not attempted to flatten out such differences, seeing them instead as a way of giving testimony to the richness of modern theology. Our only request was that contributors work descriptively, rather than prescriptively. That way, even the differences of opinion that exist would not become an issue.

For Further Reading

Ford, David, ed. *The Modern Theologians: An Introduction to Christian Theology in the Twentieth Century*. 2nd ed. Cambridge, MA: Blackwell, 1997.

Grenz, Stanley J., and Roger E. Olson. *20th-Century Theology: God and the World in a Transitional Age*. Downers Grove, IL: InterVarsity, 1992.

Heron, Alasdair I. C. *A Century of Protestant Theology*. Philadelphia: Westminster, 1980.

Jones, Gareth. *The Blackwell Companion to Modern Theology*. Malden, MA: Blackwell, 2004.

Livingston, James C. *Modern Christian Thought*. Vol. 1, *The Enlightenment and the Nineteenth Century*. 2nd ed. Upper Saddle River, NJ: Prentice Hall, 1997.

————, and Francis Schüssler Fiorenza. *Modern Christian Thought*. Vol. 2, *The Twentieth Century*. 2nd ed. Upper Saddle River, NJ: Prentice Hall, 1997.

Webster, J. B., Kathryn Tanner, and Iain R. Torrance. *The Oxford Handbook of Systematic Theology*. Oxford Handbooks. Oxford: Oxford University Press, 2007.

Wilson, John Elbert. *Introduction to Modern Theology: Trajectories in the German Tradition*. 1st ed. Louisville: Westminster John Knox, 2007.

2

. . .

THE TRINITY

Fred Sanders

W hat are they saying about the Trinity?" asked Roman Catholic theologian Anne Hunt in the title of her 1998 book about recent developments in trinitarian theology.[1] Hunt's book was part of Paulist
Press's *What Are They Saying About . . .* series, featuring short volumes that keep
readers up to date on topics in theology and biblical studies. It was a replacement volume for Joseph Bracken's 1979 entry in the series, which had also been
titled *What Are They Saying about the Trinity?*[2] The point is that theologians
keep on talking, and what "they," the theologians, were saying about the Trinity
in the late 1970s was not the same as what they were saying in the late 1990s.
In fact, the doctrine of the Trinity has been the subject of the most lively and
most rapidly developing conversation in modern theology.[3] That such an ancient
and established doctrine should be the subject of such vigorous contemporary
discussion is striking. It has even become common to talk about the doctrine of
the Trinity as having made a comeback from a long period of neglect.

1. Anne Hunt, *What Are They Saying about the Trinity?* (Mahwah, NJ: Paulist Press, 1998).
2. Joseph Bracken, *What Are They Saying about the Trinity?* (Mahwah, NJ: Paulist Press,
1979).
3. The Lutheran journal *Dialog* tracked a particularly active phase of the conversation in
a series of articles: Ted Peters, "Trinity Talk," parts 1 and 2, in *Dialog: A Journal of Theology*
26, no. 1 (Winter 1987): 44–48, and no. 2 (Spring 1987): 133–38; Fred Sanders, "Trinity Talk,
Again," in *Dialog* 44, no. 3 (Fall 2005): 264–72.

Commentators on modern theology often describe this surge of interest in all things trinitarian as a fairly recent phenomenon. Roger E. Olson, for instance, names the years after 1940 in particular as the time of "one of the greatest surprises of twentieth century theology": "the resurgence of interest in and renewal of reflection on the doctrine of the Trinity."[4] There has unquestionably been a spike in the number of publications, conferences, and general excitement about the doctrine in the second half of the twentieth century.[5] If the sheer volume of books and articles is the measure of a renaissance, then there has been one since about 1970.[6] "They" are saying more and more about the Trinity.

But if we speak of a renaissance of trinitarianism in modern theology, and especially if we celebrate it, we should be careful to set its starting point accurately. It is not just in the last half-century that the Trinity has been a special focus of concern. Modern interest in the Trinity began about two centuries ago. If the doctrine suffered a period of neglect, that period was as far back as the seventeenth to eighteenth centuries, when the rationalistic skepticism of the critical Enlightenment reached a high point and had not yet faced a creative challenge. In that early modern period, antitrinitarian groups like the Socinians put forth their arguments vigorously. They found a readier reception, because the general intellectual climate of the Enlightenment was opposed to all revealed doctrines. What the Enlightenment considered reasonable was a universally available natural religion that admitted no more content than the existence of a god, duty to others, and justice after death.[7] This was the intellectual climate in which it became possible for public figures like Thomas Jefferson to mock "the incomprehensible jargon of the Trinitarian arithmetic." The charge was that the modern age had arrived, and the Trinity seemed like a very premodern doctrine, ready to be jettisoned.

By about 1800, though, around the time of the Romantic reaction to the Enlightenment, the doctrine had been recast in distinctively modern ways. Romanticism resists precise definition, but it has been called an international cultural force that "began as a cluster of movements and became the spirit

4. Roger E. Olson, "The Triumphs and Tragedies of Twentieth Century Christian Theology," *Christian Scholars Review* 29, no. 4 (Summer 2000): 665.
5. Good recent summaries of the vast literature can be found in Stanley J. Grenz, *Rediscovering the Triune God: The Trinity in Contemporary Theology* (Minneapolis: Fortress, 2004), and Veli-Matti Kärkkäinen, *The Trinity: Global Perspectives* (Louisville: Westminster John Knox, 2007).
6. As early as 1952, however, a prescient observer like Claude Welch could see a resurgence underway. See his thorough survey *In This Name: The Doctrine of the Trinity in Contemporary Theology* (New York: Scribner, 1952), 3–122.
7. For the major figures in "the critical Enlightenment," such as Reimarus, Semler, and Lessing, see the chapter with that name in Samuel L. Powell, *The Trinity in German Thought* (Cambridge: Cambridge University Press, 2001), 60–96. For the British scene, see "The Rise, Growth, and Danger of Socinianisme," in Philip Dixon's *Nice and Hot Disputes: The Doctrine of the Trinity in the Seventeenth Century* (London: T&T Clark, 2003), 34–65.

of an age," and it arose between 1789 and 1815.[8] It was a rather Romantic doctrine of the Trinity that made its way into the modern age. The Trinity, that is, had been reinterpreted in light of three epochal Romantic ideas: world history, human experience, and the retrieval of the past. These are the major intellectual forces that would shape modern trinitarianism down to our own time. This chapter will survey modern trinitarianism under these three headings: history, experience, and retrieval.

The Trinity and History

The leading thinkers of the critical Enlightenment were committed to reason, by which they meant a set of necessary truths in a realm above historical flux, best typified by mathematical and logical relations.[9] Truths of reason were contrasted with mere matters of fact: facts might happen to be true in this world, but the truths of reason were necessarily true for all possible worlds. The rationality of the Enlightenment had a pristine, ahistorical character, which made for great gains in clarity, but which also opened a gap between rationality and worldly reality. G. E. Lessing (1729–1781) felt the crisis keenly, and stated it as an axiom: "Accidental truths of history can never become the proofs of necessary truths of reason." Especially in matters of religion, it seemed that events taking place in world history could never be more than historically probable, and thus could never succeed in carrying metaphysical significance. Faced with the Christian claim that God was definitively revealed in the historical life of Christ, Lessing spoke for the crisis of Enlightenment rationality when he admitted that even if Christ had risen from the dead, "to jump from that historical truth to a quite different class of truths" was impossible. "That, then, is the ugly, broad ditch which I cannot get across."[10] With the historical Jesus on one side of the divide, and divinity on the other side, the Trinity was strictly unthinkable. Some sort of supreme being might be compatible with Enlightenment reason, but not the Father, Son, and Spirit of traditional Christian faith.

Hegel: The Trinity as Absolute Spirit Coming to Itself

It was G. W. F. Hegel (1770–1831) who took up the task of reconciling reason and history in a grand philosophical synthesis that he habitually elaborated

8. Jacques Barzun, *From Dawn to Decadence: 500 Years of Western Cultural Life* (New York: HarperCollins, 2000), 465.

9. For all their differences, the rationalists (following Descartes) and the empiricists (following Locke, but most explicitly Hume) shared this characteristic inability to reckon with history. For a nuanced argument about the Enlightenment's ahistorical tendencies, see Ernst Cassirer, *The Philosophy of the Enlightenment* (Boston: Beacon, 1951), 197–209.

10. "On the Proof of the Spirit and of Power," in *Lessing's Theological Writings*, ed. Henry Chadwick (Stanford: Stanford University Press, 1956), 53–55.

in trinitarian terms. For philosophical reasons of his own, Hegel set out to broaden the very definition of reason to encompass the historical. "Reason," he declared, "is the law of the world, and . . . therefore, in world history, things have come about rationally."[11] The historical flux in which all real things have their being was not an obstacle to reason according to Hegel, but was the very place where the philosopher could trace the path of reason as it made its way from abstract ideals to concrete realities. "The time has finally come," said Hegel with confidence that his own system was a step forward in the progress of philosophy, "to understand also the rich product of creative Reason which is world history."[12]

Hegel was an idealist, basing his entire system on the ultimate reality of mental entities and cultivating metaphysical speculation in a grand style. But where previous varieties of idealism had been subjective, Hegel's was absolute and objective: the crucial thing for him was that the ideal was not one thought among others, nor was it merely a thought at all. The ideal, for Hegel, was ultimately the real. That is, the ideal became concrete reality in the course of world history, giving rise to cultures and epochs and philosophies, art and music and languages, as it developed and elaborated itself. Hegel's system, in other words, can be categorized as a form of absolute, objective idealism.

Hegel's thought defies brief summaries, but one way of thinking about world history according to Hegel is that it is the ultimate coming-of-age story. His masterpiece, the *Phenomenology of Spirit*, has been called "a kind of *Bildungsroman* (a novel that portrays a character's growth, acculturation, and philosophical development), but one where the protagonist is 'consciousness.'"[13] Coming of age is no straight or easy path for this hero whom we can call consciousness, or spirit, or thought, or the real, or the absolute and objective ideal. To develop its potential and unfold its powers, it has to pass through an ordeal in which it seems in danger of losing itself. Pure thought is something that emerges from abstraction, posits itself in the form of something actual, and reintegrates abstraction and actuality into one living whole called Spirit. Absolute reality undergoes what Hegel called diremption (*Entzweiung*), affirming itself by positing an other and then overcoming the estrangement.

What this dialectic of diremption and reconciliation has to do with the Trinity seemed obvious to Hegel. The doctrine of the Trinity is a kind of pictorial representation, at the level of religious myth, of the structure of the ultimate spiritual reality that encompasses absolutely everything. It was Hegel's task to make that structure explicit. Charles Taylor claims that "the dogma of the Trinity is ideal for Hegel's purposes." It is a system in which

11. G. W. F. Hegel, *Reason in History: A General Introduction to the Philosophy of History*, trans. Robert S. Hartman (New York: Prentice Hall, 1995), 11.

12. Ibid., 18.

13. Craig B. Matarrese, *Starting with Hegel* (London: Continuum, 2010), 52. See Hegel, *The Phenomenology of Spirit*, trans. A. V. Miller (Oxford: Oxford University Press, 1977).

the Universal goes out of itself, undergoes self-diremption and engenders the particular (the Father begets the Son before all ages); and the particular nevertheless returns to unity with the Universal in a common life (the Holy Spirit proceeds from Father and Son and unites them). Thus Hegel sees deep speculative meaning in the notion of an eternal Trinity, a play of love in the absolute itself.[14]

Instead of being a doctrine hung on the horns of the Enlightenment dilemma between universal truths and contingent facts, for Hegel the Trinity became the principle of the unity between the two, and the grammar of universal truth's self-communication in history. To make his case for a trinitarianism that had metaphysical implications, Hegel sometimes availed himself of the traditional religious language of trinitarianism, and sometimes paraphrased it into his increasingly idiosyncratic metaphysical jargon. "When the time was fulfilled, God sent his Son," he quoted from Gal. 4:4, and then offered the Hegelian paraphrase: "When the need for Spirit came into existence, Spirit manifested the reconciliation."[15]

Hegel's own intentions are hard to discern: Was he a Christian apologist claiming ultimate truth for the church's doctrine of the Trinity, or an atheist who pillaged trinitarian terminology to say something altogether different? Interpreters are divided. But Hegel's influence on modern trinitarianism has been so pervasive as to be nearly inescapable. His work established a style for modern trinitarianism, according to which the doctrine is grounded in the dynamics of world process.

Moltmann: The Suffering, Open Trinity

The way this Hegelian heritage has played out in more recent trinitarian theology is obvious if we turn to one of its most creative and influential advocates, Jürgen Moltmann. Moltmann's starting point was an intentionally radical account of the cross of Christ, which he described as the event of God's self-abandonment in history. As he worked out this fundamental commitment, Moltmann recognized that it demanded a robust, and thoroughly historicized, doctrine of the Trinity: "The doctrine of the Trinity is the conceptual framework that is necessary if we are to understand this history of Christ as being the history of God."[16] Classical, premodern theology had consistently argued that God in his own divine nature is impassible and incapable of falling into suffering. The incarnation, on the traditional view, was God the Son participating in human suffering, but not experiencing suffering in the divine nature.

14. Charles Taylor, *Hegel* (Cambridge: Cambridge University Press, 1975), 489.
15. *Vorlesungen über die Philosophie der Religion*, ed. Georg Lasson (Leipzig: F. Meiner, 1925–1930), 1:121; cited in Stephen Crites, "The Gospel according to Hegel," *Journal of Religion* 46, no. 2 (April 1966): 246–63.
16. Moltmann, "The Trinitarian History of God," in *The Future of Creation* (Philadelphia: Fortress, 1979), 81.

Moltmann self-consciously sets himself against the tradition and teaches "the pathos of God," a doctrine of divine suffering. In order to describe the death of Christ as the saving work of "the human, crucified God," Moltmann asserts that "the theology of the cross must be the doctrine of the Trinity and the doctrine of the Trinity must be the theology of the cross."[17]

What this entailed for an overall theology became clear with Moltmann's 1981 book *The Trinity and the Kingdom*. In that book, he declares that "the history of the world is the history of God's suffering." "If a person once feels the infinite passion of God's love," says Moltmann, "then he understands the mystery of the triune God. God suffers with us—God suffers from us—God suffers for us."[18] In Moltmann's hands, the doctrine of the Trinity becomes a theology of the redemptive suffering of God in human history. In order to heal his creatures, God has opened himself to their suffering and made it his own, internalizing it so that only by delivering himself from the exile of history will he deliver them also. "The theology of God's passion leads to the idea of God's self-subjection to suffering. It therefore also has to arrive at the idea of God's eschatological self-deliverance."[19] This account of salvation has the Hegelian family likeness; it is another version of redemption by diremption.

History obviously matters for this sort of doctrine of the Trinity, and Moltmann emphasizes its importance strikingly, portraying the entire Western metaphysical tradition from Plato to Barth as a series of efforts to contrast the realm of being with the realm of becoming, keeping God on one side of the divide and the world on the other.[20] Moltmann thinks that this divide makes it impossible to confess the Christian God—God with us—since it begins with the eternal, immanent Trinity located safely in the realm of being, and sees only a ghostly reflection of that real Trinity down here with us under conditions of finitude and in the processes of becoming. Such a God would be closed off from real fellowship with creatures, and Moltmann takes the doctrine of the Trinity to be a declaration of God's openness to the world, openness for real relationship.

Moltmann even rejects the classic descriptions of God's unity as being too one-sided, because they are biased against history. If God is one because he is the supreme substance, or if he is one because he is the absolute subject, then his unity is already established before the doctrine of the Trinity is taken into account. Instead, Moltmann describes God's unity as a perichoretic (mutually indwelling) unity of the fellowship of the three persons in the history of salvation. God is one, in other words, because "the unity of the Father, the Son and the Spirit is . . . the eschatological question about the consummation

17. Jürgen Moltmann, *The Crucified God* (New York: Harper & Row, 1974), 241.
18. Jürgen Moltmann, *The Trinity and the Kingdom: The Doctrine of God* (New York: Harper & Row, 1981), 4.
19. Ibid., 60.
20. Ibid., 158–59.

of the trinitarian history of God."[21] Moltmann obviously has an instinct for finding the edges of traditional doctrines, and his treatment of the unity of the Trinity leads him to innovations like an unprecedentedly social doctrine of the Trinity, a rejection of a metaphysical-political construct he identifies as monotheism, and a pantheistic account of God's relationship to the world. Some of these positions are idiosyncratic to Moltmann's maverick temperament, no doubt, but most of them are driven by his decision "to develop a historical doctrine of the Trinity" from "the history of Jesus the Son."[22]

Pannenberg: The Historical Self-Actualization of the Trinity

Moltmann's trinitarianism is not just historical but eschatological. Yet ever since his breakout book *Theology of Hope*, Moltmann tried to find a balance between two different meanings of eschatology: an orientation toward an open future on the one hand, and an orientation toward a definitively ultimate conclusion on the other. Moltmann's contemporary Wolfhart Pannenberg is much more decisively invested in the priority of the latter orientation. For Pannenberg, the whole point of biblical eschatology is that it brings all things to definitive completion. Eschatology is temporal holism. Pannenberg views being itself as historical, but only because it is truly on its way to a definite state of completion.

The doctrine of the Trinity is central to Pannenberg's thought precisely because it is a working out of the tensions of his eschatological ontology. Early in his career, Pannenberg framed this idea in a famously controversial way. Having argued that the concept of God's being was bound up with the concept of God as the all-determining power, Pannenberg pointed out that during the course of history, God does not appear to be determining all things. Therefore, until the coming of God's kingdom, his very existence remains dubious because it is not enacted. God without his kingdom is not God. For this reason, as Pannenberg put it, "it is necessary to say that, in a restricted but important sense, God does not yet exist."[23] Pannenberg could state this claim more expansively, as he did in his *Systematic Theology*, where he argued that "only with the consummation of the world in the kingdom of God does God's love reach its goal and the doctrine of God reach its conclusion."[24] The realization that God rules with love and power will only occur when time is taken up into and included in eternity, which is to say, when the kingdom of God comes.[25] At this point the temporal whole will be fully present, and the

21. Ibid., 149.
22. Ibid., 19.
23. Wolfhart Pannenberg, *Theology and the Kingdom of God* (Philadelphia: Westminster, 1969), 56.
24. Wolfhart Pannenberg, *Systematic Theology* (Grand Rapids: Eerdmans, 1991), 1:447.
25. Ibid., 3:595–607.

events of history, having passed through judgment, will become eternal. But Pannenberg only elaborates his full position when he brings the doctrine of the Trinity to the task. The missions of the Son and the Spirit into world history, he claims, are the central events of God establishing his kingdom. So the fullness of the being of God the Trinity apparently waits on the course of world history, the consummation of salvation history in the eschatological work of the Son and Spirit, and the coming of the kingdom in the future.

Pannenberg seems to be quite aware of the doctrinal and metaphysical dangers involved in linking the being of the Triune God to history so directly. Integrating the divine life into the historical reality of the world tends toward pantheism, and Pannenberg is eager to ward off that danger. He argues, "Refuted herewith is the idea of a divine becoming in history, as though the trinitarian God were the result of history and achieved reality only with its eschatological consummation."[26] Although such divine becoming might appear to be taking place from our point of view, what actually happens is that "the eschatological consummation is only the locus of the decision that the trinitarian God is always the true God from eternity to eternity."[27]

Whenever Pannenberg talks from two points of view, he shows some comfort with a broadly Platonic ontology in which an eternal reality is manifested under the changing conditions of history. In Pannenberg's case, that eternal reality lies in a real future rather than in a strictly atemporal world above. But once Pannenberg admits a stable eternity, how can he square it with the notion of a divine reality fully engaged in the process of history, a God for whom history really counts? Pannenberg admits that this can only come about if we develop "a concept of God which can grasp," in one unified conceptual framework, "not only the transcendence of the divine being and his immanence in the world but also the eternal self-identity of God and the debatability of his truth in the process of history, along with the decision made concerning it by the consummation of history."[28] Pannenberg piles up a lot of ideas in sentences like this, but the main thing to notice is that he piles them up in the ultimate future, which is the locus of God's decision that determines reality.

Another way Pannenberg makes this point is to talk about God's self-actualization. "God actualizes himself in the world by his coming into it," he says.[29] Only God is capable of self-actualization, since in order to actualize oneself, one would have to already be somebody who is identical with the somebody who is to be actualized. This is what the eternal God does in the course of world history: "The idea of self-actualization transcends our measure as finite beings. . . . Nevertheless, the relation of the immanent to the

26. Ibid., 1:331.
27. Ibid.
28. Ibid., 333.
29. Ibid., 390.

economic Trinity, of God's inner trinitarian life to his acts in salvation history inasmuch as these are not external to his deity but express his presence in the world, may very well be described as self-actualization. For here the subject and result are the same, as the expression demands."[30] Once again, it is the historical action of the Son and Spirit in the world that enables Pannenberg to think of God's very being as intimately connected to the outcome of world history. But much more clearly than Moltmann, Pannenberg also succeeds in using trinitarian categories to recognize the antecedent reality of God:

> It is certainly true that the trinitarian God in the history of salvation is the same God as in his eternal life. But there is also a necessary distinction that maintains the priority of the eternal communion of the triune God over that communion's explication in the history of salvation. Without that distinction, the reality of the one God tends to be dissolved into the process of the world.[31]

If this futurist metaphysic is convincing, the doctrine of the Trinity allows Pannenberg to have his historical-ontological cake and eat it too.

Jenson: Three Characters in the Story of God

One other trinitarian theologian who has given priority to history is the American Lutheran Robert W. Jenson, whose work is a kind of narrative theology that rises to the level of making metaphysical claims. Jenson's early book *The Triune Identity* argued that "Father, Son, and Holy Spirit" is the name of God.[32] In his later work he argues that "the primal systematic function of trinitarian teaching is to *identify* the *theos* in 'theology.'"[33] This God-given tool for identifying God becomes, for Jenson, the basic equipment for a revisionist metaphysic, an ontology in which the central role is played by narrativity. Identity, according to Jenson, is something that is narrated in a history, and a history is something that has closure. This narrative closure applies also to God: "Since the biblical God can truly be identified by narrative, his hypostatic being, his self-identity, is constituted in dramatic coherence."[34] It is the death and resurrection of Christ that provide the dramatically coherent narrative of the identity of God. The doctrine of the Trinity is what specifies the content of that narrative and picks out its three characters: "It is the very function of trinitarian propositions to say

---

30. Ibid., 392.

31. Wolfhart Pannenberg, "Books in Review: Robert W. Jenson, *Systematic Theology*: Volumes I & II," *First Things*, no. 103 (May 2000): 49–53.

32. Robert W. Jenson, *The Triune Identity: God according to the Gospel* (Philadelphia: Fortress, 1982).

33. Robert W. Jenson, *Systematic Theology*, vol. 1, *The Triune God* (New York: Oxford University Press, 1997), 60. Emphasis in the original.

34. Ibid., 64.

that the relations that appear in the biblical narrative between Father, Son, and Spirit are the truth about God himself."[35] Jenson has much in common with Moltmann and Pannenberg, but his emphasis on the narrative surface of revelation sets him apart. It is important to note that Jenson is not simply ignoring metaphysics or seeking to change the subject from being to stories. Instead, he is installing story as the central ontological category. Jenson claims that narrativity is ontological, because in its highest form it is the identity of the Trinity.

The theologians considered above share a commitment to history that shapes their trinitarianism. It is instructive to contrast their approaches with a group of modern theologians who made an opposite decision about the role of history for the Christian faith. Emerging from the historical-critical fires of the nineteenth century, theologians like Wilhelm Herrmann were concerned to minimize history's claim by arguing that faith must not be thought of as mere assent to historical data, but must be grounded in the inner life of Jesus as pictured in the New Testament. Paul Tillich shared that desire to secure a historical safe zone for Christian faith. He joked with his classes, "I do not wish the telephone in my office to ring and to hear from some New Testament colleague: 'Paulus, our research has now finally removed the object of your ultimate concern; we cannot find your Jesus anywhere.'"[36] Tillich (like Bultmann in this regard) made use of certain existential motifs to remove Christian commitment from a merely historical foundation, basing faith instead on resources that faith itself could guarantee. For Tillich, the biblical picture of Christ is true, whether it corresponded to anything historical or not. Modern theologies that made this basic decision about history tended to find themselves cut off from the motive that impelled serious reflection on the Trinity in other sectors of modern theology. Tillich has a theology of religious symbolism that permits some rather thin reflection on trinitarian dynamics; Bultmann can make almost nothing of the doctrine. This underdevelopment of the doctrine among thinkers who made a different choice about how to handle the challenge of history simply underlines how history exerts formative influence on the shape of modern trinitarianism. A complete survey of the way the doctrine of the Trinity was enlivened in the modern period by reflection on history, movement, and the world process would have to include many more figures and schools of thought. The works of process theology, open theism, and the revival of panentheism in philosophical theology deserve to be considered under this heading, as do numerous theologians who are less influenced by Hegelian patterns of thought, but are nevertheless committed to history.[37]

35. Ibid., 150.
36. As quoted by Langdon Gilkey in *Gilkey on Tillich* (New York: Crossroad, 1990), 151.
37. For instance, Bruno Forte, *The Trinity as History: Saga of the Christian God* (New York: Alba House, 1989).

The Trinity and Experience

The second major category that enlivened trinitarianism and gave it a modern form is the category of experience. Around the time of the rise of Romanticism, it began to seem to many people that truths had to come within the range of personal experience before they could be meaningful. Once again, this was in reaction against the Enlightenment depiction of truth as an objective body of facts that were true whether they were experienced or not. Though the requirement that truth be a matter of experience did not immediately favor the doctrine of the Trinity, it soon became a key element of how the doctrine was to be stated in the modern period.

Schleiermacher: The Capstone of the Christian Consciousness

Friedrich Schleiermacher stands at the head of the category of experience. Schleiermacher had a Pietistic upbringing, but developed into the first great modern theologian. In standard accounts of how the Trinity came to be neglected in modern thought, Schleiermacher typically receives much of the blame. He famously placed the doctrine in the last few pages of his influential work *The Christian Faith*, making it something of an appendix to the main work.[38] To understand why the doctrine would be located there, we must understand how Schleiermacher constructed his system. For him, Christianity is "essentially distinguished from other faiths by the fact that in it everything is related to the redemption accomplished by Jesus of Nazareth."[39] Schleiermacher's theology was entirely centered on that redemption, or rather on the knowledge of that redemption, meaning the contents of the self-consciousness of the redeemed. The theologian's task was to unpack and articulate the Christian's self-consciousness of being redeemed: "We shall exhaust the whole compass of Christian doctrine if we consider the facts of the religious self-consciousness, first, as they are presupposed by the antithesis expressed in the concept of redemption, and secondly, as they are determined by that antithesis."[40]

To "exhaust the whole compass of Christian doctrine" by analyzing redemption (what redemption presupposes, and what it brings about) may seem to run the risk of reducing theology to a study of salvation. But Schleiermacher's method was expansive enough to include much besides salvation. The Christian consciousness of redemption presupposes concepts such as God's holiness, righteousness, love, and wisdom; the opposing negative states of evil and sin; and the transition between them by way of Christ and the church through rebirth and sanctification. These concepts, further, presuppose others:

38. Friedrich Schleiermacher, *The Christian Faith*, 2nd ed. (Edinburgh: T&T Clark, 1930), 738–51.
39. Ibid., 52.
40. Ibid., 123.

creation and preservation, an original state of human perfection, and the divine attributes of eternity, omnipresence, omnipotence, and omniscience. Even angels and devils can be given a place within the redemption-centered project of *The Christian Faith*, although only a bit tentatively, since their alleged operations are so far at the periphery of the Christian consciousness of redemption that angelology "never enters into the sphere of Christian doctrine proper."[41]

The Trinity, however, could not be admitted to the doctrinal system proper, because it is not directly implicated in redemption. "It is not an immediate utterance concerning the Christian self-consciousness but only a combination of several such utterances."[42] Piecing together doctrines to construct more elaborate doctrines was something Schleiermacher regarded with horror, because it led out from the living center of the faith to the arid regions of theological formulations, where dogmaticians do their deadening work. Schleiermacher had long since rejected that approach in his *Speeches*: "Among those systematizers there is less than anywhere, a devout watching and listening to discover in their own hearts what they are to describe. They would rather reckon with symbols."[43] The young Romantic may have grown up to write a big book of doctrine, but he continued his "devout watching and listening" and never betrayed his basic insight or became one of "those systematizers" content to "reckon with symbols."

Because the Trinity could not be directly connected to redemption, Schleiermacher placed it well outside the life-giving core of *The Christian Faith*. In the heading of the section where he finally treated it, Schleiermacher pointed out that the doctrine of the Trinity could not be considered an issue that was "finally settled," because after all it "did not receive any fresh treatment when the Protestant Church was set up; and so there must still be in store for it a transformation which will go back to its very beginnings."[44] Schleiermacher considered it obvious that if the Trinity were implicated in the *evangel*, the *evangelisch* (that is, Protestant) awakening of the sixteenth century would have transformed and deepened it as it had everything central to Christian redemption.

For these reasons, Schleiermacher is not usually reckoned among the champions of the modern doctrine of the Trinity. He did in fact push it to the margin of his system for reasons that were very important to him. But he also set the terms and declared the conditions under which the doctrine could reemerge in the modern period, with a "transformation which will go back to its very

---

41. Ibid., 156.

42. Ibid., 738.

43. Friedrich Schleiermacher, *On Religion: Speeches to Its Cultured Despisers* (1799; New York: Harper & Bros., 1958), 52.

44. Schleiermacher, *Christian Faith*, 747. I have changed the standard translation here at the word "Evangelical," which Schleiermacher manifestly meant in the sense of "Protestant."

beginnings." For well over a century, the doctrine remained dormant wherever Schleiermacher's influence was felt. But when it reemerged from hibernation, it would be as a doctrine of Christian experience.

LaCugna: The Trinity as Mystery of Salvation

In her influential book *God for Us: The Trinity and Christian Life*, Catherine Mowry LaCugna's opening thesis is that "the doctrine of the Trinity is ultimately a practical doctrine with radical consequences for the Christian life."[45] LaCugna argues that the history of trinitarian theology is the history of an increasing alienation from the doctrine's original soteriological and doxological position; it is the story of "the emergence and defeat of the doctrine of the Trinity."[46] The doctrine emerged in the first place as an explanation of how God's relationship to us in salvation history (*oikonomia*) reveals and is grounded in the eternal being of God (*theologia*). As it increasingly came to be a description of God *in se*, however, trinitarian theology grew speculative and unrelated to Christian experience, and finally issued in a doctrine of God that had no internal links to the doctrine of salvation. She traces this non-soteriological doctrine of God to its underlying "metaphysics of substance; the pursuit of what God is 'in se,' what God is 'in Godself' or 'by Godself.'"[47] According to LaCugna, the central challenge faced by trinitarian theology in the modern period is reconnecting the doctrine of God to the doctrine of salvation. The doctrine of the Trinity is the place to demonstrate that "theology is inseparable from soteriology, and *vice versa*."[48]

LaCugna attempted to carry out this agenda by transcending the distinction between God in himself and God in salvation. She described a larger view of God's ways with the world, a view in which "there is neither an economic nor an immanent Trinity; there is only the *oikonomia* that is the concrete realization of the mystery of *theologia* in time, space, history, and personality."[49] The book *God for Us* is aptly titled, since on LaCugna's view of the Trinity, God is for us, without remainder. The opening page has the suggestive sentence, "The life of God—precisely because God is triune—does not belong to God alone."[50] One of the things this turns out to mean is that, doctrinally speaking, "the doctrine of the Trinity is not ultimately a teaching about 'God' but a teaching about God's life with us and our life with each other."[51]

45. Catherine Mowry LaCugna, *God for Us: The Trinity and Christian Life* (San Francisco: HarperCollins, 1991), 1.
46. Ibid., 8.
47. Ibid., 3.
48. Ibid., 211.
49. Ibid., 223.
50. Ibid., 1.
51. Ibid., 228.

LaCugna's development of trinitarian theology in light of the experience of salvation seems to some critics to be a complete conflation, a collapsing of the being of God into the experience of salvation in the economy. But whether she succeeded or not, LaCugna at least intended to safeguard God's mystery and eternity. "Trinitarian theology is not merely a summary of our experience of God," she cautions. "It is this, but it also is a statement, however partial, about the mystery of God's eternal being."[52] For LaCugna, there simply is no option to think about "God in himself," so what is often called the immanent Trinity can only be discerned as the divine mystery inherent in the economic Trinity. LaCugna declares that in a well-ordered trinitarian theology, "divine self-sufficiency is exposed as a philosophical myth," and that "the God conceived as a self-enclosed, exclusively self-related triad of persons does not exist."[53] Finally, sounding a feminist note not often heard in her publications, LaCugna argues that the notion of a self-contained Trinity is a projection, an idolatrous self-enlargement of "the idea of person as self-sufficient, self-possessing individual, which is perhaps the ultimate male fantasy."[54]

Elizabeth Johnson: Naming toward the Triune God from Women's Experience

Feminist theology was not, for several decades, a likely quarter in which to seek dialogue on trinitarian theology. The first generations of feminist theologians tended to identify this doctrine as self-evidently problematic. Ranging from Mary Daly's 1973 *Beyond God the Father* to Rosemary Radford Ruether's 1983 *Sexism and God-Talk: Toward a Feminist Theology*, the bare fact of language about Father and Son seemed to mark the doctrine as a boys' club; it was viewed as a provocation to feminists, and they responded to it with subversion and parody. But the category of experience has been crucial for feminist theology, and this eventually brought the experiential Trinity of modern theology within range of the feminist project. Ruether, for example, declares experience to be the bedrock of all theological reflection, with the supposedly objective sources like Scripture and tradition being nothing more than codified experience. Feminist theology, on this account, uses women's experience as the criterion of what counts as "usable tradition" in the larger Christian tradition. When it comes to the Trinity, the question is essentially Schleiermacher's, with a feminist turn: Are women conscious of an experience of the Triune God?

The most developed and fruitful affirmative answer is Elizabeth Johnson's *She Who Is: The Mystery of God in Feminist Theological Discourse*. Johnson views the Christian community's religious language as formative and

52. Ibid., 4.
53. Ibid., 397.
54. Ibid., 398.

instrumental. "The symbol of God functions," she says: our concept of God shapes our worldview and our conduct.[55] Johnson does not object to the use of male metaphors for God altogether, but she does object to them being used "exclusively, literally, and patriarchally," as they have been in the Christian church.[56] Her goal in *She Who Is* is to supplement that masculine imagery with feminine imagery, "to speak a good word about the mystery of God recognizable within the contours of Christian faith that will serve the emancipatory praxis of women and men, to the benefit of all creation, both human beings and the earth."[57]

Though Johnson's project is intentionally revisionist, her work is deeply informed by the traditional trinitarian categories. She takes up each of the three persons and expounds them in feminine imagery, using the wisdom terminology of Sophia as a kind of master metaphor. The first person, accordingly, is Mother-Sophia (who mothers the universe, establishes the mercy of justice, and nurtures growth toward maturity); the second person is Jesus-Sophia (who is not just a human savior but a cosmic deliverer, is in solidarity with the oppressed, and whose incarnation affirms the body and sacramentality); and the third is Spirit-Sophia (who gives life, empowers, graces, and befriends). But Johnson actually reverses the traditional order and begins her exposition with the Spirit, precisely because the work of the third person is the point of deepest experiential contact, and thus the best starting point. Theology, on Johnson's account, is a project of naming toward God analogically from human experience.[58] "The God of inexhaustible mystery who is inexpressibly other is also with the world in the flesh of history, and is furthermore closer to us than we are to ourselves. Sophia-God is beyond, with, and within the world; behind, with, and ahead of us; above, alongside, and around us."[59] As Johnson moves through the three persons and considers the one Triune God in experiential, feminist-Sophia categories, she arrives at many of the same positions we have seen in Moltmann and others: a panentheistic relation of God to the world, and a strong stance on God as a fellow-sufferer in the pain of the oppressed.

The result of Johnson's feminist investigation of trinitarian theology is a Trinity deeply resonant with the experience of women. This refashioning of the doctrine was made possible by the modern turn to experience, the same

55. Elizabeth A. Johnson, *She Who Is: The Mystery of God in Feminist Theological Discourse* (New York: Crossroad, 1992), 4, 5, 36 passim.

56. Ibid., 33.

57. Ibid., 8.

58. There is an extensive discussion internal to feminist theology about the legitimacy of essentializing "women's experience." For an analysis of Johnson and essentialism, see Kathryn Greene-McCreight, *Feminist Reconstructions of Christian Doctrine: Narrative Analysis and Appraisal* (New York: Oxford University Press, 2000), 112–17.

59. Johnson, *She Who Is*, 191.

turn which also brought the doctrine of the Trinity within range of a number of other liberationist theological projects. Leonardo Boff, for example, describes the Trinity as the perfect society and appeals to it as a model and a critique of human order: "Society offends the trinity by organizing itself on a basis of inequality."[60] The turn to experience has also been an invitation to theologians from many cultures to explore the doctrine afresh: Indian, African, and Asian Christian authors have made connections between trinitarian theology and their cultural backgrounds.[61] Another obvious extension of the project of applying the Trinity to human experience is the recent rush to relevance in trinitarian theology. The most sophisticated and promising approach to the Trinity in experiential terms is the work of Sarah Coakley, whose investigations of contemplative prayer in the church fathers and in contemporary spirituality have found an "ineluctably tri-faceted" component of religious experience. Coakley has been answering the question, "Can God be experienced as Trinity?" with a nuanced Yes, and claims that this experience is actually the "soft underbelly" of the origin of the doctrine of the Trinity,[62] as well as an important resource for contemporary faith and thought.

Karl Rahner: A Synthesis of Experience and History

Karl Rahner is one of the most important thinkers in the doctrine of the Trinity's modern career. It is possible to tell the whole story of trinitarian theology from 1960 on as the story of how Rahner's work was accepted, rejected, or modified.[63] We have already had to gloss over his influence on several figures in this thematic survey (an influence that is especially marked in Pannenberg and LaCugna) in order to reserve him for this key role synthesizing the streams of history and experience. Rahner's lament over the doctrine of the Trinity's neglect in "the catechism of head and heart" is the classic starting point of dozens of books on the Trinity. Rahner warned that if the doctrine were to be deleted from the textbooks and the histories of doctrine, there would be little change in the life or thoughts of the average Christian, and that much of Christian literature, sadly subtrinitarian as it was, would remain unaltered. In

---

60. Leonardo Boff, *Trinity and Society* (London: Burns and Oates, 1988), 236.

61. For a survey that intentionally highlights cultural diversity, see Veli-Matti Kärkkäinen, *The Trinity: Global Perspectives* (Louisville: Westminster John Knox, 2007). Kärkkäinen devotes chapters to Leonardo Boff and Justo González (Latin American and Hispanic authors), Jung Young Lee and Raimundo Panikkar (Asian theologians), and C. Nyamiti and A. O. Ogbonnaya (African theologians).

62. A great early essay is Sarah Coakley, "Can God Be Experienced as Trinity?" *Modern Churchman* 28, no. 2 (1986): 11–23. Coakley's many-sided project appears in numerous articles, and she promises a kind of systematic theological summary in the forthcoming *God, Sexuality and the Self: An Essay "On the Trinity."*

63. I have done this in *The Image of the Immanent Trinity: Rahner's Rule and the Theological Interpretation of Scripture* (New York: Peter Lang, 2001).

systematic theology, the doctrine had shrunk to an obligatory short chapter safely contained within the much more important treatise on the one God, where it is dutifully discussed and then "never brought up again," giving no shape or power to the rest of the doctrines.

But for this thematic survey, we consider Rahner not as the chronological source of certain lines of influence, but as the synthesis of the two major themes studied so far. Karl Rahner's overall theological project, which can be called transcendental Thomism, is devoted to synthesizing experience and history.[64] He taught that ultimate truth manifests itself in two ways to humans: first, as the transcendent condition of all possible experience, and second, as an actual historical entity to be encountered. The first claim is very abstract, but Rahner considers it his central message as a theologian. Summarizing his masterpiece, *Foundations of Christian Faith*, Rahner said, "I really only want to tell the reader something very simple: Human persons in every age, always and everywhere, whether they realize it and reflect on it or not, are in relationship with the unutterable mystery of human life that we call God."[65] But because humanity is also physically and historically actual, this transcendental openness to grace will be matched to a historical entity that presents itself to us concretely in world history. That entity is the man Jesus Christ, whose ministry is present in an ongoing way in the church and sacraments. When these two meet, salvation is present. God communicates himself in experience as such, and in a particular history.

These categories come to life in Rahner's trinitarian theology, where they are roughly correlated with the omnipresent Spirit and the incarnate Son. It is the proper office of the Holy Spirit to pervade all human experience as its horizon and term, and it is the proper office of the Son to become incarnate and stand among us as the presence of God in a particular. Where Augustine started a tradition of mapping the Son and the Spirit onto the psychological categories of knowledge and love, Rahner intentionally mapped them onto salvation history and existential experience, respectively.

Rahner's theology is highly philosophical in character, and its main elements can only be described in detail by taking up his major philosophical influences: Thomas Aquinas, Kant, Heidegger, and more. But in line with this

---

64. "Transcendental Thomism" is a modern transformation of the theology of Thomas Aquinas. It was a style of thought that arose in the early twentieth century, "initiated by such remarkable interpeters as Pierre Rousselot and Joseph Maréchal," and based on the conviction that "Thomas had to be reread in the light of modern philosophical considerations." The most important modern thinker to be grappled with was Kant, whose "analysis of experience is 'transcendental,' in the sense of getting behind actual experience to lay bare the conditions which make it possible at all" (Fergus Kerr, *After Aquinas: Versions of Thomism* [Oxford: Blackwell: 2002], 208).

65. Paul Imhof and Herbert Biallowons, eds., *Karl Rahner in Dialogue: Conversations and Interviews 1965–1982* (New York: Crossroad, 1986), 147. He is describing his own book *Foundations of Christian Faith: An Introduction to the Idea of Christianity* (London: Darton, Longman & Todd, 1978).

synthesis of history and experience, Rahner also proposed a methodological approach to trinitarianism that has been his greatest legacy for the doctrine. When we consider the Trinity in itself, he argued, we must always begin with the manifestations of the Son and Spirit in the economy of salvation. These two missions are ultimate, because in them the Trinity appears in the history of the world, and they are revelations of the eternal Trinity in itself.

Together on their mission from the Father, the Son and Spirit constitute the economic Trinity. But there is no discrepancy, and hardly even a distinction, between the Trinity we meet here in the gospel story (the economic Trinity) and the eternal Trinity in itself (the immanent Trinity). There is no gap, no inconsistency, between the Trinity in itself and the Trinity in salvation history. Rahner summed this up in what he called his fundamental axiom (*Grundaxiom*), which interpreters have called "Rahner's Rule": "The economic Trinity is the immanent Triinity, and the immanent Trinity is the economic Trinity."

Applying this axiom consistently, Rahner was led to insist that the person of the Trinity who became incarnate was not only the eternal Son, but was necessarily the Son. No other person of the Trinity could have become incarnate. This is not just because, as voices in the tradition have long argued, it is appropriate to the Son's character to be sent and to become incarnate, but because, in Rahner's terms, the economic logos is the immanent logos, and vice versa. Applying the axiom to the Holy Spirit, Rahner argued that the presence of the Holy Spirit in the economy of salvation (whether as the Spirit of Pentecost binding the church together, or the indwelling of God in the faithful heart as uncreated grace) is a clear and direct extension of the inner-divine role of the Spirit in the immanent Trinity. Rahner's use of his own rule pulls together the economic Trinity and the immanent Trinity, but also pulls together the modern emphases on history and experience, the *historia salutis* and the *ordo salutis*. In Rahner's theology, it also becomes apparent that the approaches to the Trinity through history and experience converge in focusing attention so much on the economic Trinity that it becomes somewhat difficult to talk about the immanent Trinity.

The Trinity and Retrieval

The standard account of the trinitarian renaissance of the twentieth century is a tale of two Karls: Karl Rahner, the Jesuit theologian whose trinitarian thought we have just met, and Karl Barth, the Swiss Protestant theologian whose work we now come to. Barth's influence in trinitarian theology is certainly vast and made a major difference on the theological scene. When Barth announced programmatically in 1931 that the doctrine of the Trinity would be foundational and central to his *Church Dogmatics*, he was intentionally moving against the untrinitarian tide of liberal Protestantism. The doctrine of the Trinity was widely considered to have outlived any usefulness it might have ever had, and a strategy of polite neglect was moving it to the very margin of Christian discourse. When Barth brandished the teaching as his starting point, he was accused of having taken counsel with reactionary confessionalists and the most entrenched, conservative sorts of Roman Catholics. In the preface to the first volume of the *Dogmatics*, he admitted that he was open to "the charge . . . that historically, formally and materially," he was "now going the way of scholasticism." He continued, "I obviously regard the doctrine of the early Church as in some sense normative. I deal explicitly with the doctrine of the Trinity, and even with that of the Virgin Birth. The last-named alone is obviously enough to lead many contemporaries to suspect me of crypto-Catholicism. What am I to say?"[66] The question "What am I to say?" was rhetorical, because Barth was certainly not at a loss for words. The thousands of pages of *Dogmatics* he would generate in the coming decades were themselves a demonstration that turning to the Trinity gave theology everything it needed to keep talking with confidence. As Hans Frei and John Webster have pointed out, "Barth was reinstating a theological language which had fallen into disrepair, and doing so by using the language in a lengthy and leisurely fashion."[67] Retrieving and elaborating the ancient doctrine of the Trinity in late modernity, Barth was insisting that "not merely the most important but also the most relevant and beautiful problems in dogmatics begin at the very point where the fable of 'unprofitable scholasticism' and the slogan about the 'Greek thinking of the fathers' persuade us that we ought to stop."[68] Losing interest in this central Christian doctrine (along with other unfashionable doctrines like the virgin birth) was one of the chief symptoms of the disease of theological liberalism:

> Shall I . . . bemoan the constantly increasing confusion, tedium and irrelevance of modern Protestantism, which, probably along with the Trinity and the Virgin Birth, has lost an entire third dimension—the dimension of what for once, though not confusing it with religious and moral earnestness, we may describe as mystery—with the result that it has been punished with all kinds of worthless substitutes.[69]

In other words, Barth's championing of the doctrine of the Trinity was self-consciously a form of theology as retrieval of the endangered past. As such it

---

66. Karl Barth, *Church Dogmatics* I/1, xiii.

67. John Webster, *Karl Barth* (London: Continuum, 2000), 50. Webster is paraphrasing Frei's insight in "Eberhard Busch's Biography of Karl Barth," in *Types of Christian Theology* (New Haven: Yale University Press, 1992),158.

68. Barth, *Church Dogmatics* I/1, xiv.

69. Ibid.

represents the third major trend giving modern trinitarianism its particular shape.

Retrieval, says John Webster, is "a *mode* of theology, an attitude of mind and a way of approaching theological tasks," rather than a distinct school of thought. Various kinds of modern theologians have turned to projects of retrieval for a whole range of different reasons:

> These theologies are differently occasioned: some are generated by dissatisfaction with the commanding role played by critical philosophy or by historical and hermeneutical theory in mainstream modern theology; some derive more directly from captivation by the object of doctrinal reflection as unsurpassably true, good, and beautiful. All, however, tend to agree that mainstream theological response to seventeenth- and eighteenth-century critiques of the Christian religion and Christian religious reflection needlessly distanced theology both from its given object and from the legacies of its past.[70]

Considered in light of the broader cultural reaction of Romanticism against the critical Enlightenment, the motif of retrieval can be seen in any of the creative arts that found inspiration in repristinating medieval resources. The revival of trinitarian thought, especially as we see it in someone like Barth, cannot be reduced to a Romantic urge to return to the Middle Ages. But it shares in the spirit of protest against the thinness of critical modernism.

Barth's own deployment of the doctrine of the Trinity can be summarized briefly. He linked the doctrine closely to all his other characteristic themes, especially Christology and revelation. Barth begins with the fundamental assertion that taking Christian faith seriously demands that we base our understanding of God on the revelation in Jesus Christ; in other words, God must be as we see him revealed in Christ. There can be no "revelation gap" between God and Jesus, such that somewhere in the unrevealed mystery behind the God of Jesus Christ lurks the "real, absolute God." Barth then unfolds his doctrine of the Trinity from the fact of the revelation in Jesus Christ: God is Trinity in himself, and no less so in his revelation, and then once again equally so in the effect of his revelation. To put it in the densest form: "God reveals himself as Lord." God himself, through himself, reveals himself, as Lord. Stated thus briefly, Barth's Trinity doctrine can seem to be unfolded analytically from the structure of the concept of revelation. But Barth filled out this schema richly with abundant scriptural material drawn not from the concept of "revealer, revelation, and revealedness," but from the actions of God in the history of salvation. And by moving the doctrine of the Trinity to the front of his system, engaging it with his central ideas, Barth restored the doctrine to its

---

70. John Webster, "Theologies of Retrieval," in John Webster, Kathryn Tanner, and Iain Torrance, *The Oxford Handbook of Systematic Theology* (Oxford: Oxford University Press, 2007), 584. Webster briefly discusses the Trinity in the project of retrieval on pages 594–95.

original place in the structure of Christian faith: as the hermeneutical key to theological discourse rather than as one more problematic puzzle in need of explanation and justification.

Of Barth's three major contributions (closing the revelation gap, unfolding the doctrine of the Trinity from the concept of revelation, and using the Trinity as hermeneutical key), the first and last have been widely influential and have set the tone of the ensuing conversation. Fewer people have been able to follow Barth in treating the doctrine as an immediate implication of the fact of revelation. But the most important legacy of Karl Barth for modern trinitarianism is the confidence and consistency with which he carried out the remarkable act of retrieval.

Great as Barth's achievement was, it would be too much to say, as is often said, that Karl Barth simply brought back the doctrine of the Trinity. That would be insulting to the various theological communities who never lost track of the doctrine in the first place, and therefore could not have it brought back. As Colin Gunton has pointed out with reference to modern theology, "In all periods there have been competent theologians, Catholic and Protestant alike, who have continued to work with traditional trinitarian categories while being aware of the reasons that have led others to question, modify or reject traditional orthodoxy."[71] Or as John Webster says, "It is not that the doctrine ever disappeared from view (it is basic to Roman Catholic school dogmatics and massively present in, for example, Protestant dogmaticians like Dorner and Bavinck)."[72] Rather, Barth put the Trinity back on the agenda of self-consciously modern theology, specifically among the liberal mainstream of academic theology in Europe and America, and specifically among those for whom history and experience were decisive modern categories dictating the conditions of Christian thought. What Barth accomplished was to leverage his own credibility as a decidedly modern theologian, in touch with all the right academic interlocutors and able to draw the attention of academic practitioners, in order to put the classic doctrine of the Trinity in terms that could engage that subculture. He scored such a direct hit that it has become common to say that he revived the doctrine altogether.

A good index of how well Barth succeeded in drawing attention to this retrieved doctrine is the way liberal theologians of the time responded. The German-American theologian Wilhelm Pauck published in 1931 an interpretation of what Barth was up to, under the title *Karl Barth: Prophet of a New Christianity?* To Pauck's mind, Barth was almost, but not quite, the prophet of something new. Pauck applauded Barth's existential interpretation of revelation (though he described it in terms that would be more comfortable for

71. Colin Gunton, "The Trinity in Modern Theology," in *The Companion Encyclopedia of Theology* (London: Routledge, 1995), 937.
72. Webster, "Theologies of Retrieval," 595.

Tillich than for Barth). What Pauck could not accept was the large amount
of traditional material that kept cropping up in the *Dogmatics*:

> Barth . . . throws himself with all the intellectual passion that he can command
> into these old doctrines of the Church, desiring to think them through from
> the point of view of the revelation of God. He does not, however, do his task
> well. He acts altogether too often in a way which hides his real interest. The
> impression which every unprejudiced reader must derive from his discussion
> on revelation, is that a clever and exceedingly eloquent theologian has applied
> himself to the old forms of theological thought with a profound emotional
> intellectualism, trying almost beyond the power of his capacity to understand
> them. As if it were really a matter of life and death, that as members of the
> church of the Twentieth Century—we should accept the dogma of the Trinity![73]

For this kind of academic theological culture, Barth's retrieval of the doctrine
of the Trinity was epochal. It would be possible to show how Barth employed
the categories of history and experience in giving his trinitarian theology a
distinctively modern contour, and we could have considered Barth's work
instructively under each of those categories. But it is worth remembering that
Barth's trinitarianism shook up the modern theological world simply by being
a retrieval of a classic central theme of the Bible and the Christian tradition.
Theologians like Pauck dug in and resisted: "We deny that it is necessary that,
in our efforts for a new expression of the Christian faith, we occupy ourselves
with the Trinity and Christology. We would then commit the same mistake
that Barth makes in his *Dogmatics*."[74] Whatever mistakes Barth made in his
Dogmatics, his retrieval of the Trinity has turned out to be the most forward-
looking of his major decisions.

As for the "competent theologians" whom Colin Gunton alluded to—
"Catholic and Protestant alike, who have continued to work with traditional
trinitarian categories" all throughout the modern period—it is hard to say what
they failed to provide in their trinitarian theology. Everything that is routinely
praised as belonging to the excitement of the trinitarian revival of recent times
is fairly easy to find in those older sources, and there does not seem to be any
chronological gap during which serious theological voices were not holding
forth on the doctrine of the Trinity with faithfulness and creativity. If we are
looking for a treatment of the Trinity that recognizes it as the core content of
the continuity of the Christian faith, we can find it in the British Methodist
William Burt Pope (1822–1903):

> The doctrine of the ever-blessed Trinity is essential to Christianity; there is no
> Theology, there is no Christology without it. . . . This has been the catholic

73. Wilhelm Pauck, *Karl Barth: Prophet of a New Christianity?* (New York: Harper, 1931), 189.
74. Ibid., 201.

belief, as the catholic interpretation of Scripture. Whatever exception may be taken to dogmatic definitions, the eternal underlying truth is the life of the Christian revelation.[75]

If we are looking for a recognition that the doctrine is eminently practical, and is not just a revealed mystery cobbled together in propositional form, we can find it in the American Presbyterian Charles Hodge (1797–1878):

> Truth is in order to holiness. God does not make known his being and attributes to teach men science, but to bring them to the saving knowledge of Himself. The doctrines of the Bible are, therefore, intimately connected with religion, or the life of God in the soul. . . . This is specially true of the doctrine of the Trinity. It is a great mistake to regard that doctrine as a mere speculative or abstract truth, concerning the constitution of the Godhead, with which we have no practical concern, or which we are required to believe simply because it is revealed.[76]

If we are looking for a recognition that the doctrine is organic and integral, revealed progressively in divine actions in history but also emerging directly from Christian experience, we can find it in Dutch Calvinist Herman Bavinck (1854–1921):

> The doctrine of the Trinity makes God known to us as the truly living God, over against the cold abstractions of Deism and the confusions of pantheism. A doctrine of creation—God related to but not identified with the cosmos—can only be maintained on a trinitarian basis. In fact, the entire Christian belief system stands or falls with the confession of God's Trinity. It is the core of the Christian faith, the root of all its dogmas, the basic content of the new covenant. The development of trinitarian dogma was never primarily a metaphysical question but a religious one. It is in the doctrine of the Trinity that we feel the heartbeat of God's entire revelation for the redemption of humanity.[77]

And if we are looking for the doctrine of the Trinity as the theological factor that identifies Christian doctrine as Christian, that specifies who the God of the Bible is and therefore what is biblical about any of the individual doctrines, we can find it in the American Episcopalian Francis J. Hall (who published from 1908 to 1922):

> The doctrine of the Trinity is the interpretive principle of all Christian doctrine, the ultimate basis of Christian ideals and hopes, and the most vital and inspiring of all the truths which human minds can contemplate. . . . The doctrine of the

75. William Burt Pope, *Compendium of Christian Theology* (New York: Phillips & Hunt, 1881), 1:284.
76. Charles Hodge, *Systematic Theology* (Grand Rapids: Eerdmans, 1995), 1:443.
77. Herman Bavinck, *Reformed Dogmatics* (Grand Rapids: Baker Academic, 2004), 2:260.

Trinity must occupy the central place in any sound or adequate conception of spiritual realities. It constitutes the postulate of the doctrines of the Incarnation, of the Atonement, of the Church, of justification and salvation, and of the coming kingdom of God. If it were shown to be false, these doctrines would have to be modified beyond recognition, and Christianity would become something quite other than it actually is.[78]

In light of these and many other voices that were speaking throughout the entire period under question, we should be careful how we talk about retrieval when it comes to the Trinity. There is an oft-told tale of how the doctrine of the Trinity was marginalized in the modern period, until a heroic rescue was performed by one of the Karls (Barth or Rahner). But for theologians like Pope, Hodge, Bavinck, and Hall, as for most Christians, there was no need for an absolute retrieval of a completely lost doctrine. Retrieval is a normal part of responsible theological method, and theologians were actively engaged in a kind of low-level, ordinary retrieval throughout the modern period, a retrieval so incremental as to be indistinguishable from conservation.

Jaroslav Pelikan has said that "the modern period in the history of Christian doctrine may be defined as the time when doctrines that had been assumed more than debated for most of Christian history were themselves called into question: the idea of revelation, the uniqueness of Christ, the authority of scripture, the expectation of life after death, even the very transcendence of God."[79] Defined in this way, of course, the doctrine of the Trinity faced major challenges in the modern period. But as we have seen, its crisis point was near the end of the critical phase of the Enlightenment, and by the dawn of the nineteenth century, Christian theology had begun to transpose the traditional doctrine into modern categories like history and experience. Those modern categories often had a distorting influence on the doctrine, pressing the content of the doctrine of the Trinity into new forms that did not succeed in maintaining continuity with the great tradition or faithfulness to the revelation in Scripture. It was especially difficult to confess the freedom of God over creation and salvation, for example, when the motifs of world history and human experience came to dominate the expression of the doctrine of God. But the modern categories also provided a great opportunity for an unforeseen development and elaboration of the doctrine of the Trinity. Premodern theology simply had not pondered its trinitarian resources in the suggestive terms of history and experience, and the modern forms of trinitarianism brought to light new resources previously unglimpsed. At the very least, the level of widespread doctrinal excitement over the Trinity became a new and invigorating element

78. Francis J. Hall, *Dogmatic Theology* (London: Longmans, Green, 1910), 4:2–3.
79. Jaroslav Pelikan, *The Christian Tradition: A History of the Development of Doctrine*, vol. 5, *Christian Doctrine and Modern Culture (Since 1700)* (Chicago: University of Chicago Press, 1989), viii.

of late twentieth-century discourse, and it shows no signs of abating. As trinitarian theology continues to be discussed and developed, theologians will do well to carry on the modern trinitarian project by articulating this classic Christian doctrine in such a way that the doctrine is not an opaque monolith of inherited terminology, but is transparent to history, transparent to human experience, and transparent to its biblical foundation.

For Further Reading

Barth, Karl. *Church Dogmatics*. Vol. I/1, *The Doctrine of the Word of God*. Vol. IV/1, *The Doctrine of Reconciliation*. Edited by G. W. Bromiley and T. F. Torrance. Translated by G. W. Bromiley. Edinburgh: T&T Clark, 1975.

Jenson, Robert W. *Systematic Theology*. Vol. 1, *The Triune God*. New York: Oxford University Press, 1997.

Johnson, Elizabeth. *She Who Is: The Mystery of God in Feminist Theological Discourse*. New York: Crossroad, 1992.

LaCugna, Catherine Mowry. *God for Us: The Trinity and Christian Life*. San Francisco: HarperCollins, 1991.

Levering, Matthew. *Scripture and Metaphysics: Aquinas and the Renewal of Trinitarian Theology*. Oxford: Blackwell, 2004.

Molnar, Paul. *Divine Freedom and the Doctrine of the Immanent Trinity*. London: T&T Clark, 2002.

Moltmann, Jürgen. *The Trinity and the Kingdom: The Doctrine of God*. New York: Harper & Row, 1981.

Pannenberg, Wolfhart. *Systematic Theology*. Vol. 1. Grand Rapids: Eerdmans, 1991.

Powell, Samuel M. *The Trinity in German Thought*. Cambridge: Cambridge University Press, 2001.

Rahner, Karl. *The Trinity*. New York: Herder & Herder, 1997.

3

· · ·

DIVINE ATTRIBUTES

STEPHEN R. HOLMES

Introduction

In 1879, Isaak Dorner wrote this:

> The doctrine of the Divine Attributes leads back to the Trinity as it were to its underlying truth. In order to be the actual and Absolute Primary Life, Knowledge, and Goodness, the Godhead must be thought as Self-originating and Self-conscious, just as He must be thought as voluntary Love. This is only possible by the Godhead's eternally distinguishing Himself from Himself, and always returning to Himself from His other Self, that is, by God's being triune. Just as God must be trinitarian in all His attributes, so also by means of the Trinity the divine attributes first harmoniously coalesce into the Unity. . . . The eternal result of the eternal Self-discrimination of God from Himself, together with the equally eternal re-entrance into Himself is the *Organism of the Absolute divine Personality*.[1]

Dorner had earlier dealt with "the general idea of God" and analyzed the attributes that he supposed to be necessary to a divine being; he had then examined the doctrine of the Trinity in its biblical basis and historical development.

1. Isaak A. Dorner, *A System of Christian Doctrine*, vol. 1, trans. Alfred Cave (Edinburgh: T&T Clark, 1880), 412; emphasis in original.

The paragraph quoted is the opening summary of his own positive doctrine of the specifically Christian idea of God as Trinity, a discussion that will, on Dorner's telling, turn on a rejection of the idea, dominant for fifteen centuries, of God as "absolute substance," and its replacement with a vision of God as "absolute personality."

A divine attribute is any term that adequately completes the sentence "God is . . ."; classically, lists of divine attributes would include such terms as goodness, love, omnipotence, eternity, and so on. A doctrine of the divine attributes is a proposal concerning how these terms work as descriptions of God, and of which terms are necessary and appropriate to number among the attributes. Dorner, in the quotation above, lists life, knowledge, goodness, self-origination, self-consciousness, and love as proper divine attributes. He claims there is a precedence to the divine possession of an attribute (God is "actual and absolute Primary . . . Goodness"; any created experience of goodness is thus secondary and derivative), that the attributes are trinitarian, and that in God the various attributes form a unity. Each of these claims might be challenged, but together they form (the beginnings of) a doctrine of the divine attributes. Dorner manages, in these few—although admittedly somewhat tortuous—lines, to either reflect or prefigure almost all of the significant issues in the doctrine of the divine attributes over the past two centuries, a time when the doctrine, relatively settled before that period, has become profoundly questioned and controversial.

It will already be obvious that some sort of account of divine attributes is fundamental not just to theology but to Christian devotion. Hymnody and liturgy, echoing biblical material, celebrate divine attributes in praise. Songs announce God's holiness and omnipotence ("Holy, holy, holy! Lord God Almighty!"—Reginald Heber), his beauty and majesty ("My God how beautiful thou art, thy majesty how bright"—F. W. Faber), and his love and mercy ("God is love, let heaven adore him"—Timothy Rees; "There's a wideness in God's mercy"—F. W. Faber), among many other perfections. Prayers similarly confess God's perfections in praise, and also recollect God's omnipotence and plead his love and mercy in seeking forgiveness for the one praying ("but you are the same Lord, whose nature is always to have mercy"—the "Prayer of Humble Access" from the Eucharist service in the *Book of Common Prayer*), or in intercession for the world. While extempore private devotion is, by its very nature, not susceptible to careful analysis, it seems reasonable to claim that here again there is an instinctive recollection of God's perfections in praise, and a similarly instinctive appeal to God's nature in petition. In all of this, some sort of doctrine of the divine attributes is assumed. God's perfections are real and can be named and understood and celebrated and pleaded.

The same assumptions may be found already in Scripture. The praise recorded in Scripture routinely revolves around celebrations of the divine attributes: Isaiah the prophet hears angels calling one to another, "Holy, holy, holy is the LORD of hosts" (Isa. 6:3); at the end of his life King David is recorded as publicly declaring, "Yours, O LORD, is the greatness and the power and the glory and the victory and the majesty" (1 Chron. 29:11); when interceding for the cities on the plain, Abraham pleads God's justice on their behalf and expects to be heard: "Shall not the Judge of all the earth do what is just?" (Gen. 18:25).

The Settled Doctrine of Early Modernity

As already noted, at the beginning of the period on which this essay focuses, the doctrine of the divine attributes was relatively settled. This had not always been the case; indeed, perhaps the most famous debate of medieval theology had centered on this doctrine, that between "nominalism" and "realism." The question concerned the ontological status of universals (terms that express the collective essence of something: "humanity," "redness," "chairness"): Are these mere names given by us to refer to a commonality we happen to have noticed, or are they real essences that somehow communicate their nature to members of the class? Are we human beings because we all somehow share in a real thing called "humanity," or are we merely a bunch of particulars, which for convenience we group together in a class we invent and call "humanity"?

The medieval philosophers believed that this was at root a debate over the status of the divine attributes. The problem of universals becomes interesting when one considers a concept such as "goodness" or "justice": Is an action good and just because there is some universal standard against which it may be judged, or is it good and just only because we have chosen to call it so? Clearly the former position is attractive; otherwise we might call evil good without any possibility of complaint. However, if we call God good, does that mean that there is a standard of goodness external to God to which he must conform? If not, could we just as properly call God evil? Neither position is attractive, and so the debate raged.

In the turmoil of the Reformation and the wars of religion that followed, however, that debate was set aside. It is difficult to claim that it was solved, as no new distinction or argument was offered that was widely accepted; at best we might suggest that a solution that was already available in the tradition before the debate began—the Thomistic claim, codified in the doctrine of divine simplicity, that God is identical with his attributes—was recognized as being adequate, and so perhaps as rendering two centuries of debate unnecessary.[2] (The argument, in the terms used above, runs something like this: if God is identical with his attributes, then the standard of goodness is God himself, thus it is neither something "above" God, nor merely arbitrary.) Whether this

---

2. The post-Reformation scholastic systems assumed this solution to be correct on every side, save the Socinians.

is a correct reading or not, from the sixteenth to the eighteenth century, in the orthodox scholastic systems of Roman, Lutheran, and Reformed theologians alike, there was a general agreement as to how to speak about the divine attributes.[3]

The core of this settled doctrine may be summed up in the claim that the attributes of God are essential to the being/life of God. This is (almost) never true for created objects: we might truly claim that "Jane is wise," or that "it is a hot day today," or that "Lake Superior is large." There presumably was, however, a time when Jane was not wise, and yet she was still Jane; it is possible to imagine today not being hot and still being today; changes to global weather patterns might one day make Lake Superior dry up to the point where it is a small pond. In contrast, the claim "God is wise/good/omnipresent" is not susceptible to such questions or thought experiments: wisdom, goodness, and omnipresence are each (a part of) what it is to be God.

This claim is further defined by three other assertions: an assertion of the perfection of each of the divine attributes, an assertion of their primacy over created instantiations of the same quality, and an assertion of their unity with each other. First, *created attributes are generally not perfect*: Jane presumably could grow wiser, today could have been hotter, and Lake Superior could become larger. God is utterly wise and good, and cannot grow more so (I take it that this level of perfection is already contained in the idea of omnipresence, but if not, the point applies there also). God's attributes are perfect, and so cannot increase. Second, when we assert both that Jane is wise and that God is wise, there is clearly a question of priority: Is wisdom a human quality that we project onto God or an aspect of the divine perfection of which we see echoes in certain created beings? The classical doctrine emphatically asserted the latter. *God's attributes are the primary and original instances of the qualities named, and any created approximation to that quality is secondary and derivative.* Wisdom is what God possesses; insofar as there is a distant echo of God's perfection in Jane's practices of moral reasoning, we call Jane "wise." Third, *God's life is perfectly coherent and united*: God is never torn, with his mercy demanding he act one way and his justice demanding he act another; instead, mercy and justice (and wisdom, goodness, omnipresence, . . .) are each partial reflections of the one perfect life of God. God's attributes are united and harmonious, not several and opposed. After making these

---

3. It is striking that on this subject, even when in controversial mode, the dogmaticians found little to disagree about. To take a representative example, in his *Institutes of Elenctic Theology*, F. Turretin has twenty-two questions concerning the divine attributes; twelve have no named opponents, and nine more are directed at the Socinians (i.e., early Unitarians). The only issue where Turretin can find any disagreement with other Trinitarian dogmaticians is in denying the idea of "middle knowledge," against the Jesuits and Remonstrants. See Francis Turretin, *Institutes of Elenctic Theology*, trans. George Musgrave Giger, ed. James T. Dennison Jr. (Phillipsburg, NJ: P&R, 1992), 1:169–253.

points, a doctrine of the divine attributes would generally culminate with an attempt to name an adequate set of attributes to capture all the nuances of God's perfection. Such, in brief summary, was the settled classical doctrine.

Epistemological Questioning and the Appeal to Experience

The first blow to this synthesis came with the profound epistemological questioning of the eighteenth century. There is not space here to rehearse the story, but it culminates with a profound philosophical skepticism, coupled with a generally accepted common-sense pragmatism. For the first, the crowning figure is Kant, and the claim is that all of our knowledge is confined to the "phenomenal" realm—we know things as they appear to us, filtered through our senses and our mental categories; what they are in themselves (the "noumenal" realm) is necessarily opaque to us. We might observe certain patterns, but (as Hume had argued[4]) unless we can reduce the pattern to something that is logically necessary, we have no good reason to assume that it will continue. We have no good reason, Kant suggests, to even assume that the pattern is in (noumenal) reality, and not an artifact of our organs of perception.

The logical conclusion of such ideas (particularly if we ask what reason we have for assuming, as Kant did seem to assume, that all human beings share similar organs of perception) is an extreme skepticism of the form that has recently become fashionable under the name of postmodernism. What prevented these conclusions from being drawn in the eighteenth century would seem to be a basic empirical pragmatism. This is not a triumph of Locke's empirical program—Hume's denials were targeted specifically at Locke, and are philosophically devastating—so much as a willingness to set aside unanswerable philosophical doubts on the basis of the impressive success of natural science. Boats float, airplanes fly, and internal combustion engines power rapid travel in motor cars; it might well be, as Hume claimed, that the only reason we believe these things is that it "costs us too much pains" to think otherwise, but most of us still gratefully make use of the possibilities for travel afforded by the modern world.

The extent of this pragmatic solution (or evasion) is, however, profoundly limited. It offers nothing to moral or metaphysical reasoning, and so nothing to theology. It is this intellectual impasse that marks the beginnings of recognizably modern theology. While through the nineteenth and even twentieth

---

4. Hume points out very simply that unless we know the mechanisms that cause things to happen, past experience cannot be a reliable guide to the future. His classic example is the rising of the sun (*Enquiry concerning Human Understanding*, 4.1). Why then do we continue to base our lives on such false assumptions? In Hume's own words, "If we believe, that fire warms, or water refreshes, 'tis only because it costs us too much pains to think otherwise" (*Treatise of Human Nature*, 1.4.7).

centuries it is possible to find able writers who rehearse and refine older debates with no apparent recognition of this challenge, modern dogmatics in its intellectually serious forms has been endlessly concerned with the question of how, in the face of the apparent impossibility of attaining knowledge of the metaphysical realm, theology may continue.[5]

The first great figure, offering a radically new proposal that sets the agenda for almost everything that follows, is, of course, Schleiermacher, whose proposal for reconstruction was based on redefining theology as the analysis of religious experience. This has a striking effect on Schleiermacher's account of the divine attributes; as he puts it in his own summary of his introduction of the subject, "All attributes which we ascribe to God are to be taken as denoting not something special in God, but only something special on the manner in which the feeling of absolute dependence is to be related to Him."[6] For Schleiermacher, and for much theology that follows him, a doctrine of the divine attributes is not an answer to the question "Who is God?" so much as an account of our experience of the divine. This shift of the point of reference of the doctrine, from the eternal divine life to the economy, has become endemic in modern theology.

The reasons for this shift are various. Sometimes, particularly in the Kantian-influenced theologians of the nineteenth century, the concern is precisely the impossibility of knowledge of anything metaphysical. Slogans concerning the unknowability of the divine essence could easily be borrowed from the history of theology, which, in its most extreme moments, had indeed given in to the same temptation.[7] (The claim that the divine essence is unknowable is a standard one, of course, but the adequacy of divine attributes to refer to the divine essence was defended by *an account of analogy, of which more later.*) J. A. L. Wegscheider, for example, who was finally deposed from his

5. This is not to say that "conservative" theologies are less "modern" or less "intellectually serious" than mediating or liberal theologies; it is possible to face up to these challenges and find solutions that reaffirm traditional theological claims (just as it is possible to dismiss such traditional theological claims as the doctrine of the Trinity with no knowledge of the epistemological challenges bequeathed by Kant). It seems a fair criterion to me, however, that for a theological proposal to be considered intellectually serious post-Kant, it must display at least some awareness of, and a proposal for dealing with, the challenges to the very possibility of theology that have been posed.

6. Friedrich Schleiermacher, *The Christian Faith*, trans. H. R. Mackintosh and J. S. Stewart (Edinburgh: T&T Clark, 1928), 194.

7. The influence of Pseudo-Dionysius was important in this regard, and indeed decisive in the distinction, taught by St. Gregory Palamas, and so enshrined in Eastern Orthodox tradition, that the essence of God remains unknown, and all that is known are the divine energies. The same question was repeatedly raised in the West but, prior to Schleiermacher, the claim that knowledge of the attributes of God is true knowledge of the essence of God was repeatedly defended, as for instance in the condemnation of Gilbert de la Porrée at the Synod of Reims (1148), or Pope John XXII's condemnation in 1329 of the claim, attributed to Meister Eckhart, that "no distinction in the very essence of God can be, or can be known" in *In agro dominico.*

university chair for rationalism, claimed that speaking of a multiplicity of attributes, rather than simply of the idea of perfect, absolute substance, was necessarily anthropomorphism, and a feature—albeit an inevitable one—of the imperfection of our knowledge.[8] In his view, human knowledge of the divine essence is simply unavailable, and a doctrine of the divine attributes, which traditionally had been a careful and measured account of precisely such knowledge, must therefore either be set aside or be redefined to speak about some subject that is a possible object of human cognition.

In the twentieth century, the desire to make the gospel history an account of the internal life of God—again, more on this later—makes the distinction under discussion somewhat meaningless; if (crudely put) the divine economy is God's essence,[9] then there is little point in arguing whether the language of attributes refers to the essence or the economy. Nevertheless, even theologians careful to avoid this identification, and certainly careful to avoid letting Kant define their intellectual options, seem to follow this Schleiermacherian turn, consciously or unconsciously. Emil Brunner was hardly captive to Kant or Schleiermacher, and yet he will conclude his treatment of the divine attributes with the claim, "In Himself, however, God is not the Almighty, the Omniscient, the Righteous One; this is what He is in relation to the world which He has created."[10] Consider even John Webster, concluding a book on holiness: "Holiness is thus God's personal moral relation to his creatures."[11]

This debate might seem somewhat abstract, but it in fact has profound implications. Isaak Dorner, with whom I began, makes the point precisely and strongly: if the divine attributes do not refer somehow to the divine essence, God "would display not Himself, but something else different to Himself, and

8. J. A. L. Wegscheider, *Institutiones Theologiae Christianae Dogmaticae* (1815; repr., Halle, 1833), 247–48.

9. "God is what happens to Jesus and the world" (Robert W. Jenson, *Systematic Theology* [Oxford: Oxford University Press, 1997], 1:221); Jürgen Moltmann's doctrine of the Trinity leads him to assert, "The scarlet thread that runs through the biblical testimonies might be called the history of the kingdom of God. . . . It does not merely run its course on earth—which is to say outside God himself—as dogmatic tradition ever since Augustine has maintained. . . . It takes place in its earthly mode within the Trinity itself" (*Trinity and Kingdom of God: The Doctrine of God*, trans. M. Kohl [London: SCM, 1981], 95). These testimonies could be multiplied.

10. Emil Brunner, *Dogmatics*, vol. 1, *The Christian Doctrine of God*, trans. Olive Wyon (London: Lutterworth, 1949), 247. Brunner seems in fact to believe in two classes of divine attributes: those that describe God *in se* ("God in Himself is the Holy One," 247), and those referred to in the quotation above, which describe God's relations with the world.

11. John Webster, *Holiness* (London: SCM, 2003), 100. This reference might be considered somewhat unfair in that, in the paragraphs around, Webster is unquestionably concerned to protect the claim that holiness is both a statement about who God is and how God acts; in some ways, this makes the cited definition the more striking, however—a careful and brilliant theologian, aware of the danger, still slips back into "Schleiermacherian" language in offering a lapidary definition.

substituted for Himself."[12] When we name God as love, is it God we name, or merely his "public persona," so to speak? Is God in fact not utter love in himself, but only acts as such toward us? Is there a "God behind God," unknown and unknowable? Teaching this is certainly not the positive intent of Schleiermacher (or indeed of St. Gregory Palamas), but the doctrine that the divine attributes refer to the economy and not the divine essence raises this as a possibility.

One theologian who did want to teach something like this was Thomasius, whose commitment to developing a kenotic Christology, in which the divine Logos lays down certain divine attributes in becoming incarnate, led him to postulate a class of divine attributes which God could take up or lay down at will. He distinguished between "immanent," or essential, divine attributes and "relative" divine attributes, which he describes as those "in which the immanent divine attributes are outwardly manifested and make their appearance."[13] That is, Thomasius sees many of the classical divine perfections as not actually divine perfections at all, but (his term) divine "modes of being." In the incarnation, the eternal Son continues to be God, but in a different mode, a different way.

The question raised by this is how we differentiate between those attributes that are in fact essential and those that are merely relative and so could perhaps be reexpressed. While Thomasius was mainly concerned with attributes such as omniscience and omnipresence, we might ask, If God can choose whether to be good or merciful or not, on what basis does he make the choice? We again have a hidden God, whose character and purposes are unknowable. Thomasius's response would be that goodness belongs to the class of divine attributes that are intrinsic to God's life, and so cannot be laid down. Attributes, for him, are expressions of a being's life that arise only in relationship with another being;[14] this is saved from being a Schleiermacherian restriction of the attributes to the economy by an assertion that certain attributes are manifested in the intra-Triune relations ("immanent" attributes), and others only in the God-world relation ("relative" attributes). Thomasius would presumably claim that goodness fell into the former category, whereas omniscience falls into the latter; it is not clear, however, on what grounds such an insight may be claimed,[15] and there seems little doubt that mercy can only be a relative attribute on these terms. It was open to God to be implacable,

12. Dorner, *Christian Doctrine*, 1:195.

13. Thomasius, "Christ's Person and Work," trans. Claude Welch, in *God and Incarnation in Mid-Nineteenth Century German Theology*, ed. Claude Welch (New York: Oxford University Press, 1965), 70.

14. On which see Welch's discussion: *God and Incarnation*, 67–69n10.

15. The most that can be proved from an appeal to the gospel history is that the divine Logos did not, in fact, choose to cease to be good in becoming incarnate; to argue from this "did not" to a "could not" seems difficult without further data within Thomasius's logic. Dorner, with whom I began, criticized Thomasius sharply on just this point—see *Christian Doctrine*, 3:266–67.

rather than merciful; why did he choose the latter way and not the former? Because of an inscrutable decision of self-actualization in the incarnation. God's true character, the reason for the incarnation, the basis of the gospel hope—all remain hidden.[16]

From Being to Person: The Nature of God and the Question of Divine Attributes

One solution to this problem, offered in detail by a later British defender of kenotic Christology, P. T. Forsyth, is to suggest that the answer lies in the immutability of divine personality. In Forsyth's language, God cannot change his "moral" attributes, such as goodness, but can lay down his metaphysical attributes, such as omnipotence.[17] Forsyth is working out of a controlling theological intuition, borrowed from Dorner,[18] that God, and so ultimate reality, is more adequately understood as moral than metaphysical. This reflects Dorner's turn, which I noted in my introduction, from seeing God as absolute substance to seeing God as absolute personality.[19] If this shift can be accomplished thoroughly and convincingly, then perhaps the kenoticism of Thomasius—and indeed Forsyth—might be sustained.[20]

16. Thomasius's major works have not been translated, to the best of my knowledge. For helpful recent analyses of Thomasius in English, see Welch, *God and Incarnation*; Thomas R. Thompson, "Nineteenth-Century Kenotic Christology," in C. Stephen Evans, ed., *Exploring Kenotic Christology: The Self-Emptying of God* (Oxford: Oxford University Press, 2006), 74–111, esp. 78–85; Ronald J. Feenstra, "Reconsidering Kenotic Christology," in *Trinity, Incarnation, and Atonement: Philosophical and Theological Essays*, ed. Ronald J. Feenstra and Cornelius Plantinga Jr. (Notre Dame: University of Notre Dame Press, 1989), 128–52, esp. 129–33.

17. This is a slight oversimplification of Forsyth's position. He views all divine attributes as moral, speaking of "the less ethical attributes like omniscience, omnipotence, or ubiquity" (*The Person and Place of Jesus Christ* [London: Independent Press, 1946], 295); indeed, he views the attempt to "moralize" dogma, interpreting metaphysics as the expression of personality, as the highest goal of modern theology (*Person and Place*, 213–24). He finally seems to suggest that what I have called the "moral" attributes are true attributes of God, whereas the "metaphysical" attributes are consequences of the true attributes.

18. For evidence of Dorner's influence on Forsyth, see Leslie McCurdy, *Attributes and Atonement: The Holy Love of God in the Theology of P. T. Forsyth* (Carlisle, UK: Paternoster, 1999), 5–7. McCurdy focuses simply on the definition of God as "Holy Love" here, and so does not explicitly recognize either the centrality of a turn from metaphysical to moral conceptions of deity (a point which is made elsewhere in his book), or the dependence of this central Forsythian move on Dorner (a point which is absent).

19. For an excellent examination of this theme in Dorner, see Jonathan Norgate, *Isaak A. Dorner: The Triune God and the Gospel of Salvation* (London: T&T Clark, 2009), 10–52.

20. Forsyth's relegation of the metaphysical attributes to mere consequences of the real attributes probably makes his system more defensible, but at the same time more of a departure from traditional Christian faith. If omnipotence is a mere consequence of more central moral attributes, then it is easier to imagine how it may be set aside—but such a relegation of the title of "the Almighty" for God seems a significant move from classical Christian talk about God.

Forsyth and Dorner—and others—had in their sights a tradition of theology that defined God as *ens perfectissimum*, "most perfect being." This conception was in fact relatively recent—Leibniz might be the first thinker to deploy it as the central claim concerning God. The classical earlier claim, in Aquinas and many others, was that God is *actus purus sine ulla potentia* ("pure activity lacking any unfulfilled potential"); this was supplemented with a claim that God's being is his act, which at least implied an *ens perfectissimum* account, but that was not the fundamental claim. I suspect that the difference is important in connection with the problem perceived by Dorner and Forsyth: "perfect being" seems a much more static account of the nature of the divine than "pure act."

That said, Dorner and Forsyth witness to an impatience with metaphysical definitions of God that chimed well with the general philosophical context after Kant. Wilhelm Herrmann, for instance, whose influence on his student Karl Barth was significant, took Kant's epistemological revolution to be a demonstration that any attempt to argue from the phenomenal to the noumenal, or from physics to metaphysics, was impossible. Just so, natural theology was excluded in principle, and there could be no general science of the divine, no metaphysics—instead only knowledge granted by direct revelation.[21] Herrmann—and Barth after him—represents a particularly radical version of a very general assumption, at least in nineteenth-century German theology. (Albrecht Ritschl also repudiated starting with metaphysics instead of revelation, but assumed that a final synthesis of natural and revealed knowledge was both possible and desirable.[22]) When this is coupled with the Romantic sensibilities of nineteenth-century Europe, the emergence of a desire to move the doctrine of God from a metaphysical study to a personal encounter is not surprising.

In the twentieth century, this move has become entangled with another nineteenth-century claim, concerning the Greek "infection" of Christianity in its formative periods. The deep origin of this idea is probably F. C. Baur's elaborate account of Catholic Christianity as the result of a Hegelian synthesis between Jewish thesis and Hellenistic antithesis; this positive sense of a Hegelian synthesis has been completely lost, however, by the time the idea is taken up by Ritschl and von Harnack (briefly Herrmann's colleague at Marburg, 1886–1888, before taking up his more famous post in Berlin). Instead, Greek influences, including a focus on metaphysical speculation and a complex system of ritual, are seen as damaging accretions to the original, simple, and ethical religion of Jesus.

21. As far as I am aware, Herrmann has not been translated into English. A brief but helpful account of this aspect of his theology may be found in Mark D. Chapman, "'Theology within the Walls': Wilhelm Herrmann's Religious Reality," *Neue Zeitschrift für Systematische Theologie und Religionsphilosophie* 34 (1992): 69–84.

22. See, e.g., Ritschl, *Three Essays*, trans. Philip Hefner (Philadelphia: Fortress, 1972), 150–217.

Such accounts of Christian origins are no longer regarded as remotely credible historically, but they have left a strangely resilient legacy in dogmatics. The idea of damaging Hellenistic accretions is still regularly deployed in various ways, sometimes as if it were an established fact of scholarship (for an example, see the quotation from Gunton, below), more happily when an alternative genealogy is offered. (For an example of the latter, consider Robert Jenson's account: the discourse we call "philosophy" is, on Jenson's telling, the demythologized remains of Olympian theology; however, there is a constant temptation—thoroughly surrendered to in the eighteenth-century "Enlightenment"—to see it as something different, a "rational" discourse, universally available and authoritative, that is thus able to judge and control biblical-theological claims.[23])

The language of Greek "infection" of biblical religion is regularly advanced as a reason to be suspicious of a certain set of traditional, metaphysical attributes of God, including simplicity, aseity (the idea that God is solely self-caused—"*a se*"), impassibility (of which more below), immutability, and eternity. When coupled with the shift to a more "personal" understanding of God, this potentially has far-reaching consequences for a doctrine of the divine attributes. "Metaphysical" attributes become profoundly suspect as improperly derived and also inappropriate to the general account of God being offered. If they are retained at all in such a context, they are relegated to a very minor place in the system. For a particularly stark statement of the claim, consider Colin Gunton: "The impersonal attributes come from Greece, the Greek philosophical tradition; the personal ones come from the Bible and don't appear to be consistent with them."[24] The same point may be found in Moltmann,[25] or, in more measured form, in Pannenberg[26] or Barth.[27]

The Denial of Analogy: Speaking about God in Terms of the Divine Attributes

The metaphysical language can also be found, perhaps surprisingly, in a very conservative near-contemporary of Dorner and Forsyth, the Princeton theologian Charles Hodge. His writings at first sight might seem like an example

23. Jenson, *Systematic Theology*, 1:8–11.
24. Colin E. Gunton, *The Barth Lectures*, ed. P. H. Brazier (London: T&T Clark, 2007), 94. This is, to be fair, a posthumously published transcript of a lecture, and so perhaps a blunter statement than Gunton would have offered in public by choice; however, the same point, albeit in more nuanced language, is made in (e.g.) *Act and Being* (London: SCM, 2003), 39–54.
25. See, e.g., *The Trinity and the Kingdom*.
26. Wolfhart Pannenberg, "The Appropriation of the Philosophical Concept of God as a Dogmatic Problem of Early Christian Theology," in *Basic Questions in Theology*, trans. George H. Kehm (London: SCM, 1971), 2:119–83.
27. Barth, *Church Dogmatics* II/1, 329–30.

of the problem they perceived. Hodge claimed, remarkably ambitiously, that "probably the best definition of God ever penned by man is that given in the 'Westminster Catechism': 'God is a Spirit, infinite, eternal, and unchangeable in his being, wisdom, power, holiness, justice, goodness, and truth.'"[28] While personal/moral language is not absent—"wisdom," "holiness," "goodness"—it would be easy to understand a reader interpreting the definition as fundamentally metaphysical, and so imagining that Hodge, so often profoundly and aggressively conservative in his theology, is here an example of the older dogmatics that Dorner and Forsyth sought to replace.

Such an interpretation would, surprisingly, be unfair to Hodge, however. It is true that for the writers of the Catechism, the opening affirmation that "God is a Spirit" functions mostly as a denial of corporeality, and so of presence restricted locally, and of change—it is a metaphysical claim. But Hodge, by contrast, invested the idea with more positive, and personal, content. He more than once uses the doctrine of human creation in the *imago Dei* to draw an analogy between our experience of spirituality and God's being, suggesting that possession of intellect, volition, and affection is intrinsic to being spirit.[29] This seems a deliberate development of the doctrine he inherited, which generally noted intellect and volition in the divine life. Hodge's addition of feeling (or sensibility, or affection) is introduced explicitly in deference to contemporary psychology, and a concern for a less philosophical, more biblical, doctrine of God;[30] Schleiermacher's turn to experience as the basis of theology is nowhere mentioned in this discussion, but is surely relevant.

Hodge indeed stressed what he called the personality of God as an antidote to pantheism, which he saw as endemic in contemporary German theology.[31] So concerned was he to avoid this, that he did away with any traditional doctrine of analogy and insisted that our knowledge of God's perfections is different in extent from God's own knowledge, but not different in kind. This is a profoundly radical theological move, as Hodge must have known, and yet he repeatedly insists on it. Speaking of God's knowledge, he insists first that divine knowledge is different "in its modes and objects" from human knowledge, but is not different "in its essential nature." He then expands this point to a general doctrine of divine perfections: "We must remove from our conceptions of the divine attributes all the limitations and imperfections which belong to the corresponding attributes in us; but we are not to destroy their nature."[32] Indeed, he even seems to suggest that our experience of knowing is

28. Charles Hodge, *Systematic Theology* (Grand Rapids: Eerdmans, 1960), 1:367, quoting q. 4 of the Westminster Shorter Catechism.
29. See, e.g., *Systematic Theology*, 1:371 or 1:424–25.
30. Ibid., 376–80.
31. Ibid., 424–26.
32. Ibid., 396.

basic, and God conforms himself to it: "God, therefore, does and can know in the ordinary and proper sense of the word."[33]

Hodge's reasons for this radical doctrine are, I suppose, apologetic: his account of the divine perfections is constructed in dialogue with those who would deny the possibility of any existence or knowledge of divine perfections at all. Hodge was hardly a profound philosopher, and it seems likely that he was not aware of the full ramifications of this move: he seems to think that he may maintain a traditional doctrine of divine simplicity without any particular defense, for instance, which seems to me impossible once analogy is denied.[34]

Duns Scotus had famously insisted that analogy could not survive without some point of underlying univocity, of course,[35] and the doctrine of analogy has been increasingly out of fashion in recent decades. On the one hand, there are many, following Dorner and Forsyth in the turn to more personal doctrines of God, who have found in personal and relational language the key point of contact between the divine and created orders. John Zizioulas's influential work *Being as Communion: Studies in Personhood and the Church*[36] claims (surely wrongly) to find this position in the fourth-century Cappadocian Fathers;[37] and the recent "trinitarian revival" has seen many writers adopting his claims with enormous enthusiasm. I will return to this later.

The doctrine of analogy is also sidelined or denied in another well-populated area of recent theological discussion in English-language theology: "perfect being theology." Ironically, this can look very much like a re-presentation of the very tradition that Dorner was reacting against, although that is probably an unfair characterization. Perfect being theology starts simply with the affirmation that God is a perfect being, and assumes that it is possible to draw deductions about the divine perfections from that claim (Herrmann would not have been happy with this procedure). From Dorner's day onward, this mode of argument would have been largely confined to a Roman Catholic neo-scholastic tradition of natural theology, which held that God's existence and at least some of God's perfections were demonstrable by the natural light of

33. Ibid.
34. Hodge affirms simplicity (1.370–74) as taught by Turretin, a doctrine in which the attributes differ *virtualiter* (virtually), but not *realiter* (really). That is, there is a certain basis in God's eternal life for the distinction we perceive in the divine perfections. This account as stated is traditional and orthodox, and (as I suppose Hodge well knew) can be found in Thomas Aquinas as much as in Turretin; but Aquinas links it quite closely with his account of analogy to preserve the logic of it.
35. The relevant text is in the *Oxford Commentary*; for a translation of the key passage, see Allan Wolter, *Duns Scotus: Philosophical Writings* (Edinburgh: Thomas Nelson, 1962), 15–25.
36. John D. Zizioulas, *Being as Communion: Studies in Personhood and the Church* (Crestwood, NY: St. Vladimir's Seminary Press, 1985).
37. Zizioulas almost completely ignores the context of the development of Cappadocian thought in the debate with Eunomius, which turned on questions of the way language could refer to God, on which see further below.

reason and that St. Thomas Aquinas had demonstrated this fully and finally, so that all that was necessary was an understanding of his logic.[38]

This neo-Thomist philosophy was heavily emphasized by the Vatican around the beginning of the twentieth century as a response to the modernist crisis. It reached its height, perhaps, in the imposition of the infamous "Twenty-Four Thomistic Theses" imposed by Pius X in 1914. Thesis 22, for example, in what now reads as almost a parody of Aquinas's "Five Ways," argues that the existence, perfection, intelligence, spirituality, and omnicausality of God are adequately demonstrable from observing the created order.[39]

Since about 1970, however, perfect being theology has enjoyed an enormous renaissance within the analytic tradition of the philosophy of religion. Major scholars such as Alvin Plantinga[40] or Richard Swinburne[41] have led the way in producing a school of philosophers working in the analytic tradition who are committed to exploring, and often to defending, classical themes in Christian doctrine.[42] Accounts of the divine perfections have been important in this work, both as the subject of investigation in themselves and as data to be deployed in other investigations.

To take these in reverse order, two of the most energetic debates in this tradition have concerned the coherence of classical trinitarianism[43] and the

---

38. For the classic statement from the twentieth century, see Reginald Garrigou-Lagrange, *Dieu: Son existence et sa nature; Solution Thomiste des antinomies agnostiques*, 2 vols. (Paris: Beauchesne, 1950). (The first edition had been published in 1919; eighteen editions in three decades speaks of the enormous popularity of a book that is now, like its author, all but forgotten.) Garrigou-Lagrange treats the divine perfections in the second volume. On Garrigou-Lagrange, see Richard Peddicord, *The Sacred Monster of Thomism: An Introduction to the Life and Legacy of Reginald Garrigou-Lagrange* (South Bend, IN: St. Augustine's Press, 2005). He retired from the Angelicum as recently as 1960, having there supervised the doctoral studies of Karol Wojtyla, who was to become Pope John Paul II.

39. It reads: *Deum esse neque immediata intuitione percipimus, neque a priori demonstramus, sed utique a posteriori, hoc est, per ea quae facta sunt, ducto argumento ab effectibus ad causam: videlicet, a rebus quae moventur ad sui motus principium et primum motorem immobilem; a processu rerum mundanarum e causis inter se subordinatis, ad primam causam incausatam; a corruptibilibus quae aequaliter se habent ad esse et non esse, ad ens absolute necessarium; ab iis quae secundum minoratas perfectiones essendi, vivendi, intelligendi, plus et minus sunt, vivunt, intelligunt, ad eum qui est maxime intelligens, maxime vivens, maxime ens; denique, ab ordine universi ad intellectum separatum qui res ordinavit, disposuit, et dirigit ad finem.*

40. See, e.g., Alvin Plantinga, *Does God Have a Nature?* (Milwaukee: Marquette University Press, 1980).

41. See Richard Swinburne, *The Existence of God* (Oxford: Oxford University Press, 1991).

42. Interesting new methodological proposals mark a new stage in the maturity of this endeavor. See Oliver D. Crisp and Michael Rea, eds., *Analytic Theology* (Oxford: Oxford University Press, 2009), or Thomas G. Flint and Michael Rea, eds., *The Oxford Handbook to Philosophical Theology* (Oxford: Oxford University Press, 2009).

43. For an excellent and representative account of different analytic approaches to trinitarian doctrine, see Thomas McCall and Michael C. Rea, eds., *Philosophical and Theological Essays on the Trinity* (Oxford: Oxford University Press, 2009).

possibility of an account of eternal punishment.[44] In each case, the debates regularly turn on appeals to and discussions about the meanings of particular divine attributes. To cite examples almost at random, Leftow criticizes social trinitarian thought because it necessarily denies that God is omniscient and omnipotent,[45] while Walls addresses problems concerning the doctrine of hell raised by omniscience, omnipotence, and divine goodness.[46] In each case, the task of offering an analytic definition of the divine attributes named becomes an important part of the argument.

Turning to areas where the divine attributes have been the subject of discussion, there has been a certain amount of agreement within recent analytic philosophy that, for a being to be classed as perfect, it must be possessed, at least, of omnipotence, omniscience, and omnibenevolence (perfect goodness); each of these has been analyzed extensively, and there seems to be an emerging agreement that coherent accounts can be offered. Other traditional attributes have been more contentious, notably, eternity, simplicity, and aseity. Each can find its defenders, but in each case strong criticisms concerning coherence have been mounted that are regarded by many as at best unanswered and possibly unanswerable.[47]

Rather than considering these debates in detail, it is perhaps worth pausing at the level of methodology. The central task of analytic work is to attain to conceptual clarity; if words are carefully defined and equally carefully used, then sense will emerge. There is no question that this is a procedure in deep conformity with aspects of the Christian theological tradition; it is the essence of St. Thomas's intellectual endeavor, for instance, to strive for clarity of meaning and expression. However, St. Thomas balances this with a profound appreciation of the fundamental mystery of the divine life. We are not able to achieve analytic clarity when we speak of God's essence; instead, all our language is necessarily analogical, a halting gesturing toward a luminous truth that shines too brightly for us ever to see it clearly.[48]

44. For summaries of the debate, see, variously, Jonathan L. Kvanvig, *The Problem of Hell* (New York: Oxford University Press, 1993); Jerry L. Walls, *Hell: The Logic of Damnation* (Notre Dame, IN: University of Notre Dame Press, 1992); and (more recently), Joel Buenting, ed., *The Problem of Hell: A Philosophical Anthology* (Farnham, UK: Ashgate, 2010).

45. Brian Leftow, "Anti Social Trinitarianism," in McCall and Rea, *Philosophical and Theological Essays*, 52–88. Cf. the recent response from William Hasker, "Objections to Social Trinitarianism," *Religious Studies* 46 (2010): 429–31.

46. Walls, *Logic of Damnation*, 33–111.

47. For a summary of the arguments, see Katherin A. Rogers, *Perfect Being Theology* (Edinburgh: Edinburgh University Press, 2000).

48. Thomas's most famous, but far from only, description of analogy is in q. 11 of the *Summa Theologiae Prima Pars*. For an excellent discussion of his teaching on the subject, see Laurence Paul Hemming, "*Analogia non Entis sed Entitatis*: The Ontological Consequences of the Doctrine of Analogy," *International Journal of Systematic Theology* 6 (2004): 118–29, and Hemming's further development of his thesis in *Postmodernity's Transcending: Devaluing God* (Notre Dame, IN: University of Notre Dame Press, 2005). I find Hemming's account wholly

The centrality of this limitation may be seen from its importance in the defining of orthodox trinitarian doctrine in the fourth century. The heresiarch Eunomius taught that words corresponded directly with concepts (a theory of language borrowed from the Neoplatonists of his day), so that, if God was properly called "ungenerate," the Son, being generate, could not be God. In response, the Cappadocian fathers developed an account of how human language refers to divine reality that stressed the difficulty and uncertainty of the reference. Theology is a work of *epinoia*, of hesitant creative construction of language that succeeds in partial but accurate reference to the unspeakable reality of God.

In classical doctrines of the divine perfections, this doctrine of analogy plays an important part in defining how differing divine attributes are related. At the heart of this is the doctrine of divine simplicity. "Simplicity" is, traditionally, a central divine attribute that claims that God is in no way composite or divided. This conditions the accounts of all other divine attributes, which are clearly multiple. So we claim that God is variously good, just, loving, omnipotent, eternal, and so on, whereas the doctrine of divine simplicity insists that God is in fact just God, and that our multiple perceptions are primarily a feature of our inability to grasp or articulate divine perfection. This can become important, for instance, in discussions of salvation. A popular soteriological narrative speaks of a clash between God's justice and God's love, mercy, or goodness, which are reconciled by the atonement;[49] under the rubric of simplicity, such an opposing of two divine attributes must always be wrong.

There is a standard analytic "disproof" of divine simplicity that picks up on this use, while ignoring the warning concerning analogy above, and that thus illustrates the potential problems with recent perfect being theology. Simplicity, it is claimed, teaches that God is identical with his attributes, but if God is identical with his love, and God is identical with his omnipresence, it seems to follow that God's love is identical with God's omnipresence, which is obviously meaningless. The answer to this point is to insist on the partial, hesitant, and analogical nature of the language being used. Neat syllogisms like this one simply cannot be constructed out of analogical language.

This does not mean, of course, that the desire for conceptual clarity that lies at the heart of most recent analytical theology of religion is misplaced, only that there is a need to be aware of the limits of language, of the places where, as with Eunomius, precision in reference is a misleading pretense rather than a gain in clarity. As noted already, St. Thomas is an outstanding example

---

convincing, but for some criticisms, see Victor Salas, "The Ontology of Analogy in Aquinas: A Response to Laurence Hemming," *Heythrop Journal* 50 (2009): 635–47.

49. Consider Elizabeth Clephane's hymn, "Beneath the Cross of Jesus": "O safe and happy shelter, O refuge tried and sweet—O trysting place, where heaven's love and heaven's justice meet."

of how a drive for conceptual clarity and a proper appreciation of mystery can cheerfully coexist.[50]

The Perfections and the Doctrine of the Trinity

The desire to find some language that is not hesitant and analogical when applied to God goes wider than just the contemporary analytic tradition. As noted earlier in passing, much recent theology associated with what has become known as the "trinitarian revival" looks to categories of "person" and "relationship" as points of contact between the divine and the created.[51] This recognizably draws on the turn to the personal championed by Dorner and Forsyth, but with a crucial distinction: whereas for Dorner and Forsyth the perfection of personhood was found in the one God, for more recent writers, the ancient decision to term the three hypostases as "persons" has led to a willingness to apply modern (post-Romantic) accounts of personhood to Father, Son, and Spirit individually.[52] Each divine hypostasis is possessed of unassailable personal interiority, and in the loving sharing of this personal essence, God happens.

It is perhaps surprising that the problems raised by this radical redefinition of trinitarian doctrine for a doctrine of the divine attributes are more formal than material. It can still be held that God is perfectly just, good, omnipresent, eternal, and so on; the claim of the *Quincumque vult* (the Athanasian Creed) that "there are not three eternals, but one eternal" must be discarded, but this seems bearable to those who hold this doctrine. In popular presentation, it rather invites the ancient error that different divine persons instantiate different divine perfections (as when salvation is discussed in terms of a loving Son turning aside the wrath of a holy Father), but this can surely be guarded against with sufficient care.

Some particular attributes fare rather more badly under this sort of scheme: it is difficult to see how the doctrine of simplicity might be retained; aseity (the claim that God is self-caused; "*a se*") also becomes difficult: the Father might be *a se*, but Son and Spirit are, respectively, begotten of the Father and spirated by the Father (and the Son). These, however, are the impersonal, negative, metaphysical attributes that have so often been claimed to be Greek

---

50. For an excellent demonstration of this, see Karen E. Kilby, "Aquinas, the Trinity and the Limits of Understanding," *International Journal of Systematic Theology* 7 (2005): 414–27.

51. The classic statement of this case remains Zizioulas, *Being as Communion*. Many other studies have followed the same route, however.

52. Barth's desire to term the hypostases "modes of being" (*Seinsweisen*) rather than "persons" follows Dorner and is based precisely on a fear that this move might seem plausible because of the accident of language. See *CD* I/1, 351–60; see especially the small print discussing the views of Anton Günther and Richard Grützmacher on 357; see Dorner, *Christian Doctrine*, 1:410–11, 448–53.

accretions to the gospel, rather than authentic theological constructions. They have been jettisoned with as much alacrity as celebration by many recent theologians.

The most radical and yet most common version of this modern tradition makes a further move, however: having located the Son as a distinct personal being over against the Father, it seems natural to collapse the difficult and counterintuitive strictures of classical Christology, and to read the gospel narrative of the interactions of the Jewish man Jesus of Nazareth with the One he called Father as the history of the inner life of the Trinity.[53] This is in contrast to a Chalcedonian and later conciliar tradition that insisted that human actions—such as prayer or suffering—remained properties of the human nature, which was indissolubly united to the divine nature in the hypostatic union. So, for instance, we find the Cyrillian claim that "impassibly, he suffered in the flesh," or the so-called *extra Calvinisticum*, in fact merely a restatement of historic orthodoxy: the assertion that the divine Son did not cease to fill and rule the universe when he became incarnate.

If the human career of Jesus of Nazareth is the internal history of God, many of the traditional attributes must be radically redefined, or completely discarded. God's eternity might be retrievable, but only by a significantly revised account of what "eternity" is; Jesus of Nazareth, rather obviously, did not live his life in a timeless eternal now.[54] The passion of Christ becomes the suffering of a crucified God, and so divine impassibility must be done away with.[55] Immutability, similarly, is untenable if the gospel narratives are read in this way. The list could be extended.

What is noticeable, however, is that the list is composed entirely of the negative, metaphysical, or "Greek" attributes, which were already being relativized by Forsyth's insistence of God's holy personality, tested for logical coherence by analytic philosophers, and criticized by Harnackian accounts of history that stressed the differences between Hebrew and Hellenistic mind-sets. Over the last two centuries, the classical doctrine of the divine attributes has been subject to a "perfect storm" of seemingly unrelated challenges that have made it appear completely untenable to anyone without a clear grasp of the shifts in the history of ideas that have gone on. This can lead to a belief that the doctrine

53. See n10 in this chapter for some examples.

54. Barth's fascinating account of eternity, including the claim that eternity does not negate time, but encompasses it (*CD* II/1, 612), was moving in a rather different direction, but offered perhaps the beginnings of an invitation for a move like this.

55. The classic statement is Jürgen Moltmann, *The Crucified God* (London: SCM, 1974); for a telling defense of the traditional position, see Thomas G. Weinandy, *Does God Suffer?* (Edinburgh: T&T Clark, 2000). Impassibility has been one of the most challenged of the traditional attributes since 1945, with the (appropriate, of course) horror at the revelation of the depths of suffering in the Nazi concentration camps leading many, many theologians to insist that a denial of God's experience of suffering is now untenable. The argument is emotionally and rhetorically powerful, but logically lacking.

has had its day, even by fairly conservative theologians.[56] In this essay, I have attempted to sketch some of the revisionist proposals that have been offered to rescue and reconstruct the doctrine; I have also indicated what I regard as compelling reasons to discount each one of the challenges and to hold, with a degree at least of untroubled serenity, to the unfashionable doctrines of our scholastic forebears.

For Further Reading

Barth, Karl. *Church Dogmatics* II/1, secs. 29–31. Edinburgh: T&T Clark, 1957.

Bavinck, Herman. *Reformed Dogmatics*. Vol. 2, *God and Creation*, 95–255. Translated by John Vreind. Grand Rapids: Baker Academic, 2004.

Gunton, Colin E. *Act and Being: Towards a Theology of the Divine Attributes.* London: SCM, 2002.

Moltmann, Jürgen. *The Crucified God*. London: SCM, 1974.

Pannenberg, Wolfhart. *Systematic Theology*. Vol. 1, 337–448. Grand Rapids: Eerdmans, 1991.

Plantinga, Alvin. *Does God Have a Nature?* Milwaukee: Marquette University Press, 1980.

Rogers, Katherin A. *Perfect Being Theology*. Edinburgh: Edinburgh University Press, 2000.

Schleiermacher, Friedrich. *The Christian Faith*, 35, 79–85, 164–69. Translated by H. R. Mackintosh and J. S. Stewart. Edinburgh: T&T Clark, 1928.

Weinandy, Thomas G. *Does God Suffer?* Edinburgh: T&T Clark, 2000.

---

56. "The attempt now easily assumes a comic air. . . . It is absurd to ask What are God's (six? seven? or one hundred?) perfections? . . . What can be retained from the traditional doctrine is the attempt to state the method of deriving predicates for use with 'God' and the discussion of a sampling of cases." Robert W. Jenson, "The Triune God," in *Christian Dogmatics*, ed. Carl E. Braaten and Robert W. Jenson (Philadelphia: Fortress, 1984), 1:181.

4

. . .

SCRIPTURE AND HERMENEUTICS

Daniel J. Treier

Like it or not—and many moderns have not—all Christian theology inter-
acts with preceding tradition(s). Making sense of "modern" doctrines
accordingly requires beginning with perceptions of that "premodern"
perspective to which they respond. This is especially true for doctrines of
Scripture and approaches to hermeneutics (the study of human understanding, especially in the interpretation of texts). Many modern theologians define themselves through new, uniquely "critical" attention to concerns about
knowledge (epistemology). Indeed, this modern preoccupation with how we
know led to the very invention of "hermeneutics," as well as, arguably, to the
concept of a "doctrine" of Scripture. Thus, the present chapter basically tells
a story, narrating epistemological developments that influenced approaches
to Scripture over the last two centuries. However, the story also has a moral:
how we imagine the nature and importance of human redemption influences
how we understand the Bible—despite modern efforts to evade the classic
Christian concept of salvation.

Precursors

Premodern theologians generally did not argue for biblical authority as such,
but assumed it in preaching, catechizing, and so forth. Until the Protestant

Reformation, the Scriptures shaped church life as means of grace without much epistemological hand-wringing.[1] No doctrine of Scripture appears in the early creeds; even the canonical status of certain apocryphal books remained fuzzy until Protestants rejected them and Roman Catholics reacted by formally accepting them. Saint Augustine's *De doctrina christiana* was the dominant hermeneutical work for a millennium.[2]

Yet the humanist learning of the Renaissance along with the Reformation fractured the perceived unity of Scripture and tradition. Rival churches within the West increased rival claims to political authority as well. Revolts within and wars between nations had religious components.[3] Within the church, in addition to Protestant-Catholic polemics, arose Protestant fragmentation itself. Hence violence and skepticism set the context for Enlightenment rejection of churchly claims to divine revelation, in favor of appeals to universal reason. Reason and revelation had already begun to seem distinct as sources of knowledge in medieval scholasticism. Later Protestant scholastic theologies tended to frontload treatment of revelation, further highlighting epistemological starting points. Hence revelation and reason changed from distinct to separate or even opposite entities.[4] Scripture and tradition became rivals to each other's authority, threatening human freedom and social order; they also came to be treated as merely contingent cultural artifacts from particular historical settings.

Historical Criticism

Such treatment points to the first and most dominant precursor of modern biblical hermeneutics, "historical criticism," which "seeks to answer a basic question: to what historical circumstances does this text refer, and out of what

1. For a version of this story that rejects treating Scripture as an epistemological criterion for evaluating truth claims, see William J. Abraham, *Canon and Criterion in Christian Theology* (Oxford: Clarendon, 1999); William J. Abraham, Jason E. Vickers, and Natalie B. Van Kirk, *Canonical Theism: A Proposal for Theology and the Church* (Grand Rapids: Eerdmans, 2008).

2. Saint Augustine, *On Christian Teaching*, trans. R. P. H. Green (Oxford: Oxford University Press, 1997). Augustine explored the "use" of "things" as "signs" to know and "enjoy" God. Such a semiotic view has implications beyond the use of Scripture, for interpreting all of creation. This leads Oliver Davies to claim that "the consummate representative of a premodern Christian hermeneutic is not in fact a theologian but a writer," namely, Dante Alighieri with his *Divine Comedy* ("Hermeneutics," in *Oxford Handbook of Systematic Theology*, ed. John Webster, Kathryn Tanner, and Iain Torrance [Oxford: Oxford University Press, 2007], 499).

3. Enlightenment supporters often portray themselves pursuing universal reason while limiting religion for the sake of peace. William T. Cavanaugh, however, has contradicted this picture in *Theopolitical Imagination: Christian Practices of Space and Time* (London: T&T Clark, 2003).

4. This construal energizes "Radical Orthodoxy"; see especially John Montag, "Revelation: The False Legacy of Suárez," chap. 2 in *Radical Orthodoxy: A New Theology*, ed. John Milbank, Catherine Pickstock, and Graham Ward (New York: Routledge, 1999).

historical circumstances did it emerge?"[5] Lorenzo Valla's demonstration in 1440 that the *Donation of Constantine* was spurious, rather than an authentic fourth-century document, is a key marker in the movement toward newly critical study of history. But the challenge of historical criticism became acute for Scripture somewhat later, when figures such as Baruch Spinoza, Hermann Samuel Reimarus, and David Friedrich Strauss claimed to relegate the texts to purely human phenomena while rejecting their witness to divine revelation, miracles, and the like.

At that point historical criticism functioned as a worldview, not just a set of interpretative methods, and did battle royal with Augustinianism.[6] Augustine's representative teaching involved original sin and the resulting need for authority via government and church, along with divine providence. By contrast, historical criticism reflected the political project of classical, Enlightenment liberalism, in which the fundamental goal becomes the autonomy of the self. As liberal anthropology applies to biblical interpretation, the goal is an "objective outsider who exercises disinterested awareness, uncovers the facts, and pronounces final judgment."[7] The essence of "critical" study is each individual not taking for granted anyone else's say-so—at least the church's or the Bible's—whether regarding a text's meaning or a life's destiny.

For Baruch Spinoza (1632–1677) and Hermann Samuel Reimarus (1694–1768), the Bible's story could be reduced to political relationships, since "the essence of institutional religion is the priestly manipulation of the fear of the gods by means of dogma and ritual."[8] Historical criticism is necessary for ideological liberation of individuals to pursue their own ideals. These anthropological optimists seemed rebellious early in their pursuit of nonecclesiastical Christendom, but by 1900 they became the new establishment: cultural Protestantism, with private religion.[9] Despite a contrary minority tradition that sought to use historical-critical methods for churchly, even Augustinian ends,[10] three results of historical criticism dominated.

(1) *There emerged a separation of the Bible from dogma and theology.* Johann P. Gabler's 1787 lecture, "An Oration on the Proper Distinction between Biblical and Dogmatic Theology and the Specific Objectives of Each," provides a handy reference point. Gabler wanted to preserve the integrity of the primitive religious ideas of biblical writers. He distinguished religion from theology, and historically conditioned statements from timeless truths. The

5. Richard E. Burnett, "Historical Criticism," in *Dictionary for Theological Interpretation of the Bible*, ed. Kevin J. Vanhoozer (Grand Rapids: Baker Academic/London: SPCK, 2005), 290, dealing primarily with the broader, widely used sense of the term.
6. Roy A. Harrisville and Walter Sundberg, *The Bible in Modern Culture*, 2nd ed. (Grand Rapids: Eerdmans, 2002), 5.
7. Ibid.
8. Ibid., 332.
9. Ibid., 334.
10. Ibid., 336–37.

Bible contains both; "pure" biblical theology would differentiate between the pure ancient religion pointing to perennial truths and other, contemporary theological formulations. This would offer dogmatics a sure foundation.[11]

(2) *There emerged developmental accounts of biblical theology*, modeled on the Hegelian dialectic of thesis-antithesis-synthesis. An influential example would be F. C. Baur's construal of basic conflict between Petrine (more Jewish) and Pauline (more Greek) schools in the New Testament church, from which the synthesis of early Catholicism eventually emerged. These accounts presumed greater theological conflict than traditional Christianity allowed for, in addition to historical progression usually based on anthropological optimism. In other words, the apostles and biblical texts themselves conflict, but over time humans make intellectual and religious progress.

(3) *There also emerged tendencies toward a "Hellenization thesis,"* most notably in Adolf von Harnack's multivolume *History of Dogma*. In such accounts, Christian doctrine evolved from simpler Jewish forms toward more complex Greek ones. This could be seen as tragic, for it coincided with the development of ever-higher christologies leading to Nicaea and Chalcedon, affirming Jesus's full divinity. For many biblical scholars influenced by this, early Jewish simplicity has been equated with the purity of the "historical Jesus"—critically recovered—over against later dogmatic and liturgical accretions of the "Christ of faith."[12] Yet in the long run, evolutionary accounts of religion remained positive, with developments leading ultimately to the modern Western culture supported by the critical scholars themselves. On this paradigm, earlier, "Greek" dogmatic accretions had to be stripped away, but not in favor of Jewish concreteness. Rather, elements of Jesus had to be highlighted in which he lived and taught pure moral religion in accord with the modern fashions of universal reason and individual autonomy.

General Hermeneutics and the Liberal Tradition

The interface between historical criticism and such (supposedly universal) rational criteria points toward the modern development of "general"

---

11. C. Kavin Rowe and Richard B. Hays, "Biblical Studies," in Webster et al., *Oxford Handbook of Systematic Theology*, 441; for Gabler's text, see John Sandys-Wunsch and Laurence Eldredge, "J. P. Gabler and the Distinction between Biblical and Dogmatic Theology: Translation, Commentary, and Discussion of His Originality," *Scottish Journal of Theology* 33, no. 2 (1980): 133–58.

12. Many theologians further rue the tragedy of attributing the philosophically derived characteristics of an Unmoved Mover or Most Perfect Being to the God of Israel. Recent historical scholarship critiques the Hellenization thesis, although to explain why is beyond the scope of this essay. See, e.g., Paul L. Gavrilyuk, *The Suffering of the Impassible God: The Dialectics of Patristic Thought* (Oxford: Oxford University Press, 2006); Matthew Levering, *Scripture and Metaphysics: Aquinas and the Renewal of Trinitarian Theology* (Oxford: Blackwell, 2004); and other sources they reference.

hermeneutics. By highlighting the influence of culture in both directions, the Enlightenment created a fracture not only between the Bible and theology but also between the Bible and the Word of God.[13] The Bible's authority no longer lay in shaping theology, but rather in fostering a new concept, "culture": "As the Bible was separated from universal theological truth—and reconfigured as a particular cultural document—and as theology itself conformed to an ideal of religious culture, the nation in effect stepped in to guarantee the cohesiveness of (religious) community."[14] The political implications were quite specific for Jews: a paradigmatic thinker, Friedrich Schleiermacher, rarely preached from the Old Testament and thoroughly "excluded all Jewish custom and the entire Old Testament from the purview of Christian theology."[15]

Eventually these German developments exported themselves to England, where Sheehan likewise summarizes the trends: "toward a normative ideal of culture, toward a cultural Bible, toward a cultural religion, toward a sanitized Christianity."[16] As culture and Christianity became coextensive, they could also be seen as rivals—one rendering the other unnecessary. In the usual modern vision of secularization, "religion plays the role of the hapless onion, whose layers are constantly peeled away to make a secular soup."[17] Yet what actually occurred was productive transformation: the creation of the Bible-as-literature, the font of a "canon" of "Western culture." There was no simple modern turn to unbelief, but instead the creation of "religion" treated as a source that philology could study in charting a people's language and mind-set.

Though valorizing a particular culture, purveyors of the Enlightenment Bible nevertheless pursued a general account of human understanding; there was a developmental scale on which Western culture(s) ranked highly. Hans Frei helpfully explores this interface of general hermeneutics with historical criticism by way of Christology.[18] Premodern biblical interpretation, roughly until John Calvin, read the Gospels as "realistic narratives" depicting the identity of Jesus Christ as an acting subject. For classic, churchly interpreters, the "literal

13. Jonathan Sheehan, *The Enlightenment Bible: Translation, Scholarship, Culture* (Princeton: Princeton University Press, 2005), 90.

14. Ibid., 233.

15. Ibid., 234. Schleiermacher "seems only to have preached on the Old Testament when such texts were specifically stipulated for special worship services by order of the king" (Jeffrey Hensley, "Friedrich Schleiermacher," in *Christian Theologies of Scripture: A Comparative Introduction*, ed. Justin S. Holcomb [New York: New York University Press, 2006], 182n34). Immanuel Kant even spoke of the euthanasia of Judaism in favor of "pure moral religion," in *The Conflict of the Faculties*, trans. Mary J. Gregor (1798; repr., New York: Abaris, 1979), 95 (which I first discovered on a handout from J. Kameron Carter).

16. Sheehan, *Enlightenment Bible*, 255.

17. Ibid., 260.

18. See *The Eclipse of Biblical Narrative* (New Haven: Yale University Press, 1974), 104: "General (not theologically privileged) hermeneutics and biblical-historical criticism grew up together, and historical criticism by and large was the dominant partner."

sense" of the narratives and "historical reference" were identical; stories about miracles, for example, were about miracles, not abstract themes like hope or new life (with the events themselves being reinterpreted or denied). In other words, there was only one world—plotted by the biblical story line. Reading Scripture was done figurally (even for a literalist like Calvin): one found one's place in the symbolic world narrated by the text as a whole.

But the rise of modern historical consciousness meant that now there were two worlds—biblical history and actual history—needing correlation. Conservatives claimed that they matched (the biblical narrative became "historical" not just "realistic")—often trying to prove this case-by-case. For so-called liberals, the options became enormously complicated. Frei demonstrates that many, except for some empirically minded British deists, rejected historicity but rescued the narratives' religious value by relating Jesus Christ to some other conceptual scheme (such as morality or supreme God-consciousness).[19] Christian self-description lost out;[20] hermeneutics became the vehicle through which scholars rescued the Bible's truth by changing its meaning.

Not only did biblical stories no longer refer to actual happenings, but they also no longer cohered with each other. The canon splintered into numerous contextual fragments furthering interests of particular communities. Thus the church's approach changed, for liberals and conservatives alike. Classic figural reading meant reading biblical stories literally in a realistic sense and a canonical context. In a modern context, figural reading came to mean non-literal reading, while literal interpretation pursued grammatical and historical precision in individual contexts only.[21]

Friedrich Schleiermacher

As historical criticism became the arbiter of truth, it shaped what the texts could mean if they would have religious value. This leads us to study Schleiermacher and the twin traditions associated with him—general hermeneutics and liberal theology—in more detail. For historical criticism and apologetic responses gave crucial impetus to general hermeneutics vis-à-vis the Bible.[22]

In his dogmatic theology, Schleiermacher locates Scripture in the major portion devoted to consciousness of sin and grace, as an aspect of grace whereby the church subsists alongside the world. Holy Scripture is the first of six "essential and invariable features" of the church. Yet its authority *"cannot be the foundation of faith in Christ; rather must the latter be presupposed before*

19. Frei, "Biblical Hermeneutics and Religious Apologetics," chap. 6 in *Eclipse*, esp. 113–23.
20. See Hans W. Frei, *Types of Christian Theology*, ed. George Hunsinger and William C. Placher (New Haven: Yale University Press, 1992).
21. Frei, *Eclipse*, 7.
22. See especially ibid., 124.

a peculiar authority can be granted to Holy Scripture."[23] Proving Scripture's authority rationally would reserve it for an elite intellectual group, contradicting the universal possibility of faith as well as perhaps the element of faith in which one senses need for redemption. Like the apostles, we must believe in Christ before we can see Scripture in a particular way. Precautions must be taken "to avoid the impression that a doctrine must belong to Christianity because it is contained in Scripture, whereas in point of fact it is only contained in Scripture because it belongs to Christianity."[24]

Schleiermacher next explores biblical authority vis-à-vis theology: "The Holy Scriptures of the New Testament are, on the one hand, the first member in the series, ever since continued, of presentations of the Christian Faith; on the other hand, they are the norm for all succeeding presentations."[25] Note again the omission of the Old Testament. In fact, the church's historical development involves eradication of "Jewish and pagan views and maxims," for "their antagonism to the Christian spirit could only be recognized gradually."[26] Hence a distinction is necessary between the canonical and the apocryphal, even within Scripture itself: the apocryphal are elements of church presentations that must be purged; the canonical are elements that truly reflect "the living intuition of Christ." Authority is not uniform across the Scriptures, but proportional to the writers' attainment of canonical elements.

> Nor is it meant that every later presentation must be uniformly derived from the Canon or be germinally contained in it from the first. For since the Spirit was poured out on all flesh, no age can be without its own originality in Christian thinking. Yet, on the one hand, nothing can be regarded as a pure product of the Christian Spirit except so far as it can be shown to be in harmony with the original products; on the other, no later product possesses equal authority with the original writings when it is a question of guaranteeing the Christian character of some particular presentation or of exposing its unchristian elements.[27]

A balancing act ensues. Early, biblical presentations should contain the most deeply canonical elements. But the later, developed church should have purged more apocryphal elements in favor of a wider dispersion of the canonical. This principle applies to recognition of canonical books as well, even to "the different grades of normative authority to be conceded to particular portions of Scripture": "the judgment of the Church is only approximating ever more

23. Friedrich Schleiermacher, *The Christian Faith*, ed. H. R. Mackintosh and J. S. Stewart (London: T&T Clark, 1999), 591; emphasis in the original.
24. Ibid., 593.
25. Ibid., 594.
26. Ibid., 595.
27. Ibid., 596.

closely to a complete expulsion of the apocryphal and the pure preservation of the canonical."[28]

Therefore, "the peculiar inspiration of the Apostles is not something that belongs exclusively to the books of the New Testament. These books only share in it; and inspiration in this narrower sense, conditioned as it is by the purity and completeness of the apostolic grasp of Christianity, covers the whole of the official apostolic activity thence derived."[29] Schleiermacher's enemy throughout is an "utterly dead scholasticism" drawing lines of demarcation between the author or intention and the written word—even between Scripture and other books: "It at once follows that we must reject the suggestion that in virtue of their divine inspiration the sacred books demand a hermeneutical and critical treatment different from one guided by the rules which obtain elsewhere."[30] The apostles differ from later church presenters—even all other humans—not in kind but only in degree of intuition regarding revelation in Jesus Christ. If scholastic theologians could not agree on whether to tie inspiration to the impulse to write, the ideas formed, or the very words written, then why not relate it to the entirety of life?[31] The text is not the point anyway: "You are right to despise the paltry imitators who derive their religion wholly from someone else, or cling to a dead document by which they swear and from which they draw proof. *Every holy writing is merely a mausoleum of religion*, a monument that a great spirit was there that no longer exists."[32]

Hence general hermeneutics aimed to recover and celebrate the human spirit: as Benjamin Jowett put it in 1860, the Bible must be read like any other book.[33] In Schleiermacher's view—and the story is frequently told like this even today—premodern hermeneutics consisted chiefly in rules for solving particular problems of biblical interpretation. There was no larger philosophical framework correlating this activity with other cultural engagements.[34] Yet the human creative spirit lay at the core of Schleiermacher's interests. The

28. Ibid., 603.
29. Ibid., 599.
30. Ibid., 600.
31. See Harrisville and Sundberg, *Bible in Modern Culture*, 72n17.
32. Friedrich Schleiermacher, *On Religion: Speeches to Its Cultured Despisers*, trans. Richard Crouter (Cambridge: Cambridge University Press, 1988), 134 (emphasis added), cited in Sheehan, *Enlightenment Bible*, 229.
33. Benjamin Jowett, "On the Interpretation of Scripture," in *Essays and Reviews: The 1860 Text and Its Reading*, ed. Victor Shea and William Whitla (Charlottesville: University Press of Virginia, 2000), esp. 482.
34. This is somewhat questionable since premodern Christians only undertook biblical interpretation within a larger set of commitments about God and the world, as Augustine's *De doctrina christiana* illustrates (so Jens Zimmermann, *Recovering Theological Hermeneutics: An Incarnational-Trinitarian Theory of Interpretation* [Grand Rapids: Baker Academic, 2004], although he may overestimate the extent to which these qualify formally as "hermeneutics").

knowledge most interesting to him was shared intuition between friends;[35] he particularly cherished the feelings (not necessarily "emotions") arising in response to music.[36] This highlights the pivotal role of empathy with the author: associated with formulating the "hermeneutical circle" (movement back and forth between the part and the whole of a text to refine interpretation), Schleiermacher even proposed "understanding the author better than he understood himself," an archetypally Romantic notion of interpretation. The crucial goal was recognition of and shared participation in the unfolding of human genius. Schleiermacher was first to wrestle with "the theoretical and practical implications" of this set of problems:[37] the nature of what it means to understand anything at all, not just handling isolated misunderstanding; the need to address both grammatical and psychological dimensions of interpretation, understanding both a system of language and the author as its user in context; and so forth. The goal is reproducing the process of the author's thoughts, trying to enjoy the creative human spirit in action.

Because of this—universal?—focus on the particularity of the human spirit, "only historical interpretation can do justice to the rootedness of the New Testament authors in their time and place."[38] The phenomena are such that the Holy Spirit must have chosen not to produce Scripture in a "totally miraculous way"; instead "every element must be treated as purely human, and the action of the Spirit was only to produce the inner impulse."[39] Thus to honor the Spirit's work is to reject dogmatic imposition of assumptions about biblical inspiration, applying only general rules one would use for any text.[40]

After Schleiermacher

Despite disagreements, Schleiermacher set the paradigmatic terms for decades—particularly in the German university, where hermeneutics became a way of rejuvenating the humanities, relative to the natural sciences, as sources for knowledge.[41] One version of the story highlights "the difference between understanding the subject matter of a text (Hegel) and understanding the

35. Anthony C. Thiselton, *New Horizons in Hermeneutics* (Grand Rapids: Zondervan, 1992), 210.

36. See Friedrich Schleiermacher, *Christmas Eve: Dialogue on the Incarnation*, trans. Terrence N. Tice (Richmond: John Knox, 1967).

37. Thiselton, *New Horizons*, 204.

38. Friedrich Schleiermacher, *Hermeneutics: The Handwritten Manuscripts*, AAR Texts and Translations, ed. Heinz Kimmerle, trans. James Duke and Jack Forstman (Missoula, MT: Scholars Press, 1977), 1:104.

39. Ibid., 106.

40. Ibid., 107.

41. To explore hermeneutical discussions see Kurt Mueller-Vollmer, ed., *The Hermeneutics Reader* (New York: Continuum, 1989).

subjectivity of the text's author (Schleiermacher)."[42] In many ways this is an early form of the distinction between Edmund Husserl's (Schleiermacher) and Martin Heidegger's (Hegel) traditions of phenomenology (a philosophical approach focusing on the structure and contents of consciousness). For Schleiermacher/Husserl, transcendental interpretation moves backward to share an author's mind-set; for Hegel/Heidegger, ontological hermeneutics moves forward to appropriate a text in a new historical moment. Hans-Georg Gadamer (1900–2002), the twentieth century's most influential hermeneutical philosopher, favored the latter, ontological tradition, as do most Christian literary scholars today, though many caricature and wrongly neglect Schleiermacher.[43] The literary trend warns against

> a type of theology that wants to adopt only a historical attitude toward religion; [this type of theology] has an abundance of cognition, though only of a historical kind. This cognition is no concern of ours, for if the cognition were merely historical, we would have to compare such theologians with countinghouse clerks, who keep the ledgers and accounts of other people's wealth, a wealth that passes through their hands without their retaining any of it, clerks who act only for others without acquiring assets of their own.[44]

Following the path of Hegel and Heidegger rather than Schleiermacher and Husserl, Gadamer criticizes the modern obsession with methodological clarity and scientific certainty. Instead, truth happens in events of disclosure.[45] Interpretation is not just a scientific enterprise in which we "explain" the text or its origin and determine meaning on that basis. To "understand" a text involves existential application in particular contexts.

Yet Gadamer is no relativist, as analogies illustrate. Reading a text is like playing a game: certain actions only become meaningful within context; one responds within the play instead of endlessly analyzing every move in isolation. Similarly, texts act upon us in ways that influence possibilities for response; meaning arises without waiting for our separate initiative as human subjects. We respond within the flow of encountering the text rather than acting upon a neutral object. Focus on application does not mean we can or should do to a text anything we want. There is a form of objectivity the text exerts upon us.

Reading a text is also like having a conversation: the text "speaks" and we respond, or we ask a question for the text to answer. Negotiation occurs between the "horizons" of the text and the reader as to what the subject matter

42. Gerald L. Bruns, *Hermeneutics Ancient and Modern* (New Haven: Yale University Press, 1995), 152.

43. Thiselton, *New Horizons*, 23, 197, 204–36, 267, 558–61.

44. G. W. F. Hegel, *Lectures on the Philosophy of Religion*, trans. R. F. Brown (Berkeley: University of California Press, 1984), 1:128, quoted in Bruns, *Hermeneutics*, 150.

45. Hans-Georg Gadamer, *Truth and Method*, trans. Joel Weinsheimer and Donald G. Marshall, 2nd ed. (New York: Continuum, 1989).

of the conversation will be. A "fusion of horizons" results: overlap between what the text addresses and what the reader seeks in an existential situation. Again, the text has its say, while a dimension of understanding remains relative to the later context.

Of course, we do not simply leap from our horizon back over intervening history into the author's horizon or the text's original context. A text generates a "history of effects" (*Wirkungsgeschichte*) accumulating through language and affecting subsequent readings—intentionally or unintentionally, for good or ill. This traditioning process links us back to the text itself and those elements of its context carried along through history. Hence, for example, one can no longer read Rom. 4 on "justification by faith" apart from Luther's influence. Even if one has never heard of Luther, nevertheless his interpretation of Paul so shaped Western culture that translations and linguistic connotations of words bear its marks.

Gadamer's recovery of understanding as responsive agency within the flow of history has been inspirational to many, rescuing texts from certain kinds of historicism and scientism. However, others—from critical theorists like Jürgen Habermas to "postmodern" deconstructionists like Jacques Derrida—have rejected Gadamer's thought, viewing it as naively positive about tradition and/ or entirely too negative about critical methodologies. In any case, it is clear that to some degree "the hermeneutical circle . . . is never purely philological, that is, it is not simply an exegetical movement between the parts and the whole of a text that is present before us as an object. Instead, it is an ontological movement between the text and our situation as interpreters of it."[46]

Subsequently, Paul Ricoeur (1913–2005) mediated between various approaches.[47] Ricoeur speaks of a threefold hermeneutical arc: an initial moment of *understanding* (a first, naive encounter with the text), a critical moment of *explanation*, and then a refigured moment of *application* (a "second naïveté"). Upon hearing a biblical parable, for instance, a person might be existentially grabbed by how God's grace creates new possibilities for authentic living. But this "understanding" needs to be subject to "explanation," a critical moment that involves not merely suspicion about societal power structures, but also very careful exegetical study. Finally, though, a "hermeneutic of trust" must be more fundamental than the necessary critical "suspicion," and so application becomes possible alongside explanation. The regulating prin-

46. Bruns, *Hermeneutics*, 4.
47. See Dan R. Stiver, "Method," and Kevin J. Vanhoozer, "Ricoeur, Paul," in *Dictionary for Theological Interpretation of the Bible*, 510–12, 692–95. Most relevant to biblical hermeneutics are Paul Ricoeur, *Essays on Biblical Interpretation*, ed. Lewis S. Mudge (Philadelphia: Fortress, 1980); *Figuring the Sacred: Religion, Narrative, and Imagination*, ed. Mark I. Wallace, trans. David Pellauer (Minneapolis: Fortress, 1995); André Lacocque and Paul Ricoeur, *Thinking Biblically: Exegetical and Hermeneutical Studies*, trans. David Pellauer (Chicago: University of Chicago Press, 1998).

ciple is not recovery of the original context or the author's intention(s), but the text's "sense" (semantic features especially—words, grammar, and such) enabling "reference" to reality by projecting a "world" to inhabit—a way of living. Ricoeur's importance lies not only in rejuvenating elements of Schleiermacher's hermeneutical legacy, but also in attending specifically to biblical interpretation.[48]

We can draw together the threads here by noting that Schleiermacher is father not only of general hermeneutics but also of modern ("liberal") theology. The two coincide regarding anthropology, focusing on the human spirit. Schleiermacher reconfigured Christian teaching to acknowledge Kant's critical epistemological turn, while addressing the concerns of his artistic friends that this turn reduced all of cultural life to low-level morality available to universal reason. Thus Schleiermacher described Christian faith as a particular form of "religion" treated as a distinct, universal locus of human experience—concerned with a "feeling of absolute dependence":

> God is immediately present to the human subject, but not isolatable as an object of direct thought. Rather, God is "co-given" with our experience of the world and ourselves. Any theological statements we might make are *post facto* rationalizations of such co-givenness in experience, because what is co-given remains essentially beyond or above reason.
>
> What unites the various strands of the liberal Protestant project—whether historically, rationally, or experientially based claims to discern God's being and truth—is the conviction that access to the divine is in one way or another a natural phenomenon.[49]

David Tracy offers a prominent, more recent, and Roman Catholic exemplar of this project. Influenced by Gadamer and Ricoeur among others, he treats Scripture as a "classic" text shaping moments of imaginative possibility as Shakespeare might.[50] Liberal theologies ever since, however much they vary from Schleiermacher's particulars, tend to share the mix of historical criticism and philosophical commitment according to which Christian faith correlates with something culturally universal.[51]

48. For an overview of general hermeneutics vis-à-vis Scripture, see Anthony C. Thiselton, "Biblical Studies and Theoretical Hermeneutics," in *Cambridge Companion to Biblical Interpretation*, ed. John Barton (Cambridge: Cambridge University Press, 1998), 95–113, and Thiselton, "Biblical Interpretation," in *The Modern Theologians: An Introduction to Christian Theology since 1918*, ed. David Ford with Rachel Muers, 3rd ed. (Oxford: Blackwell, 2005), 287–304.
49. Ben Quash, "Revelation," in Webster et al., *Oxford Handbook of Systematic Theology*, 329.
50. For an overview, see David Tracy, "Theological Method," in *Christian Theology: An Introduction to Its Traditions and Tasks*, ed. Peter C. Hodgson and Robert H. King, 2nd ed. (Minneapolis: Fortress, 1994), 35–60. Tracy speaks of "mutually critical correlations" between interpretations of the text and culture.
51. In Frei's pungent words, "Modern mediating theology gives an impression of constantly building, tearing down, rebuilding, and tearing down again the same edifice" (*Eclipse*, 129).

Early Dogmatic Responses

Conservative dogmatic responses reaffirmed the respective post-Reformation theologies of the Western churches.[52] For the Roman Catholic Church, the First Vatican Council (1869–1870) reaffirmed the pope's recent *Syllabus of Errors*, in which various Enlightenment-style ideologies were rejected. The council also formalized papal infallibility, in which the pope cannot err when speaking *ex cathedra*—definitively for the whole church on faith and morals. Although this occurred sparingly—only twice, concerning Marian dogmas—its formalization set the church's face against modernity while setting in stone a strong role for tradition and the magisterium vis-à-vis Scripture.

Protestants likewise strengthened affirmations of infallibility, yet pertaining to Scripture itself. Princeton theologian Charles Hodge began his *Systematic Theology*, completed in 1873, by treating theology as a science dealing with facts about God, all contained in the Scriptures. After critiquing rationalism, mysticism, and the Roman Catholic magisterium, Hodge expounded the Protestant rule of faith. Among the "adverse theories" opposed was Schleiermacher's. Hodge affirmed the infallibility of Scripture because it is the Word of God by inspiration, which "was an influence of the Holy Spirit on the minds of certain select men, which rendered them the organs of God for the infallible communication of his mind and will. They were in such a sense the organs of God, that what they said God said."[53] This divine influence is distinct from general providence and personal spiritual illumination, as well as revelation—which all may have occurred before the writing of the knowledge by inspiration, or not at all when writers were without new, direct divine knowledge.

Hodge appealed to the usual proofs such as 2 Pet. 1:21 and 2 Tim. 3:16, plus 1 Thess. 2:13, where the apostolic message is indeed God's Word. "Infallibility" is repeatedly equated with this "divine authority" of Scripture's teaching. All its books are alike infallible, in all content, not just in "moral and religious truths."[54] Inspiration is thus "plenary" as well as "verbal," dealing with all the words, not just ideas that could be abstracted from them. Hodge suggested that many object to this doctrine because they reject the very possibility of providence—a personal God exhaustively ordering world affairs while making creaturely action meaningful.[55] Nevertheless, God's influence did not obliterate human peculiarities.

52. Eastern Orthodox churches treat Scripture as a primary aspect of tradition, composed further of ecumenical councils (also infallible), the Sacred Liturgy, and so forth. These churches have largely not developed systematic theologies in the Western sense, often claiming thereby to bypass modernity. Thus they have not undertaken the sort of epistemological definition characteristic of the subject of this essay.
53. Charles Hodge, *Systematic Theology* (Grand Rapids: Eerdmans, 1993), 1:154.
54. Ibid., 163.
55. Ibid., 168.

Hodge acknowledged apparent contradictions within Scripture, plus between Scripture and history or science. Yet few alleged errors remain without reasonable explanation, and "no sane man would deny that the Parthenon was built of marble, even if here and there a speck of sandstone should be detected in its structure."[56] Moreover, we must always distinguish both between present theories and actual facts, and between biblical teaching itself and our interpretations.

In 1881 Benjamin Breckinridge Warfield, another Princeton theologian, coauthored a defense of biblical inerrancy with Hodge's son. He continued to defend tirelessly the understanding of scriptural authority he found consistent with Calvinism, the Westminster Confession of Faith, and ultimately the heritage of the church.[57] On the European continent, L. Gaussen of Geneva defended a similar view as early as 1840.[58] The German Isaak Dorner exemplified a relatively conservative, mediating view that nevertheless restricted biblical infallibility to the spiritual message within the author's revealed vision.[59]

Karl Barth, "Neo-Orthodoxy," and the "New Hermeneutic"

Between liberalism and evangelicalism stands Karl Barth, arguably the twentieth century's greatest theologian. In 1915, as a pastor, Barth was distressed that the liberal verities of his teachers did not help him preach, and that those very theologians supported the German war effort. Beginning to rediscover the Bible, he launched his Romans commentary, famously labeled a "bombshell dropped on the playground of the theologians." Many have viewed Barth's *Der Römerbrief* not really as a commentary, but as a virtuoso performance of theology or spiritualized interpretation. Yet, in his original preface, Barth wrote that "if we rightly understand ourselves, our problems are the problems of Paul." He affirmed that "the historical-critical method of Biblical investigation has its rightful place," though he acknowledged, "Were I driven to choose between it and the venerable doctrine of Inspiration, I should without hesitation adopt the latter, which has a broader, deeper, more important justification."[60]

---

56. Ibid., 170.

57. The most relevant articles were published posthumously as *The Inspiration and Authority of the Bible*, ed. Samuel G. Craig (Philadelphia: Presbyterian and Reformed, 1948).

58. *La Théopneustie, ou pleine inspiration des saintes écritures*, published in English as *The Inspiration of the Holy Scriptures* (Chicago: Moody, 1949).

59. See *A System of Christian Doctrine*, trans. Alfred Cave and J. S. Banks (Edinburgh: T&T Clark, 1888), 2:196. Dorner affirmed the authors' full humanity by suggesting that in inspiration they do not lose self- or God-consciousness but only perhaps aspects of world-consciousness (184–85). Inspiration is a process happening to the writers before it affects their writings; the difference between what happens to these writers and the illumination of later Christians is not a matter of degree, but of mediation—the biblical writers are progenitors for others (191).

60. Karl Barth, preface to the first edition, in Karl Barth, *The Epistle to the Romans*, trans. Edwyn C. Hoskyns, 6th ed. (Oxford: Oxford University Press, 1933), 1. His retention of historical criticism is emphasized in Bruce L. McCormack, "Historical-Criticism and Dogmatic Interest in

It is not as if Barth was unaware of hermeneutical developments. Yet Barth emphasized exegesis, dealing with the actual content—a principle apparently held for all texts, not just Scripture.[61] According to Richard Burnett, four commitments follow. First, Barth focused on the "subject matter" or "substance" of the text as having hermeneutical control. Hence, second, he held that one must enter into or participate in its meaning. The starting point is theological rather than anthropological: we do not read "religiously," as a practice located in a pious feature of generic humanity; instead of conjuring empathy for the author's mind-set, we respond to divine gift. Third, then, one must read "with more attention and love" than do the modern scientists, the mere historical critics. Fourth, Barth insisted "upon a reading of the Bible that is more in accordance with 'the meaning of the Bible itself.'"[62]

Barth kept the Bible's language and content together, instead of using hermeneutics as a justification for moving behind the text or translating its words into general, rational principles held on other grounds. This is not to deny the importance of textual criticism in particular.[63] Still, historical criticism is only preparatory for interpretation: servant, not master. The subject matter must have freedom to speak. Therefore, Barth prioritized paraphrase: what the text says must be restated in other words, making use of concepts contemporary to the interpreter. For Barth the model exegete is Calvin, however different their work might appear to us. From Calvin we learn a type of criticism that takes the humanity of the biblical text seriously, though keeping its subject matter primary.[64]

Barth's innovative doctrines of revelation and Scripture are additionally striking. Despite the modern scandal over its (ir)rationality, Barth embraced trinitarian theology with revelation as its root. God as the subject of revelation (Revealer) is the Father; God as the act of revelation itself (Revealed) is the Son; God as the effect of revelation (Revealedness) is the Holy Spirit. As self-revealing, God is identical with his Word so that revelation is not a minus or an other from God but a repetition. This Word takes a threefold form: the

---

Karl Barth's Theological Exegesis of the New Testament," *Lutheran Quarterly* 5, n. s. (Summer 1991): 211–25, though complicated in practice (Mary Kathleen Cunningham, "Karl Barth," in Holcomb, *Christian Theologies of Scripture*, 183–201).

61. Richard E. Burnett, *Karl Barth's Theological Exegesis: The Hermeneutical Principles of the Römerbrief Period* (Grand Rapids: Eerdmans, 2004), 64.

62. Ibid., 221.

63. See, e.g., Barth's preface to the second edition, in Barth, *Epistle to the Romans*, 6–7.

64. Burnett, *Karl Barth's Theological Exegesis*, chap. 6. Romans was by no means Barth's only biblical preoccupation. Not only is his *Church Dogmatics* saturated with scriptural exegesis (studies of which continue to increase), but Barth also taught courses on numerous biblical texts and held a combined chair in Dogmatics and New Testament Exegesis for a time. See Bruce L. McCormack, "The Significance of Karl Barth's Theological Exegesis of Philippians," in Karl Barth, *Epistle to the Philippians: 40th Anniversary Edition*, trans. James W. Leitch (Louisville: Westminster John Knox, 2002), v–vi.

Word revealed is Jesus Christ; the Word written is Scripture; and then the Word is preached in various ways. This means that there is only indirect identity between Scripture and the Word of God, which is preeminently Jesus Christ, God himself personally; Scripture becomes the Word of God when made effective by the Holy Spirit. Yet the identity is real: Barth's only analogy for this is the Triune God, with the three forms corresponding to three persons.[65]

Indirect identity accords with the dialectical nature of revelation. On one hand, revelation unveils—God making himself known to humans via creaturely media, ultimately taking human nature in Jesus Christ. Yet revelation simultaneously veils—to the degree that finite, creaturely form is involved, humans cannot fully grasp thereby what God, their Creator, is like. Quite apart from the difficulties of recognizing Jesus's true identity, those to whom he came could not have fully grasped the character of the Infinite, obscured in human form: "We ought to speak of God. We are human, however, and so cannot speak of God. We ought therefore to recognize both our obligation and our inability and by that very recognition give God the glory."[66]

Proponents of verbal, plenary inspiration predictably objected. Cornelius Van Til of Westminster Seminary, heir of the Hodge-Warfield legacy, wrote an acerbic critique that shaped evangelical responses for decades.[67] Barth was on this view a purveyor of existential encounter. Such evangelicals rightly recognized that Barth did not hold biblical inerrancy in their fashion. However, they did not understand Barth's approach to ontology, in which something becomes what it is by divine acts in relation; thus Barth could say that Scripture is the Word of God in a sense.[68] A fairer criticism might have opposed Barth's too strongly stressing the Protestant principle that the finite is incapable of the infinite: God's freedom need not preclude the characteristic bond with the Word of God that Scripture claims for itself.[69]

65. See Karl Barth, *Church Dogmatics*, trans. G. W. Bromiley (Edinburgh: T&T Clark, 1975), I/1, esp. 121.

66. Karl Barth, "The Word of God and the Task of the Ministry," in *The Word of God and the Word of Man*, trans. Douglas Horton (London: Hodder & Stoughton, 1928), 186.

67. Cornelius Van Til, *Christianity and Barthianism* (Grand Rapids: Baker, 1962).

68. Bruce L. McCormack, "The Being of Holy Scripture Is in Becoming: Karl Barth in Conversation with American Evangelical Criticism," in *Evangelicals and Scripture: Tradition, Authority and Hermeneutics*, ed. Vincent Bacote, Laura C. Miguélez, and Dennis L. Okholm (Downers Grove, IL: InterVarsity, 2004), 55–75. Christology is distinctly important: "If it would be wrong to say of the humanity of Jesus Christ that it is, as such, the *direct* revelation of God (and on the soil of Reformed Christology, Barth had to refute this possibility), then how can we say this of Scripture?" (63).

69. Evangelicals need not reject the idea that Scripture is a witness to revelation; McCormack highlights Warfield's own qualitative distinction between Jesus Christ as revelation and other means (62–63). Instead debate should focus on whether to discuss the Bible "as such" and then adopt "dynamic infallibilism," as McCormack terms it—whether one should thereby hold irresistible grace and an actualistic approach to ontology. G. C. Berkouwer questions Barth's critique of the traditional view as static and his association of God's Word with miracle, believing that

Some liberals, too, overemphasized the dialectical, apparently existential elements of Barth's doctrine of Scripture. From both sides he was labeled "neo-orthodox" along with several others—whether in celebration or derision.[70] While there were allies such as Dietrich Bonhoeffer in the composition of the Barmen Declaration, affirming the authority of Christ according to Scripture over against Hitler's German state, there were hardly any theologians in comprehensive agreement with Barth.

Another important thinker, Rudolf Bultmann, further illustrates why the family label "neo-orthodox" is inappropriate. Bultmann famously asked, "Is exegesis without presuppositions possible?" If this means without presupposing the results of one's exegesis, then his answer was yes. But no exegete is a *tabula rasa*, or blank slate; every exegete approaches a text with questions, at minimum with specific ways of raising questions, and thus with some concept of what the text addresses. Moreover, "the one presupposition that cannot be dismissed is *the historical method* of interrogating the text."[71] This means that history has unity as a closed system of causes and effects; while free human decisions prevent this history from simply operating in law-like fashion, nevertheless, even human effects have causes to explore in terms of motives.

Historical science, according to Bultmann, must translate biblical texts, mired in mythological assertions, into their real content. Myth objectifies authentic human reality (which Bultmann understood in terms of his colleague Heidegger's existential philosophy) and dramatizes it in otherworldly terms. Thus "demythologization" is required to peel off the mythological husk of biblical material and get to the kernel of *kerygma* underneath—God's gospel message proclaiming to humans their need for authentic existence. "History as a factual science cannot, as the biblical scriptures do, speak of the intervening activity of God in the course of history. It can only perceive belief in God's activity, but not God Himself, as a historical phenomenon."[72] Since God is not an objectifiable worldly phenomenon, we can only speak of God via understanding our own existence.

Apparent similarities between Barth and Bultmann concern this dialectical reality, the human inability to objectify God. But Barth believed in a

---

this overemphasizes divine hiddenness and minimizes the Old Testament (*Modern Uncertainty and Christian Faith* [Grand Rapids: Eerdmans, 1953], esp. 17–18).

70. See, e.g., Douglas John Hall, *Remembered Voices: Reclaiming the Legacy of "Neo-Orthodoxy"* (Louisville: Westminster John Knox, 1998). But Barth apparently disavowed the concept: "As I see it, Evangelical Germany will sooner or later have to see another dividing and regrouping directed no less against Bultmann than Communism; and it may be—but who can say?—that the *Church Dogmatics* will have some part to play in this respect. At any rate, if it is read with understanding it will not contribute either in Germany or elsewhere to the formation of a 'Neo-Orthodoxy'" (preface [1950], *Church Dogmatics* III/3, xii).

71. Rudolf Bultmann, "Is Exegesis without Presuppositions Possible?" in Mueller-Vollmer, *Hermeneutics Reader*, 243; emphasis in the original.

72. Rudolf Bultmann, "The Problem of Demythologizing," in Mueller-Vollmer, *Hermeneutics Reader*, 252.

transcendent element of divine revelation, having to do with the freedom of a personal God, in a way that Bultmann did not. Over time this became clear, as Bultmann's New Testament scholarship promoted form criticism. According to his version, we cannot use the Bible to know anything about Jesus himself but only to study forms of the faith of the church. Actual knowledge about Jesus would thwart the existential demand for faith. Bultmann's legacy helped to foster the "New Hermeneutic," which blended emphasis on hearing the Word of God with literary "New Criticism," in which the text must be studied structurally without regard to authorial intention.[73] Though profound in New Testament scholarship for a time, Bultmann's influence now seems to be fading.[74] Barth, meanwhile, considerably galvanized contemporary "postliberalism" and "theological interpretation of Scripture."

Vatican II

Loosely parallel to Barth's creative reappropriation of classic Protestant tradition, twentieth-century Catholic theologians undertook *ressourcement*, recovering the church fathers and their Scripture-soaked theology over against more rigid, arid versions of scholastic Thomism. Henri de Lubac recovered the precritical approach to spiritual exegesis in particular.[75] These theologians were not uncontroversial, appearing initially to threaten the stability of the church's rejection of the Enlightenment.[76]

Eventually, though, they paved the way for the Second Vatican Council (1962–1965). Concerning Scripture, the important result was *Dei Verbum*, the *Dogmatic Constitution on Divine Revelation*. The document reaffirmed the church's emerging openness to careful use of historical-critical methods and its newly promoted use of vernacular Bible translations. Its doctrine of biblical inspiration appears traditional, containing a hint of inerrancy, although without the prominence or complexity of the evangelical concept.[77]

---

73. For an excellent snapshot of the New Hermeneutic see Francis Watson, "The Scope of Hermeneutics," in *The Cambridge Companion to Christian Doctrine*, ed. Colin E. Gunton (Cambridge: Cambridge University Press, 1997), 66. See also Watson's "The Bible," in *The Cambridge Companion to Karl Barth*, ed. John Webster (Cambridge: Cambridge University Press, 2000), 57–71.

74. A defender of Bultmann's instincts—along with Schleiermacher and Ricoeur—over against Barth is Werner Jeanrond, *Theological Hermeneutics: Development and Significance* (New York: Crossroad, 1991).

75. Henri de Lubac, *Exégèse Médiévale: Les Quatre Sense de l'Écriture*, 4 vols. (Paris: Aubier, 1959–1964). The first three volumes have been translated into English as *Medieval Exegesis: The Four Senses of Scripture* (Grand Rapids: Eerdmans, 1998, 2000, 2009).

76. See Fergus Kerr, *Twentieth-Century Catholic Theologians* (Oxford: Blackwell, 2007).

77. See *Dei Verbum* 3.12, available online at the Vatican website, http://www.vatican.va/archive/hist_councils/ii_vatican_council/documents/vat-ii_const_19651118_dei-verbum_en.html.

A crucial development concerns the relation between Scripture and tradition. The Council of Trent had been seen as teaching a "two-source theory," with some beliefs or practices taught by Scripture and others by tradition. Vatican II seemingly reinterpreted Trent in favor of a "one-source theory" that starts more clearly where Barth does: with Jesus Christ as divine Revelation.[78] Scripture is the inspired verbal witness to this Word, which tradition faithfully hands down:

> 9. Hence there exists a close connection and communication between sacred tradition and Sacred Scripture. For both of them, flowing from the same divine wellspring, in a certain way merge into a unity and tend toward the same end. . . . Therefore both sacred tradition and Sacred Scripture are to be accepted and venerated with the same sense of loyalty and reverence.
>
> 10. Sacred tradition and Sacred Scripture form one sacred deposit of the word of God, committed to the Church. . . . But the task of authentically interpreting the word of God, whether written or handed on, has been entrusted exclusively to the living teaching office of the Church, whose authority is exercised in the name of Jesus Christ.[79]

Insofar as tradition does not constitute a fully independent source, this is a more Protestant-friendly position, although still rejecting *sola scriptura*.[80] Nevertheless, Catholics have continued to engage the Bible, critical scholarship, and ecumenical opportunities in new ways during the ensuing decades.

Evangelical Debates over Biblical Inerrancy[81]

Evangelicals such as Carl F. H. Henry likewise maintained the identity of the Bible with God's Word along with the "propositional" character of divine revelation: Scripture contains cognitive content, claims that are either true or false.[82]

78. Two-source versus one-source is a model influenced by Heiko A. Oberman's discussion of Tradition I and Tradition II in *The Harvest of Medieval Theology: Gabriel Biel and the Late Medieval Nominalism* (Grand Rapids: Baker Academic, 2000), chap. 11. On Trent's debate see Donald S. Prudlo, "Scripture and Theology in Early Modern Catholicism," in Holcomb, *Christian Theologies of Scripture*, 143.

79. *Dei Verbum* 2.9–10.

80. For a summary of developments, see Avery Cardinal Dulles, SJ, "Revelation, Scripture, and Tradition," in *Your Word Is Truth: A Project of Evangelicals and Catholics Together*, ed. Charles Colson and Richard John Neuhaus (Grand Rapids: Eerdmans, 2002), 35–58; on *sola scriptura*, see Thomas G. Guarino, "Catholic Reflections on Discerning the Truth of Sacred Scripture," in *Your Word Is Truth*, 79–101.

81. Portions of this section depend upon Daniel J. Treier, "Scripture and Hermeneutics," in *The Cambridge Companion to Evangelical Theology*, ed. Timothy Larsen and Daniel J. Treier (Cambridge: Cambridge University Press, 2007), 35–49.

82. Carl F. H. Henry, *God, Revelation, and Authority*, 6 vols. (Waco, TX: Word, 1976–1983); for a more contemporary formulation balancing the propositional and personal, the fixed and

At best (admittedly with popular aberrations), evangelicals reject a "dictation" theory of inspiration, in which God directly communicates every word as if the writers were nothing more than impersonal divine pens. God communicates through human investigation and structuring of material (e.g., Luke 1:1–4), linguistic styles (e.g., compare Mark and Hebrews), personalities and histories (e.g., psalms, apocalypses, and prophetic writings), and so on. For many, an analogy between the "living Word" Jesus Christ and the written Word seems helpful: the Son is fully God yet embraces full humanity; likewise Scripture's fully divine revelation is spoken by fully embracing human communication.

Yet the comprehensive nature of inspiration became a matter of debate again in the middle of the twentieth century. From Princetonian roots, many conservative Protestants committed themselves to the Bible's "inerrancy," which continued as the self-understanding of new evangelicals such as Henry when, in the 1940s, they revived that label to redirect fundamentalism. Controversy ensued in the 1960s, however, when the flagship evangelical seminary, Fuller, revised its doctrinal statement to allow for limited inerrancy—Scripture is infallible on matters of faith and practice, but possibly in error concerning history, science, and the like—with some faculty influenced by their understanding of Barth. In the 1970s, as the "battle for the Bible" intensified, Jack Rogers and Donald McKim asserted that a form of this limited inerrancy position was the closest contemporary heir of traditional Protestantism.[83] John Woodbridge of Trinity Evangelical Divinity School (revitalized as an academically rigorous, inerrantist alternative to Fuller) responded with a rejection of their work on historical grounds.[84] Meanwhile, the International Council on Biblical Inerrancy produced the "Chicago Statement," which defined this aspect of the doctrine of Scripture for many American evangelicals.

The inerrancy of Scripture means "that when all the facts become known, they will demonstrate that the Bible in its original autographs and correctly interpreted is entirely true and never false in all it affirms, whether that relates to doctrine or ethics or to the social, physical, or life sciences."[85] It does not, however, require the Bible to speak with technical precision that excludes phenomenological description; to contain verbatim quotation of the Old Testament

---

the dynamic, see Kevin J. Vanhoozer, "God's Mighty Speech-Acts: The Doctrine of Scripture Today," in *A Pathway into the Holy Scripture*, ed. Philip E. Satterthwaite and David F. Wright (Grand Rapids: Eerdmans, 1994), 143–81.

83. Harold Lindsell, *The Battle for the Bible* (Grand Rapids: Zondervan, 1976); Jack B. Rogers and Donald K. McKim, *The Authority and Interpretation of the Bible: An Historical Approach* (San Francisco: Harper & Row, 1979).

84. John Woodbridge, *Biblical Authority: A Critique of the Rogers/McKim Proposal* (Grand Rapids: Zondervan, 1982). Thomas Buchan argues that all three books—Lindsell, Rogers/ McKim, Woodbridge—reflect forms of anachronism in "Inerrancy as Inheritance? Competing Genealogies of Biblical Authority," in Bacote et al., *Evangelicals and Scripture*, 42–54.

85. Paul D. Feinberg, "Bible, Inerrancy and Infallibility of," in *Evangelical Dictionary of Theology*, ed. Walter A. Elwell, 2nd ed. (Grand Rapids: Baker, 2001), 156.

in the New or literalist agreement between parallel accounts; or to lack unclear passages, recording of sinful acts or errant claims, quotations from noninspired authors, or historical perspective. Inerrancy certainly does not extend to interpretations of Scripture, and therefore does not imply that evangelicals presently know all the answers to challenging historical-critical questions. But inerrancy does entail that there can finally be neither outright conflicts within Scripture's teaching (rightly interpreted in canonical context), nor contradictions between Scripture and genuine science or other human knowledge. Thus, careful attention must be paid to the diverse ways that literary genres relate to truth claims. Conflict over inerrancy has not defined evangelicalism elsewhere as in the United States, or found an embrace among all its theological traditions.[86] There is increasing distinction between particular epistemologies or apologetics and commitment to the trustworthiness of Scripture itself.[87]

Meanwhile, secular thinker E. D. Hirsch Jr. dominated conservative Protestant hermeneutics for decades.[88] To distinguish between valid and invalid interpretations, the only possible standard, he argued, is authorial intention. Readers cannot recover an author's psychology or motivations.[89] But they can begin with a sense of the text's genre before examining details, refining an interpretation that reliably approximates the meaning as expressed. Many have seen Hirsch's view as a way to preserve the Bible's authority, distinguishing between its objective single meaning, the interpreter's subjective understanding, and the many possible applications that are somewhat relative to the reading context. Hirsch's attack upon Gadamer influenced conservative rejections of that figure as a relativist.[90]

Probably the chief evangelical tension over biblical hermeneutics concerns the contemporary role of the Holy Spirit in the reader(s), relative to Scripture's meaning as written text(s). To what extent is the latter fixed by the Spirit's already-completed witness to God's final Word spoken in Jesus Christ? That is, how do the implications of inspiration set parameters for the Spirit's work of "illumination"?

86. E.g., Stanley J. Grenz, "Nurturing the Soul, Informing the Mind: The Genesis of the Evangelical Scripture Principle," and Donald W. Dayton, "The Pietist Theological Critique of Biblical Inerrancy," in Bacote et al., *Evangelicals and Scripture*, 21–41, 76–89.

87. On this more positive theological word, see Paul Helm and Carl R. Trueman, eds., *The Trustworthiness of God: Perspectives on the Nature of Scripture* (Grand Rapids: Eerdmans, 2002).

88. Especially *Validity in Interpretation* (New Haven: Yale University Press, 1967).

89. Such an aspiration is associated with the "intentional fallacy," as sometimes is Hirsch; see Kevin J. Vanhoozer, "Intention/Intentional Fallacy," in *Dictionary for Theological Interpretation of the Bible*, 327–30.

90. Roger Lundin, *From Nature to Experience: The American Search for Cultural Authority* (Lanham, MD: Rowman & Littlefield, 2005), 158. Hirsch's later work acknowledged other interpretive aims besides validity, weakening his earlier position. However, conservative Protestant admirers largely ignored this. It should be noted that many nonconservative biblical scholars also approximate Hirschian hermeneutics.

This tension relates to other trends. Increasing emphasis upon biblical diversity, especially its literary genres, has brought recognition of different models for Scripture's authority within the texts themselves.[91] Second-person address to God, as in the Psalms, functions differently than omniscient narrative that may describe God in the third person, which is different still from the oracular model of God as first-person speaker in the Prophets.

Moreover, some contemporary theologians have emphasized more the Holy Spirit and the present, rather than the Logos and the past, when constructing a doctrine of revelation. Rather than its ontology, emphasis lies upon Scripture's "functioning" dynamically for sanctification by the Holy Spirit. In this regard the work of David Kelsey is particularly influential concerning the variety of theologians' actual practices in appealing to the Bible.[92] Whereas traditional theologies placed the doctrine of Scripture at the front, among "prolegomena," or introductory words justifying theology methodologically, today some, such as Stanley Grenz, place the doctrine toward the end, under the Spirit's community-forming work.[93] The popular incarnational analogy between the divine-human Christ and a divine-human Bible is now subject to controversy as well.[94]

Hence variety proliferates. Appreciation for Gadamer among scholars in general now affects theologians. Consequently, evangelicals today also interact with broader developments described below, including ideological criticism and postliberal theology, while having significant presence within the movement advocating "theological interpretation of Scripture."

Ideological Criticism and Globalization

Rereading the story of salvation against both liberal and evangelical theologies are a host of advocacy approaches. Latin American liberation theology provides a foundational example. Liberation theologians read the Bible from the perspective of the poor and marginalized, with focal attention upon structural evil rather than personal sin. Narratives such as the Exodus offer principal paradigms for advancing God's kingdom on earth. Though still tending to

91. John Goldingay, *Models for Scripture* (Grand Rapids: Eerdmans, 1994).

92. See David H. Kelsey, *The Uses of Scripture in Recent Theology* (Philadelphia: Fortress, 1975), reissued as *Proving Doctrine* (Harrisburg, PA: Trinity, 1999); the responses in Robert K. Johnston, ed., *The Use of the Bible in Theology: Evangelical Options* (Atlanta: John Knox, 1985) are only partially satisfying. Most recently, therefore, see Kevin J. Vanhoozer, *The Drama of Doctrine: A Canonical-Linguistic Approach to Theology* (Louisville: Westminster John Knox, 2005).

93. *Theology for the Community of God* (Nashville: Broadman & Holman, 1994).

94. On the challenges, see Stephen E. Fowl, "Scripture," in Webster et al., *Oxford Handbook of Systematic Theology*, 352; on the controversy, track reception of Peter Enns, *Inspiration and Incarnation: Evangelicals and the Problem of the Old Testament* (Grand Rapids: Baker Academic, 2005).

speak of theology as critical reflection, liberation theologians insist that this be "critical reflection on praxis," undertaken in the midst of the church and its work for justice. Thus epistemology as such takes a back seat, intertwined with ethics and eschatology.

A "hermeneutic of suspicion" is exercised concerning ecclesiastical and theological structures as well as the biblical texts themselves. Feminist theology exemplifies various possibilities: some reinterpret the Christian tradition; others try to redeem it, mining for treasure useful to reform while minimizing harmful elements; still others reject the tradition outright. Native Americans complicate references to the Exodus, noting how often the early European settlers of America appealed to the conquest narratives of the Promised Land. Biblical stories work out differently from the perspective of the Canaanites or someone like Hagar. Black theology offers a poignant case regarding the ways in which scholarly opportunity was systematically denied to a group with ongoing consequences—not just for the people in question, but for the very nature of biblical interpretation itself.[95]

Slavery, poverty, and sexuality are only some of the questions culture raises for biblical interpretation. Liberals speak of "correlation" between text and context, whereas evangelicals speak of "contextualization" regarding the text's application within context; yet these paradigms are breaking down. Among other inadequacies, they presume "one-size-fits-all" relationships between the Bible and culture, whereas actually an entire series of complex negotiations takes place.[96]

The dominant contemporary challenge of globalization remains susceptible to various definitions, with two primary hermeneutical manifestations. First, postcolonial theory claims to provide a "postmodern" replacement for liberation theology, critiquing the latter as too concerned with the poor themselves to oppose their monotheistic religion and authoritative Bible.[97]

95. See Cain Hope Felder, ed., *Stony the Road We Trod: African American Biblical Interpretation* (Minneapolis: Fortress, 1991). This gave rise to "double-voiced" interpretation addressing both now and not yet, according to Lewis V. Baldwin and Stephen W. Murphy, "Scripture in the African-American Christian Tradition," in Holcomb, *Christian Theologies of Scripture*, 282–99.

96. Compare the controversies within mainline Protestant churches over sexual ethics with evangelical debate regarding William J. Webb, *Slaves, Women and Homosexuals: Exploring the Hermeneutics of Cultural Analysis* (Downers Grove, IL: InterVarsity, 2001). See also Pamela D. H. Cochran, "Scripture, Feminism, and Sexuality," in *Christian Theologies of Scripture*, 261–81.

97. R. S. Sugirtharajah, "Introduction: Still at the Margins," in *Voices from the Margin: Interpreting the Bible in the Third World*, ed. R. S. Sugirtharajah, 3rd ed. (Maryknoll, NY: Orbis, 2006), 5. For more general accounts of postmodernity's hermeneutical effects see Kevin J. Vanhoozer, "Scripture and Tradition," in *The Cambridge Companion to Postmodern Theology*, ed. Kevin J. Vanhoozer (Cambridge: Cambridge University Press, 2003), 149–69, as well as Dan R. Stiver, "Theological Method," 170–85. Note the emphasis on fluidity of identity but also on hypermodernity in Gerard Loughlin, "Postmodern Scripture," in Holcomb, *Christian Theologies of Scripture*, 300–322.

Postcolonial theorizing comes from academics unapologetically advocating particular political perspectives.[98] Postcolonial theorists engage in "subaltern" studies, describing conditions or approaches on behalf of poor people and marginalized groups. But the identities of the theorists themselves are hybrid, since frequently they have made it to the Western academy or at least enjoyed enough privilege to engage in intellectual life wherever they are.

Accordingly they are unafraid to criticize global South Christians for "making the same Bible an uncaring, mean-spirited and cruel book by using it uncritically," while simultaneously asserting that "the imposition of one's culture on others is plainly unacceptable."[99] Yet others can ask of the postcolonialists, Is not their Western form of religious pluralism as institutionalized in academic culture an imposition upon those who do not wish to see the Bible "as an entertaining narrative devoid of its ecclesiastical and dogmatic functions"?[100] Postcolonial theory is therefore in a bind: useful in helping Christians to recognize human finitude and fallenness in our theological understanding, but tending to assume the normative absence of divine revelation—ironically a sort of intellectual colonialism.

Hence encountering globalization means, secondly, accounting for the clever quip that, while intellectuals advocate a preferential option for the poor, the poor themselves prefer Pentecostalism. Bible readers in the global South, now on the radar screen of Western scholars, gravitate toward different portions of Scripture than "Western" readers—the Old Testament, Hebrews, and James, among others. They sense greater immediacy to biblical texts and contexts, recognizing common political struggles and expectations of radical divine intervention with which Westerners do not readily resonate.[101]

These Christians find themselves on the front lines of interaction with other religions.[102] Modern theology usually sought to compare these faiths with general categories such as "religion," placing "scripture" in such a class as if all faiths have sacred texts functioning in similar ways. But as the world "gets smaller," scholars must acknowledge particularity more carefully, so general categories break down. Still, the modern West has affected how people of all religions read their sacred texts, weakening traditional practices.[103] Another

98. For a recent example of addressing a political theme, see R. S. Sugirtharajah, *The Bible and Empire: Postcolonial Explorations* (Cambridge: Cambridge University Press, 2005).

99. R. S. Sugirtharajah, "Afterword: The Future Imperfect," in *Voices from the Margin*, 495.

100. Ibid., 496.

101. Among scholars specializing in this field are Lamin Sanneh, Andrew Walls, and Philip Jenkins. Jenkins provides the best hermeneutical description in *The New Faces of Christianity: Believing the Bible in the Global South* (Oxford: Oxford University Press, 2006).

102. For examples see Timothy C. Tennent, *Theology in the Context of World Christianity* (Grand Rapids: Zondervan, 2007).

103. For comparative work demonstrating this, by a scholar attentive to religious particularity and Christian theology, see Paul J. Griffiths, *Religious Reading: The Place of Reading in the Practice of Religion* (Oxford: Oxford University Press, 1999).

facet of interreligious encounter is the recent development of "scriptural reasoning." This movement involves meetings in which Christians, Jews, and Muslims read each other's scriptural texts together.[104] The goal is not simply the increase of mutual understanding, but also greater awareness of one's own tradition by encountering its strangeness relative to others'. The practice holds promise for moving interreligious dialogue beyond its tendency to require checking distinctive beliefs at the door.

Postliberalism and Theological Interpretation of Scripture

Such integrity for the Christian tradition has been a key concern of so-called postliberal theology. Earlier we explored the contributions of two figures, Frei and Kelsey. Another associated figure is George Lindbeck, who brought the term into wide usage with *The Nature of Doctrine: Religion and Theology in a Postliberal Age.*[105] Lindbeck rejected both the conservative tendency to identify doctrine with cognitive propositional content and the liberal tendency to identify doctrine with symbolic expressions of experience (in which the real truth is explained philosophically). According to Lindbeck, doctrine is "cultural-linguistic," like the second-order grammatical rules for proper first-order religious speech, such as prayer. Doctrine teaches Christian citizenship in the church.

Here the important point is what Lindbeck calls "intratextuality," in which "the text absorbs the world" rather than vice versa. Lindbeck resists the liberal translation of Christian language into some general scheme held on other grounds (the world absorbing the text). Influenced by Frei's focus on biblical narrative, Lindbeck urges Christians to have the text's framework determine the cultural-linguistic symbolic lenses through which to view everything else. Imagine the difference between a sermon on the book of Nehemiah regarding "successful leadership" and another on "servanthood": the former would be extratextual, the latter intratextual.

Lindbeck is not calling for stodgy conservatism in which only the Bible would influence theology. Neither would his Yale colleagues Frei or Kelsey. Moreover, these figures had significant disagreements among themselves, as did their legions of graduate students. Hence there is considerable debate over whether a "Yale School" exists, what might be the meaning of the "narrative theology" associated with it, and whether postliberalism is a coherent concept. Nevertheless, it galvanized an ecumenical set of relationships pursuing

104. See David F. Ford and C. C. Pecknold, eds., *The Promise of Scriptural Reasoning* (Oxford: Blackwell, 2006).

105. *The Nature of Doctrine: Religion and Theology in a Postliberal Age* (Louisville: Westminster John Knox, 1984).

"generous orthodoxy" by taking the Bible and Christian tradition seriously when engaging Christ and culture.[106]

Postliberal theologians, following Lindbeck, also pay close attention to Christian-Jewish relations. Concerned to maintain an integral relationship between the church and its founding sources, they affirm the importance of the Old Testament for Christian identity. They thus recognize God's irrevocable promises to the Jewish people along with the need for Christians to repent of and resist "supersessionism." It may seem odd to connect reaffirmation of Christian particularity with greater attentiveness to Judaism, but the Rule of faith vigorously commits Christians to worshiping the God of Israel as revealed in Jesus Christ.

Several so-called postliberal figures have been active in another movement, advocating "theological interpretation of Scripture."[107] What unites these advocates is criticism of historical criticism—at least its hegemony and effects on the church. Since everyone interprets with perspective(s), it is appropriate to undertake biblical exegesis with churchly interests—which ultimately are concerned with hearing the Word of God. Beyond this basic theme, the dominant foci are canon, creed, and context or culture. Concerning canon, theological exegesis highlights the need to read texts as part of the Bible's overall narrative and in relation to other passages, along with awareness of the process by which the church has received and transmitted these authoritative texts.[108] Concerning creed, theological exegesis refers specifically to reading Scripture within

106. Celebrating rapprochement between postliberals and postconservatives is John R. Franke, "Theologies of Scripture in the Nineteenth and Twentieth Centuries: An Introduction," in Holcomb, *Christian Theologies of Scripture*, 163—where this is the capstone of a trajectory of key figures parallel to the present account: Schleiermacher, Barth, Balthasar, and Frei (on Frei's rejection of "story theology" see Mike Higton, "Hans Frei," in ibid., 232). Denying the coherence of a Yale School including both Frei and Lindbeck (calling Lindbeck neoliberal) is George Hunsinger, "Postliberal Theology," in Vanhoozer, *Cambridge Companion to Postmodern Theology*, 42–57. Tying Frei and Lindbeck more closely to each other and to the liberal tradition of someone like Niebuhr, thus contesting postliberalism from a different angle, see Paul J. DeHart, *The Trial of the Witnesses: The Rise and Decline of Postliberal Theology*, Challenges in Contemporary Theology (Oxford: Blackwell, 2006). See also representative essays in James J. Buckley and David S. Yeago, eds., *Knowing the Triune God: The Work of the Spirit in the Practices of the Church* (Grand Rapids: Eerdmans, 2001); Christopher R. Seitz, ed., *Nicene Christianity: The Future for a New Ecumenism* (Grand Rapids: Brazos, 2002).

107. For representative works see Vanhoozer, *Dictionary for Theological Interpretation of the Bible,* and Stephen E. Fowl, ed., *The Theological Interpretation of Scripture: Classic and Contemporary Readings* (Oxford: Blackwell, 1997). For a survey see Daniel J. Treier, *Introducing Theological Interpretation of Scripture: Recovering a Christian Practice* (Grand Rapids: Baker Academic, 2008), from which elements of this chapter are taken. On the relationship between postliberalism and theological interpretation of Scripture, see Daniel J. Treier, "What Is Theological Interpretation? An Ecclesiological Reduction," *International Journal of Systematic Theology* 12, no. 2 (April 2010): 144–61.

108. The former is basically what the Protestant Reformers meant by the "analogy of faith"; the latter stems from the "canonical approach" taken by Brevard S. Childs—still another Yale

the Rule of faith and then more broadly to recovering precritical, spiritual, exegetical practices, plus possibly deploying particular doctrinal traditions.[109] Concerning context or culture, theological exegesis affirms the need to ask wide-ranging questions regarding the church in the world, even allowing critical perspectives to open up fresh readings. Despite all these agreements, there is considerable variety among advocates of theological exegesis over how much to engage the disciplines of biblical theology and general hermeneutics, and over whether to emphasize author, text, or reader most prominently.

Conclusion: Imagining Scripture vis-à-vis Redemption

Modern theology is so varied—or, some might say, fragmented—that it is difficult to generalize regarding Scripture and hermeneutics. Yet, if this essay has demonstrated nothing else, it should be clear that modern theologians perceived a need to spend time and energy on these prolegomena in unprecedented ways. To some degree this exacerbated trends beginning in both medieval and Protestant "scholastic" theologies. But the requirement to set forth clearly one's method became all the more definitive for modernity when joined with the tendency to use general, philosophical criteria for measuring theology's intellectual integrity. In that case, prolegomena are not so much the *first* words said in actually doing theology as the words said *beforehand*—spoken while appealing to other foundations.

Thus modern theology, in Jeffrey Stout's oft-cited phrase, fell into clearing its throat without going on to say anything. Put differently, theologians went around, hat in hand, begging for academic respectability. Such defensiveness is now abating, to a degree, as liberationist and global South theologians orient themselves to audiences other than the academy and as others recover the nerve to focus on Scripture and the church fathers, Christian theology's classic sources.

Traditional doctrines and uses of Scripture today profit from the greater attention to trinitarian theology necessitated by this recovery. Efforts to locate understanding of the Bible "in the economy of salvation"[110] and with respect to "sanctification" as the work of the Triune God pay dividends in more balanced understandings of "revelation" and "inspiration,"[111] even as older

---

scholar. See Christopher Seitz, "Canonical Approach," in Vanhoozer, *Dictionary for Theological Interpretation of the Bible*, 100–102.

109. Two seminal essays are David C. Steinmetz, "The Superiority of Pre-Critical Exegesis," and David S. Yeago, "The New Testament and the Nicene Dogma: A Contribution to the Recovery of Theological Exegesis," in Fowl, *Theological Interpretation of Scripture*, 26–38, 87–100.

110. Telford Work, *Living and Active: Scripture in the Economy of Salvation*, Sacra Doctrina (Grand Rapids: Eerdmans, 2002).

111. John Webster, *Holy Scripture: A Dogmatic Sketch*, Current Issues in Theology (Cambridge: Cambridge University Press, 2003).

formulations are revitalized.[112] These discussions often involve and contribute
to philosophical and literary hermeneutics at the same time, with particular
regard to speech-act theory.[113] Yet, partly at Barth's instigation, these engagements are rooted creatively in trinitarian theology rather than defensively
borrowing from outside Christian faith.

Liberal accounts of Scripture similarly rest on theological premises, especially concerning redemptive ends. The "house of authority" associated with
the Protestant Scripture principle and papal infallibility has crumbled, on this
view, due not only to historical criticism but also to rejection of the classical
salvation-history scheme. Its particularity leads to triumphalism that modern universality must exclude, and the sedimented nature of classic sources
is inappropriate to churchly existence understood in terms of contemporary
dynamism and human freedom. Thus a functional account of scriptural authority lends itself to the exercise of a neglected faculty, the imagination.[114]

Acknowledging the need to recover this aesthetic dimension is the sprawling oeuvre of Hans Urs von Balthasar. Paying distinctive attention to form,
Balthasar urges never-ending engagement with the inexhaustible richness
of biblical texts as rooted in God's triune love: "Theologians err when they
suppose they can extract the essentials of faith's object from the scriptures as
though they were juicing an orange."[115] Balthasar recovers a venerable tradition according to which, along with Jesus and the church, Scripture is a form
of Christ's body into which there is divine *kenosis*.[116]

Acknowledging the inevitability of theologians approaching the biblical text
with imaginative construals of what to look for, as Kelsey has shown, Kevin

112. E.g., Timothy Ward, *Word and Supplement: Speech Acts, Biblical Texts, and the Suf-
ficiency of Scripture* (Oxford: Oxford University Press, 2002); Kevin J. Vanhoozer, "Triune
Discourse: Theological Reflections on the Claim that God Speaks," in *Trinitarian Theology for
the Church: Scripture, Community, Worship*, ed. Daniel J. Treier and David Lauber (Downers
Grove, IL: InterVarsity, 2009), chaps. 1–2.

113. E.g., Kevin J. Vanhoozer, *Is There a Meaning in This Text? The Bible, the Reader,
and the Morality of Literary Knowledge* (Grand Rapids: Zondervan, 1998); the Scripture and
Hermeneutics series led by Craig Bartholomew (Grand Rapids: Zondervan/Carlisle, UK: Paternoster). For a wider survey, see Daniel J. Treier, "Theological Hermeneutics, Contemporary," in
Vanhoozer, *Dictionary for Theological Interpretation of the Bible*, 787–93. Speech-act theory
explores meaning in terms of the force of authorial action in speaking (e.g., promising), not
just the ideational content. Vanhoozer borrows it in theological key to construct a doctrine
of Scripture vis-à-vis God's covenantal drama. Others such as Richard S. Briggs apply it only
to certain "strong" actions (again, e.g., promising) in particular texts, but not as a general
theory; see *Words in Action: Speech Act Theory and Biblical Interpretation* (Edinburgh: T&T
Clark, 2004).

114. See Edward Farley and Peter C. Hodgson, "Scripture and Tradition," in *Christian
Theology*, esp. 72–76.

115. W. T. Dickens, "Hans Urs von Balthasar," in Holcomb, *Christian Theologies of Scripture*, 205.

116. Dickens, "Hans Urs von Balthasar," 209–10.

Vanhoozer appropriates the biblical drama of redemption. The imagination must be shaped canonically rather than culturally, being elicited by Scripture's literary forms.[117] However much the modern conservative-liberal two-party system can be overcome, in the end theology still prioritizes either God and the Word of God or else the human.[118] Modernity too often chose the latter, refusing to acknowledge the human need for salvation.

As we move ahead, great treasures lie in recognizing hermeneutical dimensions of the biblical narrative, placing accounts of the divine Word and its human hearing within that framework. If potential danger lurks on this treasure hunt, it is probably the opportunity to obscure the scriptural economy of salvation itself with abstract "trinitarian" fancies that continue the modern trend of Christians bowing to alien authorities. What this essay has shown is that imaginative construals of divine and human action are inevitably at play when approaching biblical interpretation. Even to know what we mean by "Scripture" requires a narrative framework oriented by some notion of redemption—and our need.

For Further Reading

Bacote, Vincent, Laura C. Miguélez, and Dennis L. Okholm, eds. *Evangelicals and Scripture: Tradition, Authority and Hermeneutics*. Downers Grove, IL: InterVarsity, 2004.

Bartholomew, Craig, ed. Scripture and Hermeneutics series. Grand Rapids: Zondervan/Carlisle, UK: Paternoster, 2000–2008.

Burnett, Richard E. *Karl Barth's Theological Exegesis: The Hermeneutical Principles of the Römerbrief Period*. Grand Rapids: Eerdmans, 2004.

Frei, Hans W. *The Eclipse of Biblical Narrative*. New Haven: Yale University Press, 1974.

Harrisville, Roy A., and Walter Sundberg. *The Bible in Modern Culture*. 2nd ed. Grand Rapids: Eerdmans, 2002.

Holcomb, Justin S., ed. *Christian Theologies of Scripture: A Comparative Introduction*. New York: New York University Press, 2006.

Jenkins, Philip. *The New Faces of Christianity: Believing the Bible in the Global South*. Oxford: Oxford University Press, 2006.

117. Besides *Drama of Doctrine*, see Kevin J. Vanhoozer, *First Theology: God, Scripture and Hermeneutics* (Downers Grove, IL: InterVarsity, 2002).

118. Mark Alan Bowald demonstrates the nearly universal exclusion of divine action from modern hermeneutics in *Rendering the Word in Theological Hermeneutics: Mapping Divine and Human Agency* (Aldershot, UK: Ashgate, 2007). Matthew Levering compatibly explores approaches to history vis-à-vis divine realities in *Participatory Biblical Exegesis: A Theology of Biblical Interpretation* (Notre Dame, IN: University of Notre Dame Press, 2008).

Sheehan, Jonathan. *The Enlightenment Bible: Translation, Scholarship, Culture*. Princeton: Princeton University Press, 2005.

Thiselton, Anthony C. *New Horizons in Hermeneutics*. Grand Rapids: Zondervan, 1992.

Treier, Daniel J. *Introducing Theological Interpretation of Scripture: Recovering a Christian Practice*. Grand Rapids: Baker Academic, 2008.

Vanhoozer, Kevin J., ed. *Dictionary for Theological Interpretation of the Bible*. Grand Rapids: Baker Academic/London: SPCK, 2005.

Webster, John. *Holy Scripture: A Dogmatic Sketch*. Current Issues in Theology. Cambridge: Cambridge University Press, 2003.

Work, Telford. *Living and Active: Scripture in the Economy of Salvation*. Sacra Doctrina. Grand Rapids: Eerdmans, 2002.

5

. . .

CREATION

KATHERINE SONDEREGGER

In a poem of rare mystery and power, the English poet William Blake muses about a creature enigmatically titled "the Tyger." Brawny and terrible, the Tyger's "fearful symmetry" is forged in some terrible, unearthly furnace, sinews and eyes and heart hammered out in the fire of some "distant deep." Looking back on his delicate *Songs of Innocence*, Blake asks the haunting question about this fearsome Tyger, "Did he who made the lamb make thee?" Is this Maker, who, Prometheus-like, "seized the fire" to bring to life this terrible thing, the very Creator of heaven and earth? Was his fiery act of manufacture a creation? And like the Lord God of Genesis, did this Maker "smile his work to see?" Blake does not answer his own questions; perhaps he considered the *Songs of Experience* from which the Tyger is drawn to raise questions unanswerable within the life of sorrow and fear and sin we know all too well.[1]

Blake could not answer these questions, it seems, but perhaps he could lend us his framework to explore the doctrine he adumbrates so finely: the doctrine of creation in the modern age. A child and architect of the modern, Blake sensed in his poetic imagination the elements of the modern doctrine of creation in the West. The Tyger sets out a vision, dark and brooding, of a world that is at once natural and distorted, familiar and alien, and of a Maker

---

1. William Blake, "The Tyger," from *Songs of Experience*, and "The Lamb," from *Songs of Innocence*, in *Poetry in English*, ed. W. Taylor and D. Hall (New York: Macmillan) 252, 247.

at once Lord of grace and a stranger, a creator and a terrible power. Here we see the themes that will carry us from the brink of the modern—the late Enlightenment and burgeoning Romanticism—to the suffering heart of the "terrible century," the twentieth, and the dawn of our day, the twenty-first. We can summarize these elements this way: (1) the theme of the natural, (2) the theme of the artifact, and (3) the theme of genesis.

As we see even in Blake's poem, these elements cannot be kept wholly apart; they are mutually defining and reinforcing. In modern theologies of creation, the elements of nature, artifact, and genesis cut across many modern theologians—Catholic and Protestant, liberal and evangelical—and many widely varied doctrines of creation—from an extended reflection on the place of Spirit in matter, to problems of the knowledge of God in creation, to a theory of development within nature and species, to an exploration of cause and temporality with the act of creation and the Creator himself. They will touch on ethics as well as dogma, on the history of doctrine as well as defense of church teaching, on exegesis, modern science, and radical reworking and rejection of past doctrine.

The doctrine of creation in the modern era sought to understand—as did ages past—just what we mean by "nature"; but even more, and with more originality, the modern era sought to understand what we mean by "the natural." And, although the category of the "artifact" is as old as Aristotle, in our modern era the artifact, and even more, "the artificial," took its bearings from the notion of the natural on one hand and the rise of the manufactured and the technological on the other. This dialectical pair, the natural and the artificial, placed within the framework of a divine genesis of the cosmos, set the stage for the modern doctrine of creation, as we will see in theologians as diverse as Friedrich Schleiermacher and Karl Rahner, William Paley and Sallie McFague, and the diverse theologians of the nineteenth-century Council of the Roman Catholic Church, known commonly as Vatican I. As with most dialectical pairs, this one—the natural and the artificial—rests on a deeper, or higher, unity: the beginning, or "genesis," of all things.

The doctrine of creation most broadly and traditionally treats the absolute origin of all things as from God, and the prominence of our third theme, "genesis," marks the modern era as fully traditional in the midst of its many innovations. To be sure, "genesis" in the nineteenth and twentieth centuries could hardly speak with the confident tones of earlier eras. From the rise of modern astronomy to the carbon-dating of our earth and the development of present-day animal species, the genesis of all things from God has found itself in the midst of pitched battles over the place and cogency of Christian doctrine in an intellectual climate dominated by the exact sciences and driven by the fear of them. It will take all our concentration to set out this element in the modern doctrine of creation without falling prey to the old and discredited story of "religion against science" on one hand and the newer, but hardly more persuasive, story of science as the confident and supreme champion of the entire field. In the unifying element of "genesis" we will examine, certainly, the theologians who undertake the painstaking and often painful encounter of Scripture and doctrine with Darwin and Einstein, with paleontology and quantum mechanics. But we will also examine, beyond these attempts at defense and rapprochement, those theologians of creation who seek to express Christian teaching positively in fresh and imaginative ways through the idiom of physics and genetic evolution. Under the rubric of genesis we will encounter theologians spanning all divisions and periods of modern theology, from the philosophical theologians Immanuel Kant and William Temple, to the progressive authors of *Essays and Reviews*, to scientifically minded writers such as Charles Hodge, John Locke, and Wolfhart Pannenberg.

In sum, we will see the theologians of our modern and postmodern age strive to confess the doctrine of creation in a world that remembers Blake's natural Lamb of Innocence but cannot forget the Tyger that roams freely in our day, the natural Lamb and the artificial Tyger, each in its own way mysterious and demanding, each in its own way dependent upon the genesis of the Almighty Maker of heaven and earth.

The Genesis of the Natural World

Almost all Christian theologians agree that God created or is the absolute genesis of the world; but hardly any two agree on just what creation or the natural creature might be. In our era, this disagreement has grown acute. The modern concept of the creation springs from several sources—as do the grounds of disagreement: The development of Newtonian mechanics laid out a new account of created nature and its laws; the rise of great cities and their mighty industries left a society yearning for the world of nature. The venerable argument from design enjoyed a heightened influence from the intricate discoveries of naturalists; the natural became a law for ethics and a dynamism leading to and crowned by grace. Natural theology offered many a royal road to knowledge of God; a theology of nature awakened in others a fresh commitment to the natural environment. And for each of these positions on the natural creation, a dedicated opponent can be found right at hand. We will not find, at survey's end, a modern consensus on creation or the natural. The variations are too great; the disagreements, too sharp and unrepentant. Yet these theologians hold in common a deep background conviction, that God created nature, and, for just this reason, the natural is to be prized as gift and sign of God's work *ad extra*, his gracious act toward that which is not God. From this background unity will spring an ethical imperative to live a human life on earth that recognizes and honors creation as the gracious and fertile gift of God.

The Terms of the Debate

Both the higher unity and the deep divisions in the understanding of God's genesis of creaturely nature point to an original and rather unexpected question: When God created all that is, just what is it that he made? Aspects of this question are not new, of course. As we will see, traditional elements will emerge throughout the discussion of this topic. But in the main, this is a modern question, raised by modern science and the philosophy that accompanies it. Although this topic will return in different guise when we discuss the modern conception of nature and the natural, it belongs here as the *precondition* for any discussion of creation itself. The identity of that reality God created—its fundamental character—sets the terms of the debate over creation, and no exchange among modern theologians of creation can be intelligible apart from this conceptual underpinning. Just as Descartes's analysis of the nature and relation of body and mind set the terms of all modern debate about the mind and its relation to the brain, whether Cartesian or no, so the fundamental analysis of the creaturely sets the terms of debate about the natural, whether Christian or no. It is the lens through which all modern, Western theologians, and their opponents, see the world.

So, just what is it that God creates in the beginning of all things? The instinctive response of most Christians through the centuries has been rather straightforward and filled with sturdy common sense: God makes all the things we see on our earth and all that belongs to the starry heavens that stretch out beyond our earthly sight. It is just this insight that is quietly affirmed in a straightforward, or "plain," reading of Genesis. Greater and lesser lights; waters beyond the heavens and on the earth; swarming creatures of all sorts and winged birds; fruit-bearing trees; men and women, and all animals; and light itself: all these are made by the Lord God, and fashioned into a garden fit for the human creatures to tend and to flourish within. As we will see, this stout affirmation of God's will to create *things*, animate and inanimate, will lead to complex and painful encounters with the science of the present age. Yet it is the plainest and to many the most compelling answer to the question before us, *Just what did God make when he created the world?* And it is not without defenders of a very sophisticated sort in this age and in the past. To express this commonsense insight in more scholastic and philosophical language, we would say: God created, without any prior material or aid—*ex nihilo*—complete or "whole substances," the inert and living matter, the animals and organisms, the planets and stars in their courses, and the measureless galaxies that make our world a cosmos. It is this language of "whole substance" that will find its way into the documents of Vatican I (1869) and its controversial definitions of nature and grace. In the first decree of Vatican I—the *Canons of the Dogmatic Constitution of the Catholic Faith*—we read the following stout affirmation of a traditional Latin doctrine of creation: "If anyone does not confess that the world and all things which are contained in it, both spiritual and material, were produced, according to their whole substance, out of nothing by God, let him be anathema."[2] But the roots of this council reach much further back, back to the greatest scholastic theologian in the West, Thomas Aquinas.

Thomas gives voice to the commonsense tradition in his doctrine of creation, relying on Aristotle's notion of substance—itself a complex concept with its own history—when he asserts that God created the world in one, simple, motionless act, bringing out of nothing whole substances, both matter and form.[3] Now Thomas knew perfectly well that the cosmos was filled with more than objects, living or inert; he knew that the world of things was qualified by innumerable properties or characteristics, and he recognized that certain immaterial realities—ideas, values, numbers, and time itself—governed much of what we call our world. These were also created by God, Thomas firmly concludes, but they receive a special delimitation: they are "con-created" by God, as these properties, or *qualia*, accompany all that is.

To advert to more modern terminology, and putting J. L. Austin's phrase to rather other purposes, we could say, in this commonsense reading, that God creates "moderate-sized dry goods"[4] when he turns outward to make finite reality. Such a conception significantly affects the doctrine of creation in all its parts. When we encounter debates over Darwin's theory of evolution, say, or Heisenberg's theory of thermodynamics, or, in another dimension, astrophysical accounts of the Big Bang, we see modern theologians of the "moderate-sized-dry-goods" school attempting to square their doctrines with these scientific accounts *as they relate to visible, tangible objects.* In their doctrines of creation they are "antireductionists." The *scopus*, or goal, of God's creative will, that is, is directed toward *objects*; the debate, for these theologians, *assumes* this goal and from this presumption turns to the questions that remain on the composition of objects and their creaturely origin and destiny. For this reason, the evolution of the species posed the greatest threat to these theologians' doctrine: natural selection concerns and presupposes medium-sized objects in all its varying interpretations.

Of lesser danger to this school are the theories of modern quantum mechanics or astrophysical origin and collapse, for these theories are seen only to touch on the parts or elements of physical reality that compose objects, and not the objects themselves. A kind of "instrumental cause" is assigned to these theories of subatomic or cosmic physics: God may make use of these particles and their behavior to achieve his goal, the creation of medium-sized objects in a harmonious universe. Just as a carpenter may make use of a hammer or level to set out the framing for a house, so God may make use of these

---

2. *The Decrees of the First Vatican Council*, Dogmatic Constitution of the Catholic Faith, Canon 1, found at the Vatican website, http://www.papalencyclicals.net/Councils/ecum20.htm.
3. *Summa Theologiae* Ia.45.2.2.
4. J. L. Austin, *Sense and Sensibilia* (Oxford: Clarendon, 1962), 8.

physical elements and laws to create all animate and inanimate things, and in both cases, the instruments drop out of sight when the finished house, or cosmos, is complete. (The modern German philosopher Martin Heidegger made a similar point about the metaphysical status of instruments, *die Wären*, in his path-breaking work, *Being and Time*; and in a different key, the Austrian philosopher Ludwig Wittgenstein made an analogous point about objects embedded in practices or "language games.") In all cases, the *telos*, or goal, of God's creative will is the finite object, and the Creator's sustaining and judging and governing of the cosmos will be measured by the divine decree concerning the things, not the elements, of this world.

"Not so," others argue. For these other theologians, the *scopus* of God's creative will is the *fundamental particle or law* that will then result in visible and finite objects. God's intention or aim, we might say, is toward the *infinitesimal*, and the medium-sized objects that emerge from these particulars and their relations are the outworking or, more daring still, the *epiphenomena* of these deep realities. As with the "medium-sized-dry-goods" school, so with this school (we might call it "reductionist"): there are both ancient and modern philosophical and scientific correlates. To find our ancient corollaries we must reach back to the very roots of the Western philosophical tradition, to the "pre-Socratic" philosophers of Attic Greece.

Ancient indeed is the human impulse to discover the deepest reality or fundament of the world. Many of the earliest philosophers—as do their modern counterparts—held that the foundation of things could be uncovered by going *deeper*, moving down through the layers of the known and visible world to a hidden and truer element that is the basis of all things. For such thinkers, all things are, *in reality*, one thing; though the cosmos appears diverse, it can properly be reduced to one element, one particle or kind. Heraclitus taught that the world, in its deepest and truest sense, was fire. As there is no flame without motion, so the cosmos as a whole at its deepest reality is change—ceaseless motion and alteration. To be sure, many things in this cosmos appear static, permanent, unshakeable; but it is just this appearance to eye and commonsense experience or measurement that must be set aside and seen through to its deeper identity. (A parallel but inverted schema can be seen in Parmenides, for whom Being is eternal and all change an illusion.) Common to reductive accounts of creation, ancient and modern, is this appeal to the *conceptual* reality of all things, at once deeper and higher than anything our senses and instruments can record. Democritus began a long line of analysis in Western thought when he sought the fundament of reality in "atoms," those parts of whole objects that could be divided no longer. These were "simples," the deepest and truest building blocks of reality.

A second form of simplicity proved far more troublesome for the doctrine of the world's creation in time, however. In its wake, this form of simplicity provided another ground for fearing that the world is eternal. We might think of this as a second root of the reductionist impulse in the medieval concept of nature itself. Much to the dismay of modern interpreters such as Colin Gunton,[5] the notion of the simple carried over into Christian doctrines of created or "material" objects, in Thomas and other Augustinian theologians. All created things, these medievals said, were composed of an utterly simple yet utterly inferior kind of stuff titled "prime matter": without form or definition, it was "close to nothing," in Augustine's fateful phrase, and just so could enter into the composition of every created thing. We should be quick to note, however, that such reductionism remains an impulse only, as, for these thinkers, created objects are far more than their matter—indeed their reality lies not in matter at all but in their definition or "form."

When we turn to our era, however, we see the strong resurgence of full-throated reductionism in philosophical and scientific circles, and its downward pressure on the doctrine of creation. Consider that architect of the English Enlightenment, John Locke. In his *Reasonableness of Christianity*, Locke affirms—though in passing—the doctrine of creation and God as Almighty Creator to be the bedrock of rational religion. Locke's Christianity is hardly traditional or dogmatic, however, despite this conventional nod toward the doctrine of creation. Famous to the *Reasonableness*, after all, is Locke's confident assertion that nothing more is required of the Christian than to assent to the teaching that "Jesus is the Messiah," an assertion considered "reductionist" already in Locke's own day. "Rational religion" was certainly reductionist in just this sense—the fewer dogmas the better. Yet the reductionist commitment of modern philosophy does not properly pertain to elements of Christian creedal belief. Properly, reductionism in its full power pertains to worldly ontology, to the theory that enumerates the kinds and qualities of finite, created things. For John Locke, a certain form of reductionism in creaturely substance makes our knowledge of creation, and the aims of the Creator, deeply mysterious. Locke-interpretation is notoriously vexed, so we must tread carefully here. But his positions—however interpreted—are so vital to modern conceptions of epistemology, metaphysics, and religion that we must hazard a reading all the same.

In his *Essay in Human Understanding*, Locke draws a famous distinction between the substance, or, literally, the underlying reality of a thing, on one hand—"it is that which I know not what"—and, on the other, its appearances to our eyes and thought—its host of "primary and secondary qualities." Objects are congeries of *qualities* as they strike our senses and awaken our intellect. Two sorts can be intellectually discerned: primary qualities, which inhere in their substance apart from our sensing them; and secondary qualities, which depend upon our encountering the object and judging it. Locke seemed to think that extension—Descartes's great property of matter—belonged to

5. Colin Gunton, *The Triune Creator* (Grand Rapids: Eerdmans, 1998), esp. chap. 2, 14–40.

primary *qualia*, but added solidity and impulse as "objective" properties of things. Secondary *qualia* consist in the properties we most common-sensibly associate with things: color and taste and texture, even utility. Already, the notion of "primary quality" reduces objects to elements—"atoms" or, perhaps, "corpuscles"—that fall outside human sight and touch. But the deepest reality of an object lies far deeper, in the unifying concept of "substance," a reality so metaphysically hidden that we can know just nothing about it. A great gulf is here fixed between our experience of the world and its deepest reality, a gulf that will in time be known as philosophical "idealism," though its earliest advocates, Locke and George Berkeley, were considered to be classical empiricists. The stern transcendence and hiddenness of substance in Locke's reflections lead him to teach that God's providence equips us to see the world after a human and creaturely fashion, and graciously shields us from sensing the world as would a powerful telescope or perfect microscope—a monstrous and debilitating power for a finite, human creature. Yet the goal of God's creative will is the substance, with its primary properties—the deep and true unity of all things—and it is just this that we can conceive through reflection, but never encounter or know.

Such ideas live on in the "philosopher of Lutheranism," Immanuel Kant. For Kant, the world of medium-sized objects could be understood and known only by retaining clearly in the mind a distinction or schema that separates the truest reality of a thing from its appearance to the senses. That distinction is Kant's celebrated contrast of the "noumena" versus the "phenomena" in every act of knowing. Kant does not deny that we have certain and trustworthy knowledge of the world; indeed his critical philosophy presses every lever to achieve such certainty under the conditions of modern scientific thought. Yet, like Locke, Kant's distinction between "things in themselves"—of which we can know strictly nothing—and "things for us" forces Kant to radical positions that threaten the foundations of his very campaign. So radical is Kant's denial of the experience (and so, the knowledge) of the deep underlying substratum of objects that it is not clear whether in the *Critique of Pure Reason* Kant affirms a particular substance underlying each object, or whether, in the end, he must affirm that there can be only one "Noumenon," an utterly uniform Simple or Prime Matter that supports each object and its qualities.[6]

Puzzles of this kind led Kant to express reservations about most traditional metaphysical and theological categories, from the doctrine of the soul to the doctrine of *creatio ex nihilo*. Dogmatic doctrines of this sort must be relegated to a realm of moral and intellectual usefulness: these ideas regulate and limit our thought, so that, in Kant's celebrated trio, we can recognize "what we can know; what we can hope; and what we can do." Kantianism, then, is reductive

---

6. Immanuel Kant, *The Critique of Pure Reason*, trans. N. K. Smith (New York: St. Martin's Press, 1929), 1.2, "The Deduction of the Pure Concepts of Understanding."

in a critical sense: the truest reality of the world lies underneath what we encounter and know; we cannot know it but can only infer and point to it; it may be in reality but one substance; and we cannot properly know but rather believe and postulate that God, as Creator, willed and sustains it in being.

Modern scientific accounts of the physical laws of finite objects do not stray so far from Kantianism, though in a strong and reductive sense. Consider the modern thermodynamic concept of the cosmos. Here we find a reductionism so thoroughgoing that to apply it directly to the doctrine of creation would entail an altogether symbolic or "mythic" reading of Genesis. That is because the objects named in the Creation narratives could scarcely constitute the goal of an omniscient Creator; rather, the Author of the physical laws of the universe would aim instead at the deep and universal reality of the cosmos: *energy*. Matter, for these physicists, is a form of heat or energy; from the largest visible object to the tiniest subatomic particle, energy constitutes the building block and deepest reality. Indeed, the very notion of an object or thing is revised in such quantum physics. All physical things are composed of atoms, these scientists tell us, and these atoms, far from representing Democritus's simples, are themselves divisible into particles, each bundles of energy. Atoms, molecules, compounds organic and inorganic, elements, minerals, gases and liquids: all are forms of energy, joined together by chemical bonds that are themselves forces of energy. To break down and decay, to cook and slice and boil, to eat and digest, to separate in nuclear fission—in all these acts, energy is released, and, in the latter, tremendous, annihilating energy, a power that has reshaped modern politics and modern war.

Parallel to such descriptions of the object as energy is the modern notion of force field, a notion associated with Michael Faraday and put to great dogmatic use by the modern Lutheran theologian, Wolfhart Pannenberg.[7] For Faraday, the force field expressed the unique properties of magnetism, a power fascinating to the early scientific naturalists. Magnets attracted iron filings in *patterns* drawn around the magnets' poles. These patterns marked the outer reaches of a field where magnetic force would register and attract. Later physicists generalized Faraday's findings to the cosmos as a whole: the universe was an interlocking structure formed by the forces of energy in relation and repulsion to each other. The world of things is revolutionized. No longer freestanding or independent, no longer discrete substances—however counted and conceived—creaturely objects are now "nodes" in a web of energy, places of density where energy has coalesced and become visible to the naked eye. This web of relation that gives rise to objects, scarcely conceivable

7. Wolfhart Pannenberg, *Systematic Theology*, vol. 1, trans. G. Bromiley (Grand Rapids: Eerdmans, 1991). See also Thomas Torrance, *Ground and Grammar of Theology: Consonance between Theology and Science* (Edinburgh: T&T Clark, 2005), and Alister McGrath, *A Fine-Tuned Universe: The Quest for God in Science and Theology*, Gifford Lectures, 2009 (Louisville: Westminster John Knox, 2009).

to earlier generations, has now become the fundament of all finite reality, the energy that drives the universe in all its parts. Reductionism could hardly find a greater partisan than these theoretical physicists. The Heraclitean fire returns now under the idiom and concept of energy and its forces. One step remains.

In modern philosophy of science, or in metaphysics, reductionism is laid out as a complete theory of the cosmos and all things within it. For these philosophers, particularly in the Anglo-American analytic tradition, all objects, organic and inorganic, all artifacts and culture, every thought and hope and belief, all matter living and inert must be in fact and reality a collection of subatomic particles. For metaphysicians such as W. V. O. Quine or philosophers of mind such as Jaegwon Kim, every thing that is and every thought conceived and held must be traced back to these particles, either in element and molecule, or in brains and their chemical structure and state.[8] The biochemical account of the physical universe, sketched above, has become in these philosophers a metaphysical *theory*, a complete doctrine of everything. In the philosophy of mind, such philosophers are "physicalists"; in metaphysics, "reductive" or "eliminative materialists." It is important, and difficult, to see just how radical this position is.

If we were to count up all the things in this world, these philosophers say, we would count no trees, no rocks nor birds, no kitchen chairs nor dessert plates, no Sistine Chapel, no Michelangelo. That is not because such things do not *matter* to these philosophers; far from it! Rather, these beings and objects belong to a human, cultural, and linguistic world that we might call "phenomenal," following Kant, or "intentional," following the physicalist Daniel Dennett.[9] But such artifacts and conventions and practices, if they are to belong to a true and scientific account of the world, must be seen for what *in truth* they are: a collection of particles "arranged thing-wise."

Should any such philosopher be a Christian, he or she would affirm that the Creator God—wholly omniscient, wholly immaterial and transcendent—would create this realm of quarks and positrons and electrons, and would decree the physical laws that would govern their ordering and organizing as the medium-sized objects human beings see and prize, love and fear. The cosmos such a God would create would be exhausted in the infinitesimal particles of energy that compose, structure, and cause the universe with all its parts.

With the help of these philosophers we reach the antipodes of our commonsense readers of Genesis and their antireductive kin. This array, from the theologians and philosophers of ordinary objects, to the scientists of modern quantum mechanics, to the philosophers that translate their findings into metaphysics, all contribute an answer to the background question, *When*

---

8. See for example, W. V. O. Quine, *Ontological Relativity and Other Essays* (New York: Columbia University Press, 1969), and J. Kim, *Mind in a Physical World* (Cambridge, MA: MIT Press, 1998).

9. Daniel Dennett, *The Intentional Stance* (Cambridge, MA: MIT Press, 1996).

God created the world, just what did he create? From medium-sized objects, to prime matter, to quarks and positrons, the presuppositions that will inform and clarify our main subject at hand are now in place, and we return directly to our first broad analytic category: the Genesis of the natural world.

Genesis in a Scientific Age

"Those who tried to bring Jesus to life at the call of love, found it a cruel task to be honest," Albert Schweitzer wrote in his elegiac introduction to *The Quest of the Historical Jesus.* "The critical study of the life of Jesus," Schweitzer concluded, "has been for theology a school of honesty. The world had never seen before, and will never see again, a struggle for truth so full of pain and renunciation as that of which the Lives of Jesus of the last hundred years contain the cryptic record."[10] So we might say of the Christian struggle to reconcile the doctrine of creation with modern science.

Historians of science are quick to point out—and right to do so—that the rise of modern science cannot be seen simply as a heroic rebellion against the hidebound reaction of dogma. Great historical events are much more complex than that. Most early modern scientists were Christians; many themselves clergy. Newton and Priestley, Paley and Harvey, Descartes and even the young Darwin were devout men, and saw their discoveries as royal roads into the high mystery of God's genesis of the world. As we will see when we turn to the theology of Karl Rahner, science in its modern empirical and professional form *depends* upon the doctrine of creation and its sharp dividing line between the Creator and everything created. Yet there is no denying that the pain Schweitzer noted in modern German theology scrapes across the Christian mind—even today—when it considers the teachings of modern science.

Most Christians in the modern era have taken in stride scientific findings when applied to medicine or agriculture or urban life: Christians too hope for a medical breakthrough in the curing of disease, or breathe easier when a camera discovers miners trapped deep within a collapsing shaft, or feel relief when finally the lights spring back to life after a major storm. The technological reach of modern science—though in itself a worry for many Christian ecologists—has not been seen on the whole as a threat to Christian dogma. But it is otherwise with cosmology—modern astrophysical accounts of the genesis of the universe—and with evolution—the modern biological account of the genesis of animal and human species on our earth. These are neuralgic points in the modern Christian doctrine of creation, and many, in the English-speaking world especially, when they hear of the scientific doctrine of the origin of all things and of humankind, still find it "a cruel task to be honest." Any survey of Christian theology in the modern era will need to address this painful task,

---

10. Albert Schweitzer, *The Quest of the Historical Jesus,* trans. W. Montgomery (New York: Macmillan, 1961), 5.

and, most of all, explore why this "school for honesty" still enrolls so many students in our English-speaking world.

We begin with William Paley, the Christian naturalist and author of the widely admired *Natural Theology*. Written at the beginning of our era (1801), Paley's *Natural Theology* was the standard textbook in divinity across the English-speaking world. The subtitle to this work, *Evidences of the Existence and Attributes of the Deity*, gives a clue to the book's power: drawing on the evidence of the natural world, Paley sets out a fresh argument for the existence and character of the Creator. Paley asks us to imagine that the world is something like an *artifact*—in his famous example, a pocket watch—and that the very complexity and richness of this artifact points to its being made for a *purpose*. The world, Paley suggests, is *intentional*: the delicate and ingenious intricacy of the eye or ear; the remarkable flourishing of each animal in its niche; the order and power of muscle and sinew and spine; the complex interweaving of animate and inanimate life, of planets in their courses and of the entire universe—all these natural phenomena, he says, can be most fully and coherently explained by a powerful and purposeful Deity, or, in modern idiom, an "Intelligent Designer."

Two themes central to our task in this chapter spring to mind. Relying upon a widely admired archetype, Joseph Butler, bishop of Durham, Paley argued his case by way of analogy: the creation should be seen *as* an artifact, or, *analogous to* an artifact. Note that an analogy as used by Butler and Paley does not make a deductive or "scientific demonstration." Rather, an analogy invites a comparison: the world may best be understood as something like an ornate and self-reproducing watch. We consider the elements at work in a mechanism, then see how this analogy illuminates the natural world we humans inhabit and represent. Any such analogy contains *dissimilarity* as well: the organic and animal world cannot be a machine in any straightforward sense. A fox is not turned out on a lathe, or riveted together from sheet metal parts, or driven by a steam engine. These dissimilarities show that Paley and others who rely upon analogy in theological argument expect readers to consider only what is fitting in the likeness, and shear off the rest. Like an argument from probability—common among Intelligent Design advocates—the argument from analogy cannot compel assent as does, say, an algebraic equation. Rather, it invites a way of seeing that is coherent, fruitful, and insightful. The relation between theology and science can be strengthened and deepened, such Christian naturalists argue, when the proper paradigm and example is conjured up and put to work.

Now, I think most Christians would say to such analogies: well and good. They might even consider the current arguments based upon statistical probability—think how exponentially improbable a world of our kind truly is!—a welcome innovation in the traditional cosmological argument, or, as this argument is often termed, the argument from design. But there is no mistaking the air of *retreat* that hovers over these innovations. It is one thing, after all, to assert, as did Thomas Aquinas in his famous Five Ways, that the existence of God can be *demonstrated* by deep reflections upon the structure of the cosmos.[11] It is another thing altogether to say that the logical and empirical demonstrations of natural theology can no longer be advanced, and in its place must stand a suggestion, an analogy, an invitation, or a probability. To medieval apologists such a move would appear to be a concession, and it is the sting of such a charge that fuels the animosity and high rhetoric of current debates over cosmology, scientific theory, and Intelligent Design. A parallel concession accompanies the modern doctrine of theological knowledge after Kant, David Hume, and Gottfried Lessing launched their various attacks on scholastic theology: Friedrich Schleiermacher is without doubt a towering figure in modern Christian theology, but his concession to Kant's critical philosophy has given him the title Father of Liberal Theology—and that has not always been a compliment. When we consider the painful struggle of Christians to understand, respond to, and incorporate the modern findings of natural science, we must remember that the *form* of theological argument influences the debate as much as the content.

The second theme sounded in Paley's treatise—like the first motif of analogy—strikes a painful note, though for an altogether different reason. No modern reader of Paley's *Natural Theology* can miss the uncanny resemblance of Paley's description of natural adaptation to Darwin's work on the origin of the species. Formally they are the same. Paley begins the scientific portion of the work by a close and technical description of the animal and reptile eye, brimming over with an early modern naturalist's love of exacting detail and minute observation of the function of each element. It is this element of function or purpose, after all, that drives the engine of analogy. Paley suggests that such a wonderful mechanism could have been designed, built, and sustained only by a Deity, a benevolent, omniscient, and provident God. Only God could make such a fruitful, harmonious, successful, and lovely world! In fateful language, Paley writes that a design or artifact *implies* a Designer. But it is just this implicator that Darwin denies.

Like Paley, Darwin was an amateur naturalist, a vocation open to the broad public in the early, unprofessionalized days of empirical science. In Darwin's early days of travel and close observation of nature, there was little difference between Paley's description of a sense organ, say, and Darwin's description, from the South Sea Islands, of a bird's colorful feathers, adorning the strutting male. In each, a detailed observation points to and undergirds function and purpose: the biological mechanism is remarkable, they both say, for the power it has to make the creature flourish in its habitat and raise its young. But the *explanation* of that function underwent revolutionary treatment at

11. *Summa Theologiae* Ia.2.2.

Darwin's hands. Darwin proposed that the fundamental analogy between a mechanism and its designer need no longer apply.

What David Hume cautiously suggested in his *Dialogues on Natural Religion*, Darwin boldly stated: the extraordinary fittingness of animals to their niche could be explained in a wholly naturalistic, intrinsic, and this-worldly fashion. An inner dynamism of the animal itself could account for the adaptation, flourishing, and reproduction of creatures apart from any Creator, however conceived. LaPlace's threat to Napoleon—"I have no need of the hypothesis of God"—is now made good. The world and its inhabitants can be cogently and, its advocates say, exhaustively explained by the adaptation of populations to changing conditions. That power of adaptation is called natural selection. Darwin's theory of natural selection[12] is one of the great breakthroughs of modern science, and like breakthroughs in human psychology and human politics, it is one of the defining ideas of the modern age.

Like any great idea and movement, the theory of evolution rests upon the work of many, before and since Darwin. Since Darwin, evolutionary biologists have investigated the part played in the mechanism of natural selection by cellular genes and their mutations. The adaptation of living things to their environment is now most broadly explained through a deeper, underlying force: the division, replication, and alteration of fundamental proteins arranged into long, twisted strands—DNA—and, bundled in turn, into genes stretched along an organism's chromosomes. The aim of living beings—to flourish in their habitat and to reproduce—is now popularly transferred *downward* to the genetic level. The self-interest of animals is now appropriated to their genes: the "selfish gene" now drives organisms to live long, be fruitful, and multiply. Of course professional scientists recognize that agency—the power to decide or act or strive—belongs only to conscious beings; no mere chemical or compound could in fact be "selfish." Yet the influence of analogy is felt even here. Popular accounts of natural selection, and the place of genetic mutation within it, are not infrequently "personified." It seems that even in fully naturalistic accounts, the notion of an intelligent designer or agent cannot be resisted completely.

A Christian doctrine of creation must take seriously, of course, the post-Darwinian theories of natural selection. But these all pale before the scientific revolution that preceded Darwin: the naturalistic account of the origin of the world proposed by early modern geologists. It is sometimes thought that Darwin and the theory of the Big Bang caused Christians their greatest worry in the traditional doctrine of creation. These do indeed pose challenges, painful challenges, for the older, familiar, and commonsense doctrines of creation *ex nihilo*. But these are mere aftershocks to the primary eruption in the early modern era: the geologists' challenge to "Mosaic cosmology," the seven-day

---

12. See, for example, Charles Darwin, *On the Origin of Species* (London: John Murray, 1859).

creation narrated in the opening books of Genesis. Early modern geologists developed, from fossil records, excavation of rock formations, and measurement of layers within the earth's crust, a cosmology that argued the earth could not have been formed in the sequence laid out in Genesis, nor in its span of days, nor could the planet be as young as most early modern Christians reckoned it to be. The geologists' cosmology, unlike earlier scientific discoveries of Galileo and Copernicus, touched the veracity, accuracy, and credibility of a prominent and complete segment of the Bible: the influential, powerful, and foundational account of creation in six days, the Hexameron, in Gen. 1. It is common in our day—and duly mentioned (though rejected) by a theologian as traditionalist as Charles Hodge—to regard the opening account of the world's creation in Genesis as a form of *myth* or religious legend. So common is this response that we rarely recognize that the category of myth does not *answer* the problem of the Mosaic cosmology but rather *repeats* it. "Myth," in traditional terms, is the history of the gods: deities become visible and active in our world. In compressed form, "myth" is the story of a cold war waged between traditionalist readings of Genesis and early modern science.

Consider, once again, the theology of Charles Hodge. A theologian of wide learning and sophistication, Hodge represented a sturdy and traditional Reformed orthodoxy. His *Systematic Theology*[13] summed up what historians term the "Princeton theology," a rigorous defense of older teaching among American evangelicals. Traditional he is, and classical too, but hardly backward-looking! A glance at his *Systematics* reveals Hodge's deep reading in the philosophy, natural science, and history of the most advanced intellectuals in Europe and the United States of Hodge's day. We might profitably compare Hodge to the early twentieth-century Thomist Reginald Garrigou-Lagrange. Though differing, to be sure, in churchmanship—Garrigou-Lagrange was a Roman Catholic, Hodge a Presbyterian—Hodge shares with Garrigou-Lagrange the confident belief that Christian dogma can meet any intellectual challenge and is fully equal to the demands of a modern, scientific, and skeptical age. Hodge brings this refreshing boldness to his doctrine of creation.

Hodge stoutly defends a traditional, commonsense reading of Genesis. "Genera and species," he contends, "are permanent. A fish never becomes a bird, nor a bird a quadruped." Hodge concedes that a modern wind is blowing through that settled certainty: "Modern theorists have indeed questioned these facts," he says, "but they [the permanence of genus and species] still are admitted by the great body of scientific men, and the evidence in their favour is overwhelming to the ordinary mind."[14] Not content with this straightforward

13. Charles Hodge, *Systematic Theology*, 3 vols. (1871–1873; repr., Peabody, MA: Hendrickson, 2008).

14. Ibid., 1:212.

defense of the direct, divine creation of the species, Hodge summarizes his confidence in the veracity of Holy Scripture in a ringing phrase: "As the Bible is of God, it is certain that there can be no conflict between the teachings of the Scriptures and the facts of science."[15] Hodge adduces the work of a contemporary scientist at Yale University, James Dana, who in his *Manual of Geology* proposed an ingenuous and elaborate schema for reconciling the findings of nineteenth-century geology with the Mosaic cosmology. The long and somber history of Christian accommodation to science begins with this work of "harmonization." Hodge repeats an idea already old in the nineteenth century: that "day" in Gen. 1 cannot mean a twenty-four-hour cycle. Instead it must mean something like a "cosmological event," organized loosely in Hodge's and Dana's accounting into the inorganic and organic eras, each composed of three cosmological "days." When such adjustments are made, Hodge asserts, "faith, though at first staggered, . . . rejoice[d] to find that the Bible, and the Bible alone of all ancient books, was in full accord with these stupendous revelations of science."[16]

Not so do the authors of *Essays and Reviews* rejoice in the Bible and its "full accord with these stupendous revelations of science."[17] Published a full generation before Hodge's *Systematics*—in 1860, a mere year after Darwin's *Origin of Species*—these Anglican divines proposed a more radical, and more chastened, tutorial in the Christian's school for honesty. The essayists were no mere parish clergy: Frederick Temple was headmaster of the Rugby School, a prominent private school in England, and later the Archbishop of Canterbury, the Church of England's highest prelate; Baden Powell was an Oxford don and Anglican priest; Benjamin Jowett a famed classicist in Oxford and celebrated translator of Plato; Mark Pattison, tutor and rector of Lincoln College in Oxford. With one exception, these men were priests of the Church of England and represented its most advanced, influential, and sophisticated face. The seven essays they edited—*Essays and Reviews*—became an immediate flash point; the work was caricatured as "Seven against Christ" by its detractors. Though little read now, the work mesmerized the English-reading public because it boldly grasped the nettle: the Christian doctrine of creation would have to find new footings in a world of modern science. Harmonization could no longer be considered credible, they argued. Pitiable indeed, they said, were attempts to do so by such earnest Christians as Dana or Hodge. In its place came a full-throated embrace of evolution or development as the very structure of the cosmos and the silent hand of the Creator. The natural world of inorganic and organic reality develops and changes; species evolve and begin fresh animal kinds; religious society and its

---

15. Ibid., 573.
16. Ibid., 573–74.
17. F. Temple et al., *Essays and Reviews* (London: John W. Parker, 1860).

Holy Scriptures develop and advance, from its earliest primitive insights into the elevated teachings of Christ; human cultures and mores evolve, gradually becoming more spiritual, more insightful, more orderly and noble. Far from fearing the results of the new science, these authors applauded modern geology and biology as opening Christian eyes to the divine pattern underlying all things: to grow, to change, to rise from nature to Spirit, to evolve into the "full stature of Christ."

So powerful was this alliance with doctrines of development and evolution that William Temple, son of the essayist Frederick Temple, and himself later a distinguished Archbishop of Canterbury, entitled his vision of the cosmos "World Process" and included in the Gifford Lectures (*Nature, Man and God*) an extended commentary on Alfred Whitehead, the father of process theology.[18] And Wolfhart Pannenberg, in his recent writings on religion and science, compliments the English-speaking world for offering a theology that early on forged a new and fruitful path for accommodating, acknowledging, and advancing a fully scientific doctrine of creation.[19]

The story of this element, genesis, and its encounter with modern cosmology and evolutionary biology, remains unfinished: even today Christians add chapters to this account. Any robust doctrine of creation lays hold of the world that truly is: it is *this* world and not a cloudy fiction over which the Lord God rules and from nothing creates. However Christians—and others—understand, analyze, and discover that the world must figure in a doctrine of the genesis of all things. How this is done in a faithful, confident, and honest fashion is the work of present-day theologians of creation; and it is a taxing, exhilarating, and worthy work.

We turn now to our second and third broad themes in the modern doctrine of creation: the natural and its wake, the artificial.

The Natural and the Artificial

The German idealist G. W. F. Hegel is notoriously taxing on his readers; but for our purposes, at least, the prize is worth the struggle. In his *Lectures on the Philosophy of Religion*,[20] Hegel lays out a philosophy of nature that at once sums up his most characteristic and innovative ideas, and represents the broad, modern debate over nature as the work of God. Here is how Hegel—in customary dense and technical obscurity—sets out the natural as an idea within Christianity, "The Consummate Religion":

18. William Temple, *Nature, Man and God*, Gifford Lectures, 1932–1934.

19. Wolfhart Pannenberg, *Toward a Theology of Nature* (Louisville: Westminster John Knox, 1993), chap. 2, 29–49.

20. G. W. F. Hegel, *Lectures on the Philosophy of Religion*, ed. P. Hodgson (Berkeley: University of California Press, 1988).

The act of differentiation [within the Eternal Being] is only a movement, a play of love with itself, which does not arrive at the seriousness of other-being, of separation and rupture. . . . Otherness is requisite in order that there may be difference; it is necessary that what is distinguished should be the otherness as an entity.[21]

This remarkable passage depicts the world as the "other" (*heteron*) of God, an existent that takes its character—its nature—from the fact that it is not-God: it is "determinate, limited, negative." To be natural, Hegel tells us, is on one hand to exist as independent, autonomous, distinct. But for just the very same reason, nature exists, on the other hand, as "separate," "fallen," "ruptured." Creation is at once, in Hegel's pregnant phrase, "estranged," or "alienated," and—by "passing over" its separation and sin through love—"reconciled" to God. Because nature is not-God, it is not Spirit (*Geist*); it is even "outside the truth": "nature knows nothing of Spirit." Yet, because nature is also known and conceived of by human intellects, it contains "understanding and reason" within it: it cannot be outside of God, who is Reason or Truth itself. Nature in its fullest and dialectical reality is two-sided, complex, growing, alive. It bears contradictions within itself, and by virtue of the Spirit, finite and Infinite, it unifies those contradictions—*sublates* them—into a higher unity that integrates yet preserves the distinctions themselves. Nature is not Spirit—indeed, it is "untruth"—yet in the fuller reality that is Truth itself, nature "passes over" into Spirit, is reconciled to it, and Spirit takes into itself its alienated other, becoming Absolute, the Absolute Spirit. This, in Hegel's idiom, is the history of the cosmos, the development of a complex, vital, and total reality Hegel calls the Idea. Just as the eternal Son is the Word or Reason (*logos*) of the Father, so the world is itself the Other of Spirit: both are distinct yet One. (As in many other areas of Christian dogmatics, Hegel here sees much further than his more conventional theological peers. He notes, as they do not, the deep, inner structure between Christology and creation, and it is this insight that powers much twentieth-century Christology in the West.) The legacy Hegel's idealism leaves for the doctrine of creation is this: nature is at once godless—estranged and lying in darkness—and filled with the truth of God, reconciled, luminous, and very good.

Now, in lesser hands, such teaching would be reduced to a kind of distaste or ambivalence for the natural—an ambivalence we will encounter once again in the discussion of our third category, the artificial. But it is not in fact in Hegel's hands a form of indecision or uncertainty about the natural we encounter here: Hegel is far too metaphysical, far too preoccupied with the higher reality of things, to settle for such an interior and subjective state of affairs. Idealists, though certainly absorbed by the relation of "thought" to "being," do not

21. Ibid., 434.

share our current hesitation about speaking about "objective reality." Indeed, their very program is dedicated to a high-scale realism, in which every thing that is, is shown, manifested, as the intelligible. In Hegel's celebrated maxim: the real is the rational. Such confidence in both metaphysics and epistemology gives modern (that is, not postmodern) doctrines of creation their rich and elevated conceptuality and their daring exploitation of the natural as both godless and the created mediator of the very presence of God.

Karl Rahner, the twentieth-century Austrian Jesuit and neo-Thomist, is a direct heir of this expansive metaphysics, both idealist and Kantian: nature presses on to the horizon of all being, to its goal in the luminous Self-presence of God, the Creator who remains, in his radical intelligibility, absolute Mystery. *Foundations of the Christian Faith*,[22] though not properly a systematic theology, presents Rahner's analysis of nature in a compressed and rounded way. The entire cosmos, Rahner tells us in this work, is "denuminized," borrowing Weber's fateful phrase. "Insofar as the world, established by God in his freedom, does indeed have its origin in him, but not in the way in which God possesses himself, it really is not God. It is seen correctly, therefore, not as 'holy nature' but as the material for the creative power of man."[23] This radical demythologizing of the world, Rahner says, is "decisive for the Christian understanding of existence."[24] Yet we are not to see in this deflationary account of nature only a call for human beings to exercise their stewardship and mastery over the world. Something more radical is in view here. Rahner dares to say: "As ineffable and incomprehensible presupposition, as ground and abyss, as ineffable mystery, God cannot be found in his world."[25] Here is nature as separation, rupture, even estrangement. "[God] does not seem to be able to enter into the world with which we have to do because he would thereby become what he is not: an individual existent alongside of which there are others which he is not. . . . By definition God does not seem able to be within the world. If someone says too quickly that he does not need to, that he is always to be thought of as beyond the world, he has probably not yet felt this really radical difficulty."[26]

Our task in this section of our chapter is to pursue "this really radical difficulty." Though not unheard of in earlier Christian theologies, the vivid sense of nature as godless belongs distinctly to our modern era. In the main, modern doctrines of creation find nature to be godless in two senses, distinct but not entirely separate from one another. On one hand, Christians have gained an increasing respect for nature as a law-bound, integrated whole;

22. Karl Rahner, *Foundations of Christian Faith*, trans. W. Dych (New York: Crossroad, 1978).

23. Ibid., 80.

24. Ibid.

25. Ibid., 81.

26. Ibid.

and on the other, they have been scarred throughout the modern era by the corrosion of suffering, evil, and death in nature and by human nature. Both make the presence of Creator within the creation difficult to justify and trust, morally and dogmatically. To speak in Hegel's idiom for a moment, we could say that nature is on one hand *distinct* from God, and on the other, *estranged* or *alienated* from him. The problem of evil is certainly familiar—sickeningly so for us moderns—and its effects on Christian teaching are widely known. So we may well begin with our first arm of the disjunction—the natural world as distinct from God—as needing closer attention; then we will return to the problem of the estrangement of nature from the goodness of God.

The pride of place, then, belongs to nature as distinct and separate from God. Now this is what Rahner and Max Weber intend by their phrase, the "de-numinizing" (*Entmythologiserung*) of nature,[27] and it is, as Rahner notes, central to the modern human experience of the world. Modern Westerners, by and large, consider the world an area governed by the law of efficient causality, and sufficient, by itself, to account for the events taking place within it. Friedrich Schleiermacher gave voice to this view of the cosmos when he spoke of the world in *The Christian Faith* as the *Naturzusammenhangen*, the integrated and relatively autonomous "causal nexus."[28] (We must say "relatively autonomous" here because Schleiermacher, a devout Christian, recognized the world as utterly or "absolutely dependent" on God, the Primal Cause.) In a different key, David Hume, the Scottish philosopher, sounded this same theme when, in a famous and fateful essay, he called miracles a "violation of the laws of nature" and for just that reason, incredible.

All these figures are setting out in fancy dress a rather commonplace view of modern persons, that everything within our natural world can be explained, sufficiently explained, by the actions and interactions of physical objects and forces within it. It is not simply that we modern Westerners explain a red sunset by amounts of particulates in the air, or a car's backfiring by a faulty fuel injector, and then we are done with it, though to be sure these are instances of the modern worldview. It is also, and more profoundly, a confidence that physical laws can *fully* or at least *sufficiently* account for any natural event in our world.

When rivers are polluted or food contaminated, when energy must be harnessed from sun or wind, when disease runs rampant and must be contained, when earthquakes or drought threaten, when novel or inexplicable events unfold, or when ordinary human practices such as marriage or political elections fall on hard times—in all these cases, modern Westerners expect that the root causes of such events will be uncovered, sometimes by science, sometimes by

27. Max Weber, *The Sociology of Religion*, trans. E. Fischoff (Boston: Beacon, 1993).
28. Friedrich Schleiermacher, *The Christian Faith*, trans. H. R. Mackintosh and J. S. Stewart (Philadelphia: Fortress, 1928), §§46, 47.

reporters or historians or officials of some kind, and the event corralled and
explained and brought under human control. We should be careful to see that
such expectations—what the theologian Rudolf Bultmann called the "scientific
world-view"—do not necessarily rule out divine agency or presence. Not at
all! Indeed many modern Christians find themselves adverting to doctrines of
particular providence or miracles when speaking about natural, human events
such as physical healing or the ending of war. The understanding of nature
as godless—an integrated and autonomous whole—does not in fact demand
atheism, as Bultmann knew very well. Rather, it demands that the relation
of cause to effect, of problem to solution, of need to remedy be understood
fundamentally as this-worldly, and adequately if not exhaustively explained in
this way. Unlike the medievals, modern people, including modern Christians,
do not need to speak the name of God in order to understand and explain
the events that surround them.

To borrow from Rahner once again, we would say that God is not "an
existent" within our natural world—he would not be one of the individuals
counted in a whole inventory of natural reality—and so is not required for
any adequate explanation of the natural. It is this absence of God from the
necessary elements of explanation and cause that prompts Colin Gunton, in
part at least, to consider the modern era a time of "mechanical causality" in
which "impersonal causes" are now understood to stand behind every event,
even the humane and personal. We can say that "nature" and "the natural"
have become distinct and separate from God, and our understanding of them
rides free of theological teaching.

We have a more familiar but more daunting task when we turn to the second
arm of our disjunction, the natural world as godless because of the unnatural
within it. Here we encounter the theme we have termed "the artificial" in
the modern doctrine of creation. Modern Christians face an explosion of
the artificial in their world. To be sure, every human age has fashioned new
machinery, new weapons, new factories and chemicals for use in culture, in
the arts, in medicine, and most soberly, in war. Even Aristotle in his path-
breaking reflection on nature found a prominent place for the artifact. But
the modern Christian lives in an age of the artificial, or, in the language of
some commentators, in an age of technology. A technological invention poses
special problems for a Christian doctrine of creation. On one hand, of course,
a machine, however sophisticated, cannot exist apart from the natural: an
artifact just is nature under human hands and ingenuity. And on the other
hand, a machine threatens to undo nature, to overmaster it, and to despoil
it. The human intellect, itself natural, appears to unmake itself, by devising
technologies that threaten nature itself. Little wonder that Hegel's dialectic
speaks with such power to modern intellectuals!

Consider briefly an example of the power, the complexity, and the danger of the artificial, one touched on briefly before. Modern technology has

revolutionized mining: no longer must miners climb down deep into shafts, boring out coal for the modern, insatiable hunger for energy. Today mining engineers and their machines can *remove* the entire upper crust of a coal vein—"mountain top removal"—to expose the vein of coal to air, to open-pit extraction and shipping. These machines then permit a pile of rock face to be fashioned into a new covering—an artificial mountain. Now we would say, on one hand, that nothing is natural about mining: it is a human artificial practice, bent on powering many other artifacts, through the artificial combustion of coal. Yet Christians have felt increasingly restive about the *extent* and *quality* of this technological innovation. Is it consistent with the doctrine of creation—especially its created goodness—to destroy, scar, and refashion an entire mountain ridge, even, or especially, if it proves to be efficient? What can be the long-term consequences of such startling and permanent environment destruction? How will it affect the species given over to our care, the beasts of the field, the winged birds, and the things that creep upon the earth?

Christian ecological theologians such as Sallie McFague would reply thus: we are sinning against the very goodness of creation.[29] Rather than viewing and receiving creation with a "loving eye," McFague argues, we moderns seek to master and control nature, to exploit it for our own ends, to exhaust it in our insatiable drive to possess and to consume. Of course we Christians might counsel restraint. Asceticism and self-discipline have long been held to be virtues of the sanctified life. Yet McFague and others argue that merely holding back, or doing without—as worthy as these may be in an individual's discipleship—cannot in fact counter the breadth, power, and scope of modern technology. The "planetary agenda," as environmental theologians term this wide-ranging analysis of technological destruction, cannot be prosecuted by small remedies such as recycling paper or turning off water taps. Rather, a modern Christian doctrine of creation, these theologians argue, must reconceive nature itself, loving it for its own sake, and organizing human life and its artifacts to serve, preserve, and enhance nature, not undo it. This revolution, they say, will require a fresh theology of nature that affirms a deeper commitment by Christians to creation: we should act, they counsel, not merely because all life depends upon the earth and its health, but because nature, *in itself*, in its own intrinsic reality, is good—indeed, as Genesis teaches, very good.

The natural and the artificial, then, belong together, for evil and for good. As any social revolution teaches, the "natural" itself, especially in human society, cannot be easily discovered, nor readily distinguished from the artifact of convention and intolerance that passes all too readily for the natural and the given. What struck a Roman or Victorian moralist as natural, and God's own design, may strike a modern Christian as artificial and oppressive. Yet

---

29. See, for example, Sallie McFague, *The Body of God* (Minneapolis: Fortress, 1993) and *Super, Natural Christians* (Minneapolis: Fortress, 1997).

the hunger for the natural, the open land, the unsettled, the unmade and unspoiled, the basic and the primal: these are the elements of nature, a nature given and shaped and sustained by a provident God, that Christians in our age find tantalizing, vanishing, and deeply eloquent of the Lord God who speaks the world into being.

Conclusion

William Blake introduced our themes for a modern doctrine of creation: of the Tyger, burning bright, sinewy and terrible, an artifact forged in an industrial age; and of the Lamb, innocent and mild, born in some distant garden when nature was young. The modern doctrine of creation has encountered both animals in its complex journey through the thought forms, philosophy, and science of our world. Christians have struggled to understand the very foundation of the world—its composition and character—and have sought, at times at great cost, to find God's presence, design, and will in the ordering of nature's laws, growth, and creatures. They have witnessed over two long and often brutal centuries the godforsakenness of a world seemingly left to its own cruel self-destruction in war and famine and despoliation. Yet Christians have remained faithful to the doctrine of creation's central tenet: that God is the absolute origin of all that is; that what God has fashioned is wonderfully made and rich in divine benevolence; and that human life, however ordered and however wayward, receives from this natural world a grace and gift fresh each morning. The challenges to this doctrine have been severe in our modern age; and yet the tenacity, resilience, and creativity of Christian theologians continue to sustain and enrich this doctrine for the church's proclamation. It is a great task to show how the heavens tell the glory of God, and the doctrine of creation, in this age and every age, is the church's song of praise to that glory.

For Further Reading

Barth, Karl. *Church Dogmatics*. Vol. III, *The Doctrine of Creation*. Translated by G. W. Bromiley and T. F. Torrance. Edinburgh: T&T Clark, 1960–1961.

Bavinck, Herman. *Reformed Dogmatics*. Volume 2, *God and Creation*. Translated by J. Vriend. Grand Rapids: Baker Academic, 2004.

Gunton, Colin. *The Triune Creator*. Grand Rapids: Eerdmans, 1998.

Hegel, G. W. F. *Lectures on the Philosophy of Religion*. One-volume edition. Translated by R. F. Brown, P. C. Hanson, and J. M. Stewart. Berkeley: University of California Press, 1988.

Hodge, Charles. *Systematic Theology*. Volume 1. Peabody, MA: Hendrickson, 2008.

McFague, Sallie. *Super, Natural Christians*. Minneapolis: Fortress, 1997.

Polkinghorne, John. *Science and Theology*. Minneapolis: Augsburg Fortress, 1998.

Rahner, Karl. *Foundations of Christian Faith*. Translated by W. Dych. New York: Crossroad, 1978.

Schleiermacher, Friedrich. *The Christian Faith*. Translated by H. R. Mackintosh and J. S. Stewart. Philadelphia: Fortress, 1928.

Temple, William. *Nature, Man, and God*. The Gifford Lectures, 1932–1934. Whitefish, MT: Kessinger, 2003.

6

. . .

ANTHROPOLOGY

KELLY M. KAPIC

Introduction

The psalmist cries out, "O LORD, what is man [אָדָם *'adam*] that you regard him, or the son of man [אֱנוֹשׁ *'enowsh*] that you think of him?" (Ps. 144:3; cf. Job 7:17; Ps. 8:4; Heb. 2:6). Thus the psalmist asks what it means to be human, to stand before God and the rest of creation. Prayed and echoed through the ages, this question easily births other questions: Who am I? What if I am not a "man," but a woman? From whence did I come and where is humanity going? Why do I think and do the things I do? Who am I if I live on the margins and no one, not even God, regards me? How am I related to others, to the earth? What does *being* human really mean?

Christian theology has a built-in tension to questions about *being* human. Paul Tillich (1886–1965), for example, comments that "man's existence has the character of self-contradiction or estrangement," and therefore our explorations of theology and the human person must account for the duality of this contradiction, "one side dealing with man as he essentially is (and ought to be) and the other dealing with what he is in his self-estranged existence (and should not be)."[1] Tillich's point is that to understand humanity theologically

---

1. Paul Tillich, *Systematic Theology*, 3 vols. (Chicago: University of Chicago Press, 1951), 1:66. Cf. Paul Tillich, *The Eternal Now* (New York: Scribner, 1963), esp. chap. 4.

121

one necessarily moves between the "realm of creation" and the "realm of salvation." Reinhold Niebuhr (1892–1971) echoed this sentiment during an interview with Mike Wallace in 1958 on national television: "The truth about man [is] that he has a curious kind of dignity, but also a curious kind of misery that these forms of agnosticism [as opposed to Christianity] don't understand."[2] His point was that the Christian faith has unique resources to understand the human person in her complexity as created, fallen, and yet redeemed in Christ. Such a tension must be kept in mind in our review of anthropology.

This chapter will highlight a few key discussions that have been exceptionally significant for shaping modern theological anthropology. First, we will discuss the shift to a more holistic conception of the human that developed over the last two centuries in parallel with similar concerns in philosophy and science. Second, we will examine recent attempts to ground anthropology in Christology and the Trinity.

Attempts at a More Holistic Human

Classic debates about human persons often treated our physicality (i.e., embodiment) as of negligible importance. What really determined "a person" was some particular faculty that distinguishes us from the rest of nature, and the older debates often gave reason that honor.[3] Far too often, these discussions reduced being human somehow to cognitive skills that mark humans as of a higher being than the animals. But increasingly this way of imaging and defining humans has become suspect, so that by the end of the twentieth century such a conception became the minority view. Anthropological discussions now consistently highlight the interplay of various faculties, the organic connection between humanity and the rest of the earth, and the complexity and interconnections of the "mind" and "body." "I" cannot simply be my mind. Understanding this shift to human wholeness requires that we review some key discussions.

Living in Kant's Wake: The Mind and Human Particularity

Although many still believe that ancient Western Christianity is primarily to blame for reducing our humanity to mere rationality, this oversimplifies a complex story to the point of falsehood. Generalizations of this kind can

2. Reinhold Niebuhr, *The Mike Wallace Interview*, April 27, 1958, Harry Ransom Center, The University of Texas at Austin, www.hrc.utexas.edu/multimedia/video/2008/wallace/niebuhr _reinhold.html. This basic insight is spelled out at length in his classic 1939 Gifford Lectures, published as Reinhold Niebuhr, *The Nature and Destiny of Man: A Christian Interpretation* (New York: Scribner, 1949).
3. E.g., Aristotle's *De Anima* 2.3 (414b8–11) and 3.4 (429a10–18) identifies the power of rational thought as the "part" of the soul that sets humans apart from all other animals.

normally be debunked by reading a scholar who specializes in the work of the theologian being criticized (e.g., Irenaeus, Augustine, Aquinas, Calvin); researchers show that these theologians had a far more nuanced and holistic view of human persons than textbooks often attribute to them.[4] So are patristic and medieval churchmen really to blame for such reductionist views of human persons that became so prominent in modern history? I have my doubts, although these theologians had a consistent tendency to give primacy to the intellect. Still, this primacy provided theological validation and stimulus for advances in science and inquiries in philosophy, exploring the question, who am I? in fresh ways. Such "advances" in modernity, however, tended to cultivate an environment that divided "theology" from "anthropology."

In many ways it was the work of such diverse philosophers as Descartes, Locke, Hume, and Kant that really gave shape to new concepts about being human, fostering ideas that deeply influenced the church starting early in the 1600s and continuing since then. Fundamentally, to be human came to be identified with the ability to doubt, to think, and then to will. Consequently, humanity came to be viewed primarily in terms of individual ability to reason and exercise volition, providing a theoretical ground for human dignity, freedom, and power. Kant's memorable answer to "What is Enlightenment?" in 1784 displays the spirit of his age:

> Enlightenment is man's emergence from his self-incurred immaturity. Immaturity is the inability to use one's own understanding without the guidance of another. This immaturity is self-incurred if its cause is not lack of understanding, but lack of resolution and courage to use it without guidance of another. The motto of enlightenment is therefore: *Sapere aude!* [Dare to know!] *Have courage to use your own understanding.*[5]

Thus, the more "enlightened" one becomes, the more human, so to speak, one becomes.[6] In his emphasis on the courageous exercise of autonomous reason, Kant advances the modern embrace of starkly individualist accounts of humanity formulated earlier by Descartes, Locke, and Hume. Descartes's search for a solid epistemological foundation led him to flirt with solipsism: he could

---

4. For fuller treatments, see, e.g., Gustaf Wingren, *Man and the Incarnation: A Study of the Biblical Theology of Irenaeus*, trans. Ross Mackenzie (London: Oliver & Boyd, 1959); Stephen J. Duffy, "Anthropology," in *Augustine through the Ages: An Encyclopedia*, ed. Allan Fitzgerald and John C. Cavadini (Grand Rapids: Eerdmans, 1999), 24–31; James Lehrberger, "The Anthropology of Aquinas's 'De Ente Et Essentia,'" *The Review of Metaphysics* 51 (1998): 829–47; T. F. Torrance, *Calvin's Doctrine of Man* (London: Lutterworth, 1997).

5. Immanuel Kant, "An Answer to the Question: 'What Is Enlightenment?'" in *Kant: Political Writings*, ed. H. S. Reiss, trans. H. B. Nisbet (Cambridge: Cambridge University Press, 1991), 54.

6. Cf. G. E. Lessing's *The Education of the Human Race* (1778), where humanity is seen as a single individual who is growing in reason through history, reaching maturity with the Enlightenment.

be sure that his soul (alone) existed so long as he was thinking. Ominously for the development of theological anthropology, Descartes is sure about his mind/soul's existence, but not of his body's actuality. Escaping disembodied solipsism takes some work. The first *other* he finds is God, but his body and other people remain all but out of reach to the end of his *Meditations on First Philosophy*.[7] Locke's *Essay concerning Human Understanding* and Hume's *Treatise concerning Human Nature* pursue empiricist solutions to epistemological problems, but like Descartes they *start* from the conviction that humans are solitary thinking things. In keeping with this Enlightenment individualism Kant celebrates the image of the autonomous human figure as valuable—even noble—for voluntarily acting in splendid isolation. Thus he provides part of the crucial backdrop for modern theological anthropology—the individual elevated in nineteenth-century philosophy, but then called into question more and more in the twentieth.[8]

Kant does not portray human existence as Cartesian disembodied rationalism, because experience constitutes an important part of it. Experience is possible, however, only because of a priori intuitions and categories brought to experience by an active rather than passive mind.[9] Kant's "Copernican Revolution" (that a priori concepts make experience possible, rather than that experience makes a priori concepts possible) provided theologians not simply with a possible advance (a way to preserve the necessity of moral laws, for example), but also with new problems. Built into Kant's approach was a kind of ambiguity: he insists on the *objectivity* of empirical judgments, but at the same time emphasizes the necessary contribution of the subjective individual mind.[10] Even as later theologians often reacted against the inherent individualizing tendency in Enlightenment philosophy, Kant's epistemology paved the way for others to appreciate human subjectivity to a degree often

7. René Descartes, *Meditations*. The self as a disembodied soul occurs in Meditation II, God in Meditation III, while his body and other minds are (almost) recovered in Meditation VI.

8. Consequently, such an emphasis on the "self," it will be argued, actually undermines what it means to be a person, but these observations are only truly developed in the middle of the twentieth century, not in the nineteenth. E.g., John Macmurray's seminal Gifford Lectures at the University of Glasgow, delivered in 1953–1954, which published as *The Form of the Personal*, vol. 1, *The Self as Agent* (1957), and vol. 2, *Persons in Relation* (1961). More recently, see Charles Taylor, *Sources of the Self: The Making of the Modern Identity* (Cambridge, MA: Harvard University Press, 1989).

9. Rather than constructing concepts such as *space* or *causal necessity* out of passive experiences of space or cause-effect connections, Kant held that experience depends upon our being hard-wired to construct our experience in terms of necessary (a priori) concepts such as space and causal necessity. For his fullest statement examining the capacities of reason, see Immanuel Kant, *Critique of Pure Reason*, ed. Paul Guyer and Allen W. Wood, in *The Cambridge Edition of the Works of Immanuel Kant* (Cambridge: Cambridge University Press, 1998). A priori categories or intuition that carry out this interpretation include everything from time and space to the concepts of quantity, quality, relation, and modality.

10. Macmurray, *Form of the Personal*, 1:51–61.

ignored in classic theological anthropology. Kant himself likely would have been dismayed to see the effect that his work had in promoting subjectivity over the next two centuries. Although his revolutionary system emphasized the role of the individual mind in the constructing of experience (the phenomenal world), he held that the shaping intuitions and categories were identical in every mature human mind. In his *Prolegomena to Any Future Metaphysics* he states that our knowledge of phenomena is *objective* because we all construct the same phenomena. He insists that all we could ever have meant by "objective" reality is "intersubjective" reality: the same experiences produced by subjective processes that are the same in every mature person. Not long after Kant's work, however, others abandoned the expectation that everyone constructs the world of experience in exactly the same way. More and more commentators eventually concluded that we construct or interpret the world according to principles that differ from culture to culture, gender to gender, or according to socioeconomic class.

Kant's impact on theological anthropology is not limited to his revolutionary approach to objectivity and subjectivity. His work also continued an Enlightenment push to place the solitary human self at the center of every discourse. John Macmurray observed in his seminal Gifford lectures of 1953, "Modern philosophy is characteristically *egocentric*. I mean no more than this: that firstly, it takes the Self as its starting point, and not God, or the world or the community; and that, secondly, the Self is an individual in isolation, an ego or 'I', never a 'thou.'"[11] Though this oversimplifies the issue, Kant follows the lead of Descartes and Hume in furthering a shift that moves the starting point of anthropology from God's creative Logos and sustaining Spirit to the human mind. Looking into the mirror, we no longer expect to see a reflection of God's image, but a courageous picture of ourselves. *I* interpret my experience, *I* make sense of the world, and thus the ego is *who I am*. This assumption about our identity dominated philosophical anthropology for the following centuries. While greatly developing and modifying (and, some would argue, corrupting) Kant's original proposal, various theologians and philosophers argued that the mind's centrality in shaping our understanding of the world requires that we view our humanity more and more in terms of our distinctiveness.

Kant shifted the ground of anthropology so that its central question becomes, How do our individual minds shape our experiences of the world, determining our knowledge and lives? And if the individual mind is distinctive and unique in making sense of our experiences and identity, how might our differences rather than similarities play into concepts of the self as well as our concepts of others? Later commentators will ask, Isn't it naive for Kant to think that the mind simply brings indifferent categories to the task

11. Ibid., 31; emphasis in the original.

of constructing experience? Don't hidden biases and blinders also play a significant role? Isn't it also odd that Kant makes this constructive process the
work of a coldly dispassionate, disembodied intellectual power? More on these
questions later, but first we turn to the man sometimes known as the father
of modern Protestant theology.[12]

Schleiermacher and the Feeling of Absolute Dependence

It has been said that Friedrich Schleiermacher learned how to think from
Kant and how to feel from the Moravian Brethren with whom he grew up.[13]
While he voraciously read and absorbed Kant, he did so critically, even anticipating the need to take human embodiment more seriously. In Schleiermacher's assessment, as summarized by Thandeka, "Kant overlooked the fact
that we are *beings* who think," for thinking takes place as part of our fuller
"organic nature."[14] However, Schleiermacher's development of the importance
of embodiment primarily meant stressing the role of "feeling" or "intuition"
(*Gefühl*). Whereas Kant wanted to separate the theoretical from the practical, Schleiermacher wanted to bring them together. Kant's "transcendental
unity of apperception" for the self was inadequate: Schleiermacher attempts
to bring knowing, doing, and feeling together.[15] In this way he created space
for "piety," which he believed should be at the heart of properly conceived
humanity.

Part of Schleiermacher's aim in his early apologetic work *On Religion*
(1799) is to locate a point of connection with the "cultured despisers" of
Christianity, for they are part of a common humanity. "Religion's essence,"
he writes, "is neither thinking nor acting, but intuition and feeling."[16] He

12. I would like to thank my colleague and friend William C. Davis for his valuable help in
the above section, particularly in dealing with Kant.
13. Thandeka, *The Embodied Self: Friedrich Schleiermacher's Solution to Kant's Problem
of the Empirical Self*, SUNY Series in Philosophy (Albany: State University of New York Press,
1995), 15.
14. Ibid., 19. She adds, "Kant characterized human beings as coordinated acts of thinking
without acknowledging that this coordinated activity takes place in our organic nature."
15. Friedrich Schleiermacher, *The Christian Faith*, ed. H. R. Mackintosh and J. S. Stewart
(Edinburgh: T&T Clark, 1999), e.g., 5–18 passim. He writes, "Knowing and being exist for us
only in relation to one another. Being is the known, and knowing knows that which is." Schleiermacher, *Ethik*, ed. Hans-Joachim Birkner (1812/13; repr., Hamburg: Meiner, 1981), 192; quoted
by Andreas Ardnt, "Schleiermacher: Dialectic and Transcendental Philosophy, Relationship to
Hegel," in *Schleiermacher, the Study of Religion, and the Future of Theology: A Transatlantic
Dialogue*, ed. Brent W. Sockness and Wilhelm Gräb (Berlin: Walter de Gruyter, 2010), 359. See
also Frans Jozef van Beek, "Depth of Self-Awareness and Breadth of Vision: Joining Reflection
and Interpretation," in *Theology after Liberalism: A Reader*, ed. J. B. Webster and George P.
Schner (Malden, MA: Blackwell, 2000), 257–302, esp. 261–62.
16. Friedrich Schleiermacher, *On Religion: Speeches to Its Cultured Despisers*, trans. Richard
Crouter (New York: Cambridge University Press, 1993), 102.

believed he could paint a picture of human experience that would resonate with his readers. They should cultivate an "intuition of the universe" where the finite is taken to the infinite, not so much by thinking, but by intuition and feeling.[17] To use a phrase from his later, more mature work, *The Christian Faith* (1830–1831), people must come to "the feeling of absolute dependence."[18] Here one encounters the interconnected dynamic between the self and the universe, and thus between the individual and God. Writing well over a century later, Wolfhart Pannenberg concluded that even amid Schleiermacher's many missteps, his sophisticated emphasis on feeling continues to be relevant for anthropology. Rather than fragmenting religious feelings within the larger set of human experience, Schleiermacher understood that the "peculiar character [of religious feelings] consists . . . in the fact that in them the wholeness of human life which is always present in feeling as such" is central, not peripheral.[19] Consequently, all doctrine can be explained as putting words to "the Christian religious affections."[20] Such a radical move relocates anthropology: it is no longer one *locus* amid others, but it is now *the* avenue through which all *loci* are understood.

By pointing to the transcendent even as he focuses on the self, Schleiermacher creatively links his theology and anthropology in religious "feeling." Humans were created with this connection, this sense of the divine that is not merely rational. Even though he concludes that the necessary information for a "historical picture" of the creation narratives in Scripture "is wanting," Schleiermacher isn't worried. Such historical details are not relevant to understanding human existence, and they are not the point of the ancient story.[21] Rather than seek a scientific account of some primal paradise, we are to discover that humanity was designed to live with this "God-consciousness" as fundamental to "our physical and bodily organism," linking humans with the rest of God's handiwork.[22] Before the fall, "God-consciousness appears as already present,"

17. Human intuitions and feelings should never be separated. Schleiermacher, *On Religion*, 104–13. Modifying the famous Kantian dictum, Schleiermacher concludes, "Intuition without feeling is nothing and can have neither the proper origin nor the proper force; feeling without intuition is also nothing; both are therefore something only when and because they are originally one and unseparated." Schleiermacher, *On Religion*, 112. The Kantian dictum read: "Thoughts without content are empty, intuitions without concepts are blind." *Critique of Pure Reason*, A51, cited by Crouter in Schleiermacher, *On Religion*, 112n20.

18. Schleiermacher, *Christian Faith*, 12–18.

19. Wolfhart Pannenberg, *Anthropology in Theological Perspective*, 1st ed. (Philadelphia: Westminster, 1985), 251.

20. Schleiermacher, *Christian Faith*, 76.

21. Ibid., 150–51, 250.

22. Ibid., 252. Cf. "Each person knows that he is also a part and a creation of the universe, that its divine work and life reveals itself also in him. He thus looks on himself as an object worthy of the intuition of others. . . . Everything human is holy, for everything is divine." Schleiermacher, *On Religion*, 188.

something given, not something that develops.[23] Unfortunately, for various reasons (which he categorizes under the headings of "sin" and "evil") common human experience testifies to a brokenness and anxiety, and thus the need for "the consciousness of grace." Sin manifests itself in "alienation from God," partly "having its source in ourselves" and partly "having its source outside our being"; but where fellowship with God is known, this "we call Grace."[24]

While all humanity should live with an absolute sense of dependence, only Jesus Christ experienced it without wavering, and so his life reveals our true humanity. The uniqueness of Jesus Christ as Redeemer is bound up with the idea that we should "regard Him as the one in Whom the creation of human nature, which up to this point had existed only in a provisional state, was perfected."[25] Sinless Jesus is not merely like others, but his life ("person") and action ("work") carry a divine dignity so that he "assumes believers into the power of His God-consciousness," the great manifestation of his redemptive action.[26] Such a christological orientation for discovering the truth about humanity has strong methodological similarities with the later approach taken by Karl Barth, though the Swiss theologian developed his theology in a very different way.

The genius of Schleiermacher's system is that he takes his anthropological emphases and pulls his entire theology through this grid. Arguably this creates an anthropocentric theology, since he consciously grounds his methods in human experience. This understandably provoked many questions. For example, Ludwig Feuerbach (1804–1872), a one-time student of Schleiermacher, later turned this perspective on its head, concluding that there really is *no theology* at all, since it is all ultimately reducible to anthropology.[27] God is nothing more than the projection of human desires and feelings, but not a reality in itself. Nodding in Schleiermacher's direction, Dutch theologian G. C. Berkouwer later commented that "theological anthropocentrism is always a more serious danger than secular anthropocentrism, since we, from the very meaning of *theo*logy, might expect that it would not misunderstand man as *centrum*."[28] Karl Barth, especially in his younger years, also chastened

23. Schleiermacher, *Christian Faith*, 249. Underlying the intellect and will, then, is "our immediate self-consciousness," and here we are to experience an absolute sense of dependence upon the divine.

24. I have here blended together quotes and images from Schleiermacher, *Christian Faith*, 262, 279; cf. 259–324.

25. Schleiermacher, *Christian Faith*, 374.

26. For more on this see ibid., 361–65, 377–424, 425–75.

27. Ludwig Feuerbach, *The Essence of Christianity* (1841; repr., New York: Barnes & Noble, 2004). Van Austin Harvey makes a somewhat similar link between Schleiermacher and Feuerbach in his *Feuerbach and the Interpretation of Religion*, Cambridge Studies in Religion and Critical Thought 1 (Cambridge: Cambridge University Press, 1995), 196.

28. G. C. Berkouwer, *Man: The Image of God*, Studies in Dogmatics (Grand Rapids: Eerdmans, 1962), 355.

Schleiermacher with his famous quip: "One can not speak of God simply by speaking of man in a loud voice," since doing so means you will misunderstand *both* God and man.[29] Finally, Paul Tillich worried that Schleiermacher's language and emphasis on "feeling," which he admits was commonly misunderstood, nevertheless contributed to the exodus of men from German churches.[30] Although this appears to me an unfair charge to level against Schleiermacher, it is fair to say that his proposal to orient all religion, and consequently the truth of theology, to *Gefühl* does widen the canvas on which theological anthropology will be painted by including more than rationality and will as the core of being human.

The Sciences and Human Formation: Darwin and Freud

Although philosophers like Kant reshaped concepts of the human person, it is arguable that far more significant contributions to that change came from other sciences. Space limits our discussion to two such scientists, but their impact on anthropology is huge. Jerome S. Bruner comments, "Two figures stand out massively as the architects of our present day conception of man: Darwin and Freud."[31] They produced a further shift in anthropology that contributed—intentionally or not—to the growing chasm between theology and anthropology.

At the start of the nineteenth century, William Paley published his *Natural Theology* (1802), claiming that scientific observation displays that everything hints at an ultimate Designer. From the perfectly suited fins for fish or wings for birds, all aspects of this world point back to a Creator, to God himself.[32] The noblest example of this was humanity, which mirrored God's image. By the middle of the century, Charles Darwin's *Origin of Species* (1859) made similar observations about the amazing details and interconnections one observes in nature, but came to a different conclusion from Paley's: all of the apparent "design" features one sees in this universe point *back* (but not necessarily *beyond*). Such "design" actually betrays a slow but organic process *within* history.[33] Through "natural selection" animals evolve, and man fits

29. Karl Barth, "The Word of God and the Task of the Ministry," in *The Word of God and the Word of Man* (New York: Harper, 1957), 195–96. He continues, "What Luther and Calvin, Kierkegaard and Jeremiah all understood was what Schleiermacher never possessed, a clear and direct apprehension of the truth that man is made to serve God and not God to serve man," 196.

30. Paul Tillich, *A History of Christian Thought: From Its Judaic and Hellenistic Origins to Existentialism*, ed. Carl E. Braaten (New York: Simon & Schuster, 1972), 393.

31. Jerome S. Bruner, "The Freudian Conception of Man and the Continuity of Nature," *Daedalus* 87, no. 1 (1958): 78.

32. William Paley, *Natural Theology: Or, Evidence of the Existence and Attributes of the Deity, Collected from the Appearances of Nature*, ed. Matthew Eddy and David M. Knight (Oxford: Oxford University Press, 2006).

33. For more on the connection between Paley and Darwin and the social and theological shift this represents, see David N. Livingstone, *Darwin's Forgotten Defenders: The Encounter*

within this animal world rather than outside of it. Darwinian assumptions sparked the public imagination (and sometimes fury), but more importantly, they provided a theoretical basis for explaining the empirical sciences without reference to the supernatural. This set anthropology on a completely new track. Physicality (i.e., one's organic connection to the rest of creation), far from being neglected, became the aspect of humanity given the most attention. Morton Levitt, recognizing Darwin's impact on later thinkers, writes, "With certainty, it can be said that Darwin revolutionized man's concept of himself by making him a part of nature. It thus followed that the study of man could take place along naturalistic lines."[34] One no longer needs to study the sacred book of Scripture to know that which makes humanity unique. Now one can simply study the book of nature.

Through science we could now learn not merely of human origins, but also about the constitution of human nature. Whereas Darwin concerned himself with our physical origins, Sigmund Freud (1856–1939) observed the complexity of our psyche, emphasizing human subjectivity. As Friedel Weinert rightly states, "Freud belongs to a handful of thinkers in the Western tradition, whose impact on the way we think has been as significant as his contribution to science has been judged insignificant."[35] Freud's development of psychoanalysis has a controversial history, both in scholarship and in popular media. What Freud really contributed might better be thought of in terms of a new language, the role of symbol, and a new openness to mental and emotional complexity.[36] For example, Freud writes, "The ego is not master in its own house," for there are forces—an unconscious or subconscious—that move and shape us in surprising and hidden ways.[37] Most famously, Freud explored human sexuality, giving it a determinant prominence never admitted before. His answers may not have been satisfying, but his questions were undeniably fascinating and linger with us to this day.

Freud's name symbolizes some deep shifts in conceptions of the human self and the growing sense that our natures are actually far less "reasonable" than the Enlightenment seemed to assume. Freud moves us further down the path toward including new factors (e.g., sexuality, ethnicity, socioeconomics) in the discussion of theological anthropology, and thus toward emphasizing the particularity of each person over our commonality. Phillip Rieff argues

---

between Evangelical Theology and Evolutionary Thought (Grand Rapids: Eerdmans, 1987), 3–7, 48–51. Cf. Taylor, *Sources of the Self*, 403–4.

34. Morton Levitt, *Freud and Dewey on the Nature of Man* (New York: Philosophical Library, 1960), 76.

35. Friedel Weinert, *Copernicus, Darwin, and Freud: Revolutions in the History and Philosophy of Science* (Oxford: Wiley-Blackwell, 2009), 185.

36. Cf. Paul Ricoeur, *Freud and Philosophy*, trans. Denis Savage (New Haven: Yale University Press, 1970), 3–56.

37. Sigmund Freud, *Introductory Lectures on Psychoanalysis* (1916; repr., New York: Penguin, 1991), 284–85, quoted by Weinert, *Copernicus, Darwin, and Freud*, 186.

that Freud caused a massive shift in cultural assumptions so that now we think of one's psychology as constituting the center of personhood. As a result, therapeutic concerns rule popular attitudes toward the human person, with the result for theological anthropology that sin and wholeness are now conceived almost entirely under this rubric of pathology.[38] In contrast with Schleiermacher, Freud did not look to the divine since he thought liberation *from* transcendence was necessary in order to discover human nature. His approach could flourish in a world that Darwin had explained in terms of survival instincts, unconscious desires, and naturalistic process. All of this serves as the necessary backdrop for the moves that later theologians made in their anthropological proposals.

Christian Anthropology and the Scientists

Navigating between the two books of God (Scripture and nature), theologians have both learned from and reacted against scientists and each other. A few representative examples will demonstrate the variety of their results.

Bridging the nineteenth and twentieth centuries, German Protestant theologian Ernst Troeltsch (1865–1923) was one of the last proponents of classic theological liberalism. His massive project *The Christian Faith*[39] was based on his 1912–1913 lectures at the University of Heidelberg. Arguing for the place of "Christian" or "religious anthropology," as distinct from scientific anthropology, Troeltsch wanted theology to be able to contribute to the conversation. Since the religious approach focuses on the "soul as spirit and personality," something not dealt with by "exact sciences," there was still room for a theological contribution. Theology should not focus on sociological or psychological approaches to anthropology, but rather the personality of the soul: "soul" here is primarily understood in terms of *the ultimate destiny of uniting with God*. Consequently, "the religious concept of the soul has absolutely *nothing* to do with the scientific anthropology and experimental psychology; it is rather an object of faith."[40] Here is comprehension beyond what is provided by empirical science. As he later writes, "The soul can only be thought, not empirically displayed! This unified center of the personality, where life joins forces with moral freedom, is an *idea*!"[41] Troeltsch's anthropological ordering admits that the general and scientific observations about being human are more basic than the religious ones, and therefore such statements

38. Philip Rieff, *The Triumph of the Therapeutic: Uses of Faith after Freud* (Chicago: University of Chicago Press, 1987).
39. I.e., *Glaubenslehre*, a title echoing Schleiermacher's project with the same name.
40. Ernst Troeltsch, *The Christian Faith*, ed. Gertrud Le Fort, trans. Garrett E. Paul, Fortress Texts in Modern Theology (Minneapolis: Fortress, 1991), 225. Emphasis in the original.
41. Ibid., 227. Emphasis in the original.

of faith "cannot correct anthropology on a solely religious basis."[42] The book of nature trumps the book of Scripture. He makes space for theology within anthropology while still showing deference to the scientific endeavors of the day. Scripture does not, according to Troeltsch, give us insight into human origins or the composition of the human person; these are matters for modern science, which only after they are deduced can then be "illuminated by a religious interpretation and valuation of the soul."[43] Confessing that this is a relatively novel approach that has grown out of "modern" theology, he explicitly admits that this constitutes "a decisive departure from traditional scholastic dogmatics."[44] Yet he insists that science, while not needing to conform to religious statements, needs to leave room for the religious in anthropology, specifically with regard to the soul.

Troeltsch argued that the Christian understanding of the image of God should not be expressed in terms of human beginnings, but in terms of human ends. The image of God does not consist in a pristine beginning, but "signifies struggle, becoming, a longing and yearning for completion," which necessarily then recognizes the importance of development.[45] He believed that the Enlightenment's greatest achievement was the discovery or invention of "autonomy," which has had immense influence on modern anthropology and ethics.[46] Perfection, for Christians, should not be a discussion about the past, but a view to the future—the goal for which we strive. The phrase "image of God" refers to "the Christian ideal of personality, which firmly derives its content from the person of Jesus."[47] His orientation toward the future is consistent with his strong affirmation of life after death, which he also sees as a ground for the religious significance of the present. Here his example is Goethe, however, rather than Jesus: Troeltsch argues that great courage is needed to affirm immortality, but that alone is what can make "great heroism possible."[48] Thus Christian anthropology affirms the tension of living between the beginning and the end, and what inhabits this space is the realm of ethics. Religious anthropology seeks to nurture the soul in kingdom values of "love and spirit, or the self-sanctification of the soul for

42. Ibid.
43. Ibid., 226.
44. Ibid.
45. Ibid., 237.
46. Cf. Mark D. Chapman, *Ernst Troeltsch and Liberal Theology: Religion and Cultural Synthesis in Wilhelmine Germany*, Christian Theology in Context (New York: Oxford University Press, 2001), 156.
47. Troeltsch, *Christian Faith,* 237. It should be mentioned here that although Troeltsch's Christology is normally considered to be the end of nineteenth-century liberal Protestantism, Sarah Coakley carefully argues for a much more nuanced reading of him on this point: Sarah Coakley, *Christ without Absolutes: A Study of the Christology of Ernst Troeltsch* (New York: Oxford University Press, 1988).
48. Troeltsch, *Christian Faith,* 240.

God and the binding of souls together in him."[49] We are to live courageously as we move into the future.

Not everyone was so enthusiastic about the new scientific influence beginning to dominate theological anthropology. From 1903 to 1904 James Orr gave the L. P. Stone Foundation lectures at Princeton. Orr had great concerns that those who accepted this modernist thinking were also required to significantly revise (and in his opinion, make deficient) the Christian view of God, humanity, and sin. Focusing on the latter two, Orr believed that accepting "current anthropological theories" compromised the Christians' view of sin.[50] This was devastating, he reasoned, because it distorted a biblical view of humanity, which also meant losing the orthodox doctrine of redemption. Misunderstanding humanity meant misunderstanding the whole Christian story. He saw the church's growing embarrassment about and neglect of (or outright reaction against) the doctrine of the atonement as evidence of this shift in anthropology. Orr recognized that the evolutionary theory of his day was not merely explaining the process of human origins, but also proposing a new theology of human existence: the new faith at the end of the nineteenth century proclaimed that humanity was ascending, getting better, moving up the chain of being. "The myth of the fall of man is replaced by the scientific theory of the ascent of man."[51] Such evolutionary views tended to make God "superfluous" and called into question the biblical doctrine of human distinctness as bearing God's image. It would not be until after two world wars that such optimistic views of humanity would become widely questioned again.

Orr's reaction is a good example of the uneasiness that evolutionary doctrine provoked in conservative theological circles, and yet noteworthy Princeton theologians like Charles Hodge (1797–1878) and B. B. Warfield (1851–1921) were surprisingly conversant with and open to the growing scientific discussion about evolution and human origins.[52] While Hodge rejected evolution for scientific as well as theological reasons, Warfield showed more receptivity. He believed, like his Scottish counterpart James Orr, that evolutionary processes could be a way of explaining God's larger creation, although they seemed problematic for understanding the special creation and dignity of humanity.[53] The underlying concern was that contemporary scientific observations about humanity seemed to rest on unexamined naturalistic philosophical

49. Ibid.

50. James Orr, *God's Image in Man and Its Defacement in the Light of Modern Denials* (London: Hodder & Stoughton, 1905), 11.

51. Ibid., 14.

52. See especially Charles Hodge, *What Is Darwinism? And Other Writings on Science and Religion*, ed. Mark A. Noll and David N. Livingstone (Grand Rapids: Baker Books, 1994); Benjamin Breckinridge Warfield, *Evolution, Scripture, and Science: Selected Writings*, ed. Mark A. Noll and David N. Livingstone (Grand Rapids: Baker Books, 2000).

53. Cf. Mark A. Noll, *The Scandal of the Evangelical Mind* (Grand Rapids: Eerdmans, 1994), 177–208.

presuppositions. Theologians such as Warfield and Orr could imagine legitimate readings of Scripture that account for some form of organic evolutionary progression, but they could not abide reductionist attempts to replace God's special creation of humanity with a merely naturalistic reading of the data.

In the first half of the twentieth century conservative evangelicals, especially in America, hardened their views against the implications of evolution and what they thought it would mean for their anthropology, as shown in the infamous *Fundamentals* published in 1917. Conservatives soon widely regarded the evolutionary teaching as antithetical to orthodoxy. To compromise here was to compromise human dignity and scriptural integrity. Dyson Hague, writing on the first chapters of Genesis for the *Fundamentals*, captures the feelings of this group:

> Man was created, not evolved. . . . When you read what some writers, professedly religious, say about man and his bestial origin your shoulders unconsciously droop; your head hangs down; your heart feels sick. Your self-respect has received a blow. When you read Genesis, your shoulders straighten, your chest emerges. You feel proud to be that thing that is called man.[54]

There was no question here that the Bible opposed the idea that humans had evolved, though it allowed development in the nonhuman creation. Nevertheless, evolution of humanity is a "garish theory," for it undercuts human significance as God's unique creation.

Later fundamentalist evangelicals went farther, often arguing for a very young earth (less than ten thousand years old), no organic evolution of any kind, and growing distrust of the natural sciences. Consequently, their anthropology became almost wholly dictated by a certain interpretation of Scripture that became known as "creationism."[55] This theology often became so consumed with defending a literal and detailed historicity of Gen. 1–3 that, ironically, it risked losing the *theological* significance of these passages.[56] Such

---

54. Dyson Hague, "The Doctrinal Value of the First Chapter of Genesis," in *The Fundamentals: A Testimony of the Truth*, ed. R. A. Torrey (Grand Rapids: Baker Books, 2003), 1:280.

55. Ronald L. Numbers, *The Creationists: From Scientific Creationism to Intelligent Design*, expanded ed. (Cambridge, MA: Harvard University Press, 2006).

56. David H. Kelsey, in his magisterial work that serves as the culmination of thirty years of reflection on theological anthropology, concludes that we should "privilege canonical wisdom literature" rather than Gen. 1–3 when giving shape to our "remarks about God relating creatively to all that is not God." David H. Kelsey, *Eccentric Existence: A Theological Anthropology*, 2 vols. (Louisville: Westminster John Knox, 2009), 1:176–214. He uses Wisdom literature to then shape his proposal. Kelsey's concerns about rightly treating Gen. 1–3, especially in light of the whole Pentateuch, are heavily influenced by Claus Westermann in his numerous writings on Genesis. E.g., Claus Westermann, *Genesis 1–11: A Commentary* (Minneapolis: Augsburg, 1984) and *Creation* (London: SPCK, 1974). For a summary of what Kelsey thinks we can say about God's creation of human creatures, based on Job 10 and with Gen. 1:1–2:25 in the background, he gives a helpful list (see Kelsey, *Eccentric Existence*, 1:208).

an approach has always run the risk of letting modern scientific discussions actually govern and dominate the ancient text, rather than the other way around, the very deficiency with which they charge their opponents.

But plenty of other theologians certainly did let evolutionary theory affect their theological anthropology. Priest Pierre Teilhard de Chardin, who was also trained in geology and paleontology, upset many in the Catholic church with his attempts to bring humankind into the story of the cosmos in a way that appeared to compromise classic Augustinian doctrines of humanity and sin. Amid the evolving universe, humans are a vital step in the growing complexity of higher levels of consciousness: with this movement in mind, Teilhard emphasized the cosmic pull forward to the "Omega"[57] and the promise of "superlife," adding a more mystical and eschatological bent to his theological anthropology.[58] To know humanity in light of evolution, then, meant looking forward as much as it meant looking backward; to see humankind as part of a larger cosmic movement of progress rather than digression. This view encouraged an optimistic anthropology that played down the classic conceptions of how sin affects us and our relation to God, others, and even the universe.

The dance between theology and science, and how anthropology emerges from these two sources, continues to be a debate. Few ideas capture this tension more than debates regarding the body and soul, as hinted at above. Some form of dualism between the soul and body had been assumed through most of the history of the church, with the soul distinguishing the human as the pinnacle of God's creation. But for the last one hundred and fifty years, more and more theologians began to question—or at least reenvision—the dualism that reigned in Christian anthropology.[59] As Karl Barth memorably wrote, the human person "is not only soul that 'has' a body which perhaps it might not have, but he is bodily soul, as he is also besouled body."[60] Many have rejected older forms of dualism, offering new theological alternatives such as "nonreductive physicalism" or "dual-aspect monism." These attempts aim to recognize the complexity of the human organism without at the same time abandoning theology for an utterly materialistic anthropology.[61] Whether such attempts succeed remains up for debate. Nevertheless, even those who affirm

57. "Omega" appears to be associated with God and more particularly with the unity of all things in Christ.

58. Cf. Pierre Teilhard de Chardin, *The Human Phenomenon*, trans. Sarah Appleton-Weber, new ed. (Brighton, UK: Sussex Academic, 2003). Pierre Teilhard de Chardin, *The Future of Man*, 1st American ed. (New York: Harper & Row, 1964).

59. For a listing of the various approaches in short form, begin with Marc Cortez, *Theological Anthropology: A Guide for the Perplexed* (London: T&T Clark, 2010), 68–97.

60. Karl Barth, *Church Dogmatics* III/2, 350.

61. E.g., Warren S. Brown, Nancey C. Murphy, and H. Newton Malony, *Whatever Happened to the Soul? Scientific and Theological Portraits of Human Nature*, Theology and the Sciences (Minneapolis: Fortress, 1998).

some form of more classic dualism now emphasize embodiment to a degree that premodern theology often did not. All of this is best understood in light of the history of scientific influences on anthropology.

The Human Person in Context: The Importance of Particularity?

Another consequence of the efforts to present a holistic view of humanity is the growing appreciation in theological anthropology for the importance of context and history (for good or ill). Ray S. Anderson captures the underlying concern: "Human nature is creaturely life experienced as personal, social, sexual, and spiritual life under divine determination, judgments, and promise." Sin, then, represents "a failure to live humanly in every area of social, personal, sexual, and spiritual life."[62] To live "humanly" means to be in relation, to have a history, and to be an embodied person. Thus, particularity is a legitimate part of one's humanity, for there is no humanity that is not particular.

Attempts at constructing an anthropology, therefore, need to observe not simply the similarities among all humankind, but also our differences. This in turn leads us to ask if traditional theological anthropology has far too often reflected latent prejudices and blind spots. How, for example, does (or should) being a Jew or Greek, a slave or free person, a male or female shape our conception of being human? The theological concern is that unquestioned prejudices about human "nature" might have been previously assumed to have divine and creational sanction, when in fact they do not. Could such previous anthropological claims (e.g., the primacy of reason) say less about normative creation and more about the power structures and biases behind earlier theological formulations? These concerns have shown that theological anthropology needs to work against assumptions that create dehumanizing hierarchies and discriminations.

The second half of the twentieth century saw a growing chorus of voices concerned that Christian anthropology had heretofore been unconsciously prejudiced toward the white, male, educated, affluent individual, and that it had devalued insights into human existence that would be discovered if theologians enlarged their observations beyond such a selective lot. Maybe it had neglected experiences and emotions, or undervalued personal and family histories that shape us and contribute in profound ways to our human nature. While not fully embracing feminist poststructuralism, Donna Teevan, for example, believes that those critiques are valuable for drawing our attention to the way language, subjectivity, and politics interrelate. Such appraisals offer "a powerful critique of ahistorical approaches to theological anthropology," and at the same time they highlight the challenges that arise when some try to

---

62. Ray Sherman Anderson, "Theological Anthropology," in *The Blackwell Companion to Modern Theology*, ed. Gareth Jones (Malden, MA: Blackwell, 2004), 89.

make "women's experience central to feminist theology."[63] Simply replacing the male prejudice with a female prejudice does not escape the problem, but only perpetuates it. She pursues a more "socially grounded sense of humanity," viewing "human subjectivity as historically conditioned but not entirely socially constructed."[64] Such a view has a sympathetic audience in contemporary theology.

One further example will suffice, as we see some of these concerns linked back to more general creation. Anne M. Clifford argues for an interconnection between emphases on the female and those on nature. Representing "Ecofeminism," Clifford worries that "for most of the modern period" theologians have focused their anthropology on human existence and history, approaching it through the lens of promised salvation and "sociopolitical emancipation." She worries that the "particularity of women's experience and relationship with God" is lost, or at least downplayed by this male-dominated discourse. Furthermore, nature itself becomes a "timeless and static backdrop," and by neglecting both nature and women, theological anthropology is inescapably skewed.[65] Growing out of a patriarchal history, she worries that hierarchical ordering of the male/female and body/soul dualistic patterns have damaged the anthropological significance of both women and nature.[66] Instead, she advocates a Christian anthropology that grows out of solidarity: this represents a unified effort that seeks "not to erase difference, be that the differences among peoples of different cultures, races and classes or the differences between humans and other life forms."[67] Humans (or "earthlings") come from and are dependent on the earth. Rather than "human" meaning "man," this approach is thought to present a more full-orbed anthropology than previously encountered in male-dominated Christian history.

Others have likewise emphasized constructing anthropology in a more contextual manner than that used earlier. Liberation theology, broadly understood, can claim that anthropology should not simply be a question about the past, but about the possibilities of the future, since "the purpose of those who participate in the process of liberation is to 'create a new humanity.'"[68] They ask not simply who we are, but who we should be. That is the human question. Yet for Gustavo Gutiérrez, this is not merely a political revolution, but the claim made possible because of the incarnate Word, for here we see

63. Donna Teevan, "Challenges to the Role of Theological Anthropology in Feminist Theologies," *Theological Studies* 64 (2003): 582–97.
64. Ibid., 596.
65. Anne M. Clifford, "When Being Human Becomes Truly Earthy: An Ecofeminist Proposal for Solidarity," in *In the Embrace of God: Feminist Approaches to Theological Anthropology*, ed. Ann Elizabeth O'Hara Graff (Maryknoll, NY: Orbis, 1995), 177; cf. 173–89.
66. Ibid., 178–80.
67. Ibid., 185.
68. Gustavo Gutiérrez, *A Theology of Liberation: History, Politics, and Salvation* (Maryknoll, NY: Orbis, 1988), 106.

God with us as the new creation, and genuine hope is exemplified. "Both God's presence and our encounter with God lead humanity forward, but we celebrate them in the present in eschatological joy."[69] This sense of openness, possibility, and danger is also reflected by liberation theologians Ivone Gebara and María Clara Bingemer, who write, "A human being is not primarily a definition or essence, but a history marked by space and time. A human being is not initially good and then depraved, or initially perverse and saved later; the human is this complex reality, full of division and conflict, whose nature is both limited and unlimited."[70] Complexity of past and present, individual and social, hope and despair, struggle and perseverance governs this conception of anthropology. Human beings must be understood in this complex web, rather than in terms of an ahistorical or decontextualized definition offered by philosophers or classically minded theologians. To be human is never less than standing before God and one's neighbor, with dignity and responsibility, connected to and distinct from them.

While some have spent their time trying to develop their anthropology by paying more attention to the empirical world and science, or to the particularities of human creatures, other theologians in the twentieth century believed these led to dead ends; instead, they decided to head in an entirely different direction.

Anthropology: Grounded in Christology and the Trinity?

Karl Barth: Anthropology Founded on Christology

Amid the new emphasis on human origins and scientific insight that dominated the twentieth century, Karl Barth is probably the most prominent example of a theologian who moved in a very different direction—not because he was plagued by doubts about scientific discoveries regarding human origins, but because he did not consider them theologically significant for the development of Christian anthropology. His methods and approach to theological anthropology, however, were equally revolutionary.

Put simply, Barth argues that we should begin our anthropological discussion with the second Adam, Jesus the Christ, rather than the first Adam, because only Jesus Christ reveals "real man" (his term) and therefore the contradiction of sin that plagues him and his world. In Barth's language, we know humanity—theologically—just as we know God, namely, by looking at Jesus, the incarnate Word of God. God speaks to humanity, and the Word "discloses his purposes" to humanity alone within God's cosmos: only from

69. Ibid.
70. Ivone Gebara and María Clara Bingemer, "Mary," in *Systematic Theology: Perspectives from Liberation Theology*, ed. Jon Sobrino and Ignacio Ellacuria (London: SCM, 1993), 165–66; cf. 165–77.

the Word can humanity know itself.[71] There is no question that God is the Creator and Lord of everything, but humanity alone is summoned, spoken to, and called to respond in a distinct relationship with Yahweh.[72] Barth is not against science, with its "precise information and relevant data," but such scientific conclusions *assume* human existence and reality—they are a human endeavor after all.[73] Barth's theological anthropology, on the other hand, does not simply see humanity as determined by the cosmos—though he does not deny such organic determination—but as determined by God's relationship with him: "Man is made an object of theological knowledge by the fact that his relationship to God is revealed to us in the Word of God";[74] indeed, humanity receives the Word because humanity is "summoned." For Barth this means "summoned because chosen," and only as "summoned" is humanity "real," for here humanity is "awakened" and "claimed."[75] This emphasis on the Word originates in his Christology and takes us to the "human nature of Jesus" in particular. While we don't have time here to unpack its multilayered and suggestive anthropology, we do need to highlight a few of the more relevant points.

First, Barth argues that a theological anthropology "means nothing more nor less than the founding of anthropology on Christology."[76] As Daniel Price has observed, while orthodox theologians and ministers proclaim that when we look to Jesus Christ we see the God who is, Barth also argues that in Jesus we also "find out who we are."[77] To use Barth's words, "Jesus is man as God willed and created him. What constitutes true human nature in us depends upon what it is in Him."[78] Barth is not trying here to describe the human constitution as composed of various faculties, but instead as consisting in a distinct relationship to God grounded in the Word made flesh. "What precedes human being as a being summoned by the Word of God is simply God and His Word; God in the existence of the man Jesus. . . . We are men

71. Barth, *CD* III/2, 16–19.

72. As he writes later, "Man is the creaturely being which is addressed, called and summoned by God. He is the being among all others of whom we know that God has directly made Himself known to him, revealing Himself and His will and therefore the meaning and destiny of man's own being." Ibid., 149.

73. Ibid., 24. Cf. Barth's later discussion on the question of human nature as approached from an apologetics viewpoint in much of modern theology, in which he begins by raising particular concerns about naturalism and the limits of "self-perception" (ibid., 79–96, 200).

74. Ibid., 19. See III/2, sec. 43 throughout for this dynamic distinction between other anthropologies and theological anthropology.

75. Ibid., 150.

76. Ibid., 44. Cf., e.g., *CD* II/1, 155–56; III/2, 552–53, 571. See also the correspondence from Pannenberg (9 May 1965) in reaction to Barth regarding the relationship between Christology and anthropology, in Karl Barth et al., *Letters, 1961–1968* (Edinburgh: T&T Clark, 1981), 350–51.

77. Daniel J. Price, *Karl Barth's Anthropology in Light of Modern Thought* (Grand Rapids: Eerdmans, 2001), 19.

78. *CD* III/2, 50.

as God is our Creator, and speaks as such with that one man as His Word."[79] Barth grounds human existence in the reality of the Word made flesh, rather than in an ancient ancestor. In this way he resists anthropocentric theologies while still centering his theology on a particular man—the man Jesus Christ, God's Revelation. While not all will agree that his approach is successful, most theologians concur that by grounding his anthropology in Christology, Barth is doing something fresh. His work continues to deserve serious consideration, as well as analysis as to whether he was successful or not. The most well-known critics of this christological grounding of his anthropology are Emil Brunner and G. C. Berkouwer, but others have continued to echo some of these early objections even as they acknowledge his contribution.[80]

Second, Barth warns against simply deducing anthropology from Christology in a crude and overly direct fashion.[81] The incarnate Lord does not become generic humanity, but the man Jesus, a real and particular human. To know humanity, beyond superficial appearances and mistaken a priori assumptions, one needs to know the nature of Jesus, for he alone reveals the true nature of humanity: "This man is man."[82] One danger in theology is the temptation to compromise the true and full humanity of Jesus, thus also compromising our understanding of authentic humanity and our connection with him. Jesus was a *particular* man, and in this way God becomes man, the man for us. For such reasons as these Barth states that the Son of God assumed our "fallen human nature" (although without committing sin) rather than an unfallen nature. Barth even suspects that the latter doesn't really exist. By becoming man, the real man, he took sinful human flesh, redeeming and freeing it from sin.

Third, in the humanity of Jesus we discover the paradox and promise of humanity. Barth basically agrees with Tillich's observation that a study of human nature must include the contradiction between creation and sin, between brokenness and redemption, although his development of the idea is very different from Tillich's. The human nature of Jesus presents both judgment and hope. "The human nature of Jesus spares and forbids us our own," because here we encounter a dialectic: the end of sin and the reality of forgiveness and grace are found in Jesus.[83] In Jesus alone, in his human nature, we discover a human nature without sin, at peace with God, and thus free of the "self-contradiction" and the "self-deception" that we so long to escape from. "The sinlessness, purity and freedom of human nature in Jesus

79. Ibid., 151.

80. Henri A. G. Blocher argues that "Barth's decision to ground his anthropology on Christology constitutes the most original feature of his treatment." Henri Blocher, "Karl Barth's Anthropology," in *Karl Barth and Evangelical Theology: Convergences and Divergences*, ed. Sung Wook Chung (Grand Rapids: Baker Academic, 2006), 101.

81. E.g., *CD* I/1, 131; III/2, 71–72, 222.

82. *CD* III/2, 43.

83. Ibid., 47.

consist precisely in the fact that, laden with the sin which is alien to His own nature, He causes Himself to be condemned and rejected with us. Thus the sin of our human nature is not only covered by Him but rightfully removed and destroyed."[84] Elsewhere he adds, "God's nature consists in the fact that as He freely shows mercy, so He will again show mercy," and that nature is made "effective and visible" ultimately "in the fact that He has mercy on the man Jesus and in Him on all men by becoming man Himself, by taking up and taking away man's burden in order to clothe man with His own glory."[85] We look to Jesus, the one who takes our sin, who brings reconciliation, who brings "judicial pardon," to see humanity as created and redeemed by God.[86] Further, not only is Jesus true human; he is also true God, and therefore human fellowship with God is always and only understood as occurring in Jesus. In Jesus alone do we have dignity and our promised forgiveness, for he is the living God, the one who is the true Prophet, Priest, and King, the great Representative and Giver, the lone Mediator between God and humanity. Barth works from the particular man Jesus, rather than from a priori, general, philosophical abstractions about human nature, examining Jesus as "a man," and not just "His humanity."[87]

Fourth, the humanity of Jesus is relational—he is for others. Not only does the divinity of Jesus present us as "man for God," but "his humanity can and must be described . . . that He is man for man, for other men, His fellows."[88] Jesus is always understood to be the man for others, not in part or accidentally, "but originally, exclusively and totally": that is who he is.[89] Barth emphasizes here that Jesus's humanity is from the beginning and always about his fellow humanity: "His orientation to others and reciprocal relationship with them are not accidental, external or subsequent, but primary, internal and necessary."[90] Jesus's embodiment of the two chief commandments—to love God and to love one's neighbor—displays and establishes our real humanity. To be human is to be for and with one's fellow humans. Thus, for example, Barth creatively explores the biblically and philosophically suggestive phrase "I am," concluding that it could be paraphrased as "I am in encounter."[91] This is not an occasional encounter, preceded and followed by isolation. Rather, "at the very root of my being and from the very first I am in encounter with the being of the Thou," and this necessarily takes a person to his or her fellow humanity. As a corollary, he says, "we must oppose humanity without

84. Ibid., 48.
85. *CD* II/2, 219.
86. *CD* III/2, 49.
87. Ibid.
88. Ibid., 208.
89. Ibid.
90. Ibid., 210.
91. Ibid., 247.

the fellow-man."[92] Expounding some varieties of this opposition, he discusses the dehumanizing effects of isolation, petty bureaucracy, the failure to look another in the eyes, and the failure to engage in mutual hearing, speaking, or helping others in need. "Human being is not human if it does not include this being for another."[93] Humanity, real "Man," is summoned by God in love with fellow humans.[94]

While much more could be said regarding Barth's anthropology, we have seen the results of his work grounding it on theology, particularly upon his Christology, but also clearly related to his doctrine of the Triune God. Other theologians have connected anthropology to the doctrine of the Trinity, and many of them have drawn from Barth.

More Recent Trinitarian Emphases

In 1894 J. R. Illingworth delivered the Bampton Lectures, giving them the title *Personality: Human and Divine.*[95] Arguing against the Unitarians, who seem to believe their conception of God is simpler and thus more persuasive than the mysterious Trinity, Illingworth wrote that the Trinity "moves in the direction of conceivability, for the simple reason that it is the very thing towards which our own personality points. Our own personality is triune."[96] Reminiscent of Augustine in some ways, Illingworth described the human personality as grounded in a threefold form of subject, object, and their relation. This form specifies "relation" as a dynamic that cannot be realized by a singular entity in isolation. A human needs that which is beyond or outside the individual (e.g., human relations like family) in order to be complete. God, on the other hand, does not need something external to realize that dynamic, since he has all the necessary conditions within himself: "a Trinity in Unity; a social God with all the conditions of personal existence internal to Himself."[97] The Triune God is personal in himself and then to others, whereas people are personal only as they engage others. In other words, there is similarity of some kind between the divine person(s) and the human person. This opens the

92. Ibid.

93. Ibid., 260.

94. Colin Gunton used to remind me, following the lead of Barth, that "man" is a unique theological word and should not always be avoided. "Man" has the rare ability to convey both particularity and universality. Such dual function is often employed by Barth, for example, as he illumines links between anthropology and Christology.

95. Christoph Schwöbel and Brian L. Horne first brought this work to my attention, each engaging and summarizing it in helpful ways in Christoph Schwöbel and Colin E. Gunton, *Persons, Divine and Human: King's College Essays in Theological Anthropology* (Edinburgh: T&T Clark, 1991), 1–3, 65–67.

96. J. R. Illingworth, *Personality, Human and Divine* (London: Macmillan, 1894), 74. Also quoted by Schwöbel and Gunton, *Persons, Divine and Human*, 2.

97. Illingworth, *Personality*, 75.

door for exploring such comparative reflection, which can prove profoundly illuminating—about God and/or about us.

Nearing the end of the twentieth century, the emphasis on the doctrine of the Trinity did not disappear but instead grew, partly as a result of the thundering influence of Karl Barth. While all do not agree with Barth's anthropology, he profoundly reshaped the conversation toward coordinating one's doctrine of God, and Christology in particular, with anthropology. In fact, the last quarter of the twentieth century saw work on this connection really flourish, though not without serious criticism. Attempts to connect anthropology with the Trinity continued in such books as the multiauthored *Persons: Divine and Human* (1991) and Stanley Grenz's volume *The Social God and the Relational Self* (2001). Similarly, Leonardo Boff examines the connection between the individual and the social or political sphere necessarily inhabited by humans in *Trinity and Society* (1988). Boff explores how divine triunity provides the basis for "all liberation" of humanity, with special concern and promise given to the poor—those whose dignity (and one might add their humanity) is often undermined by sinful social structures. In other words, the Trinity provides the basis for understanding real human social existence. There is a growing momentum for linking the Trinity to anthropology, and this includes a range of topics from human psychology to sociology, informing and transforming theologians' understanding of human *being*.

John Zizioulas: Being—Divine and Human

Few have been as suggestive and influential in examining the relationship between anthropology and the Trinity as the Greek theologian John D. Zizioulas, metropolitan bishop of Pergamon. Zizioulas's work is inspired by the early fathers, especially Athanasius and the Cappadocians (Basil the Great, Gregory of Nazianzus, Gregory of Nyssa). While some dispute his interpretation of these patristic sources, what matters in our survey is not his accuracy in handling the historical data but the resulting picture of human existence. *Being as Communion* (1985) remains Zizioulas's most important contribution in this discussion, though his more recent *Communion and Otherness* (2006) has filled in his reflections and provided more fuel for the fire.[98]

For Zizioulas, questions of ontology (*being*), particularly as they are related to anthropology, cannot be separated from questions about God. To

---

98. John D. Zizioulas, *Being as Communion: Studies in Personhood and the Church*, Contemporary Greek Theologians 4 (Crestwood, NY: St. Vladimir's Seminary Press, 1985); John D. Zizioulas, *Communion and Otherness: Further Studies in Personhood and the Church*, ed. Paul McPartland (London: T&T Clark, 2006). The heart of his original work grows out of his earlier essays in the French volume *L'Etre Ecclésial*, Perspective Orthodoxe 3 (Genève: Labor et Fides, 1981). See also his essay "On Being a Person: Towards an Ontology of Personhood," in Schwöbel and Gunton, *Persons, Divine and Human*, 33–46.

understand what it means "to be" should not be a philosophical question one answers by isolating an individual *thing*, deleting as much as you can from that thing, and then hoping you will discover a hidden essence. Instead, ontology begins with the Source of all Being, the eternal Triune God. The *being* of God as Father, Son, and Spirit—not some hidden essence—is the appropriate starting point for ontological discussion. This method counters problems arising when theologians start their anthropologies not with the Creator, but with creation in isolation. God is personal, not because of some abstract "substance" but because he is Father, eternally begetting the Son, and bringing forth the Spirit.[99] Consequently, for God (Father, Son, and Spirit), to *be* is to *be in communion*. God exists in this triune love and freedom, and thus all creatures, especially those created in his image, have their ontological basis in relation to the abiding, eternal, triune love and communion, rather than in some implanted "being" within them.

This basic observation, combined with choosing the doctrine of the Trinity as starting point, sets off all manner of implications for anthropology. The order in which Zizioulas chooses to address and connect theological questions gives his anthropology its distinctive form and content, beginning as he does with God, then moving to ecclesiology, and then to anthropology, circling around to soteriology. The human remains always dependent, not self-existent. "Between the being of God and that of man remains the gulf of creaturehood, and creaturehood means precisely this: the being of each human person is *given* to him."[100] Thus our being is "given" and upheld continuously, not a static gift that is independently ours. Specifically, we "are" as derivative images of God's original "I am."

Rather than adopt the reductionist methods of material science, defining humanity only in terms of its distinctions from other members of the kingdom *animalia*, Zizioulas speaks of being human primarily in ecclesial and salvific terms.

> From the fact that a human being is a member of the Church, he becomes an "image of God," he exists as God Himself exists, he takes on God's "way of being." . . . It is a way of relationship with the world, with other people and with God, an event of communion, and that is why it cannot be realized as the achievement of an individual, but only as an ecclesial fact.[101]

Zizioulas takes this position because he is more interested in *relations* than in individualistic physical composition—personhood (*hypostasis*) is the key.[102]

99. E.g., Zizioulas, *Being as Communion*, 44–49.
100. Ibid., 47.
101. Ibid., 15. Cf. the following: "The fact that man in the Church is the 'image of God' is due to the *economy* of the Holy Trinity, that is, the work of Christ and the Spirit in *history*" (ibid., 19).
102. Without doubt he does retain a strong affirmation of human physicality, which he will relate especially to eucharistic ideas.

The survival of "personhood" is necessarily related to divinization (*theosis*), which implies "participation not in the nature or substance of God, but in His personal existence."[103] One does not take on some divine substance, but rather enters into divine-human relations. Thus, "the goal of salvation is that the personal life which is realized in God should be realized on the level of human existence. Consequently, salvation is identified with the realization of personhood in man."[104] Notice here the fourfold connection that he makes among the Trinity, anthropology, ecclesiology, and soteriology.

Zizioulas admits that his theory, defining the "image of God" in terms of the church, could call into question the humanity of those outside the church. When asked if his theory means that those outside the church do not carry the image of God, Zizioulas responds that the church fathers always recognized two different modes of existence: (1) the hypostasis of biological existence and (2) the hypostasis of ecclesial existence. The former is common to all, but it points beyond itself, for an individual without the ecclesial is a "tragic figure." Sin and the fall represent human resistance to our "being dependent on communion," and so we require the truth and communion of God manifested in the body of Christ.[105] Only in the church, constituted by baptism and then Eucharist, is one reborn from above—and this is the good news for us. Here is real personhood. The biological is realized only within the church, which is why the early fathers view the church as a Mother. The argument does not deny the biological aspect of humanity, but argues only that our *being* attains its fullness in a nonbiological way, namely, by our spiritual communion in the church: "to endow it with real being, to give it a true ontology, that is, eternal life."[106] Thus this "hypostatic expression of the human person" is the only way to unite genuine liberation and community.

Even so, this human personhood can only fully be understood eschatologically, for the ecclesial person's daily existence doesn't really look all that different from the biological. This is because the ecclesial does not abolish the biological but introduces the eschatological to human existence. "Man appears to exist in his ecclesial identity not as that which he is but as that which he will be."[107] This takes us to what he calls a "sacramental or eucharistic hypostasis." That is, in the Eucharist we lose the biological restraints of our families according to the flesh, for the Eucharist transcends the exclusivity of biological categories by joining us to the entire body of Christ. Consequently, "the truth and the ontology of the person belong to the future, are images of the future."[108]

103. Zizioulas, *Being as Communion*, 49–50.
104. Ibid., 50.
105. Ibid., 102.
106. Ibid., 63.
107. Ibid., 59.
108. Ibid., 62.

This ecclesial framework connects us not only to God but also to other Christians. "The mystery of being a person lies in the fact that here otherness and communion are not in contradiction but coincide."[109] That is, our union is not that of uniformity, but a union of otherness in the connection of love— this is "truth as communion." Thus understood, human personhood affirms otherness without division. Sin divides, bringing fragmentation, isolation, and so on. "A human being left to himself cannot be a person."[110]

The Trinitarian Approach to Anthropology Broadly Affirmed

From 1983 to 1988 a study commission of the British Council of Churches met to explore the significance of the Trinity for doctrine today. The group included members from a diversity of denominations: Roman Catholics and Orthodox, Baptist and Quaker, Church of England and United Reformed, and so on. The report tied anthropology to the Trinity and drew specific implications for the church and society. It noted several trends that had gained power over the popular mind-set in the last two to three hundred years and that posed a huge challenge to Christian anthropology at the end of the twentieth century. Post-Enlightenment individualism, for example, which tends to define the human in terms of faculties (e.g., mind or body), offers autonomy; in truth, however, it actually produces isolation and longings that undermine the fullness of being human. Collectivism, on the other hand, subordinates the individual to the group and thus undermines freedom and flattens out distinctness among its members in an effort to achieve unity.[111] We need our freedom and distinctness to love the other genuinely.

According to the study commission, appreciating the way that the Triune God is personal provides a countercultural and yet promising pattern for society and the relations of its particular members. "God as Trinity is neither an impersonal collectivity, nor a collection of individuals, nor a unitary, solitary being. The three persons of the Trinity are joined in a free and loving relationship of communion."[112] An anthropology derived from trinitarian theology must maintain two points, argues the commission: (1) it must "preserve the particularity and uniqueness of every person," and (2) it must not allow particularity to oppose or undermine social relations, but rather to "show how the being of the particular derives from its relatedness to other particulars."[113]

109. Ibid., 106.
110. Ibid., 107.
111. Cf. the more fully fleshed out cultural critique and theological proposal by Colin Gunton, a member of the commission, in his book *The One, the Three and the Many: God, Creation and the Culture of Modernity: The Bampton Lectures 1992* (Cambridge: Cambridge University Press, 1993).
112. British Council of Churches, *The Forgotten Trinity: The Report of the BCC Study Commission on Trinitarian Doctrine Today* (London: British Council of Churches, 1989), 2:28–29.
113. Ibid., 1:21.

It sees relationality and reciprocity at the heart of personal being. "Human personhood is realizable in the present through the Spirit in the Church and in other forms of true community. We are thus enabled to say that true personhood is the gift of God."[114] In conclusion, the commission believes its main contribution comes from the idea that only in understanding the Triune God can we properly understand ourselves and each other, "our freedom to be with and for each other; our relations which yet respect the otherness, particularity and uniqueness of every human person; and the communion which may be realized through our free and particular relatedness."[115]

For all the strengths of using "relationality" as a key to understand human "personhood," concerns with possible shortcomings are growing louder, not diminishing.[116] Whether making such a direct analogy between the immanent Trinity (God *ad intra*) and human social relations is warranted, it has greatly stimulated conversations in theological anthropology over recent decades.[117] While theologians differ widely in their claims of how one should use trinitarian perspectives or presuppositions in anthropology, they tend to agree that any theological anthropology must take account of them in some way.[118]

Conclusion

This essay has covered a fair amount of ground.[119] Responding to the Enlightenment and to other movements since then, theologians have drawn from an increasing variety of sources in their attempts to present a more accurate and useful anthropology by making it more holistic. Human creatures are complex physical and psychological beings who are best understood in relation to

114. Ibid., 22.

115. Ibid., 25.

116. See, e.g., Edward Russell, "Reconsidering Relational Anthropology: A Critical Assessment of John Zizioulas's Theological Anthropology," *International Journal of Systematic Theology* 5, no. 2 (2003): 168–86; Harriet A. Harris, "Should We Say That Personhood Is Relational?" *Scottish Journal of Theology* 51, no. 2 (1998): 214–34; Julian N. Hartt, "The Situation of the Believer," in *Faith and Ethics: The Theology of H. Richard Niebuhr*, ed. Paul Ramsey (New York: Harper, 1957), 225–45; Alistair I. McFadyen, "The Trinity and Human Individuality: Conditions for Relevance," *Theology* 95 (1992): 10–18.

117. E.g., Gary Deddo's recent article, "Neighbors in Racial Reconciliation: The Contribution of a Trinitarian Theological Anthropology," *Cultural Encounters* 3, no. 2 (2007): 27–46.

118. See this theme throughout both volumes of Kelsey's work *Eccentric Existence*. Cf. Alistair I. McFadyen, *The Call to Personhood: A Christian Theory of the Individual in Social Relationships* (Cambridge: Cambridge University Press, 1990); Ian A. McFarland, *Difference and Identity: A Theological Anthropology* (Cleveland: Pilgrim, 2001); Tom Smail, *Like Father, Like Son: The Trinity Imaged in our Humanity* (Grand Rapids: Eerdmans, 2006); John Webster, "The Human Person," in *The Cambridge Companion to Postmodern Theology*, ed. Kevin J. Vanhoozer (Cambridge: Cambridge University Press, 2003), 219–34.

119. I would like to thank Cameron Moran, William C. Davis, and John Yates for their helpful feedback on earlier versions of this essay.

their Triune Creator and fellow creatures. The psalmist's question "What is man, that you are mindful of him?" continues to open more and more layers of questions to this day, and there is no sign that this will end anytime in the near future.

For Further Reading

Barth, Karl. *Church Dogmatics* III/2. Edited by G. W. Bromiley and T. F. Torrance. Edinburgh: T&T Clark, 1960.

Berkouwer, G. C. *Man: The Image of God*. Studies in Dogmatics. Grand Rapids: Eerdmans, 1962.

Kelsey, David H. *Eccentric Existence: A Theological Anthropology*. 1st ed. 2 vols. Louisville: Westminster John Knox, 2009.

Macmurray, John. *The Form of the Personal*. Vol. 1, *The Self as Agent*. Vol. 2, *Persons in Relation*. Gifford Lectures, 1953–1954. London: Faber & Faber, 1957.

McFadyen, Alistair I. *The Call to Personhood: A Christian Theory of the Individual in Social Relationships*. Cambridge: Cambridge University Press, 1990.

Niebuhr, Reinhold. *The Nature and Destiny of Man: A Christian Interpretation*. New York: Scribner, 1949.

Pannenberg, Wolfhart. *Anthropology in Theological Perspective*. 1st ed. Philadelphia: Westminster, 1985.

Schwöbel, Christoph, and Colin E. Gunton. *Persons, Divine and Human: King's College Essays in Theological Anthropology*. Edinburgh: T&T Clark, 1991.

Taylor, Charles. *Sources of the Self: The Making of the Modern Identity*. Cambridge, MA: Harvard University Press, 1989.

Webster, John. "The Human Person." In *The Cambridge Companion to Postmodern Theology*, edited by Kevin J. Vanhoozer, 219–34. Cambridge: Cambridge University Press, 2003.

Zizioulas, John D. *Being as Communion: Studies in Personhood and the Church*. Contemporary Greek Theologians 4. Crestwood, NY: St. Vladimir's Seminary Press, 1985.

7

. . .

THE PERSON OF CHRIST

Bruce L. McCormack

Introduction

The subject matter treated under the heading of the "person" of Christ in classical Protestant theology had to do with the ontological constitution of the Mediator.[1] The question of ontological constitution was by then a very old one, having been a focal point of attention in the early church. A settlement of the often rancorous debates that had sprung up from time to time over the proper solution to this problem was achieved in the fifth century by the Council of Chalcedon (451). In the millennium that separated the Protestant Reformation from that council, the Chalcedonian Definition had been the subject of a great deal of interpretive labor, above all in the time of Maximus the Confessor (d. 662) and again in the high Middle Ages. This process of mediation certainly left its mark on the Reformed wing of the Reformation especially. The Lutherans were more innovative.

The question to which Chalcedon addressed itself was this: How is it that Jesus Christ was fully God ("consubstantial with the Father as regards his

---

1. I mention Protestant theology here at the outset because *modern* theology was Protestant before it saw the emergence of Catholic forms as well. Due to limitations of space in this chapter—and the need to enter more deeply into the figures treated than is customary in textbooks—I will confine my attention here to a handful of leading Protestants. But Catholic modernism is a subject of interest in its own right.

divinity") and fully human ("consubstantial with us as regards his humanity")? To ask the *how* question—how it is that Jesus Christ could be both God and human at the same time—is to inquire into the nature of his being. It is to ask, what *kind* of being is this?—which is one of the most basic questions that can be asked in ontological reflection. "Ontology," after all, is the question of being, of what is real and how it is real.

That the ontological constitution of the Mediator should have become a question at all is due to the witness of the earliest Christians as found in the New Testament. Paul gives the question classical expression in his confession that Jesus Christ "was descended from David according to the flesh and was declared to be Son of God in power according to the spirit of holiness by his resurrection from the dead" (Rom. 1:3–4). In this passage, there is at least a hint of the "two-natures" *logic* (if not the categories) that would come to dominate early church reflection on Christology. Taken by itself, that might not have been sufficient to lead to the dogma of the church, but it did not stand alone. Of the greatest importance where pre-Chalcedonian christological reflection was concerned was the Logos-concept drawn from the prologue to John's Gospel (1:1–18). The idea of the "preexistence" of the Logos set forth in the prologue was given further support in the language of God's "sending" of his Son into this world scattered through the New Testament witness (cf. Matt. 10:40; Mark 9:37; Luke 4:43; 9:48; Rom. 8:3; Gal. 4:4, *inter alia*) as well as in the claim that God's Son played a role in creation (John. 1:3; Col. 1:16; Heb. 1:2). But it is not just as the "preexistent" Son that Jesus Christ performed functions that were thought at the time to belong uniquely to God. It is the man Jesus who claims for himself "the power to grant forgiveness."[2] The trend of such affirmations lay clearly in the direction of the participation of Jesus of Nazareth in the *identity* of the God of Israel[3]—a point underscored by intertextual allusions that made Jesus to be the object of claims made in the Old Testament by Yahweh with respect to himself (see, e.g., Phil. 2:10–11; cf. Isa. 45:23). All of this had to lead, eventually, to a solution like that found in Chalcedon.

But are the terms, the basic categories, employed by Chalcedon the most adequate for bearing witness to the being of the Mediator? Modern Christology was born in a reaction not so much against the theological values that sought expression in and through those categories as against the categories themselves. We make a huge mistake at the outset if we understand modern

2. Arthur M. Wainwright, *The Trinity in the New Testament* (London: SPCK, 1962), 162.
3. The language employed here is that of Richard Bauckham, *Jesus and the God of Israel: "God Crucified" and Other Studies on the New Testament's Christology of Divine Identity* (Grand Rapids: Eerdmans, 2008). See also Larry W. Hurtado, *Lord Jesus Christ: Devotion to Jesus in Earliest Christianity* (Grand Rapids: Eerdmans, 2003); Larry W. Hurtado, *How on Earth Did Jesus Become a God? Historical Questions about Earliest Christian Devotion to Jesus* (Grand Rapids: Eerdmans, 2005).

Christology as simply a repudiation of the dogma of the church. Initially, at least, it was anything but that.

To understand what is at stake in modern Christology, what the major issues and most important questions were and are, an attempt to survey the results of the many studies written in the last two hundred years would be less than helpful. What is needed is focused attention on the truly groundbreaking works, those theologians and philosophers who were opening up the paths on which others would later find themselves.

The story begins with the two thinkers most responsible for the creation of modern Christology: Friedrich Schleiermacher and Georg Wilhelm Friedrich Hegel. But before we turn to them, we would do well to have some understanding of the church's dogma and its evolution in the millennium prior to the Reformation. We should also pause to examine the reception of orthodox Christology in the Reformation period. For those who laid the foundations of distinctively modern Christology were seeking to work *within* the logic of Chalcedon, even as they revised its basic categories. And they did so with an eye fixed upon the confessions of their own Protestant churches.

From Chalcedon to the Reformation: The Evolution of Orthodox Christology

On the Relation of Chalcedon to Constantinople III

Because the formulation of the Chalcedonian Definition is considerably simplified in the Protestant confessions, it is important to understand it first in its original, more expansive form.

> So, following the saintly fathers, we all with one voice teach the confession of one and the same Son, our Lord Jesus Christ: the same perfect in divinity and perfect in humanity, the same truly God and truly man, of a rational soul and body; consubstantial [*homoousion*] with the Father as regards his divinity, and the same consubstantial [*homoousion*] with us as regards his humanity; like us in all respects except for sin; begotten before the ages from the Father as regards His divinity, and in the last days the same for us and for our salvation from Mary, the virgin God-bearer [*theotokou*] as regards his humanity; one and the same Christ, Son, Lord, only-begotten, acknowledged in two natures [*physein*] which undergo no confusion, no change, no division, no separation; at no point was the difference between the natures taken away through the union, but rather the property of both natures is preserved and comes together into a single person [*prosōpon*] and a single subsistent being [*hypostasin*]; he is not parted or divided into two persons, but is one and the same only-begotten Son, God, Word, Lord Jesus Christ, just as the prophets taught from the beginning

about him, and as the Lord Jesus Christ himself instructed us, and as the creed
of the fathers handed it down to us.[4]

What is most significant for our purposes here are the terms employed. Three
terms especially merit mention: "natures," "person," and "hypostasis." "Nature" (*physis*) is the most easily defined. A "nature" is a catalogue of properties
that provide a description of what a thing or person is. It is, in other words,
an answer to the question of "what-ness." "Person" and "hypostasis" are a
bit more difficult. It helps that they are used here as virtual synonyms. Each
interprets the meaning of the other. To speak of a "hypostasis" is to speak of
the concrete realization (or "instantiation") of a catalogue of properties. It
is to point to a specific exemplification of a catalogue of properties and say,
"there is one, right there," or (as in this case in which we are speaking of two
sets of properties) "there He is!" It is, therefore, an answer to the question of
"that-ness." The word "person," on the other hand, is derived from the Greek
prosōpon, which literally meant "face." It had to do with how a person or
thing presents itself, how it appears. In saying that there is but one *prosōpon*
in the God-human, the bishops were saying that he presents to us a single
"face"—and the reason for this is that there is but one "hypostasis"—a single
concretization of both natures—which the fathers clearly identified with the
"only-begotten Son, God, Word, Lord Jesus Christ." The One who "for us
and our salvation came down from heaven" (as the Nicene-Constantinopolitan
Creed has it) is the One in whom both "natures" were "hypostasized" (or
made concretely real). The two natures come together *in him*. Thus the simplified form of the definition which we find in most Protestant confessions is
justified—"two natures *in* one Person."[5]

But a problem emerges at the point at which we begin to consider the
question of how the God-human acts and who it is that performs those acts.
There is only one "person" that has been directly identified with the preexistent Logos. He it is who assumes human nature. He it is who continues (after
the assumption) to act in and through it. Indeed, there is here, to use more
modern terminology, but a single "subject" who acts through and upon the
human "nature." Cyril of Alexandria, whose Christology was affirmed in all
of its most significant features by the bishops at Chalcedon, understood the
human "nature" to be the "economic instrument" of the Logos.[6]

4. Norman P. Tanner, SJ, *Decrees of the Ecumenical Councils*, vol.1, *Nicaea I to Lateran V*
(Washington, DC: Sheed & Ward and Georgetown University Press, 1990), 85, 87 (p. 86 contains
the Greek and Latin texts).
5. Cf. (on the Lutheran side) the *Solid Declaration*, 8.2, and (on the Reformed side) the
Tetrapolitan Confession, chap. 2; the First Confession of Basel, art. 4; the First Helvetic Confession, art. 11; the French Confession, art. 15; the Scots Confesson, chap. 8; the Belgic Confession,
art. 19; the Second Helvetic Confession, chap. 11.
6. John McGuckin, *Saint Cyril of Alexandria and the Christological Controversy* (Crestwood, NY: St. Vladimir's Seminary Press, 2004), 184.

The human nature is, therefore, not conceived as an independently acting dynamic (a distinct person who self-activates) but as the manner of action of an independent and omnipotent power—that of the Logos; and to the Logos alone can be attributed the authorship of, and responsibility for, all its actions. This last principle is the flagship of Cyril's whole argument. There can only be one creative subject, one personal reality, in the incarnate Lord; and that subject is the divine Logos who has made a human nature his own.[7]

It is, therefore, the Logos who "activates" the mind and will ascribed to the man Jesus. The logical question to ask here is this: How meaningful is the ascription to Christ of a full and complete human "nature" (including a human mind and will) if that "nature" cannot function as ours does? To put a finer point on it, what good is having all the right "equipment" if it is never allowed to function normally? And by "normally," I do not mean sinfully; I just mean "naturally" (in accordance with created "nature"). If the human nature of Christ was never allowed to function *naturally*, is not human nature suppressed and finally set aside? Surely, even sinless obedience is self-activated. On the other hand, if we were to say that sinless obedience is self-activated, then the man Jesus looks less and less like the "instrument" of the Logos's activity. And it looks more and more as if we are thinking of two "subjects" rather than just one. So how do we affirm the self-activating character of the man Jesus without giving rise to two subjects?

It was almost inevitable that the Chalcedonian Definition should be subjected to further scrutiny. The question of "whether action belonged to the hypostasis and was therefore single or whether it belonged to the natures and was therefore double had not occurred to the church fathers"[8] in the fifth century. A rancorous debate on this question among those committed to Chalcedonian orthodoxy broke out in the seventh century. The Sixth Ecumenical Council (Constantinople III) decided the question in 681 on the side of action belonging to natures. In Jesus Christ, there are "two natural volitions or wills . . . and two natural principles of action."[9] Since these two wills are never "in opposition," the unity of the Person is not an issue. The human will is always and at every point in subjection to his divine will (which is shared with the Father and the Spirit). It does not resist or struggle against the divine will.[10]

Clearly, the human nature is now seen to function naturally—which means that the instrumentalization of the human defended by Cyril has been altered. The subjection of the human will of Jesus Christ to his divine will is a matter of self-movement. Thus, the "two natural wills and principles of action

7. Ibid., 186.
8. Jaroslav Pelikan, *The Christian Tradition*, vol. 2, *The Spirit of Eastern Christendom (600–1700)* (Chicago: University of Chicago Press, 1974), 64.
9. Tanner, *Decrees of the Ecumenical Councils*, 1:128.
10. Ibid.

meet in correspondence for the salvation of the human race."[11] And yet, the work performed by the God-human in and through his two natures is one as a consequence of the subjection of the human to the divine. "Each nature wills and performs the things that are proper to it in a communion with the other."[12] Thus, the result of divine-human action is always singular in nature. There are not two works but one work of the one God-human in and through both natures. Whether the agreement of the two wills took place always and everywhere without struggle would become a point of contention in the modern period. But it is clear enough what led the council to this conclusion. They intended a deepening and a clarifying of Chalcedon, even if what they produced was in some ways a critical correction.

Before we depart from Constantinople III, it should be observed that an ambiguity has been introduced where the "person" is concerned. Earlier, I noted that Chalcedon had made "person" to be synonymous with "hypostasis"—with both being identified with the preexistent Logos. The natures subsist in the person. But now there is a tendency to think in the other direction. The "person" subsists in and through his two natures. "We acknowledge the miracles and the sufferings are of one and the same [person?], according to one or the other of the two natures *out of which he is and in which he has his being.*"[13] In back of this ambiguity lies the affirmation of a "composite hypostasis" (*synthetos hypostasis*)—language that goes back to Apollinaris, was revived by Leontius, and was made to be orthodox by Maximus the Confessor.[14] At the very least, it has to be said that such language would seem to make the "person" to be "the whole Christ" (composed of divine and human natures) rather than being equated with the "hypostasis" that is the preexistent Logos. And that ambiguity leaves us with a bit of a puzzle. If both natures subsist in the Logos, are the attributes of both natures rightly ascribed to him or are they rightly ascribed to the whole Christ? As we are about to see, this ambiguity would play an important role in the debates that would unfold in the Reformation period.

To round out this discussion, it is important to observe that although the problem of instrumentalization had been solved, the solution had its own

11. Ibid., 129–30.
12. Ibid., 129.
13. Ibid. (emphasis added). Cf. Thomas Aquinas, *Summa Theologiae* IIIa.2.4 (Cambridge: Cambridge University Press, 2006), 53: "The person or hypostasis of Christ can be viewed in two ways. As it is in itself, it is completely simple, just as is the nature of the Word. But considered under the aspect of person or hypostasis, which means subsisting in some nature, the person of Christ subsists in two natures. Hence, although there is a single subsisting reality there, the style of subsisting is double. He is thus called a composite person in that one reality subsists in two natures."
14. Cf. St. John of Damascus, "An Exact Exposition of the Orthodox Faith," in *Writings* (Washington, DC: Catholic University of America Press, 1958), 282: "And the Person of the Word which formerly had been simple was made composite."

drawbacks. Schleiermacher put the point well. "But if Christ has two wills, then the unity of the person is no more than apparent, even if we try to conserve it by saying that the two wills always will the same thing. For what this results in is only agreement, not unity; and, in fact, to answer the problem thus is always simply to return to the division of Christ."[15] That this argument proved cogent in the long run had to do with the fact that "natures" could no longer be understood solely in terms of capacities abstracted from existing individuals. What modern theologians would add to the concept of the human person was self-consciousness and the personality development it made possible. Being a human "person" was seen as a matter of maturation that entailed striving and becoming. If, then, the human "nature" of Jesus was equipped (as Constantinople III insisted) with a natural will and a natural principle of action, the human "nature" looks even more like a second "subject" than ever it had in the early church. For that reason, Schleiermacher's objections were taken very seriously throughout the nineteenth century and on into the twentieth.

Development and Reaction in the Protestant Reformation

The Reformed and Lutheran wings of the magisterial Reformation were divided initially by a disagreement over the nature of Christ's presence in the Lord's Supper. The Reformed understood that presence to be spiritual in nature; the Lutherans understood it in terms of a local, physical presence of the body and blood of Christ "in, with and under" the elements of bread and wine. In order to explain how the body of Christ (risen, ascended, and seated at the right hand of the Father) could be physically present in the elements of more than one eucharistic celebration simultaneously, the Lutherans advanced an innovative understanding of the nature and effects of the hypostatic union. Thus, arguments over the Lord's Supper quickly devolved into a christological debate, one that continues to divide these two great communions today.

The official Lutheran position established in the *Book of Concord* maintained that the most important consequence of the hypostatic union was an intimate communion of the two natures, each with the other. The two natures are not simply placed alongside of each other "as if two boards were glued together."[16] No, this "indescribable communion" was well described by the ancients in terms of the analogies of a rod of iron that is permeated at every point by the fire that heats it up to the point of glowing and by the union of soul and body in the human being.[17]

---

15. Friedrich Schleiermacher, *The Christian Faith*, trans. H. R. Mackintosh and J. S. Stewart (Philadelphia: Fortress, 1976), 394.

16. *Epitome* 8.5 in Robert Kolb and Timothy J. Wengert, eds., *The Book of Concord: The Confessions of the Evangelical Lutheran Church* (Minneapolis: Fortress, 2000), 510.

17. Ibid.

The Lutheran teaching was novel to this extent: their intensive focus on the "communion of natures" led them to posit a new subclass of the "communication of attributes" that was based directly upon it (rather than simply upon the hypostatic union as such). They held that the divine attributes of omnipotence, omniscience, and omnipresence were "communicated" to the human nature. This "genus of majesty" (as it was called in the sixteenth century) then provided a basis for asserting the presence of the physical body of Christ (which was localized in heaven) in the elements of bread and wine in eucharistic celebrations (on earth).

Now the Lutherans were very careful to insist that the natures are not transformed essentially by their communion. "Neither is one [nature] transformed into the other. Rather, each retains its own essential characteristics, which never become the characteristics of the other nature."[18] Thus, divine characteristics never become predicates of the human nature as such—even though the human nature is granted a share in them.

The Reformed were only able to hear in all of this an illegitimate mixing of the natures (which had already been ruled out of court by the Chalcedonian "without confusion" and "without change"). Or, to put it another way, they heard in this a composition of the natures rather than the "composite hypostasis" of Constantinople III. The Lutherans rejected such criticism and insisted on the dynamism of the participation in question, which allowed for no transformation of one nature into the other.

For their part, the Reformed (precisely in their efforts to contradict this teaching) laid the emphasis on the Chalcedonian phrase "at no point was the difference between the natures taken away through the union, but rather the property of both natures is preserved."[19] They did not deny that the hypostatic union had to result in a communion of natures, but they rejected all analogies to it that seemed to require that such communion be understood along the lines of a penetration or permeation of either nature by the other (including, most especially, that of an iron rod in fire). For that reason, they also rejected any "communication of attributes" based on the communion itself (which meant, in practice, a firm rejection of the "genus of majesty"). They restricted the "communication of attributes" to a "communication" of the attributes to the "person"—by which, in most cases, they meant "the whole Christ." Expressed in this way, the "communication" could be understood synecdochally

18. *Epitome* 8.2 in ibid., 510.
19. See above, n. 4. For the sake of comparison, one example will suffice. The French Confession, art. 15, reads: "We believe that in one person . . . the two natures are actually and inseparably joined and united, and yet each remains in its proper character: so that in this union the divine nature, retaining its attributes, remained uncreated, infinite, and all-pervading; and the human nature remained finite, having its form, measure, and attributes; and although Jesus Christ, in rising from the dead, bestowed immortality upon his body, yet he did not take from it the truth of its nature, and we so consider him in his divinity that we do not despoil him of his humanity."

(the ascription to a whole of that which is proper only to a part). The Lutherans were able to hear in this only a violation of the "without division" and "without separation" of Chalcedon and, therefore, an undermining of the unity of the person. They too could affirm a "communication" of the attributes of both natures to the whole person, but it was finally the additional "genus of majesty" that secured (in their view) the proper understanding of the unity of the person.

Taking a step back, it must be said that both sides to this disagreement had some degree of legitimate purchase on Chalcedon. Like the seventh-century debates, this one took place between defenders of Chalcedonian orthodoxy. The use of pejorative labels like "Nestorian" and "Eutychian" by the Reformers when speaking of their opponents tended to conceal this fact and brought credit to neither side.

The Makers of Modern Christology: Schleiermacher and Hegel

Thus far, we have seen that Chalcedonian orthodoxy was not a single position but a number of permutations on the meaning of a basic formula. The questions to which it gave rise were many, and the answers given by even its most ardent defenders were disputed (by other equally ardent defenders). The modern period saw a transformation in the categories employed to explain the basic values that came to expression in the formula, but no abandonment of those values. We begin with Schleiermacher.

Friedrich Schleiermacher (1768–1834)

Schleiermacher is sometimes referred to as "the father of modern theology." That is a half-truth. Hegel is more thoroughly modern than he. Schleiermacher was something of a transitional figure, a person who still clung to the ancient conception of God as simple, impassible, and, indeed, ineffable. Hegel would challenge each of these points and in so doing step more clearly into the modern world. Moreover, it is precisely because he remained committed to divine impassibility that Schleiermacher was not a "panentheist." There could be, he believed, no reciprocity in the God-human relation (let alone the God-world relation), for reciprocity would effectively annul the "feeling of absolute dependence" that he believed to be basic to all religious consciousness in human beings.[20]

For Schleiermacher, human beings are relatively free and relatively dependent on all persons and things in the universe no matter how remote they may be in space. On God alone are they *absolutely* dependent. God is, thus, the Whence of the "feeling of absolute dependence." But then this also means that

20. Schleiermacher, *Christian Faith*, 12–26.

God cannot enter into the world he has created. To enter into the world, to act within the "system of nature,"[21]would be to act as one finite cause among others. Were God to do this, we would then be relatively free and relatively dependent upon him, and the "feeling of absolute dependence" would have been destroyed. God cannot do this and still be God. Schleiermacher's conclusion is that God acts toward and upon the world but not in it. God's activity is singular and directed continuously to the "system of nature" as a whole. Creation, providence, and redemption are thus a singular activity; redemption results from the providential arrangement of all things, an arrangement that is itself the result of a continuous, ever-present, and unchanging divine causality. The divine causality is certainly effective in the world, but effective from a point "outside" of it, as One who transcends the world absolutely. Expressed metaphorically: God cannot enter into the world, but God can "encounter" the world. He can "touch it" at a single mathematical point, a null point at which "the supernatural becomes natural" (i.e., divine causality passes over into and becomes natural laws of operation, including the natural laws of human development).[22]

This understanding of the God-world relation has a significant implication where Christology is concerned. There can be no incarnation in the traditional sense of the divine Logos entering into this world from outside of it. But that does not mean that Schleiermacher has no account of the incarnation of God in an individual life; far from it. In fact, he would like to do justice to all of the theological values that came to expression in the orthodox Christology of the ancient church if he possibly can.[23]

Schleiermacher understands Jesus as the man in whom there existed a "vital receptivity"[24] to the divine causality that is at work in and through all persons and things, a receptivity so pure as to enable him to realize perfectly in himself the presence of God to and in him. Thus, in him, the feeling of absolute dependence became a constantly potent God-consciousness that "was a real

21. Ibid., 138–39.
22. The phrase "the supernatural becoming natural" is used at a number of points in *The Christian Faith*; see 365, 430, 434, 492, 526, 537, 552, and 553. Schleiermacher also touches upon its importance in his second open letter to his friend Friedrich Lücke: "Whenever I speak of the supernatural, I do so with reference to whatever comes first, but afterwards it becomes secondly something natural. Thus creation is supernatural, but it afterwards becomes the natural order. Likewise, in his origin, Christ is supernatural, but he also becomes natural, as a genuine human being. The Holy Spirit and the Christian church can be treated in the same way." See Friedrich D. E. Schleiermacher, *On the Glaubenslehre*, trans. James Duke and Francis Fiorenza (Atlanta: Scholars Press, 1981), 89.
23. Schleiermacher, *Christian Faith*, 374. Schleiermacher understands these values to consist in the "exclusive dignity" (divinity) and "peculiar activity" (humanity) of Christ. The goal of Christology, he says, is "to describe Christ in such a way *(frater, consubstantialis nobis)* that in the new corporate life a vital fellowship between us and Him should be possible, and, at the same time, that the existence of God in Him shall be expressed in the clearest way" (ibid., 391).
24. Ibid., 387.

being of God in him."[25] Moreover, the fact that there is this pure receptivity in him is itself the result of the divine causality. God has so arranged things that the perfect union of divine causality with an individual in time is the telos toward which all of his creative and providential activity had been directed. In him, the completion of the creation of human nature has taken place. He is the Second Adam, the completion of creation, and it is only because he is this that he is also the Redeemer.

This is a point that is often missed by Schleiermacher's critics who are only able to find in him a horizontal line of reflection that traces the Christian experience of redemption back to its source in the Redeemer. The truth is that Schleiermacher's Christology lives at the intersection of two lines, a vertical first and only then a horizontal. The vertical line is his version of the doctrine of the incarnation. The divine "essence," Schleiermacher says, unites itself with human nature in Christ.[26] It is because this is so that Schleiermacher's Christology can *sound almost Apollinarian*. "The existence of God in the Redeemer is posited as the innermost fundamental power within Him, from which every activity proceeds and which holds every element together; everything human (in Him) forms only the organism for this fundamental power."[27] There is an important difference, though, between Schleiermacher and any early church theologian like Apollinaris. Consistent with his emphatic rejection of deism and his belief that the divine causality is operative continuously (so that it is present in any given moment of time), Schleiermacher understands the uniting of the divine "essence" with human nature in Jesus to be progressive and, indeed, gradual. It is not complete in the conception by the Holy Ghost (as the old orthodoxy maintained). And this allowed him already to make room for personality development in Jesus at a point in time *before* historical reconstructions of the life of Jesus had made it necessary! It was only as Jesus's "higher powers" (reason and will) developed that the uniting activity could produce that redemptive power that would emanate from him to those who came after. To be sure, the uniting activity was present in such a way that it kept him preserved from sin at every point—but always in a manner congruent with his stage of human development.[28]

Perfect passivity in relation to the uniting activity of God results in pure activity in relation to all the persons and things encountered by Jesus. This is what it means to speak of a perfectly potent God-consciousness in Jesus: he was able, in an unbroken fashion, to join his God-consciousness to all the stimuli mediated to him by his sensible life. In that his God-consciousness dominated or brought all of these stimuli into subjection to itself, he was

25. Ibid., 385. It should be noted that I have here revised the translation found in the introductory paragraph with which Schleiermacher opens §94.
26. Ibid., 739.
27. Ibid., 397.
28. Ibid., 383.

able to remain free from sin. It is because he is sinless that he is the Redeemer. Human sinfulness is overcome in him, in his divine-human being. The power of this overcoming is self-communicating; it is the power of love that seeks to unite itself with others. It reaches out beyond itself, drawing others who come after him into its power, awakening and empowering the consciousness of God that is latent in them so that they come to experience the grace of redemption. This is the aspect of Schleiermacher's Christology that is least understood by his critics. Since Schleiermacher refuses to attach greater dignity to the Redeemer than is necessary to explain the redemption we experience,[29] it is all too often assumed that the difference between Christ and ourselves can only be a difference of degree, not of kind. What is missed is the fact that it is precisely in his redeeming activity that *he is the replication in human form of the pure activity which God is*—an incarnation of God by any other name. And he alone can be this. It is in him alone that the creation of human nature is made complete (in his pure receptivity to God). This is something that can only happen once. Therefore, Christ is utterly unique, and what takes place in him is final (in the sense of being unrepeatable) and universal in its significance.

If, now, it be objected that because (by Schleiermacher's definition) we cannot be absolutely dependent on anything found in the system of nature but only relatively free and relatively dependent, the answer must be a dialectical one. We are not absolutely dependent on him with regard to his humanity as such but with regard to the inmost divine power at work in and through him, a power that (in its outworking) has been thoroughly naturalized and has taken place through laws of natural human development. Thus, the feeling of absolute dependence is preserved even as we are made to be absolutely dependent upon Jesus.

Georg Wilhelm Friedrich Hegel (1770–1831)

Hegel was a colleague of Schleiermacher's at the University of Berlin during the last thirteen years of his life. Theirs was an often stormy, contentious relationship. That story has been well told and need not concern us here.[30] Suffice it to say that although Hegel understood himself as a philosopher and not as a theologian, he was capable of presenting himself in lectures to his students as the champion of an older orthodox theology that the Christian theologians of

29. Ibid., 375.
30. See Richard Crouter, "Hegel and Schleiermacher at Berlin: A Many-Sided Debate," in *Friedrich Schleiermacher: Between Enlightenment and Romanticism* (Cambridge: Cambridge University Press, 2005). What was at issue in the conflict between Hegel and Schleiermacher as Hegel saw it was Schleiermacher's attempt to overcome the subject-object split created by Kant's epistemology by means of "mystical intuition and feeling." See ibid., 91. Hegel wanted to address the same problem rationally, by finding the ground of that split in reason itself. For his part, Schleiermacher found the absolutist tendencies resident in Hegel's rationalism imperialistic and at odds with his own ideal that a university should promote a diversity of perspectives (ibid., 88–89).

his time had wrongly neglected or dismissed.[31] He could do this, even if a bit tongue-in-cheek, because he firmly believed that "the content of philosophy, its need and interest, is wholly in common with that of religion. The object of religion, like that of philosophy, is the eternal truth, God and nothing but God and the explication of God. Philosophy is only explicating *itself* when it explicates religion, and when it explicates itself it is explicating religion."[32]

One of the central goals of Hegel's philosophy was to overcome the split between the human subject and the objects of her knowledge that had been created by Kant's epistemology. He did so by finding in God the ground of both, an originating point of identity.

For Hegel, the history of the world is the history of the unfolding of divine Self-consciousness. In order for the being of God to be fully realized, God must come to know himself in an "other"—which is himself. This takes place in that God "posits" himself over against himself, a second "moment" in the divine being. This is Hegel's version of the "eternal generation" of the Son. Notice that this act of Self-positing is no less necessary on Hegel's view than eternal generation had been for the ancients. Where he differs from the ancients is in the fact that his "other" turns out initially to be the world—which makes the act of creating to be necessary for God. Hegel refers to the act of Self-positing as an "essential determination" of God.[33]

But creation is not finally adequate to serve as the "other" in and through which God comes to full Self-consciousness. Consciousness is spiritual activity; the "other" through whom God comes to know himself must himself be a self-conscious being. And, in fact, he must be a finite subject. God is infinite; therefore, that which is "other" than himself can only be finite. So God becomes a human being. What Hegel has accomplished to this point is to set forth a new version of the ancient Logos Christology. The second "person" of the Trinity is a human being.

Jesus of Nazareth is, at one and the same time, the Self-revelation of God and the One in whom the alienation produced by God's act of going forth from himself is overcome and God is reconciled in and with himself. Why alienation? Because the act of Self-positing is an act in which God places

31. G. W. F. Hegel, *Lectures on the Philosophy of Religion*, one-volume edition, *The Lectures of 1827*, ed. Peter C. Hodgson (Oxford: Clarendon, 2006), 82, 85: "In recent theology very few of the dogmas of the earlier system of ecclesiastical confessions have survived or at least retained the importance attributed to them, and others have not been put in their place. . . . For though Christ as reconciler and savior is still constantly made the focus of faith, nevertheless what formerly was called in orthodox dogmatics the work of salvation has taken on a significance so strongly psychological and very prosaic that only the semblance of the ancient doctrine of the church remains. . . . Philosophy no longer has to face the reproach that it devalues the dogmas. Instead it suffers the reproach of containing within itself too much of the teachings of the church, 'more than the generally prevailing theology of our time.'"

32. Ibid., 78–79.
33. Ibid., 454.

himself over against himself as finite. God is "separated" from himself in becoming finite. God is himself even in this separation, but the substantial unity joining God and his "other" is only "implicit" as long as it does not become a conscious fact in the other. And this cannot happen until God has fully embraced "otherness"—that is, the experience of death, of radical negation, which is proper to all things finite. And so Jesus must die, and must do so as an event in God's own life.

Having reached the extreme limit of finitude and taken that limit up into his own life, God is then able to return to himself, so to speak. In that the dead Jesus is raised, God's act of Self-revelation is made complete. The substantial unity that had joined God to Jesus (and in him, to all humanity) in and through the "infinite anguish"[34] of separation is now made "explicit" (or fully manifest). The God who identifies himself with the crucified Jesus by raising him from the dead is the God who is made known as Self-sacrificial love, a love that goes to any extreme to be reconciled with the object of his love. And in that all of this is revealed to those who follow Jesus, their knowledge of God is made to be the vehicle of God's own Self-knowledge. God knows himself in and through their knowledge of him. This is the third "moment," the Spirit of communion and love that animates the church, which is founded in the resurrection.

Clearly Hegel has moved well beyond the "two natures" Christology of Chalcedon—which he rather caustically refers to as a "monstrous compound."[35] And yet he has retained something of the originating impulse that led to the formation of the orthodox Christology, namely, the direct identification of the "person" of Christ with the divine Subject. The fact that he makes this divine Subject to be human (full stop) is certainly novel but has at least this much to commend it: it allows for growth and development in the human Jesus (something which Constantinople III had denied). In this way, Hegel contributed directly to the emergence of historical-critical investigation into the life of Jesus.

But making God to be the Subject of a human life up to and including the experience of death also had the effect of introducing mutability into the concept of God. To be sure, this is not the stuff of twentieth-century "panentheism," with its understanding of the reciprocal-relatedness of God and the world. There is no reciprocity here. Indeed, the becoming of God in time is already "hardwired" into the being of God "from the beginning" insofar as the Self-positing activity of God is itself the consequence of an "essential determination."[36] God, we might say, is immutably what he is precisely in his mutability and passibility—because his being predetermines the outcome.

34. Ibid.
35. Ibid., 457.
36. Ibid., 454. Or as Spinoza put it, "The eternal and infinite being . . . acts by the same necessity whereby it exists." See Roger Mason, *The God of Spinoza: A Philosophical Study* (Cambridge: Cambridge University Press, 1997), 25.

After Hegel's death, his followers divided into a left wing and a right wing.[37] The point of division had to do with the question of whether God's "other" had to be an individual human being or whether it might not be preferable to see humanity collectively as God's "other." The left wing followed David Friedrich Strauss in affirming the second possibility (and, thereby, denying to Jesus a uniqueness or finality by means of which he might be qualitatively distinguished from his fellow human beings). The right wing, led by Philip Marheineke (a colleague of Schleiermacher's in the theological faculty at the University of Berlin), upheld the more strictly theological reading of Hegel. This remains a much-disputed question even today. My own conviction is that Marheineke had the best of the argument. If "death" marks the extreme limit of finitude and death is the experience of the individual, then God had to become a single human being.

Before taking our leave of Schleiermacher and Hegel, it is worth pointing out one item of belief that they held in common (albeit for quite different reasons). For both, the triunity of God is the consequence of the divine act of relating to the world in Christ and through the church. The Trinity is an eschatological rather than a protological reality. And that means, as Schleiermacher put it, God is not differentiated in himself in independence of his union with Christ and with the church.[38]

Kenotic Christology

"Kenotic" Christology was the creation of conservative Lutheran theologians at the University of Erlangen in Germany in the 1840s. The leading figure here was Gottfried Thomasius (1802–1875). The motivation was to preserve, as far as possible, the confessional Lutheran teaching with respect to the "genus of majesty." By the 1840s, investigation into the life of Jesus had made it increasingly difficult to maintain that Jesus of Nazareth had shared in the divine attributes of omnipotence, omniscience, and omnipresence (even in the dynamic way suggested by the Formula of Concord). The real sticking point was the issue of "personality development" (which included not only the self-understanding of Jesus but also his understanding of his mission—which on some accounts changed in the course of his public ministry). But there was also a new realism with regard to Jesus's intense struggle (in Gethsemane, especially) to remain obedient to the will of his Father. How could these features of the Gospel testimony be reconciled to the kind of "divinized" humanity that both the ancient church and the Lutheran Christology in particular had taught?

37. See Claude Welch, *Protestant Thought in the Nineteenth Century* (New Haven: Yale University Press, 1974), 1:104–5, 141–42.
    38. Schleiermacher, *Christian Faith*, 739.

Thomasius's solution to this problem was to suggest that, as a precondition to uniting himself with human nature in the incarnation, the Logos divested himself of those divine attributes deemed incompatible with the normal functioning of the human mind and will (i.e., omnipotence, omniscience, and omnipresence). He called this divestment "kenosis"—the noun form of the Greek verb that appears in the first half of the so-called Christ hymn in Phil. 2. Verses 5–7 (NRSV) read as follows: "Let the same mind be in you that was in Christ Jesus, who, though he was in the form of God, did not regard equality with God as something to be exploited, but *emptied [ekenōsen]* himself, taking the form of a slave, being born in human likeness." Such divestment was understood, however, to have been a temporary measure. As resurrected and ascended, the Logos took up once again the attributes he had laid aside and exercised them to the full—which meant that the participation of the man Jesus in them spoken of by the Formula of Concord began only at that point.

Critics of Thomasius's proposal were quick to point out that all the divine attributes belong to God essentially and that a divestment of any of them would mean change in the Logos; it would make the Logos mutable. And that, in turn, would destroy the essential unity of the Son with the Father and the Holy Spirit. To this, Thomasius had an answer—one that pointed to a fairly massive revision in the received understanding of God's being.

Thomasius introduced a distinction between attributes that are "essential" to God (i.e., those without which God would not be God) and attributes that are "relative" (those he "acquires" only because he freely decided to create a world).[39] To the first class belong truth, holiness, and love. To the second class belong God's omnipotence, omniscience, and omnipresence—attributes that are "relative" because they only arise in God as a consequence of the relation in which he stands to the world he created.

Did this distinction solve all the problems surrounding the Lutheran "genus of majesty"? The answer must be a cautious yes. Thomasius had postponed the interpenetration of natures to the "state of exaltation" so that he could now make space for a carefully delimited use of historical science in reconstructing the life of Jesus. That certainly addressed a central difficulty in the Lutheran reception of Chalcedon. But it failed to address the problems resident in the Chalcedonian Definition itself.

The real problem created by the definition had already been posed by that archcritic of Christian faith, David Friedrich Strauss. In a two-volume work published in 1840 and 1841, Strauss had argued that the two-natures doctrine had been rendered incoherent at the point at which Gregory of Nazianzus had insisted (over against Apollinaris) that the human nature was complete

---

39. Gottfried Thomasius, "Christ's Person and Work," in *God and Incarnation in Mid-Nineteenth Century German Theology*, ed. Claude Welch (New York: Oxford University Press, 1965), 66–72.

(i.e., that it was equipped with a human mind and a human will). For in that moment, the "two natures" were made into "two personalities." The problem, Strauss argued, is that it is impossible to understand two personalities (one infinite and the other finite) as capable of forming a single "person" (or "subject").[40] The one will always cancel the other out so that one alone can be person-forming—which is why, he said, the bishops at Chalcedon made the Logos (clothed in his divine nature) alone to be person-forming. But this only serves to underscore the fact that human personality under these conditions is suppressed and cannot function properly. If, for example, the "person" of Christ knew all things by an immediate act of eternal intuition (and given the equation of the "person" with the eternal Logos, this must be the case), then it is impossible that this "person" should also learn things discursively (through a process of discovery).

Clearly, Thomasius felt the force of this argument. In his efforts to address this issue, he took a fateful step. He suggested that the divine "self-consciousness" was also surrendered by the Logos in becoming incarnate[41]—so that the problem of an infinite self-consciousness and a finite self-consciousness coexisting in the same "person" was eliminated. The reason this was a problem is that divine self-consciousness was regarded even by Thomasius as basic to the truth, holiness, and love that God "essentially" is—which made divine Self-consciousness too to be "essential." Isaak August Dorner (1809–1884) put the problem this way: How could the love of God for the human race that animated Jesus of Nazareth and made possible his self-sacrificial, self-giving way of being in the world even be thinkable in the absence of the divine self-consciousness?[42] The point is that not even Thomasius himself was able to maintain the distinction between "essential" and "relative" attributes with anything like consistency. And there were other problems as well—as Dorner made clear. To strip the divine of anything essential to it was to reduce divine nature to human nature with the result that the hypostatic union now became (in effect) a union of two human natures—which could not possibly achieve a unity of "person."[43] Moreover, a temporary divestment of divine attributes would yield a theophany (i.e., an "appearing" of God in a medium that remains other than himself) but not yet an incarnation.[44]

40. David Friedrich Strauss, *Die christliche Glaubenslehre in ihrer geschichtlichen Entwicklung und im Kampfe mit der modernen Wissenschaft* (Tübingen: C. F. Osiander/Stuttgart: F. H. Köhler, 1841), 2:105, cf. 112–13.

41. Gottfried Thomasius, *Beiträge zur kirchlichen Christologie* (Erlangen: Verlag von Theodore Bläsing, 1845), 94–95.

42. I. A. Dorner, "Rezension von G. Thomasius, *Beiträge zur kirchlichen Christologie*," *Allgemeines Repertorium für die theologische Literatur und kirchliche Statistik* 5 (1846): 42; Dorner, *Entwicklungsgeschichte der Lehre von der Person Christi von den ältesten auf die neueste* (Berlin: Gustav Schlawitz, 1853), pt. 2.

43. Dorner, "Rezension von G. Thomasius," 44.

44. Dorner, *Entwicklungsgeschichte*, 1270.

Though Dorner's own Christology was anything but "kenotic," it too sought to provide an answer to the challenge posed by Strauss (while upholding the central aims of the Lutheran confession) and for that reason deserves mention here. His solution was to adopt Schleiermacher's strategy of a gradual uniting of divine and human, so that the human self-consciousness of Jesus was given sufficient room to develop naturally from childhood to adulthood. For him, no divestment of anything proper to God was needed. A gradual Self-communication took place, which resulted in a single divine-human personality in the exaltation of Christ.

Both Thomasius and Dorner were seeking to work *within* the Chalcedonian framework. Not only its logic, but its categories too have here been retained. That both did so under the conditions of modernity is also clear. The days when such efforts could be undertaken were, however, numbered. Even as Dorner was completing work on his own systematic theology, the antimetaphysical stance of the Ritschlian school was sweeping aside both classical Christology and the alternatives offered by Schleiermacher and Hegel.

Albrecht Ritschl (1822–1889)

Albrecht Ritschl's theology belongs to a world that passed away in World War I. For that reason, it has often been interpreted in the worst light possible and to this day remains inaccessible to those who choose to see it in this light. Such readings make it difficult to understand how it could have been celebrated in its day not only in Germany but also in Great Britain and the United States. The truth is that in its major methodological commitments, it anticipated the moves made (in their differing ways) by Karl Barth as well as by a fair number of political theologies in the late twentieth century.

Ritschl began his career in the field of New Testament studies. Having written a second dissertation in that field under the guidance of F. C. Baur, he was quite naturally attached for a time not only to Baur himself but also to Hegel (Baur's primary philosophical influence). That meant in practice a strong commitment to historical research informed by a drive to find unity in historical developments (in the form of the evolution of Hegel's Absolute Spirit). In 1856, Ritschl would abandon both of these commitments, and his relationship with Baur was permanently ruptured.[45] A contributing factor was Ritschl's growing uneasiness with a theology dominated by philosophical commitments—a development that may have had something to do with changes occurring within the discipline of philosophy itself. Hegel's star descended in dramatic fashion after the abortive 1848 revolution (which left many in Germany suspicious of totalizing explanations that were often called upon

45. See Philip Hefner, "Albrecht Ritschl: An Introduction," in Albrecht Ritschl, *Three Essays* (Philadelphia: Fortress, 1972), 6–8.

in the service of entrenched political and social interests). Ritschl himself passed through a "liberal" phase before becoming a conservative supporter of Bismarck in the 1860s.

In any event, Ritschl's constructive theology was built on a foundation laid in historical work. What he did was to elaborate a Christology "from below." That is to say, he took as his starting point the results of a historical investigation into the life of Jesus carried out by those belonging to the community formed by the reception of revelation. The reception of revelation—and with that, the experience of justification/reconciliation—provides the hermeneutical lens through which God's saving work in Christ is understood.

For Ritschl, what lay at the heart of Jesus's earthly ministry was his proclamation of the kingdom of God. Jesus understood it to be his unique calling to announce the coming of the kingdom and, in doing so, to inaugurate a process that would lead to its realization in this world. Ritschl defined the kingdom as "the organization of humanity through action inspired by love."[46] The goal of God's redemptive activity in this world, in other words, is moral in nature. The human race will one day be unified not through "the common exercise of worship"[47] (i.e., as "church") but as an ethical commonwealth characterized by love of the neighbor. The conception of Christian piety embedded in this understanding of the coming kingdom is worldly in nature; the Christian life is lived before God in the world, not in separation or withdrawal from it. Not surprisingly, the church exists only to put itself out of business. When the world has come fully under the reign of God, there will be no further need for a church, for the kingdom will have been fully realized.

What is the Christology that arises on the soil of this understanding of Jesus's inauguration of the kingdom of God? To rightly understand the person of Christ, one must begin with Jesus's fidelity to his calling. Jesus's trust and confidence in God led him to place himself completely under the Father's gracious rule, thereby enacting in himself the reign of God in this world. His "divinity" consisted precisely in this: the perfect unity of his will with the will of his Father. It is this unity of wills that made him to be the unique and final revelation of God.[48] He was the founder of the Christian religion not because he brought a new law[49] or because he set up his teachings as "doctrines" to which assent must be given[50] but because he was, in himself, the Self-revelation of God and the One in whom God's electing purposes to found a moral commonwealth of free persons ("children of God") was made effective in time.[51]

46. Albrecht Ritschl, *Justification and Reconciliation*, vol. 3, trans. H. R. Mackintosh and A. B. Macaulay (Edinburgh: T&T Clark, 1900), 12.
47. Ibid.
48. Ibid., 389.
49. Ibid., 413.
50. Ibid., 393.
51. Ibid., 13.

Is such an account of Jesus's "divinity" adequate? Well, it has to be acknowledged that, for Ritschl, Jesus is all that God is—or can be known to be. He was very much opposed to speculative metaphysics. For him, what a thing is cannot be found in anything lying in back of or beneath the thing (in a "substance"). The same is true of persons. Both are given to us to be known in the nexus of the relations in which they exist. By contrast, the general ideas we form about things in order to classify them and order them to one another have no reality; they are only ideas.[52] Applied to our knowledge of God, this means that God is real only in the relation he establishes with us in Christ. God is what he is in the act of giving himself to be known by us. The being of God is therefore rightly understood in terms of that "loving will" to give himself to "that community he elected before the creation of the world."[53] What God is essentially is love. But that is precisely what Jesus is as well. In that his will is perfectly conformed to the loving will of God, he is God in the flesh. One does not need metaphysics to explain this. One does not need to affirm the preexistence of the Son or an abstract doctrine of the Trinity or the two-natures doctrine to affirm that Jesus is the perfect revelation of God. It is not only superfluous to add anything to what Jesus is (since what Jesus is, God is); it is meaningless. In Ritschl's view, we cannot attach any reality to the ideas generated by means of metaphysical speculation.

Ritschl was not the first resolutely "postmetaphysical"[54] theologian. That honor probably belongs to Wilhelm Herrmann. Herrmann was the first theologian of the (then) student generation to attach himself to the "Ritschlian

52. Albrecht Ritschl, "Theology and Metaphysics," in *Three Essays*, 182–84.
53. Ibid., 164.
54. The word "metaphysical" has often been taken as synonymous with "ontological." It is not used so here in this essay. "Metaphysics" is a way of speaking about transcendent (supramundane) realities, which begins with general concepts rather than concrete particulars. A move is made from a general concept (often a totality that has been abstracted from the individuals of which it is composed) such as "world" or "humanity." The problem is that a totality is only an idea; it is not given to us directly to know. We do not encounter it anywhere. It is simply postulated in order to introduce and explain the unity of a group of items. As such, it lacks reality. And, therefore, the attempt to provide an ultimate explanation of the real involves a use of inferential reasoning, which abstracts from these general concepts to a putatively "real" ground of them that has no more reality than the concepts with which one began. That it is also possible to construct an ontology (an account of what is real and how the things we encounter are real in distinction one from another) on the basis of an individual is a possibility made necessary by the belief that Jesus Christ is God incarnate. In him, that which "deity" is and that which "humanity" is are "universals" made concretely real *in an individual*. Therefore, the attempt to think about the nature of God and the nature of the human on the basis of a starting point in a single individual is not metaphysical (since it does not draw inferences from general concepts). But it does result in an account of divine and human being, which means that it is ontological. I call such an ontology that is grounded solely and strictly in Christology "postmetaphysical" because it is an option that was only recognized after the failings of both classical and modern metaphysics had become clear.

school," and Ritschl himself learned a great deal from him.[55] But it was Ritschl who had the greater impact, especially outside of Germany. Ritschl does not quite say what the later Karl Barth would say, namely, that God is what God does. But it would be right to say that his theological epistemology presses in the direction of something like the theological ontology made explicit in the later volumes of Barth's *Church Dogmatics*.

The weakness of Ritschl's approach to Christology in particular becomes clear when we pose to it the question of its adequacy as measured by the New Testament. Few today would be willing to affirm the cultural optimism that suffused Ritschl's work, and I doubt anyone would agree with his depiction of the message and the person of Christ. And yet many today use a similar approach—a "historical" reading of Jesus's way to the cross—to fund politically driven christologies, which provide a stark contrast to Ritschl's "throne and altar" conservatism. The content of Ritschl's theology may not remain, but he remains the unseen guest presiding over the exegetical/theological performances of a good many liberationists and feminists. But the fact that Ritschl's method can give rise to such dramatically different results ought to give us pause. No matter how much we may prefer the hermeneutical location of the liberationists to Ritschl's, a method that could lead just as well to either is not finally capable of helping us make the move from the descriptive to the prescriptive, that is, from a description of what is deemed "helpful" in preferred sites to the kind of engagement with the truth-question that can be compelling to those in other places and times. For the latter, a theological ontology is going to be needed sooner or later, one that is more developed and consistent with the New Testament witness to the full reality of Christ than what Ritschl was able to provide.

Karl Barth (1886–1968)

The later Christology[56] of Karl Barth was formed out of close engagement with the terminological distinctions of the Chalcedonian Definition. But his categories of reflection were not finally theirs. Barth "actualized"[57] the

55. On the complex nature of the relationship between Ritschl's thought and that of his younger friend Wilhelm Herrmann, see Bruce L. McCormack, *Karl Barth's Critically Realistic Dialectical Theology: Its Genesis and Development, 1909–1936* (Oxford: Clarendon, 1995), 51–54.

56. Barth also took up the subject matter of Christology from the standpoint of its contribution to his doctrine of revelation in I/2. But he did this at a point in his theological development when he had yet to revise his doctrine of election and to find in that doctrine the ontological ground of his Christology. He returned to the subject matter of Christology more fully in volume IV (which is also his most complete treatment). It is the Christology of volume IV that I refer to as "later." *CD* I/1 continues to set forth the "early Christology" that Barth first worked out in his lecture on dogmatics in Göttingen in the mid-1920s.

57. Karl Barth, *Church Dogmatics* IV/2, 105.

"natures"—which meant that the category of history had replaced that of abstract definitions of the shared properties of a thing or person. And he replaced the abstract metaphysical conception of the "person" employed at Chalcedon (and which still haunted Constantinople III) with an understanding of the "person" as the result of the history of God's Self-identification with the man Jesus in his history, the continuous (not gradual) uniting of the Son of God with the man Jesus to form one "composite person."[58] In what follows, we will explain the meaning of these claims.

The first thing we need to recognize is that Barth's later Christology was made possible by his revision of the doctrine of election that he carried out in *Church Dogmatics* II/2. Though a fair bit of the theological ontology that he then began to elaborate had been anticipated in earlier volumes, it was only at this point that the grounding of his ontology in an eternal act of divine Self-determination (i.e., election) was put in place and made effective in the construction of the doctrines treated subsequently. Why did he speak of *Self*-determination? Because the content of the divine election was not only that God should do something in Christ but that he should *be* something in him. The meaning of election, as Barth understands it, is that God chose to be God as the man Jesus. That is to say, God eternally chose to subject himself to the human experience of divine judgment that would fall upon Christ in his passion and death in the place of sinful humans who merited destruction. That God could do this, that he could make himself the Subject of a human life and death without undergoing change on the level of his being is made by Barth to be a function of the fact that the eternal act of Self-determination is a determination of what God is "essentially."[59] It is a "determination" that makes its content to be "proper" or "essential" to God.[60] In any event, from this point on in the *Church Dogmatics*, election is seen as providing the ontological ground of Barth's later Christology, and his later Christology is the epistemic ground of his doctrine of election. And in making Christology to be the epistemic ground of the doctrine of election, Barth also bid a firm farewell to all metaphysical conceptions of the divine being-in-act. His is a postmetaphysical Christology that finds its focus in narrated history of Jesus of Nazareth as attested in the New Testament and never looks away from it. Nothing may be said of God that does not find its ground here alone.

With this understanding of election and its relation to Christology in place, we are now in a better position to understand the Christology itself. Barth makes the activity of the eternal Son in relation to the man Jesus to consist in ontic receptivity, in an ongoing act of identification with the man Jesus through which he makes the latter's history to be his history. "The Subject Jesus

---

58. Barth himself did not employ this phrase. But it is wholly apt for describing the results of his understanding of the person of Christ.
59. See on this point Barth, *CD* IV/2, 84–85.
60. Ibid., IV/1, 200–201.

Christ is this history."[61] Applied to this understanding, the older terminology of a "composite person" takes on new meaning. The "person" is made to be composite not through adding something to a divine being that is complete in itself without reference to the human. No, the second "person" of the Trinity is himself "composite"; in himself he already is, by way of anticipation (as founded in election), what he will become in time through ontological receptivity. Thus, "Jesus Christ" (i.e., the God-human in his divine-human unity) is the identity of the second "person" of the Trinity—not only in time but also "in himself" (when, as yet, there was no creation standing in need of redemption).

It should be clear that what Barth has done is to dispense with the metaphysical conception of the "person" of Christ altogether. There is no "person" somehow "beneath" the two natures as that in which they "subsist." The two "natures"—really, divine and human *being*—are made one in a single human history.

Barth's achievement in the realm of Christology can be evaluated and better understood by means of a quick comparison with the other models we have already treated. Like Dorner, Barth substitutes hypostatic uniting for hypostatic union. Unlike Dorner, he does not postpone the formation of a single divine-human person to the so-called state of exaltation but makes it an ongoing historical reality. Like Hegel, Barth has elaborated a model that allows him to make God to be the Subject of a human life, of the suffering and death that mean the destruction of the sinner. Unlike Hegel (who lacked Barth's doctrine of election), Barth understands God to be, already in himself (in his second "mode of being" as Son) what he will become in time. Triunity, for him, is not the result of the historical process but its presupposition (in the divine election). Like Ritschl, Barth has advanced a postmetaphysical account of Christ (and, indeed, of God). Unlike Ritschl, Barth did not have to dispense with the "preexistence" of the Son and the protological Trinity that is its corollary. And, finally, Barth has upheld the logic of Chalcedon. He has affirmed that Jesus Christ is fully divine and fully human in one person.

Conclusion: Christology after Barth

If "Christology" is concerned with the ontological constitution of the Mediator, then it is a real question how much of what has been written on and about Jesus Christ since Barth is truly "christological." Many have simply bracketed off such questions and concentrated their attention on Jesus's message or his way of being in the world, as though to address ontological questions must inevitably embroil one in fruitless metaphysical speculation. If Barth has taught us anything, it is that this is not the case; theological ontology can be

61. Ibid., IV/2, 107.

constructed on the basis of the narrated history of Jesus of Nazareth without the help of metaphysics. The best "post-Barthian" theologians understood this and proceeded in a way reminiscent of Barth (Piet Schoonenberg, Jürgen Moltmann, and Hans Urs von Balthasar, among others)[62]—or they sought in varying ways to revise metaphysics so as to make its results commensurate with historical investigation into the life, death, and even the resurrection of Jesus (Wolfhart Pannenberg, Walter Kasper, and Jon Sobrino).[63] Still, many today take for granted a complete identification of ontology with metaphysics and give up on both, thereby turning the doctrine of the person of Christ into a less than convincing treatment of his work that lacks the reality-referential character of christologies more attentive to questions surrounding theological ontology. In any event, their work belongs more properly to the chapter on the work of Christ found in this volume.

Christology after Barth has demonstrated clearly that permutations on the basic approaches treated in this chapter are possible. But the fact that these are permutations on basic paradigms suggests that the student who has mastered the paradigms will be well prepared to understand more recent developments.

For Further Reading

Boff, Leonardo. *Jesus Christ Liberator: A Critical Christology for Our Times*. Maryknoll, NY: Orbis, 1978.

Crisp, Oliver. *Divinity and Humanity*. Cambridge: Cambridge University Press, 2007.

Davis, Stephen, Daniel Kendall, SJ, and Gerald O'Collins, SJ, eds. *The Incarnation: An Interdisciplinary Symposium on the Incarnation of the Son of God*. Oxford: Oxford University Press, 2002.

Evans, C. Stephen, ed. *Exploring Kenotic Christology: The Self-Emptying of God*. Vancouver: Regent College Publishing, 2009.

Hector, Kevin W. "Actualism and Incarnation: The High Christology of Friedrich Schleiermacher." *International Journal of Systematic Theology* 8 (2006): 307–22.

Hodgson, Peter C. *Hegel and Christian Theology: A Reading on the Lectures of the Philosophy of Religion*. Oxford: Oxford University Press, 2005.

---

62. See Piet Schoonenberg, *The Christ: A Study of the God-Man Relationship in the Whole of Creation and in Jesus Christ* (New York: Herder & Herder, 1971); Jürgen Moltmann, *The Crucified God: The Cross of Christ as the Foundation and Criticism of Christian Theology* (San Francisco: Harper & Row, 1974); Hans Urs von Balthasar, *Theo-Drama: Theological Dramatic Theory*, vol. 3, *Dramatis Personae: Persons in Christ* (San Francisco: Ignatius, 1992).

63. Wolfhart Pannenberg, *Jesus—God and Man* (Philadelphia: Westminster, 1968); Walter Kasper, *Jesus the Christ* (New York: Paulist Press, 1974); Jon Sobrino, SJ, *Christology at the Crossroads: A Latin American Approach* (Maryknoll, NY: Orbis, 1978).

Jenson, Robert W. *Systematic Theology*. Vol. 1, *The Triune God*. New York: Oxford University Press, 1997.

Johnson, Elizabeth A. *Consider Jesus: Waves of Renewal in Christology*. 2nd ed. New York: Crossroad, 2000.

Kärkkäinen, Veli-Matti. *Christology: A Global Introduction*. Grand Rapids: Baker Academic, 2003.

Marsh, Clive. "Christocentricity and Community as Norms for Biblical Theology." In *Ritschl in Retrospect: History, Community, and Science*, 51–72. Edited by Darrell Jodock. Philadelphia: Fortress, 1995.

McCormack, Bruce L. "Karl Barth's Christology as Resource for a Reformed Version of Kenoticism." *International Journal of Systematic Theology* 8 (2006): 243–51.

———. "Karl Barth's Historicized Christology: Just How 'Chalcedonian' Is It?" In *Orthodox and Modern: Studies in the Theology of Karl Barth*, 201–33. Grand Rapids: Baker Academic, 2008.

Norgate, Jonathan. *Isaak A. Dorner: The Triune God and the Gospel of Salvation*. London: T&T Clark, 2009.

Sanders, Fred, and Klaus Issler. *Jesus in Trinitarian Perspective: An Introductory Christology*. Nashville: B & H, 2007.

Tanner, Kathryn. *Christ the Key*. Cambridge: Cambridge University Press, 2010.

8

• • •

ATONEMENT

KEVIN J. VANHOOZER

Introduction

The term "atonement" speaks to the heart of the relationship between God and human beings, signaling the process of "making at one" (i.e., at-one-ment) that restores right relations between parties that have for some reason fallen out. Arguably, the cross marks that spot in Scripture to which the prophets look forward and the apostles look back: the place where God was reconciling the world to himself (2 Cor. 5:19). Forgiveness through atonement is "the essential of evangelical Christianity," the central revolutionary divine act that orients and fulfills world history.[1] If the Gospels are "passion narratives with long introductions,"[2] then is Christian theology essentially atonement theory with long doctrinal prefaces? One early twentieth-century treatise affirmed the cross to be "the focus of revelation, the point at which we see deepest into the truth of God, and come most completely under its power. For those who recognize it at all it is Christianity in brief; it concentrates in itself, as in a germ of infinite potency, all that the wisdom, power, and love of God mean in relation to sinful men."[3]

---

1. P. T. Forsyth, *The Cruciality of the Cross* (Grand Rapids; Eerdmans, 1973), 1.
2. Martin Kähler, *The So-Called Historical Jesus and the Historic, Biblical Christ* (Philadelphia: Fortress, 1964), 80n11.
3. James Denney, *The Atonement and the Modern Mind* (London: Hodder & Stoughton, 1903), 1–2.

The New Testament contains an abundance of linguistic resources for proclaiming the saving significance of Jesus's death—metaphors drawn, for example, from the temple (e.g., sacrifice), battlefield (e.g., victory), commerce (e.g., redemption), and law court (e.g., justification). This may be one reason why there is no "dogma"—no single orthodox formulation—of the atonement, as Robert Jenson has observed (and perhaps overstated): "If you deny that Christ is 'of one being with the Father,' or that the Son and Jesus are but one hypostasis, you are formally a heretic. But you can deny any explanation of how the atonement works, or all of them together, or even deny that any explanation is possible, and be a perfectly orthodox believer."[4] Scripture's multiple metaphors and tradition's attitude of laissez-faire have consequently given rise to a proliferation of theories of the atonement, especially in modernity.

Jesus's cross stands not only at the climax of redemptive history but at the theological crossroads where a number of crucial Christian doctrines intersect. Indeed, perhaps no other doctrine is a better microcosm or barometer for the cultural and intellectual sea changes that ripple through theology than the doctrine of the atonement. How we conceive the atonement "determines more than anything else our conceptions of God, of man, of history, and even of nature"[5]—and vice versa. The significance of the cross is tied up with (1) the doctrine of God, (2) the gospel, and (3) biblical interpretation. Hence the doctrine of the atonement affects, and in turn is affected by, the core of "first theology" (i.e., the doctrine of God that informs one's theological hermeneutics). In this, church tradition agrees with the apostle Paul: "For I delivered to you as of first importance what I also received: that Christ died for our sins" (1 Cor. 15:3). The atonement is the heart of the gospel, the "keystone of the Christian system,"[6] the "Holy of Holies of Christian theology."[7]

What follows is an attempt to highlight seven major trajectories in modern discussions about the saving significance of Jesus's death on a cross. The story begins in polarization (i.e., one theory vs. another) but ends in pluralization (i.e., many metaphors/models working together). Note that the seven trajectories do not represent seven distinct "types" of theories, just different conversations. At the same time, there is some overlap between these conversations; certain theologians (e.g., Barth, Moltmann) could well have appeared under more than one heading. Running throughout the various conversations is a unifying concern, namely, how best to understand Jesus's death as

4. Robert Jenson, "On the Doctrine of the Atonement," *Princeton Seminary Bulletin* 27, no. 2 (2006): 100.

5. Denney, *Atonement*, 1.

6. B. B. Warfield, introduction to Junius B. Remensnyder, *The Atonement and Modern Thought* (Philadelphia: Lutheran Publication Society, 1905), x.

7. Robert H. Culpepper, *Interpreting the Atonement* (Grand Rapids: Eerdmans, 1966), 11.

a *gospel*—the power of God for salvation (Rom. 1:16)—good news "greater than which none better can be conceived."[8]

The (Re)Turn to the Subject: The Spirituality and Sociopolitics of Jesus

> Christ also suffered for you, leaving you an example, so that you might follow in his steps.
>
> 1 Pet. 2:21

Among the most important questions to be asked of any theory of atonement are (1) Who needs to be reconciled to whom? and (2) How does Jesus's death bring about reconciliation? The questions really concern where to locate the complication: "Where did the difficulty lie that was to be overcome by Redemption? Was it in forgiving the penitent, or in producing the penitence that could be forgiven? Was it in God or in man, in the Divine conscience or the human?"[9] Anselm and Abelard gave two contrasting answers to these questions in the twelfth century that have dominated the discussion for nearly a millennium. Indeed, Gustaf Aulén dubbed these opposing theories the "objective" and "subjective" models of the atonement, respectively.[10] Anselm argued that the cross satisfied God's honor; Jesus's death is an event in the past that effects a change in God by setting the world order objectively to right. By way of contrast, Aulén viewed Abelard as arguing that the cross displays the love of God that moves sinners to repentance; Jesus's death saves through its influence in the present. Aulén's own view of the matter was that neither Anselm nor Abelard does justice to the "classic" view of the fathers, namely that the cross is the linchpin in God's rescue operation that saves sinners from evil powers.

To a large extent, subsequent theologians have recycled and refurbished these earlier models, with varying degrees of contextual sensitivity. The Reformers and post-Reformation theologians worked a penal variation on Anselm, contending that Jesus's death satisfied not God's honor but his justice. These views tended to stress the saving significance of Jesus's death as a past

8. The phrase "than which none better can be conceived" is drawn from Anselm's proof for the existence of God. Atonement theories able to articulate our understanding of the gospel in the best way possible for a particular context have what Peter Schmiechen calls "evangelical value" (*Saving Power: Theories of Atonement and Forms of the Church* [Grand Rapids: Eerdmans, 2005], 7).

9. P. T. Forsyth, in Frédéric Louis Godet, ed., *The Atonement in Modern Religious Thought: A Theological Symposium*, 2nd ed. (New York: Thomas Whitaker Bible House, 1902), 77.

10. See Gustaf Aulén, *Christus Victor: An Historical Study of the Three Main Types of the Idea of the Atonement* (New York: Macmillan, 1969).

event (redemption *accomplished*) to which a subjective moment—repentance—was an appendix (redemption *applied*). In modernity the pendulum has swung to the other side, with many atonement theories beginning at the subjective end—the human response to God in the present—and only then discovering an objective moment as the catalyst of human response. As Kant worked a "turn to the subject" in philosophy, so the rise of psychology and history (i.e., the human sciences) led theologians to turn their attention to human subjectivity. The nineteenth-century concern with human consciousness and experience, coupled with the tendency to reject divine retributive justice and affirm God's love, led to a second coming as it were of Abelard's moral influence theory.[11]

Communicating the Consciousness of Forgiveness: Friedrich Schleiermacher and Adolf von Harnack

Writing in the wake of Kant's critique of reason, Schleiermacher (1768–1834), the "father of modern theology," made Christianity a function of religious feeling, and doctrine a matter of setting forth religious feelings or consciousness in speech. All human beings have an inherent God-consciousness (i.e., the feeling of absolute dependence). However, this awareness of being "spirit" comes into conflict with the "flesh," namely, our consciousness of our lower, animal nature. Jesus is the Christ because his "God-consciousness" is so potent that he is able to communicate it to others: "The Redeemer assumes believers into the power of his God-consciousness, and this is His redemptive activity."[12]

Schleiermacher also says that "the Redeemer assumes the believers into the fellowship of His unclouded blessedness, and this is His reconciling activity."[13] The point is that Jesus saves through his effectual spiritual formation, that is, by communicating his experience and steadfast consciousness of God the loving Father to others.[14] Conspicuous by its absence, however, is any mention of Jesus's death being an atoning sacrifice. What most impresses Schleiermacher instead is how even suffering and death were unable to snuff out the Son's communion with the Father. Moreover, as Jesus influenced his disciples, so the community continues to mediate his influence through its attitude-transforming corporate God-consciousness. In the words of one critic: "Thus does Christ's redeeming work consist in administering a tonic to the

11. Or perhaps "third," if one counts Socinus's appeal to Abelard against the Reformers' understanding of penal substitution.
12. Friedrich Schleiermacher, *The Christian Faith*, trans. H. R. Mackintosh and J. S. Stewart (Edinburgh: T&T Clark, 1928), 425.
13. Ibid., 431.
14. That Schleiermacher is working a modern variation on an Abelardian theme is evident from his reference to Christ's work as "that person-forming divine influence upon human nature" (*Christian Faith*, 427).

spiritually enfeebled rather than, as the New Testament teaches, making an atonement for the sinfully helpless."[15]

Adolf von Harnack (1851–1930) represents much late nineteenth- and early twentieth-century Protestant liberal thinking on the subject of atonement. In light of modern psychology, history, and philosophy, how can one consider a person who lived eighteen hundred years earlier to be a redeemer for today? Harnack's famous 1900 lectures on "The Essence of Christianity" maintained that the good news of Jesus Christ concerns the universal fatherhood of God, the brotherhood of man, and the infinite value of the soul. God is the redeemer because he helps people to live higher, holier lives through the teachings and example of Jesus, the definitive prophet who not only taught but also embodied God's word. For Harnack, the sole purpose of Jesus's death was to convince sinners "that forgiving Love is mightier than the Justice before which they tremble."[16] To believe this is to be reconciled: coming to believe in a mercy mightier than judgment is the actuality of atonement. What counts about the blood shed on the cross is "the sacred impression of this divine fact upon the soul."[17]

The Turn to the Intersubjective: Albrecht Ritschl

With Albrecht Ritschl (1822–1889) we might speak of a corporate variation on an "Abelardian" theme, moving from individual to social morality—a turn to the *intersubjective*, as it were. He was "the 'characteristic' man of the period, the embodiment of the late nineteenth century's effort to hold together personal faith, scientific history, and ethical demand."[18] God is known not in himself but in his reconciling effects, and these take place not in the individual's conscience but in the believing community. Ritschl compared Christianity to an ellipse, with justification and reconciliation as one focus and the kingdom of God as the other. Jesus is the founder of a moral commonwealth—the church, a community of reconciliation—whose task in turn is the transformation of society into the kingdom of God: "the organization of humanity through action inspired by love."[19] Though sin frustrates God's purpose to form a family, Christ's life and death communicate rather than enable the Father's familial love. Justification and reconciliation—the forgiveness of sins—occur in the church as the consciousness of guilt (which is the real punishment for sin) dissipates in the love of God that radiates from the

15. H. D. McDonald, *The Atonement of the Death of Christ: In Faith, Revelation and History* (Grand Rapids: Baker, 1985), 214.

16. Harnack in Godet, *Atonement in Modern Religious Thought*, 123.

17. Ibid., 124.

18. Claude Welch, *Protestant Thought in the Nineteenth Century* (New Haven: Yale University Press, 1985), 2:2.

19. Albrecht Ritschl, *The Christian Doctrine of Justification and Reconciliation*, ed. H. R. Mackintosh and A. B. Macaulay, 2nd ed. (New York: Scribner, 1902), 13.

Son. Sacrifice is not a means for removing guilt but a gift given to sustain a relationship. Ritschl thus recasts the work of Christ from a legal category to one of moral or familial fellowship. Atonement happens as one experiences forgiveness in and through the communion of saints. Jesus *dies* to fulfill his vocation and *saves* by communicating his vocation to others.

More recently, Theodore Jennings has called for a political theology of the cross.[20] Like Schleiermacher and Ritschl, he is looking for language that will make the cross intelligible to modern ears tired of worn-out mystic or cultic (i.e., sacrificial) language. He prefers instead to speak of the "theopolitical" significance of the cross. Atonement is real because the cross makes a difference, not inwardly in one's consciousness but outwardly in the public square. As a public event, the cross is a miscarriage of justice, but its effect is to break down social barriers between Jew and Greek, male and female, management and labor. God does not will Jesus's death. On the contrary: "The [power] structures crucify because they falsely believe that they are willed by God."[21] Jennings's turn to the (inter)subjective, like that of the other theologians here treated, assumes that the problem to be overcome through the cross is our enmity toward God, not God's toward us. In so doing, he confuses the underlying problem (alienation from God) with its outward symptom (broken political structure). The actuality of atonement is social in nature; the cross redeems insofar as it overcomes enmity toward God and occasions community-forming fruit. The cross points toward both an alternate way of life—a new politics—and its cost. Such is Jennings's "nonreligious" or secular view of atonement, where what fundamentally matters is not *interpreting* Christ's death but *using* it to confront the tyrannical powers that militate against the sociopolitics of Jesus.[22]

From Substitution to Representation: Incarnation as Atonement

> Truly, I say to you, today you will be with me in Paradise.
>
> Luke 23:43

The theologians we have just considered took issue with the idea of satisfaction. A second development in atonement theology objects to the idea of substitution, and to its concomitant focus exclusively on Jesus's death,

---

20. See his *Transforming Atonement: A Political Theology of the Cross* (Minneapolis: Fortress, 2009).

21. Ibid., 215.

22. Cf. Scot McKnight's suggestion that the "praxis" of atonement is a matter of participating in God's project of forming a community in which his will is done (*A Community Called Atonement* [Nashville: Abingdon, 2007], Part Four, "Atonement as Praxis").

preferring instead the more inclusive concept of representation and a focus on Jesus's life. Does the story of Jesus Christ focus on a life that ends in death, or a death that ends a life? In contrast to traditional theories that allegedly espouse a "narrow" understanding of atonement that limits it to what Jesus accomplished on the cross, theologians who make up this second trajectory champion a broader understanding of atonement that includes the life and resurrection of Jesus too: "We need a category of representative action, which describes a work of Christ for men so altogether great and inclusive that they cannot accomplish it for themselves, but which, far from being external to themselves, and therefore substitutionary, is a vital factor in their approach to God, because in it they can participate."[23] Participation—in Jesus's life, death, and new life—is the operative concept.[24] It is not that Jesus suffers so much as acts in our place: he is our representative, not our substitute. It is not only his death but also his entire incarnate life that is ultimately of saving significance.

Representative Flesh: Edward Irving

The nineteenth-century Scottish theologian Edward Irving (1792–1834) held that Christ's atoning representation of sinners began as early as conception, when he assumed *fallen* human flesh, a belief that led to the Church of Scotland's charging him with heresy. Irving's aim was to provide an alternative to what he called "Stock-Exchange divinity" where Jesus pays the debt of human sin. Sin "is not a thing, not a creature, but it is the state of a creature."[25] One cannot make at-one-ment simply by balancing the moral books. On the contrary, as Colin Gunton says, "The Son of God has given himself to be where we are so that we might be where he is, participants in the life of God."[26] Christ's self-giving therefore begins with the decision to take on fallen flesh: "The *humiliation* was the sacrifice . . . the *being made flesh*."[27] Indeed, atonement begins to take place as the Holy Spirit puts sinful flesh to death in Christ. This happens as the Son offers his life, through the power of the Spirit, in total obedience to the Father. Atonement happens first in Jesus's own body, where the Spirit does not "punish" but transforms sinful human flesh. Jesus's

---

23. Vincent Taylor, *The Atonement in New Testament Teaching* (London: Epworth Press, 1954), 198. In context, Taylor is referring to McLeod Campbell (see below), but his remark also applies more broadly to others in this second trajectory.

24. As I suggest toward the end of the present section, "participation" brings Western atonement theology closer to Eastern Orthodox notions of "deification" or *theosis*, where the emphasis is on partaking of the divine nature.

25. Edward Irving, *The Collected Writings of Edward Irving* (London: Alexander Strahan, 1865), 5:218.

26. Colin Gunton, *The Actuality of Atonement* (Grand Rapids: Eerdmans, 1989), 140.

27. Irving, *Collected Writings*, 5:270. For an overview of the debate, and its significance, see Kelly M. Kapic, "The Son's Assumption of a Human Nature: A Call for Clarity," *International Journal of Systematic Theology* 3, no. 2 (2001): 154–66.

active human obedience is transferable to sinners because the Son is priest—a representative who acts on our behalf. At his resurrection, the one who gives his life becomes life-giving spirit (1 Cor. 15:45). As the Spirit enabled Christ to defeat sin, so Christ enables sinful human beings to participate in his victory by giving them the Spirit.

Representative Repentance: J. McLeod Campbell

The teaching of J. McLeod Campbell (1800–1872) deviated, as did Irving's, from the received orthodoxy of the Church of Scotland, eventually leading to the revocation of his license to minister. Campbell afterwards ministered to an independent congregation and continued to develop his views, eventually publishing them in his 1856 work *The Nature of the Atonement*.[28] Driving his proposal was a pastoral concern for his congregation's understanding of the God of the gospel, in whom there is a priority of love over law. The Father forgives sinners not because of but *before* the atonement. God is not Judge first and Father second, but Father first and forever.

The gospel is not a demand for what humans have to do to be right with God, even when the "to do" in question is "repent and believe" (i.e., exercise faith). Rather, the gospel concerns what God in Christ first does for us in grace. It is just here that we come to what is distinctive about Campbell's view: "The Son's dealing with the Father in relation to our sins [took] the form of a perfect confession of our sins. This confession [was] *a perfect 'Amen' in humanity to the judgment of God on the sin of man*."[29] Christ's high-priestly "Amen" satisfies divine justice by offering a perfect repentance.[30] More pointedly: Christ's "Amen" actualizes atonement: "*In that response* sin is conquered, God is satisfied, and we are called to be partakers through Christ in eternal life."[31] No one comes to the Father but through the vicarious humanity of Jesus Christ: we participate in the one true response to the Father that summarizes both his life and death.[32]

"Jesus wept" (John 11:35). Yes, but for McLeod Campbell they were tears of representative penitence, not substitutionary penance. Indeed, Campbell tends

---

28. See the new edition with an introduction by James B. Torrance (Eugene, OR: Wipf & Stock, 1996).

29. Campbell, *Nature of the Atonement*, 118–19. Emphasis in the original.

30. Jesus here satisfies God by offering perfect contrition, not by undergoing punishment. Leanne Van Dyk argues that Campbell's alternative to traditional satisfaction theories offers a promising way forward for Reformed theology. See her "Toward a New Typology of Reformed Doctrines of Atonement," in *Towards the Future of Reformed Theology: Tasks, Topics, Traditions*, ed. David Willis and Michael Welker (Grand Rapids: Eerdmans, 1989), 225–38.

31. Van Dyk, "Toward a New Typology," 229.

32. James B. Torrance, introduction to Campbell, *Nature of the Atonement*, 11. Torrance also says: "Participation is . . . a key word in McLeod Campbell's theology. The Son of God has participated in our humanity, that through the Spirit we might participate in his Sonship and communion with the Father" (14).

to think that the most extreme suffering of Christ took place in the garden, not on the cross.[33] This is problematic in the eyes of his orthodox critics, for Scripture identifies the efficacy of atonement with Jesus's shed blood (Rom. 3:25), not his sorrowful soul (Matt. 26:38). In the final analysis, it is not clear why, for Campbell, it was *necessary* for Jesus to suffer and die.

Representative Mediation: T. F. Torrance

T. F. Torrance (1913–2007) goes even further in his insistence on the atoning quality of the incarnation itself in order to refute what he terms the "Latin heresy," namely, the idea that Jesus's work is separate from or external to his person. The incarnation must be more than an instrumental means of atoning death. Drawing upon Athanasius's notion that the Son is *homoousios* with (of the same being as) the Father, Torrance argues that the incarnation is intrinsically redemptive. Because the Son has really and truly assumed human nature, there is a union of natures, a hypostatic union, in the person of the Son. Reconciliation is not a matter of some judicial or commercial transaction between God and humanity; rather, it is ontological incorporation of humanity into the Son's very being. Here, too, the accent falls not upon substitution but representation: Jesus Christ is the "real" man into whom other men and women are incorporated. The "wondrous exchange" for Torrance is thoroughly ontological: Christ "[became] what we are that we might become what he is."[34]

What, then, of the historical cross and the work of Christ? According to Torrance, Christ accomplishes his atoning reconciliation not in his death per se but *within* his whole being and life, which includes both death and resurrection. He *is* the mediator: "He is in his own incarnate person the reality and content of the atoning redemption that he mediated."[35] God deals with the guilt and corruption of sinful humanity in the person of the Son, in whom our sinful humanity is joined to, and hence exalted by, the divine nature. Sinful humanity becomes sanctified, in other words, precisely by being joined to the divine being (including history) of Jesus Christ: "From his birth to his death and resurrection on our behalf he sanctified what he assumed through his own self-consecration as incarnate Son to the Father."[36] The hypostatic union (i.e., incarnation) is thus a reconciling union (i.e., atonement). In Torrance's words: "The incarnation and the atonement [have] to be thought together in terms of their intrinsic coherence in the divine-human Person of the Mediator. . . . The incarnation [is] seen to be essentially redemptive and redemption [is] seen to

33. For an elaboration of this point, see Campbell, *Nature of the Atonement*, chap. 11.
34. T. F. Torrance, *The Trinitarian Faith: The Evangelical Theology of the Ancient Catholic Church* (Edinburgh: T&T Clark, 1988), 179.
35. Elmer M. Colyer, *How to Read T. F. Torrance: Understanding His Trinitarian and Scientific Theology* (Downers Grove, IL: InterVarsity, 2001), 89.
36. T. F. Torrance, *The Mediation of Christ* (Edinburgh: T&T Clark, 1992), 41.

be inherently incarnational or ontological. Union with God in and through Jesus Christ who is of one and the same being with God belongs to the inner heart of the atonement."[37] In sum: the incarnation or hypostatic union *is* the actuality of atonement.[38]

From Identification to Deification: No Participation without Ontological Representation?

Torrance helps us to see just how divergent are our first two trajectories. Atonement in the first case is a function of Jesus as a moral exemplar. This ethical *imitatio Christi* pales in comparison, however, to the ontological *participatio* that characterizes this second trajectory that we are now considering.[39] Indeed, Torrance so emphasizes the inclusive nature of Jesus's incarnation (in which there is not only a "recapitulation" but a "summation" of human history) that atonement becomes a function of our absorption into his personal being. Union and communion with Christ here approximate what in Greek Orthodoxy is called *theosis* or deification, which means not "becoming God" but "being drawn much more deeply into the relationships in which God exists as a Trinity of love."[40] A number of contemporary atonement theories—in particular those that emphasize the whole of Jesus's incarnate life and not his death only—work with this broader view of atonement as involving not simply the remission of sins but the restoration of right relationships.

Deification is a "nontransactional" notion of salvation for which the most important watchword is participation, not propitiation. It is therefore a natural end to theories that view the incarnation itself as the actuality of atonement. The key element such theories seek to uphold is the idea that Jesus's death and resurrection are the culmination of a life lived in identity with sinful humanity. By identifying with human life (i.e., becoming one with it), Jesus also heals it—makes ontological repairs, not penal reparations.[41] While it may be premature to say "there is no East or West" in theology, there is some

37. Torrance, *Trinitarian Faith*, 159.
38. See also T. F. Torrance, *Atonement: The Person and Work of Christ*, ed. Robert Walker (Downers Grove, IL: InterVarsity, 2009), and "The Atonement: The Singularity of Christ and the Finality of the Cross," in *Universalism and the Doctrine of Hell*, ed. Nigel M. de S. Cameron (Grand Rapids: Baker, 1993), 225–56.
39. I contemplated making *theosis* or deification an independent trajectory, but decided in the end that it is the capstone as it were of discussions of the atonement that stress the saving significance of the hypostatic union, that is, of Jesus becoming as we are so that we could become as he is.
40. Paul S. Fiddes, "Salvation," in *The Oxford Handbook of Systematic Theology*, ed. John Webster, Kathryn Tanner, and Iain Torrance (Oxford: Oxford University Press, 2007), 176.
41. Cf. Bruce R. Reichenbach, "Healing View," in *The Nature of the Atonement: Four Views*, ed. James Beilby and Paul R. Eddy (Downers Grove, IL: InterVarsity, 2006), 117–42.

indication that the recent "incarnation as atonement" views are converging with the older *theosis* tradition.

Scot McKnight's position is an interesting case in point. On his view, atonement refers to God's work in Christ to create a human society in which God's will is done on earth as it is in heaven. The atonement restores humans as "Eikons" (i.e., icons, images)—those who are able actively to image God's rule: "The atonement is designed by God to restore cracked Eikons into glory-producing Eikons by participation in the perfect Eikon."[42] Jesus participates in our humanity so that we may participate in his. Here, too, the logic of atonement is "identification for incorporation."[43] The outstanding question for such theories concerns the conditions for incorporation: what, if anything, must I *do* in order to participate?

Must There Be Blood? The Nonviolent Atonement

> Pilate said to them, "Take him yourselves and crucify him, for I find no guilt in him."
>
> John 19:6

A third development in atonement theology joins the first two in questioning the necessity of Jesus's bloody death as a condition for putting humanity right with God, though the focus now is on rejecting *sacrifice* as well as *satisfaction* and *substitution*. The three ideas are related, for sacrifice is often viewed as a substitute satisfaction. Hence this third trajectory, like the first two, takes issue with the notion of penal substitution. Unlike the first two developments, however, this one has its roots firmly in the twentieth century and its appreciation of the role of social context on theological reflection. The overriding concern is to dissociate God from the idea of redemptive violence. Accordingly, proponents of this trajectory object in the strongest terms to the idea that, in order to save us, God requires a bloody death. The emphasis here is negative (i.e., protesting the unjust nature of sacrifice), though, as we shall see, the theologians in our fourth category go on to offer positive accounts of the liberating effect of Jesus's death without thereby sanctioning violence.

The Cross in Gender and Racial Oppression

Twentieth-century theologians have detected what they take to be a direct link between the way in which traditional atonement theology interprets the cross of Christ and contemporary patterns of social and racial abuse. The

42. McKnight, *Community Called Atonement*, 3.
43. Ibid., 109–10.

connecting link in each case—feminist, black, and liberation theology—is the notion that God uses sacrificial suffering for good.[44] Feminist theologians in particular have insisted that "lifting high the cross" contributes both to victim passivity and violent oppression by giving them divine sanction. They do not want to see Jesus's suffering on the cross used to legitimate slavery or women's subordination and therefore deny the cross any sense of divine imprimatur. Joanne Carlson Brown and Rebecca Parker, in their oft-cited article "For God So Loved the World," say, "Christianity is an abusive theology that glorifies suffering. . . . We must do away with the atonement, this idea of a blood sin upon the whole human race."[45] They further (and controversially) characterize the notion that God sent the Son to suffer and die as "divine child abuse."[46]

The theologians involved in this third conversation insist that God never employs violence for redemptive purposes. God is not the author of Jesus's death; on the contrary, God is a loving father who does not need to punish one child before he can love the rest. The problem is not sin as individual guilt so much as sin as systemic evil (i.e., racism, sexism, imperialism). The cross is an instrument of state torture, not the linchpin in a divine plan of salvation. Jesus did not come to suffer and die but to announce the good news to the poor and liberty to the oppressed. Jesus's death was the consequence of this challenge to the dominant powers of the day. To suggest that God willed the death of the Son is to legitimate the idea that there can be a "good" suffering: "Until this image is shattered it will be almost impossible to create a just society."[47] From such a liberationist perspective, the fatal flaw of the substitutionary sacrificial death of Jesus is that it does nothing to challenge, much less to change, the unjust structures of the status quo.[48] Overturning those structures is precisely the point of exhibiting Jesus as a scapegoat.

Must There Be Scapegoats? René Girard

The Day of Atonement in ancient Israel featured two goats: one is killed as a sacrifice; the other is sent into the wilderness to carry away Israel's guilt (Lev. 16:15–22). According to the literary critic René Girard (b. 1923), this is a prime instance of the scapegoat phenomenon that, in his view, lies at the very origin of culture and religion.

44. See esp. the essays in part 1 of Marit Trelstad, ed., *Cross Examinations: Readings on the Meaning of the Cross Today* (Minneapolis: Augsburg Fortress, 2006).

45. Joanne Carlson Brown and Rebecca Parker, "For God So Loved the World," in *Christianity, Patriarchy and Abuse: A Feminist Critique*, ed. Joanne Carlson Brown and Carole R. Bohn (New York: Pilgrim, 1989), 26.

46. Ibid., 2.

47. Ibid., 8–9.

48. So Rita Nakashima Brock, *Journeys by Heart: A Christology of Erotic Power* (New York: Crossroad, 1988), 57.

Girard believes that all human interaction involves "mimetic rivalry": we want what we see other people having (e.g., food, sexual partners, land), and we're willing to compete for it. Violence is often the result. Newton's law of motion has a counterpart in the human realm: for every violent action there is an equal and (sometimes greater) opposite reaction. The problem of culture, of humans living together, is how to stop the violence from escalating to the breaking point of society. Enter the scapegoat. Girard believes that sacrifice restores peace by transferring hostility to a third party on the margins of the group. This third party becomes the scapegoat who is sacrificed (i.e., killed, exiled, punished) for the sake of restoring peace: "The purpose of the sacrifice is to restore harmony to the community, to reinforce the social fabric."[49] The solution to bad group violence is "good" violence directed at an individual. For Girard, then, the dark secret of culture and religion alike is that each is founded on an act of collective violence against a victim whose guilt is unquestioned.[50]

The power behind the scapegoat mechanism is not divine but demonic: it is Satan—the accuser—who both instigates and benefits from the idea that there is a good violence. In Girard's view, Christianity has too often collaborated with the powers and principalities, especially when it turns the cross of Christ into an object lesson on the redemptive effects of violence. Yet the true intent of the Gospels (and the uniqueness of genuine Christianity) is not to legitimate but *expose* the scapegoat mechanism as the satanic device it is. The authors seek not to justify the idea of sacred violence but to end it once for all, thus breaking the cycle of violence (i.e., an eye for an eye). God demands nonviolence, not sacrifice. From this perspective, the idea that Jesus's death was necessary to satisfy God has got the wrong end of the cross. The Gospels defang the scapegoat mechanism by showing Jesus the scapegoat to be wholly undeserving of his fate, thereby dissipating the illusion of sacred violence together with the notion that God willed his death. According to Girard, Jesus had to die not as a sacrifice but as a prophet who paid the ultimate price by confronting the powers and speaking the truth: "I will utter things hidden since the creation of the world" (Matt. 13:35 NIV).[51]

Several theologians have enthusiastically taken up Girard's ideas. Raymund Schwager goes to great lengths to show that the Bible never depicts God as advocating violence or even retributive justice.[52] "Have I any pleasure in the

49. René Girard, in James G. Williams, ed., *The Girard Reader* (New York: Crossroad, 1996), 78.

50. See his *Violence and the Sacred* (Baltimore: Johns Hopkins University Press, 1977) and *The Scapegoat* (Baltimore: Johns Hopkins University Press, 1986).

51. See, further, Girard, *Things Hidden since the Foundation of the World: Research Undertaken in Collaboration with J.–M. Oughourlian and G. Lefort* (Stanford: Stanford University Press, 1987) and *I See Satan Fall like Lightning* (Maryknoll, NY: Orbis, 2001).

52. Raymund Schwager, *Must There Be Scapegoats? Violence and Redemption in the Bible* (San Francisco: Harper & Row, 1987).

death of the wicked, says the Lord God?" (Ezek. 18:23). The cross not only exposes the scapegoat mechanism but demonstrates that God continues to love even when his love, embodied in Jesus, is violently rejected: "The full exposure of violence robs ritual sacrifices of any meaning."[53] To translate this Girardian idea in terms of Luther's "wondrous exchange," God returns violence with *nonviolence*.

S. Mark Heim has written what is to date the most important North American appropriation of Girard's ideas: *Saved from Sacrifice: A Theology of the Cross*.[54] Heim argues that the Bible does not commend bloody sacrifice but rather interprets the cross as the event to end all sacrifice (i.e., sacred violence). The saving act of God is overlaid on the sinful human act: it is the very idea that we achieve peace by wreaking violence on victims that we need to be saved from. One might therefore say with regard to Jesus's death on a cross: "you (Jews and Romans) meant it for sacrifice, but God meant it for good" (cf. Gen. 50:20). The effect of the cross is not to placate God but to vacate the myth that we can solve violence by working more violence. As such, the cross is aimed at disarming the powers and principalities of the myth of "good" violence. In so doing, the victims become visible as victims, not scapegoats. Heim goes further than Girard in acknowledging the cross as necessary not simply to expose the scapegoat mechanism but to point the way to communal living without sacrifice.[55]

Girard's critics think that he makes only a negative gesture: the cross saves not by instituting something positive (i.e., a new practice), but simply by refusing an old one (i.e., scapegoating). William Placher observes, "It all still sounds too much like gnosticism to me. Our problem, according to Girard and Heim, was that we did not understand something. The solution is to realize the truth and therefore live differently."[56] Others wonder whether Girard's bloodless account passes the acid test of any doctrine of atonement, namely, explaining the *necessity* of Jesus's suffering and death (Luke 9:22).[57]

Christus Victor Recapitulated: The Cross "after Christendom"

Father, forgive them, for they know not what they do.

Luke 23:34

53. Ibid., 202.
54. *Saved from Sacrifice* (Grand Rapids: Eerdmans, 2006).
55. See also Robert Hamerton-Kelly, *Sacred Violence: Paul's Hermeneutics of the Cross* (Minneapolis: Fortress, 1992).
56. William C. Placher, "Why the Cross?" *Christian Century*, December 12, 2006, 39.
57. Cf. Michael Winter's complaint that modern theologians (1) agree that the Bible never explains how sacrifice achieves its results, but (2) are themselves largely unable to explain the necessity of Jesus's suffering and death (*The Atonement* [London: Geoffrey Chapman, 1995], 37).

Theologians in this fourth trajectory follow those in the third in decisively repudiating the idea of redemptive violence. The defining feature of this fourth group is their somewhat paradoxical attempt to describe God's victory over evil on the cross in nonviolent terms. Accordingly, this fourth trajectory could be described as a "demythologizing" recapitulation of the patristic victory motif, inasmuch as it views the powers and principalities vanquished by the cross as cultural rather than cosmic forces. Christ wrestled not against flesh and blood, but against social and political powers, both institutional (e.g., an oppressive Roman state) and ideological (e.g., Jewish ethnocentrism). The cross is simply the last stage of Jesus's broader lifelong struggle against oppressive satanic forces. Consequently, theologians in this fourth stream tend to emphasize the saving significance of the whole of Jesus's life. Jesus lived the life that God originally intended humanity should live. In doing human history over, but this time the right way, Jesus puts things right and makes peace.

The Cross as God's Victory: Gustaf Aulén

It was Gustaf Aulén (1879–1977), in his 1931 publication *Christus Victor*, who first recovered what he called the "classic" or "dramatic" view of the atonement. On Aulén's view, salvation involves more than the removal of guilt. Sinners are saved not by being declared innocent but by sharing in the victory of God over the power of evil, and even death itself. God saves as the mighty warrior incarnate who, in defeating the evil powers, removes the very cause of judgment. Jesus Christ's victory makes atonement (i.e., brings about reconciliation).

"Victory" Expanded and Pacified: Walter Wink and J. Denny Weaver

A number of contemporary theologians have critically appropriated Aulén's victory motif, working, like Aulén, with Irenaeus's recapitulation view (according to which Christ gains the victory through obedient living and dying) but in a more pacifist direction. The result is a nonviolent variation on a *Christus Victor* theme. Like the preceding trajectories, this one too rejects the idea that God requires retributive justice before he can forgive sinners. It is not that God uses violence (i.e., Jesus's bloody death) to make atonement but rather that Jesus's death is the way God deals with violence. In the words of John Yoder: "Every major strand of the New Testament, each in its own way, interprets the acceptance by Jesus of the violence of the cross as the means, necessary and sufficient, of God's victory over the rebellious powers."[58]

58. John Yoder, "Theological Critique of Violence," *New Conversations* 16 (1994): 6. See also the essays in Brad Jersak and Michael Hardin, eds., *Stricken by God? Nonviolent Identification and the Victory of Christ* (Grand Rapids: Eerdmans, 2007).

Walter Wink (b. 1935) associates violence not with God's victory but with the oppressive "powers and principalities" from which God seeks to release us.[59] Wink understands the evil powers to be both spiritual and institutional: sociopolitical forces inclined to oppose the rule of God. Human history is the dramatic conflict between the powers that dominate the world and the coming reign of God that received its decisive embodiment in the person of Jesus Christ ("thy will be done"). Sensing a threat to their dominion, the powers rose up to crush Jesus and his way. However, the victim exposed the powers by exposing their essential violence: "By submitting to the authority of the Powers, Jesus acknowledged their necessity but rejected the legitimacy of their pretentious claims. He submitted to their power to execute him, but in so doing relativized, de-absolutized, de-idolized them."[60] Jesus conquers the powers by remaining true to his way—the living out of God's rule and God's love—refusing to compromise with violence or to act from fear of death: "When he was reviled, he did not revile in return; when he suffered, he did not threaten" (1 Pet. 2:23). In sum, Jesus defeats the powers precisely by engaging them nonviolently: "We are liberated, not by striking back at what enslaves us—for even striking back reveals that we are still determined by its violent ethos—but by dying out from under its jurisdiction and command."[61]

J. Denny Weaver's 2001 publication *The Nonviolent Atonement*[62] adds "narrative" to the notion of *Christus Victor*, emphasizing the role of Jesus's life as well as death in his struggle against and victory over the evil powers of this world.[63] Weaver argues that the church lost interest in the *Christus Victor* model after the Constantinian power-sharing arrangement of the fourth century. What powers can Christians oppose in Christendom, where the church

59. Walter Wink, *Engaging the Powers: Discernment and Resistance in a World of Domination* (Minneapolis: Fortress, 1992).

60. Ibid., 142. Cf. Ben F. Meyer: "Jesus did not aim to be repudiated and killed; he aimed to charge with meaning his being repudiated and killed" (*The Aims of Jesus* [London: SCM, 1979], 218).

61. Ibid. 157. Elsewhere in the book (e.g., 227), Wink does contemplate employing "nonviolent" coercion to oppose the powers. Like the other themes currently under discussion, the notion of a nonviolent atonement that liberates the oppressed names not a single theory but a recurring theme in recent atonement theology. In addition to the theologians discussed here, Moltmann (along with many liberation theologians) takes issue with traditional views of the atonement that focus on individual sins and encourage the poor to take up their cross (i.e., accept suffering passively) rather than to oppose oppressive sociopolitical forces nonviolently. Liberationist models emphasize the atoning efficacy of the whole of Jesus's history, especially his concerns for the poor and the outcast. For an argument for viewing "liberationist" models of atonement as distinct from the *Christus Victor* approach, however, see Marit Trelstad's introduction to *Cross Examinations*, 14–15.

62. *The Nonviolent Atonement* (Grand Rapids: Eerdmans, 2001).

63. Weaver distinguishes his own position from Girard's: "Narrative *Christus Victor* has more focus on the entire scope of Jesus's mission to make the reign of God visible" (*Nonviolent Atonement*, 49).

holds the spiritual and temporal reins? The implication is that the two swords go hand in hand with the idea of the cross as the locus of divine retribution and redemptive violence.

Weaver sides with feminist, womanist, and black theology in protesting Christianity's unequal yoking with white patriarchal power. Jesus's death overcomes the powers—oppressive systems of social injustice—not by dying but by living in a certain way (hence the significance of Jesus's narrative). Jesus displays the victory of the age to come over the present evil age in his life, death, and resurrection. To be saved is to be liberated from anything to do with these violent powers, and liberated for the (narrative) way of Jesus Christ. This way is not that of the passive victim but of nonviolent forgiveness, witnessing to the reign of God by affirming the humanity of the oppressed and by exposing structures and systems that theoretically or practically deny it. Jesus's refusal to respond to violence is a chosen act, not a helpless surrender.

The whole of Jesus's life, then, as well as his death, narrates in bodily form the reign of God as it confronts, and defeats, the reign of evil (Satan). The resurrection is the victory of God, and an invitation to participate in Jesus's way, truth, and life. Weaver sees this pattern continued in the book of Revelation where "the confrontation of the church and empire [is] depicted symbolically [as] a nonviolent confrontation."[64] Christians present their bodies as living sacrifices to God (Rom. 12:1), as did Jesus, not by making blood payment to satisfy guilt but rather as a ritual of dedication and self-giving to God.[65] In sum, the cross is not a satisfaction of God's justice but a sign of service to God's peacemaking cause.[66] One question that critics of this view press home concerns the uniqueness of Jesus's work: Have there not been other martyrs who similarly forgave those who trespassed against them?

The Cross as an Event in God's Being

> My God, my God, why hast thou forsaken me?
>
> Matt. 27:46 KJV

There is another, more radical way of responding to criticisms of the cross as a violent substitutionary sacrifice that satisfies God's justice. Earlier we spoke of Jesus as man representing rather than substituting for humanity. Theologians in this fifth trajectory view the cross as an event not only in the history of Jesus but also in the very history of God (i.e., the relationships of

64. Weaver, *Nonviolent Atonement*, 32.

65. Ibid., 59.

66. See Brad Jersak's related "nonviolent identification" approach outlined in "Nonviolent Identification and the Victory of Christ," in *Stricken by God?* 18–53, esp. 32–33.

Father, Son, and Spirit). As such, the death of Jesus affects God's own life. Stated differently: the efficacy of the atoning act is internal, not external, to God's own being. While the various theologians treated under this heading agree that atonement is a moment in God's triune being, they differ with respect to their understandings of the divine ontology, especially as concerns (1) the God-world relationship and (2) the relationship of the economic and immanent Trinity.

Atonement and the "Death" of God: G. W. F. Hegel and Jürgen Moltmann

Though Hegel (1770–1831) rarely figures in surveys of the atonement, he was arguably the first to radicalize Luther's theology of the cross. Hegel treats the incarnation-crucifixion-resurrection as a historical representation that he then presses into metaphysical service in his complex account of the historical self-unfolding of Absolute Spirit (Subject, not "substance"): the emergence of self-consciousness and the reconciliation of opposites (i.e., self/other). In a dialectical nutshell, *Geist*—the divine Spirit or Mind—must go out of (i.e., die to) itself as Absolute in order to come back to itself (i.e., achieve self-consciousness).[67] The Gospel story represents the way in which the divine mind (i.e., Logos) enters into the world of time and physicality in order ultimately to return to itself.[68] Hegel works this out in trinitarian fashion such that the incarnation, crucifixion, and resurrection are episodes in God's trinitarian life, a history in which *Geist* or Absolute Spirit comes to be fully self-aware through the mediation of the finite human spirit (i.e., collective consciousness). Gunton rightly comments that while Hegel retains the language of traditional atonement theology—its *form*—he has radically revised its *content*.[69]

At the heart of Hegel's gospel (and metaphysics) is the theme of overcoming estrangement—to be precise, the alienation of infinite and finite, God and world. Note, however, that the problem (i.e., that which has to be reconciled) is finitude, not fallenness. Accordingly, the solution required is less personal than philosophical: How can we think of the finite and infinite together? Hegel sees the answer in symbolic-logical form in the incarnation: in Christ, the fullness of the infinite divine Idea dwelt in finite human form. There is an "absolute identity" of finite and infinite spirit. Moreover, for God to become human is already to effect a reconciliation: the Absolute enters into finitude,

---

67. "The universal has to pass into actuality through the particular. Spirit is known 'in itself' only because it has appeared 'for itself' and 'in and for itself' in history" (Welch, *Protestant Thought*, 93).

68. For an introduction to Hegel's thought and its theological significance, see Cyril O'Regan, *The Heterodox Hegel* (Albany, NY: State University of New York Press, 1994), and Merold Westphal, "Hegel," in *The Blackwell Companion to Modern Theology*, ed. Gareth Jones (Oxford: Blackwell, 1997), 293–310.

69. Gunton, *Actuality of Atonement*, 19.

negation, and death in order to absorb them into the divine being. In this is love, what God *is*: the actuality of reconciliation, the healing of opposites, and opposition.

The good news of the unity of the divine and human is historically "proved" by Jesus's death and resurrection. Death, the ultimate form of finitude, is absorbed by God's being, thus negating the negation (i.e., the estrangement of the finite from the infinite). Not for nothing, then, has Hegel's notion of Jesus's atoning death been described as a "speculative Good Friday," a transitional moment in the emergence of Absolute Spirit.[70]

The outstanding question for Hegel is whether Jesus's death is only a cipher for a metaphysical atonement embedded in the entire world process, or a unique event in the concrete history of both God and humanity. Does Jesus's death actually bring about something new (i.e., reconciliation) or rather reveal that the finite and infinite are already one—or accomplish the former by means of the latter?

Jürgen Moltmann (b. 1930) presents the cross as a moment in the history of the trinitarian God as well, though the framework he employs for doing so is eschatological rather than metaphysical. Writing after the horrors of World War II, Moltmann wants to exorcise the ghost of Greek philosophy, in particular its notion that God's transcendence immunizes him from suffering. He refuses to think of God as impassible and apathetic. God is not "above" the world but "around" it: God created the world by making a space within himself, emptying or retracting himself to make room for others.[71] The triune God is in relationship to himself and also to the world, human and nonhuman alike.

Moltmann understands the cross as a death "in" God as opposed to the death "of" God. Accordingly, the significance of the cross is as much a matter for the doctrine of God as it is of atonement: the Son suffers forsakenness and death, and this experience is taken up into God's own experience. In the event of the cross, the Father forsakes the Son in order to show his solidarity with all abandoned persons. Further, while the Son suffers death, the Father suffers the death of his Son. The cross is thus a disruption in the trinitarian life: "At the cross the relationships within the being of God himself were broken."[72] In Moltmann's words: the event of the cross is one in which "God

---

70. Those who confess Christ confess the oneness or identity of finite and infinite Spirit. For Hegel, the resurrection represents the fact that now the whole community, and not only one individual, has God's spirit: "The name 'Holy Spirit' refers to the unifying and liberating power of divine love arising from infinite anguish—the same love that was objectively represented on the cross of Christ but that now works inwardly, subjectively, building up a new human community" (Peter C. Hodgson, "Hegel," in *Nineteenth Century Religious Thought in the West*, ed. Ninian Smart et al. [Cambridge: Cambridge University Press, 1985], 1:106).

71. The technical term for this picture of the God-world relationship is "panentheism" (i.e., the world ["all"] is in God, but God is greater than the world).

72. Paul S. Fiddes, *Past Event and Present Salvation: The Christian Idea of Atonement* (Louisville: Westminster John Knox, 1989), 218.

abandoned God."[73] The cross defines God's reconciling love in terms of God's willingness to suffer such that "the self-sacrifice of love must be God's eternal nature."[74] Paul Fiddes's summary is apt: "The transcendence of a suffering God can only be understood as a transcendent suffering, not a transcendence beyond suffering."[75]

For Moltmann, the cross defines God's nature in terms of a suffering love that takes the whole of created history into itself. The cross and resurrection are not events outside of but intrinsic to the divine trinitarian life. God's acts in history (*ad extra*) constitute his life as Father, Son, and Spirit. The cross thus marks the spot, not of the actuality of atonement, but rather of the actuality of God's triune being. The Son's death defines the Triune God as a loving fellowship open to and in solidarity with the world. It pertains to atonement only in the sense that it defines God as a being who is willing to suffer even godforsakenness out of his love for others.[76] In this sense, Moltmann's view of the cross may be better classified under theodicy rather than atonement.

Atonement and Divine Self-Determination: Karl Barth

Not all ontological accounts of the atonement are in thrall to metaphysics. Karl Barth (1886–1968) insists that God determines his own being when, in eternity, he decides to enter into covenant fellowship with human creatures. Contra Hegel, Barth argues that God's self-differentiation—his decision to share his life with humanity—is a free and gracious act, not a necessary step toward self-realization. Whereas Hegel sees God's being as becoming through the process of world history, Barth works a novel variation on a Reformed theme, insisting that God's being is self-chosen in an eternal act of predestination. Hence God is already in himself what he wills to be in time for us: the economic actualizes the immanent Trinity. Stated differently: the incarnation and atonement accomplish in time God's eternal self-determining decision to be "for us."

God's eternal election—his self-determination as "for us" and his determination of humanity as "for him"—is enacted in the history of Jesus Christ. It is not simply that Christ does something that saves humanity, but rather that he *is* the grace of God made flesh. Christ is the decree; the history of Jesus is

73. *Crucified God*, 244. Cf. Moltmann's colleague Eberhard Jüngel: "God himself takes place in Jesus' God-forsakenness and death" (*God as the Mystery of the World* [Grand Rapids: Eerdmans, 1983], 370).
74. Jürgen Moltmann, *The Trinity and the Kingdom of God: The Doctrine of God* (London: SCM, 1981), 32.
75. Fiddes, *Creative Suffering of God*, 143.
76. Richard Bauckham highlights the dialectical nature of Moltmann's interpretation of the cross and resurrection in terms of death and life, the absence and presence of God, the way the world is now and the way God promises to make it ("Jürgen Moltmann," in *The Modern Theologians*, ed. David F. Ford and Rachel Muers, 3rd ed. [Oxford: Blackwell, 2005], 148–49).

the history of the covenant, the outworking in time of God's decision to be our God. Jesus is "God with us," God's-being-in-reconciling-activity: "What unites God and us men is the fact that He does not will to be God without us."[77] Hence, for Barth, reconciliation (his preferred term for atonement) involves both the Son's person and work, for everything that Jesus is, does, and suffers enacts God's covenant faithfulness, God's very being. Indeed, Barth describes the history of Jesus Christ in three ways: he is the divine Son who humbles himself, the man from Nazareth whom the Father exalts, and the one in whom God and humanity enact a common history. Hence "the atonement is history," the singular history that defines God, humanity, and their covenantal relationship.[78]

The highpoint of Barth's massive study of reconciliation is paragraph 59, "The Obedience of the Son of God." There is "high humility"[79] in God's predestining himself to be "for us." In his sovereignty, God chooses to give himself, yet this choice also accords with God's own life, in which the Son freely chooses obedience.[80] Ultimately, the Son chooses both to elect and condemn himself: the incarnate Son is "the Judge judged in our place." God thus "declared Himself guilty of the contradiction against Him in which man was involved."[81] The history of Jesus Christ, which encompasses his death on the cross, is the actualization of God's eternal self-determination to be "for us"—by bearing and thereby doing away with our sinful existence and "old self" (Rom. 6:6)—which is simultaneously the actualization of God's primordial decision to give himself in love for lost human creatures. The cross is not a contingency plan but part of the content of God's self-determination to be our God and to embrace humanity as his covenant partner.

Sin is the refusal of God's determination to love us and of his determination of us as his beloved. Jesus's death on the cross does not merely provide satisfaction for the sinner's guilt but destroys sin itself.[82] The extent of God's love—the cost of the cross to God's own being—is nowhere better seen than

---

77. Karl Barth, *Church Dogmatics* IV/1, *The Doctrine of Reconciliation* (Edinburgh: T&T Clark, 1956), 7.

78. Ibid., 157. Robert Jenson radicalizes the history of Jesus Christ by viewing it not as the event that enacts God's electing purpose, but as the event that constitutes God's triune identity: the gospel history of Jesus Christ "itself determines who and what God is" (*Systematic Theology*, vol. 1, *The Triune God* [New York: Oxford University Press, 1997], 165).

79. Ibid., 159.

80. Cf. Hans Urs von Balthasar's related idea that the ultimate ground of atonement resides in a "primal kenosis" that characterizes God's immanent trinitarian being (*Theo-Drama: Theological Dramatic Theory*, vol. 4, *The Action* [San Francisco: Ignatius, 1994], 324–32).

81. Barth, *CD* II/2, 164.

82. Cf. Garry J. Williams's comment that Barth affirms the idea of Jesus's death as a satisfaction not of God's hostility to sin but rather of God's love, which is satisfied only by the destruction of sinful man on the cross ("Karl Barth and the Doctrine of the Atonement," in *Engaging with Barth: Contemporary Evangelical Critiques*, ed. David Gibson and Daniel Strange [Nottingham, UK: Inter-Varsity, 2008], 246).

in light of Barth's treatment of Jesus's descent into hell, a theme that von Balthasar also develops in his theology of Holy Saturday. The basic idea is that, in experiencing hell—the full measure of God's wrath—Jesus dies the "second death" (Rev. 20:6; 21:8) as well as the first.[83]

The event of Jesus Christ is therefore nothing less than the beginning of a new humanity: "This creating and grounding of a human subject which is new in relation to God and therefore in itself is, in fact, the event of the atonement made in Jesus Christ."[84] The resurrection is the Father's verdict that Jesus's death really did negate sinful humanity. Human being *is* (i.e., is *real*) only insofar as it is caught up in the history of the covenant. The actuality of atonement is nothing less than the creation of a new humanity, a matter of ontological participation in Jesus's history: "Jesus Christ is the atonement."[85] Reconciliation is therefore the free and gracious act of God that draws us into the history of Jesus Christ, into the Son's fellowship with the Father in and through the Spirit.

Critics object that if reconciliation is identical with the event of Jesus Christ, and if this event determines both the being of God and of humanity, then (1) all other human action is covenantally insignificant, and (2) no one is outside the covenant, hence the extent of the atonement (i.e., salvation) must be universal. In response, Barth's defenders argue that God's grace does not negate but establishes the significance of human action and freedom by demanding that we correspond in all that we say and do to our divine determination as human covenant partners. Our vocation is actively to become (subjectively) what we are (objectively) in Christ.[86]

The Umpire Strikes Back: Penal Substitution Despised and Defended

It is finished.

John 19:30

The sixth trajectory is in fact more of an ebb and flow, a back and forth debate over the concept of penal substitution that has occurred in regular waves throughout the modern period since the mid-nineteenth century, when Charles Hodge (1797–1878) and others argued that sin could be forgiven

---

83. See David Lauber, *Barth on the Descent into Hell: God, Atonement and the Christian Life* (Aldershot, UK: Ashgate, 2004), and Alan E. Lewis, *Between Cross and Resurrection: A Theology of Holy Saturday* (Grand Rapids: Eerdmans, 2001).

84. Barth, *CD* IV/1, 89.

85. Ibid., 34.

86. See, further, Adam Neder, *Participation in Christ: An Entry into Karl Barth's "Church Dogmatics"* (Louisville: Westminster John Knox, 2009), chap. 4, esp. the distinction between *de jure* and *de facto* participation in Christ (46).

"only on the ground of a forensic penal satisfaction."[87] One merit of the penal substitution view is the clarity and conciseness with which it is able to answer the question, "Why did Jesus have to die?" The answer: in order to bear the condemnation (penal) in our place (substitution). While defenders of penal substitution affirmed divine justice and human guilt, its detractors (some of whom we have described above in the first three trajectories) emphasized divine love and human repentance. The "first wave" of the debate made penal substitution and the necessity of Jesus's bloody death the point "which ultimately divide[d] interpreters of Christianity into evangelical and non-evangelical."[88]

A second wave in the mid-twentieth century broke on the exegetical front. C. H. Dodd (1884–1973), a leading British New Testament scholar and chair of the committee that produced the New English Bible, argued on lexical grounds against the traditional translation of "propitiation" for the Greek *hilasterion* word group (Rom. 3:25; Heb. 2:17; 1 John 2:2; 4:10). It is not as though the blood placates a wrathful God (as though a loving God needed to be appeased) but rather that God's "wrath" is a way of speaking about expiation, indicating the impersonal process (i.e., cleansing) by which sin is removed. Leon Morris (1914–2006) marshaled an arsenal of counterevidence to rebut Dodd's view that God's wrath is a figure of speech rather than "the stern reaction of the divine nature towards evil."[89]

A "third wave" of protest, aimed at the apparent conflict between the divine retribution implied by penal substitution and the love of God, emerged not only from so-called liberals but also from the ranks of evangelicalism itself. Certain evangelicals from both sides of the Atlantic have wondered whether penal substitution is a biblical idea or, less radically, if it should be the controlling model for understanding the significance of Jesus's death.[90]

The Critics: Penal Substitution as Sub-Evangelical

Critics of penal substitution raise both methodological and material objections. Some question the priority given to one metaphor/model over others in the New Testament. Others claim that penal substitution, together with its harsh economy of exchange, stems as much from modern Western culture and society as it does from the Bible itself if not more so. Turning to the content itself, many complain that it wrongly depicts God as requiring, like Shylock,

87. Charles Hodge, *Systematic Theology* (New York: Scribner, 1872), 2:488.

88. Denney, *Atonement and the Modern Mind*, 82.

89. Leon Morris, *The Apostolic Preaching of the Cross*, 3rd ed. (Grand Rapids: Eerdmans, 1965), 150.

90. See, for example, Joel B. Green and Mark D. Baker, *Recovering the Scandal of the Cross: Atonement in the New Testament and Contemporary Contexts* (Downers Grove, IL: InterVarsity, 2000); John Goldingay, ed., *Atonement Today* (London: SPCK, 1995); Derek Tidball, David Hilborn, and Justin Thacker, eds., *The Atonement Debate* (Grand Rapids: Zondervan, 2008).

his pound of flesh before he can forgive sin.[91] Others complain that the idea of God the Father punishing his innocent Son is a miscarriage of justice, perhaps even an instance of divine child abuse. Still others are concerned that this model reduces our relationship with God to legal categories. These objections are not new, but the idea of paying the penalty for someone else has become less plausible in the cultural logic of late capitalism. In contemporary parlance, "God is love" means unconditional acceptance; violent retribution is no longer a sign of a civilized state, much less deity, but barbarism.

Anglo-American Evangelicalism

In the latter decades of the twentieth century, both J. I. Packer (b. 1926) and John Stott (1921–2011) were representative of the evangelical stance on penal substitution. Packer's classic 1973 Tyndale Biblical Theology lecture, "What Did the Cross Achieve? The Logic of Penal Substitution," is a magisterial statement of the position.[92] Packer presents penal substitution as a distinguishing feature of evangelicalism, part of its Reformation inheritance. He roots his defense of the principle of substitution in Scripture: Christ "died for us" (Rom. 5:8) and became a curse "for us" (Gal. 3:13). That Christ's substitution was penal—a propitiation that takes away divine judicial wrath—is no abstract forensic notion but rather the result of God's very personal, loving will to suffer divine retribution in our place. Stott similarly insists that the Bible "everywhere views human death not as a *natural* but as a *penal* event."[93] Strictly speaking, we must not say that the Father punishes the Son, "for both God and Christ were subjects not objects, taking the initiative together to save sinners."[94] Neither Packer nor Stott acknowledges any contradiction between divine retribution and redemptive love.

That some evangelicals have joined the chorus of criticism against penal substitution has led others more vociferously to defend it. What began as a ripple of opposition against liberalism has become in the late twentieth and early twenty-first centuries a growing tide, especially in the pool of Reformed-leaning Anglo-American evangelicals. The last decade has seen at least three multiauthor volumes appear defending various aspects of penal substitution, the most recent of which responds to no fewer than twenty-six objections concerning everything from its biblical credentials and alleged cultural conditioning to its presuppositions about God and its alleged complicity with violence and injustice.[95]

---

91. See William Shakespeare, *The Merchant of Venice* 4.1.304–7.

92. *Tyndale Bulletin* 25 (1974): 3–45. See also the essays in J. I. Packer and Mark Dever, *In My Place Condemned He Stood* (Wheaton: Crossway, 2007).

93. John R. W. Stott, *The Cross of Christ* (Downers Grove, IL: InterVarsity, 1986), 65.

94. Ibid., 151.

95. See, for example, David Peterson, ed., *Where Wrath and Mercy Meet: Proclaiming the Atonement Today; Papers from the Fourth Oak Hill College Annual School of Theology* (Carlisle, UK: Paternoster, 2001); Charles E. Hill and Frank A. James, eds., *The Glory of the Atonement:*

Current debates in Anglo-American evangelicalism concern the relative (or absolute) centrality of penal substitution. According to Stephen Holmes, British evangelicals have traditionally held to penal substitution as one of many models for thinking about the atonement, though some believe that it is the most important. He suggests that, beginning in the late nineteenth century, theologians like George Smeaton insisted "on penal substitution as the one and only correct way of talking about the atonement."[96] The outstanding question for evangelicals on both sides of the Atlantic now concerns not only the legitimacy of penal substitution but its centrality: is it merely one among many possible models, first among equals, or the one true explanation?

The "Unified" Atonement: Nonreductive Crucicentrism

Father, into your hands I commit my spirit!

Luke 23:46

The final trajectory we here consider responds to the question left hanging in the previous section by emphatically stressing the need to do justice to multiple valid insights into the meaning of Jesus's death "for us." This last group of theologians affirms the importance of attending to the many metaphors and categories to be found in Scripture and tradition, but not to the extent of Joel Green's "kaleidoscopic" view, where no single model enjoys primacy and the "many" trumps the "one."[97] Instead, they strive for a new harmonization or "unified" theory that focuses on Jesus's work as mediator of a new covenant in an explicitly trinitarian framework.

Trinitarian Approaches

"United they stand, divided they fall" could well be Robert Sherman's watchword, for he contends in *King, Priest, and Prophet*[98] that the various atonement theories are mutually supportive, not mutually exclusive. The problem with earlier theories, in Sherman's opinion, is their reductionist impulse;

Biblical, Historical and Practical Perspectives (Downers Grove, IL: InterVarsity, 2004); Steve Jeffery, Michael Ovey, and Andrew Sach, *Pierced for Our Transgressions: Rediscovering the Glory of Penal Substitution* (Wheaton: Crossway, 2007).

96. See Stephen R. Holmes, "Ransomed, Healed, Restored, Forgiven: Evangelical Accounts of the Atonement," in Tidball, Hilborn, and Thacker, *Atonement Debate*, 276.

97. Joel B. Green, "Kaleidoscopic View," in Beilby and Eddy, *Atonement: Four Views*, 157–85. Cf. Peter Schmiechen, who believes that the best way to demonstrate the breadth of Christian witness to the fullness of Christ is to maintain ten distinct atonement theories (*Saving Power*, 2).

98. Robert Sherman, *King, Priest, and Prophet: A Trinitarian Theology of Atonement* (New York: T&T Clark, 2004).

each focuses on only one aspect of God's reconciling work. The solution is to view the Son's atoning work in relationship to the Father and Spirit: "One can understand adequately neither Christ's multifaceted reconciliation . . . nor that reconciliation's fundamental unity as God's gracious act apart from the Trinity."[99] Sherman's constructive theological proposal suggests that we should recognize "a certain correspondence and mutual support" among the three persons of the Trinity, the three offices of Christ (i.e., the *munus triplex* consisting of prophet, priest, king), and the three commonly recognized models of his atoning work (moral exemplar, vicarious sacrifice, *Christus Victor*). Specifically, he argues that the almighty Father corresponds with the royal work of the Son and the victory motif, that vicarious sacrifice goes with the priestly work of the Son, and that moral example best fits Christ's prophetic work and the illumining work of the Holy Spirit.

Recapitulative

The integrative motif in Hans Boersma's *Violence, Hospitality, and the Cross: Reappropriating the Atonement Tradition*[100] is not the Trinity but rather Irenaeus's model of recapitulation, under which Boersma subsumes Aulén's three types in the hope of providing an "ecumenical grounding" for atonement theology. Recapitulation leads to reconciliation as the Son redoes Israel's history and all of human history, making straight the crooked and healing the human condition as it were from the inside, fulfilling the *imago Dei* in which human beings are created through his obedience as prophet, priest, and king. In this light, the violence of the cross is less a reflex of divine retribution than a necessary means for preserving the integrity of God's purpose for creation. God's concern for creation's *shalom* entails his rejection of evil (i.e., that which is opposed to the created order). Jesus's atoning work—his recapitulating Adam's and Israel's respective "exiles"—makes restoration possible and is ultimately an expression of God's hospitality toward sinners.

Mediatorial

Alan Spence's *The Promise of Peace: A Unified Theory of Atonement*[101] aspires to be a comprehensive "unified" theory, the equivalent in theology of the physicists' $e = mc^2$. Spence believes he has found it in the idea of Christ's mediatorial work that overcomes our alienation from God: "*The Son became as we are so that he might, on our behalf, make peace with God.*"[102] He also claims that his

99. Ibid., 9. Sherman points to Jesus's baptism as involving all three persons of the Trinity, whereas I have chosen to cite as the epigraph to this section Jesus's last word on the cross.
100. Grand Rapids: Baker Academic, 2004.
101. New York: T&T Clark, 2006.
102. Spence, "A Unified Theory of the Atonement," *International Journal of Systematic Theology* 6 (2004): 420; emphasis in the original.

theory better accounts for the significance of Jesus's action as the one uniquely anointed with the Spirit to serve as prophet, priest, and king. God's overarching purpose for his covenant relationship with humanity is peace. Though the Bible uses victory language to speak of the peacemaking cross, Spence holds that the mediatorial rather than *Christus Victor* theory provides the better explanation of how God makes good on his covenant promise to be our God.

A Way Forward? The Atonement as Triune Covenantal Mediation

We conclude with a few notes toward any future nonreductive theory of atonement, building on the insights of the three views just presented. With Sherman, we should affirm the importance of trinitarian theology, for the God who reconciles is Father, Son, and Spirit. Moreover, God is all that he is—all holy, all loving, all just, all merciful—in all that he does. The cross, as the sum of divine wisdom, displays all the divine perfections. With Spence, we should affirm that the entire drama of redemption is set in motion by God's covenant promise that he will be ours and we his. With Boersma, we should affirm that the incarnate Son is the executive agent of God's covenant purpose, and that the three offices that compose the Son's overarching vocation and identity as the "Christ" are themselves covenantal. The cross is the climax of the history of the Son's covenantal mediation, the culmination of the whole triune economy of redemption. The shed blood is a graphic sign that God has proved faithful to his Abrahamic promise (Gen. 17) precisely by undergoing the sanctions, legal (i.e., death by execution) and relational (i.e., exile), for covenant disobedience (Deut. 28:15–68). By dying for us, Jesus makes possible new and expanded "in-law" relationships (Rom. 5:15–19; 8:15), giving us a share in his Sonship.[103]

How can it be good news (i.e., "gospel") that at the heart of Christianity is the announcement of the bloody death and resurrection of an innocent man? To paraphrase the first line of the famous hymn: *How* can it be? The various atonement theories we have surveyed attempt to respond precisely to this question, explaining how Jesus's death can be redemptive. In the final analysis, however, no single doctrinal formulation conveys everything that must be said about the atonement, and were every one of them to be written, the world itself could not contain them (cf. John 21:25). Even one who spent the better part of his career clarifying the biblical vocabulary of atonement, Leon Morris, acknowledges this: "Christ's atoning work is so complex and our minds are so small. We cannot take it all in. We need the positive contributions of all the theories, for each draws attention to some aspect of what Christ has done for us."[104]

103. For further elaboration of this idea, see Kevin J. Vanhoozer, "The Atonement in Postmodernity: Guilt, Goats and Gifts," in Hill and James, *Glory of the Atonement*, esp. 396–404.

104. "Atonement," in *New Dictionary of Theology*, ed. Sinclair Ferguson, David F. Wright, and J. I. Packer (Downers Grove, IL: InterVarsity, 1988), 56.

We can do no better to conclude, however, than to quote P. T. Forsyth:

The mind and soul of the Church returns to this perennial interest. The Church must always adjust its compass at the Cross. But in so returning it does not simply retrace the steps or tread the ground of those that have gone before. There is a deepening evolution of human thought in this regard. The efforts to pluck the heart from its mystery are not a series of assaults renewed with blind and dogged courage on an impregnable hold. They form the stages of a long spiritual movement of slow battle, of arduous illumination and severe conquest. . . . The revelation of God in the Cross of Christ is its own reforming principle and its own cleansing light.[105]

For Further Reading

Beilby, James, and Paul R. Eddy, eds. *The Nature of the Atonement: Four Views.* Downers Grove, IL: InterVarsity, 2006.

Blocher, Henri. "The Sacrifice of Jesus Christ: The Current Theological Situation." *European Journal of Theology* 8 (1999): 23–36.

Boersma, Hans. *Violence, Hospitality, and the Cross: Reappropriating the Atonement Tradition.* Grand Rapids: Baker Academic, 2004.

Cole, Graham A. *God the Peacemaker: How Atonement Brings Shalom.* Downers Grove, IL: InterVarsity, 2009.

Girard, René. *I See Satan Fall like Lightning.* Maryknoll, NY: Orbis, 2001.

Gunton, Colin E. *The Actuality of Atonement: A Study of Metaphor, Rationality, and the Christian Tradition.* Grand Rapids: Eerdmans, 1989.

Hill, Charles E., and Frank A. James, eds. *The Glory of the Atonement: Biblical, Historical and Practical Perspectives.* Downers Grove, IL: InterVarsity, 2004.

Jersak, Brad, and Michael Hardin, eds. *Stricken by God? Nonviolent Identification and the Victory of Christ.* Grand Rapids: Eerdmans, 2007.

Packer, J. I., and Mark Dever. *In My Place Condemned He Stood: Celebrating the Glory of the Atonement.* Wheaton: Crossway, 2007.

Torrance, T. F. *Atonement: The Person and Work of Christ.* Downers Grove, IL: InterVarsity, 2009.

105. P. T. Forsyth in Frédéric Louis Godet, ed., *The Atonement in Modern Religious Thought: A Theological Symposium*, 3rd ed. (London: James Clarke, 1907), 52–53. I want to acknowledge, and thank, two of my PhD students in particular for their assistance: Adam Johnson for his help in brainstorming the overall structure of this essay, his comments on an earlier draft, and his reading reports on the Western front of atonement theory; Jeremy Treat for his thorough editing and critical challenges.

9

. . .

PROVIDENCE

JOHN WEBSTER

Providence: A Problem in Modern Theology?

The Christian doctrine of providence concerns God's continuing relation to the world he has created. In his work of providence, God acts upon, with, and in each particular creature and created reality as a whole. As God so acts, God preserves created reality and being, maintains its order, and directs it to the end that he has established for it. God's providence enacts his enduring love for that which he has made and shows him to be a faithful Creator.

In modern theology, providence has commonly (though not universally) been approached as a problematic doctrine, sometimes, indeed, as a doctrine in crisis. Much of this chapter will be given over to reviewing perceived problems in Christian teaching about providence and solutions proposed to them. At the outset, however, it is important to scrutinize the sense of the difficulty of the doctrine that pervades many modern treatments. In theology, as in other spheres of human life, a sense of crisis is not necessarily an accurate guide to a given situation, because it may obscure the distinction between apparent and real dilemmas and discourage us from attempting possible resolutions.

How might the difficulty of the doctrine of providence be conceived? On one account, the difficulty is to be traced to the pressure exerted upon the doctrine by a cluster of external objections; this is the more common modern understanding of the doctrine's predicament. On such an account of the matter, the doctrine finds itself in crisis to some degree because the claims it advances do not cohere with the public norms (rational, moral, political) of the wider culture in which theology operates. As a result, the doctrine has lost a measure of plausibility, and received forms of the doctrine can no longer give a publicly cogent interpretation of natural and human reality. Thus, teaching about providence is put on the back foot by—for example—skepticism about whether God's action in the world can be identified; or by fears that it may promote complacency in the face of oppressive evil; or by its apparent legitimation of static social and political order; or, most of all, by the authority of accounts of the way the world is, advanced by historians or natural scientists, that exclude or simply bypass Christian beliefs about providential order and direction.

When theological thinking about providence is shaped by perceived external problems, the solutions proposed usually take the form of adjustment of the doctrine in order to display its coherence with, or at least noncontravention of, public norms of rationality. The adjustment may involve more or less radical reworking of the doctrine, with differing levels of commitment to the wider culture and to the traditions of Christian teaching. Nevertheless, for many, the situation of the doctrine is acutely problematic, making some such modification imperative. As this is undertaken, the cultural setting of theology by which the doctrine is challenged is itself a major resource in the doctrine's reconstruction.

A rather different account of the problematic situation of the doctrine of providence identifies the primary challenges as internal rather than external. These internal challenges may be the perennial difficulties that attend the exposition of any article of Christian teaching—for example, human resistance to divine revelation—though they may take on specific contours in relation to providence, such as the need for humility and trust as prerequisites for knowing and acting in accordance with the divine ordering of the world. Or the internal challenges may have to do with how Christian theology has handled itself before its modern critics. What makes the doctrine of providence problematic may be, in part, self-alienation from its authentically Christian content, and the substitution of that content with weak or truncated versions of the doctrine. If the doctrine faces a crisis of plausibility, it may be because of internal weaknesses in modern Christian theology: the unavailability of versions of Christian teaching about providence of real sophistication and intellectual and spiritual cogency, capable of challenging their detractors; feebleness in calling into question the coarsened accounts of providence that are the targets of external critique; concession to the restrictions imposed by dominant intellectual conventions. On such an account, the crisis of the doctrine of providence is, precisely, acquiescing to the idea that the modern setting of theology constitutes such a crisis and redefines what theology can and cannot say. That being the case, the solution lies not in the doctrine's adaptation by negotiating with theology's ambient culture, but in more compelling exposition of Christian claims.

The Christian doctrine of providence is, then, an acute register of differing judgments about the tasks of modern theology. These judgments shape not only decisions about the proper sources and procedures of a theology of providence, but also the doctrine's content, proportions, and placement in relation to other doctrines. Before turning to the career of the doctrine in modern theology, however, two pieces of background need to be filled in. First, some sense of classical (premodern) formulations of Christian teaching about providence is necessary, in part to show how often both modern critics and modern defenders have operated with restricted or distorted versions of the doctrine. Second, a broad sense of the realignment of teaching about providence from the early seventeenth century is important, because the more recent history of the doctrine builds upon a reorientation that was largely complete by the middle of the nineteenth century.

Classical Approaches to Providence

We begin by identifying some elements in classical Christian teaching about providence.[1] In classical Christian theology, teaching about providence is primarily teaching about God and only derivatively teaching about the order of the world. An account of providence begins, therefore, by attending to the divine acts of providential care and governance, and by contemplating the agent of these acts. It is only in modernity that questions about the order of creation become the center of gravity of teaching about providence.

The Christian doctrine of providence is grounded in the theology of God as Triune Creator. God the Holy Trinity enjoys perfect, utterly abundant life in the mutual delight of the three persons and their ordered relations, the Father generating the Son, the Father and Son together breathing the Spirit. In this mutual love, God is from himself and is in himself complete, requiring no reality beside himself to bring his blessedness to perfection. It is this One who is the maker of heaven and earth. Because he is in himself complete, God's act of creation is an act of sheer freedom. In creating, God acts under no necessity but out of love, giving life, form, and history to a reality that is other than himself and that he does not need in order to fulfill himself. Creation is "out of nothing": not an emanation from God's own being (for then Creator and creation would be indistinct), nor a shaping of preexisting raw material (for then "creating" would be mere "forming," and the Creator merely a craftsman), but a bringing into being of that which is not God.

That which God brings into being is alive, not simply inert, but characterized by movement. This created movement is inherent to the creature but not

---

1. For an introduction to the history, see L. Scheffczyk, *Creation and Providence* (New York: Herder & Herder, 1970).

independent of the Creator. It takes place in relation to God the Creator, not apart from him. There is, in other words, a continuing relation between Creator and creation, an unfolding history in which the Creator acts upon and within created reality in such a way as to enable it to attain full realization of the life it has been given. This unfolding history is the subject matter of the doctrine of providence.

God is not simply the initial cause or manufacturer of created reality. God does not, as it were, bring creation into existence and then simply release it to follow its own path, for God is present and faithful to what he has called into being. There is a proper coexistence between Creator and creation in which God exercises his lordship for the creation's good, acting upon it to sustain and direct its life. Neither the origin of the world nor its continuation is immanent within the world; they are divine gifts to a reality that cannot constitute or order itself. Creation and providence are thus inseparable. Nevertheless, there is a proper distinction between the divine works of creation and providence. The act of creation is nonrepeatable; as a work "out of nothing" it effects the transition from nonbeing to being, and establishes the relation between Creator and creature. Providence is a different work, directed to that which has already been given life by God; it is an act of preserving rather than making. Because of this, providence is not to be thought of as continuous creation, that is, as a ceaseless repetition of the act of bringing the world into being. This not only confuses "bringing into being" and "sustaining in being," but also undermines the integrity and stability of created reality, mischaracterizing the divine act of creation by failing to grasp that it is a gift of dependent but real being and freedom in relation to God.

Providence is the enactment of God's will. The presupposition of God's providential activity in creation is the "immanent" reality of his "decree," that is, his purpose for creation that is then administered in his "transitive" or external work of providential government. Providential acts rest on foreordination. Foreordination is not simply foreknowledge but planned purpose; the "seat" of providence is not only the divine intellect by which all things are known in a single instant of comprehensive intelligence, but the divine will by which all things are determined. God's will is not, however, to be construed narrowly as unrestricted and arbitrary force, in isolation from the love, wisdom, and holiness of God. The mere fact of God's infinitely strong will is not the primary factor, but rather its purposive content. What God wills is the creature's good, not simply the creature's submission; and so what God enacts in providence is entirely consistent both with his own supreme moral excellence and with the dignity and blessedness of the creature. Indeed, to speak of God's decree, providentially executed, is to affirm that God's creatures are not at the mercy of nameless fate, for God so orders nature and history that through them he blesses creatures and directs them to perfect happiness.

The modes of God's providential activity are often identified as preservation, concurrence, and government (the three modes are not three separate divine works but the one work of providence variously apprehended and conceived). In *preservation* God acts upon and within created reality to hold it in being, maintaining by his power and goodness the order of nature and history that he has established at the act of creation. *Concurrence* specifies this preserving activity by speaking of how God's providential work is not simply a force brought to bear upon creation from outside, but is integral or interior to creation: providence works through creaturely working. In his acts of *government*, God directs creation to its goal, ensuring that the fulfillment he has purposed for it will be attained. In these acts, God operates medially, that is, through the power that he has himself bestowed upon creation. Created reality is not merely passive, for it has been given a movement of its own by which it maintains itself and moves toward its end. Providence does not eliminate but enables this creaturely movement; providence moves creation to move itself, working "interiorly" rather than as an extrinsic impulse. Providence is not merely to be thought of as maintaining a static creation, a set of unchanging natural or cultural forms. It concerns the teleology of creation: created reality is purposive or historical. Accordingly, providence is related not only backwards to the initial act of creation out of nothing, but also forward, to the saving work of God and to the eschatological future of the new creation.

All things fall within God's providential order. Nothing lies beyond the reach of his will, and his care and governance are universally operative, though not always in ways that fallen creatures can discern or find easy to trust. The scope of providence can be conceptualized by drawing distinctions between general and special providence. General providence is the care exercised by God over creation in its entirety; special providence is God's activity directed to particular recipients (such as the elect) or undertaken by extraordinary means (such as miracles).

Such in skeletal form are some of the principal features of the doctrine of providence in classical Christian divinity (a more ample historical treatment would, of course, display the variety within the commonalities). Along with the doctrine of creation, teaching about providence furnishes a systematic theological account of created reality, its natural forms and its movement through time. But though teaching about providence forms an element in Christian metaphysics, it also functions as a piece of practical theology, providing orientation and consolation to believers by instructing them in how to read the world as an ordered, not random, reality—ordered by divine love and directed by divine power for God's glory and the creature's good. Knowledge of providence is thus bound up with faith in and confession of Christ, the one who upholds the universe (Heb. 1:3), and of the Holy Spirit through whom created reality is conformed to the Father's purpose. Providence is not known simply by taking observations of the world. It requires attention to the course of nature and history formed by glad abandonment to the purpose of the creator and redeemer of all things, and by hope in the coming fulfillment of that purpose.

Rethinking Providence

From the seventeenth century on, study of history and nature came to be dominated by explanations that marginalized and sometimes excluded talk of God's intentions for and present activity upon and within the world, and that treated nature and history as largely explicable within terms of themselves, with only minimal reference to an initial divine cause. Before looking at the strains these developments placed upon Christian doctrine, mention should be made of a commanding figure of the early nineteenth century whose theology of providence both reflects and redirects modern shifts in understanding God's relation to the world, namely, Friedrich Schleiermacher. In *The Christian Faith*, Schleiermacher rejected notions of particular divine causality (whether in special providence or in miraculous divine interventions). He did so not on any "naturalist" grounds, however, but because he considered that older dogmatic accounts of providence were occasionalist or atomistic. That is, they identified particular happenings with divine activity but failed to see that created reality in its entirety is subject to a single, comprehensive divine decree, put into effect not extrinsically by occasional acts of God but intrinsically, God being the universal cause of all natural causality, the one who determines and effects "the universality of the nature-system."[2] It is an open question whether Schleiermacher is adjusting doctrine to cultural circumstance or revisiting earlier Christian models of a union between divine and natural agency. The fact that Schleiermacher's critique of classical providential thought has proved more congenial to many modern theologians than his reconstruction of teaching about providence is indicative of the character of the recent history of the doctrine, which is our next topic for examination.

The development of the doctrine of providence is much affected by shifts in the wider intellectual and civic culture in which theology operates. This general rule in the history of Christian teaching holds particularly with respect to the theology of providence because of the subject matter of that doctrine, namely, nature and history (public and personal). From the early modern period, "natural" reason claims increasing (and eventually exclusive) competence to explain nature and history with the most minimal reference to the purpose and action of a deity. The doctrine of providence, that is, is a casualty in the steady expansion of the explanatory reach of metaphysical and scientific thinking owing no allegiance to the Christian confession. A full history of

2. Friedrich Schleiermacher, *The Christian Faith*, trans. H. R. Mackintosh and J. S. Stewart (Edinburgh: T&T Clark, 1928), 173.

the Christian theology of providence would, therefore, consider not only the internal career of the doctrine but also the ways in which it is impacted and sometimes distorted by ideas about nature, history, and human institutions. Cultural and dogmatic history are inseparable.[3]

That said, it is also important to be alert to internal factors in the public decline of Christian teaching about providence. We need to ask whether the versions of the doctrine that were espoused by theologians betrayed some alienation from its authentically Christian content, and so promoted the process of decline. It has, for example, been suggested that the post-Reformation divines replace an "actualist" doctrine of providence that emphasizes God's present activity in the world by a metaphysically oriented doctrine placing excessive weight on the eternal divine counsel.[4] That particular interpretation may or may not carry; nevertheless, it is important not to overlook changes in the dogmatic conception of providence, lest we attribute its decline simply to the steady success of a metaphysics of nature and history hostile to theology.

In the modern history of the doctrine of providence, then, we have an incremental transformation from a Christian metaphysics of nature and history (including the nature and history of human creatures) toward one in which appeal to Christian beliefs about God's relation to creation comes to be considered as at best redundant and at worst destructive. This transformation is effected both by elements of internal disarray in Christian theology and by the increasing cultural prestige of ways of thinking about nature, history, and humankind critical of or indifferent to Christian providential teaching. Of the factors "internal" to theology, three related elements should be noted. First, there is a gradual "anonymization" of providence. Little significance is accorded to the identity of the agent of providence, which can be stripped down to a nameless causal force, the term "providence" itself often becoming a substitute for "God." Second, there is the "immanentization" of providence: the effects of divine maintenance of the world are considered in and for themselves, without reference to their origin in the divine counsel or to present intentional action by a divine agent. Providence means "world order." Third, there is the "generalization" of providence, so that the domain of providence is the order of nature and time considered apart from the special history of the elect. These internal shifts in Christian teaching are closely related to wider alterations in the understanding of the natural order and of human history that, in effect, weaken conceptions of nature and history as created realities sustained and directed by their Creator.

3. For some representative works here, see A. Funkenstein, *Theology and the Scientific Imagination from the Middle Ages to the Seventeenth Century* (Princeton: Princeton University Press, 1986); A. Walsham, *Providence in Early Modern England* (Oxford: Oxford University Press, 1999); G. Lloyd, *Providence Lost* (Cambridge, MA: Harvard University Press, 2008).

4. R. Bernhardt, *Was heisst "Handeln Gottes"? Eine Rekonstruktion der Lehre von der Vorsehung* (Gutersloh: Kaiser, 1999).

From the seventeenth century on, natural science and philosophy of nature made decreasing use of Christian cosmological teaching with its emphasis upon God's personal action to move created being. Two particular developments command attention. One is a conception of nature as a perfectly self-regulating mechanism, set in motion by God but requiring no continuing divine activity—a view advanced by Leibniz and, slightly later, by Wolff. This affects the doctrine of providence by restricting divine causality in respect of the universe to efficient causality: nothing more need be said of God's relation to creation than that he brought all things into being. God is no longer creation's "final" cause, that is, the one who continues to act in order to bring all things to their goal. Providential activity is eliminated, for God simply supplies the initial motion of nature, to which he bears a purely extrinsic relation. Of such a restricted account of God's involvement in the course of nature, deism is the inevitable outcome.

Another development, associated particularly with Spinoza, is a variety of pantheism, in which the term "God" signifies not the transcendent divine agent by whom all things are kept, but rather a principle within nature, nature's inner structure and dynamic. With this, the distinction between uncreated and created being, basic to classical understandings of providence, is no longer in force. Providence is merely a way of talking of the order intrinsic to nature, and does not name God's purpose and its execution.

Both deism and pantheism entail the transformation of teaching about providence into teaching about the regularity of nature; neither has need of a concept of personal divine governance. Nevertheless, it would be a mistake to think of either mechanistic philosophy or pantheism as inherently secular; neither seeks to emancipate nature from God, and both are theistic in that they think of the natural order as a mode in which the divine operates. Nevertheless, the natural theology of the later seventeenth and the eighteenth centuries promoted a precarious understanding of the providential order of the world, one which radical Enlightenment thinkers like Paul Henri Thiry Baron d'Holbach could with little effort transform into a materialist and atheist idea of nature from which all traces of God have been expelled.[5]

What of God's providential direction of human history? Classical Christian theologies of history, set out in such enduring monuments as Augustine's *City of God*, understand the course of created time to be the outworking of God's plan, an ordained and orderly history of creation, fall, redemption, and consummation. The meaning of history is elicited by attending to the works of God, through which the depth of history—its reference back to the divine plan, providentially enacted—can be discerned. As Christian dogmatics and metaphysics begin to lose their hold on Western culture from the mid-seventeenth

5. See here J. H. Brooke, *Science and Religion: Some Historical Perspectives* (Cambridge: Cambridge University Press, 1991).

century, history, like nature, comes gradually to be considered a self-contained immanent sphere: talk of God and the acts of God is no longer the sine qua non for grasping the reality of history. Where in classical Christian divinity history is a sphere in which final causes are operative (for God moves history to its proper end), it becomes common to think of the agent of history as the creature, not the Creator. History is made. It is not as it were a planned domain in which humankind is placed and summoned to act out an allotted role; rather, it is an empty space for the exercise of human spontaneity. History is the sphere of freedom.

Moreover, concentration on humankind as the prime mover of history ties in with an emphasis on the novelty and relativity of history. History is not characterized by the essential stability of its forms, but by change. Transience, not permanence, is basic to history; to live in time is not to conform to given structures but to be engaged in a process of emancipation and transformation. Within these terms, the doctrine of providence clearly requires considerable reworking. As with nature, so with history: providence is in large part "naturalized," to become a term for the internal direction of history. Thus Giambattista Vico in his account of history in his *New Science* retains the concept of providence, but its content is divine immanence within history. Somewhat later, Hegel presents an account of history as the process through which Absolute Spirit constitutes itself.

To sum up, from the seventeenth century on, study of both nature and history came to be dominated by explanations that marginalized and sometimes excluded talk of God's intentions for and present activity upon and within the world, and that treated nature and history as largely explicable within terms of themselves, with only minimal reference to an initial divine cause. Such explanations placed considerable strain upon the Christian doctrine of providence. The strain continued to be felt in the nineteenth century and beyond, and did much to determine its recent history.

Various Modern Approaches to Providence

How have modern theologians conceived of the task of a doctrine of providence? The question is important because theologians differ not only about what they take to be the content of Christian teaching, but also in their judgments about the nature of theology itself. These judgments concern such matters as the sources and norms of theology, the situation in which theology is undertaken, the audiences to which it addresses itself, the kinds of arguments that are persuasive, and the overall aim of the theological enterprise. One way of getting some purchase on these issues is to distinguish between modern theologies that are primarily internal in orientation and modern theologies whose orientation is primarily external. As with any typification, the distinction is only heuristic: no theologian matches the type exactly, and the value of the typology is simply that of drawing attention to common characteristics or points of contrast.

Modern theologies with an internal orientation find their source and norm in Scripture, along with esteemed strands of the classical Christian tradition, both Scripture and tradition being understood as media of God's self-disclosure and its reception. Scripture and tradition are preponderant sources, outweighing sources that are more recent or that are external to the Christian tradition (such as philosophy, culture, or human experience). Doctrine is a conceptual articulation of Christian reality claims, understood to correspond or testify to divine reality in a reliable though imperfect way. Accordingly, the present situation of theology is not something sheerly given, within whose terms theology has to reinvent itself or with which it must make accommodations. Theology can adopt a critical stance toward its setting, and in so doing, it finds the inheritance of Christian teaching to be a resource rather than a problem, offering a store of meanings that exceed the limited range offered by the culture in which theology finds itself. This sense that theology is not wholly enveloped by its situation goes along with a sense that the society of the church furnishes the primary audience for theology, such that reception by the community of faith is important approbation of a theological proposal. This does not necessarily reduce theology to an intramural exercise, because it can coexist with significant commitment to the missionary and apologetic tasks of theology. But it does mean that in the construction of theological teaching, the boundary between the church and the world should be kept in view, and that the direction of theology is from the church to the world and not vice versa: the church does not require the world's instruction in order to know the gospel. Arguments that persuade are arguments that at some level persuade the community of faith, the corollary being that, in the absence of faith, theological arguments are less likely to carry. The end of theology is, therefore, contemplative and catechetical, edifying the church through thought about and description of the objects of Christian faith, and only so commending or defending Christian claims.

How is the task of the doctrine of providence conceived on this account? Although, as we have seen, classical Christian teaching about providence has been marginalized in modern culture, there has been a steady stream of theological work on providence that in both approach and content is continuous with the theology that antedates those cultural developments. Sometimes this has been in the genre of school dogmatics, which by and large repeat one or other version of the tradition without much engagement with what lies beyond a quite closed ecclesial and theological circle, or which engages with modern thought only polemically. It is easy to dismiss such work as outmoded and isolationist, addressing an audience that no longer exists; but at its best, it can be an exercise in contemplative intelligence and love.[6] Others have sought to go further, retrieving, rethinking, and rearticulating the tradition rather than simply repeating it. Herman Bavinck, a great Dutch dogmatician at the turn of the nineteenth and twentieth centuries, gave a remarkably sophisticated and penetrating account of the inner structure of biblical and classical Christian teaching about providence in his *Reformed Dogmatics*.[7] His account is fully alert to the modern situation, devoting a good deal of space to detailed interaction with philosophical and scientific trends from the early modern period on, and yet retaining a sense that the church's teaching can outthink its opponents. In the next generation of Reformed thinkers, Karl Barth possessed a similar sense of the inner coherence and depth of scriptural and traditional teaching about providence, and presented it with rare descriptive cogency.[8] In Barth's case, this went along with a conviction that theology is responsible to revise tradition, not in order to bring it into alignment with modern norms, but in order to attempt greater fidelity to the content of the gospel in its biblical attestation.

What of modern theologies with an "external" orientation? These theologies tend to think of Christian doctrine as constructed in a process of negotiation with the culture(s) in which the church is set and of which the church forms part. The received teachings of Scripture and tradition are certainly essential to the constructive task, but they are only indirect means of divine self-communication—starting points rather than conclusions given in advance. Theological work on these elements involves, therefore, discernment of what comes to (often inadequate) expression in these sources, and openness to subject them to critical appraisal, that is, to treat them as sources but not necessarily as norms. Classical Christian teaching has no perennial validity; it is relative to the settings in which it was produced, and may prove insufficient in the task of articulating the Christian message in modern culture. That culture is both a source and a norm in shaping Christian teaching, and so a Christian doctrine is built up in the course of a conversation between faith and "situation" or "context." Theological construction is as much revision as it is retrieval. The audience to which the results of theological construction are directed includes both the church and the wider culture, for the boundary between church and culture is porous, the church not being simply a closed entity with its own stable and isolated cultural forms. As it directs itself to this audience, theology aims to give an imaginative construal of Christian claims in order to demonstrate their relevance and value and their coherence with whatever else is taken to be true.

6. Durable examples would include Charles Hodge, *Systematic Theology* (New York: Scribner, 1877), 1:575–616; L. Berkhof, *Systematic Theology* (London: Banner of Truth, 1958), 165–78.

7. H. Bavinck, *Reformed Dogmatics* (Grand Rapids: Baker Academic, 2004), 2:591–619.

8. Karl Barth, *Church Dogmatics* III/3 (Edinburgh: T&T Clark, 1961).

This mode of theology gathered momentum in the more liberal schools of nineteenth-century German dogmatics, as well as in earlier twentieth-century English philosophical theology, which tried to negotiate a way through evolutionary idealism (the work of William Temple is a good example).[9] Though it was in some measure eclipsed by Barth's counterproject from the 1920s to the 1950s, it has enjoyed considerable prominence in North American theology since then, especially in the tradition of "correlational" theology, which often looks to the work of the German émigré theologian Paul Tillich as an exemplary instance of theological engagement with modern culture. The most impressive treatment of providence from this perspective is an influential work by Langdon Gilkey, *Reaping the Whirlwind*, which set the parameters of theological discussion of providence for some time. The book is a reconstruction of Christian teaching about providence in light of what he takes to be prominent features of modern consciousness: human historicity and relativity, the ubiquity of change as process but not necessarily progress, history as a sphere of human agency, the inadequacy of older religious symbol systems for articulating modern experience, a contrast between classic and modern cultures. The task of a Christian doctrine of providence is not to face modern culture with an opposing account of human experience and its ambiguities, but rather to direct attention to "a dimension of ultimacy and of sacrality" within secular modernity.[10] Hence "part of the task of theology is . . . to relate traditional symbols to life-experiences, to manifest the experiential meaning of theological concepts in terms of our life world."[11] Doctrines of providence are symbols, coordinated not simply with that to which they refer but also with the situations from which they emerge; as such they are open to critical revision or translation into the framework of a modern ontology of history.

The contrast between "internal" and "external" orientations and between the tasks of "retrieval" and "revision" ought not to be too clearly drawn. But it is an aspect of the history of modern thought about providence that will keep surfacing as we turn to examine some of the topics that have been prominent in doctrinal discussion: the knowledge of providence, the God of providence, providence and the order of nature, and providence and history.

The Knowledge of Providence

How is God's providential purpose for and governance of all things known? As providence is immanentized or naturalized, there occurs a corresponding

---

9. See, for example, William Temple, *Christus Veritas* (London: Macmillan, 1924) and *Nature, Man and God* (London: Macmillan, 1934).

10. Langdon Gilkey, *Reaping the Whirlwind: A Christian Interpretation of History* (New York: Seabury, 1976), 46.

11. Ibid., 144.

shift in the way in which knowledge of providence is conceived. In premodern theology, knowledge of providence was primarily understood as "positive" or "revealed" knowledge, that is, knowledge given to creatures in the course of God's saving self-communication, and so bound up with faith as the proper creaturely response to God's presence. It is true that some considered the doctrine of providence to be a "mixed" article, known in some measure by reason as well as by faith in divine revelation. But even here, reason is not "pure" reason unassisted by divine grace, but "creaturely" reason, reason that is already by its very nature oriented to the knowledge of God, even though hampered by fallenness. Further, reason is subordinate to revelation, its in-adequacies overcome and completed by God's gift, for it is only by God's act that God's ways with the world can properly be known.

In some of the major strands of modern theology, revelation is no longer or only rarely invoked in talking about knowledge of providence. When teaching about providence, theologians from those strands locate it in the realm of natural religion, and discernment of providence is thought to require no confessional convictions. Knowledge of providence is a matter for "natural" theology, as the kind of knowledge of God that humans acquire by observing and interpreting nature and history. Knowledge of providence is not built on the basis of direct divine instruction, but is an imaginative picture of the world, a "reading" of the way the world might be taken to be. Even when the category of revelation is retained, it tends to operate indirectly, for revelation is mediated through experience of and reflection upon the world, and knowledge of providence is grounded in "a dimension of ultimacy in that experience that must be understood, illumined, and dealt with in terms of religious symbols."[12]

Alongside this, the older tradition has found compelling modern advocates such as Berkouwer[13] or Barth, both of whom reject the association of providence with preconfessional natural theology. The providential will of God for history, Barth proposes, is plain. But "it is not plain . . . because we have lifted the veil of this history and discovered its secret. It is not plain because we have perceived, planned or determined it of ourselves. It is plain because God has revealed it to us in his Word. And he himself has revealed it in the simple way in which he has revealed himself . . . as the triune God who as the Father is over us and as the Son is for us, and both in the unity in which as the Holy Spirit he creates our life as a life under and again for him."[14] Knowledge of providence is knowledge of God and the ways of God revealed by God.

Barth's reference to the connection between knowledge of providence and life under and for God leads to a further aspect of the knowledge of providence, namely its practical aspects. For classical Christian theology, knowledge of

12. Ibid., 37.
13. G. C. Berkouwer, *The Providence of God* (Grand Rapids: Eerdmans, 1952), 31–49.
14. Barth, *CD* III/3, 34.

providence is practical knowledge: it is not a theoretical view of the situation of the world and humankind within the world, but one of the skills required for and reinforced by living life in a certain direction. Knowledge of providence is not to be isolated from attitudes and behaviors, and its plausibility derives in part from its exercise and application in the trials of life, when it offers consolation and direction. Knowledge of providence can perform these functions of comfort and orientation because it refers us to the objective realities of God's antecedent purpose, present active care, and promises for the future. Attention to the practical-subjective aspects of belief in providence is widespread in modern theologies, but often with a significantly altered relation to their objective ground.

Whereas older theologies thought of faith in providence as assent to objective divine acts that generate Christian dispositions, modern theologies are characteristically less confident about access to objective knowledge (i.e., less realist). Such modern approaches are consequently more concerned to discuss how the capacities and situation of the believer shape apprehensions of God's providential presence and activity. The early twentieth-century liberal Protestant historical theologian Ernst Troeltsch illustrates this tendency well. He draws a sharp contrast between "scientific explanation of the world" and belief in providence, belief that is "purely religious" and so not grounded in objective knowledge of how the world is.[15] "Faith's absolute teleology of the world has nothing to do with the teleological concepts of natural science."[16] The reduction of faith in providence to "attitude" was a common strand in those Christian theologies of the middle part of the last century that drew upon existentialist philosophy in articulating Christian doctrine. Bultmann, for example, insists that Christian faith is properly not concerned with "universal history" (which he thought merely abstract), but with the meaning of the present moment in which the believer is summoned to responsibility.[17] Again, "liberation" theologies, which emphasize how knowledge of God is acquired in the course of sociopolitical action, propose that God's activity in history is discerned "through engagement with some form of transformative, emancipatory praxis."[18] To know providence is not to contemplate the order of the world but to experience and act in ways that are essential ingredients of the process of giving order to the world. Modern accounts of the knowledge of providence are, in short, often "idealist" in that they are concerned to elucidate the human conditions for, and limitations of, apprehension of the ways of God.

This idealism leads to differences between classical and modern theology in responding to the obscurity and hiddenness of providence. Older theology

15. Ernst Troeltsch, *The Christian Faith* (Minneapolis: Augsburg Fortress, 1991), 205.
16. Ibid., 206.
17. See R. Bultmann, *History and Eschatology* (Edinburgh: Edinburgh University Press, 1951), 154.
18. C. Hodgson, *God in History: Shapes of Freedom* (Nashville: Abingdon, 1989), 41.

accounted for the obscurity of the ways of God by, for example, referring to the inscrutability of God's will to finite, temporal creatures whose knowledge of all things is acquired over time, and who do not have command of the totality of their lives, or by speaking of the effects of sin upon our knowledge of providence. These hindrances to knowledge are in the process of being overcome by divine revelation discerned by the illuminating power of the Spirit. Modern theologies, by contrast, are less likely to appeal to revelation as bridging the gap between the infinite God and finite, fallen creatures. Furthermore, they are more likely to assume that human reason must operate without divine aid in thinking about providence, and thereby more likely to recommend tentativeness in talking of God's purposes for, and action in, the world.

The God of Providence

Who is the God who purposes the course of created reality and acts to bring his purpose into effect?

We have already seen how from the seventeenth century providence was often conceived in impersonal ways, detached from much by way of specifically Christian content: the author of the world's order is a supreme being, exercising causal power. This (at best) theistic and (at worst) deistic understanding of providence has proved remarkably durable. It remains a major element in some kinds of contemporary analytical philosophy of religion, in which the particular characteristics that Christians attribute to God are often of little interest. This is because the main topics for discussion—such as divine foreknowledge, the nature of divine action in the world, the relation between providence and human freedom or between providence and evil—have much the same shape whichever god is under discussion, and because appeal to positive doctrine is thought unlikely to illuminate philosophical quandaries. Similarly, doctrinal theologians concerned to correlate "message" and "situation" tend to give relatively scant attention to the particulars of Christian teaching about God, since it is just these particulars that are thought to inhibit the kind of engagement with culture out of which plausible Christian doctrine emerges. In such major accounts of Christian teaching about providence and history as Gilkey's *Reaping the Whirlwind* or Hodgson's *God in History*, for example, trinitarian and incarnational doctrine hardly surfaces, playing no substantial role in conceiving God's historical presence and activity, because Trinity and incarnation are unusable components of a broken "classic" model of divine providence. Part of what renders the classic model irretrievable is its investment in conceptions of divine "rule," which are incapable of supporting ideas of human freedom or the openness of history. As an alternative, Hodgson, for example, suggests talk of an immanent God—what he calls "God's shaping presence"[19]—to the articulation of which trinitarian and incarnational doctrine offers little contribution.

Other accounts of the doctrine of providence have adopted a different strategy in conceiving of the God of providence, drawing on the renewed interest in trinitarian theology that has been a prominent feature of systematic theology in recent decades. Two features of this renewal of trinitarian doctrine are important here. First, it has pressed theologians to attend to the distinctive character of Christian claims about God's identity: talk of God as Father, Son, and Spirit is not simply one version of talk of "God" or "god." Second, the doctrine of the Trinity is not an isolated piece of Christian teaching, but a doctrine that determines the entire corpus of dogmatics: with this doctrine in place, everything else looks different, including the doctrine of providence. And so the motor of teaching about providence is not ideas about nature and history, which determine what may and may not be plausibly maintained about God, but claims about God's triune identity.

A representative recent presentation of a trinitarian theology of providence can be found in Charles Wood's *The Question of Providence*.[20] The book argues (not uncontroversially) that the theistic idiom of modern accounts of providence is in part a result of the separation of the doctrines of providence and Trinity in the early Christian period, providence being shaped by material taken from pagan sources rather than by the Christian doctrine of God. One result of this was the appropriation of providence to God the Father and corresponding neglect of teaching about Christ and the Spirit in articulating God's providential relations with creation. By contrast, Wood proposes that "God relates to things 'triunely.'"[21] Wood's rejection of unitarian accounts of providence is not only directed against deist ideas of a providential supreme being, but also intended to correct strands of the Christian tradition that have emphasized that God's works in the world are indivisible. This emphasis he believes to undergird a static picture of providence as merely maintaining the way things are, stressing providential governance at the expense of its teleological aspects. In effect, then, the capacity of a doctrine of providence to furnish a reading of the human situation depends upon readiness to appeal to the inner logic of Christian teaching about the Trinity.

Two other aspects of this renewed trinitarianism are to be noted. One is that it tends to concentrate on God's providential relation to history and to have little to say about his relation to nature. Second, this salvation-historical emphasis is in turn connected to a focus on the "economic" rather than "immanent" dimensions of the doctrine of the Trinity, that is, on the external works of God rather than on God's life in himself. In terms of the doctrine

19. Hodgson, *God in History*, 235.
20. Charles Wood, *The Question of Providence* (Louisville: Westminster John Knox, 2008).
21. Ibid., 69.

of providence, this means that much more is said about providence as divine activity in creation than about the will or plan of God that the activity realizes. And this, in turn, may indicate that even theologians most invested in a distinctively Christian doctrine of God may not be as immune from cultural convention as they aspire to be.

How does God act in the world? This question has been approached in a couple of ways in modern theology. One line of investigation concerns the conceivability of divine action, and has been conducted largely by those with philosophical interests, especially but not exclusively those in the analytical tradition. Others have been interested in more direct deployment of doctrinal resources to articulate the modes of God's providential action.

Investigation of providence in modern Anglo-American philosophical theology or philosophy of religion has devoted a good deal of attention to questions of the intelligibility of talk about providence.[22] The procedures followed in such inquiries are characteristically those of conceptual and logical analysis, in order to discern what language about God's action in the events of the world adds to language about the event in and of itself, or to make sense of what it means to say that worldly happenings realize God's intentions. These investigations of intelligibility form the basis for approaches to larger philosophical topics: Does God act in the world? How are divine and human action related? Is divine determination compatible with creaturely freedom? Some doctrinal theologians are frustrated by these analytical exercises, partly because so much appears to turn on the clarification of terms and arguments, partly because they seem to work with simplified and historically uninformed accounts of the content of Christian teaching. Others are more ready to allow the value of the analysis, believing that, for example, analytical theories of action provide resources for thinking through Christian beliefs about providence in the same way that discriminating use of Platonic or Aristotelian metaphysics enabled classical Christian theologians to build up a portrait of Christian teaching.

More directly, doctrinal discussion of God's providential action has been much preoccupied with the nature of divine causality. We have already seen that a major factor in the breakdown of the doctrine of providence in modernity was restriction of God's action toward the world to that of efficient causality, as a result of which God became a remote prime mover, furnishing initial motion but only extrinsically related to the processes of nature and history. In part this is driven by models of nature and history as self-moving and self-regulating mechanisms. But it is also connected to some deep modern instincts, according to which human integrity and freedom can be preserved only if

22. See Vincent Brümmer, *Speaking of a Personal God* (Cambridge: Cambridge University Press, 1992); Mats J. Hansson, *Understanding an Act of God: An Essay in Philosophical Theology* (Uppsala: Uppsala University Press, 1991); Thomas F. Tracy, ed., *The God Who Acts: Philosophical and Theological Explorations* (University Park: Pennsylvania State University Press, 1994).

undetermined by God. The ideal of creaturely self-responsibility continues to haunt modern Christian thought, surfacing, for example, in theologies that fear that talk of divine governance is inherently oppressive and corrosive of creaturely dignity and liberty.

Some deal with this issue by accepting one or another version of the modern axiom that the integrity of creatures is incompatible with certain understandings of divine action, but arguing that in an authentically Christian doctrine of providence, God's action is neither determinist nor oppressive. In a major historical and theological study of providence, for example, Bernhardt proposes that providence is enacted "kenotically," God's providential power being made perfect in weakness as God suffers with creation.[23] Similarly, those associated with "open theism" have revived the Pelagian and Arminian tradition in which God's relation to creation includes an element of divine risk.[24] God creates beings capable of accepting or rejecting God, thereby making some of his actions contingent on creaturely actions. Moreover, God is temporal rather than timeless, and not exhaustively omniscient, since aspects of the future must wait upon as yet unrealized human choices. Both of these accounts of providence make the same basic move, that of overcoming apparent competition between divine and human action by pointing to some kind of voluntary divine self-limitation or self-restraint, through which a space for created integrity is kept open, something which it is thought classical doctrines of the divine purpose and its enactment were unable to do.

Other theologians reject modern axioms about divine and human freedom, arguing for a noncontrastive account of the action of God and creatures, in which divine and creaturely movement are directly, not inversely, proportional.[25] God's providential action does not need to be held in check in order to retain the creature's freedom, for God does not act against the creature but in and through the creature in its freedom and integrity. A major element here is retrieval of concepts of primary and secondary causality to talk of how God's acts concur with creaturely acts. These concepts were standard in medieval and post-Reformation scholastic theologies of providence, but dropped from view when divine causality was restricted to being initial and external. In the absence of this restriction, something like the following can be said: God is the first cause of all things, and only by virtue of his acts of bringing all things to be and ceaselessly maintaining all things can the creature act at all. But the fact that God produces, guides, and maintains creaturely actions

23. See Bernhardt, *Was heisst "Handeln Gottes"?*

24. A representative account can be found in John Sanders, *The God Who Risks: A Theology of Divine Providence* (Downers Grove, IL: InterVarsity, 2007).

25. See, for example, Kathryn Tanner, *God and Creation in Christian Theology* (Oxford: Blackwell, 1988); Robert Sokolowski, *The God of Faith and Reason* (Notre Dame, IN: University of Notre Dame Press, 1982); David B. Burrell, *Freedom and Creation in Three Traditions* (Notre Dame, IN: University of Notre Dame Press, 1993).

does not mean that the creature is entirely passive, and God the only agent, for omnicausality is not sole causality. It simply means that the creature is a particular kind of cause—a "secondary" or "caused" cause, a cause that mediates God's causality but is no less really active for being caused. God's providential action does not suppress the creature but sustains it. Where modern ideals of liberty assume that only purely spontaneous, self-caused action is free, theologically specified notions of secondary causality maintain that God's providential moving of the creature is not against but in fulfillment of its nature, a moving of its own movement. Providence directs the creature from within, supplying and directing the inner movement by which it lives its life at the hands of the Creator.

Having considered how theologians have thought about the divine agent of providence and the ways in which he acts, we turn to the two spheres in which providence is operative: nature and history.

Providence and the Order of Nature

From the early modern period the expansion of natural philosophy and science prompted the growth of a "naturalized" concept of nature, one in which nature is not a providentially maintained created order whose motion is moved by the presence and activity of its creator but a self-maintaining system, set in motion by a supreme cause but now moving independently. The contraction of teaching about providence in the explanation of nature was reinforced from the mid-nineteenth century by two factors. First, in the wake of Darwin's *Origin of Species* (1859), the explanatory power of evolutionary models of nature gained considerable momentum and was often judged to undermine talk of divine providence in the natural order (though it ought not to be forgotten that evolutionary theory evoked a body of sophisticated natural theology in the later nineteenth century, especially in Britain). This was because in giving a purely naturalist or physicalist account of change in nature, evolution appeared to eliminate ideas of an antecedent divine purpose or a divine goal and of present divine action. Second, the technologization of nature in modern industrial societies presupposed that nature is mere raw material for human projects of manufacture or manipulation, in effect treating natural order and forms as constraints to be overcome by the exercise of technical reason rather than as indications of divine design. In the face of the remarkable cultural prowess of natural scientific inquiry and technology, and the resulting transformation of attitudes to nature, how has the doctrine of providence fared?

One approach has been to hand over nature to natural science, withdrawing from the attempt to relate divine providence to questions of physics, biology, or cosmology, and restricting the scope of providence to history—whether history as a whole or salvation history in its social or individual dimensions.

Barth's doctrine of providence is an authoritative example of this move. For him, the subject matter of providence is God's ordering of human history as a whole toward the covenant with humankind established in Jesus Christ. The setting of providence is thus soteriology rather than the theology of created nature, and questions about natural forms and processes are quite peripheral in Barth's account. Whether this restriction of providence to the historical is to be traced to a turn to religious subjectivity in the Reformation and philosophical idealism is an open question; but that it constitutes a contraction of the scope of the doctrine is difficult to dispute.

A quite different strategy is found in attempts over at least the last forty years to deploy talk of providential divine action in ultimate (if not penultimate) explanation of natural forms and processes, thereby retaining nature within a comprehensive theology of providence. Much of the work here has not been undertaken by doctrinal theologians but by those whose interests and competencies span theology and the natural sciences. Recent debates have explored a number of possibilities. "Emergentist" theories of evolution have proved theologically suggestive, going beyond reductive physicalism in raising the possibility that natural processes are open to (and perhaps directed toward) the emergence of consciousness or moral culture. In a similar way, accounts of the universe as "fine-tuned"[26] (possessing exactly the right constants and physical laws for life to emerge) can be coordinated with a theology of creation and providential government, especially when connected to the idea of "intelligent design" of such constants by some supreme being.[27] The success of most of these arguments depends upon the viability of some sort of account of how divine action operates in, with, and under natural forms and processes. Some advance accounts of "double agency" in which an event is attributed both to a divine agent and to a natural motion. Others adopt varieties of "panentheism" in which the world has its being "in" the God who exceeds the world yet acts through its processes.[28] In something of the same direction, Pannenberg appeals to Christian teaching about the cosmic presence of the divine Logos: the divine Word is the "principle" of the historically unfolding order of nature, whose processes have a ministerial function in God's preservation and direction of all things.[29]

These approaches to the doctrine of providence may form part of a natural theology, serving as pretheological observations that, without making appeal

---

26. A. McGrath, *A Fine-Tuned Universe: The Quest for God in Science and Theology* (Louisville: Westminster John Knox, 2009).

27. W. Dembski, *Intelligent Design* (Downers Grove, IL: InterVarsity, 1999).

28. See Philip Clayton and Arthur Peacocke, eds., *In Whom We Live and Move and Have Our Being* (Grand Rapids: Eerdmans, 2004); Philip Clayton, *Adventures in the Spirit: God, World, Divine Action* (Minneapolis: Fortress, 2008).

29. Wolfhart Pannenberg, *Systematic Theology*, trans. Geoffrey W. Bromiley (Grand Rapids: Eerdmans, 1994), 2:35–136.

to supernatural divine revelation, in some measure stimulate or confirm assent to the truths of faith. As such, they require rather little by way of positive teaching about God, their intention being primarily apologetic rather than confessional. However, when understood as a theology of nature, they may be part of a doctrinal explanation of natural forms and processes that apply and extend prior teaching about God and creation. In such cases, the positive content of Christian belief is presupposed rather than left for later exposition.

Providence and History

The cultural setting for modern accounts of God's providential action in history is the twofold process of historicization and secularization of time. To speak of time as "historicized" is to say that temporal change is a primary metaphysical category, and that temporality is basic, not founded upon some prior nontemporal reality. To speak of time as "secular" is to say that the events and actions of which time is the measure are autonomous and spontaneous, and that their meaning is not to be elicited by seeing them as signs of divine order or the means by which creatures are borne toward a divine purpose. How has the doctrine of providence addressed itself to this setting?

For some—Barth is again the most cogent and imaginative example— theology is not at liberty to accept the terms of the question as posed by its setting, because its responsibilities are apportioned to it by revelation rather than context. Barth retained many affirmations of classical accounts of providence: that history is a unified whole, given coherence and extension by the eternal counsel of the Triune God of whose purpose history is the enactment; that what takes place in time is not simply the deliberations and actions of creatures, but the triumph of God as his will is executed in and through created occurrence; that history is thus both derivative and purposive, from God and for God. Nevertheless, Barth proposed wide-ranging corrections to redress what he considered inadequacies in the older theology of providence. He unearthed what he took to be a christological inadequacy, which formalized divine providential order without grasping that it is the incarnate Son who is the "epitome of the wisdom, will and power of the Father."[30] The result was a certain abstractness in talking of history as a sphere of providence and a lack of coordination between general world history and the specific salvation-historical reality of the covenant. This Barth sought to overcome by making the history of the covenant into that around which our understanding of providence is organized: the history of the covenant, with Christology, election, and soteriology at its core, illuminates the wider history of creation and providence. Only this, Barth believed, can block modern ideas of "free and

30. Barth, *CD* III/3, 35.

secular creaturely occurrence"[31] and enable theology to state how creaturely history provides the time, space, and opportunity for the unfolding of the covenant of grace and the kingdom of Jesus Christ.

In effect, Barth renewed the concept of history as providentially ordered *magnalia Dei* (mighty works of God), suffusing it with his particular christological emphasis. Many judge Barth's reworking of features of classical providential teaching to be an insufficient revision, leaving intact views of history no longer retrievable in modern cultural circumstances. Perhaps the chief problem of "classic" providential readings of history is that of "over-determination," that is, the assumption that history is a bounded reality with a fixed shape and direction, given by God's counsel and effected by God's temporal acts, and capable of being given—in principle, at least—a comprehensive explanation on the basis of divine disclosure. Two particular aspects of this critique should be noted. A first concerns the unavailability of a comprehensive view of history to contingent observers of or participants within an unfinished historical process. A strong form of this is found in "postmodern" rejections of overarching historical explanation in favor of radical historical pluralism that dissolves history into a random assemblage of revisable perspectives. Second, providential schemes of history may function ideologically, hiding relations of power by cloaking them in larger patterns of divine order that legitimate established political and economic orders, and so inhibit perception of, and action against, injustice. Doctrines of providence, in short, know too much and do too little.

By way of theological response, a range of strategies have been attempted. One—drastic—solution is to abandon any theology of providence and think of history as simply anarchic,[32] though this is more a counsel of despair than a revision of Christian teaching. Another possibility is to set out a theology of providence in a chastened voice, one less total, more provisional, in its explanatory scope.[33] Rather than deploying talk of providence to outbid the temporally unfolding character of our knowledge of ourselves, theology might be guided by the incremental nature of our knowledge of God's ways with the world, which are not grasped all at once in some instant of perception, but diachronically, through time, and never in any final way. Such a theology of providence might make its appeal to aspects of Christian doctrine such as God's infinity, which exceeds any single contingent representation, or teaching about the Spirit as the energy of historical process. Others have oriented the theology of providence around the primacy of liberating historical action. On these accounts, classical theologies of providence are complicit in a view of the

31. Ibid., 41.

32. Mark C. Taylor, *Erring: A Postmodern A/theology* (Chicago: University of Chicago Press, 1984).

33. Ben Quash, *Theology and the Drama of History*, Cambridge Studies in Christian Doctrine (Cambridge: Cambridge University Press, 2005).

world in which the social and political order is taken to be natural rather than constructed, ordered by God and so not open to change; belief in providence therefore reinforces social passivity and conformity. However, it may be that Christian symbols enable us to think of God not merely as one who wills and maintains a fixed order of things, but as one whose providence is known in his empowerment of creatures to make (and therefore to remake) history. A theology of providence would then be a "political-liberation theology as it attempts to work out an open-ended theology of history."[34]

Conclusion

Surveys of possible ways of expounding one or other element of Christian teaching risk conveying the impression that all the options are open all the time and that any doctrinal strategy can be countered by another. Such indeterminate pluralism generates indecision, irony, or skepticism. Properly speaking, examination of the various possibilities that lie open to the theologian is preliminary to, not a substitute for or a way of avoiding, the exercise of judgment. The richest, most compelling doctrines of providence, ancient or modern, have been those in which such judgment is exercised, and which, moreover, afford evidence of a range of qualities: sophisticated awareness of the theological and cultural history of Christian teaching about God's providential works; deeply formed instincts about the inner content of the doctrine and of its relations to other tracts of Christian teaching; a sense of its full scope as a theology of nature and history, which can resist reduction of the doctrine to some particular theme or application; confidence in the resources that Christian faith can bring to bear upon the matter beyond those supplied by philosophies of nature and history; careful attention to the uses (legitimate and illegitimate) of teaching about providence in understanding the natural, social, and spiritual lives of human persons. The co-presence of all these qualities in a single theological account of providence is rare. Yet together they constitute a set of criteria by which we may assess the adequacy of theological reflection on God's continuing relation to, and action within, the created order, which in his love he maintains and governs, and which he will bring to perfection.

For Further Reading

Barth, Karl. *Church Dogmatics* III/3. Edinburgh: T&T Clark, 1961.

Berkouwer, G. C. *The Providence of God*. Grand Rapids: Eerdmans, 1952.

34. Hodgson, *God in History*, 240.

Clayton, Philip. *Adventures in the Spirit: God, World, Divine Action*. Minneapolis: Fortress, 2008.

Gilkey, L. *Reaping the Whirlwind: A Christian Interpretation of History*. New York: Seabury, 1976.

Gorringe, Timothy. *God's Theatre: A Theology of Providence*. London: SCM, 1991.

Pannenberg, Wolfhart. *Systematic Theology*. Vol. 2. Translated by Geoffrey W. Bromiley. Grand Rapids: Eerdmans, 1994.

Sanders, J. *The God Who Risks: A Theology of Divine Providence*. Downers Grove, IL: InterVarsity, 2007.

Scheffczyk, L. *Creation and Providence*. New York: Herder & Herder, 1970.

Tracy, T. F. *The God Who Acts: Philosophical and Theological Explorations*. University Park: Pennsylvania State University Press, 1994.

Wood, C. M. *The Question of Providence*. Louisville: Westminster John Knox, 2008.

10

. . .

PNEUMATOLOGY

Telford Work

Introduction: Surveying the Spirit in the Late Modern World

Theologians in the modern era inherited the patristic tradition on the Holy
Spirit's divinity, the medieval tradition on the Holy Spirit's presence to and
in the church, and the Reformation-era tradition on the Holy Spirit's justifying and sanctifying activities. Classic doctrines, all; and all have continued
to dominate Christian theology to the present day. Yet the Enlightenment
had ushered in a radical rethinking of what it means to be human, and the
scientific revolution had ushered in a radical rethinking of how to understand
the universe. The saga of modern pneumatology is largely a story of how
theology struggled to account and compensate for these shifts. We see an
interplay of a variety of long-consolidated theological traditions, a few new
ones, and an intimidating range of cultural shifts that continually reshape the
church's local landscapes.[1]

1. These struggles were already well underway by the era of this volume's concern (roughly
the past 150–200 years). Many were already fundamentally concluded—not to the satisfaction
of all parties, of course, but certainly to the satisfaction of the various camps whose convictions remain those of their early modern champions: Wesleyans with their developed doctrines
of experienced justification and sanctification, liberals who interpret theological claims in the
experiential categories of Schleiermacher, and so on. As the Christian faith spreads worldwide
with unprecedented scope and speed, these schools are more influential now than in their heydays.

This essay arranges the projects that are happening everywhere in modernity's recent world in an actual map of modern pneumatology. Its point is not to determine the normative place for reflection on the Holy Spirit, but to inform us about the wide variety of theological reflections in the modern era about the Holy Spirit, who is their object. A map of our country does not say which province or city is best. It shows where we live, tells us who our neighbors are, reminds us where we grew up, and goes some way to explaining why we are the way we are.

But how should such a map represent these forces and traditions? What kind of theological cartography can make recent pneumatology more navigable? We could color in states or provinces—a sprawling Catholic Texas, a Vermont of process theology, a Pentecostal Quebec—and then describe regional traits, local heroes, and migration patterns. But surveying a scene as complicated as ours would grow tedious, cataloguing the interrelationships would become hopelessly complicated, and the borders we drew would train us against seeing the broad regional commonalities. Another option would be to draw a topical map, clustering common concerns such as the Spirit's justice, restoration, gifts of life, power, revelation, and intimate presence, like the transitional ecological zones of a topographic rendering. Yet many of those concerns spring up all over our territories, not just in one region. Few theologians, let alone churches and traditions, really focus on just one topic, or even one stable cluster. Pentecostals seek order too, just as Calvinists invite the Spirit's transformation.

Instead, we will sketch a map like a seismic survey that identifies a variety of social forces[2] shaping modern pneumatology such as technology, culture, philosophy, and especially ecclesiology. In an era of such vast changes, this broad focus suggests a map of a frontier territory rather than settled domains, with familiar landmarks, rugged country, distant lands, complicated interactions, flux, plenty of unknowns—and, in and through all of it, a *mission*, laid out before us like the vast Roman world into which the Spirit propelled Jesus's designated witnesses (Luke 24:48–49).

Other dynamics were playing out in the modern era whose ramifications for modern theologies are of more strictly recent influence. The ever-changing industrial revolution transformed our physical and economic relationships with one another, with those near and far, with the earth, and with our own bodies. Ideologies arose and swept the world, altering not only theological imaginations but world history. Scientific thinking turned toward more and more of the human domain, generating whole disciplines that did not even exist around, say, 1850, such as sociology and psychology. Congregations' ways of life have changed, and their habits and thinking along with them. These forces have shaped recent thinking on the Holy Spirit in both stark and subtle ways—even if only by creating new settings for the old convictions.

2. Focusing on intellectual forces, LeRon Shults offers an enlightening map of intersections between contemporary pneumatology and the developing philosophical conceptions of matter, person, and force. F. LeRon Shults, "Current Trends in Pneumatology," in *Spirit and Spirituality* (Copenhagen: University of Copenhagen Press, 2007), 20–38.

Such a portrait leaves much concealed that a different kind of map might expose. Yet it reveals a number of significant features of the complicated theological world of the past century and a half.[3]

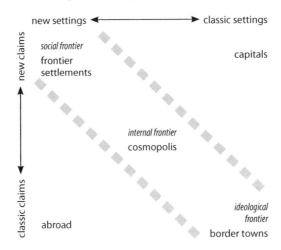

This map will help us plot five sorts of modern pneumatology:

1. We start with the gospel's "**capitals**": long-established ecclesial settings where classic claims rule.
2. Next we travel "**abroad**" to new social and ideological settings in which the Spirit is understood in different terms than in orthodox Christian tradition.
3. Then we backtrack to the "**frontier settlements**" of the gospel's *social frontier*—the modern era's new social settings in which traditional Christian life and faith have taken root.

3. In some ways this grid resembles H. Richard Niebuhr's popular typological spectrum of "Christ and culture" (*Christ and Culture* [New York: Harper, 1956]), but it better respects the dynamic forces at work in both domains. The nineteenth and twentieth centuries saw both awakenings and upheavals in dominantly Christian societies. At the same time, the faith migrated to new locations worldwide—emerging industrial landscapes as well as foreign civilizations— and intellectual ferment at home as well as cultural influences from abroad shaped Christian imaginations. (Niebuhr's typology would have worked better as a typology of eschatologies relating "church and world.")

This grid also bears resemblances to Frei's types of Christian theology (*Types of Christian Theology* [New Haven: Yale University Press, 1994]). However, Frei's types seem difficult to locate on this grid and no longer fall along a neat line. Frei's types 1 and 3 would seem to lie at the bottom of the grid, with 3 on the right. Type 5 arguably belongs along the top, tending toward the right. Types 2 and 4 seem to scatter diagonally along the frontiers rather than falling at precise points. The mismatch occurs because so much more is going on in recent theology than just an encounter between theology and philosophy (or any one field), and the results are too messy to fit along Frei's spectrum. A whole world is changing, along with the innumerable little worlds within it.

4. We cross over to another frontier, the *ideological*, whose "**border towns**" are shaped as much by residents' reactions to modernity's new claims about the Spirit as by their own theological heritages.

5. Finally we visit the center of the map, an *internal frontier* where the new world and the old interact and intermingle and shape a "**cosmopolis**," whose faith and theological imagination incorporate and react to features of both classic and modern life.

In each quadrant we will (a) identify *a predecessor* whose influence marks the pneumatology done in that place, (b) note several prominent and influential *figures and schools of thought* there, (c) draw *generalizations* and find *a representative figure*, and, finally, (d) ask *who the Holy Spirit is* as manifested there. Then we can conclude by considering briefly whether the overall picture has overarching pneumatological significance.

1. Pneumatology in Capitals

Historical theology displays a bias toward new developments by highlighting them; these innovations, after all, are what distinguish an era. This bias tempts us to overlook some of the most important movements in recent pneumatology: to go *nowhere*, or else to go back to the theological milestones of earlier eras.

The eighteenth- and nineteenth-century Christian world was implacably separated into divided confessional traditions, so we can point to no one common predecessor who inspired traditionalist pneumatology across the church's various theological capitals. Each tradition had its own. One representative predecessor, whose influence in later American Christianity is uncontested, is Jonathan Edwards. The leader of America's First Great Awakening began and remained firmly in the Westminster tradition of English Puritan Calvinism, helping weave its threads into the durable fabric of American Christian thought and spirituality. Where pneumatology is concerned, we can add that Edwards's account of "the distinguishing marks of the work of the Spirit of God" influenced, among many others, a young John Wesley, who in 1738 was developing his pneumatological understanding of personal and ecclesial revival.[4] However, even the capitals of nineteenth-century American theology were provincial backwaters compared to their counterparts in the Old World. So this analysis focuses on Europe.

In response to the challenges of modernism, nineteenth-century Catholic neo-scholasticism relied on formalized positions and methods from the medieval scholastics—above all, Thomas Aquinas, whose theological style had become effectively canonical for Roman Catholics. Pope Leo XIII commended

---

4. Albert Outler, *John Wesley* (New York: Oxford University Press, 1964), 15, cited in Winfield H. Bevins, "The Historical Development of Wesley's Doctrine of the Spirit," *Wesleyan Theological Journal* 41, no. 2 (Fall 2006): 161–81.

the neo-scholastic approach in his 1879 encyclical *Aeterni Patris*. This recharged the Roman Church's appreciation of the Holy Spirit with the rich resources of Augustinian-Thomistic classic Western pneumatology.[5]

When a number of Catholic theologians found neo-scholasticism's formalism stale and unsatisfying, they turned back even further, to the giants of the patristic era. Their "turn to the sources" came to be known as the *ressourcement* movement. Leaders such as Hans Urs von Balthasar, Yves Congar, Jean Daniélou, and Henri de Lubac helped revitalize Western appreciation for the groundbreaking pneumatological work of Origen, Basil of Caesarea, Gregory of Nazianzus, and Augustine. This laid one of the foundations of the renaissance of trinitarian doctrine in the twentieth century. This revival's consequences for pneumatology continue to reverberate throughout current Christian theology.

Eastern capitals were busy too. The Christian East had always prized its patristic heritage and cultivated its memory with unparalleled devotion. Orthodox theology is not always as conservative as it can be made out to be; Russian Orthodox theology in particular carried on sustained conversations between Byzantine and Slavic tradition on the one hand and modernity on the other. Still, the vigor with which Orthodox theologians developed and defended convictions from the Cappadocian fathers to Gregory Palamas and John of Damascus kept these voices vital in twentieth century orthodoxy, as well as powerfully accessible to the Western Christians who were drawn into those conversations.

Where the Holy Spirit was concerned, this legacy was constantly felt along the fault lines between the Augustinian and Cappadocian doctrines of the Spirit's procession. Vladimir Lossky and many other Orthodox theologians regularly alleged that Western scholasticism depersonified the Holy Spirit by misconstruing his relations of origin as the Father's and Son's shared nature, and reasserted the classic Eastern doctrine of the Spirit's single procession from the Father. Their critiques have been heard by a growing audience of sympathetic Westerners, effectively reopening the question of the *filioque* in some Western circles.

Another modern impact for traditional Orthodox pneumatology concerns tradition itself. The issue of authority has dominated Western theology since the Great Schism (1054). Its eras can practically be named in terms of battles over the authority of the bishop of Rome and his *curia*, the authority of civil governors, the authority of reason, the authority of Scripture, the authority of individual conscience, and the authority of the community.[6] Champions of

5. For a helpful treatment see Ralph del Colle, *Christ and the Spirit: Spirit-Christology in Trinitarian Perspective* (New York: Oxford University Press, 1994), particularly chap. 2, "Christ and the Spirit: Spirit-Christology in the Neo-Scholastic Tradition," 34–63.

6. See William F. Abraham, *Canon and Criterion in Christian Theology: From the Fathers to Feminism* (New York: Oxford University Press, 2002).

each often described its force in pneumatic terms: the magisterium exercises its teaching office as a *charism* of the Holy Spirit, the Bible is inspired and therefore authoritative, and so on. Here the Orthodox contribution was, above all, to reassert its long-standing conviction that holy tradition in its entirety is the Spirit's work and legacy. Dumitru Staniloae puts it concisely: "Church, tradition, and Scripture are woven into a whole, and the work of the Spirit is the soul of this integral unity."[7] Authority is not vested in one location, or in a simple hierarchy with the pope or the Scripture or the local community at the top; authority describes Jesus's sacramental presence throughout the whole body and life of the church, whose saints, liturgy, leaders, Scriptures, councils, and sacraments all manifest the light and grace of the Triune God. This perspective has proven attractive to a number of Westerners, particularly evangelicals, who have tired of the old disagreements.[8]

Some Protestants were going back to their sources too. John Calvin was ever popular reading in Protestant capitals. His power as a systematic thinker, channeled through heirs such as Charles Hodge, Herman Bavinck, Louis Berkhof, and Hyung Nong Park made Reformed thinking a center of theological gravity that pulled evangelicals into its orbit from everywhere on its wide confessional spectrum. Reformed theology has a robust, if sometimes underappreciated, pneumatology, which understands the Holy Spirit to be the agent who accomplishes God's ongoing work in the world.[9] The Spirit inspires the apostles and prophets and illuminates the minds of those who hear their message. He confirms the truth of the gospel as only God's internal witness can. His word and sacraments kindle faith in believers, applying the grace of Christ that alone turns God's elect into God's holy ones. His fruit of love, joy, and peace animates the church's worship, and his law disciplines decent and orderly communities.

Pietism (here an umbrella term for movements stressing that authentic relationships with God must be vital and actual, not just formal) was another dependable force for modern Protestant renewal. Theologically robust Pietism is pneumatic at its heart, insisting that the personal Spirit effects not just formal faith in forensic righteousness but rebirth into truly personal relationships with God in Jesus Christ. Carried into worshipers' hearts and congregational lives through prayers, hymns, meetings, revivals, catechisms, and devotional guides, modern Pietism claimed little that had not already been said by Philipp Spener

7. Dumitru Staniloae, *The Experience of God*, trans. Ioan Ionita and Robert Barringer (Brookline, MA: Holy Cross Orthodox Press, 1994), 55.
8. For a further development of this argument see Telford Work, "Gusty Winds, or a Jet Stream? Charismatics and Orthodox on the Spirit of Tradition," delivered at a joint session of the Evangelical Theology and Orthodox Theology groups at the 1999 annual conference of the American Academy of Religion, http://www.westmont.edu/~work/lectures/GustyWinds.html.
9. See Philip Walker Butin, *Revelation, Redemption, and Response: Calvin's Trinitarian Understanding of the Divine-Human Relationship* (New York: Oxford University Press, 1995).

in the seventeenth century and the Wesleys in the eighteenth. It facilitated a knowledge of the Holy Spirit and a respect for his dominical discipline that refreshed (and sometimes splintered) generations of Lutherans, Anglicans, Reformed, Baptists, Methodists, and Adventists. Pietism is, if not the heart of worldwide evangelicalism, certainly one of its chambers.

The pneumatological convictions of all these traditionalists remain immensely influential in conservative circles of Catholics, Orthodox, and Protestants in America. They are even more influential in the growing churches of the global South that have begun to dominate their worldwide communions and set their agendas. With a few massive exceptions, such as the world's charismatic and Pentecostal Wesleyans, Christians of the twenty-first century will tend to understand the Holy Spirit along lines set out before the seventeenth century.

One other return to the sources deserves mention here: biblical studies. "Grammatical-historical exegesis" and much historical-critical exegesis investigate the meaning of biblical texts in their original historical contexts. Historians and biblical scholars have recovered a level of knowledge of first-century Judaism and its Greco-Roman world that is probably surpassed only by those generations themselves. Such rediscoveries have sometimes called settled traditions into question, so we will visit biblical pneumatology again in the other sections of this analysis. However, after two centuries of often overly skeptical historical criticism, responsible scholarly historiography has also overturned a number of fashionable but flimsy revisionisms while also broadly confirming and reinforcing earlier traditional stances. As a result, one important function of biblical pneumatology in the past 150–200 years has been to reassert, with greater scholarly precision and sophistication, many of the classic claims of the past. Jewish pneumatologies in the centuries leading up to Jesus and the apostles make a particularly informative backdrop for interpreting the New Testament's different portrayals of the Holy Spirit.[10] Richard Bauckham appeals to recovered Jewish doctrines of God and God's Spirit in arguing that Jews excluded divine mediator figures such as angels from God's identity. By identifying Christ with God, then, the New Testament church was claiming nothing less than full divinity for Jesus.[11] Nicene trinitarianism is thus not a development away from apostolic Christology as

10. Robert Menzies situates Luke-Acts firmly within the prophetic stream of early Jewish pneumatology, in which the Spirit of the Lord bequeaths vision and inspires speech upon God's anointed messengers. *The Development of Early Christian Pneumatology with Special Reference to Luke-Acts*, Journal for the Study of the New Testament Supplement 54 (Sheffield: JSOT Press, 1991). Gordon Fee locates Paul's more explicitly soteriological pneumatology in the Old Testament's eschatological promises of the gift of the Spirit's presence in and among God's people. See *God's Empowering Presence: The Holy Spirit in the Letters of Paul* (Peabody, MA: Hendrickson, 1994).

11. Richard Bauckham, *God Crucified: Monotheism and Christology in the New Testament* (Grand Rapids: Eerdmans, 1998).

sometimes alleged, but a translation of the original Jewish church's teaching into Hellenistic categories of essence and personhood.

The stubborn theological issue of the Spirit's procession has done more than polarize East and West. It has driven ecumenically minded theologians and organizations in the twentieth century to draw on the common "great tradition" to reconceive the Holy Spirit's personhood in ways that respect the stances of their divided camps.[12] Spirit-Christology rethinks the Spirit's relationship to the Son even more ambitiously by retracing the role each plays in the ministry of the other in the economy of salvation, finding an explicitly pneumatological dimension to Christ's work of redemption and even a necessary reciprocity between the two.[13] These scholars and leaders sometimes recruit voices from outside the tradition,[14] but the source of the radical impulse is often within the tradition itself—as Martin Luther and many others discovered. This is the case for biblical scholar James D. G. Dunn's work tracing the early church's experience of Christ and the Spirit.[15] The sometimes radical edge of conservative biblicism demonstrates that theology in the capitals may not just preserve the past.

We might personify traditionalist schools of pneumatology in the figure of John Henry Newman, leader of the Oxford Movement. Newman's encounter with the Bible and Reformed orthodoxy as a child and with Augustine around 1840 helped impress on him a Catholic vision in which the Spirit develops Christ's church from its apostolic infancy to its mature stature.[16] He strengthened English Catholicism immensely—not through innovative theology, concessions to liberalism, nor sensitivity to the nineteenth-century *Zeitgeist*, but through a deliberate retrieval of theological wisdom from the church's first five centuries, along with sheer steadfastness in the face of opposition. Newman's counterparts in every Christian tradition assure that, whatever else happens, one of the most powerful dynamics in future theology is sure to be continuity with the past and present.

---

12. Catholic ecumenists produced such a study in 1995 of "The Greek and the Latin Traditions regarding the Procession of the Holy Spirit," claiming more common ground for ecumenical convergence than is often recognized.

13. Del Colle, *Christ and the Spirit*, 3–4.

14. Aristotle, Hegel, and others inform the striking trinitarian proposals of ecumenical evangelical catholic Robert Jenson. See his *Systematic Theology*, 2 vols. (New York: Oxford University Press, 1997 and 2001), in particular 1:146–61. Moltmann's Spirit Christology qualifies as well; it appears below among "pneumatology in the cosmopolis."

15. James D. G. Dunn, *Christology in the Making: A New Testament Inquiry into the Origins of the Doctrine of the Incarnation*, 2nd ed. (Grand Rapids: Eerdmans, 1994) and *The Christ and the Spirit*, 2 vols. (Grand Rapids: Eerdmans, 1997–1998).

16. The role of pneumatology in the development of holy tradition is understated in *Essay on the Development of Doctrine*, but explicit and prominent elsewhere, for instance in the sources to which Newman appeals for the trustworthiness of the "consensus of the faithful" in *On Consulting the Faithful in Matters of Doctrine*. For both essays see John Henry Newman, *Conscience, Consensus, and the Development of Doctrine* (New York: Doubleday, 1992).

There is one final matter to consider in this section: here in the gospel's capitals, what does all this thinking show the Holy Spirit to be? These developments cannot define him, but they do *manifest* him. The Holy Spirit is the Lord, alive in the living church. In theology's capitals we see the seven spirits before God's throne, whom the Son of Man holds and sends out to all the earth (Rev. 1:4; 3:1; 5:6)—the Spirit of the Son who abides in his body of disciples (1 John 4:13) to remind them of everything he teaches (John 14:26).

2. Pneumatology Abroad

Imperial Britain's elites barely tolerated Catholics in Newman's day. Both the Soviet bloc and humanist Western Europe were inhospitable environments for Orthodox and Catholic *ressourcement*. Defensive American traditionalists had to reassert "fundamentals" of the faith in response to modernist intellectual incursions. Often what was pressing in upon these centers of Christianity was a "beyond": a world moving out of the church, already emigrated into secularism, or not yet reached with the gospel.[17] Modern pneumatology was happening there too, even among secular imaginations who rejected Christianity's core assumptions.

A number of predecessors tower over this quadrant of our map, setting the terms for its pneumatology. For the sake of economy, this analysis will focus on one: Georg W. F. Hegel. With his Christian commitments and philosophical ambitions, Hegel himself belongs in a border town or the cosmopolis of our map's middle. Yet his philosophy is seminal for modern Western imaginations in the secularity "abroad." As his influence spread, his system with its totalizing qualities and progressive pneumatology came to shape even visions antithetical to Christianity. Many dispensed with Hegel's theology of a Triune God in the process of becoming and turned Hegel's cosmology into a nearly inverted Platonism: the material world does not emanate *from* a prior and superior spiritual order, but progresses *through* historical processes of self-realization to attain its perfection as *Geist*—what could be called "Mind" or "Spirit."[18]

Communism, transcendentalism, social scientism, and liberal democracy are just four of the ways *Geist* could manifest itself, depending on the philosopher. Karl Marx took history's self-realization to be the resolution of social contradictions in a workers' paradise—a kingdom of God without God, whose *Geist* is society itself. Ralph Waldo Emerson found in Hegel's "Progressive God" the grounds for accepting past human evolution and driving

17. Theology that is recognizable as pneumatology and relevant to this analysis seems to need at least some interaction with the Christian tradition. So the *unevangelized* "beyond" is out of this section's scope.

18. David F. Ford, *The Modern Theologians*, 2nd ed. (Malden, MA: Blackwell, 1997), 9–10.

humanity to become "a triumphant and faultless race."[19] Emile Durkheim drew on Hegelians to imagine human knowledge culminating in the universal cosmopolitan truth that arises out of the integration of humanity's diverse collective representations of reality.[20] Since for Durkheim a society's gods are its collective self-representation, this cosmopolitan unification is *Geist* itself—the spirit of self-realized society.[21] When the Soviet Union collapsed, economist Francis Fukuyama proclaimed a Hegelian "end of history" in which Hegel's Absolute Idea turns out to be human freedom exercised through liberal democracy and global capitalism.[22]

Thus Hegel's *Geist*, ever more tightly anchored to humanity, haunts the consciousness of the modern progressive West. Secularists cut it free from the God of Israel, where it becomes the triumphant (or tragic) human spirit. Many Christian progressives on the political left and right identify it *as* the spirit of God—a god of liberty, prosperity, or solidarity with the oppressed.

Hegel is not the only voice of pneumatology abroad. While his theology of history and thus his pneumatology are fundamentally teleological, persistent objections to every Hegelian schema have come from *dysteleological* visionaries—those who see *no* point to history, no inevitable or even possible progress, no transcendent resolution to the universe's complexities and contradictions, and no overarching goodness or badness. Here "spirit" cannot be singular and universal. What "spirits" there are in a dysteleological universe must be contingent and plural; so they inevitably come into conflict.

For Nietzsche these spirits are individual wills vying for power. For Freud they are the dark psychological forces that drive single minds and whole civilizations. Among humanity's countless groups and subgroups they are the countless human structures that Paul calls *stoicheia* or "elements" of the world (Gal. 4:3) and that Walter Wink associates with the New Testament's powers and principalities.[23] For neo-Darwinians, who posit a never-ending

---

19. William H. Gilman et al., eds., *The Journals and Miscellaneous Notebooks of Ralph Waldo Emerson* (Cambridge: Harvard University Press, 1960), 11:263.

20. Peter Knapp, "The Question of Hegelian Influence on Durkheim's Sociology," *Sociological Inquiry* 55 (1985): 1–15, cited in Deniz Tekiner, "German Idealist Foundations of Durkheim's Sociology and Teleology of Knowledge," *Theory and Science* (2002), International Consortium for the Advancement of Academic Publication, http://theoryandscience.icaap.org/content /vol003.001/tekiner.html.

21. It might be pointed out that in a world characterized by sin, this cosmopolitan self-representation would not be the Holy Spirit but the adversary that John calls "the ruler of this world" (e.g., John 12:31; 14:30; 16:11).

22. Francis Fukuyama, *The End of History and the Last Man* (New York: Free Press, 1992). Fukuyama's direct influence has mainly come through the counterarguments he provoked. However, he speaks for many who see progress and even a kind of historical finality in the evolution of global democratic capitalism and welfare-statism. Most Western political parties since the Cold War have promoted variations of this common vision.

23. See, most succinctly, Walter Wink, *The Powers That Be: Theology for a New Millennium* (New York: Doubleday, 1998).

biological flux in a world of change and adaptation, they can be the ephemeral species themselves, their ecosystems, the whole evolving biosphere, genes, or individual specimens.

The world's spirits are thus embedded in an eternal struggle with one another and with the world that creates and destroys them. The cosmology of dysteleological modernity is pluralist, pagan, and ultimately nihilist.[24] Ambition, shame, and envy rule the lives of individuals, families, empires, oppressed peoples, cultures, gangs, parties, and businesses—not because of original sin, because that has been dismissed out of hand,[25] but because it is simply how things are. The power of this vision is as immense as its varieties are innumerable. Only a few prominent ones need mentioning: Social Darwinism makes "survival of the fittest" into a social ethic, to the point of imposing empire upon and even sterilizing the weak. National Socialism elevates the honor of a *Volk* (a people or race) above all human decency. Corporatism forges alliances between ruling parties and business, labor, and advocacy groups. Environmentalism weighs the conviction that ecological destruction ill serves humanity against its suspicion that the real problem is humanity itself. Prejudice marginalizes whole groups in order to privilege others; meritocracy tries to defuse it by setting achievers against one another in a competition for access to power; affirmative action and then multiculturalism have turned the tables on the old winners in the name of justice.

Modern pneumatology abroad lies "outside" of Christian contemplation and analysis of the Holy Spirit.[26] Yet it is a mistake to imagine either place as aloof from the other (1 John 4:1–6). Theological capitals and foreign lands have often been overlapping, not separate worlds. Insiders worked with outsiders always in view, and often under their scornful eyes (or over their heads, depending on who held power at the time). As many abroad had upbringings in the church, so many traditionalists came to the inside only after spending years as skeptics. The Pietism that refreshed modern Western Christianity also produced the "atheistic pietism" that today characterizes moralistic but secular societies.[27]

Martin Heidegger may be the best figure to personify such a conflicted cultural landscape. He oscillated between constructing a Spirit of cosmic history, fleeing it, and deifying the fleeting and shadowy spirits of this world.

---

24. Lesslie Newbigin, *The Gospel in a Pluralist Society* (Grand Rapids: Eerdmans, 1989), 220; Robert W. Jenson, "Much Ado about Nothingness," in *Sin, Death, and the Devil*, ed. Carl E. Braaten and Robert W. Jenson (Grand Rapids: Eerdmans, 2000), 1–6.

25. Alan Jacobs, *Original Sin: A Cultural History* (San Francisco: Harper, 2008).

26. The term *beyond* seems odd when it describes increasingly dominant mind-sets in parts of what were once firmly Christian societies: universities, principal cities, mass media, educational systems, and civic institutions. However, that is to take the societies themselves as central, not the new creation that outlasts them.

27. The term may have been coined by W. H. Mallock in *Atheism and the Value of Life: Five Studies in Contemporary Literature* (London: Bentley, 1884), 160.

That's quite a journey! Jacques Derrida sought a window into Heidegger's philosophical development by tracing his changing regard for Hegel's category of *Geist*.[28] In Heidegger's earlier work, Derrida finds avoidance and suspicion of the term, with its Hegelian connotations of grand divine unification. Then, from 1933 to 1935—as he joined the National Socialist Party—Heidegger embraced *Geist* as resolve and a will to knowledge, and as the spiritual world of a people nourished in land and blood. *Geist*'s goal was no longer a Hegelian perfection of the cosmos but was bound to a particular people's identity and culture. Derrida notes that both when Heidegger is avoiding the term and when he is using it, another, transcendent *Geist* haunts his work. Heidegger characterizes it as a world-unifying *and* people-gathering *pneuma* of divine presence. Finally, in the 1950s, Heidegger translates *Geist* not in these earlier Hegelian ways, nor as *pneuma* (or anything else in the "Platonic-Christian epoch" he wanted to extricate it from) but *Flamme*, immolating fire, Being-outside-Itself.[29]

So Heidegger moved from rejecting Hegel, to substituting a demonic Aryan sociological alternative, to tentatively embracing a teleological pneumatology, and finally to describing a consuming transcendence that puts things to an end and so begins other things (echoing, Derrida suggests, the fiery Spirit of the Hebrew prophets). The turbulence of Heidegger's sometime pneumatology, tracked in Derrida's own maddening jargon of ambivalence, characterizes the chaos abroad.[30]

Who is the Spirit abroad? Still the Holy Spirit, of course. No theology or cosmology can change that. And still the Spirit of wisdom (Isa. 11:2) whose mundane truth all the world can recognize and acknowledge (1 Kings 4:29–34). Yet where God's truth is suppressed (Rom. 1:18–19) the Spirit haunts rather than indwells, as the Spirit of truth whom the world does not know or see and cannot accept (John 14:17). Other stories and categories direct the imaginations of outsiders who sense his presence and power, sometimes revealing his qualities yet concealing his full identity as the Spirit of the Son. He consigns us to our darkness even while graciously luring us toward the light.

These interactions set up frontiers between the capitals of Christian pneumatology and the territory abroad. We are now ready to map these meeting places.

3. Pneumatology in Frontier Settlements

Some of the messengers who brought the gospel to fresh places and peoples were missionaries obeying the Great Commission. Others were accidental and

---

28. Jacques Derrida, *Of Spirit: Heidegger and the Question* (Chicago: University of Chicago Press, 1991).

29. See David Ferrell Krell, *Daimon Life: Heidegger and Life-Philosophy* (Bloomington, IN: Indiana University Press, 1992), 265–87.

30. This is not to deny chaos in any other part of our grid.

even unconscious evangelists: relatives, neighbors, coworkers, travelers, or refugees. They carried the news of God's kingdom into new settings, making social frontiers where classical expressions of Christian faith can colonize or be replicated, but can also take new forms and resonate in new ways.

As Hegel towers over pneumatology abroad, so the Holy Spirit's modern social frontier has an early and influential settler in John Wesley. Wesley was a revivalist, not a missionary—an eighteenth-century Anglican Pietist who seems more at home in a capital city than here on the frontier. Yet Wesleyan faith proved to be particularly well suited to carrying the gospel into new social environments. Its zeal channeled incredible energy into spreading the message and renewing the church. Its ecclesiological pragmatism allowed liturgy, church structures, and private practices to spread as well as adapt in rapidly changing situations. It was Wesleyan piety, not the rurally developed Anglican parish culture, that could flourish in England's newly industrialized cities and America's immigrant cultures. Wesleyan sensibilities even generated a liturgical style that James F. White calls "the frontier tradition" in American worship.[31] Its Arminian soteriology and stress on both personal and social holiness encouraged steadfast focus on the lost and the beleaguered, and on the Spirit who transforms them. By the mid-nineteenth century these qualities of Wesleyan spirituality had already diffused into other Protestant traditions and pushed the Christian witness out from its center and into long-unreached, newly emerging, and nearly forsaken sectors across the world, yielding a considerable harvest in our era.

In which new settings do we find classic claims being translated, repeated, contextualized, and newly applied?

The first and most obvious set of answers includes sub-Saharan Africa, south and east Asia, and a number of other places where renewed Christian mission (sometimes irenic and fraternal, sometimes strident and colonialist) planted the seeds of today's massive churches there.[32] These churches are not merely Western transplants. They inculturate Christian life and faith into both their indigenous cultures and the emerging global "third culture"[33] that increasingly gives every city and suburb in the world something of a common feel. While some of their thought is better classified among the cosmopolitan theologies we will examine below, most tend to have strong traditionalist tendencies: loyalty to the liturgical forms and theological convictions of their confessions, often literalistic interpretations of the Bible, and conservative morals. They

31. James F. White, *A Brief History of Christian Worship* (Nashville: Abingdon, 1993), 146.
32. A captivating Catholic account of contextualized mission among the Masai of Tanzania is Vincent Donovan, *Christianity Rediscovered* (Maryknoll, NY: Orbis, 2003).
33. Sociologist Ruth Hill Useem's term "Third Culture Kid" refers to a child growing up in a foreign culture because of expatriate working parents. For a contemporary Christian usage, see Dave Gibbons, *The Monkey and the Fish: Liquid Leadership for a Third-Culture Church* (Grand Rapids: Zondervan, 2009).

basically reproduce classical faith in a new cultural idiom, and even recover neglected biblical themes and revisit issues, crises, and developments from Christianity's first centuries.

For instance, African and Chinese churches have incorporated affirmations, adaptations, or critiques of ancestral veneration practices; these as well as aboriginal Australian and American Christians have developed angelologies and pneumatologies of the creator Spirit to extents that go far beyond today's withered Western counterparts. Church disputes over the role of ancestors evoke ancient biblical struggles over household gods and ancestral patrons. Affirmations of the creator Spirit over the hegemony of technology are reminiscent of Irenaeus against the Gnostics. Korean Minjung theology's calls for justice to the poor echo the prophets and early church. These churches also share a more pronounced stress on the Holy Spirit's healing power and presence, often understanding the Spirit's power to be mediated through baptism and other sacramental rituals—a baptismal theology that looks more like the north African and Greco-Roman theologies of the first few centuries than any contemporary Western counterpart.[34]

The familiar issues and stances in these contextualized churches make their work resonate beyond their cultures. Early twentieth-century pioneers such as Ní Tuosheng (Watchman Nee) and house church leader Wang Mingdao[35] have followings in the United States, especially among traditionalists who recognize them as kindred spirits. Charismatic prayer ministries in the West admire and imitate the Korean morning prayer movement that began with Gil Sun-Joo.[36]

The patterns that repeatedly emerge across the world suggest that each frontier settlement is not restricted to one place or culture but is a presently emerging global culture. White American evangelicals and liberals often have more in common with their counterparts in the global South than they do with one another.

Within this global culture subsist many smaller new settings in which classic claims are seldom heard. One of them is the modern research university. Launched in Berlin in the nineteenth century, its architects struggled to articulate a convincing rationale for its faculty of theology.[37] In the end, they failed. Theology faculties have migrated—often under escort—to the margins of the lives of their campuses. Most survived institutionally by turning themselves into departments studying religion as a field of scientific, historical, or comparative

34. Veli-Matti Kärkkäinen, "Pneumatology," in *Global Dictionary of Theology*, ed. William A. Dyrness et al. (Downers Grove, IL: InterVarsity, 2008), 667.
35. See, for instance, Thomas Harvey, *Acquainted with Grief: Wang Mingdao's Stand for the Persecuted Church in China* (Grand Rapids: Brazos, 2002).
36. Moonjang Lee, "Asian Theology," in Dyrness et al., *Global Dictionary of Theology*, 74, and S. W. Chung, "Korean Theology," in ibid., 461.
37. See David Kelsey, *Between Athens and Berlin: The Theological Education Debate* (Grand Rapids: Eerdmans, 1993).

inquiry. As this happened, outspoken Christians became disciplinary orphans and even ridiculed minorities in now normatively secular academic environments. In response, campus ministries—both denominational outreaches and nondenominational organizations such as InterVarsity Christian Fellowship, the World Student Christian Federation, and Campus Crusade for Christ—rose to support and reassert Christian faith in collegiate contexts. These ministries are doing more than just saving souls and growing churches. They are evangelizing the secular meritocratic elite who have been the principal architects of the global technological culture itself—and thus fostering the creation of yet another contextualized Christianity.

Outreach on university campuses is being matched by Christian outreaches in the arts, high tech, politics, business, militaries, trades, and professions. Churches, parachurches, and orders have sponsored many of these. However, outreach due to believers' personal initiative to their own informal social circles has also been rising rapidly.[38] Believers from the United States to China to Indonesia have grown impatient with institutional ministries and ventured out on their own. They have begun Bible studies, prayer circles, cell churches, and volunteer efforts in workplaces and neighborhoods. Underneath this "community-based ministry" approach is a missional pneumatology indebted to sixteenth-century free-church ecclesiology, which trusts that God provides spiritual gifts to meet the needs of all local congregations—"wherever two or three are gathered" (Matt. 18:20). These communities rely explicitly on the Holy Spirit to mediate Christ's leadership of their missions.

Each time the gospel takes root in one of these social circles, the good news finds expression in an additional idiom, critiques and remakes the world, and ushers in new creation in the Spirit's power. The modern academy's frontier settlements have spurred the rise of a new theological genre: interdisciplinary theologies constructed by disciples at these crossroads. Among the more traditional of these are C. S. Lewis, patron saint of evangelicals, working in theology and literature; Pope John Paul II, theorizing about theology and political economy at the conclusion of the Cold War; a whole constellation of scientist-theologians interrelating the faith with physics, psychology, biology, and the rest of the sciences;[39] and others cross-examining theology and the various arts. Theologian Robert Barron, for example, draws on the literature of Dante Alighieri, William Faulkner, Flannery O'Connor, and others to

38. George Barna chronicles the trend in the United States in *Revolution* (Carol Stream, IL: Tyndale, 2005).
39. For an informative and accessible primer, see Larry Witham, *The Measure of God: Our Century-Long Struggle to Reconcile Science and Religion* (San Francisco: Harper, 2006), a history of the Gifford Lectures that serves as a tour of natural theology's intersections with the natural, behavioral, and social sciences.

articulate, contextualize, and refresh a basically traditional Catholic theology.[40] (These voices' more innovative counterparts tend to be synthesizers whose work we will examine below in the two other frontiers of our map.)

Because of the Holy Spirit's roles in creation, life, providence, redemption, communication, and eschaton, these interdisciplinary projects soon gain direct relevance for modern pneumatology. Jeremy Begbie affirms David Bentley Hart's contention that the music of J. S. Bach reveals "the uncontainable and infinite 'inventiveness' of the Holy Spirit at work in the world."[41] Begbie's and Barron's appeals to these other disciplines are not mere illustrations for pedagogy's sake. They are source material for translating theological claims: signs and parables of the kingdom for the spiritually discerning to see and trust.

These discourses can have a prophetic edge to them when they subject the disciplines of the modern world to the gospel's judgment and deliverance. The prophetic tone of interdisciplinary theology is nowhere more pronounced than within a movement among mainly British theologians called Radical Orthodoxy. Its principals, foremost among them John Milbank, draw primarily on sources from the Anglican and Catholic capitals to restore theology to its own terms, return it to the center of academic intellectual inquiry, and thereby bring the social sciences in particular back into its informing and transforming sphere.[42] Since this is not about restoring a premodern university but evangelizing a postmodern one by speaking its own blunt academic idiom, Milbank's project stands as a bold retranslation of classic theological claims, including the Augustinian doctrine of the Holy Spirit, in a new setting.[43]

Mother Teresa is a compelling figure who personifies the Spirit's frontier settlements. Called and gifted by the Holy Spirit in 1946 to lead the Missionaries of Charity, she left her cloister to live with the poor of Calcutta. Her ministry was not a radical departure from previous Catholic practice. Her theology was not some bold new vision of the gospel, but reflected her church's holy tradition. Her account of the Holy Spirit's involvement in her work and through her coworkers' lives was conventional.[44] Even her failings

40. Robert Barron, *And Now I See: A Theology of Transformation* (New York: Crossroad, 1998) and *The Strangest Way: Walking the Christian Path* (Maryknoll, NY: Orbis, 2002).

41. Jeremy Begbie, *Resounding Truth: Christian Wisdom in the World of Music* (Grand Rapids: Baker, 2007), 137.

42. John Milbank, *Theology and Social Theory* (Malden, MA: Blackwell, 1993).

43. Milbank's postmodern pneumatology is developed in *The Word Made Strange: Theology, Language, Culture* (Malden, MA: Blackwell, 1997), 171–218. For a critique of the authenticity of Radical Orthodoxy's overall project, see R. R. Reno, "The Radical Orthodoxy Project," in *In the Ruins of the Church: Sustaining Faith in an Age of Diminished Christianity* (Grand Rapids: Brazos, 2002), 63–81.

44. The constitution of the Missionaries of Charity states, "Our religious family started when our foundress, Mother Teresa Bogaxhiu, was inspired by the Holy Spirit with a special charism on the 10th of September, 1946. This inspiration . . . means that the Holy Spirit communicates God's will to Mother" (Eileen Egan, "Polar Opposites? Remembering the Kindred Spirits of

were ordinary. Yet her life communicated and embodied Christian faith far beyond Christian circles. Insiders, outsiders, and frontier settlers alike from across denominations, religions, nations, languages, and ideologies all saw Jesus, and recognized him *as* Jesus, in the Missionaries of Charity.

Who is the Holy Spirit we see moving in these frontier settlements? He is the one who comes to convict the world regarding sin and justice and judgment (John 16:8). He came to Jesus's disciples when their risen Lord breathed on them, having sent them onward on his mission (John 20:21–23). Wherever they come, the Spirit comes.

4. Pneumatology in Border Towns

Frontier settlements are a people's early excursions, and incursions, into one another's territory. Over time the newly acquainted peoples get to know one another and even begin to understand each other. As cultural exchanges become more regular and bidirectional, some frontier settlements give way to established border towns. As Ciudad Juárez, Mexico, and El Paso, Texas, face one another on opposite sides of the Rio Grande, so well-acquainted insiders and outsiders to the kingdom have long faced one another in theological equivalents. They distinguish themselves over against one another, yet also absorb one another's sensibilities.

The theology that goes on here has long been a favorite among Christian intellectual historians. This may be because sustained exposure to the secular academy sensitizes and then desensitizes Christian academics to forms of life across that border. The Christian academy is a kind of border town in its own right, fluent in the dialects of both the church and the university. Having grown used to the once-shocking ways of intellectuals, its products are tempted to look down on the church's monolinguals and envy the world's.

An archetypical predecessor here is Friedrich Schleiermacher, father of liberalism at the dawn of the nineteenth century. His attempts to draw Christianity's "cultured despisers" back into the fold suggest an emissary from the capital or a frontier settler. Yet Schleiermacher's approach was radical. He rejected his family's Moravian Pietism for rationalism, losing his faith in college and returning to Christian practice only by reframing Christian faith in terms of the epistemic presuppositions of Immanuel Kant and other modernists. By the middle of the nineteenth century, liberalism's border-town theology was making major inroads in Western Christian traditions. It dominated European and American Christianity by the early twentieth century, and continued to do so despite emphatic attempts to defeat it by Catholics, fundamentalists, and postliberals.

If Western Christian pneumatology already suffered from an attenuated appreciation of the Spirit's person and work, modernity only intensified the

---

Dorothy Day and Mother Teresa," *Catholic Peace Voice*, Fall 1997, http://www.catholicworker.org/roundtable/essaytext.cfm?Number=36).

problem. The Renaissance enterprises of scientific inquiry and critical history hardened into modern naturalism, historicism, and skepticism. From within the confines of the era's Newtonian paradigms of creation as a closed system of causes and effects, every improvement in the knowledge of natural physical and social processes seemed to make less room for the Holy Spirit's work. The result was a "Spirit of the gaps," whose activity was relegated to the shrinking realms that learning had not yet penetrated.

In response, liberals tended to accept both this knowledge and the Newtonian (and Kantian) presuppositions that interpreted it, and to cede ground on which their ancestors had once stood. The following is just a sampling of pneumatologically relevant revisions: historical critics of church history, the tradition history of the Bible, and biblical events undermined both the Catholic sense of holy tradition and the Catholic and Protestant doctrines of direct biblical inspiration. Ernst Troeltsch and Rudolf Bultmann privatized a faith that had once been essentially public, confining its pneumatic new creation to the inner worlds of believers and treating the visible church as a mere human institution rather than the Holy Spirit's living temple.[45] Generations of deists dismissed miracles in the present age and explained away the definitive miracles of the Christian past, even the Spirit's virginal conception and resurrection of Jesus. Harry Emerson Fosdick, called the greatest liberal American preacher of the twentieth century, not only rejected all these traditional doctrines but regarded substitutionary atonement (which Heb. 9:14 envisions as an offering mediated by the Spirit) as an artifact of unredeemed thinking. Adolf von Harnack considered sacramental theology a pagan accretion;[46] the more orthodox Edward Schillebeeckx treated sacraments in terms of their subjective effects on believers, as a personal encounter with Christ.[47] Walter Rauschenbusch, leader of the social gospel movement, embraced an evolutionary anthropology that treated sin not as a condition in which humanity lies enslaved and dead apart from the Spirit's reviving grace, but merely as the accumulated weight of past sins that believers must struggle against.[48] These add up to a massive—and often dubiously trinitarian—revision of orthodox Christian faith, with a radically different scope for the Spirit's work. Paul Tillich exemplifies the systematic form of this vision. For Tillich, who followed Schleiermacher's lead and consigned the issue of God's threeness to an appendix of his systematic theology, the Holy Spirit is not a person in any orthodox sense but "the Spiritual Presence," a meaning-giving symbol for the divine life.[49]

45. Robert Morgan, "Rudolf Bultmann," in Ford, *The Modern Theologians*, 74–75.
46. Adolf von Harnack, *Outlines of the History of Dogma* (London: Hodder & Stoughton, 1901), 195.
47. Robert J. Schreiter, "Edward Schillebeeckx," in Ford, *The Modern Theologians*, 153.
48. Christopher H. Evans, *The Kingdom Is Always but Coming: A Life of Walter Rauschenbusch* (Grand Rapids: Eerdmans, 2004), 107–8.
49. Pneumatology is a similarly minor theme in another border-town movement, twentieth-century process theology. For instance, it is scarcely mentioned in John B. Cobb and David

Whether radically as in Tillich, or more moderately in a variety of liberal Catholics and Protestants,[50] the power of modern paradigms and presuppositions compelled thinkers to reenvision theology even while they tended to conserve Christian vocabularies and liturgical forms. Liberalism provoked a number of reactions; we will highlight three.

Conservatives typically reacted by defending at all cost the claims that methodological naturalism seemed to be taking away. They insisted on the historicity of past miraculous "violations" of the laws of physics. They defended the supernatural divine power and character of the Word and sacraments. They affirmed the church as the earthly locus of Christ's salvation and the Spirit's redeeming work. They refuted textual and external evidence for the human histories of the biblical writings and asserted their propositional inerrancy. They rationalized or discounted the earlier racist, sexist, and colonialist injustices of their holy traditions. And they denied accumulating evidence for the evolution of species. When one of these approaches failed, conservatives might flee to the other side of the nature/supernature dichotomy and identify the natural and historical *as* the spiritual—thus turning the Spirit into the sprite of environmental conservation, the patron of our desires for freedom and prosperity, or the dispenser of psychic therapy.

The theological apex of this reaction was American fundamentalism, which sought to recover five of these fundamentals in spite of modernist arguments against them. Conservatives could articulate these as claims that sometimes superficially, sometimes deeply, matched the classic claims being made in capitals and frontier settlements. Yet even if they were, these were still border-town visions, always framed in reaction to the city on the other side of the border and in suspicion or envy of sympathizers who resided within its own city limits. Fundamentalism's Holy Spirit had many of the features of classic Protestant faith, yet maintained a sectarian edge: "Whoever knows God listens to us; but whoever is not from God does not listen to us. This is how we recognize the Spirit of truth and the spirit of falsehood" (1 John 4:6 NIV).

A second important reaction to liberalism began with Karl Barth and developed into postliberalism. Barth's theology is one part *ressourcement*, returning to the giants of Reformation theology to rebuild evangelical theology after liberalism, one part concession to the long Western obsession with epistemology

---

Ray Griffin, *Process Theology: An Introductory Exposition* (Philadelphia: Westminster John Knox, 1976). Yet process theologian Norman Pittenger offers an account of the Holy Spirit very similar to Tillich's in *The Holy Spirit* (Philadelphia: United Church Press, 1974). This suggests that liberal Protestantism and more radical theologies such as process theology share both a common formative milieu and a willingness to revise the meanings of traditional Christian terms radically without necessarily dispensing with the terms themselves or the liturgical forms in which they are used.

50. Frei lists a number of these in the first three types of his *Types of Christian Theology* (28–38).

by prioritizing the doctrine of revelation, one part rejection of common Catholic, Pietist, neo-Protestant, and fundamentalist approaches that Barth found inimical to the gospel of grace through faith alone, and one part prophetic critique of modernity and any other compromise of the gospel through unswerving loyalty to the principle of *solus christus*. This puts Barth and the postliberals who followed him closer to the middle right of our map than most of the border-town theologies we have already examined. Yet Barthian theology has a border-town character and agenda. Its fixation on modernity (understandable given Barth's own history and postliberals' later contexts), its frustrating struggles to free dogmatics from Kantian epistemological shackles, and its concessions to the twentieth-century *Zeitgeist* (especially pronounced in its politics and vulnerability to universalism) all describe a theology for a church harried by the world.

Barth's theology does emancipate the Holy Spirit from captivity to human subjectivity. But some judge his pneumatology to have done so by subordinating the Spirit's work in creation and every other sphere to the soteriological.[51] Moreover, to keep theology fixed on Jesus Christ, Barth arguably treats the Spirit as a mere adjunct or power of the Son's salvation.[52] Consequently, his pneumatology ends up narrower than either Luther's or Calvin's. Rather than a liberal or conservative Spirit of the gaps, he leaves gaps of the Spirit, which both friendly and rival pneumatologies have endeavored to fill.[53]

A third response to liberalism was the liberationist strand of theology. This arose in nineteenth-century Christian and secular social activism, expanded in the social gospel movement, energized the Second Vatican Council's *Gaudium et Spes* and the broader Catholic *Aggiornamento* movement, and radicalized as liberation theology. Of our three strands of responses, this one is most sympathetic to liberalism, because it shares a deeper set of presuppositions and habits. Liberation theology appeals to an impressive list of texts from across the Scriptures and later tradition demonstrating God's regard for the stranger, the powerless, the weak, and the oppressed. Yet the principle for its analysis of injustice and thus Christ's remedy comes from the social-scientific analysis of Karl Marx and its many cognates, not canonical tradition. In liberationist epistemology the oppressed gain a privileged epistemological status, and their experiences of oppression and liberation become definitive for the scope of salvation and the mission of the church.[54] Traditional

---

51. Eugene F. Rogers Jr., *After the Spirit: A Constructive Pneumatology from Resources outside the Modern West* (Grand Rapids: Eerdmans, 2005), 19–20.

52. Robert Jenson, "You Wonder Where the Spirit Went," *Pro Ecclesia* 2 (1993): 296–304.

53. Jenson does just this in *Systematic Theology*; so does Rogers in the rest of *After the Spirit*. Many others just return to anthropology.

54. An acute and succinct analysis of the substructure of liberation theology is Joseph Cardinal Ratzinger, "Instruction on Certain Aspects of the 'Theology of Liberation,'" Congregation for

Christian teachings are appropriated selectively according to how well they fit this framework, becoming illustrative proof texts rather than substantive theological sources.

Border-town theologies can be as motivated by a desire to give up as a desire to embrace. In the battle between liberals and postliberals over the theological priority of anthropology versus Christology, the *filioque* debate has taken on new significance. One of the factors making the *filioque* less popular among liberals is, as Barth noticed, its demand for integrating pneumatology with Christology. Given the Spirit's role as revealer of God's truth, the *filioque* therefore reinforces the classical dogma that one knows the Father only through the Son (Matt. 11:27). This is an obstacle for liberal advocates of religious pluralism, who wish to affirm that God can be truly and redemptively known through a variety of religious traditions.[55] Religious pluralists prefer to treat Jesus as the agent through whom God is revealed to Christians, and the Spirit as the agent through whom God is revealed in other religions. Since 1968 the World Council of Churches (WCC) has even pursued this strategy, which its secretary Konrad Raiser misleadingly labels "trinitarian," over against the so-called christological paradigm of church unity and mission that had focused the WCC's earlier efforts.[56] The Spirit then becomes the god present in all the world's spiritualities, whose divine work requires no coherence with the work of Jesus Christ. The danger here was noted long before, for instance in the 1933 Bethel Declaration authored by Dietrich Bonhoeffer.[57] Bonhoeffer, Barth, and others insisted on the *filioque* in their resistance to the frank paganism of Nazi Germany's "German Christians." The *Holy* Spirit is the Spirit of Father *and the Son*.

True doctrine ought to be useful. But should its perceived usefulness in a particular context really drive our allegiance? The "filioque" is a claim about God's internal relations. If considerations such as Christ's centrality or religious coexistence tempt us to affirm or deny it, if we yield to consequences rather than the sheer force of the apostolic faith, then we are feeling the pressure of life in a border town.

Perhaps the best choice for a representative border-town theologian is not a liberal icon like Tillich, a fundamentalist icon like B. B. Warfield, or

---

the Doctrine of the Faith, http://www.vatican.va/roman_curia/congregations/cfaith/documents/rc_con_cfaith_doc_19840806_theology-liberation_en.html.

55. See, among others, Paul F. Knitter, *No Other Name? A Critical Survey of Christian Attitudes toward the World Religions* (Maryknoll, NY: Orbis, 1985).

56. Lesslie Newbigin, "The Trinity as Public Truth," in *The Trinity in a Pluralistic Age: Theological Essays on Culture and Religion*, ed. Kevin J. Vanhoozer (Grand Rapids: Eerdmans, 1997), 7.

57. Dietrich Bonhoeffer, *Dietrich Bonhoeffer Works*, ed. Wayne Whitson Floyd Jr. (Minneapolis: Fortress, 1998–2009), 12:399 and 13:48, cited in Benjamin Myers, "Why I (Still) Confess the Filioque," Faith and Theology, October 25, 2009, http://faith-theology.blogspot.com/2009/10/why-i-still-confess-filioque.html.

a postliberal icon like Barth, but a feminist theologian. Feminist theology juggles an intimidating set of considerations from across our map's boundaries. The feminist movement itself has roots in both Christian tradition and secular progressivism. Biblical and holy tradition both offer vital resources for appreciating both women's and men's full significance to God; yet they also embody the often oppressive patriarchal structures through which that appreciation was historically given. The liberationist paradigm that promises social justice, and for these theologians generally defines it, comes from the "Masters of Suspicion" (Marx, Nietzsche, Freud, Durkheim, and the like) across the border, channeled through modern sociology to the contemporary social consciousness especially of the Western political left. Feminists have tended to draw pragmatically and unapologetically from a variety of anthropologies—relational ones, transcendentalist ones, individualist ones, and collectivist ones—according to how well they serve the causes of women's liberation and gender equality. For Christians the matter of gender also extends beyond human creaturely life to the language of God: both the history and threat of oppression and the history and promise of justice haunt the church's liturgy, prayer, imagination, dogma, Scripture, saints, leaders, and strangers, and above all its deity.[58] If ever there was a border-town theology, Christian feminist theologies would qualify.

Elizabeth Johnson is a fitting representative of the movement, negotiating these vexing factors skillfully and firmly within the liberal tradition of Kant and Schleiermacher that prioritizes human experience.[59] She describes a Trinity of Spirit-Sophia, Jesus-Sophia, and Mother-Sophia—terms culled from Christian tradition but rearranged to privilege feminine imagery. The principle of this selection and transposition is standard in feminist theology: the privileged epistemological status of women's interpreted experience of liberation.[60] Wisdom, heretofore associated primarily with the Son, is now identified with the divine essence shared among the persons. This shift is as radical as moving *logos* (which in John 1 is practically equivalent to *sophia*) from distinguishing the Son to describing the Godhead: Spirit-Word, Jesus-Word, Father-Word.[61] The result is a Spirit whose relations with Jesus are

58. Gendered terms are used for many languages' pronouns for God, for the names of the triune persons, and for the bigendered images for God that permeate the biblical witness and subsequent tradition. At the same time, gendered language even more vividly describes forbidden idols that would construct the God of Israel as any created thing.

59. Elizabeth A. Johnson, *She Who Is: The Mystery of God in Feminist Theological Discourse* (New York: Crossroad, 1994), 76.

60. Johnson's hermeneutical principle in drawing on Scripture and tradition is "interpretation guided by a liberating impulse" in a community constituted by shared "struggle for emancipation from sexism" (ibid., 77). The goal is thus definitive.

61. Why couldn't another consistently feminine term, *agape* (Hebrew *ahabah*, Latin *caritas*) have been similarly unpacked without having to migrate from a *hypostasis* to essence, given the biblical (1 John 4) and traditional warrants for identifying it with the Godhead? Surely it has

subsumed into her relations with all humanity.[62] This suggests a move in the modalistic direction that haunts much liberal Christian theology. Johnson relegates most of her treatment of inner-trinitarian relations to her critical review of the classical theological tradition, and with human experience as the evidentiary basis for Johnson's reflective work on the Trinity, there is little to go on. When it comes time to speak constructively of the Spirit, Johnson describes her as "Spirit-Sophia, friend, sister, mother, and grandmother *of the world.*"[63] It is not surprising when she later downgrades the word "Trinity" itself to a simile,[64] prefers a model because it best encourages human social justice,[65] and concludes again with relationships *to* creation rather than the persons' relations to one another revealed *in* creation.[66] She calls the figure of Spirit-Wisdom and her two divine complements "the mystery of triune Holy Wisdom as *imago feminae*," flouting the warning of her cross-town rival Barth that "one cannot speak of God simply by speaking of man"—or woman—"in a loud voice."[67] Johnson exemplifies border-town consciousness in both her patient and painstaking investigation of her Catholic tradition in critical deference to the liberal modern category of liberation, and her often subtle but radical reworking of that tradition as a practitioner rather than an emigrant or expatriate.[68]

And who is the Holy Spirit in these tense and exhilarating border towns? He or she is the mysterious one who blows where he or she wills (John 3:8), amidst a tempest of other spirits whose confused and contradictory testimonies are a worldly cacophony (1 John 4:1–3). The Spirit's origin and goal may be mysterious to those blown about and reborn (John 3:8). Yet such witnesses learn to perceive as the Spirit testifies, not always politely or gladly, to those in Christ's churches who are listening (1 John 4:2–6; Rev. 3:6). The Spirit displayed here is the patient leader, Torah and wisdom giver, and prophetic juror of an ancient border nation called Israel.

We have traversed each quadrant of modern pneumatology's map. One area remains: its middle.

---

a deeper history in women's experiences of liberation than the category of wisdom. Perhaps it is the subsequent Latin tradition's shift to *amor*, a masculine term. At any rate, Johnson is far more guarded about the term's potential (ibid., 143).

62. Ibid., 140, in the context of 133–46.
63. Ibid., 146, emphasis added.
64. Ibid., 205.
65. Ibid., 209.
66. Ibid., 211–15.
67. Karl Barth, *The Word of God and the Word of Man* (New York: Harper, 1957), 195–96.
68. For a helpful comparative analysis of Johnson's pneumatology see Helen Bergin, "Feminist Voices on the Spirit of God," *Journal of Women Scholars of Religion and Theology* 5 (December 2005), http://wsrt.asn.au/web_images/bergin.pdf. For a survey of feminist pneumatologies see Nicola Slee, "The Holy Spirit and Spirituality," in *The Cambridge Companion to Feminist Theology*, ed. Susan Frank Parsons (New York: Cambridge, 2002), 171–89.

5. Pneumatology in the Cosmopolis

In the strict sense, everything but the very edges of a map is its middle. The four areas we have described are obviously not corners where *every* claim is classic or new and where *every* setting is either church or world. Nevertheless, we could describe the preponderant qualities of each place for modern pneumatology in terms of its proximity to one of those corners.

Some places on this map are better described in terms of distance from any one corner.[69] One, the cosmopolis, lies in the very middle of our grid. Its real-world counterpart is arguably the most significant emerging social setting across the globe.[70] Across the world, cities are being flooded with immigrants from the countryside and abroad. Residents, torn from the tribal and family relationships that had sustained them, face economies and living situations that call for new skill sets. They also face similarly bewildered neighbors from backgrounds just as incomprehensible. Their frontier is internal.

Where contemporary pneumatology is concerned, an important cosmopolitan predecessor is John Locke. Locke's enormous influence on the course of deism might suggest another location for him elsewhere in our grid. Yet his belief in miracles and supernatural revelation, particularly that of the Bible, distinguished him from deists. Moreover, both Richard Hooker and the Bible critically influenced his theological imagination. At the same time, Locke's empiricism, natural theology, and Arian Christology and pneumatology[71] departed from tradition.[72] The result is a surprising amalgam of conventional Protestant claims concerning the Holy Spirit and rejection of historic orthodoxy. What could hold these disparate things together was a *governing pragmatism* and an *eclecticism* that distinguish the synthetic (some would say incoherent) cosmopolitan imagination from both the totalizing Enlightenment mind-set in parts abroad and the reactionary paradigm of the border town.

Locke's idiosyncratic pneumatology is by no means the only possible modern hybrid. Several other recent synthetic visions practically dominate global Christianity today.

The first is Pentecostalism. Theologically, Pentecostalism draws on the strong pneumatology of the Reformed tradition and the nineteenth century's

---

69. Some of these are what urban planners call "zones of transition"—areas moving from one kind of cityscape to another. Yesterday's frontier settlement might be tomorrow's border town or capital, or if borders shift it might even be assimilated into another country. Repeatedly we encountered figures who lived in one place but influenced or migrated to others.

70. The cosmopolis is not a new phenomenon; ancient Rome probably qualified as one. What may be new in our day, however, is the uniformity of the global culture that has been emerging ever since the Industrial Revolution transformed transportation, communication, and international trade. There is enough commonality in this "third culture" to let us call the world's sprawling metropolises *the* cosmopolis.

71. See Victor Nuovo, ed., *John Locke: Writings on Religion* (New York: Oxford University Press, 2002), 25–28.

72. John Orr, *English Deism: Its Roots and Its Fruits* (Grand Rapids: Eerdmans, 1934), 108.

increasingly involved Wesleyan catalogues of sanctification, which affirmed second and even third blessings of the Spirit. Philosophically, modern propositionalism feeds a literalistic Pentecostal biblical hermeneutic like that of Adventism and fundamentalism. But this is not the extent of its cosmopolitanism.

Pentecostals spoke in tongues at the Azusa Street revival of 1906. Interpreting the experience yielded pneumatologies with several striking features. The Spirit is the one who intends and grants a saving relationship with a particular existential shape (intimacy expressed through tongues) and vocational result (anointing to powerful ministry).[73] Pentecostal theology has many traditionalist features, but its pneumatology is both distinct and more pronounced than in conservative Wesleyan or Reformed theology. It shares fundamentalism's dependence on modern propositionalism and on the premillennial eschatology built on it;[74] however, the Spirit's outpouring sidelined that premillennial framework and centered charismatic communities elsewhere. The Azusa Street revival was not just another revival but a restoration. Its "full gospel" shaped a distinctive missional ethic for the closing days of the present age that is less defensive than border-town fundamentalism. And its Holy Spirit is not just a person; he is a personality.

The variety of these influences attests to a (Lockean?) eclecticism that matches a similar cosmopolitan pragmatism in Pentecostal liturgy, polity, and missionary strategy. These features give Pentecostal faith a cultural adaptability that helped it take root and flourish just about everywhere it was planted, from indigenous churches where its practices resonated with local sensibilities to non-Pentecostal Christian traditions (with the charismatic revival of the 1960s). One century after its official birth, one third of the world's Christians may be Pentecostal and charismatic.

Adaptability is not incidental to Pentecostal pneumatology. The movement's apparent lack of theological discipline can perplex systematic theologians

73. The reasoning works like this: Because the Bible's unified witness means that tongues in Acts must be the same prophetic and devotional tongues as those in 1 Corinthians, they represent a unique spiritual gift that signifies a normative relationship with God. This gift is God's promised "latter rain," affording a special relationship with the Holy Spirit that mediated Christ's intended relationship with humanity as savior, healer, sanctifier, and soon coming king. Glossolalia's apparent earlier absence implies that the 1906 event was a new Pentecost that had inaugurated a restoration of the church that had slumbered, or worse, since the age of the apostles. The prominence of this gift here and there in the book of Acts makes tongues necessary evidence of being filled with the Holy Spirit, a relationship many regard as constitutive of being saved and anointed to faithful service in the kingdom. See Donald Dayton, *Theological Roots of Pentecostalism* (Peabody, MA: Hendrickson, 1987), cited in D. William Faupel, "The Restoration Vision in Pentecostalism," *Christian Century* 107, no. 29 (October 17, 1990): 938–41. For one of many narratives of early Pentecostal history see Samuel Escobar, *The New Global Mission: The Gospel from Everywhere to Everyone* (Downers Grove, IL: InterVarsity, 2003), 113–16.

74. See Robert Anderson, *Vision of the Disinherited: The Making of American Pentecostalism* (Malden, MA: Hendrickson, 1979), cited in Faupel, "Restoration Vision in Pentecostalism," 938.

from other traditions. But the discipline is elsewhere, in the pneumatology behind these practices. Pentecostals regard their flexibility and diversity as the newness of the Spirit's new creation. Amos Yong contends that Pentecostal pneumatology is well suited to respecting the local particularities of churches in the new global context, rather than subsuming their witness into a deceptively uniform theology.[75]

A second influential set of cosmopolitan pneumatologies is eclectic in a different way. Many Western Christians ground some aspects of their vision (often doctrines of sin, salvation, and church) in the gospel, but ground others (often creation, anthropology, and ethics) in "natural law." Calvinists may mistake this bifurcation as their necessary distinction between common and special grace; Lutherans may take it as their gospel/law dichotomy or Christ's "two kingdoms"; Catholics may see revealed theology contrasted with natural theology.[76] But the real pattern is Locke's. Western civil religions and folk theologies amalgamate Christian and secular traditions in ways that honor both, but only partially. In the public realm, natural theology and empiricism reign. Christian specificity is confined to an ideological ghetto, while empiricism and its vague natural theology rule the cosmopolis from behind their castle walls. The word "God" becomes a public term that even presidents may use in official discourse; the name "Jesus" belongs in congregational sermons; and the term "Holy Spirit" is best whispered in private, or at least candlelight. This impulse comes so naturally to Americans that it must be deliberately pointed out to us, and we need even more strenuous training to keep from reading it into the New Testament. It is not pragmatism that arbitrates between these two separate orders. Nor is it Augustine's much maligned doctrine of the Trinity. With further historical training we will learn to see the same principle in the spirituality of the Gnostics and the spiritualists of the Radical Reformation. Their Holy Spirit works to free the spiritual aspects of spiritual beings from the fetters of a material world governed by a different set of rules, and perhaps even a different god. This Holy Spirit is about our souls rather than our bodies—a still small voice uttering classified communiqués, a mystery accessible only to mystics, a sanctifier but not a creator.

Third, a number of theologians are cosmopolitan simply in the breadth of their influences. They mine a variety of sources, inside and outside the tradition, out of a habitual respect for both. This can do violence to one or both disciplines, or it can produce elegant syntheses such as Wolfhart Pannenberg's appropriation of modern historiography.[77] In North American evangelicalism

75. Amos Yong, *The Spirit Poured Out on All Flesh: Pentecostalism and the Possibility of Global Theology* (Grand Rapids: Baker Academic, 2005), 18.

76. Of course, some loyalists of each of these schools adopt a Gnostic bifurcation of their faith they mistakenly regard as a true heir to their Reformation tradition.

77. Pannenberg's theological vision is developed most extensively in *Systematic Theology*, trans. Geoffrey Bromiley, 3 vols. (Grand Rapids: Eerdmans, 1988–1993). For Pannenberg, "the

one can appreciate Clark Pinnock's pneumatology[78] and theology more generally as commuting between cosmopolis and capitals, and the Emergent Church movement as conducting pneumatological investigations[79] between cosmopolis and border towns.

Finally, some of the interdisciplinary theologians we placed in frontier settlements have counterparts here. These are loyal both to the logics of their disciplines and the logic of the faith, refusing to silence either field's voice even when the two seem to conflict. As Thomas Aquinas brought Islamized Aristotelian philosophy into a true critical exchange with medieval Augustinian theology, so physicist-turned-churchman John Polkinghorne turns the resources of both contemporary physics and Anglican Christianity to the issue of divine action. He finds quantum mechanics an appropriate warrant for seeing not a deistic world of deterministic causes and effects but a universe structurally open to un-self-caused quantum events. The traditional dogmas of creation, incarnation, and resurrection offer theological language for what God does with that structural openness. The two testimonies together suggest that creation is sacramentally designed by and for the Holy Spirit, and thus indicative of his character and work.[80] It may be too optimistic to say that Polkinghorne's account really does justice to both the apostolic tradition and contemporary physics, but it is too critical to say he has simply domesticated either one to the other.

No one representative of cosmopolitan theology will call to mind both a John Polkinghorne and husband-and-wife Pentecostal pastors in a storefront church. However, a number of sophisticated and stimulating figures in cosmopolitan pneumatology are drawn to both of these types and many more. One of these is Jürgen Moltmann, a disciple of Karl Barth who has made eschatology rather than revelation the dominant category of his theology. Since eschatology describes God's apocalyptic renewal of creation, the topics, disciplines, and practices that concern the aspects of creation that are most directly being renewed are central to his theological reflection. History, sociology, psychology, and the natural sciences are all disciplinary partners of systematic theology that are indispensable to Moltmann's task. The Holy Spirit thus understood becomes "the divine wellspring of life—the source of

---

dynamic of the divine Spirit [is] as a working field linked to time and space—to time by the power of the future that gives creatures their own present and duration, and to space by the simultaneity of creatures in their duration" (2:104).

78. Clark Pinnock, *Flame of Love: A Theology of the Holy Spirit* (Downers Grove, IL: InterVarsity, 1996).

79. For instance, Patrick Oden, "An Emerging Pneumatology: Jürgen Moltmann and the Emerging Church in Conversation," *Journal of Pentecostal Theology* 18, no. 2 (2009): 263–84.

80. John C. Polkinghorne, *Science and Providence: God's Interaction with the World* (West Conshohocken, PA: Templeton, 2005), 38, 45, 106. For an appreciation and critique, see Telford Work, "The Science Division: Pneumatological Relations and Christian Disunity in Theology," *Zygon: Journal of Religion and Science* 43, no. 4 (December 2008): 897–908.

life created, life preserved and life daily renewed, and finally the source of eternal life of all created being."[81]

Moltmann's results are too shaped by theological categories to please many historians, sociologists, and scientists; like many cosmopolitan theologians, his work is of serious interest only to believers. And his results are often too indebted to these other disciplines' metaphysics to please theologians, who complain when Moltmann's proposals violate important theological (and here pneumatological) rules. For instance, Moltmann's social trinitarianism, which construes the Spirit as one of three centers of consciousness, arguably owes too much to prevailing psychological notions of the self. His historicism "imports" Christ's suffering into the eternal life of the Triune God in ways that suggest a revival of theopaschitism, the heresy that construes the divine nature, and thus the Holy Spirit, as subject to suffering.[82] Moltmann endorses a divine regard for creation and a pneumatic relationship to it (a little too motivated, one suspects, by political affinities and revulsions)[83] that looks less like the pervasive apocalyptic eschatology of the New Testament and more like the philosophical panentheism for which he has long received (sometimes unjustified) criticism.[84] And so on. Moltmann's Holy Spirit has all the familiarity and strangeness of the cosmopolis, and of God seen through cosmopolitan eyes.

What does cosmopolitan theology suggest about the Holy Spirit? That he makes connections. He cries "Come!" along with the bride: not just inviting Jesus to come and restore the earth filled with violence and idolatry, but inviting the violent and idolatrous to come join the callers, who have drunk the water of life (Rev. 22:17). The Spirit is the one who leads even John the prophet, whose book of Revelation might seem the least cosmopolitan vision in the whole Bible, to perceive a new earth dawning in his own day[85] in which

81. Jürgen Moltmann, *The Spirit of Life: A Universal Affirmation* (Minneapolis: Fortress, 1991), 82.
82. See Michael Ward, "Theopaschitism: Is Jesus Christ Able or Unable to Suffer in His Divine Nature?" in *Heresies and How to Avoid Them: Why It Matters What Christians Believe*, ed. Ben Quash and Michael Ward (Peabody, MA: Hendrickson, 2007), 59–72. For a more satisfactory treatment, see Hans Urs von Balthasar, *Mysterium Paschale: The Mystery of Easter* (San Francisco: Ignatius, 2005).
83. The extent of Moltmann's engagement with a variety of "millenarian" eschatological visions and his consequent rejection of a number of orthodox features of "apocalyptic eschatology" in *The Coming of God: Christian Eschatology* (Minneapolis: Fortress, 2004) suggest a preoccupation with the contemporary situation rather than the church's biblical and traditional witness. Indeed, they suggest that Moltmann lives along cosmopolis's border-town fringes.
84. See Jürgen Moltmann, *In the End—The Beginning: The Life of Hope* (Minneapolis: Fortress, 2004).
85. The "new heavens and new earth" language of Rev. 21 draws on Isa. 65, which describes a preresurrection order (Isa. 65:20). Its new Jerusalem still has walls, gates, and an outside (21:12–21) in which live sinners and the unclean (21:27). It seems to describe a present age in which the enduring church invites the nations to come and be healed (22:2, 14–15)—an era *before* the last

the godless nations may bring their treasure and their kings may bring their glory and honor (Rev. 21:24–26). New Jerusalem's gated walls are an open border housing a multicultural milieu: a border town that is becoming an eschatological cosmopolis. Its open invitation has stood since Jesus secretly journeyed to the old and doomed cosmopolis of Jerusalem to call on its worshipers to believe in him and become sources of the Spirit (John 7:37–39).

Conclusion: Pneumatology on the Map

What are we to make of all this? Some will be looking for clues for which sector is the one right place for pneumatology, or which is the author's personal favorite.[86] That is to miss the point.[87] There *are* theological border towns and frontier settlements, capitals and the burgeoning cosmopolis, and places beyond the Christian tradition; and their residents *will* all think about God from wherever they are.

So it is not just one of these locations that shows us who the Spirit is. The Spirit is the Spirit everywhere. Not like an elephant that is only partially known by each of the blind men who interpret what little they can feel, but as one who can appear distinctly in a given context. To make this point we have drawn on the New Testament's Johannine material to characterize the one Spirit of all five areas.

We might also draw on the Acts of the Apostles, a work with such import for pneumatology that some call it "the Acts of the Holy Spirit." Its characters would be at home in each quadrant and the middle of our map.

James, custodian of the apostles' tradition after Peter's departure from Jerusalem, and ever mindful of its Old Testament heritage and loyalists (Acts 15:19–29), does pneumatology in his young tradition's capital. Two very different figures exemplify pneumatology on the outside: Simon subsumes the Spirit into the categories of magic into which he was immersed as a Samaritan

---

judgment described in Rev. 20:11–15. A "present day" Rev. 21:1–22:5 thus leads more naturally into the postscript and exhortations of Rev. 22:6–21. For a helpful introduction to Revelation's many temporal cycles and sequential shifts backward see Craig R. Koester, *Revelation and the End of All Things* (Grand Rapids: Eerdmans, 2001).

86. For readers who would be distracted by not knowing, I admire some of each place's theologians, but my own sympathies and loyalties run along the top edge and down somewhat into the middle. I am a migrant from liberal Protestantism to evangelicalism and specifically Pentecostalism, worshiping most happily at a low-key, missional Pentecostal church in Los Angeles.

87. A map drawn fairly will reflect the cartographer's opinions but need not suggest or express favoritism. Of course, where a map is centered and bounded influences the reader's perceptions and can be a clue to the cartographer's biases. Saul Steinberg's famous cover of *The New Yorker* of March 29, 1976, titled "View of the World from 9th Avenue," does drive home the postmodern point that mapmaking is never objective.

magician (8:9–24), while the Ephesian disciples of John have not even heard of the Holy Spirit (19:1–4).

Peter is Acts's leading frontier theologian of the Spirit. Pentecost's authoritative interpreter (2:14–40) is the very capital of the tradition from its beginning (1:13–22), yet he brings the gospel into every kind of new place as Acts's narrative unfolds.[88] Stephen and the party of the Pharisees both represent pneumatology in border towns. Stephen, a Spirit-filled Hellenistic Jew, was both an apt servant of a neglected sector of the church (and an inspirer of belief among Jerusalem's worshiping priests, Acts 6:7) and an excoriating critic of Jerusalem's parochial and undiscerning rulers (6:8–8:1). By contrast, the party of the Pharisees know the Holy Spirit so exclusively through the inspired Torah that they cannot at first appreciate what the Spirit has been doing among either the gentiles or their own people (15:4–12). Acts's and the whole New Testament's most cosmopolitan thinker is Paul. A master of rabbinical Pharisaism, Hellenistic epistolary, and Greco-Roman diatribe, Messiah's apostle to the gentiles skillfully retells the traditions of Jesus in the forms and categories of skeptical and receptive Jews and pagans, incredulous Athenian philosophers, and bemused rulers, and fearlessly theorizes about what the Spirit's outpouring among the gentiles means for salvation history.

Luke and the Fourth Evangelist know what the later church has received from them and remembered. The Holy Spirit is the Lord of the whole world and each of its ages, and our grid is itself the product and the domain of God's unfolding missional work of new creation. That we could map John's verses or Acts's witnesses on it demonstrates perhaps the most important finding for an exercise in mapping modern pneumatology. Above all, it is simply *pneumatology*, whose object remains the same as ever.

For Further Reading

Del Colle, Ralph. *Christ and the Spirit: Spirit-Christology in Trinitarian Perspective*. New York: Oxford University Press, 1994.

Heron, Alasdair. *The Holy Spirit*. Philadelphia: Westminster, 1996.

Jenson, Robert W. *Systematic Theology*. 2 vols. New York: Oxford University Press, 1997 and 2001.

Johnson, Elizabeth A. *She Who Is: The Mystery of God in Feminist Theological Discourse*. New York: Crossroad, 1994.

88. Among these are Jewish expatriates (2:14–40); then Jerusalem's outcasts (3:1–10), crowds, rulers, and everyone else there (3:1–4:20; 5:28); then questionable Samaritan believers (8:14–23) and the surrounding Jewish country (9:32–35). Next Peter becomes the prophet and vanguard of the cultural revolution of the gentiles' incorporation into the church (10:1–11:18), the experience of which revolutionizes his missional theology (15:7–11). Peter's journeys to Antioch (Gal. 2:11–14) and Rome (1 Pet. 5:13) are assumed but not attested in Acts.

Moltmann, Jürgen. *The Spirit of Life: A Universal Affirmation*. Minneapolis: Fortress, 1991.

Pannenberg, Wolfhart. *Systematic Theology*. Translated by Geoffrey Bromiley. 3 vols. Grand Rapids: Eerdmans, 1988–1993.

Pinnock, Clark. *Flame of Love: A Theology of the Holy Spirit*. Downers Grove, IL: InterVarsity, 1996.

Shults, F. LeRon. "Current Trends in Pneumatology." In *Spirit and Spirituality*, 20–38. Copenhagen: University of Copenhagen Press, 2007.

Witham, Larry. *The Measure of God: Our Century-Long Struggle to Reconcile Science and Religion*. San Francisco: Harper, 2006.

Yong, Amos. *The Spirit Poured Out on All Flesh: Pentecostalism and the Possibility of Global Theology*. Grand Rapids: Baker Academic, 2005.

11

. . .

SOTERIOLOGY

RICHARD LINTS

Preliminaries

Mapping modern theology reminds one of the interconnections among all of the major theological topics. To speak of salvation, as this essay will, is to speak in large measure in the Christian tradition of the God who saves, and so all of the prior discussions about the nature and character of God come into play in any discussion of soteriology. The distinctive shape of salvation in the Christian tradition is undoubtedly directly related to Jesus Christ, whose life, death, and resurrection play the central role in salvation. In other words, Christology can never be very distant from a discussion of soteriology in Christian theology. The power and presence of the Holy Spirit form the inevitable backdrop for discussions of God's work in saving humans in the world. So the work of the Holy Spirit in creation and redemption must be integrally related if our understanding of salvation is to have the depth and theological richness it deserves. And whatever else may be said about salvation, human identity and purpose serve as the locus around which soteriology must swirl. More recent discussions of soteriology have reminded us, as did the ancient discussions, that salvation is bound up with the nature of the church (ecclesiology) and is played out across all of time (eschatology). In other words, all of the major theological topics are connected in one way or another to soteriology.[1]

1. An older but still helpful introduction to the theological shape of salvation is H. D. Mac-Donald, *Salvation* (Westchester, IL: Crossway, 1982). See also G. C. Berkouwer's two volumes

If this is so, three options are available to us. We might, with a certain humility, despair of any intelligible discussion of salvation, since it rightly ought to include every other theological topic. We might, by contrast (and with some degree of arrogance), suppose that every theological topic is being adequately addressed in our discussion of salvation. Or finally, and the tack taken here, we might opt for a little false humility and overconfidence mixed together. We will simply get on with the task at hand as best we can, recognizing the enormous amount that must inevitably be left unsaid, but also with the confidence that faith requires us to say something even if we cannot say everything.[2]

In the background of our discussion of soteriology must also be the place of our inherited traditions of discourse as they frame the contemporary map of theology.[3] Protestants have tended to think through the categories of justification and sanctification. The Roman Catholic tradition has often seen salvation through the lens of transformation and renewal. Eastern Orthodox traditions have emphasized participation and deification. It would be unfair to all three traditions to suppose that they have not had vigorous internal discussions and disagreements across the ages relative to these tendencies. And, further, it would be unfair to suppose that we now stand in a privileged position at the beginning of the twenty-first century that enables us, by contrast to these traditions, to simply add all three of these emphases into one neat little package. The historic debates within and across these traditions will not simply go away by an all-too-easy theological paradigm of inclusion.[4]

Finally, an important theological and pastoral caution ought to be expressed. Talk about salvation is not equivalent to salvation itself. Knowing about God is not the same as knowing God. Understanding the conceptual categories through which God speaks of salvation is not the same as being renewed, reconciled, and redeemed by God. Yet salvation is not so mysterious that it transcends in its entirety all our attempts to understand it and articulate it, and therefore safeguard it from misunderstandings.

---

on salvation in his series in dogmatics, *Faith and Justification*, trans. Lewis B. Smedes (Grand Rapids: Eerdmans, 1954), and *Faith and Sanctification*, trans. John Vriend (Grand Rapids: Eerdmans, 1952).

2. Karl Barth writes, "The reality of the relation of revelation in which Jesus Christ stands on the one side and our faith and obedience on the other is equivalent to the fact that our knowledge of God in this relation is the knowledge of his mystery, of the limit that he has set for our knowledge, of the need to ask concerning him." *The Göttingen Dogmatics*, ed. Hannelotte Reiffen, trans. Geoffrey Bromiley (Grand Rapids: Eerdmans, 1990), 1:332.

3. On the relationship of theology to diverse Christian traditions see David Buschart, *Exploring Protestant Traditions: An Invitation to Theological Hospitality* (Downers Grove, IL: InterVarsity, 2006).

4. On this point see Geoffrey Wainwright, "Schisms, Heresies and the Gospel: Wesleyan Reflections on Evangelical Truth and Ecclesial Unity," in *Ancient and Postmodern Christianity: Paleo-Orthodoxy in the 21st Century: Essays in Honor of Thomas C. Oden*, ed. Christopher Hall and Kenneth Tanner (Downers Grove, IL: InterVarsity, 2002), 183–97.

Introduction

Salvation is one among many terms in the Bible to describe the work of God to renew, redeem, and reconcile a fallen humanity with consequences for all of the created order. The language of salvation should be distinguished from the doctrine of salvation. The term "salvation" in the ancient context was a medical term referring to healing or the restoration to well-being (cf. Acts 28:27–28). A doctrine of salvation refers to the whole plethora of conceptual frameworks through which the problem of humankind is understood as solved by divine action. As a specific term in the Bible, "salvation" links together by way of analogy the physical healing of a diseased body and the spiritual healing of a corrupted human nature.[5] In this narrow semantic range, the term "salvation" in Scripture calls attention to the restorative dimensions of God's grace extended to sinners.

In theological discourse, the "doctrine of salvation" refers to the breadth of divine actions in renewing, redeeming, and reconciling a fallen humanity and is not limited to the medical metaphor. It is God who saves, and humans and the created order who are saved. The breadth of terms to depict this action and the wider meaning of those terms in the web of theological discourse is the purview of this essay. The doctrine of salvation collects under one umbrella the various ways in which these divine actions are described across the canon of Scripture. It also draws attention to the connections and tensions between the varied ways the canon speaks of these actions.[6]

Theologians have distinguished the means of salvation (Christ's life, death, and resurrection) and salvation itself (creatures and the created order being reconciled, redeemed, and renewed). Atonement and salvation are the theological categories that designate this difference respectively. Christ's death and resurrection, in some sense, effect the saving of sinners. His death and resurrection serve as the means of salvation. Christ's death and resurrection can also be spoken of in their own right as the defeat of death and the gift of life. It is Christ's death and resurrection and the gift of the Spirit that mark the turning of the ages whereby God has set in motion the new creation in which all things eventually will be made new in a way that we now only understand as "through a glass darkly." Salvation is accomplished by means of Christ's life, death, and his subsequent resurrection in which death itself is defeated and life is given. These great redemptive historical events

5. Ellen Charry uses this medical metaphor to instructively inform her entire theological paradigm in *By the Renewing of Your Minds: The Pastoral Function of Christian Doctrine* (New York: Oxford University Press, 1997).

6. A careful word study on the terms the New Testament uses to depict salvation is John Murray, *Redemption: Accomplished and Applied* (Grand Rapids: Eerdmans, 1955). A more technical though less theological work on these same issues is Jan van der Watt, ed., *Salvation in the New Testament: Perspectives on Soteriology* (Leiden: Brill, 2005).

form the specific shape of salvation. The apostle Paul can write, "If we have been united to Christ in death like this, we shall also be united to him in the resurrection" (Rom. 6:5). Death's defeat and the gift of life are "salvation" for the created order.

The Gospel and Salvation

"Salvation in Christ" is often shorthand for the full breadth of the gospel of Jesus Christ. In Scripture, this gospel is the good news that God has redeemed humans through Jesus. Stretched across the canon, the good news endures from the Alpha to the Omega of creation.[7] Enveloping not only our own conversion story, the good news is also a narrative encompassing the whole of creation. Salvation is not simply about "getting to heaven," nor "avoiding hell"—though there are undoubtedly implications for life after the grave in the gospel. All of history is embedded in the greater reality of the gospel.

The gospel is narrated as the story that begins at Gen. 1 and runs all the way through Rev. 22. Important dimensions of the gospel are lost when any part of the story from Genesis to Revelation is omitted. When Luke records, "And beginning with Moses and with all the prophets He [Jesus] explained to them the things concerning Himself in all the Scriptures" (Luke 24:27 NAS), the claim is being made that the story of Jesus is the story of the whole Bible.[8] And the whole Bible is the whole gospel. Even as Jesus is the glue that holds the whole story together, so the gospel is the glue that holds the Bible together.[9]

This strongly suggests the "story" is not a simple story, nor can it be held in its entirety in any short summary.[10] Begging us to embrace a complex narrative, the gospel finally puts its hearers into an alternative reality, a reality that resists reductionist attempts to capture its essence easily and cleanly. It "spills over" any articulation of its nature and character. And yet the New Testament

7. On the canonical shape of salvation see Michael S. Horton, *Covenant and Salvation: Union with Christ* (Louisville: Westminster John Knox, 2007), and Christopher J. H. Wright, *Salvation Belongs to Our God: Celebrating the Bible's Central Story* (Downers Grove, IL: InterVarsity, 2007).

8. On christological readings of Scripture see Royce Gordon Gruenler, "Old Testament Gospel as Prologue to New Testament Gospel," in *Creator, Redeemer, Consummator: A Festschrift for Meredith G. Kline*, ed. Howard Griffith and John R. Muether (Jackson, MS: Reformed Academic Press, 2000), 95–104.

9. See Craig G. Bartholomew and Michael Goheen, *The Drama of Scripture: Finding Our Place in the Biblical Story* (Grand Rapids: Baker Academic, 2004).

10. On the importance of story and narrative to the project of interpreting Scripture see Craig Bartholomew and Mike Goheen, "Story and Biblical Theology," in *Out of Egypt: Biblical Theology and Biblical Interpretation*, ed. Craig Bartholomew (Milton Keynes, UK: Paternoster, 2004), 144–71.

speaks in the vernacular of first-century Judaism to depict the simplicity of the gospel and the costliness of embracing it.[11]

Using different word pictures to articulate the breadth and depth of the gospel, the Bible presents a multicolored tapestry. Legal language (justification, punishment, judgment) illuminates the fundamentally moral character of redemption. Temple language (atonement, sacrifice, sanctification) highlights the mystery of the universal presence of God as creator interwoven into the local presence of God as redeemer. Familial language (adoption, bride and bridegroom, reconciliation) explores the central relational quality of God's dealing with his creatures. Terms associated with the marketplace (redemption and possession) capture the dynamic of God's ownership of his people in all of life.[12] These and many more word pictures help us to appreciate the all-encompassing character of the gospel.[13]

In all of its various streams, the Christian church has historically affirmed the full participation of the Triune God in salvation. The gospel is predicated on the love of the Father, effected through the death and resurrection of the Son, and applied through the Spirit. Trinitarian relations are not incidental to any depiction of salvation, but ought to retain a centrality in the discussion of salvation just as they are central to the Scriptures themselves.[14]

Affirming from the beginning the trinitarian shape of salvation argues against reducing salvation to an individual event or to an objective corporate event. Salvation is not merely getting into a subjectively experienced relationship between oneself and God. Neither is salvation strictly about belonging to

11. N. T. Wright's massive three-volume study *Christian Origins and the Question of God* (Minneapolis: Fortress, 1992) is the best contemporary treatment of the concrete historical context through which the New Testament authors understood Jesus Christ.

12. On legal imagery see Henri Blocher, "Justification of the Ungodly (*Sola Fide*): Theological Reflections," in *Justification and Variegated Nomism*, vol. 2, *The Paradoxes of Paul*, ed. D. A. Carson, Peter T. O'Brien, and Mark A. Seifrid (Grand Rapids: Baker Academic, 2004), 465–500. On temple imagery see G. K. Beale, *The Temple and the Church's Mission: A Biblical Theology of the Temple* (Downers Grove, IL: InterVarsity, 2004). On familial and relational imagery see C. F. D. Moule, *Forgiveness and Reconciliation: And Other New Testament Themes* (London: SPCK, 1998). Scott Hahn, *A Father Who Keeps His Promises: God's Covenant Love in Scripture* (Ann Arbor, MI: Servant Publications, 1998), connects the familial themes with the language of covenant. On marketplace imagery, see Dale Martin, *Slavery as Salvation: The Metaphor of Slavery in Pauline Christianity* (New Haven: Yale University Press, 1990).

13. A helpful though limited attempt to understand the variety of models of salvation in relationship to each other is John McIntyre, *Models of Soteriology* (Edinburgh: T&T Clark, 1992). A more instructive attempt at developing the New Testament metaphors for salvation into a cohesive whole is Gordon Fee, "Paul and the Metaphors for Salvation: Some Reflections on Pauline Soteriology," in *Redemption: An Interdisciplinary Symposium on Christ as Redeemer*, ed. Stephen T. Davis, Daniel Kendall, and Gerald O'Collins (Oxford: Oxford University Press, 2004), 43–67.

14. See John Webster, "The Place of the Doctrine of Justification," in *What Is Justification About?* ed. Michael Weinrich and John Burgess (Grand Rapids: Eerdmans, 2009), 35–55, for an interesting argument about the relation of soteriology to the doctrine of the Trinity.

a church of like-minded people. Salvation concerns individuals-in-community. Covenant language throughout the Scriptures underscores this tension inherent in God's actions of salvation. God's act of restoring us into a covenant relationship with him also puts us into a differently ordered (i.e., covenantal) relationship with all others who are reconciled to God.[15]

Salvation across the Twentieth Century

Paradigms of salvation at the close of the nineteenth century in Europe and North America inevitably fell into two camps—*transformationist soteriologies* and *relational soteriologies*.[16] These represented tendencies rather than exhaustive depictions of salvation. Transformationist notions of salvation draw attention to the manner in which Jesus transformed those who followed him. They focus on the way humans are transformed by divine grace and then themselves participate in the transformation of the whole created order. Relational notions of salvation highlight the manner in which faith in Jesus brought his disciples into a different relation to God. They point to the way in which the divine-human relationship is reconciled and renewed. These divine-human relationships are also described in covenantal ways in Scripture. Salvation could then be described as the restoration of covenant membership by those who have broken covenant with God.

If pressed too far, these generalizations break down. Transformationist soteriologies in the nineteenth century supposed that the transformation of individuals by the gospel surely impacted their relation to God while relational soteriologies of the same period inevitably discussed the implications of Christianity upon the character of those who believed it. The central divide, however, still stood. Was the primary impact of the death and resurrection of Christ upon (1) the relationship of individuals to God, or was it principally upon (2) the interior transformation of character in those individuals?[17] In the sections to follow, these two different soteriological traditions are traced chronologically across the nineteenth and twentieth centuries. A concluding section chronicles and describes the recent interest in the ancient participationist soteriologies most often associated with Eastern Orthodoxy.

15. See Joel B. Green, *Salvation* (St. Louis: Chalice, 2003) for an emphasis upon the communal dimensions of salvation. See Meredith Kline, *By Oath Consigned* (Grand Rapids: Eerdmans, 1968), for a distinctively theological account of covenant signs and membership.

16. Paul Fiddes, "Salvation," in *The Oxford Handbook of Systematic Theology*, ed. John Webster, Kathryn Tanner, and Iain Torrance (New York: Oxford University Press, 2007), 176–96, lays out this distinction clearly, but then reduces relational soteriologies to largely transformational soteriologies.

17. Transformational soteriologies are closely connected to what are called exemplar theories of the atonement, as relational soteriologies are associated with penal notions of the atonement.

Transformation Soteriologies and German Liberalism

Transformationist soteriologies were represented at the beginning and the end of the nineteenth century respectively by Friedrich Schleiermacher and Albrecht Ritschl. Schleiermacher's *The Christian Faith* (1822)[18] and Ritschl's *The Christian Doctrine of Justification and Reconciliation* (1874)[19] stand as supremely influential works of Protestant theology of the period and reshaped much of the discussion of soteriology in European Christianity. In different but analogous ways, both Schleiermacher and Ritschl were deeply indebted to the revisioning of Christology then current in the nineteenth century, and they stand as paradigm representations of transformation soteriologies. Christological creeds of the great tradition were increasingly viewed with suspicion in many quarters, and in particular their peculiarly sharp commitment to a full-orbed two-natures understanding of Jesus's identity. Theologically, the "fully human/fully divine" formula no longer seemed feasible in light of the growing historicist sensibilities of the age. In many circles, the emphasis upon historical development entailed a renewed examination of the humanity of Jesus, and, in some sense, a decreased interest in the claims about his deity. The prevailing naturalism then beginning to seep into many of the literate quarters of European culture exerted a disproportionate influence upon the religious studies guild in the German universities of this time. Schleiermacher and Ritschl were influential on this trajectory even as they were deeply influenced by the growing historicist scholarship of their day.[20]

Schleiermacher was keenly sensitive to the criticisms leveled at Christianity by its "cultured despisers" and thought that Christianity could be refashioned or contextualized in such a way as to avoid giving unnecessary offense.[21] On these grounds he supposed that the Christian faith ought to be articulated as a religion whose most profound orientation was the transformation of human

18. Friedrich Schleiermacher, *The Christian Faith*, 2 vols., ed. H. R. Macintosh and J. S. Stewart (New York: Harper Torchbooks, 1963).

19. Albrecht Ritschl, *The Christian Doctrine of Justification and Reconciliation: The Positive Development of the Doctrine*, English translation, ed. H. R. Macintosh and A. B. Macaulay (Eugene, OR: Wipf & Stock, 2004).

20. A largely sympathetic overview of nineteenth-century liberal theology can be found in Peter Hodgson, *Liberal Theology: A Radical Vision* (Minneapolis: Fortress, 2007). A more critical but still perceptive rehearsal of liberal theology in the nineteenth and twentieth centuries is found in Hendrikus Berkhof, *Two Hundred Years of Theology: Report of a Personal Journey* (Grand Rapids: Eerdmans, 1989). On the peculiar shape of liberal theology because of the context of the German university, see Thomas A. Howard, *Protestant Theology and the Making of the Modern German University* (New York: Oxford University Press, 2006).

21. Schleiermacher's classic work in this regard is *On Religion: Speeches to Its Cultured Despisers*, trans. and ed. Richard Crouter, 2nd ed. (1799; repr., New York: Cambridge University Press, 1996).

experience.[22] By virtue of a common consciousness of the divine, all humans inevitably strive toward a fuller explanation and evaluation of their innate dependence upon the divine (or at least upon their perception of the divine). That which is in the human driven by this God-consciousness is eternal, though each human can reasonably repudiate the eternal. But in that repudiation, these eternal realities also fade away and humanity loses its virtue. For Schleiermacher, there was no more clear and full exposition of this God-consciousness than Jesus. In Jesus the fullness of all the experiential realities of God was displayed and lived.[23] It was Jesus in whom lay the hopes of humanity, as the one who pointed the way toward a civilization of compassion. Through a communion with Jesus made possible by faith, each person could enter more fully into their potential. Here was salvation for Schleiermacher. Not in the sense of a salvation from an eternal punishment for sin, but rather a salvation into the fullness of divine compassion and love.[24] It was a salvation largely focused around earthly realities rather than "beyond the grave" concerns.

In Ritschl, these earthly realities about which salvation was concerned were identifiable as the kingdom of God. The nature and character of the kingdom of God were most fully realized in the person and life of Jesus Christ. Sin is the active opposition to the in-breaking of the kingdom of God on earth. Sin is systemic and arises in the context of humans participating in the "associations of evil."[25] There is no intrinsic connection between the sin of Adam (original sin) and the sin of humans in the contemporary context. The result of sin is a guilty conscience rather than actual guilt before a divine and heavenly court. It is the guilty conscience that must "relearn" the habits and tendencies of the kingdom of God. Relearning those habits is what Ritschl means by salvation. Fully displaying God's kingdom in their lives is the goal of those who have been saved by God.

For Ritschl, Christ's death is not a penal satisfaction of divine wrath on the basis of which individuals are justified. Rather the death of Christ is the full revelation of God's love for humankind, and in this sense serves as the basis of justification and reconciliation. Ritschl spoke of justification as by "faith alone," but in sharp contrast to what traditional Protestant theologians had meant by those terms. In Ritschl's framework, justification arose by trusting in God's love.[26] It was on the basis of this trust in divine love that alienation

---

22. Schleiermacher writes, "If it be the essence of redemption that the God-consciousness already present in human nature, though feeble and repressed, becomes stimulated and made dominant by the entrance of the living influence of Christ, the individual on whom this influence is exercised attains a religious personality not his before" (*Christian Faith*, 2:476).

23. *Christian Faith*, vol. 2, §§93–94.

24. Ibid., §§109–10.

25. Ritschl, *Justification and Reconciliation*, 335–40.

26. Ritschl writes, "This new direction of the will toward God which is evoked by reconciliation is faith" (ibid., 100).

from God, principally noticed by an unrelieved feeling of guilt, would finally be removed. Trusting in God was the solution (i.e., salvation) to being alienated by one's own guilty conscience. It was not God who was alienated from sinners, but rather sinners who were alienated from God in virtue of their guilty conscience.

Finally, we should acknowledge that Ritschl was quite critical of the individualistic orientation of soteriology in Protestant Orthodoxy. He decried the individualistic notions of salvation embedded in much Protestant theology because they inevitably drew attention away from the corporate dimensions of love as the *summum bonum* of the Christian faith.[27] "The Christian community is God's supreme end in the world."[28] Love was always directed at another, which entailed that love demanded a community in order to be lived. Thinking about salvation primarily against the backdrop of entry into heaven or hell undermined the communal nature of love and its primary context in the church. For Ritschl, recovering the essentially social nature of justification and reconciliation was of paramount importance for the modern church.[29]

Relational Soteriology and Protestant Orthodoxy

Relational soteriologies were ably represented in the nineteenth century by a variety of Protestant orthodox voices. We select just two such representatives of the period. Charles Hodge and John Williamson Nevin stood within diverse streams of Protestant orthodoxy and outside of the mainstream German theological scholarship of the period. Hodge was the single most influential voice in nineteenth-century America, having trained nearly three thousand students in a remarkable fifty-year teaching career at Princeton Theological Seminary (1822–1872).[30] His *Systematic Theology* remained the standard theological text at many American seminaries for better than a half century after his death in 1878.[31] Hodge's work summarized much of Protestant

27. Ritschl writes, "The mystical conception of the scheme of salvation which completely isolates the individual from connection with the Church, has gained a place within the sphere of the Reformed Church as well as the Lutherans" (ibid., 112).

28. Ibid., 464.

29. A helpful collection of essays covering the breadth of Ritschl's work and influence is Darrell Jodock, ed., *Ritschl in Retrospect: History, Community, and Science* (Minneapolis: Fortress, 1995).

30. A good overview of Hodge's life and career can be found in David F. Wells, "Charles Hodge," in *Reformed Theology in America: A History of Its Modern Development*, ed. David F. Wells (Grand Rapids: Eerdmans, 1985), 36–59. The deeply personal biography written of Hodge by his son, Archibald Alexander Hodge, is quite illuminating: *The Life of Charles Hodge* (New York: Scribner, 1880).

31. On Hodge's relation to the theology of Old Princeton in the nineteenth century, see Mark Noll's splendid introductory essay to Mark Noll, ed., *The Princeton Theology: 1812–1921* (Grand Rapids: Baker Books, 1983), 9–47.

history and used standard distinctions to characterize soteriology. Part 3 of his *Systematic Theology* neatly categorized soteriology under the categories of regeneration, justification, and sanctification.[32] Regeneration referred to the work of the Holy Spirit in awakening the human heart on account of which an individual would exercise faith.[33] Faith was the instrument through which individuals took hold of Christ. The result was a change in their legal standing before God from guilty to innocent. Justification was the forensic declaration of God that sinners were no longer guilty before the eternal judgment seat on the basis of the finished work of Christ.[34] Faith, which was the instrumental cause of justification, was sustained by the Holy Spirit assuredly in the process of sanctification.[35] Hodge's approach served as the model of soteriology for conservative Protestants throughout much of the nineteenth century and well into the twentieth century.

Nevin, like Hodge, was deeply embedded in Protestant orthodoxy. He was professor at the small German Reformed seminary in Mercersburg, Pennsylvania, during the middle decades of the nineteenth century.[36] Unlike Hodge, Nevin emphasized the living spiritual union between Christ and the believer as the central framework of soteriology.[37] Nevin had supposed that American revivalism had placed undue emphasis upon the subjective disposition of the human will in conversion. Revivalists of the period had one principal criterion as they thought about influencing the will: efficiency.[38] Whatever means promoted a change in the will, according to the revivalist heritage, could and should be exploited for the purpose of salvation. By contrast, Nevin railed against the individualism inherent in this system, and rather supposed that the church had been ordained as the ordinary means through which sinners came to salvation in Christ.[39] Having read Schleiermacher, Nevin likewise thought of salvation in communal terms rather than individual ones. God's

32. Charles Hodge, *Systematic Theology* (1872–1873; repr., Grand Rapids: Eerdmans, 1981).
33. Ibid., chap. 15, secs. 1 and 3.
34. Ibid., chap. 17, secs. 2–5.
35. Ibid., chap. 16, secs. 2, 7–8.
36. The best social-cultural biography of Nevin is D. G. Hart, *John Williamson Nevin: High Church Calvinist* (Phillipsburg, NJ: P&R, 2005). The best intellectual biography of Nevin is Richard E. Wentz, *John Williamson Nevin: American Theologian* (Oxford: Oxford University Press, 1997).
37. "Where we are said to be of the same life with Jesus . . . it is not on the ground merely of a joint participation with him in the nature of Adam, but on the ground of our participation in his own nature as a higher order of life." Nevin, *The Mystical Presence: The Reformed or Calvinistic Doctrine of the Holy Eucharist* (Philadelphia: J. B. Lippincott, 1846), 54.
38. On the tradition of revivalism in nineteenth-century America see Charles E. Hambrick-Stowe, *Charles G. Finney and the Spirit of American Evangelicalism* (Grand Rapids: Eerdmans, 1996).
39. See Nevin, "The Anxious Bench—A Tract for the Times" (1843), reprinted in *Anxious Bench, AntiChrist, and the Sermon on Catholic Unity*, ed. Augustine Thompson (Eugene, OR: Wipf & Stock, 2000).

election concerned the community of God's covenant people. However, Nevin further supposed the gift of the Holy Spirit was the means of producing that holy union between Christ and his church, rather than being intrinsic to human nature.[40] Following Hodge in thinking of justification in forensic terms, Nevin employed the language of "union" as a far more dominant motif through which salvation could be understood.[41] And since the church was the ordinary means of effecting this union in the power of the Spirit, Nevin was also drawn to sacramental understandings of church power.[42] There has been a renewal of interest in the Mercersburg theology in our own day, in no small measure owing to the sacramental soteriology of Nevin.[43] It ought not be forgotten that Nevin saw himself standing in the tradition of Calvin on this point, and expressed deep misgivings about Hodge's purely forensic renderings of soteriology.

Karl Barth and Soteriology

Early in the twentieth century, the indomitable presence of Karl Barth began to be felt throughout much of Protestantism. His peculiar genius did not lie in the area of soteriology, but as with so much of Protestant theology after Barth, a considerable amount of contemporary soteriology lies within the shadow of Barth's work in the area.[44] A profound change in mood was set in place across European intellectual circles with the onset of the two world wars, which quite literally devastated an entire continent.[45] Against this backdrop, Barth was

40. See Nevin, "The Natural and Supernatural," *Mercersberg Review* 11 (1850): 176–210.

41. This was especially apparent in Nevin's dispute with Hodge regarding the presence of Christ in the Eucharist. See Nevin, *The Mystical Presence.*

42. Nevin writes, "Christ's presence in the world is in and by his Mystical Body, the Church. As a real human presence, carrying in itself the power of a new life for the race in general, it is no abstraction or object of thought merely, but a glorious living Reality, continuously at work, in an organic historical way, in the world's constitution." "Christ and the Church," in *The Mercersburg Theology,* ed. James Hastings Nichols (New York: Oxford University Press, 1966), 89.

43. See Jonathan Bonomo, *Incarnation and Sacrament: The Eucharistic Controversy between Charles Hodge and John Williamson Nevin* (Eugene, OR: Wipf & Stock, 2010), and Adam Bornemann, *The Man of Faith and the Perfection of Nature: The Sociopolitical Dimensions of John Williamson Nevin's Theology of Incarnation* (Eugene, OR: Wipf & Stock, forthcoming).

44. The entire book IV of Barth's *Church Dogmatics* is devoted to the doctrine of reconciliation. It is treated there not simply as one of the loci among others, but rather as the full consummation of Barth's earlier discussion of the Trinity. On this point see chap. 6, "Reconciliation," in John Webster, *Karl Barth* (New York: Continuum, 2000).

45. The historical theological contexts of early twentieth-century Europe are well described by A. I. C. Heron, *A Century of Protestant Thought* (Philadelphia: Westminster, 1980); Jaroslav Pelikan, *The Christian Tradition: A History of the Development of Doctrine,* vol. 5, *Christian Doctrine and Modern Culture (since 1700)* (Chicago: University of Chicago Press, 1991); and Stanley Grenz and Roger Olson, *20th-Century Theology: God and the World in a Transitional Age* (Downers Grove, IL: InterVarsity, 1992).

the most prescient of the European theologians to recognize the provocative truth behind the devastation.[46] Human nature could no longer be interpreted in largely optimistic terms. The depth and reality of human corruption must be taken seriously and must give way to a more profound doctrine of reconciliation between humankind and God. Jettisoning the pervasive inclination toward transformationist soteriologies in German theological circles, Barth supposed that the only terms worth appropriating in our grasp of salvation were the terms that God himself had laid out.

In contrast to Jesus Christ, according to Barth, fallen humankind from eternity—and not merely in time—stood in opposition to God with their own pride, sloth, and disorder at the heart of their identity.[47] In this state, humankind stood under divine judgment, the divine "No."[48] Humans could not save themselves from this judgment. Salvation must originate solely in the work of the sovereign Triune God, and the divine judgment must be fully meted out if God is to remain God. For Barth, it is Christ who stands in the place of condemned humankind, and it is humankind who now stands in the place of the beloved Son of the living God.

As with the church fathers, with Barth there is an ontological connection between the divine and the human in the incarnation of Christ. As a man, Christ genuinely suffered the wrath of God on behalf of humankind. In his humanity he is ontologically connected to all humankind. As God, Christ genuinely gives to humankind the very life of God in the resurrection. It is the union of the God/Man that effectively reconciles sinful humanity with the living God. What takes place in the narrative of Jesus Christ is actually counted as the narrative of humankind, though there is no ontological union between Jesus as divine and the rest of humankind.[49] There is no hint that humans are deified for Barth as there was in many of the church fathers. There is also no change in God, but only the changed relationship of humans to God. Since God had purposed from all eternity to save humankind in Christ, God is always favorably disposed toward humankind. The relational change that takes place in salvation is the reconciliation of humankind to God, not God to humankind.

Barth's doctrine of "reconciliation" is complex, moving along the narrative plotline of humiliation (incarnation and death) and exaltation (resurrection

---

46. Barth's role in the break from the German liberal theological tradition is summarized well in Gary J. Dorrien, *The Barthian Revolt in Modern Theology* (Louisville: Westminster John Knox, 2000).

47. This contrast is most forcefully stated in *Church Dogmatics* IV/2, 378–402.

48. "By sin man puts himself in the wrong in relation to God. He makes himself impossible as the creature and covenant-partner of God. He compromises his existence. For he has no right as sinner. He is only in the wrong" (*CD* IV/1, 528).

49. This is Bruce McCormack's contention in "Participation in God, Yes, Deification, No: Two Modern Protestant Responses to an Ancient Question," in *Denkwurdiges Geheimnis: Beiträge zur Gotteslehre*, ed. Ingolf Dalferth, Johannes Fischer, and Hans-Peter Groshans (Tübingen: Mohr Siebeck, 2004), 347–74.

and ascension) while in some sense locating that narrative in the eternal being of God.[50] He makes use of standard Protestant language of the obedience of Christ that leads Jesus to the cross, on the basis of which God accounts him righteous and then credits this righteousness to sinners. However, the "crediting righteous" is not the lens through which reconciliation is viewed, but rather one of the refractions through which the splendor of reconciliation can be appreciated more fully. The emphasis is less on the mechanism of reconciliation, as such, than the agent of reconciliation, Jesus Christ. In Jesus Christ, truth exposes the falsehoods of sin. His mercy exposes the hubris of sin. Christ's victory over death exposes the slothfulness and cynicism of sin. Jesus Christ is the gospel in whom there is reconciliation.[51] To put it in reverse, the gospel is God's work of reconciling all things to himself in Christ.[52]

Salvation as Liberation

Looking now at transformationist soteriologies in the twentieth century, it is safe to say that those of greatest significance are those we identify with liberation theologies: Latino, black, and feminist streams in particular. They gain their strength in the aftermath of that tumultuous decade, the 1960s.[53] In Latin America the originating influence was the Second Vatican Council (1961–1964). Black theology emerged in the aftermath of the civil rights movement in the United States. The feminist streams of liberation theology gained prominence with the emergence of the second feminist movement of the early 1960s. Each of these movements deserves particular attention in its own right.[54] The peculiar historical circumstances in which they arose are critical to their unique identities, and the voices that articulated their core visions cannot be reduced to simple abstractions. The "lived" nature of these movements is part of the fabric of their theologies, and most assuredly at the center of their soteriologies. There are "family resemblances" among these diverse movements, and what is to follow will trace out some of these

50. A crisp summary description of Barth's soteriology can be found in Colin Gunton, "Salvation," in *Cambridge Companion to Karl Barth*, ed. John Webster (Cambridge: Cambridge University Press, 2000), 143–58.

51. "We have not to overlook the sharp line which now separates the old that is made past in Him and the new that is already present in Him, a line which is drawn by the fact that He is with us and for us" (*CD* IV/2, 266).

52. A longer treatment of Barth on salvation is Donald G. Bloesch, *Jesus Is Victor! Karl Barth's Doctrine of Salvation* (Nashville: Abingdon, 1978).

53. Historical theological background on the 1960s can be found in Richard Lints, *Progressive and Conservative Religious Ideologies: The Tumultuous Decade of the 1960s* (Aldershot, UK: Ashgate, 2010).

54. A helpful overview of all the traditions of liberation theology can be found in Paul E. Sigmund, *Liberation Theology at the Crossroads: Democracy or Revolution?* (New York: Oxford University Press, 1990).

important family resemblances in soteriology. Throughout we will try to be sensitive to the unique and peculiar contributions of the diverse streams and voices of each movement.

These movements gained steam because of the perception of entrenched oppression peculiar to their own historical and geographic locations. The immediate impetus for Latin American liberation theology was the staggering poverty of vast segments of a region where the church historically had been on the side of the Crown. The church had not stood in solidarity with ordinary citizens, nor most especially with those on the bottom of the economic ladder.[55] Theologians in the movement rejected the categories of development tied to the perpetuation of a liberal economy and adopted instead a Marxist analysis of poverty and wealth.[56] Central to Marxist theory is the conviction that those who own the means of production will create political structures in which wealth is concentrated in the hands of a few. This provided tools to expose the failure of mainstream theologies of development and their purported claim that the great wealth at the top of the economic ladder would eventually trickle down to those below with sufficient patience. Great disillusionment emerged among the impoverished in the 1960s as a result of various political coups in Latin and South America defending the wealthy against the poor. Along with the systematic suppression of various freedom movements, these circumstances brought a completely new conceptualization of the situation. Latin American liberation theologians were convinced that poverty was caused by a few and that history inevitably manifested the struggle of the oppressed against their oppressors.[57] Many of these theologians also saw themselves as furthering the work of the Second Vatican Council as it was expressed in the social encyclicals (particularly *Populorum Progessio* and *Gaudium et Spes*) while critical of many of the dictatorial regimes long allied with the Vatican in supporting Catholicism in the region. This dialectical relationship to the Roman Catholic Church was very significant in the development of soteriological themes throughout the movement.[58]

Black theology was more nearly connected with the writings of a single person, James Cone, but like Latin American liberation theology, black theology emerged out of the reality of entrenched economic inequalities across a whole

55. The most influential early work of Latin American liberation theology is Gustavo Gutiérrez, *A Theology of Liberation: History, Politics, and Salvation* (Maryknoll, NY: Orbis, 1973).

56. Gutiérrez's extensive critique of economic developmentalism is found in ibid., chap. 6, 82–88.

57. See Leonardo Boff and Clodovis Boff, *Introducing Liberation Theology*, trans. Paul Burns (Maryknoll, NY: Orbis, 1987).

58. Harvey Cox, *The Silencing of Leonardo Boff: The Vatican and the Future of World Christianity* (Oak Park, IL: Meyerstone Books, 1988), traces the history of the relationship between the Vatican and liberation theology in the context of the enforced discipline of Leonardo Boff by the Vatican.

race of people.[59] Profound feelings of oppression among African Americans
brought the civil rights movement to life in the 1950s and early 1960s. Before
the Vietnam War and the politics of protest that accompanied it, there was
no more major cultural upheaval in the era than that associated with the civil
rights movement.[60] It overturned the optimism of modern secularity that
supposed all the nation's problems could be solved with greater attention to
technique and organization, even as the movement itself was catapulted into
existence in the first place by the hope which that same modern secularity
held out for a nation of free individuals who by their efforts could achieve
material prosperity. The civil rights movement brought with it the beginnings
of "identity politics," in which race (and class to a lesser extent) was a defining element of one's orientation in the world and of one's relationship to the
rest of society. Ongoing struggles for civil rights also cast grave doubts on the
notion of an objective American perspective that could speak for all and that
represented every citizen. As America learned painfully through the struggle,
not all perspectives were created equal and not all Americans experienced life
in equal ways.

Feminist theology grew in the same soil with black theology in the early
1960s. Many of the significant players of the second feminist movement had
been active participants in the civil rights movement and would also be at
the center of the antiwar movements in the United States in the 1960s.[61] The
first feminist movement ("women's rights movement," as it was originally
known), started as early as the 1830s, became intertwined with the struggle
to abolish slavery, and resulted in the proposal for the Nineteenth Amendment, introduced in Congress in 1878. This proposed amendment remained
a controversial issue for over forty years, during which the women's rights
movement became strongly militant, conducting campaigns and demonstrations for congressional passage of the amendment and then for ratification by
the states. That same spirit emerged again in the early 1960s, set off by Betty
Friedan's famous denunciation of the "feminine mystique," her term for the
identification of womanhood with the roles of wife and mother.[62] Within the
home women with more and more education found that they had less and less
to do. Despite the baby boom, their families were smaller than their grand-
mothers' had been. Technology abbreviated the physical labor of housework

59. See James Cone, *A Black Theology of Liberation* (Philadelphia: Lippincott, 1970;
Maryknoll, NY: Orbis, 1986).

60. The best general introduction to the civil rights movement is Robert Wiesbrot, *Freedom
Bound: A History of America's Civil Rights Movement* (New York: Norton, 1990). The best
theological account of the movement is Charles Marsh, *God's Long Summer: Stories of Faith
and Civil Rights* (Princeton: Princeton University Press, 1997).

61. The best historical account of the origins of the feminist movement is Sara Evans,
*Personal Politics: The Roots of Women's Liberation in the Civil Rights Movement and the New
Left* (New York: Random House, 1979).

62. See Betty Friedan, *The Feminine Mystique* (New York: Dell, 1963).

while consumer items complicated and, in effect, expanded it again. Laundry could be done by an automatic machine, but it required the appropriate detergents, bleaches, and rinses to meet changing standards of cleanliness. Children spent their days in school and afternoon at the playground, but a model mother had to be constantly available—both physically, to drive car pools, lead Scout troops, entertain bored children, and emotionally, to avoid inflicting irreparable psychic damage. There were no monetary rewards to this calling, and it gave rise to an increasing sense of boredom. Here was the real oppression decried by the second feminist movement. A wife's dignity seemed nonexistent in the modern household of chores and became entirely parasitical upon her husband's social and economic status.[63] It was against this "silent oppression" that feminist theologians aimed their chief theological artillery.

In each of these movements the language of "liberation" came to the fore as the conceptual place-marker for the older theological language of "salvation." The experience of women or blacks or the poor served as the fundamental theological touchstone. Salvation was defined in terms of liberation from these peculiar forms of oppression. Though disagreeing in some of the particulars, Latin American liberation theologians, black theologians, and feminist theologians share several soteriological tendencies. These "family resemblances" are the reason why all three movements eventually came to be grouped as liberation theologies. We will continue that usage despite the particularities that make each distinctive.

Freedom from oppression was at the core of the concept of liberation. Oppression was defined in terms of sexism, racism, and economic discrimination. Put in positive terms, liberation can also be defined as humanization, the process by which people discover and realize forms of common life that contribute to human flourishing.[64] The goal of all genuine liberation is for people to be treated as subjects and not as objects of manipulation. Liberation contributes to the shaping of a community that encourages the humanization process. Persons become what they authentically desire to be, analogous to what psychologists refer to as self-actualization. Impossible apart from the community of liberated persons, the divine work is radically this-worldly in orientation. God's mission is coextensive with the series of human choices by which persons find their fundamental identity and dignity.[65]

These notions of liberation have a deeply social or corporate character to them. Frustrated with the ever-present corrupting individualism in modern society,

63. A thoughtful account of the cultural forces at work in the origins of early feminism is Christopher Lasch, *Women and the Common Life: Love, Marriage and Feminism* (New York: Norton, 1997).
64. This is especially clear in feminist theology. See Letty M. Russell, *Human Liberation in a Feminist Perspective: A Theology* (Philadelphia: Westminster, 1974).
65. Gutiérrez writes, "Salvation is not something otherworldly. . . . The center of God's salvific design is Jesus Christ who by his death and resurrection transforms the universe and makes it possible for man to reach fulfillment as a human being" (*Theology of Liberation*, 151).

liberation theologians questioned the foundations of the social and political order of the modern world and the modern West in particular. Their ideological critique was rooted in the conviction that Western individualism was dehumanizing because it isolated people from their natural social structures. It permitted and even encouraged oppression because it created systems wherein individuals reigned supreme over all else, even over other individuals.[66] The executive climbing the corporate ladder must of necessity trample over others in order to keep climbing. In a world where everyone is out to claim their own, invariably others are oppressed in the achievement of that goal. This oppression typically falls along either social (i.e., racial, sexual, and ethnic) or economic (i.e., class) lines.

These soteriologies included the conviction that the biblical message for the present age demanded the liberation of all people. One ought no longer to draw lines of distinction between those inside and outside the church but now between oppressed and oppressors. Sexism or racism or economic discrimination as the defining evil leads inevitably to these transformationist notions of salvation as liberation. As part of the theological project, other forms of ideological critique functioned as descriptive means to illuminate the deep structures of oppression. Liberation can never be reduced to mere individual freedoms, but must contain the elements of systemic change and reorientation.[67] This analysis of social systems is not provided by the tools of theology but rather is underwritten by postcolonial political theory, deconstructionist literary theory, and other critical ideologies that provide a means to display the entrenched social and political order of the West. Theology then becomes the means of explaining the process by which this may be worked out.

Relational Soteriologies and Justification

If transformationist soteriologies have been most forcefully defended by liberation theologies, relational soteriologies in the second half of the twentieth century have been dominated by discussion about justification. That discussion has largely been shaped by the diverse interpretive trajectories of the history of theological discussion on justification prior to the twentieth century. Somewhat unique among the other theological loci, contemporary developments of the doctrine of justification have largely been framed in conversation with and against long-standing traditions of interpretation.[68]

66. Feminist theologies were particularly critical of hierarchies of authority wherein individuals held power over other individuals. See Letty M. Russell, *Household of Freedom: Authority in Feminist Theology* (Philadelphia: Westminster, 1987).

67. This is especially clear in Latin American liberation theology. See Jon Sobrino, *Spirituality of Liberation: Toward Political Holiness* (Maryknoll, NY: Orbis, 1988).

68. On the history of the development of the doctrine of justification, see the two-volume work by Alister E. McGrath, *Iustitia Dei: A History of the Christian Doctrine of Justification* (Cambridge: Cambridge University Press, 2005).

Did Luther and/or later Lutheranism capture the breadth of the biblical material on salvation? Was the depiction of justification by faith alone peculiar to Reformation-era discussions, or was it a part of the great tradition? What role did theologies of merit play in Reformation-era discussions of justification? Was justification the central dogma, a central doctrine, or an important theme of soteriology in Protestant history? How do current Protestant–Roman Catholic discussions on justification interpret or reinterpret historic conflicts between Protestants and Roman Catholics? Where do Anabaptist and Wesleyan traditions feed into the evangelical consensus on salvation across the twentieth century? How does the Eastern Orthodox (relative) silence on the doctrine of justification relate to the Protestant–Roman Catholic dialogues and controversies on justification?[69]

Each of these questions has helped frame the contemporary theological discussions about justification—that doctrine, Luther claimed, by which the church stands or falls.[70] The familiar Protestant theological narrative supposed that Luther was consumed by an anxiety in the face of a holy and righteous God. This sense of dread reached a climax, according to Luther, as he struggled through the precise meaning of Rom. 1:17, "For in it the righteousness of God is revealed through faith for faith; as it is written, 'He who through faith is righteous shall live.'" In an emotional encounter with the text and ultimately with God himself, Luther concluded that a sinner is justified through faith alone. Divine righteousness was no longer an enemy but an ally because of the cross of Christ. "The righteousness of God is that by which the righteous lives by a gift of God, namely by faith."[71] Luther asserted that justification is *imputed* (counted as ours) on the basis of an alien righteousness—namely, the righteousness of Christ. It is a declaration of God that though humans remain sinners, they are justified sinners. "By a wonderful exchange our sins are no longer ours but Christ's, and the righteousness of Christ is not Christ's but ours. He has emptied himself of his righteousness that he might clothe us with it."[72]

As we know, Luther's "discovery" of justification by faith was not joyously received in official quarters of Western Christendom. Luther and his doctrine were repudiated at the Council of Trent (1545–1563). This council more than any other defined the Protestant controversy, and the terms by which theologians still speak of the controversy continue to emerge in large measure from the canons of Trent. Forty-four particular and sixty-one general assemblies were devoted to examining the question of justification. The final decree that

69. A helpful introduction to soteriology amidst all of the diverse Christian traditions can be found in Rienk Lanooy, ed., *For Us and For Our Salvation: Seven Perspectives on Christian Soteriology* (Utrecht: Interuniversitair Instituut voor Missiologie en Oecumenica, 1994).

70. There is an interesting literature debate as to whether Luther framed the issue in precisely this way. For the best account see McGrath, *Iustitia Dei*, 1:vii.

71. Martin Luther, *Works* (St. Louis: Concordia, 1955–1986), 34:336.

72. Ibid., 5:608.

resulted underwent three successive editions. These long discussions can be in part explained by the doctrinal uncertainty on justification in the pre-Reformation era of Catholicism. The council concluded that justification was "the grace of God by which an unjust person becomes just"; that is, "it is not only the remission of sins, but also the sanctification and renewal of the inner man by the voluntary acceptance of the grace and of the gifts whereby the unjust man becomes just, the enemy a friend."[73] Trent affirmed that righteousness must *inhere* in the individual rather than merely be imputed. There can be no mere "legal fiction" whereby God declares the unrighteous righteous on the basis of someone else's (Jesus's) righteousness.

Framing of the debate in this manner has reverberated into the twentieth century and serves as the touchstone for most current discussion. It would, however, be unfair to the prior four centuries to suppose that theological discussion simply repristinated the Reformation era debates. Rich and subtle theological tomes on a host of topics related to justification abounded in the centuries after the sixteenth century, but unfortunately that discussion was lost on much of the theological guild of the twentieth century. New perspectives were new only to those who weren't familiar with the conflicted discussions of prior centuries. Added to this confusion was the evangelical resistance to theological traditions in anything but superficial ways, and the opposite though reinforcing tendencies of liberal Protestants to be freed from the traditions of earlier Protestants.

It is somewhat arbitrary to isolate specific episodes in the twentieth century by which the prior theological consensus on justification began to crumble. Surely the Second Vatican Council (1961–1964) signaled a new era in ecumenical discussions between Rome and the major bodies of Protestantism.[74] The consequent forty years of official ecumenical dialogues have resulted in several groundbreaking accords between Rome and individual Protestant denominations or coalitions of denominations.[75] Of particular concern to the debates on justification is the *Joint Declaration on the Doctrine of Justification* by the Lutheran World Federation and the Roman Catholic Church in 1999.[76] It was not an ordinarily styled confession, but rather a series of statements that outlined the debates about justification in terms of mutual appreciation rather than official condemnation.[77] The preamble suggestively says,

73. Sixth Session, sec. 7, *The Canons and Decrees of the Sacred and Oecumenical Council of Trent*, trans. J. Waterworth (London: Dolman, 1848).

74. An early perceptive study of the Second Vatican Council is G. C. Berkouwer, *The Second Vatican Council and the New Catholicism*, trans. Lewis B. Smedes (Grand Rapids: Eerdmans, 1965).

75. A helpful overview of these discussions from the Protestant perspective can be found in Mark Noll and Carolyn Nystrom, *Is the Reformation Over? An Evangelical Assessment of Contemporary Roman Catholicism* (Grand Rapids: Baker Academic, 2005).

76. *Joint Declaration on the Doctrine of Justification: The Lutheran World Federation and the Roman Catholic Church* (Grand Rapids: Eerdmans, 2000).

77. The best treatment of the *Joint Declaration* in historical perspective is Anthony N. S. Lane, *Justification by Faith in Catholic-Protestant Dialogue* (New York: T&T Clark, 2006).

The subscribing Lutheran churches and the Roman Catholic Church are now able to articulate a common understanding of our justification by God's grace through faith in Christ. It does not cover all that either church teaches about justification; it does encompass a consensus on basic truths of the doctrine of justification and shows that the remaining differences in its explication are no longer the occasion for doctrinal condemnations. (Preamble, para. 5)

It is striking that the *Joint Declaration* could affirm, "By grace alone, in faith in Christ's saving work and not because of merits on our part, we are accepted by God. Whatever in the justified precedes or follows the free gift of faith is neither the basis of justification nor merits it."[78] The clear indication was that justification had been loosed from its moorings in the medieval framework of merit. Whatever else justification was, it was not the result of any merit on the part of sinners. Equally striking was the silence on the precise meaning of justification by the Lutherans. There was barely a mention of *sola fide* in the document, nor of the disputes about imputation. Was justification by faith alone or not? Was righteousness the sort of thing about which it was appropriate to say that it could be "counted on behalf of sinners"? Answers to these questions remained ambiguous.

An accord on the historically divisive issue of justification was likely reached in the *Joint Declaration* because of the common commitment to a christocentric rendering of salvation. Throughout, the emphasis was upon "Christ who is our righteousness" rather than upon the recipients or the means of that righteousness. Such a christocentric cast allowed Catholics to affirm that "justifying grace never becomes a human possession to which one could appeal over against God," while yet maintaining the inherent righteousness of Christ indwelling believers.[79] Righteousness is not a possession of the believer but always and only a possession of God. Inherent in believers, nonetheless righteousness does not belong to them.

The christocentric cast allowed Lutherans to define justification in part as "being made righteous" and thereby to downplay the forensic character of earlier Lutheran confessional statements about justification. Justification is about the forgiveness of sins and the gift of life, rather than an explicitly legal declaration of God about the covenantal status of sinners. Attention was drawn to Christ, on account of whom the declaration of forgiveness is made. Therefore, "only in union with Christ is one's life renewed."[80]

In retrospect, the *Joint Declaration* was much more conflicted than many originally supposed and much more than appeared on the surface of the

78. *Joint Declaration*, 3.15.
79. *Joint Declaration*, 4.3.27. Cf. Henri Blocher, "The Lutheran-Catholic Declaration on Justification," in *Justification in Perspective: Historical Developments and Contemporary Challenges*, ed. Bruce McCormack (Grand Rapids: Baker Academic, 2006), 197–217.
80. *Joint Declaration*, 4.2.23.

document. Merely a month prior to the official signing of the *Joint Declaration*, when the official Catholic response was delivered, it nearly derailed the entire accord.[81] It raised serious doubts as to whether the Catholic Church would officially affirm the Lutheran positions on justification as articulated in the *Joint Declaration*. And if those could not be affirmed, then the anathemas could not be removed. Strangely, however, the Roman Catholic magisterium permitted the *Joint Declaration* to go forward, and there is considerable speculation as to why it did. Perhaps Avery Dulles's words come the closest to comprehending the papal reluctance about the doctrinal convergence and yet papal affirmation of the document that declared the convergence. In a well-known response, Cardinal Dulles wrote,

> These considerations [regarding a common witness to the world] I think, are behind the eagerness of the Catholic Church, at the very highest level, to sign the Joint Declaration, even while recognizing that theologians have not yet been able to establish how, or to what extent, certain Lutheran positions can be reconciled with official Catholic teaching. It is not enough to say that we have different frameworks of discourse. It is necessary to establish that Lutheran proclamation and Catholic speculation are both legitimate derivatives of the same gospel, and therefore compatible.[82]

There were dialogues between Rome and other Protestant bodies during the decades following Vatican II. The Anglican–Roman Catholic dialogues (ARCIC I & II) as well as the Evangelical-Catholic dialogues (ECT I & II) addressed the issue of justification at length, but not with the binding character of the *Joint Declaration*, nor with the dynamic tension of the *Joint Declaration*.[83] The Catholic-Orthodox dialogues left the issue of justification almost entirely off the table. Undoubtedly the most important for soteriology have been the Lutheran–Roman Catholic dialogues.

A primary locus of attention prior to Vatican II and which therefore stands prior to these ecumenical dialogues on justification was Hans Küng's influential work, *Justification*.[84] Its subtitle, *The Doctrine of Karl Barth and a Catholic Reflection*, suggestively put Roman Catholicism in dialogue with the central

---

81. For an insightful commentary on the internal discussions among Catholics, including the official Catholic response, see Avery Dulles, "Two Languages of Salvation: The Lutheran-Catholic Joint Declaration," in *First Things*, no. 98 (December 1999): 25–30.

82. Ibid., 29.

83. The ARCIC documents can be found in *Rome and Canterbury: The Final ARCIC Report* (Oxford: Latimer House, 1982). The ECT documents can be found as follows: ECT I, "The Christian Mission in the Third Millenium," *First Things* (May 1994): 15–21; ECT II, "The Gift of Salvation," *Christianity Today*, December 8, 1997, 35–37.

84. Hans Küng, *Justification: The Doctrine of Karl Barth and a Catholic Reflection*, trans. Thomas Collins, Edmund Tolk, and David Granskou (1957; repr., Philadelphia: Westminster, 1981).

Protestant theologian of the twentieth century. Küng's contention was that the historic divisions over the doctrine of justification were primarily caused by two dialectically opposed but intrinsically compatible forms of discourse. Comparing the tendencies of the two theological traditions, Küng wrote, "No particular gradient (tradition) ought to claim absolute authority; the water can pour into the valley by many different routes."[85] On Küng's rendering, only the Scriptures are the "all encompassing ocean, alive and yet at rest." For the next four decades, the ecumenical dialogues inevitably had to wrestle with this vexing question of diverse theological discourses, all of which allege to have originated from the Scriptures.

This issue of the "language" of salvation was put forcefully on the table by a peculiar trajectory in New Testament studies, which we have now come familiarly (and unfairly) to call the New Perspective. It is peculiar only in the sense that New Testament exegetes purporting to stay close only to the text of Scripture have in fact offered a grand synthesis of biblical theology at odds with some of the Protestant trajectories on justification. Reacting against popular stereotypes of the Lutheran doctrine of justification in the 1950s, Krister Stendahl repudiated subjectivist notions of Luther's guilty conscience as the key to understanding the New Testament materials.[86] Stendahl supposed that Luther cemented the "introspective turn" into Western Christianity, and the result was an overly individualized, subjective rendering of the Christian faith. Stendahl may have mistaken Bultmann for Luther; nonetheless, he caused many to wonder whether Protestant traditions had misappropriated the New Testament's language of justification because of prior cultural commitments.

The narrative of the New Perspective has been well told and can only be rehearsed here in brief.[87] A reassessment of first-century (i.e., Second Temple) Judaism in the work of E. P. Sanders, *Paul and Palestinian Judaism*, initiated the movement.[88] Sanders's contention was that the pattern of religion found among the Jews of Jesus's day was fundamentally concerned with the historical covenant Yahweh had made with the Jews at Sinai. Sanders used the term "covenantal nomism" to describe this pattern of religion wherein Israel's chief concern was not works righteousness, as Luther supposed, but rather fidelity to the covenant stipulations on the basis of which God would remain

85. Ibid., 278.

86. Cf. Krister Stendahl, "The Apostle Paul and the Introspective Conscience of the West," in *Harvard Theological Review* 56, no. 3 (1963): 199–215.

87. The two best critical overviews of the New Perspective are Francis Watson, *Paul, Judaism and the Gentiles: Beyond the New Perspective* (Grand Rapids: Eerdmans, 2007), and Seyoon Kim, *Paul and the New Perspective: Second Thoughts on the Origin of Paul's Gospel* (Grand Rapids: Eerdmans, 2001). The fullest bibliography of the New Perspective can be found in Michael Bird, *The Saving Righteousness of God: Studies on Paul, Justification and the New Perspective* (Milton Keynes, UK: Paternoster, 2007).

88. E. P. Sanders, *Paul and Palestinian Judaism: A Comparison of Patterns of Religion* (London: SCM, 1977).

faithful to Israel. Serving as an expression of the covenant with God, the law primarily spelled out what was appropriate conduct in the covenant. God required obedience to the law not as a condition of entry into the covenant, but rather as the criterion for continuing in the covenant. Jews entered the covenant solely by the grace of God. Staying in the covenant, however, was a matter of obedience. In this regard the hope of salvation for Jews rested upon their status as members of God's covenant people. Sanders was also convinced that the sharp division between the apostle Paul and the Jews of his day as alleged by much of Western Christianity across the centuries was more apparent than factual. Paul, like most first-century Jews, was loyal to the covenant and differed simply on the question of the messiah. Was Jesus the savior of Jews and gentiles or not? That was the dividing question between Paul and the Jews. They did not disagree about "getting in by grace, and staying in by obedience."

James Dunn and N. T. Wright are perhaps the most influential of the New Perspective authors, extending Sanders's reassessment of Second Temple Judaism in distinctively theological ways.[89] Dunn has argued that the phrase "the righteousness of God" in the New Testament ought to be understood as a place-marker for divine faithfulness—most concretely, God's faithfulness to the covenant with the Jews.[90] From this angle, the older Protestant-Catholic debates about justification are somewhat beside the point. Justification is neither about reckoning people as righteous (Protestants) or making people righteous (Catholic). Divine righteousness/faithfulness is the reality that God is faithful to his people, and when these people come into this reality they cannot help but be changed by it. Divine righteousness is not a legal or forensic term as such, and so the questions about people having or lacking sufficient righteousness as they appear before the tribunal of the divine court is to misunderstand Paul, according to Dunn.

N. T. Wright's contribution to the New Perspective is long and complex. As with Dunn and Sanders, Wright has insisted that the Old Testament backgrounds are essential if we are to understand Jesus correctly. Second Temple Judaism is the immediate historical context for understanding Jesus, but Wright has trenchantly argued that every one of the apostles, as well as most of the Jews of Jesus's day, interpreted the events of the first century against the backdrop of Torah. These first five books of Scripture provided the theological framework to interpret contemporary events, and so it was not accidental that Jesus's apostles would interpret his messianic mission as a second exodus.

---

89. The collected essays of Dunn across the whole development of the New Perspective can be found in James D. G. Dunn, *The New Perspective on Paul* (Grand Rapids: Eerdmans, 2008). Wright's best summary of the New Perspective is N. T. Wright, *What St. Paul Really Said: Was Paul of Tarsus the Real Founder of Christianity?* (Grand Rapids: Eerdmans, 1997).

90. See James D. G. Dunn, *Jesus, Paul, and the Law: Studies in Mark and Galatians* (Louisville: Westminster John Knox, 1990).

Jesus was bringing God's covenant people back from exile into the immediate presence of God. The real problem for Jews in the first century was not an alleged conviction that they could earn God's favor by being morally upright, but rather their commitment to a perverted nationalism by which they supposed the long awaited exodus applied only to Jews. Both the Jews and the apostles believed that entry into the covenant was by grace alone. In dispute was the issue as to who was in covenant with God. The apostles claimed that all those who trust in Jesus as their Messiah would be saved. They did not have any mechanism in mind by which Jesus's perfect obedience was counted as their obedience and by which salvation could be merited.

> If we use the language of the law court, it makes no sense whatever to say that the judge imputes, imparts, bequeaths, conveys or otherwise transfers his righteousness to either the plaintiff or the defendant. Righteousness is not an object, a substance or a gas which can be passed around the courtroom.[91]

According to Wright, Jesus died as the representative Messiah of Israel. He was vindicated or justified by the resurrection. Faithful even in death, Jesus was not abandoned to the grave by the Father, but brought back to life. And being brought back to life, Jesus also brought those who believe in him back from exile. The principal message is not that Jesus suffered the curse of the law on our behalf, nor that his righteousness is imputed to us, enabling us to be reckoned by God as innocent and holy. Rather, the good news is that Jesus rescued his people from exile and they dwell in the presence of the living God.

Wright has (rightly) expressed misgivings about the notion of a uniform New Perspective movement in which all the members agree to a simple, quick, and easy digestible summary.[92] The work of Sanders, Dunn, and Wright is massive, complex, and quite diverse. These scholars have done the Christian community great service in asking afresh important historical and theological questions and not permitting the canon of Scripture to be left simply to the dustbin of historical enquiry. But while reminding us that history and theology must go hand in hand, and while making us more sympathetic to the actual historical context of first-century Judaism, they have been less successful in appropriating the history of interpretation across the centuries, often misunderstanding or misrepresenting leading theologians in the history of the church.[93] Neither have

91. Wright, *What St. Paul Really Said*, 98.
92. Wright's recent work, *Justification: God's Plan and Paul's Vision* (Downers Grove, IL: InterVarsity, 2009), includes an autobiographical account of the New Perspective in which Wright makes it clear that it is improper to speak of a coherent and cohesive movement. See chap. 1.
93. Wright often writes as if the whole of the Christian tradition has misunderstood the gospel and he alone has got it right. "In ways that the Western tradition, Catholic and Protestant, Lutheran and Calvinist—yes, and Anglican too!—has often failed to recognize, Scripture forms a massive and powerful story whose climax is the coming into the world of the unique Son of the one true Creator God, and, above all, his death for sins and his bodily resurrection from the

they forged nor do they allege to have forged a consensus in New Testament scholarship about the exact contours of Pauline soteriology. Rather, they have reinvigorated age-old discussions about the immediate historical context of Pauline soteriology as well as the canonical shape of that soteriology.

Soteriology and Union with Christ

It is not an uncommon claim today that the primary umbrella under which the New Testament places its doctrine of salvation is "union with Christ." Being united to Christ is the key to understand the ways in which salvation plays out. That "union" could be understood in a multitude of ways: as a union by faith (by faith believers are united to Christ), as a relational union (having a personal relationship with Christ), as a mystical union (believers are united to Christ in the Spirit), as an ontological union (believers share in the divine nature), as a cosmic victory over the powers of darkness that unites believers to Christ, as a legal union with Christ (by which he suffers the punishment owing to sinners and they in turn are legally accounted innocent), as a familial union (being adopted into the family of God), or as a covenant union (believers are brought into covenant with God).[94] In other words, there are a host of contexts in which the New Testament uses the language of being "in Christ." As Michael Horton helpfully writes,

> The theme of union with Christ brings together the temporal tenses of our salvation—past, present, and future—as well as the objective and subjective, historical and existential, corporate and individual, forensic and transformative, and a unilateral gift that establishes a reciprocal relationship of faithful speaking and answering with the covenant as the nucleus of cosmic renewal.[95]

Some ninety times the little phrase "in Christ" appears in the New Testament and seems to point at the reality that Christ is the key to salvation, and that this "key" is rich and profound enough to require many diverse facets to be illuminated. In mapping modern theology, however, the emphasis upon union with Christ has often been framed over and against imputation and infusion. When union with Christ is understood in distinction from relational and transformationist soteriologies, the consequent notion of salvation is referred to as participationist. An influential representative of contemporary participationist soteriology is the New Finnish school. Its central voice, Tuomo Mannermaa,

---

dead," *Justification*, 250. It is unfortunate that Wright has not wrestled with the breadth and depth of historical discussions in which this very issue has been central.

94. A helpful discussion of the variety of ways in which the language of union functions is Veli-Matti Kärkkäinen, *One with God: Salvation as Deification and Justification* (Collegeville, MN: Liturgical Press, 2004).

95. Michael Horton, *Covenant and Salvation* (Louisville: Westminster John Knox, 2007), 131.

has argued at considerable length that Luther himself was far more interested in participationist accounts of soteriology, in which "union with Christ" was central, than had previously been allowed.[96] So much so that it may be said of Luther that he should not be classified among the Lutherans on the doctrine of salvation. Calvin likewise has come under critical scrutiny, and T. F. Torrance has argued in recent decades that Calvin's loyalty to the "mystical union" at the heart of salvation was far greater than his commitment to the forensic pictures of justification.[97] It is likely a false dilemma to read into either Luther or Calvin the choice of "union" or "justification." However, it is vital to reckon with the way in which discussion of "union" language has forged strange new alliances in modern theology, wherein Luther is regarded in some circles as closer to Eastern Orthodoxy than he is to Protestant orthodoxy, and Calvin is pitted against the Reformed tradition. These interpretations of the Protestant Reformers concern us only insofar as they illuminate the map of soteriology in the contemporary context.[98]

Whatever else Christ does on the sinner's behalf, it is by being brought into union with Christ that the benefits of his life, death, and resurrection pass onto us. The question persists, though, how do these benefits "pass on" to believers? Both participationist and forensic accounts of salvation start with the assumption that God is the one from whom salvation begins, and that the originating intentions of salvation have to do with the divine character as opposed to salvation being a "plan B" after the apparent "mistake" of human sin and corruption. In other words, it has been a recurrent theme in contemporary soteriology to emphasize divine life (in participationist soteriologies) and divine justice (in forensic soteriologies) as the framework within which doctrines of salvation fit. To put it simply, the eternal God is the starting point for salvation. It is God who saves; it is creatures who are saved. Locating the nature and character of salvation in God in the first place protects salvation from becoming a human project in which God may (or may not) participate. In what follows, we draw attention to prominent participationist accounts of soteriology in Eastern Orthodoxy and in the revisionist Lutheran scholar, Tuomo Mannermaa (i.e., Finnish school). Finally we end with a brief summary of John Milbank and the movement called Radical Orthodoxy.

---

96. See most especially Tuomo Mannermaa, *Christ Present in Faith: Luther's View of Justification* (Minneapolis: Fortress, 2005).

97. See T. F. Torrance, *The Mediation of Christ* (Grand Rapids: Eerdmans, 1983).

98. By most accounts these are minority reports among Luther scholars and Calvin scholars. The revisionist interpretations of Luther and Calvin have had far greater influence in the theological guild than among historians. For a classic defense of Luther as a Lutheran see Robert Kolb, *Martin Luther: Confessor of the Faith* (New York: Oxford University Press, 2009). On Calvin see Richard A. Muller, *The Unaccommodated Calvin: Studies in the Foundation of a Theological Tradition* (New York: Oxford University Press, 2000).

Eastern Orthodoxy

It is not uncommon to suppose that *the* distinctive doctrine in Eastern Orthodoxy is "theosis." Put simply, theosis is the claim that believers participate or share in the divine nature as a consequence of salvation. Though we must safeguard against the notion that theosis functions as the central dogma among the Eastern Orthodox, it is nonetheless important to affirm that central to the Eastern Orthodox soteriologies is the claim that humans participate quite literally in the divine life. Humans, in this qualified sense, become divine. They do not take on the full range of divine attributes, but rather share in the actual divine life of the Triune God. This is often called deification. Athanasius's famous words serve as the touchstone of the doctrine: "He [the Word of God] became human that we might become God."[99] In Christ, the fullness of the divine life is interwoven with the fully constituted human nature. In the incarnation, the divine life is "shared" with humanity. The incarnation, in this sense, is the central redemptive event in Eastern Orthodoxy. However, in recent Eastern Orthodox thinkers like John Zizioulas and Dumitru Staniloae, deification must be understood not simply in the immediate temporal location of the incarnation, nor as just the primary act of redemption for humanity, but rather as the eternal intention of the creative act of God and the fulfillment of the original creation of humankind.[100] Theosis is not so much the solution to the problem of the fall of humankind, but rather the goal of creation from the very beginning. God created the world to unite it to himself.

The Eastern Orthodox often speak of theosis as an ontological or metaphysical change. Humans share in the divine being itself as opposed to merely being acquitted in a divine courtroom. Humans take on something essential to God—namely his life. On this point the center of controversy between the East and the West most often ensues. The ontological claim of theosis (participation in the divine) often carries a Neoplatonic cast whereby the creature takes on actual characteristics of the Creator, and the distinction between creature and Creator is minimized. There are various "levels" of divine life in which the creature shares. There is no fundamental ontological chasm between creature and Creator. On this rendering, the Western churches (Protestant and Catholic) parted company with Eastern Orthodoxy. They were ill-disposed to think of the creature's relation to God as one of ontological union. Protestants more often have parsed "union with Christ" as a union that is covenantal (i.e.,

99. Athanasius, *On the Incarnation of the Word*, in *The Christology of the Later Fathers*, ed. Edward Hardy (Louisville: Westminster John Knox, 1995), 54.

100. See John Zizioulas, *Being as Communion* (Crestwood, NY: St. Vladimir's Seminary Press, 1985); and *Lectures in Christian Dogmatics* (Edinburgh: T&T Clark, 2008); Dumitru Staniloae, "Image, Likeness and Deification in the Human Person," *Communio* 13, no. 1 (Spring 1986): 64–83; and *The World, Creation and Deification*, vol. 2, *The Experience of God: Orthodox Dogmatic Theology*, trans. and ed. Ioan Ionita and Robert Barringer (Brookline, MA: Holy Cross Orthodox Press, 1994).

inclusion) or legal (i.e., acquittal) or familial (i.e., adoption). Roman Catholics have tended to think of union language as pointing toward a moral union (i.e., righteousness). What Eastern Orthodoxy shares with Roman Catholicism on this point is the actual transformation (the former ontological, the latter moral) of humans as the ground of their union with God in Christ. Protestants have been cautious about these ontological and causal grammars expressing the realities of salvation in Christ. Is the actual transformation of believers prior to or antecedent to their union with Christ? Is the ground of union to be found in the transformations of believers or in the declarations of God?

As a means to protect the Creator/creature distinction, recent Eastern Orthodox writers like Vladimir Lossky and John Meyendorff have tried to revive and defend the older distinction found in Gregory Palamas (1296–1359) between the divine energies and the divine essence.[101] The divine essence is God's immutable characteristics that are not shared in any way with his creatures. God's energies refer to his actions in the world. They are not something that exists apart from God. They are God himself as he reveals himself to us. The creature is able to know God not in his divine essence, but rather because of the divine actions. These actions are manifestations of God himself in direct relationship to his creation. When persons are "saved" they are saved by a direct experience of God himself. They come into full contact with God himself, and his life becomes their life. They are not deified in the sense that they take on God's essence. This remains always hidden to them and inaccessible. Rather, they take on God's energies and are deified in this sense. God's life is their life genuinely and literally. In the Palamite tradition, everything God revealed of himself (the divine energies) in the economy of salvation is disclosed in the incarnation of Christ and is that which every true Christian inherits. The fullness of God's life in the human nature of Jesus is the very same life in which every genuine Christian shares. This is the meaning of 2 Pet. 1:4—which affirms that believers "become partakers of the divine nature."

What are the key differences between this conception of salvation in Eastern Orthodoxy and that of Western Christianity? Eastern Orthodoxy wants to see the grace of salvation as an extension of the presence of God in creation. Western Christianity (both Protestant and Catholic) has conceived of the grace of salvation as an operation of God distinct from the acts of God in creating the world. Eastern traditions have thought of salvation as on a continuum with creation, whereas the Western traditions have tended to think of salvation as a distinctively different sort of divine action from creation. Protestant orthodoxy has tended to think, in accord with the Eastern traditions, that the economy of salvation is not in the first place about the transformations of

101. Vladimir Lossky, *The Mystical Theology of the Eastern Church* (London: James Clark, 1957); John Meyendorff, *A Study of Gregory Palamas* (London: Faith Press, 1964); *Byzantine Theology* (New York: Fordham University Press, 1974).

believers, but rather about their relationship to God. Catholics in accord with the Eastern traditions have thought about the relationship of the church to God in ontological or metaphysical fashion, rather than declarative or legal. Western Christendom has also thought of Christ's death and resurrection as the defining act of salvation, whereas the Eastern Church has thought of Christ's incarnation as the defining act of salvation. Eastern Orthodox Bishop Kallistos Ware sums up,

> The cross is central, but it can only be understood in the light of what goes before—of Christ's taking up into himself of our entire human nature at his birth—and likewise in the light of what comes afterwards, the resurrection, ascension and second coming. Any theology of salvation that concentrates narrowly on the cross at the expense of the resurrection, is bound to seem unbalanced to Orthodoxy.[102]

Luther Revisited: The Finnish Influence

An important parenthetical note needs to be added to our account of the significance of theosis in modern soteriologies. There has arisen in the last twenty-five years a significant and controversial rereading of Luther on the doctrine of justification. Several Finnish and American scholars suggest that Luther (as opposed to later Lutherans) should be seen as affirming a strong doctrine of theosis, believing that the framework of theosis encompasses Luther's more important writings on justification. The most significant voice in this radical rereading of Luther is the Finnish theologian Tuomo Mannermaa.[103] While there are slight differences with Mannermaa, it is also important to signal the importance of American Lutheran theologians Carl Braaten and Robert Jenson in the revisioning of Luther's doctrine of salvation.[104] What Mannermaa has argued is that the dominant early twentieth-century German interpreters of Luther (Karl Holl most especially[105]) read Luther through a neo-Kantian lens, which unfairly left Luther without any interest in metaphysics or ontology. On this dominant German reading, Luther could not say anything about the divine being, about the real presence of Christ, or about God in the believer. At most, Luther was left with a merely forensic understanding of

---

102. Kallistos Ware, "Salvation in the Orthodox Tradition," in *For Us and for Our Salvation*, ed. Rienk Lanooy (Utrecht: Interuniversitair Instituut voor Missiologie en Oecumenica, 1994), 121.

103. See Tuomo Mannermaa, *Christ Present in Faith: Luther's View of Justification* (Minneapolis: Fortress, 2005).

104. See Carl Braaten and Robert Jenson, eds., *Union with Christ: The New Finnish Interpretation of Luther* (Grand Rapids: Eerdmans, 1998). For the definitive statement of Jenson's understanding of participation, see his *Systematic Theology* (New York: Oxford University Press, 1997–1999), esp. 2:250–69.

105. Cf. Karl Holl, *The Distinctive Elements in Christianity*, trans. Norman V. Hope (Edinburgh: T&T Clark, 1937).

justification. But according to Mannermaa and the Helsinki school, Luther had a robust ontology informed by his late medieval context. On this revised reading of Luther, the Reformer was convinced that Christ was really (i.e., ontologically) present in the believer. "In faith itself Christ himself is present."[106] There was no dichotomy in the original Luther between the forensic aspect of justification and the transformative dimensions of sanctification. Both sides of this divide are reunited by Mannermaa in Luther's understanding of the mystical union of Christ with the believer. Because of the real presence of Christ in the believer, there is no tension between the action of God whereby the sinner is declared just, and the action of God wherein this declaration is the formative reality of the sinner. Sinners become what they are declared to be because of Christ in them. Christ is genuinely present in the believer by faith in a manner that produces an ontological change in the believer. This ontological change amounts to a sharing of the divine attributes of life and love and righteousness with believers. "Christ himself, both his person and his work, is the righteousness of man before God. Faith means justification precisely on the basis of Christ's person being present in it."[107]

As there is no actual separation between Christ's person and his work, so there is no actual separation between the grounds of justification (Christ's righteousness—as really present by faith in the believer) and the grounds of sanctification (Christ's righteousness being really present in the believer). There would be no justification without the indwelling presence of Christ, nor would there be any sanctification without the indwelling presence of Christ. In classical Lutheranism, justification is prior to sanctification precisely because its grounds (the finished work of Christ) are prior to the grounds for sanctification (the ongoing work of the Spirit in the believer). For Mannermaa's Luther, the believer's righteousness is constituted not by an imputation of Christ's righteousness but by an actual ontological participation of the believer in Christ's righteousness. Jenson summarizes this new Lutheran approach to salvation:

> Faith makes righteous (1) because believing what God says fulfills the first and great commandment; (2) because the soul that hearkens to the word becomes what the word is, holy and right; and (3) because in faith the soul is united with Christ as a bride with the groom, to be "one body" with him and so possess his righteousness.[108]

There is no mention of imputation in the summary, nor any forensic or legal imagery. Salvation is what Christ is, in the believer. It is easy to see the

106. Mannermaa, *Christ Present in Faith*, 5.

107. Mannermaa, "Theosis as a Subject of Finnish Luther Research," in *Pro Ecclesia* 4, no. 1 (1995), 46.

108. Jenson, "Response" (to Tuomo Mannermaa, "Why Is Luther So Fascinating?"), in *Union with Christ*, 21.

ecumenical possibilities in this "new Luther," most especially with certain dogmatic pronouncements of Eastern Orthodoxy.[109] Additionally, Christ's righteousness is the grounds of justification for this "new Luther," though now in an ontological rather than forensic sense. In this regard, the "new Luther" remains in some important sense Protestant on the question of the moral grounds of one's justification. But unlike the "old Luther," this "new Luther" is Roman Catholic on the question of the imputation/impartation divide. The real presence of Christ is really "in us" and not merely "for us." Though Mannermaa may have opened ecumenical doors between some contemporary Lutherans and the Eastern Orthodox, those doors remain still partially closed on the question of God's being. For the Eastern Orthodox, there is still no reckoning with the full divine essence being shared with believers. Only the divine energies (actions) are "shared" with believers. Anything more would lead dangerously close to the actual equivalence between Creator and creature. However, it is precisely this equivalence "in Christ" which Mannermaa and Jenson have provocatively claimed, and which for them is the key to breaking down the modern ecumenical walls of soteriological separation.

Radical Orthodoxy: A Brief Word

Brief mention needs to be made of the theological tradition now referred to as Radical Orthodoxy.[110] It is represented by the writings of John Milbank, Catherine Pickstock, and Graham Ward, among others.[111] It is less driven by an ecumenical impulse (though it surely has some) than by a philosophical critique of modernity and the metaphysical frameworks that undergird it. The central critique of modernity is that "nature" has its own ontological space quite independent of the ontology of God. According to Milbank this leads to an exaltation of nature and eventually to nihilism in which there is no meaning or purpose because there is no God. The only alternative to nihilism for Radical Orthodoxy is a full Neoplatonic affirmation that all being partici-pates in the divine being, and only to the extent that there is participation is there being at all. Leaving aside the intricacies of the more general theological outlook, it is simply noted here that this robust affirmation of a Neoplatonist understanding of participation leads quite naturally in Radical Orthodoxy to viewing soteriology through the lens of participation. The "problem" to be resolved by Christ is the problem of taking our *eyes* off of God—losing the

---

109. It is important to note that Mannermaa's work arose in the first instance in the context of an ongoing ecumenical dialogue between the Evangelical Lutheran Church of Finland and the Russian Orthodox Church.

110. A helpful introduction to Radical Orthodoxy can be found in James K. A. Smith, *Introducing Radical Orthodoxy: Mapping a Post-Secular Theology* (Grand Rapids: Baker Academic, 2004).

111. See John Milbank, Catherine Pickstock, and Graham Ward, eds., *Radical Orthodoxy: A New Theology* (London: Routledge, 1999).

vision of God that animates our being. Redemption is the regaining of the vision of God in and through which our humanity is restored to its originating participation in the divine being. The gift of grace consists in the restoration of this vision of God by means of restoring the desire to see God for what God is. Redemption remains relatively abstract and philosophical, but still the sovereign gift of God to all of created reality. The gift and the Giver are in some important sense the same—since it is God who restores the vision and God who is the restored vision. Radical Orthodoxy has garnered a set of mixed reviews. Some have lauded their courage in abandoning the central tenets of theological naturalism. Others have been less appreciative of their embrace of Neoplatonism as the only true and genuine Christian metaphysic.

Conclusion

It is safe to say that the map of modern soteriology is far more interesting and complex at the beginning of the twenty-first century than it was at the beginning of the twentieth century. Important tensions persist, but constructive engagements have arisen across a wide range of ecclesial traditions. It is surely less than clear where the new ecumenical impulses will lead on the questions of justification and union with Christ. It is also not clear how the different traditions will continue to relate to church historical discussions and to the canon of Scripture itself.

A half century ago many theologians in the guild believed that talk of "salvation" might just have to be abandoned altogether if Christianity were to survive in the modern world. Paul Tillich famously wrote,

> Indeed it is so strange to the modern man that there is scarcely any way of making it [the doctrine of justification] intelligible to him. We have here a breaking down of tradition that has few parallels. And we should not imagine that it will be possible in some simple fashion to leap over this gulf and resume our connection with the Reformation again.[112]

Whatever else may be said, a half century later, not only have the older debates about justification come alive again, but so has talk of all the other soteriological terms. Renewed interest in God has led to a significant reconsideration of salvation as a distinctly divine act. That in turn has opened doors to think constructively and critically about the ways in which it is appropriate to talk about the divine act that constitutes the heart of the gospel of Jesus Christ. As older conflicts have been revisited about this great divine act, new tensions

---

112. Paul Tillich, *The Protestant Era* (Chicago: University of Chicago Press, 1957), 157. Quoted in Dawn DeVries, "Justification," in *The Oxford Handbook of Systematic Theology*, ed. John Webster, Kathryn Tanner, and Iain Torrance (Oxford: Oxford University Press, 2007), 198.

invariably emerged. At the very least, we should be thankful that our eyes have been lifted upward and not merely inward as we consider the salvation that is ours in Christ.

For Further Reading

Braaten, Carl E., and Robert W. Jenson, eds. *Union with Christ: The New Finnish Interpretation of Luther*. Grand Rapids: Eerdmans, 1998.

Burgess, Joseph, and Marc Kolden, eds. *By Faith Alone: Essays on Justification in Honor of Gerhard O. Forde*. Grand Rapids: Eerdmans, 2004.

Christensen, Michael J., and Jeffery A. Wittung. *Partakers of the Divine Nature: The History and Development of Deification in the Christian Traditions*. Grand Rapids: Baker Academic, 2008.

Horton, Michael S. *Covenant and Salvation: Union with Christ*. Louisville: Westminster John Knox, 2007.

Kärkkäinen, Veli-Matti. *One with God: Salvation as Deification and Justification*. Collegeville, MN: Liturgical Press, 2004.

Lanooy, Rienk, ed. *For Us and for Our Salvation: Seven Perspectives on Christian Soteriology*. Utrecht: Interuniversitair Instituut voor Missiologie en Oecumenica, 1994.

McGrath, Alister E. *Iustitia Dei: A History of the Christian Doctrine of Justification*. 3rd ed. Cambridge: Cambridge University Press, 2005.

Milbank, John. *Being Reconciled: Ontology and Pardon*. London: Routledge, 2003.

Rusch, William G., ed. *Justification and the Future of the Ecumenical Movement: The Joint Declaration on the Doctrine of Justification*. Collegeville, MN: Liturgical Press, 2003.

Staniloae, Dumitru. *The Experience of God: Orthodox Dogmatic Theology*. Vol. 2., *The World: Creation and Deification*. Brookline, MA: Holy Cross Orthodox Press, 2000.

Wright, N. T. *Justification: God's Plan and Paul's Vision*. Downers Grove, IL: InterVarsity, 2008.

12

• • •

CHRISTIAN ETHICS

BRIAN BROCK

Before There Was Christian Ethics: Setting the Stage

To grasp the uniqueness of modern Christian theology, it is crucial to understand the peculiar way that modern theologians have come to understand the relationship of theology and ethics. We must be prepared to notice how infrequently modern systematic theologians draw attention to ethical questions (especially when compared to previous generations of theologians) and how rare it is for Christian ethicists to draw directly on Christian theology. In this chapter I offer one explanation of this state of affairs from the standpoint of the discipline of Christian ethics. Practitioners of that discipline, at least as configured in the United States, have explicitly and systematically distanced themselves from traditional Christian doctrine. Explaining how systematic theology and Christian ethics could have become so estranged from one another demands we begin with a broad overview of several pivotal transitions that have repositioned Christian moral reflection over the centuries. I offer this overview in order to indicate what is peculiar about the modern profile of the discipline, which I will explicate by reference to three of its founding figures, Walter Rauschenbusch (1861–1918) and the Niebuhr brothers, H. Richard (1894–1962) and Reinhold (1892–1971). I will conclude by outlining the criticisms of the discipline levied by one of its most influential representatives,

Stanley Hauerwas (b. 1940), setting his thought, in turn, back into the larger frame with which the chapter began.

Christianity arose as a minority sect in a powerful and pagan empire. This bureaucratic and militaristic empire was shadowed by the philosophical schools carrying the cultural memory and assorted practices of the ancient Greeks; these schools were often idealized and respected as intellectually sophisticated and morally exemplary. Some of the earliest Christian writers to address moral questions, such as Clement of Alexandria (153–217), styled themselves as purveyors of a better philosophy, attempting to assume the mantle of the philosophers as the moral and intellectual paragons of pagan society. Others, such as Tertullian (145–220), rejected both the militaristic majority culture and its inner shadow of Greek philosophy, proposing instead a clear separation between Christian and all forms of pagan morality. What both types of thinker assumed was the dominance of pagan thought. They felt themselves to be defending Christianity from a minority position and conceived their account of Christian life accordingly.

In the West, at least, all this decisively changed with Augustine (354–430), whose powerful theological vision soon came to dominate the Western intellectual landscape. The crumbling of the Roman Empire and the conversion of subsequent emperors as it faded also undermined the patronage on which the philosophical schools depended. The effect was the snuffing out of the old pagan world and the rise of Christian theology as the dominant account of reality. The wide array of religions in the ancient world rested on a dominant belief in a cosmos populated with a pantheon of gods. The dissemination of Augustine's writings, however, and the cultural shifts that came to characterize what is called the Middle Ages, combined to vanquish this paganism. The new "common sense" was to be that there is only one God, the trinitarian God of the Old and New Testaments, and one church. In this new age the monasteries ended up inhabiting and reconfiguring the cultural space once held open by the communities of moral and intellectual elites that were the philosophical schools.

Centuries later, philosophy returned to the West in the monasteries, but this time as a minority voice in a Christian universe. The return of philosophy reached a critical mass in the high Middle Ages (1200–1300) in urban monasteries that had become wealthy and politically well connected. Note that to this point there was no "Christian ethics" as we know it today. In the first age of Christendom (until ca. 400), reflection about how Christians ought to live was assumed to be integral to everything Christians wrote about, as is the case in the New Testament. In the second phase of Christendom (ca. 400–1400)—often referred to as the Constantinian era because everyone was assumed to be Christian—the term "Christian" became a catchall descriptor, a vast umbrella encompassing all forms of life. Christian morality was taken as "common sense," and the only explicit discussion of the moral life during this period was to be found in monasteries and penitential manuals. The Reformation did not challenge these patterns as a whole, but sought, rather, to extend to all Christians the "higher virtues" of monastic life.

Though the changes brought about by the Renaissance and Reformation were culturally and theologically profound, the necessary conditions were still not yet in place to allow for the emergence of "Christian ethics" as a discipline that could be studied as a subject separable from exegesis and doctrinal theology. For that a final shift had to occur, a shift back to the intellectual and cultural dominance of nontheological thought. Now, however, non-Christian thought was no longer grounded in pagan philosophy, but was a new brand of philosophy emerging from the monasteries. Ironically, in this monastic setting, distinctions solidified that allowed stronger appeals to natural reason, appeals making no direct reference to God or revelation. It is from this trajectory, begun in the high Middle Ages, that the movement called the Enlightenment arose, which marked the moment of transition into the modern age. The decisive feature of this movement was not its wholesale embrace of reason understood as an entity capable of knowledge without reference to God—this had been affirmed by some Christian monks for hundreds of years[1]—but the fact that Enlightenment philosophers were not monks and made only formal avowals of revealed truth. In this philosophy, God was on the sidelines, largely called upon to guarantee the veracity of human perception. This emancipation from the church and the loosening of ties to revealed truth ultimately led to calls for an emancipation from all references to God in philosophy. At worst, God and Christianity came to be seen as the enemy of reason. The possibility of such a post-Christian rationality is the crucial feature of the third age of the West: only now can we think of the average person as neither pagan nor Christian, but secular. And only now can faith and Christian ethics appear as something that some people choose to do above and beyond what is considered generally rational and therefore moral.

It is ironic, then, that after many centuries, Christians once again found themselves assuming a minority position within an intellectual world in which non-Christian presuppositions had become dominant. If in the second phase of the Christian West philosophers were monks or clerics working in monasteries, the Enlightenment ushered in an age in which Western theologians were most often found in institutions of secular learning, such as universities; and even when located in seminaries, they were, in most cases, university trained. Only because of these developments could "Christian ethics" arise as the distinct university discipline it is today in the Protestant West.

---

1. Alasdair MacIntyre, *God, Philosophy, Universities: A Selective History of the Catholic Philosophical Tradition* (Lanham, MD: Rowman & Littlefield, 2009).

Modernity and Theology

It is no exaggeration to say that the whole configuration of modern theology is one long response to this rising tide of secular reason. Only when "secular morality" was assumed to be self-evident could Christians feel the need to justify their ethical claims without reference to doctrine and exegesis. In the ancient and medieval contexts it was clear that, in different ways, all moral claims were entailments of theological claims. In the ancient world, one's way of life was assumed to be intrinsically related to the philosophical or theological language in which it was described. Indeed, metaphysical claims were most often understood as the conceptual beliefs that sustained different ethics. The Stoics, for instance, had a cosmology that explained their ethic of rising above challenges, while the Epicureans viewed the universe as differently constructed and so espoused a life spent indulging the senses. This assumed linkage of metaphysics and ethics continued to hold in the early Middle Ages, as talk about how Christians are to live well was assumed to be an entailment of the metaphysical reality of Jesus Christ's lordship. Within this overarching agreement, however, another ancient distinction gained new prominence in the high Middle Ages, between thought conceived as separable from and superior to the questions of daily life, labeled "theoretical reason," and those forms of reasoning available even to the unlearned. "Practical reason" was understood as pertaining to all the remaining knowledge needed to live in the mutable world—the knowledge of when to reap and sow, how to judge a court case, or how to raise children.

Modernity can be understood not only as the age of secular reason, but also as the time in which a persistent gulf opened between theory and practice. Immanuel Kant (1724–1804) was to codify this distinction in ethics by separating his theory of the premises of ethical duty (now called meta-ethics) from questions about the contexts within which these duty-rules are worked out (now called special ethics, or practical reasoning).[2] Within this new separation of practical life from human theorizing about the world, it becomes possible to conceive of ethics, an account of how we are to live, as *derived* from, or reliant on, what we "know," that is, have believed in our minds. The "problem" of ethics becomes how to hold together what "natural" reason (human reason unaided by revelation) knows with the fine textures and situations of daily life. Whereas for the ancients the question was, "Which account of reality is true and so best orients one's living?" the modern question is, "How do I relate what I believe to how I live?"[3] To be a modern Christian is to experience a split

2. For his meta-ethical discussion, see Immanuel Kant, *Groundwork for the Metaphysics of Morals*, trans. and ed. Mary Gregor (1785; Cambridge: Cambridge University Press, 1998). For his approach to practical reasoning in ethics, see *The Metaphysics of Morals*, trans. and ed. Mary Gregor (1798; Cambridge: Cambridge University Press, 1996).

3. Pierre Hadot, *Philosophy as a Way of Life: Spiritual Exercises from Socrates to Foucault*, ed. and introduced by Arnold Davidson, trans. Michael Chase (Oxford: Blackwell, 1995).

between what is thought and confessed and what is lived, a split embodied in the estrangement of Christian theology and ethics.

From a theological perspective, then, "modernity" names that time in which Christians face the problem of finding an appropriate response to secular morality, as well as the temptation to claim they have a "morality" separable from their doctrinal affirmations about the reality of the work of Jesus Christ. The story of Christian ethics in the last 150–200 years is lamentable in being largely a story of succumbing to this temptation.[4] As I will soon show, most of the self-confessed practitioners of modern Christian ethics have increasingly relied on secular reason, driven by an interest in escaping from the realm of divine speaking, Scripture, doctrine, and church practice. Kant made this situation possible by persuading Christians that if humanity was to come of age it must become "autonomous," free, rational, and obedient to no one except God, defined in Pietistic terms as operating strictly within the individual's reason and conscience.[5] For example, the overwhelming impression one receives when reading the founding figures of American Christian ethics, with some marginal exceptions,[6] is that their desire was not to think in doctrinal terms at all. Their interest was in making Christianity respectable before a world that expected it to live by this Enlightenment creed. Only when it played by these rules could "Christian ethics" demonstrate its worth as a civilizing force.

By beginning with this narrative of decline I am inverting the founding narrative of the modern discipline of Christian ethics. It was, from its inception, a discipline based on the premise of modern liberal theology that Christian doctrine is a *problem* for modern Christians, that a more just church can only come about through the stripping away of accreted false beliefs. Ernst Troeltsch (1865–1923) formulated the premises that were to orient Christian ethics as a university discipline organized by the principles of autonomous reason. For him the centuries of Christian thought were taken to be a largely antiquated catalogue of ideas that needed to be supplemented in order to serve the construction of a universal ethic.[7] Insofar as those educated in the discipline engaged traditional sources, they did so using excerpted sourcebooks and with an eye to overcoming the problems they believed had been bequeathed by traditional doctrine. To lose contact with the tradition of theological thought in

---

4. This and the following two paragraphs draw on Stanley Hauerwas and Samuel Wells, "Why Christian Ethics Was Invented," chap. 3 in *The Blackwell Companion to Christian Ethics*, ed. Stanley Hauerwas and Samuel Wells (Oxford: Blackwell, 2004).

5. Immanuel Kant, *Religion within the Bounds of Mere Reason*, ed. and trans. Allen Wood and George di Giovanni (1793; Cambridge: Cambridge University Press, 1999).

6. See, for example, Paul Lehmann (1906–1994), *Ethics in a Christian Context* (New York: Harper and Row, 1963).

7. See the conclusion to volume 2, "History of the Christian Ethos," in Ernst Troeltsch, *The Social Teaching of the Christian Churches*, trans. Olive Wyon (1912; repr., Louisville: Westminster John Knox, 1992).

this way would have been paralyzing had these students not already embraced the alternative ethical framework of secular rationality.

This loss of facility with classic Christian language and doctrine had two far-reaching effects. The first was to reorient theology toward a primary concern with ideas and ethical problems. This was an inevitable result of abstracting a concept of "ethics" from the daily life of Christians in all contexts. Second, this piecemeal approach to traditional sources made it almost impossible to see how, before the modern era, Christian moral claims were always understood as entailments of doctrinal affirmations. Modern Christian ethicists were thus prone to simply misread their theological sources. To take one of many examples, the account of the role of sex in the fall that Augustine develops in book 14 of the *City of God* is almost always cited only to prove his hopelessly retrograde anthropology, a patriarchal metaphysic, and so on. The discipline of modern Christian ethics, by assuming Augustine's doctrinal and exegetical study of the fall to be fundamentally outdated, also typically refuses to see that he is raising crucial questions: How does the fall disorder our bodies and desires? What can we expect from the redemption of our bodies? Can virtue be a "habit of the body"? To note this estrangement is to bring into view that, from the perspective of Christians through the ages, creating a divide between theology and the moral life has disastrous implications.

The purpose of this essay is not to overcome this rift, but to expose it. To that end, what follows is a more detailed account of the development of Christian ethics as a university discipline in the United States. There are other stories one might also tell. In the United Kingdom, for example, the division between theoretical and practical reason became so axiomatic, and theology so associated with theoretical reason, that theology was rendered a speculative science with little interest in or connection to practical reasoning. Moral thought was relegated to "pastoral theology" and carried on in Anglican and Church of Scotland seminaries. Kenneth Kirk's *The Vision of God* is an exemplar of this tradition, with the work of F. D. Maurice[8] and William Temple[9] representing its development under the influence of the trends in liberal Protestant theology detailed below. There is likewise a continental story, driven by the strong interest in ethics of the high Enlightenment thinkers

8. Fredrick Denison Maurice is considered the founder of Christian socialism in the UK. His two main works are *The Kingdom of Christ, or Hints to a Quaker Respecting the Principles, Constitution and Ordinances of the Catholic Church*, 2 vols. (London: Darton and Clark, 1838), and *Mediaeval Philosophy; or A Treatise of Moral and Metaphysical Philosophy from the Fifth to the Fourteenth Century* (London: Macmillan, 1870). For an excellent selection of his texts and an introduction, see *Reconstructing Christian Ethics*, ed. Ellen K. Wondra (Louisville: Westminster John Knox, 1995).

9. William Temple (1881–1944), *Christianity and the State* (London: Macmillan, 1928); *Christian Faith and Life* (1931; London: SCM, 1954), and *Christianity and Social Order* (London: SCM, 1942).

such as Kant, Fichte,[10] and Hegel.[11] In this tradition of German idealism, ethics was considered integral to philosophy because without it, a "system" of thought could not be complete. Theoretical reason was still given precedence, but was conceived as necessarily encompassing practical reason in an integrated and controlling fashion. There were very thinly Christianized versions of this German tradition (Isaak Dorner),[12] and later more robustly theological versions (Karl Barth,[13] Emil Brunner,[14] Helmut Thielicke[15]). In the Low Countries, related approaches developed, as in the work of Niels Søe[16] of Denmark and the culturally influential work of the Dutch Calvinists, most notably Abraham Kuyper.[17]

That the Dutch Calvinists formulated their ethical accounts in dialogue with the scholastic Catholics of a previous generation reminds us that there is yet another story that cannot be recounted here, that of Roman Catholic moral theology. Mine will be the story of Western Protestantism, the seedbed of the English language nomenclature of "Christian ethics," and the home of its institutional development. The Catholic story is much longer and more complex, and in it the questions of the high Middle Ages and the thought of Thomas Aquinas[18] played formative roles. The Catholic discourse of moral theology has tended to orbit around the concept of natural law, which Aquinas developed in order to interlace Christian doctrine with ethics, canon law, and the penitential manuals—the textbooks for teaching priests how to weigh respective sins and assign penances in the confessional. For a contemporary exemplar of the classic scholastic approach to what Roman Catholics call moral theology, see Germain Grisez, *The Way of the Lord Jesus*,[19] and for an example of a Roman Catholic

10. Johann Gottlieb Fichte (1762–1814), *The System of Ethics: According to the Principles of the Wissenschaftslehre*, ed. and trans. Daniel Breazeale and Günter Zöller (1798; Cambridge: Cambridge University Press, 2005).

11. Georg Wilhelm Friedrich Hegel (1770–1831), *Phenomenology of Spirit*, trans. A. V. Miller (1807; Oxford: Oxford University Press, 1979); *Elements of the Philosophy of Right*, ed. and trans. Allen Wood and H. B. Nisbet (1821; Cambridge: Cambridge University Press, 1991).

12. Isaak August Dorner (1809–1884), *System of Christian Ethics* (New York: Scribner and Welford, 1881).

13. Karl Barth (1886–1968), *Ethics*, trans. Geoffrey W. Bromiley (1931; New York: Seabury, 1981); *Church Dogmatics* II/2, sec. 36, and III/4; and *The Christian Life* (1968; Grand Rapids: Eerdmans, 1981).

14. Emil Brunner (1889–1966), *The Divine Imperative* (Philadelphia: Westminster, 1932).

15. Helmut Thielicke (1908–1986), *Theological Ethics*, 3 vols. (Minneapolis: Fortress, 1958–1959).

16. Niels Hansen Søe (1895–1978), *Kristelig Etik* (Munich: Kaiser, 1957).

17. Abraham Kuyper (1837–1920), *Lectures on Calvinism* (1899; Grand Rapids: Eerdmans, 1943). Cf. James D. Bratt, ed., *Abraham Kuyper: A Centennial Reader* (Grand Rapids: Eerdmans, 1998).

18. Thomas Aquinas (1225–1274), *Summa Theologiae* IaIIae; *Commentary on Aristotle's Nicomachean Ethics* (1268–1273).

19. Germain Grisez, *The Way of the Lord Jesus*, 3 vols. (Chicago: Franciscan Herald Press, 1983–1997).

approach to moral questions that remains substantially Catholic, but which is influenced by Protestant theology, see Pope John Paul II's *Evangelium Vitae*.[20]

Christian Ethics and America

I turn now to focus more closely on the forces shaping the development of Christian ethics in the last 150 years. How, precisely, was ethics configured in the institutions formed within the presuppositions of autonomous reason? And how do Christians come to conceive the place of Christian behavior in such a landscape?

In the development of Christian ethics as a discipline in America, one striking cultural fact explains much about the nearly complete immersion of the discourse in the premises of liberal theology: its founding figures were first-generation German Americans. Walter Rauschenbusch and the Niebuhr brothers, H. Richard and Reinhold, were all children, both literally and figuratively, of German liberal Protestantism. This is of course the first irony of the story of Christian ethics in America, that its form and content were so thoroughly shaped by one very specific set of cultural and theological presuppositions arising in Protestant Europe. A second is that all three thinkers, good representatives of the tradition of German Pietism as a whole, were also steeped in a well-rounded seminary education that, on principled grounds, they were not to pass on to their students.

Walter Rauschenbusch: The Kingdom and a Social Gospel

To say that these three thinkers were representatives of German Pietism is to indicate that they affirmed and to varying extents experienced vibrant personal experiences of Christ. Walter Rauschenbusch was particularly notable in this respect, having a warm faith and a strong bent toward prayer and worship. But unlike the theology of traditional Pietists, his was sharply focused on the power of love to create social bonds. He considered Jesus the pinnacle of an Old Testament sensibility in which human goodness was presented as irreducibly social.[21] In Rauschenbusch's view, the Christians of his day were ignoring the destructive forces modern industrial life was unleashing on society. His response was to call for a renewal of a Christian love that builds social bonds and equalizes all humans to bring justice and material equality to societies. Hymn singing and prayers became central in the movement that strained in the first instance toward this unification of hearts, and which came to be called the social gospel movement.[22]

---

20. *Evangelium Vitae* (London: Catholic Truth Society, 1995).

21. These claims are drawn from chapter 2 of Walter Rauschenbusch's most influential book, *Christianity and the Social Crisis* (New York: Macmillan, 1919).

22. See Walter Rauschenbusch, *For God and the People: Prayers of the Social Awakening* (Boston: Pilgrim, 1910).

Rauschenbusch was, of course, reviving an ancient Christian sensibility: a burning passion for the welfare of the poorest in society. This passion was undergirded by his understanding of salvation as a corporate phenomenon to yield a social gospel in which caring for the poor *is* the bearing of Jesus's message. The task of Christian ethics, as the title of his 1912 book puts it, becomes *Christianizing the Social Order*. It was Rauschenbusch who established the "kingdom of God" as the leading motif in the narrower academic discipline of Christian ethics. This concept also later deeply shaped the language accessible to American social activists of all stripes. This kingdom was marked by a refusal to endorse the complacent Christianity of bourgeois Protestantism and the ascetic withdrawal he called monastic otherworldliness. "Humanity is waiting," he concluded, "for a revolutionary Christianity which will call the world evil and change it."[23] This church was to be the core agent in the saving of America.

Rauschenbusch had a classic post-Kantian account of the task of theology: the goal was to strip away the husk of centuries of Christian biblical and doctrinal misunderstanding in order to get to the kernel of the teachings of the historical Jesus. He thus uncritically accepted that the methods of historical criticism would ensure an ethically engaged church. For Rauschenbusch, Jesus Christ was the embodiment of the spirit of the Old Testament prophets, outspoken in his attention to social issues and indifferent to the ceremonial issues so apparent in vast tracts of the Old Testament. In addition, Jesus was in intimate contact with the Father, a contact that was the motivational source of his social activism. He strove for a kingdom open to all, not just the Jews, where persuasion and not force was the mode of action, and which was cleansed from the monarchal and ceremonial overtones of the Old Testament. This kingdom was not arriving with the fire and brimstone of apocalyptic judgment, but in the gradual growth of cells of mutual love and equality.

Beyond this basic Christology, Rauschenbusch was not interested in the classic doctrinal formulas about the nature of Christ.[24] His Jesus was the culminating tradition of the Old Testament prophets, whose preaching inaugurated the kingdom of God. One important aspect of Jesus's work for justice was his resistance to Old Testament monarchal conceptions of the Father in favor of a Trinity conceived in more democratic terms. In general, however, Rauschenbusch resisted the language of the Trinity, and referred to the Spirit only as the liberating force congruent with the spirit of Jesus and the prophets. This understanding of the Spirit also entailed a definition of revelation as the raising up of prophetic spirits who express the antagonism of God to the present order of things. Without making his influences explicit, Rauschenbusch

23. Rauschenbusch, *Christianity and the Social Crisis*, 91.
24. Ibid., chap. 2. See also *The Social Principles of Jesus* (New York: Association Press, 1923).

defined sin in Friedrich Schleiermacher's (1768–1834) anthropologically focused terms as the consciousness of sin. On this view the atonement rests not
on Christ's bearing of personal sin, but in his bearing the brunt of the social
sins against which he had preached. What crucified Jesus was what he had
preached against: the unjust synagogue's obsession with personal piety and
an undemocratic and exploitative state.[25]

Within this framework, Rauschenbusch's account of the kingdom of God
tended to cast the church as a barrier to the growth of the redemption of the
kingdom. One result of this suspicion was the spawning of parachurch organizations like the YMCA by the social gospel movement. Such institutions were
understood as just and democratic bearers of the gospel of the "Christianized
society," in which Christians could learn what it meant to be Christian. This
displacement of ecclesial by parachurch institutional forms also contributed
to the evolution of Christian ethics into a university discipline pursued by
those who, unlike Rauschenbusch, had not been decisively formed by life in
the churches or seminaries. These new generations of "social gospellers" might
be as personally religious as Rauschenbusch, but their faith would come to
play a much thinner methodological role in their academic work, a thinness
accompanied by an increasing ignorance of a Christian tradition they had
been taught was an obstacle to social involvement.

This loss was a direct implication of Rauschenbusch's Christology, which
drew democracy up into the doctrine of God. Jesus's familiarity with the
Father was taken to imply a democratization of the Trinity, rendering the
church the bearer of the gospel of democracy. Rauschenbusch understood
this claim as a continuation of Israel's best insights, as he found them in the
prophets' thorough repudiation of social caste and the unfair distribution of
the means of production. In this passage, Rauschenbusch gives a clear view
of his animating theological sensibilities:

> We used to see the sacred landscape through allegorical interpretation as through
> a piece of yellow bottle-glass. It was very golden and wonderful, but very much
> apart from everyday modern life. The Bible hereafter will be "the people's book"
> in a new sense. For the first time in religious history we have the possibility of
> so directing religious energy by scientific knowledge that a comprehensive and
> continuous reconstruction of social life in the name of God is within the bounds
> of human possibility.[26]

Here we can clearly see how this belief in the fundamental value of democracy,
combined with a high estimation of the social sciences, yielded a jettisoning
of the tradition of biblical exegesis as old fashioned and the harnessing of

25. For a mature synthesis of these theological themes, see Walter Rauschenbusch, *A Theology for the Social Gospel* (New York: Macmillan, 1917).
26. Rauschenbusch, *Christianity and the Social Crisis*, 209.

Christianity for the task of social progress. World War I was to cloud this serene picture, not least because it was a war against the Germany that had so shaped Rauschenbusch. He never found a good way to negotiate the tensions between his cultural homeland, from which he had drunk so deeply intellectually, and his allegiance to America. He died before the war concluded, but not without reaffirming his conviction that God was using Christian America to advance world history.[27]

H. Richard Niebuhr: Revelation and Faith in America

Many of the themes of Rauschenbusch's work continue in the work of the younger and less famous of the Niebuhr brothers, H. Richard. I am treating H. Richard before Reinhold because H. Richard stands in a middle position between Rauschenbusch's emphasis on the building up of a community of love as the primary work of the Christian ethicist and Reinhold's muting of this theme in favor of a more explicit interest in public policy and political theory. In H. Richard's work we again see the powerful admixture of theological heterodoxy and personal piety, a "God-intoxicated man."[28] He was particularly influential as a teacher, lecturing on Christian ethics at Yale from 1930 to 1962. From there he was to shape the main trajectories Christian ethics was to take in the latter half of the twentieth century, his most important students being Paul Ramsey (1913–1988) and James Gustafson (b. 1925).

H. Richard's work is best understood as a more theoretically elaborated account of Rauschenbusch's basic emphases, and began in 1929 with a book strongly critical of the church's accommodation to the world, *The Social Sources of Denominationalism*. The title indicates the continuing influence of Troeltsch's historicizing method, this time applied to strip away all the accretions of denominational factionalism to reveal the "cells" of true Christian activism. This story of a pure church was intended to orient Christians to

> build cells of those within each nation who, divorcing themselves from the program of nationalism and of capitalism, unite in a higher loyalty which transcends national and class lines of division and prepare for the future. There is no such Christian international today because radical Christianity has not arrived as yet at a program and a philosophy of history, but such cells are forming.[29]

27. The last three paragraphs draw on Stanley Hauerwas's critical analysis of Rauschenbusch in *A Better Hope: Resources for a Church Confronting Capitalism, Democracy and Postmodernity* (Grand Rapids: Brazos, 2000), chap. 5, and *Dispatches from the Front: Theological Engagements with the Secular* (Durham, NC: Duke University Press, 1994), chap. 4.

28. The phrase is from Stanley Hauerwas, "H. Richard Niebuhr," in *The Modern Theologians: An Introduction to Christian Theology since 1918*, ed. David Ford (Oxford: Blackwell, 2005), 195.

29. From H. Richard Niebuhr, "The Grace of Doing Nothing," quoted in Hauerwas, "H. Richard Niebuhr," 196.

In his mature work, *The Kingdom of God in America*, first published in 1935, H. Richard turned this method of historical unmasking on the social gospel itself, increasingly calling on an account of revelation to criticize the emphasis of the social gospel on the concept of the kingdom of God. H. Richard was becoming more aware that the Achilles heel of a highly historicist method is that one ends up having to criticize one's own views as historically derived and therefore problematic. This questioning of liberal theology seemed to ally him with the "neo-orthodoxy" of Barth, with its insistence on the priority of God's revelatory work, the speech of a God not limited by time. In *The Meaning of Revelation* (1941), H. Richard concluded that he leaned more toward Troeltsch and his emphasis on historical analysis, though nuanced by awareness of Barth's criticisms of liberal theology. What resulted was a reconfigured modern liberal theology. Now revelation is read as a stock of divinely sanctioned images or symbols through which individuals or groups might construct an intelligible account of themselves from an assumed vantage point firmly within secular rationality.

The Responsible Self: An Essay in Christian Moral Philosophy (1962) is H. Richard's most programmatic work in Christian ethics, and in it he develops his account of "man the responder." He argues that Christian ethics is not concerned primarily to develop particular moral imperatives, but with the intensification of human awareness of both other historical agents and how our actions affect others. To be responsible is not to do what is right or wrong, but what is fitting. What is fitting becomes determined by the narratives within which we find ourselves. In this way the responsible self is rendered the core term of Christian ethics. "To be a self is to have a god; to have a god is to have a history, that is, events connected in a meaningful pattern; to have one god is to have one history. God and the history of selves in community belong together in inseparable union."[30] Responsibility is defined as the human response to historical events as if they were God's action upon the agent. From this vantage point H. Richard could affirm a strong role for the church as conveyor of these images responsible for directing attention to "what is going on" in order to increase congregants' response-ability, their love of God and neighbor. His most famous book, *Christ and Culture* (1951), can be read as a Troeltschian unmasking of the historical forms of church that undermine such love.

The strength of H. Richard's account is his interest in opening Christians outward toward others by attuning them to the contextual forces that so deeply shape human interactions. But his radical monotheism[31] presents several theological difficulties, not least his insistence that historical Christianity is

30. *The Meaning of Revelation*, 80.
31. H. Richard Niebuhr, *Radical Monotheism and Western Civilization* (Lincoln, NE: University of Nebraska Press, 1960).

composed of a stock of images that must be updated to have contemporary purchase.[32] Dogmatically, he was a modalist, claiming that the Trinity named not three persons, but three moments in God's work, the creating, governing, and redeeming moments. This modalism demoted Christ to an exemplary human with a particularly strong sense of Schleiermacherian God-consciousness. The result of his emphasis on God's absolute sovereignty and transcendence, ironically, is to make the subjective and anthropocentric concept of faith more determinative than its objective referent, God. By this reduction of theology to talk about the shape of human agency, H. Richard made it the first task of Christian ethics to explain in terms of secular reason why some form of faith is humanly and universally unavoidable.[33]

Reinhold Niebuhr: Recovering Sinfulness

It is worth recalling the self-defined limits of this whole discussion by noting again the basic presuppositions of the discourse of Christian ethics, this time as expressed by Reinhold Niebuhr:

> God becomes limited by finite powers as he enters them . . . by the determinism and necessity of the fields which he enters. Here in human consciousness determinism is at its minimum. In other words, whatever other miracles may be possible (we can never establish the exact limits of this transcendence) the miracle of revelation, of conscious communion with God, is the most certainly possible.[34]

In Reinhold's theology we see the final flowering of this tradition's assumption that Christian theology must make itself acceptable to secular reason. Standing firmly within the university and secular reason, Reinhold can therefore define theology as "an effort to construct a rational and systematic view of life out of the various and sometimes contradictory myths which are associated with a single religious tradition."[35]

Reinhold's own way of doing theology in these terms was to make much use of the idea of humanity as sinful, drawing together the concepts of revelation and sin. The anxiousness of finite humans in all times and places becomes, for him, the universal marker of sin and the contact point for theological engagement. In their anxiety about their finitude humans give their loyalty to

---

32. H. Richard Niebuhr, *The Responsible Self: An Essay in Christian Moral Philosophy*, with an introduction by James Gustafson (New York: Harper & Row, 1963), appendix A.

33. Cf. H. Richard Niebuhr, *Faith on Earth: An Inquiry into the Structure of Human Faith* (New Haven: Yale University Press, 1989).

34. From his unpublished thesis, "The Validity and Certainty of Religious Knowledge," quoted in Stanley Hauerwas, *With the Grain of the Universe: The Church's Witness and Natural Theology* (London: SCM, 2002), 103.

35. Reinhold Niebuhr, *An Interpretation of Christian Ethics* (New York: Harper & Row, 1935), 13.

other finite beings, social movements, rulers, and human loves that promise
to resolve it. Jesus, or more properly the religious life, offers humans a way
out of this anxiety and the injustice it produces by allowing a "soaring of the
soul beyond the possibilities of history."[36]

In this scheme Christ is redemptive as the answer to the questions raised
by history, conceived as the work of human actors. His Christ is therefore
above history, but in being so holds out the promise of liberation from the
problem of human historical limitation. The cross is not a real event that
defines history, but a symbol for an eternal possibility that stands beyond
history as a polestar aiding human navigation within it. Hauerwas succinctly
encapsulates the ethical framework that this Christology expresses and the
cultural hermeneutic it generated, an account that bears more than a passing
resemblance to Stoicism:

> Running through Niebuhr's many examples is the same set of principles repeated
> over and over again: Finite human beings greedily seek to obtain more than their
> needs dictate, a proclivity that is made infinitely worse in collectives; therefore,
> the best one can hope for is to structure groups, societies and international
> relations in such a way that individuals and groups can be kept under relative
> control; religion illuminates this condition and provides some inspiration to do
> better, even though the full realization of its ideals are impossible in history.[37]

Though Reinhold considered Jesus's teaching and work normative for Christians, this last point indicates that he also believed the love displayed in the
crucifixion to be incompatible with political life.[38] Jesus is a symbol of love in
its eternal purity, but his example cannot and must not be directly emulated by
humans trapped within historical occurrence. Reinhold learned this "lesson"
watching what he considered ineffective nonviolent protests by factory workers
in his industrial parish. In all circumstances, what those following this transcendent justice seek is a middle way between tyranny and anarchy. Rejecting
Jesus as directly relevant for ethics, and distrusting the casuistical natural-law
approaches associated with Roman Catholic ethics, Reinhold opts for a purely
procedural account of ethics in which justice in history is reached by means
of the balancing of competing interests. He named this balancing procedure a
"realistic" approach suited to the sinful dynamics of groups. Prophetic speech

36. Reinhold Niebuhr, *Moral Man and Immoral Society: A Study in Ethics and Politics*
(New York: Scribner, 1932), 82.

37. Stanley Hauerwas and Michael Broadway, "The Irony of Reinhold Niebuhr: The Ideologi-
cal Character of 'Christian Realism,'" in *Wilderness Wanderings: Probing Twentieth-Century
Theology and Philosophy* (Boulder, CO: Westview, 1997), 51. Also see his critical analysis of
Reinhold's works in "History as Fate" in *Wilderness Wanderings* and *With the Grain of the
Universe*, chaps. 4–5.

38. See the treatment in his influential *The Nature and Destiny of Man: A Christian Interpretation*, 2 vols. (1941, 1943; repr., Louisville: Westminster John Knox, 1996), vol. 2, chap. 3.

was defined as always directed against any such groups, playing a critical func-tion rather than defending or justifying the behavior of any group. Because the church is not exempt from functioning as a self-interested political lobby, it also stands in need of limitation by the countervailing forces of other interest groups.

These political themes are succinctly outlined in a book with a subtitle that indicates Reinhold's agreement with Rauschenbusch that democracy is *the* Christian mode of social organization and government: *The Children of Light and the Children of Darkness: A Vindication of Democracy and a Critique of Its Traditional Defense*.[39] But Reinhold, in the wake of World War II, painted his theological defense of democracy in much darker colors as the government and social system best capable of dealing with the lurking self-interest that hides all ideals, for "there is no level of human moral or social achievement in which there is not some corruption of inordinate self-love."[40] This was an account that perfectly meshed with the interest-group liberalism of the postwar era. The contrast with the socialist economic assumptions of Rauschenbusch's account also became more explicit: economic justice for Reinhold is not the equal distribution of the means of production, but the limiting of the power of those owning property by the representative power of the people expressed in democratic processes.

The entire edifice of this account of Christian ethics, and of Christian faith, thus grows from an account of sin. Reinhold's account of Christian love has been translated into the unending task of helping liberal society achieve a balance of freedom and equality. "Religious faith ought therefore to be a constant fount of humility; for it ought to encourage men to moderate their natural pride and to achieve some decent consciousness of the relativity of their own statement of even the most ultimate truth. It ought to teach them that their religion is most certainly true if it recognizes the element of error and sin, of finiteness and contingency, which creeps into the statement of even the sublimest truth."[41] God does not directly intervene in a world ruled by natural laws, but he does bring about a just state of affairs by generating a moral idealism and a strong self-critical impulse. This self-critical stance, rather than any Christology, was ultimately to function as Reinhold's constructive principle. His aim was to achieve justice by fostering responsible actors who ensure that rival interests keep one another in check.

The Ire of an Insider: Stanley Hauerwas

Stanley Hauerwas is arguably the most well-known living representative of the discipline of Christian ethics, certainly in the United States. Focusing

39. Reinhold Niebuhr, *The Children of Light and the Children of Darkness: A Vindication of Democracy and a Critique of Its Traditional Defense* (New York: Scribner, 1945).
40. Ibid., 135.
41. Ibid.

on him is helpful for our purposes because throughout his career he has carefully articulated his own position in relation to his main contemporaries and precursors in the discipline. At the same time, he has been a vociferous critic of the discipline, probing and locating the points at which it has been configured to serve secular rationality. I now want to show how the major premises of his theology crystallized through a series of reactions against the tradition of American Christian ethics and its liberal theological premises.[42]

In commenting on an abandoned writing project, Hauerwas gives us a glimpse of both his affinities for the discipline and the reasons for his increasing resistance to it:

> The more I read [in preparation to write a history of Christian ethics in America], the less enthusiasm I could muster for writing the book. I think one of the reasons for my hesitation was I did not want to write so critically about people I so deeply admire. I had begun thinking about the book as an exercise in memory, but I increasingly found I was telling the story as an argument for forgetting. Every remembering, of course, is a forgetting, but the kind of forgetting entailed by the way I increasingly came to think I had to tell the story was too sad. Put differently, I find it hard to write a book about a history that I believe has come to an end.[43]

This was a judgment informed by a deep grasp of and appreciation for the tradition beginning with Rauschenbusch's social gospel. Hauerwas believes this social gospel was flawed in defining its interest in living conditions through the methodologies and assumptions of the social sciences, rendering the Christian ethicist a social scientist interested in the topic of religion.[44] H. Richard Niebuhr continued the trajectory of the social gospel, seeking a better way to articulate its main emphases without its tendency to baptize and validate human insights. But because H. Richard was also strongly influenced by the historicism of Troeltsch, he could not allow Christian ethics to inhabit its doctrinal tradition as a first-order language, but insisted the discipline devote itself to the second-order work of finding the right conceptual means to explicate the ethical implications of these first order convictions (so strongly allying Christian ethics with analytic philosophy). In a nutshell, we see here the shift from moral language that is explicitly confessional to a new Christian language that translates the supposed meaning of traditional Christian language into secular idioms like justice, rights, equality, and so on. Reinhold

42. Hauerwas regularly and openly admits this antagonism: "My enemy has always been Protestant liberalism" (*The State of the University: Academic Knowledges and the Knowledge of God* [Malden, MA: Blackwell, 2007], 38n14).

43. Hauerwas, *A Better Hope*, 67.

44. This section draws primarily on Stanley Hauerwas, "On Keeping Theological Ethics Theological," chap. 2 in *Against the Nations: War and Survival in a Liberal Society* (Minneapolis: Winston, 1985).

Niebuhr grasped several of the problematic implications of this shift and attempted to provide more substantive reasons for retaining this traditional Christian language without violating what the discipline of Christian ethics now presumed—a Kantian moral framework with its secularized language of natural law. The theological gravitas Reinhold introduced into the discipline as a reaction against the optimism of the movement took the form of a modernized doctrine of original sin. But even this revivification of some traditional Christian first-order descriptive language remained firmly set within an unquestioning acceptance of the basic claim of the social gospellers, that the subject of Christian ethics is American civil society.

The shared presumption that the primary responsibility of the discipline was to create a more moral American populace grew from the assumption of liberal Protestantism that Christianity is only useful in a modern and secularized society for the purpose of motivating a secular populace in a manner that transcends simple appeals to self-interest. The subdiscipline of medical ethics carried this presumption to its logical conclusion by assuming that this task of moralizing the populace had been effectively accomplished, relieving its practitioners of the need to make reference to the embarrassing premodern or "mythical" content of first-order Christian language.[45] As a result of these broad trends, contemporary Christian ethicists appear in public as figures struggling with the paradoxical task of articulating the insights emerging from their primary language to an audience they (perhaps mistakenly) believe either does not recognize the language, denies the validity of this language, or views it as risible.

James Gustafson summarizes this position in a thoughtful essay that struggled against the larger trajectory of the discipline by resisting its total alienation from first-order Christian language. He suggests that the church is the core audience of the Christian ethicist, while insisting that this does not absolve the Christian of communicating with unbelievers in public forums:

> In effect, the theologian moves from the particular Christian belief to a statement of their moral import in a more universal language. These statements will be

45. One of H. Richard's students, Paul Ramsey, is often called the founder of the discipline of medical ethics, the branch of Christian ethics most familiar to church people today. Ramsey might also be called the last representative of the social gospel, not because he called for the Christianizing of the social order, but because he assumed that, in America at least, it had already been achieved. In the commitment of the physician to the care of a patient's body and soul before all other considerations, Ramsey found traces of the love of Christ carried in the secular institutions of modern medicine. By demythologizing Jesus's predictions of the kingdom of God, Ramsey finds something like Kant's disinterested love, a principle that can function independently of its Christian origins. For a highly illuminating study of the cultural location and theological orientation of the American discipline of medical ethics see John H. Evans, *Playing God? Human Genetic Engineering and the Rationalization of Public Bioethical Debate* (Chicago: University of Chicago Press, 2002).

persuasive to nonreligious persons only by the cogency of the argument that is made to show that the "historical particularity" [of Christian beliefs] sheds light on principles and values that other serious moral persons also perceive and also ought to adhere to. Indeed, since the Christian theologian shares in the general moral experience of secular people, and since one facet of this work that is theologically warranted is the inferring of principles and values from common experience, he or she need not in every practical circumstance make a particular theological case for what is formulated. The theologian ought, however, to be able to make a Christian theological case if challenged to do so.[46]

This affirmation did not yet address the fact that Christian ethicists no longer had the material historical facility nor theological language to address the church in terms of its own creedal confessions, but it did, at least, suggest that they had a responsibility to do so.

These considerations suggest why the majority of practitioners of the discipline in the United States see their task as translating what is learned from the Christian tradition into nontheological discourses. But by positioning Christian ethics as a second-order discipline analyzing and translating first-order Christian language, the founders of the discipline set in motion a change in how and why future practitioners were to study the tradition of the church that had the effect of rendering them less familiar with and less interested in traditional doctrinal theology. The result was a reconfiguration of Christian ethics as the work of analyzing and testing the claims made by churches and people of faith, but finally explicitly conceived as operating wholly within the boundaries of secular reason. As James Gustafson once wrote in response to a question about how the designation "ethicist" came about, "an ethicist is a former theologian, who does not have the professional credentials of a moral philosopher."[47]

These observations suggest why, if we are to properly appreciate the landscape of contemporary Christian ethics, it is important to carefully consider the full implications of Hauerwas's observation that

> my generation was the last to assume that if you wanted to do a PhD in theology and/or Christian ethics you first had to go to seminary. Seminary training at least forced us to learn something about Scripture, historical theology, and—particularly important for those of us in ethics—nineteenth-century theology. But now people were coming into the "field" of ethics without this seminary background.[48]

Contemporary Christian ethicists thus find themselves in a dilemma: having turned to philosophical concepts to explicate the grammar of their ethical

46. James Gustafson, *Can Ethics Be Christian?* (Chicago: University of Chicago Press, 1975), 163.
47. James Gustafson, "Theology Confronts Technology and the Life Sciences," *Commonweal* 105, June 16, 1978, 386.
48. Hauerwas, *A Better Hope*, 56.

commitments, they have increasingly found themselves unable to articulate how Christian ethics can bring any distinctive content to philosophical discussions of ethics. Hauerwas's signal gift to the discipline is to have articulated the corollary that this loss of familiarity with Christian language was intertwined with the loss of any distinctive Christian lifestyle: "The reason Christian convictions have lost their power for many Christians and non-Christians alike is that many Christians, and in particular most Christian theologians, have failed to challenge the cultural accommodation of the church to the world."[49] However we may adjudge the conceptual framework of his thought (to which I will return in the last section), it is undeniable that Hauerwas's witness has been this real-time insight into the historical and theological trajectory of the discipline.

The project of translating Christian ethical claims into a secular idiom evacuated from Christian ethics anything distinctive to offer to civil society, which had, in effect, become the church of these university-based theologians.[50] Though Gustafson would not have put it in these terms, his article can be read as the incursion into the discipline of a disturbing insight. In harnessing God's name to validate its projects, Christian ethics may have forsaken its task as an organ of the church's conveying of the trinitarian God's claim on society, and ceased, in effect, to be a critical voice. What is tragic about this admission is that it exposed the utter dependence of theologians on philosophers for the generation of ethical insights. What critiques they did offer of the reigning secular rationality and morality could have been made by a theologically articulate moral theology, if it had existed, concludes Hauerwas:

> Christian thinkers, above all, should have been among the first to criticize the attempt to model the moral life primarily on the analogy of law. Instead, fearing moral anarchy, like our philosophical colleagues, Christian thinkers assumed that questions of "right" were more primary than questions of good, that principles were more fundamental than virtues, that for morality to be coherent required some one principle from which all others could be derived or tested, that the central task of moral reflection was to help us think straight about quandaries, and that we had to see the world as neatly divided into facts and values, rather than an existence filled with many valuational possibilities, some of which may well be in conflict. Perhaps most ironical, Christian theology attempted to deny the inherent historical and community-dependent nature of our moral convictions in the hopes that our "ethics" might be universally persuasive.[51]

As his career developed, Hauerwas championed these latter emphases. He did so, however, while remaining within the grammar of the social gospel

49. Hauerwas, *With the Grain of the Universe*, 216.
50. For a clear exposition of Hauerwas's reasons for considering the church of a secular age, see *The State of the University*, chap. 11.
51. Hauerwas, *Against the Nations*, 41.

that understands ethics as linked most directly to the church, defining it as a community of self-realization and social inventiveness:

> If theologians are going to contribute to reflection on the moral life in our particular situation, they will do so exactly to the extent they can capture the significance of the church for determining the nature and content of Christian ethical reflection. . . . What was original about the first Christians was not the peculiarity of their beliefs, even beliefs about Jesus, but their social inventiveness in creating a community whose like had not been seen before. . . . We need a community to direct attention toward, and sustain the insights of, those who have become more nearly good.[52]

This reformulation of the task of Christian ethics has been highly influential in opening up from within the discipline an invitation to reexamine the historical tradition of Christian ethics. It is an invitation offered via his stress that Christianity is not a set of axiomatic beliefs, but a life of discipleship, a way of living. Drawing on a Wittgensteinian (and Yale-influenced) sensibility about the interlinking of worship, habits, and virtues, Hauerwas insists that though many say "Lord, Lord," we can only know what such a confession means by way of an examination of the manner of their life as church.

The Attraction of an Outsider: John Howard Yoder

Having developed such a thorough internal critique of his own discipline, Hauerwas was ripe for a new beginning and found it exemplified in the person of John Howard Yoder (1927–1997). Yoder was a Mennonite ethicist and theologian whose intellectual and ecclesial formation took place far outside the Ivy League environment of the thinkers just surveyed (including Hauerwas). Hauerwas has often commented that though he has challenged the questions bequeathed by his liberal theological teachers, a reformulation of their questions would require not only a different set of conceptual skills, but also a different stance within the social order.[53] I now want to suggest why Hauerwas's fascination with Yoder makes sense if we grasp how Hauerwas's list of grievances against his own discipline drew him to Yoder as a witness that such a different stance within the social order was possible. Yoder embodied a tradition of rural, pastoral, and ministry-focused ecclesial formation in a manner that comprehended what Hauerwas had come to understand as the best aspects of the discipline of Christian ethics.[54]

52. Ibid., 42–43.
53. Hauerwas, *Wilderness Wanderings*, 45.
54. Hauerwas, *A Better Hope*, 67.

Late in his career Hauerwas explicitly acknowledged that his estrangement from his own discipline deeply shaped his appreciation of Yoder:

> So much depends on where you begin. Unlike Yoder, I did not begin from the margins. At least I did not begin ecclesially from the margins. I began as an outsider in mainstream Protestantism. But even as an "outsider," I am a mainstream Protestant. This "church" (that is, the mainstream Protestant church) has long been understood and justified primarily by the contribution it will make to America. Accordingly, the fundamental practices and convictions that might sustain the church as a politics sufficient to challenge the violence of the world have been absent, or relegated to religion.[55]

Yoder's Mennonite subculture embodied very different contours than established liberal Protestantism, not least in rejecting responsibility for the church to save the nation. Hauerwas's own reactions against the dominant assumptions of Christian ethics had prepared him to recognize and appreciate its distinctive position as presented in the person of Yoder. At the same time, the way Hauerwas appropriated Yoder's theology and ethic could not but be shaped by the vocabulary and emphases of the mainstream discipline in which Hauerwas was trained.

On my reading it is a mistake to overlook how Hauerwas's appropriation of Yoder is shaped by his training in liberal Protestant ways of framing questions. There are also historical grounds to suspect that Hauerwas's familiarity with Barth had also prepared him to appreciate Yoder. But Hauerwas never met Barth, and in Yoder he faced a living, embodied (and American) alternative to the social stance of the practitioners of his discipline. What Hauerwas cannot bring himself to say is that this meeting was revelatory, that in the person of Yoder, Hauerwas had his eyes opened in a concrete, historical, and therefore grace-filled confrontation with the living God. I will return to explain the reasons for this intentional refusal in the final section.

By displaying all the marks of a Christian theologian that Hauerwas had come to expect through his critical appraisal of his discipline, Yoder consummated Hauerwas's sense that liberal Protestantism, and Christian ethics specifically, had come to an end.[56] As he saw it, at least in the early days of his interactions with Yoder, *The Politics of Jesus* marked a new beginning for the discipline, one in which the first-order language of the creeds and of biblical exegesis would again be the main territory of Christian ethics. In my view such a perception of new beginnings is illuminated by thinking of it as

55. Stanley Hauerwas, in Stanley Hauerwas and Romand Coles, *Christianity, Democracy and the Radical Ordinary: Conversations between a Radical Democrat and a Christian* (Eugene, OR: Cascade, 2008), 29–30.

56. This paragraph draws on "Why *The Politics of Jesus* Is Not a Classic," chap. 8 of Hauerwas, *A Better Hope*.

analogous to Moses's view of the Promised Land, a land he has been taught to yearn for, but will not enter. Moses will only see the boundary of this Promised Land from which his people have been exiled for so long. The fertility of Hauerwas's witness lies in its explicit invitation to a whole generation trained in the tradition of Christian ethics to reconsider the richness of the first-order conversation that is the Christian doctrinal tradition.

While outspokenly critical of the assumption that the subject of Christian ethics is America, even Hauerwas could not escape his perception that Yoder represented a marginal, excluded Christian tradition. Such a judgment is no doubt true when made from within the topography of American Christianity. But behind Yoder stands the vast theological corpus of Karl Barth, with whom Yoder studied in Basel, Switzerland, and who played a central role in helping Yoder to appreciate the tradition of historical Christianity. Barth has arguably issued modernity's most resounding challenge to theological liberalism and most winsome invitation back into the rich conversation of the transtemporal communion of saints.[57] Barth's theology can hardly be called marginal within the landscape of European theology. If Yoder represented the door for Hauerwas out of "Christian ethics" and into the world of the universal church, Barth looms behind him as an invitation for those interested in living the Christian life to enter once again into the riches of the transtemporal communion of saints.

I will conclude by asking whether the genesis of Hauerwas's appreciation of Yoder in the heart of the discipline called Christian ethics has not also made it difficult to see the interconnections between Yoder and the magisterial Reformation tradition represented by Barth. While the story of Barth's emergence from the currents of liberal theology is a consistent theme of other chapters in this volume, the story of the emergence of Christian ethics in America from its captivity to liberal reason has barely begun.

Witherings and Advents

Hauerwas's interest in reinhabiting Christian language as a first-order discourse has led him to an increasing appreciation of many of the classic doctrines in Christian theology, with a primary emphasis on ecclesiology and Christology, in that order. In this concluding section I want to briefly note that one vestige of Hauerwas's training in liberal Protestantism is his nervousness about drawing attention to divine action. More pointedly, what continues to set Hauerwas apart from Barth and much of the Christian theological tradition is a resistance to admitting the concept of revelation into his theology. His most active accounts of the transformation of the church

57. See John Howard Yoder, *Karl Barth and the Problem of War* (Nashville: Abingdon, 1970).

rely on the church's remembering its proper story. Hauerwas stresses the particularity of the church's mediation of God's presence to humans, but avoids speaking of this mediation as God's own work of self-revelation.[58] For this reason he cannot avoid interpreting Barth not as a theologian of revelation, but as a pedagogue in Christian language. Learning to read Barth is thus undertaken in order to challenge secular ways of seeing the world by challenging the language we use, and "this training, which requires both intellectual and moral formation, enables Christians to see the world as it is, and not as it appears."[59] Such formulations remain determinedly within the perspective of the human subject and so within the sensibilities of liberal Protestantism. Hauerwas will go no further than "we speak, and in speaking we discover that we are caught up, together with that about which we speak, in an endeavor that must be described as metaphysical."[60]

Barth, in contrast, insists that all human interactions with other subjects must become transparent to God's work of revealing *himself*, and even more strongly, that faith is nothing more than the concrete human response to this divine in-breaking into human activities both sacred and profane. "Summoned because chosen—here we have the first definition of real man . . . to be summoned means to have heard, to have been awakened, to have to arouse one's self, to be claimed."[61] Hauerwas and Barth agree that the work of Jesus Christ demands that Christian thought begin with the particular rather than the universal, that moral deliberation in every time and place cannot proceed if the historicity of the resurrection is not taken as basic. But for Hauerwas this insight leads to the stress on the church's responsibility to ensure the visibility of God's truth,[62] whereas for Barth it becomes an assertion that every person must listen for the voice of God: "Redeemed humanity has no history except that which is with Jesus Christ, and this means that man is interesting, or more accurately, real, in his concrete and historical confrontation with the living God."[63] Though this voice has bound itself to the church and its witnesses, Barth insists that it is never reducible to it.

58. Hauerwas's most direct attempt to respond to such a criticism can be found in "The Truth about God: The Decalogue as Condition for Truthful Speech," chap. 7 in *The Doctrine of God and Theological Ethics*, ed. Alan Torrance and Michael Banner (London: T&T Clark, 2006).

59. Hauerwas, *With the Grain of the Universe*, 183.

60. Ibid., 189.

61. Karl Barth, *Church Dogmatics* III/2, 150.

62. "Witnesses must exist if Christians are to be intelligible to themselves and hopefully to those who are not Christians, just as the intelligibility of science depends in the end on the success of experiments" (*With the Grain of the Universe*, 212).

63. Karl Barth, *The Christian Life*, 19–21. At this point Barth and Yoder stand together against Hauerwas. Notice how Hauerwas directly quotes Yoder emphasizing the necessity of the address of the Spirit and the personal communication of God for the sustenance of a Christian politics but glosses the meaning of Yoder's claims without any reference to this divine agency (Hauerwas, *The State of the University*, 157n47).

Within the terms set by the Enlightenment, the main problem of Christian ethics is how we are to *know* what we should do. Kant, in setting the question up this way, answers that we are to do the thing in all times and places that is rationally and eternally true. Knowledge is gained by rational cogitation and *applied* to life. Hauerwas inverts this procedure: we know what to do because our imagination and perception are opened up by the practices of the church and the habits it bequeaths to us. Knowing is understood as a bodily knowledge that opens up into imaginative alternatives for living in the world.[64] Barth suggests that both epistemologies remain within the anthropocentric logic of modernity in that in neither framework is God allowed to appear as an agent. Barth is as insistent as Hauerwas that the church is crucial in teaching us the language, stories, and practices that help us to hear God, but he also insists that in the final analysis, this God must appear and claim individual human beings as disciples and servants.

The challenge that faces Christian ethics today is to come to terms with the triumph of the anthropological vantage point in our age. Though Barth and Hauerwas have differing opinions of the utility of habit and virtue language in Christian theology, this is not the most important difference between them. The theologically crucial conflict is over *how* Christians are to appropriately seek and describe the remaking of their habits. Hauerwas suggests that bad habits are displaced by good habits primarily by the formation of the body in the church's liturgy, thereby affirming the church as the focal point of Christian ethics. Barth thinks this inadequate for two reasons. First, as Hauerwas notes, but resists conceding,

> Barth would not agree with Lindbeck's claim that the crusader's cry *"Christus est Dominus"* while cleaving the skull of the infidel falsifies the claim. . . . Barth would see no reason why the meaning of what the crusader says should be determined by the use to which the crusader puts it. Barth certainly thinks that self-involvement is dependent on truth, but not that the truth is dependent on its self-involving character.[65]

Barth would thus insist, as Hauerwas cannot, that an apparently appropriate practice of worship or witness can be compatible with self-delusion, the phenomenon the Gospels describe as pharisaism. Hauerwas's construal of witness and emphasis on theological language thus make it difficult for Christians to gain critical distance from their worship and use of theological language.

Second, and following from this first point, Barth emphasizes the surprising and unpredictable quality of God's appearing to claim human life for his purposes. Humans have no power to construct communities that displace bad habits with good unless God first and continually breaks into the blindness

---

64. Hauerwas, *With the Grain of the Universe*, 183.
65. Ibid., 176n6.

induced by their bad habits and shows humans that they do not determine their own existence. God's faithfulness to appear is thus irreducible for Christian ethics. Hauerwas prefers to stay within the commitment of modern Christian ethics to public speech, to keep Christian language open and accessible to all who would hear, and so resists this emphasis on revelation. But Barth insists that Christian language cannot by itself do any work: only one person's voice can break the force of the habits that blind us, and this person is the one man for others, Jesus Christ. This Jesus Christ is not an idea or principle, but a person who must appear to open our eyes to other persons, to a kingdom that is more real than what we take to be reality.[66] This is an awakening with sweeping ethical implications.[67]

For Further Reading

Banner, Michael. *Christian Ethics: A Brief History*. Chichester, UK: Wiley-Blackwell, 2009.

Beckley, Harlan. *Passion for Justice: Retrieving the Legacies of Walter Rauschenbusch, John A. Ryan, and Reinhold Niebuhr*. Louisville: Westminster John Knox, 1992.

Diefenthaler, Jon. *H. Richard Niebuhr: A Lifetime of Reflections on the Church and the World*. Macon, GA: Mercer University Press, 1986.

Dorrien, Gary. *Social Ethics in the Making: Interpreting an American Tradition*. Chichester, UK: Wiley-Blackwell, 2008.

———. *Soul in Society: The Making and Renewal of Social Christianity*. Minneapolis: Fortress, 1995.

Gustafson, James. *Protestant and Roman Catholic Ethics: Prospects for Rapprochement*. Chicago: University of Chicago Press, 1978.

Long, D. Stephen. *Tragedy, Tradition, and Transformation: The Ethics of Paul Ramsey*. Boulder, CO: Westview, 1993.

Werpehowski, William. *American Protestant Ethics and the Legacy of H. Richard Niebuhr*. Washington, DC: Georgetown University Press, 2002.

---

66. Cf. Yoder, *Preface to Theology: Christology and Theological Method* (Grand Rapids: Brazos, 2002), 276, and Barth, *Church Dogmatics* III/2, sec. 47.1.

67. I am deeply grateful to Stanley Hauerwas for many discussions on the historical content of this paper, and for his gracious critical interaction.

13

. . .

PRACTICAL THEOLOGY

R ICHARD R. O SMER

The Subject Matter and Scope of Practical Theology

Practical theology is the branch of Christian theology that teaches the members of the Christian community how to perform certain practices and to embody the mission of the church in a particular social context. Its subject matter includes two central themes: "how to" and "why to." It provides concrete guidelines and models that offer practical help in how to engage in Christian practices and mission. But it also offers reflection on why such actions are important, why they serve and glorify God, and why they are best carried out along certain lines in a particular social context. The dual focus of practical theology on "how to" and "why to" commonly leads practical theologians to describe their field as both an art and a science. We can illustrate with the practice of prayer.

When prayer is the subject matter of practical theology, specific guidance is offered in how to pray. This is based on what is learned from reflection on present experience and from approaches to prayer developed in the Christian tradition on the basis of Scripture. Prayer, for example, is communication and, some might even say, communion with God. Like any relationship, it requires time and discipline. Many people find it helpful to establish a definite time, place, and pattern for this practice, which may include praying the psalms, the devotional reading of Scripture, and talking to God. Yet, it is important to listen to God, as well as speak to God. It is also important not to think of this relationship exclusively in terms of asking God for things (supplication), but to thank and praise God or simply dwell in God's presence.

In offering guidelines like these, practical theology is an art. Any thoughtful teacher of prayer or spiritual director realizes that general guidelines and models will not work with every person. A "quiet time" may work for some people, but others communicate best with God when they are surrounded by nature on a walk. As an art, practical theology offers open-ended guidelines that require reflective judgment in concrete situations. It also offers case studies, verbatims (reconstructed accounts of a pastoral conversation), and research reports that sensitize people to the particularities of concrete situations and to relevant personality and cultural differences.

In its attention to "why to," practical theology is a "science." Like the other theological disciplines, it carries out research and constructs theories, giving special attention to understanding and guiding the present life of the church as a community of practice and mission. We can clarify the "scientific" contribution of practical theology by continuing our discussion of prayer.

Research in cognitive science reveals the continuing influence throughout adulthood of cognitive models formed during the preschool years. Howard Gardner calls this the power of the "unschooled mind," the tendency to use simple "Star Wars" scripts to divide the world into good guys and bad guys or to relate to authorities as all-knowing and all-powerful parental figures.[1] Informed by this theoretical perspective, practical theologians might carry out empirical research on adults to determine the extent to which their understanding of prayer is shaped by cognitive models acquired during childhood. They also might sort out such models and attempt to explain the relational and cultural factors that appear to shape them. Why is it that some people pray to a God as a judgmental "eye in the sky," watching their every move? Why do others pray to God as a loving Father who cares about their deepest needs? Why do some spontaneously use feminine imagery in intimate conversations with God? In addressing questions like these, practical theologians enter into a dialogue with the social sciences and carry out their own empirical research. They also attempt to interpret what they discover in an explanatory framework.

Questions like those above inevitably raise normative issues. These also are a part of the "why to" of practical theology. It is particularly concerned with developing theological and ethical norms that can criticize and guide the present practices and mission of communities of faith. In developing theological norms, it enters into a dialogue with other fields of theology like biblical studies, dogmatic theology, and Christian ethics. But practical theology makes its own constructive contribution to the larger theological conversation. Drawing on

1. Howard Gardner, *The Unschooled Mind: How Children Think and How Schools Should Teach* (New York: Basic Books, 1991).

its research on Christian communities in particular social contexts, it seeks to develop norms and guidelines that are both faithful and relevant. It strives to be faithful to the authoritative sources of Christian theology; yet it also strives to develop normative proposals that are relevant to a particular sociohistorical context and that can guide the church's practices and mission in this context. We can see what this involves by continuing our examination of prayer.

Suppose a team of practical theologians discovers through empirical research on cognitive models of prayer that a large number of Christian adults use models that are highly individualistic. Prayer is about what I want and need and, occasionally, about what my family members and friends want and need, especially in times of crisis. In an American context, they might interpret this finding in light of theories of cultural individualism that explain why this pattern is so strong in this country. This finding would raise important normative questions. Should not prayer open people to God's loving concern for the world, especially those neighbors who are marginalized, vulnerable, and hurting? What implications does this have for congregations that are caught up in the resurgence of interest in Christian spirituality? Do they risk accommodating American individualism in their emphasis on prayer and spiritual formation? Does not an individualistic, inward focus undercut congregations' discernment of their missions within the mission of God, a mission of redemption and reconciliation of the world for which Christ died?

In giving answer to questions like these, American practical theologians would need to be very sensitive to developing understandings of prayer and spirituality that hold together the building-up of congregations in spiritual formation and the sending of congregations in service, witness, and social transformation. Their normative proposals would be highly contextual. In other cultural settings, the issues might be quite different. In Asian contexts informed by a strong neo-Confucian ethic, for example, duty and family loyalty might be more prominent. Practical theologians might need to stress the personal dimensions of prayer and spirituality to give individuals the psychic space to find their own selves and vocations amid the pressures of corporate identity and duty.

Enough has been said to make my point. In its attention to the theme of "why to," practical theology develops normative proposals that are both faithful and relevant. While debatable, it can be argued that practical theology is the most sensitive to context of all the theological disciplines. At least in part, its constructive contribution to the larger theological enterprise is to raise normative questions and proposals that grow out of its research on contemporary communities of faith located in particular sociohistorical contexts. It invites the other theological disciplines not to work in a vacuum but to take very seriously the audiences and contexts addressed in their work.

Thus far, the subject matter of practical theology has been portrayed as taking shape in this field's attention to the themes of "how to" and "why to."

In our examination of the practice of prayer, key tasks of this field have gradually emerged, though this has been implicit to this point. It may be helpful to identify these tasks explicitly. In practical theology, the themes of "how to" and "why to" are investigated along four different lines.[2]

- *Descriptive-Empirical*: What is going on in the practices and mission of contemporary communities of faith located in particular sociohistorical contexts?
- *Interpretive*: Why is this going on in these particular communities, and how can it best be interpreted and explained?
- *Normative*: What ought to be going on for these communities to be both faithful and relevant?
- *Pragmatic*: What practical models and principles might help these communities better embody their calling as God's people in light of their resources and circumstances?

These four tasks stand at the heart of contemporary practical theology, and we will examine them more fully at a later point in this chapter.

Describing the subject matter of practical theology with the themes of "how to" and "why to" is somewhat ambiguous. This is especially true in comparison to other fields of theology. The subject matter of dogmatic theology, for example, is church doctrine, and that of biblical studies is the sacred texts of the Christian community. What is the comparable focus of practical theology? This question has been left open to this point because the focus of practical theology has varied during the modern period. This was determined by the way different practical theologians conceptualized the scope of this field.

Some practical theologians have viewed the scope of practical theology as clergy functions. They have focused on preaching, pastoral care, Christian education, evangelism, and other leadership tasks of the ordained ministers of the church. This commonly is referred to as the *clerical paradigm* of practical theology.[3]

Others, focusing on congregations and the traditions to which they belong, have conceptualized the scope of the field differently. This is sometimes referred to as the *ecclesial paradigm* of practical theology.[4] The work of

---

2. For further discussion of these tasks, see Richard Osmer, *Practical Theology: An Introduction* (Grand Rapids: Eerdmans, 2008).

3. An example is Alexandre Vinet, *Pastoral Theology, or, the Theory of the Evangelical Ministry*, ed. and trans. T. Skinner (New York: Harper & Bros., 1853). For critical discussion of this paradigm, see Edward Farley, "Theology and Practice Outside the Clerical Paradigm," in *Practical Theology: The Emerging Field in Theology, Church, and World*, ed. D. Browning (San Francisco: Harper & Row, 1983).

4. An early American example is George Crooks and John Hurst, *Theological Encyclopedia and Methodology on the Basis of Hagenbach* (New York: Phillips & Hunt, 1884).

ordained pastors is viewed as only one form of church leadership, which also
includes nonordained professionals like Christian educators and lay leaders.
Moreover, the focus of this paradigm is not simply on leaders. It focuses on
the life of the congregation as a whole and its mission in a particular setting.
In recent decades, this paradigm has given special attention to the practices
of congregational life, often using the methods of congregational studies to
explore these practices in actual churches.[5] It also has been impacted by the
missional church discussion, which challenges congregations to reclaim their
apostolic calling as missional communities and to discover their particular
missions within God's mission.[6]

Beyond these two perspectives, others have viewed the scope of practical
theology still differently, as including the social, political, and economic systems
shaping the context of the church and impacting its mission. Primary attention
is given to the church's contribution to public life, the common good of local,
national, and international communities. Accordingly, this is often called the
public church paradigm of practical theology.[7] It has two strands that reflect
different intellectual traditions. One strand is deeply influenced by liberation,
feminist, and European political theologies. Its proponents work with a critical
theory of society, examining the ways power and economic/cultural resources
are distributed unequally by the dominant social systems, and seek to further
social transformation. The second strand draws on the traditions of philosophical pragmatism as found in the writings of William James, John Dewey, and,
more recently, Jeffrey Stout, Cornel West, and Richard Rorty. It emphasizes
the church's participation in public life, which in the contemporary world is
highly pluralistic. Thus, one of the challenges facing practical theology is to
express Christian convictions on public issues in conversations that include
many different perspectives. In democratic contexts, the capacity to debate
and discuss public issues from various perspectives is viewed as enriching the
public's ability to solve its important problems. Indeed, the contribution of

5. Two of the best introductions to the practices discussion are Dorothy C. Bass, ed., *Practicing Our Faith: A Guide For Conservation, Learning, and Growth* (San Francisco: Jossey-Bass,
1997), and Diana Butler Bass, *The Practicing Congregation: Imagining a New Old Church*
(Herndon, VA: Alban Institute, 2004). A standard resource in congregational studies is Nancy
T. Ammerman, ed., *Studying Congregations: A New Handbook* (Nashville: Abingdon, 1998).
6. The source of the missional church discussion is Lesslie Newbigin, a missionary for many
years in India who returned to England late in life to discover that his homeland was now a mission field in which many people were no longer interested in the church. An excellent overview of
Newbigin's thinking is Paul Weston, ed., *Lesslie Newbigin: Missionary Theologian—A Reader*
(Grand Rapids: Eerdmans, 2006). The best introduction to the missional church discussion
is Darrell L. Guder, ed., *Missional Church: A Vision for the Sending of the Church in North
America* (Grand Rapids: Eerdmans, 1998).
7. For the background of the public church discussion, see Martin E. Marty, *The Public
Church: Mainline, Evangelical, Catholic* (New York: Crossroad, 1981), and Cynthia D. Moe-
Lobeda, *The Public Church: For the Life of the World* (Minneapolis: Augsburg Fortress, 2004).

ideas to solving real problems determines their value—what pragmatism calls the instrumental role of ideas.

These paradigms are more fluid than portrayed above. Proponents of the public church paradigm, for example, sometimes focus on the tasks of ordained clergy, even as they locate these tasks in the broader perspective of public life. Likewise, proponents of the ecclesial paradigm often give sustained attention to cultural patterns and social systems of public life, especially if they are influenced by the missional church discussion. As used here, then, the language of paradigms provides an introductory map of the field. But as mapmakers often note, the map is not the territory. It offers a general picture of the lay of the land, but the actual territory is more complex. The same is true of our introduction to different paradigms of contemporary practical theology. The actual work of a particular practical theologian is often more complex than any clearly defined box. Yet it is helpful to have an overview of the lay of the land in order to make sense of this complexity.

Practical Theology in Historical Perspective

It also is helpful to have a historical perspective on practical theology. While the focus of this chapter is modern practical theology, a historical perspective allows us to locate this field in the longer traditions of theological reflection in the Christian community. Practical theology as a distinct branch of theology did not emerge until the modern period. Why is this the case? How was practical theology shaped by its appearance during this period? Are there older traditions of theological reflection that might need to be recovered as this field moves into the social context of postmodernity? Questions like these make a historical perspective quite important.

While practical theology did not emerge until the modern period, its subject matter has been a part of theological reflection from the very beginning of the church. As early as the letters of Paul, we find the apostle giving instructions to his congregations on how to carry out their practices and mission ("how to") and providing theological reasons on why they should do so ("why to"). First Corinthians is a good example. Over the course of this letter, Paul takes up a number of problems facing this Christian community: a man living in an incestuous relationship with his dead father's wife (1 Cor. 5), Christians taking other believers to court (1 Cor. 6), sexual conduct (1 Cor. 7), eating meat sacrificed to idols (1 Cor. 8–10), the fellowship meal accompanying the Lord's Supper (1 Cor. 11), expression of spiritual gifts, especially tongues, in the context of worship (1 Cor. 12–14). In each case, Paul provides guidelines for the actions of the community. Rarely does he command on the basis of his apostolic authority; rather, he attempts to persuade.[8] He offers theological reasons to convince the Corinthians to act in ways that better embody their identity as God's people.

Beyond the New Testament period, we find many other writings in the Christian tradition that treat the subject matter of practical theology. Augustine's *On Christian Doctrine* is a wonderful example.[9] As a former teacher of rhetoric, Augustine reflects in book 4 on what might be learned from this field for the purposes of Christian preaching. The goals of rhetoric are to teach, delight, and persuade in public speaking. In the church, Augustine argues, these goals are shaped by the unique purpose of Christian preaching. Teaching is important, for the purpose of preaching is to deepen the Christian community's understanding of Scripture and the gospel. But, obviously, preachers should strive to persuade their listeners of the truth of biblical teaching so it might take root in their lives. While there is no place for the fancy eloquence that sometimes characterized Greco-Roman rhetoric, Christian preaching may even delight its listeners. Here, Scripture serves as the preacher's model. To the well-educated Roman aristocrat, Scripture may appear poorly written and even vulgar. Yet Augustine believes that the simple language of Scripture and its stories, parables, and proverbs are a powerful form of accommodation by God to human need. It delights the ordinary reader whose heart and mind are seeking God. So, too, Christian preaching should delight its audience, not by appealing to the standards of eloquence and good taste of the elite but by allowing the truth of the gospel to shine its light into the lives of ordinary men and women.

Many additional examples of writings in which the subject matter of practical theology is present can be found in the Christian tradition. Some of these focused on the tasks of the bishops, ministers, or spiritual directors, while others were written to strengthen Christian congregations or the devotional and moral lives of individuals.[10] While the authors of these kinds of texts do not refer to their writings as practical theology, they certainly can be viewed as precursors of the field.

Practical theology emerges as a distinct field gradually over many centuries. This can be summarized briefly in three steps.[11] The first step was the separation

8. For discussion of Paul's rhetorical strategies designed to persuade his readers, see Charles B. Cousar, *The Letters of Paul* (Nashville: Abingdon, 1996), chap. 2.

9. St. Augustine, *On Christian Doctrine*, trans. D. W. Robertson (New York: Macmillan, 1958).

10. These include writings like St. Gregory the Great, *The Book of Pastoral Rule*, trans. G. Demacopoulos (Crestwood, NY: St. Vladimir's Seminary Press, 2007); *The Letters of Catherine of Siena*, trans. Suzanne Noffke (Tempe, AZ: Arizona Center for Medieval and Renaissance Studies, 2000); William Perkins, "The Whole Treatise of the Cases of Conscience," in *William Perkins, 1558–1602*, ed. Thomas Merrill (Nieuwkoop, Netherlands: B. De Graaf, 1966); Jonathan Edwards, *A Treatise concerning Religious Affections*, ed. John E. Smith (New Haven: Yale University Press, 1959).

11. I follow here my account in Richard Osmer, *A Teachable Spirit: Recovering the Teaching Office of the Church* (Louisville: Westminster John Knox, 1990), chap. 8.

of moral theology from speculative theology, or what Protestants describe as the separation of Christian ethics from dogmatic theology. Initially, this took place in Roman Catholicism and was prompted by the need to provide guidance to priests in their work as confessors who assign penance. Following the Reformation, Protestants developed a type of literature known as "cases of conscience," which helped pastors guide individuals in the moral and spiritual matters of their everyday lives. In some instances, this literature was referred to as practical theology, though this was rare.

A second step was taken by the Reformed theologian Gisbert Voetius in his five-volume work *Selectae Disputationes Theologicae*, published between 1648 and 1669.[12] Voetius noted that practical theology was occasionally identified with moral theology but argued that expanding the field to include Christian ethics, ascetic theology (the practice of the spiritual life), and ecclesiastics (church polity and the tasks of the ordained minister) would make it more useful. This understanding of practical theology began to spread during the following century.

The third and most important step was taken by the great German theologian Friedrich Schleiermacher. Schleiermacher lived at the end of the eighteenth century and beginning of the nineteenth. Throughout Europe and North America, this was a time of great social change. Democratic forms of government were established in England and the United States, and the Enlightenment took place in France. Science was making great strides in the natural sciences and, increasingly, was granted more authority in society. While many vestiges of traditional European life remained, there was a widespread sense that Europe and America were on the cusp of a new, modern age. Traditions and authorities taken for granted in the past were subject to criticism and reform.

One of the most important of these was the Christian religion. Traditional beliefs and practices were questioned. What did they really contribute to society and individuals? This was especially true among the intelligentsia. It was during this period, for example, that the so-called conflict between science and religion became a subject of intellectual discussion. This raised questions about the place of theology in higher education. From the advent of the medieval university to the rise of Reformation academies and universities, theology held a privileged place in academic institutions. With the appearance of the modern research university, this was no longer the case. The purpose of a research university was not simply to hand on the cultural heritage of the past through a liberal arts curriculum, but to produce new knowledge along the lines of modern disciplines.

12. This is translated in part in John Beardslee, ed. and trans., *Reformed Dogmatics: Seventeenth-Century Reformed Theology through the Writings of Wollebius, Voetius, and Turretin* (Grand Rapids: Baker, 1965), 265–334.

This was the context Schleiermacher faced as a key leader in the establishment of the University of Berlin. He could not simply posit the place of theology in the university by appealing to the traditional role of Christianity in Western civilization. He had to make a rational case for its contribution to society and individuals. He also had to describe the "scientific" character of theology as a modern discipline. One of the strategies Schleiermacher used to make this case was to write one of the first modern theological encyclopedias, *Brief Outline on the Study of Theology*.[13] Academic encyclopedias during this period did more than gather together information about different subjects.[14] They also described the nature of science and the relationship of its various branches. Field-specific encyclopedias, like Schleiermacher's, carried this out for a specific area of human knowledge.

Schleiermacher begins *Brief Outline* by arguing that the education of clergy is a legitimate task of the university. Like lawyers and doctors, ministers contribute to society by their leadership of the church. Schleiermacher grounds this point in his description of the important contribution that religion makes to the upbuilding (*bildung*) of culture and individuals, making a special case for the Christian religion. He also describes the "scientific" contribution of theology along the lines of modern disciplines. In a modern university, he argues, theology has three interrelated branches: philosophical, historical, and practical theology. Each field carries out research and produces specialized knowledge. Each makes a unique contribution to theology and human knowledge as a whole.

The account of three branches of theology developed by Schleiermacher was not widely accepted. But his portrait of modern theology along the lines of specialized disciplines was deeply influential. In the theological encyclopedias of other theologians, four disciplines became standard: biblical studies, church history, systematic theology, and practical theology. These fields continue to shape theological education in most American divinity schools and seminaries even today. We might call this the *encyclopedic pattern* of theology and theological education.

The strength of this pattern is the way it encourages scholars to pursue research in specialized areas and to enter into an interdisciplinary conversation with closely related fields in the natural and cultural sciences. But this is

13. Friedrich Schleiermacher, *Brief Outline on the Study of Theology*, trans. T. Tice (Richmond: John Knox, 1966). Translation of some of Schleiermacher's lectures on practical theology is found in J. Duke and H. Stone, ed., J. Duke, trans., *Christian Caring: Selections from Practical Theology* (Philadelphia: Fortress, 1988).

14. Two of the most important accounts of the incorporation of the encyclopedia into theological studies are Edward Farley, *Theologia: The Fragmentation and Unity of Theological Education* (Philadelphia: Fortress, 1983), and Charles Wood, *Vision and Discernment* (Atlanta: Scholars Press, 1985). Discussion of the encyclopedic paradigm more broadly is found in Alasdair MacIntyre, *Three Rival Versions of Moral Enquiry: Encyclopaedia, Genealogy, and Tradition* (Notre Dame, IN: University of Notre Dame Press, 1990).

its weakness as well. During the modern period, the theological disciplines have become more and more specialized, and their relationship to one another less obvious. In theological education, students taking courses in one field, like systematic theology, often have difficulty understanding how they are related to the courses of other fields, like church history, biblical studies, and practical theology. Each field is so specialized that integration across the curriculum is quite difficult.

As the modern theological disciplines became more specialized, they also frequently grew more oriented to the academy than the church. Many theologians saw their primary task as the production of "scientific" knowledge—as being scholars writing for other scholars in academic guilds. But how did their scholarship relate to the church, especially congregations? One of the ways theologians answered this question drew on the ideal of science popular during this period. Science pursues "disinterested," objective knowledge, and, thus, scholars of theology cannot worry about the effects of their research on the church. If biblical scholars, for example, raise questions about the literal interpretation of the Genesis account of creation in light of scientific theories of evolution, then they cannot worry about their impact on ordinary Christians. Likewise, if church historians discover that Luther's understanding of justification by grace through faith represents a misinterpretation of Paul's theology, then so be it. Modern scholars must be free to pursue the truth wherever it takes them.

This understanding of science as the pursuit of "disinterested," objective knowledge created certain problems for practical theology. In the encyclopedic pattern, it had the task of relating the specialized scholarship of the other theological disciplines to the church. This raised two problems that have plagued modern practical theology.

First, is it really possible for one field to achieve integration on behalf of the entire theological encyclopedia? When biblical scholars or systematic theologians pursue highly technical, "disinterested" knowledge, it is unrealistic to expect practical theology to bring these fields into a deep conversation with one another *and* to unpack their relevance for the life of the church. Integration across specialized fields has remained a perennial problem in the encyclopedic pattern, a problem that practical theology alone cannot overcome.

Second, is it wise to view practical theology as the one field where application takes place in the theological disciplines? This has been common in the encyclopedic pattern. Biblical studies, church history, and systematic theology are portrayed as "scientific" along the lines of modern disciplines, and practical theology as the field where the tasks of the pastor and the life of congregations are given direct attention. Sometimes this was portrayed as the distinction between theory and practice, and other times, as the distinction between "pure" and "applied" science. In either case, practical theology was viewed as exclusively concerned with "how to": how to preach, teach, or offer pastoral care. The sort of research and theory-building essential to "why to" were given short shrift. While many practical theologians resisted the reduction of their field to "helps and hints" for ministry, this expectation has been widespread throughout the modern period.

Practical Theology in a Postmodern Context

The encyclopedic pattern of theology inaugurated by Friedrich Schleiermacher made an important contribution in the context of modernity. It secured a place for theology in the modern research university and supported specialized scholarship by the theological disciplines. Yet the encyclopedic pattern increasingly is viewed as problematic in our postmodern intellectual and social context. Much of this stems from criticism of the model of science dominating the modern research university. Four themes have emerged in this critique.[15]

First, science—particularly natural science—no longer provides the standards and methods of all forms of scholarship. Theology, along with the arts, humanities, and cultural sciences, has both the freedom and obligation to pursue forms of rational discourse that are appropriate to its unique subject matter. Second, the tendency of the modern disciplines toward greater and greater specialization has given way to the importance of cross-disciplinary work that brings together the perspectives of a number of fields. From the human genome project to urban planning, problems are too complex to be handled by one specialized field working in isolation. In theology, hyperspecialization has given way to conversation across disciplinary lines—between different branches of theology and other forms of knowledge. Third, the older view of science as "disinterested," objective knowledge has given way to an understanding that all forms of scholarship are "interested," reflecting the interpretive traditions, values, and practical commitments of scholars. It is neither necessary nor desirable for theologians to bracket out their ecclesial commitments to achieve some false ideal of objectivity. Rather, what is called for is reflexivity: an account of the interpretive and practical precommitments that inform their work. Fourth, the older view of scientific objectivity as striving for universality and consensus has given way to an appreciation of intellectual pluralism and rational dissensus. Today, virtually every field is highly pluralistic. Psychology, for example, contains a wide variety of perspectives, including cognitive psychology, feminist psychology, psychoanalysis, sociobiology, and neuroscience. This sort of pluralism is viewed as a sign of vitality in a field. The members of a field can disagree and yet acknowledge the perspectives of others as fully rational—what is known as rational dissensus.

15. I am drawing here on the epilogue of Osmer, *Practical Theology*.

These four criticisms of the modern model of science raise important questions about the encyclopedic pattern, which was structured around the ideal of the "scientific" contribution of the modern disciplines in a research university. It is beyond the scope of this chapter to describe these questions and their possible implications for theology as a whole. Suffice it to say that the problems of integration and application that fell to practical theology in the theological encyclopedia are viewed quite differently from the perspective of postmodernity.

Perhaps most importantly all forms of theology are now viewed as grounded in and oriented toward the values and practical commitments of particular theologians. Biblical scholars and church historians are every bit as concerned about the church and public life as practical theologians. Studying biblical texts and the history of the church need not be "disinterested" in order to be "scientific." Rather, they may contribute directly to the liberation of women and minorities or to the mission of congregations, depending on the values and commitments of particular scholars. The older distinction between theory and practice or pure and applied science, which was an organizing principle of the encyclopedic pattern, no longer holds.

Moreover, the problem of integration across specialized disciplines is now viewed in new ways in both theology and theological education. The specialized disciplinary silos of the past are giving way to the importance of cross-disciplinary thinking: the ability to bring several fields into conversation with one another. This is important for pastors as well as theologians. In their leadership of congregations, pastors regularly face issues that are multidimensional and call for the perspectives of several fields and professions. Pastoral care to an alcoholic church member can illustrate what we have in mind.

As the representative of the Christian tradition, the pastor must develop a theological understanding of alcoholism. Too often in the past, church leaders have responded to alcoholics moralistically, condemning their weak willpower. Yet today we know that active alcoholics are in the grip of a disease that disables the will. The first step toward recovery is admitting that they do not have control over their drinking; any alcohol is too much for them. Christian theology offers profound interpretations of the human condition in which people are caught in the grip of forces beyond their control. Drawing on such interpretations to make sense of alcoholism theologically is an essential part of pastoral care of an alcoholic church member. A thoughtful pastor, moreover, will become familiar with the latest research on alcoholism. Today this includes research of medicine (alcoholism as a disease), biology (as a genetic predisposition), psychology (as triggered by personality factors), and anthropology (as shaped by cultural patterns like binge drinking). A pastor must also be prepared to evaluate the treatment options offered by Alcoholics Anonymous, psychotherapists, and family therapists, as well as the support and education needed by the family members of alcoholics.

Integration in this illustration is a matter of drawing on a number of fields in a responsible, informed fashion to address a complex, multidimensional issue. It requires reflexivity on the part of pastors—awareness of their own theological perspective and how it is appropriately brought into conversation with other fields and professions. The same is true of theologians as well. The isolated theological specialization of the past is giving way to an emphasis on cross-disciplinary conversation among the fields of theology and other forms of knowledge.

To summarize, a historical perspective on practical theology is important. While the subject matter of this field is as old as the church itself, it emerged gradually over many centuries as a particular form of theological reflection. Special attention has been given to modern practical theology in the context of the research university and the encyclopedic pattern of theology. As theology took the form of specialized modern disciplines, practical theology was given the tasks of integrating and applying the "scientific" knowledge of the other theological disciplines. In our postmodern intellectual context, serious questions have been raised about the continuing viability of the encyclopedic pattern and the model of science on which it was based.

This leads to a final question. If the members of all branches of theology today are concerned with practice and integration, what is the task of practical theology? Most contemporary practical theologians view the "postmodern turn" as an opportunity to clarify the particular focus of their research and theory-building. During the modern period, this field was under great pressure to confine its focus to "how to" and leave "why to" questions to other theological disciplines. Since the 1960s, practical theologians have begun to correct this imbalance. The subject matter of this field—including both "how to" and "why to"—is pursued along four lines, described briefly in the first part of this chapter:

- the *descriptive-empirical* task: empirical research on particular contexts of Christian practice in the church and public life to gain a richer understanding of what is going on;
- the *interpretive* task: interpreting research findings in frameworks that help explain why certain actions and patterns are occurring;
- the *normative* task: constructing theological and ethical norms that describe what ought to be going on in particular contexts of Christian practice; and
- the *pragmatic* task: developing practical models and principles that can guide the contemporary church in congregational and public life and support reflective judgment.

Within this framework, practical theology during the modern period may be viewed as giving primary attention to the pragmatic task. While this remains an essential part of this field, it is now one part of a larger research program.

Practical Theology Today

A sign of vitality in contemporary practical theology is the pluralism of this field. Not only do contemporary practical theologians define the scope of their field with the clerical, ecclesial, and public church paradigms, but also there is great theological variety within each of these paradigms. Moreover, practical theologians give different weight to each of the four tasks of their field and carry them out in a variety of ways.

The rich pluralism of contemporary practical theology is sometimes bewildering to students who are encountering this field for the first time. The final part of this chapter, therefore, describes some of the key decisions that practical theologians make as they carry out the four tasks of this field. This will help students spot these decisions and the reasons given to justify them. It also will help them evaluate the proposals of practical theologians in an informed manner.

Preliminary Decisions

When picking up a book on practical theology for the first time, one of the most helpful first steps is to spot the primary subject matter of the text. Is the author focusing on the tasks of clergy, the practices and mission of congregations, or the intersection of the church and public life? This provides important clues about the paradigm of practical theology guiding the text, called here the clerical, ecclesial, and public church paradigms. Often one can gain a sense of this simply by reading the table of contents.

Yet it is important that one view the initial judgment about a text as preliminary. As noted above, proponents of the public church paradigm sometimes focus on clergy tasks and congregations, and proponents of an ecclesial paradigm, on congregations' public witness in the service of their mission. In *Welcoming Children: A Practical Theology of Childhood*, for example, Joyce Ann Mercer gives great attention to the ways congregations welcome children in liturgy and Christian education.[16] At first glance, she might be located in the ecclesial paradigm. As one reads this book, however, it becomes clear that Mercer's focus on congregations is part of a larger critique of the ways global capitalism cultivates a "habitus" of consumerism among children. She engages Scripture and Christian tradition—informed by a dialogue with

16. Joyce Ann Mercer, *Welcoming Children: A Practical Theology of Childhood* (St. Louis: Chalice, 2005).

biblical studies, dogmatic theology, and feminist theory—to construct "an alternate vision of the meaning of childhood."[17] She is interested not only in the ways congregations may embody this alternative vision, but also in breaking the hold of children-as-consumers across public life—in public education, the media, families, and governmental policies. She is best located in that strand of the public church paradigm influenced by liberation, feminist, and European political theologies.

It is important to be cautious, then, in one's initial judgments about the paradigm of practical theology characterizing a particular text or author. The three paradigms identified in this chapter are best used initially as heuristic devices. They guide the exploration of a particular text, helping to identify the tradition it grows out of, until the reader has a better grasp of its central arguments and theological perspective. Only then will one be in a position to identify the methodological decisions informing the author's approach to the subject matter of this field.

The Descriptive-Empirical Task of Practical Theology

Practical theology carries out empirical research to better understand what is going on in contemporary Christian practice and mission. During the second half of the twentieth century, a revolution took place in the way social scientists understood empirical research, which affirmed the role of both quantitative and qualitative research.[18] A short review of this revolution will clarify some of the decisions practical theologians face when they carry out their own research or draw on the research of others.

When sociology and psychology first appeared at the end of the nineteenth century, they were dominated by models of research from the natural sciences. Emphasis was placed on forming clear hypotheses prior to research and verifying or falsifying them by gathering statistical data. The goal was to discover the "laws" of society and the human psyche. But this sort of qualitative research carried out primarily by cultural anthropologists was viewed as "soft" and not fully scientific. It was seen to merely describe and interpret the way of life of particular communities or individuals. Its findings could not be generalized or verified statistically and were too dependent on the subjective impressions of the researcher, who often gathered data through participant observation.

Over the past fifty years, however, qualitative research has gradually been accepted as a legitimate—some would argue even necessary—part of social science research. In part, this is due to the recognition of the limitations of quantitative research on human beings. Survey data gathered through phone calls, for example, can tell you much about broad social trends and attitudes.

17. Ibid., 5.
18. A helpful account is found in Uwe Flick, *An Introduction to Qualitative Research*, 2nd ed. (Thousand Oaks, CA: Sage, 2002).

But it has great difficulty capturing the meanings lying behind people's answers. Two people may give the same answer to a survey question, but their reasons for doing so may be quite different. This sort of variation and complexity are easily overlooked. Yet this is the strength of qualitative research. It examines a limited number of persons and communities in greater depth, paying attention to detail, processes, and complexity over an extended period of time. Today, both quantitative and qualitative research are viewed as legitimate in social science. Many researchers combine the two approaches in an approach commonly known as mixed methods research.[19] Social scientists have also become more open to action research (sometimes known as advocacy or practice-based research). Here, the goal of research is not merely to investigate a research topic but to help a community or organization change its way of doing things to better embody certain values.

When practical theologians carry out empirical research on contemporary forms of Christian practice and mission, they make certain decisions about the way they will design a research project or draw on the research of others. When reading a text on practical theology, it is important to pay close attention to the approach used and the reasons offered to justify the choice of the approach. Three examples of different types of research in practical theology may alert the reader to these decisions.

One of the most important advocates of empirical research in practical theology today is Johannes van der Ven. Across the years, he has carried out numerous research projects and written books on why such research is important in practical theology.[20] Van der Ven is currently leading an international team of scholars in carrying out research on the impact of religion on adolescents' attitudes toward human rights.[21] The approach van der Ven has chosen is quantitative, primarily using social surveys. There are three reasons for this approach. First, the research is being carried out in public school settings in order to study a population of teens with different religious affiliations and with no religious affiliation at all. Survey research is one of the least intrusive ways of gathering data in this setting. Second, van der Ven needs to gather data from a sample that is large enough to be truly representative of the broader population. Survey research is ideal for this purpose. Third, van der Ven wants to make comparisons across national contexts. This requires

19. See John Creswell, *Research Design: Qualitative, Quantitative, Mixed Methods Approaches*, 2nd ed. (Thousand Oaks, CA: Sage, 2003).

20. See, for example, Johannes A. van der Ven, *Practical Theology: An Empirical Approach* (Kampen, Netherlands: Kok Pharos, 1993).

21. For an overview, see Johannes van der Ven, J. S. Dreyer, and H. J. C. Pieterse, "Religions and Human Rights Attitudes among South African Youth in a Time of Transformation," in *Religion, Morality and Transformation*, ed. F. A. Swanepoel (Pretoria, S. Africa: Unisa, 2001), 103–34, and "Social Location of Attitudes Towards Human Rights among South African Youth," *Religion and Theology* 7 (2000): 249–83.

using the same research instrument in all settings, which is easily handled by administering the same social survey. For the purposes of his project, then, it makes good sense to use a quantitative approach.

In my book *The Teaching Ministry of Congregations*, I carried out qualitative research to explore the ways congregations in three different cultural settings carry out the teaching ministry.[22] The particular qualitative approach used was the case study, which involves interviewing, participant observation, ritual and spatial analysis, and the study of artifacts and documents. My research was not designed to verify a hypothesis or to come up with findings that could be generalized to a broader population. Rather, the goal was to look in depth at three particular communities in order to learn how, where, and why they carry out the teaching ministry.

In *Pastoral Counseling*, Seward Hiltner draws extensively on what might be called "clinical," or practice-based, research.[23] Hiltner offers numerous verbatims and cases that are taken from his practice as a pastoral counselor and from the counseling of his colleagues and students. He believes that the most important skills of pastoral counseling are learned inductively by reflecting on actual experience. Thus, he begins with reports of pastoral relationships with particular persons and only then offers principles and theories that help the reader make sense of these cases. This is the way reflective judgment is formed. Hiltner also believes practical theology as a field should take its bearings from clinical research, especially reflection on pastoral practice.[24] Reflective practice is epistemic; that is, it yields theological insights and knowledge of the human condition that cannot be gained in any other way. Hiltner describes this as a "dynamic" understanding of theology, the way theological themes can help us make sense of the tensions and equilibriums of people's lives.[25] It is a source of theological knowledge that complements the perspectives of the other fields of theology.

These three examples are illustrative of different ways contemporary practical theologians carry out empirical research. Such research is essential to gaining insight into Christian practice and mission in the present, and it is important to evaluate its quality when reading a text on practical theology. The following questions are helpful starting points. Does the author simply offer examples or illustrations of contemporary practice, or does she or he make claims based on actual empirical research? If the latter, what research approach is used? Does the author provide reasons for his or her decision to adopt this approach and note its relative strengths and limitations? If the author draws

22. Richard Osmer, *The Teaching Ministry of Congregations* (Louisville: Westminster John Knox, 2005).

23. Seward Hiltner, *Pastoral Counseling* (New York: Abingdon, 1954).

24. Seward Hiltner, *Preface to Pastoral Theology: The Ministry and Theory of Shepherding* (Nashville: Abingdon, 1958).

25. Seward Hiltner, *Theological Dynamics* (Nashville: Abingdon, 1972).

primarily on the research of others, does he or she merely cite this research or invite readers to note the general approach and methods of this project, providing insight into its strengths and limitations? These sorts of questions invite readers to pay attention to the way a particular practical theologian describes the context, practice, and mission of the contemporary church, but also to evaluate the empirical research on which such descriptions are based.

The Interpretive Task of Practical Theology

Practical theology interprets Christian practices, mission, and contexts in order to gain a richer understanding of why certain patterns and actions are taking place. In the previous section, van der Ven's research on religious affiliation and attitudes toward human rights was described. It is one thing to discover what these attitudes are—the descriptive-empirical task—and another to interpret and explain these findings. Here the task is to develop an account of *why* these attitudes are present.

Throughout the modern period, an important distinction was often made in philosophy and science between interpretation and explanation.[26] Interpretation was portrayed as the attempt to understand the *meanings* that shape human action in everyday life. Explanation was portrayed as an account of the causes of the phenomena of nature and human life in universal "laws." Sometimes, this division of interpretation and explanation was used to describe the difference between the natural and human sciences. Natural science was viewed as explaining nature, and the human sciences, as interpreting human action, which is meaningful and purposeful. Many social scientists, however, rejected this distinction between interpretation and explanation. They sought to explain human behavior along the lines of natural science by discovering the "laws" of society and the individual psyche.

While interpretation and explanation often are distinguished today, this usually is not based on the way these terms were defined during the modern period. There are many reasons for this. One of the most important reasons emerged in the philosophy of science, which now acknowledges the interpretive dimension of science, including natural science. Science works with paradigms and interpretive traditions that shape how a scientist conceptualizes and investigates phenomena.[27] Likewise, new understandings of explanation have emerged, especially in the social sciences. This is not a matter of discovering universal "laws" that apply in all times and places. Rather, it is a matter of developing an account of the preexistent structures that shape human action in a particular context and the ways human actors respond to

---

26. Richard Bernstein, *Beyond Objectivism and Relativism: Science, Hermeneutics, and Praxis* (Philadelphia: University of Pennsylvania Press, 1983).

27. One of the first to make this point was Thomas Kuhn, *The Structure of Scientific Revolutions* (Chicago: University of Chicago Press, 1962).

these structures—maintaining, revising, or rejecting them.[28] Explanation thus identifies the interplay of structure and agency in particular social contexts.

This background helps students understand and evaluate the ways contemporary practical theologians carry out the interpretive task. We will illustrate this by examining two examples of feminist practical theology: Elaine Graham's *Transforming Practice* and Leonora Tubbs Tisdale's *Preaching as Local Theology and Folk Art*.[29] Both of these practical theologians work within the public church paradigm and are deeply committed to transforming patterns of gender in the broader social context. Yet they portray and carry out the interpretive task in very different ways.

In *Transforming Practice*, Elaine Graham asks the question, How can contemporary communities of faith form beliefs and practices in our highly pluralistic, postmodern context in which communities no longer share a common metaphysical framework? She is particularly interested in helping congregations become sites of new gender patterns that move beyond patriarchy. When congregations form new patterns of Christian practice and mission beyond patriarchy, they engage in what Graham calls transforming practice. Such practice generates innovative beliefs and norms with the potential to transform the Christian tradition and contribute to the transformation of society. Graham interprets this process with the new understanding of explanation described above. Human communities and individual actors participate in the interplay of structure and agency. The preexistent structures of gender relations are quite powerful. But particular communities and individuals have the agency to respond in different ways, continuing, revising, or transforming these structures. Graham gives special attention to the diversity of ways Christian communities move beyond patriarchy. She explains this in terms of the ways these communities experience structures quite differently. Some people, for example, experience structures of race and poverty just as powerfully as others experience structures of gender. Moreover, each community will exercise agency in unique ways, developing forms of transforming practice that fit their circumstances. This not only explains the diversity of postpatriarchal Christian communities, but also points to a broader moral imperative: the importance of learning from the wisdom of other communities involved in transforming practice and not absolutizing the perspective of one's own community.

Leonora Tubbs Tisdale offers a very different portrait of the interpretive task in *Preaching as Local Theology and Folk Art*. She is especially interested in helping preachers craft sermons that take account of the culture of their particular

---

28. One of the clearest and most helpful accounts of this "new" understanding of explanation is found in Margaret Archer, *Realist Social Theory: The Morphogenic Approach* (Cambridge: Cambridge University Press, 1995).

29. Elaine Graham, *Transforming Practice: Pastoral Theology in an Age of Uncertainty* (Eugene, OR: Wipf & Stock, 1996); Leonora Tubbs Tisdale, *Preaching as Local Theology and Folk Art* (Minneapolis: Fortress, 1997).

congregations. Just as preachers explore the meaning of scriptural texts with the methods of biblical exegesis, so too must they learn to use methods for "exegeting" the congregation in all its sociocultural particularity. Otherwise, they will preach abstract sermons to a generic humanity that do not address the real-life situations of their hearers. Tisdale describes the interpretive task from the perspective of congregational studies, especially as it is informed by the methods of cultural anthropology. The goal is to interpret, not explain, a congregation's culture in all its particularity, entering into and understanding the language, symbols, and implicit norms that make up its unique way of life. Not only will this help preachers craft sermons that connect with the life experience of their hearers, but also it supports preaching that is genuinely transformational, that helps the members of a particular community imagine new forms of life that are understandable and meaningful to them. Tisdale's commitment to helping congregations move beyond patriarchy thus takes very seriously the points of pain, resistance, and possibility that are already present in a particular community. When interpreted with compassion and prophetic passion, they serve as the starting point of congregational transformation.

This brief examination of two contemporary feminist practical theologians makes it clear that even scholars who share many theological commitments can approach the interpretive task of practical theology in very different ways. When reading a particular text of practical theology, students will do well to pay attention to two kinds of issues. One sort of issue has to do with the themes that are prominent in the author's interpretation of Christian practice, mission, and context—themes like individualism, consumerism, gender relations, and so forth. A second kind of issue is the way the author conceptualizes the interpretive task. Often, this is not explicitly stated, and one will need to look closely at what the author actually does in the text. Does she or he offer in-depth exploration of particular relationships and communities to allow readers to interpret them with understanding? Or does she or he strive to explain patterns and actions in terms of the interplay of structure and agency, focusing on broad social trends and particular cases that illustrate these trends? Sometimes practical theologians do both.

The Normative Task of Practical Theology

Practical theologians develop normative perspectives to critique and guide Christian practice and mission. In our discussion of prayer at the beginning of this chapter, we drew attention to the way practical theologians are very sensitive to context in constructing theological norms. In this section, another important issue is treated: the relative weight practical theologians give to the sources of Christian theology. For our purposes, it is helpful to think of these sources as fourfold: Christian Scripture, tradition, reason, and experience. This is sometimes known at the Wesley quadrilateral, articulated by Albert Outler in his reflection on the theology of John Wesley.[30] While this model is useful in discussions of dogmatic theology and Christian ethics, it is particularly helpful in identifying normative approaches in practical theology. Almost by definition, contemporary practical theologians give attention to experience in their investigation of present practice, and to reason in their dialogue with the social sciences. The question is the authority they grant these sources in relation to Scripture and tradition. Practical theologians give different weight to these four sources of Christian theology, and examples will be noted as we move along.

Christian Scripture, obviously, has to do with the weight practical theologians give to the Bible and the strategies they use to interpret it. Some believe that Scripture is God's Word and contains the record of God's revelation. Others view the Bible as a "resource" that must be reinterpreted in every age to address contemporary problems in ways that are meaningful. Needless to say, these are very different ways of viewing the authority of Scripture and carry very different weight in normative proposals. It also is important to note the interpretive strategies that practical theologians use. Evangelical and Reformed practical theologians, for example, commonly view Scripture as the most important authority in theological reflection, the "norm of norms," but they often vary in their way of interpreting Scripture. Some interpret biblical texts in light of the Bible's christocentric focus, others focus on its narrative patterns, still others grant authority to the "literal" meaning of texts. While holding a high view of biblical authority, these practical theologians appeal to Scripture in very different ways. When reading a text on practical theology, it is important to determine the relative weight granted the Bible in the author's normative proposals, as well as the interpretive strategies he or she uses to interpret it.

Christian tradition points to the beliefs and practices emerging in the Christian community across the centuries. A practical theologian's denominational heritage frequently has great influence on the authority granted tradition. Roman Catholic and Anglican practical theologians often view the tradition as having authority equal to that of Scripture. They draw on the teachings of church councils to justify their proposals or give special weight to the sacramental and liturgical practices of the tradition. Practical theologians in denominations emerging from the Protestant Reformation commonly view tradition as subordinate to Scripture, providing hermeneutical guidance in interpreting the Bible's central teachings. Confessional traditions and ecclesial practices carry weight only as they help the contemporary church confess and embody the gospel in its own time and place. Practical theologians with Baptist and Anabaptist roots typically view tradition as carrying little weight and seek to warrant their normative proposals by appealing directly to the Bible.

---

30. For a discussion of this concept and Outler's articulation of it, see Stephen Gunter et al., *Wesley and the Quadrilateral: Renewing the Conversation* (Nashville: Abingdon, 1997).

Within these broad denominational differences, however, there is much variety in contemporary practical theology. Regardless of their denominational affiliation, for example, liberal practical theologians commonly grant little authority to tradition. They view it as something that must be reinterpreted for the faith to be meaningful and relevant in the contemporary world. Likewise, feminist practical theologians often view tradition as a source of oppression, which must be critiqued and reshaped if it is to contribute to the contemporary emancipation of women. Yet there are many practical theologians who look to tradition for normative guidance. A particularly interesting example is the retrieval of the adult catechumenate of the patristic period by Catholic, Lutheran, and United Methodist practical theologians. They approach the tradition as a source of normative practice, not ideas, which may reshape the practice of initiation in the present church. In short, practical theologians draw on tradition in their normative proposals in a wide variety of ways. While this is influenced by denominational affiliation, it also reflects the theological stance of a particular practical theologian.

Reason encompasses all of the disciplined ways a community has developed to investigate the world rationally and gain knowledge that helps it cope with its problems and advance human understanding. In the West, reason is closely identified with the arts and sciences and, over the past 150 years, with the modern scientific disciplines. Almost all practical theologians today grant authority to reason and learn from the social sciences in particular. Yet they conceptualize this authority in very different ways. Some view the authority of reason, for example, as equal to that of Scripture and Christian tradition. They attempt to correlate contemporary knowledge with the Bible and tradition, deriving their normative proposals from a conversation between these sources. Others learn from contemporary forms of reason but believe that Scripture and/or tradition are unique sources of knowledge of God, the church, and humanity. Their normative proposals give priority to the Bible and/or tradition in determining the purposes of the church and human life, and view other forms of human knowledge as auxiliary tools in achieving these purposes. The different weight granted reason as a source of theology has important implications for the interdisciplinary methods practical theologians use.[31]

Experience is conceptualized in a wide variety of ways in contemporary practical theology and given different weight. It is helpful to sort out this variety into three groups: those who look to experience as generating new theological insights and norms, those who view experience as an important part of the enculturation of the gospel, and those who view the gospel as standing in tension with experience. Examples of each group will clarify their differences.

31. For an overview of different interdisciplinary approaches, see Osmer, *Practical Theology*, chap. 3.

Liberation and feminist practical theologians view the experience of the struggling oppressed as yielding new theological insights, a perspective that harks back to liberation theology's concept of the "epistemic privilege of the poor."[32] Elaine Graham's concept of transforming practice illustrates this nicely. As we have seen, Graham argues that faith communities that are struggling to form new beliefs and practices beyond patriarchy are a source of theological insight. Feminist practical theologians, she argues, will do well to glean the wisdom of such communities in forming their normative proposals. Practical theologians informed by the Clinical Pastoral Education movement similarly view experience as a source of theological insight, harking back to Anton Boisen's idea that theology is formed by reading "living human documents," as well as sacred texts and traditions.[33] Seward Hiltner and Charles Gerkin built on this idea to portray practical theology as forging its normative proposals, at least in part, by reflecting on pastoral practice.[34]

Experience is viewed differently by those practical theologians who emphasize the enculturation of the gospel. While the gospel of Jesus Christ is granted unique authority, these practical theologians recognize that the missionary calling of the church involves helping the gospel take root in very different cultural contexts. Practical theology, then, must give attention to the unique cultural experience of communities for the gospel to be translated and embodied in their context. An excellent illustration of this position is found in the writings of Kenda Creasy Dean.[35] Building on the work of Andrew Walls, Dean argues that practical theology must hold in tension the "indigenization" principle and the "pilgrim" principle. The former takes God's self-enculturation seriously, the way the Holy Spirit enables the gospel to take shape within the *experience* of a particular culture. The latter takes seriously the ways the gospel calls every culture into question and creates a pilgrim people who witness to its transforming power. Dean explores the implications of this perspective for ministry with young people, which must take youth culture seriously and also challenge youth to live as God's pilgrim people.

Finally, some practical theologians view experience as deeply ambiguous and as standing in tension with the gospel. It is not possible to look to experience to discover what God is like or discern the purposes of human life and the church. It is filled with evil, sin, and suffering, as well as goodness

---

32. Gustavo Gutiérrez, *A Theology of Liberation: History, Politics, and Salvation*, trans. Caridad Inda and John Eagleson (London: SCM, 2001).

33. One of several places Boisen makes this point is Anton T. Boisen, *Problems in Religion and Life: A Manual for Pastors, with Outlines for the Co-Operative Study of Personal Experience in Social Situations* (Nashville: Abingdon-Cokesbury, 1946).

34. Hiltner, preface to *The Living Human Document: Re-Visioning Pastoral Counseling in a Hermeneutical Mode*, by Charles Gerkin (Nashville: Abingdon, 1984).

35. See, particularly, Kenda Creasy Dean, *Almost Christian: What the Faith of Our Teenagers Is Telling the American Church* (New York: Oxford University Press, 2010).

and beauty, and, as such, is an ambiguous source of theological knowledge. There is no bridge from human experience to knowledge of God. This gap can only be overcome by God's self-communication or revelation. An example of this position is found in the writings of the practical theologian Eduard Thurneysen, a close colleague of Karl Barth.[36] Thurneysen argues that the gospel of Jesus Christ reveals the depths of God's love, a love so powerful that it entered fully into the sin and suffering of a broken world and reconciled this world to God. This good news takes the form of proclamation, an announcement of the gospel that breaks into and stands in tension with human experience. While pastors and practical theologians must pay attention to experience in order to know how to proclaim this message in different circumstances, the message itself is not derived from experience. It is derived from God's saving actions in Christ Jesus. Moreover, because human beings remain caught in sin and death, this message can only be heard and heeded through the present activity of the Holy Spirit. It is not a simple outgrowth of their present experience.

Much attention has been paid to the normative task of practical theology because of its importance. Practical theology is a form of *theology*, not merely social science "lite" with empirical and interpretive interests. Therefore the authority practical theologians grant the sources of theology—Scripture, tradition, reason, and experience—stands at the very heart of their theological perspective. It informs both the theological method they use to construct normative proposals as well as the interdisciplinary method by which they bring practical theology into dialogue with other fields.

To recognize the way practical theologians form normative proposals, it will be helpful for students to pose certain questions to the texts they are reading. Which of the four sources of theology—Scripture, tradition, reason, and experience—is given priority? Since practical theologians, almost by definition, pay some attention to reason and experience, how are these conceptualized in the text? Are they granted authority equal to that of Scripture and/or tradition, or are they viewed as making a secondary contribution to normative proposals? Examples of different positions have been given above, and these may alert you to an author's particular perspective.

The Pragmatic Task of Practical Theology

Practical theology forms practical models and principles that offer guidance to contemporary Christian practice and mission. This has been described in terms of the theme of "how to" in the subject matter of practical theology. There are two important issues for students to keep in mind in order to understand and evaluate the way practical theologians handle this task today.

36. Eduard Thurneysen, *A Theology of Pastoral Care*, trans. J. Worthington and T. Wiser (Richmond: John Knox, 1962).

First, what is the basis of the practical models and principles that are offered? Are they based exclusively on one person's experience in one particular setting? Or are they based on a number of cases and broad empirical research? It can be quite helpful to read the account of one person's experience and the program he or she is now commending on the basis of this experience. But the limitations of this approach should be recognized. It is not clear that programs formed in this way will work in other settings, especially if these settings are very different from the author's in terms of race, ethnicity, class, denomination, and so forth. The best practical theologians today do more than share their own experience. They ground the practical models and principles of "how to" in a rich account of "why to." They also invite the reader to use reflective judgment in adapting models formed in one context to other contexts that may be quite different.

Second, does the author provide theological justification for commending particular models and principles, offering good reasons for using them in Christian practice and mission? As we have noted throughout this chapter, practical theologians today engage in a robust conversation with the social sciences. In carrying out the pragmatic task, they draw on leadership theory, psychotherapy, education, family systems theory, and other action sciences. These are helpful and important. But the question of theological appropriateness remains. Can a leadership theory developed for corporations be taken over by the church without significant changes? Does a pastor simply offer psychotherapy or crisis counseling along the lines of a therapist or social worker? What is distinctive about Christian practice and mission and how does this impact our reliance on practical models and principles developed by other fields for different purposes? Perhaps more than anything else, these questions highlight the reason practical theology today is striving to balance "how to" and "why to." Communities of faith face many challenges in the contemporary world, and it is tempting to latch on to answers that promise success, especially if they wear the mantle of science. But will this enable the church to develop forms of practice and mission that are faithful, as well as relevant and effective? A great deal hangs in the balance.

For Further Reading

Anderson, Raymond. *The Shape of Practical Theology*. Grand Rapids: Eerdmans, 2001.

Browning, Don. *A Fundamental Practical Theology: Descriptive and Strategic Proposals*. Minneapolis: Fortress, 1991.

Gerkin, Charles. *The Living Human Document: Re-Visioning Pastoral Counseling in a Hermeneutical Mode*. Nashville: Abingdon, 1984.

Graham, Elaine. *Transforming Practice: Pastoral Theology in an Age of Uncertainty*. Eugene, OR: Wipf & Stock, 1996.

Hiltner, Seward. *Preface to Pastoral Theology: The Ministry and Theory of Shepherding*. Nashville: Abingdon, 1958.

Loder, James. *The Logic of the Spirit: Human Development in Theological Perspective*. San Francisco: Jossey-Bass, 1998.

Miller-McLemore, Bonnie, and Brita L. Gill-Austern, eds. *Feminist and Womanist Pastoral Theology*. Nashville: Abingdon, 1999.

Osmer, Richard. *Practical Theology: An Introduction*. Grand Rapids: Eerdmans, 2008.

Schleiermacher, Friedrich. *Brief Outline on the Study of Theology*. Translated by T. Tice. Richmond: John Knox, 1966.

Van der Ven, Johannes A. *Practical Theology: An Empirical Approach*. Kampen, Netherlands: Kok Pharos, 1993.

14

• • •

ECCLESIOLOGY

Veli-Matti Kärkkäinen

Background and Context: The Missionary Movement as the Catalyst

While nothing can match the magnitude of the transformation in the church and ecclesiology in the sixteenth century Western church, the transition to a modern method of theology and thus a modern way of thinking about the church represents another watershed.[1]

Beginning from the Protestant Reformation, the church's institutional unity was replaced with an ever-intensifying plurality and multiformity of churches and Christian communities. While sociopolitical changes—such as the intensification of the industrial process and the massive colonialization undertakings—played a significant role in nineteenth-century church life, nothing probably compares to the role of the modern missionary movement in bringing ever-greater plurality within the church. Beginning from the end of the eighteenth century, Christianity rapidly became a world religion with a presence and outposts all over the newly developing inhabited world. Of course, the presence of the Christian church was unevenly located in the continents of Africa, Asia, and Latin America, often following either the coastlines or the paths of the colonists and merchants. Yet it is the modern missionary movement that

1. Roger Haight, SJ, *Christian Community in History*, vol. 2, *Comparative Ecclesiology* (New York: Continuum, 2005), 291.

345

laid the foundation for the current spread of the Christian church such that Christians in the global South (Africa, Asia, and Latin America) far outnumber their counterparts in the global North (Europe, North America).

Catholics and Protestants did mission differently. In the Protestant spread of the church, mission societies and entrepreneurial individuals were the key. In Catholic missions, monastic and other religious orders took the forefront. Furthermore, while the Catholic Church virtually withstood the influence of the Enlightenment until Vatican II (1962–1965), Protestant churches flung doors wide open to modernity as a result of the Enlightenment.[2] While much smaller in scale, the missionary enterprise of the Eastern Orthodox Church particularly in the eighteenth century should not be dismissed. Orthodox priests and monks traveled to Russia, Siberia, Alaska, and other places to establish significant Orthodox constituencies.[3]

Going ahead of our discussion, let us consider briefly the stage on which twentieth-century ecclesiological developments took place:

> As the twentieth century began, each of the major churches of a divided Christendom was obliged, for reasons of its own, to address anew the doctrine of the church—its place in the mind of Christ, its essential message, its nature and identity, its marks of continuity, its authority and structure, its response to its twofold mission of keeping itself "unspotted from the world" and yet of being "the salt of the earth," and above all its authentic unity despite and beyond its historic divisions.[4]

Ecclesial Traditions and Their Theological Self-Understandings

Nineteenth-Century Protestant Ecclesiologies

Unlike the Roman Catholic Church, Protestant churches embodied—and continue embodying—pluralism and multiformity. Modern Protestant theology was greatly influenced not only by the continuing effects of the Enlightenment but also by Romanticism, which emphasized imagination and creativity. Imagination helped center theological reflection about the church on the metaphors of organism, organic growth, and thus a social-organic understanding of the church.[5] For traditional Protestants, however, modern Protestant theology, particularly classical liberalism, seemed to be thin in orthodox doctrine and traditional Christian piety. Those features helped generate two kinds of

2. See Stephen B. Bevans and Roger P. Schroeder, *Constants in Context: A Theology of Mission for Today* (Maryknoll, NY: Orbis, 2004), chap. 7.
3. Ibid., 227–28.
4. Jaroslav Pelikan, *The Christian Tradition: A History of the Development of Doctrine*, vol. 5, *Christian Doctrine and Modern Culture (since 1700)* (Chicago: University of Chicago Press, 1989), 282.
5. See, further, Haight, *Christian Community*, 2:306–7.

responses from the more theologically conservative segment of the church and theology. Whereas revivalistic movements, such as Pietism, Puritanism, and Holiness Methodist movements, as well as the Awakenings on both sides of the Atlantic Ocean, sought to revitalize the "heart-religion," fundamentalist movements sought to rediscover pre-Enlightenment, precritical biblical and doctrinal stances.

While innovative in so many ways, the nineteenth-century ecclesiology of the leading nineteenth-century liberal, Friedrich Schleiermacher—as presented in his main work *The Christian Faith*[6]—continues the best tradition of *systematic* theology in that the chapter on ecclesiology, rather than being an isolated locus, is integrally related to his overall theological vision. Having explicated the meaning of God-consciousness as the constitutive part of humanity at large in the first major part, the discussion in the second major part, with a focus on a specifically *Christian* experience of God-consciousness under the rubric of sin and grace, centers on Christ and the church. The meaning of Christ's person and work for our salvation is explained from the Christian community's perspective of experience, and the discussion of the doctrine of the church "refers to the community which historically mediates the experience of Jesus Christ in history," through the lens of soteriology.[7]

For Schleiermacher, redemption, on the one hand, depends upon Christ; on the other hand, unlike the first disciples, we only have contact with the church. We can only solve this problem if we can affirm that the "influence of the fellowship in producing a like faith is none other than the influence of the personal perfection of Jesus himself."[8] The church's mediatory role comes to focus in that "the self-revelation of Christ is now mediated by those who preach him" in such a way that "the activity really proceeds from him and is essentially his own."[9]

This point also brings pneumatology into focus. Kevin W. Hector rightly notes that "the very same activity is incarnate in Christ and present in the church, which means that Christ's activity is indeed present to us in the church. We thus see one of the things that Schleiermacher's pneumatology will attempt to explain, namely, the way that God mediates Christ's activity to us through the Spirit's presence in the church."[10] The Spirit is the "medium"

6. Friedrich Schleiermacher, *The Christian Faith*, ed. H. R. Mackintosh and J. S. Stewart (1821–1822; rev. 1830–1831; repr., New York: Harper & Row, 1963).

7. Haight, *Christian Community*, 2:316.

8. Schleiermacher, *Christian Faith*, §88.

9. Schleiermacher, *Christian Faith*, §108.5. See Kevin W. Hector, "The Mediation of Christ's Normative Spirit: A Constructive Reading of Schleiermacher's Pneumatology," *Modern Theology* 24, no. 1 (2008): 1–22.

10. Hector, "Mediation of Christ's Normative Spirit," 4. For Schleiermacher's own formulation, see §125.

through which Christ continues his fellowship and unity with the church, as most fully explained in the long section 122.

Through the church Christ's redemptive mission continues in the world.[11] This will eventually lead to the sanctification of the world.[12] Echoing his Pietistic roots, Schleiermacher makes a distinction between two kinds of members in the church.[13] The church expands as more and more people come in touch with Jesus and thus move from the outer to the inner circle.[14] The doctrine of election is the Christian way of explaining why some are in the outer while others in the inner circle.[15]

Roman Catholic Ecclesiology

CHURCH AND ECCLESIOLOGY PRIOR TO VATICAN II

In the nineteenth-century Catholic Church, there was a shift toward authoritarianism as well as the adoption of a "counterculture" mentality, including resistance to modernity—so dramatically reflected in the pronouncements of Vatican Council I (1869–1870).[16] At the same time, the church tended to idealize the Christendom and the church of the Middle Ages. When it comes to the theological milieu of the nineteenth-century Catholic Church, it can be characterized as a "textbook theology mediated through the metaphysical categories of Aristotle."[17] Unlike Protestant theology, it allowed very little room for pluralism; intellectual creativity was reined in by ecclesiastical authority.

In its "First Dogmatic Constitution on the Church of Christ," Vatican I presented a view of the church as authoritarian and hierarchic, as it focused its pronouncements on the primacy of the pope, the "true vicar of Christ."[18] A "primacy of jurisdiction over the whole Church" has been given to the successor of Peter, a primacy "immediately and directly promised"[19] concerning the worldwide church[20] and to remain forever.[21] Because the power of the

11. Schleiermacher, *Christian Faith*, §124.
12. Ibid., §113.
13. Ibid.
14. Ibid., §114.
15. Ibid., §120.
16. It is significant that the Council was presided over by Pius IX, the author of the "Syllabus of Errors," the issuer of the encyclical *Quanta Qura* (1864) that sought to combat modernism and other similar views. Vatican I mentions in the introduction to Council pronouncements that the reason for its convening was the "condemnation of contemporary errors" as well as the need to define the doctrine of the church. "First Vatican Council (1869–1870)," Eternal Word Television Network, http://www.ewtn.com/library/COUNCILS/V1.htm#6.
17. Haight, *Christian Community*, 2:308.
18. "First Dogmatic Constitution on the Church of Christ" 3.1, Eternal Word Television Network http://www.ewtn.com/library/COUNCILS/V1.htm#6.
19. Ibid., 1.1.
20. Ibid., 3.1.
21. Ibid., 2.1.

bishop of Rome is "both episcopal and immediate," all have to submit to it obediently.[22] The pontiff is not only the teacher of the church—and the bishops, if needed[23]—he is also "the supreme judge of the faithful."[24] The final culmination of the establishment of the power of the pontiff is the statement on the infallibility of the pope, considered to be a "divinely revealed dogma," namely, that when the Roman pontiff speaks *ex cathedra*, that is,

> when, in the exercise of his office as shepherd and teacher of all Christians, in virtue of his supreme apostolic authority, he defines a doctrine concerning faith or morals to be held by the whole Church, he possesses, by the divine assistance promised to him in blessed Peter, that infallibility which the divine Redeemer willed his Church to enjoy in defining doctrine concerning faith or morals. Therefore, such definitions of the Roman Pontiff are of themselves, and not by the consent of the Church, irreformable.[25]

Over against—and in many ways in tension with—the official position and textbook theology, there were attempts at a more balanced way of conceiving the doctrine of the church. Prominent among them—particularly with regard to his later influence even upon Vatican II—is Johann Adam Möhler (1796–1838), named one of "the greatest ecclesiologists of the modern times."[26] According to Dennis Doyle, Möhler's view distanced itself from medieval Catholic ecclesiology and drew upon Schleiermacher's influence as well, making it thus less juridical and more mystical and organic.[27] There are two phases to Möhler's theological envisioning of the church: the former one, as presented in his *Unity in the Church*,[28] which was pneumatological in orientation[29]—but not to the exclusion of Christology[30]—and the latter one, which made a significant contribution to the developing influential Catholic

22. Ibid., 3.2.

23. Ibid., 3.6.

24. Ibid., 3.8.

25. Ibid., 4.9.

26. Peter J. Riga, "The Ecclesiology of Johann Adam Möhler," *Theological Studies* 22, no. 4 (1961): 563–64.

27. Dennis M. Doyle, "Möhler, Schleiermacher, and the Roots of Communion Ecclesiology," *Theological Studies* 57, no. 3 (1996): 478.

28. Ibid., 471. Johann Adam Möhler, *Unity in the Church or the Principle of Catholicism: Presented in the Spirit of the Church Fathers of the First Three Centuries*, ed. and trans. Peter C. Erb (Washington, DC: Catholic University of America Press, 1996).

29. Riga, "Ecclesiology," 573–77, in particular; Bradford E. Hinze, "Releasing the Power of the Spirit in a Trinitarian Ecclesiology," in *Advents of the Spirit: An Introduction to the Current Study of Pneumatology*, ed. Bradford E. Hinze and D. Lyle Dabney, Marquette Studies in Theology 30 (Milwaukee: Marquette University Press, 2001), 347–81.

30. This is wonderfully illustrated in the important article by the Jesuit ecclesiologist Philip P. Rosato, "Between Christocentrism and Pneumatocentrism: An Interpretation of Johann Adam Möhler's Ecclesiology," *Heythrop Journal* 19, no. 1 (January 1978): 46–70.

idea of the church as the continuation of the incarnation of Christ.[31] This discussion focuses on the former phase and its influence on the succeeding developments in Catholic ecclesiology.

In his *The Unity in the Church*, Möhler ties together integrally the visible and invisible nature of the church: "*One* common, true *life* forms itself through the totality of believers as a result of two factors: a spiritual power and its external organic manifestation."[32] Similarly to his modern Protestant colleagues, Möhler was fond of organic metaphors, speaking of the church in terms of growth and evolvement. This comes to the fore particularly in his pneumatological account: "Together all believers form an organic whole."[33] This is not to say that structures and hierarchy are foreign to his ecclesiology, but rather that there is an attempted balance between the inner and outer, mystical and organizational; he therefore forms an important bridge between Vatican I and II.

The continuing challenge for Roman Catholic ecclesiology as it transitioned to the last century of the second millennium—and up to today—has been the difficulty in negotiating the dilemma between traditionalists who "lament the disappearance of previously distinctive Catholic formulations and customs" and progressives who "press on towards more non-juridical, ecumenical and charismatic expressions of Catholicism."[34] The encyclical by Pope Pius X titled *Vehementer Nos* (1910) explicitly described the church as "an unequal society" with regard to the clergy and laity.[35] A significant move toward a more balanced ecclesiology was made in the 1943 encyclical *Mystici Corporis*, by Pius XII. This pronouncement takes up the challenge of christological and pneumatological orientation—the dynamic between organizational-hierarchic-clerically led and charismatic-dynamic-lay participatory orientations—and paints a picture of the church in which the two elements balance and enrich each other.[36]

THE CHURCH IN CONTEMPORARY ROMAN CATHOLIC THEOLOGY

The work of Vatican II was prepared and followed up by the important work of some leading Catholic theologians such as Karl Rahner and Hans Küng. Küng's 1967 book *The Church* is already a contemporary classic. He issued a

31. For the latter, see the important study by Michael J. Himes, *Ongoing Incarnation: Johann Adam Möhler and the Beginning of Modern Ecclesiology* (New York: Crossroad, 1997); for the shift in Möhler's theology, see Haight, *Christian Community*, 2:338–39.
32. Möhler, *Unity*, 2.1.49, 211–12; see also 2.1, 209.
33. Ibid., 1.3.26, 143.
34. Rosato, "Between Christocentrism and Pneumatocentrism," 48.
35. *Vehementer Nos* 8, at the Vatican website: http://www.vatican.va/holy_father/pius_x /encyclicals/documents/hf_p-x_enc_11021906_vehementer-nos_en.html.
36. *Mystici Corporis Christi* 17, at the Vatican website: http://www.vatican.va/holy_father /pius_xii/encyclicals/documents/hf_p-xii_enc_29061943_mystici-corporis-christi_en.html.

call for constant renewal of the church[37] and, echoing Reformers, considered the church as the communion not only of saints but also of sinners.[38] He also warned of overclericalization and stressed the importance of the charismatic gifting of the whole people of God. The significance of the charismatic element was also lifted up by his colleague Karl Rahner in the book published during the council, *The Dynamic Element in the Church*.[39]

The Second Vatican Council helped the Catholic Church to come to terms with modernity.[40] The council issued what might be the most important ecclesiological document of all times: *Lumen Gentium* (*The Dogmatic Constitution of the Church*).[41] Another key document is *Gaudium et Spes* (*The Pastoral Constitution on the Church in the Modern World*).

While the original schema emphasized the institutional nature of the church, its hierarchic structure, the priesthood and episcopacy, as well as the necessity of authority and obedience, the final version ended up looking very different.[42] *Lumen Gentium* begins with the nature of the church as a "mystery" founded by the trinitarian God (chap. 1), described as the people of God, which includes all members, ordained and lay (chap. 2), and only then speaks of "The Church as Hierarchical" (chap. 3). Immediately following is a chapter (4) on the laity, and—very importantly—"The Call to Holiness" (chap. 5), for the whole church comes before the chapter on the "Religious" (chap. 6). Then, in a dramatic reorientation from the past that looked at the Catholic Church as a "perfect society," chapter 7 speaks of the church as the "Pilgrim Church," on the way to her heavenly destiny and therefore as not yet perfect. The final chapter (8)—again after much debate—focuses on the role of Mary; the reason for attaching the teaching on the Blessed Lady as part of the ecclesiological document, rather than making it a separate document, is to highlight the church and liturgy as the proper locus of honoring the Mother of God.

In keeping with the sacramental underpinnings of all of Catholic theology, *Lumen Gentium* describes the church "in the nature of sacrament," which means that it is "a sign and instrument . . . of communion with God and of unity among all men."[43] This is truly a "catholic" vision, linking the church not only with the Triune God (as elaborated in paragraphs 2–4) but also with the whole of humanity.

37. Hans Küng, *The Church* (New York: Image Books, 1976), 341.
38. Ibid., 230.
39. Karl Rahner, *The Dynamic Element in the Church* (New York: Herder & Herder, 1964).
40. Thomas P. Rausch, *Towards a Truly Catholic Church: An Ecclesiology for the Third Millennium* (Collegeville, MN: Liturgical Press, 2005), 8–9.
41. References and citations of Vatican II documents are drawn from Austin Flannery, OP, ed., *Vatican Council II*, vol. 1, *The Conciliar and Post Conciliar Documents*, new rev. ed. (Northport, NY: Costello/Dublin, Ireland: Dominican, 1998).
42. For a lucid discussion, see Rausch, *Catholic Church*, 15–24.
43. *Lumen Gentium* 1.1.

Having defined the church as sacrament[44] and as the people of God, the document elaborates the church's hierarchical nature in the service of the growth and well-being of the church.[45] Bishops, forming a college reflecting the election of the Twelve,[46] are the leaders appointed by Christ, under the ministry of the bishop of Rome, the pope,[47] the "lasting and visible source of unity both of faith and of communion."[48] Vatican II both affirms and qualifies the power of the pope. The papal infallibility, however, is qualified and put in perspective in several ways: first of all, it is linked with the infallibility of the whole church; second, not only the pope but also the college of bishops, particularly when gathered for ecumenical council, can possess infallibility; third—while in principle valid without the reception of the church—it is said in this context that "the assent of the Church can never be lacking to such definitions" on account of the Holy Spirit's ministry; and, finally, it is affirmed that infallible pronouncements are made in conformity with revelation.[49]

Following the teaching on the hierarchy, *Lumen Gentium* brings about a remarkable theology of laity and their ministry. Having already included lay people under the people of God (chap. 2) and issuing the call to holiness to all members of the church (chap. 5), not only the ordained and religious, it speaks of the apostolate of the laity that participates in the priestly and prophetic ministry of Christ.[50] The Holy Spirit sanctifies and leads the people of God not only through the sacraments and church ministries, but also through special charisms bestowed freely on all the faithful in a variety of ways.[51]

Elaborated in the separate document *Unitatis Redintegratio*, *Lumen Gentium* opens up the doors for ecumenical work and search for unity. Unlike in the past, there is no identification of the church of Christ with the Roman Catholic Church.[52] Even though only the Eastern Church is named "church" in the theological sense, there is an acknowledgment of a number of core values shared among all Christians, such as Scripture, Christian zeal, trinitarian confession, and so forth.[53]

The church's relation to the contemporary world and culture is elaborated in great detail in the longest document, *Gaudium et Spes*, which seeks to read "the signs of the times,"[54] a favorite term at and around the council. In keep-

44. A related term, "mystery," is employed in several places, e.g., in 1.5.
45. Ibid., 3.18.
46. Ibid., 3.19.
47. Ibid., 3.22.
48. Ibid., 3.18.
49. Ibid., 3.25.
50. Ibid., 4.33–34.
51. Ibid., 2.12. For other references to charisms, see 4.30; *Apostolican Actuositatem* 1.3; and *Presbyterorium Ordinis* 2.2.9.
52. *Lumen Gentium* 1.8.
53. Ibid., 2.15.
54. *Gaudium et Spes* 4.

ing with the "catholic" vision, the council addresses here not only the church but the whole of humanity.[55]

Nostra Aetate and other documents further develop the teaching in *Lumen Gentium* of the openness of the Catholic Church to other religions: there is a kind of "hierarchy" of religions in terms of how they are related to the Catholic Church, from the Jews (the closest religion), to Muslims, then on to other monotheists, and finally to other religions. Furthermore, there is the possibility of salvation because of Christ's universal salvific work for those who have not heard the gospel but are sincerely following the light of their own religions and ethical codes.[56]

CATHOLIC BASE COMMUNITIES

One of the significant new challenges in twentieth-century Roman Catholic ecclesiology is the emergence of "base communities" in Latin America. While these communities emerged "from underneath," advocating the cause of the common people and the poor, oppressed, and underprivileged, their coming into existence was also prepared by several episcopal-hierarchic initiatives such as the Second Conference of Latin American Bishops at Medellín, Colombia (1968).

The main figure behind the Catholic base communities, Leonardo Boff, in his highly acclaimed *Ecclesiogenesis*, summarizes key features: "Slowly, but with ever-increasing intensity, we have witnessed the creation of communities in which persons actually know and recognize one another, where they can be themselves in their individuality, where they can 'have their say,' where they can be welcomed by name. And so, we see, groups and little communities have sprung up everywhere."[57] The base communities not only identify with the poor and the weakest in the society; they *are* a church of the poor, made up of poor people.

While important sociological and sociopolitical reasons—particularly the cause of the poor—lie behind the base communities, there is also a defined theologico-ecclesiological conviction. These theologians argue that base communities present more than just renewal movements within the larger church (i.e., the Roman Catholic Church). These communities represent a new ecclesiology, "ecclesiogenesis," "starting the church again."[58] It is the theological claim for the ecclesial nature of these communities that has also placed them in tension with Catholic ecclesiology and hierarchy.[59]

55. Ibid., 2.

56. *Lumen Gentium* 2.16. See also *Gaudium et Spes* 1.1.22 and *Nostra Aetate* 2, among others.

57. Leonardo Boff, *Ecclesiogenesis: The Base Communities Reinvent the Church* (Maryknoll, NY: Orbis, 1986), 1.

58. Yves Congar, "Os grupos informais na Igreja," in *Communidades eclesiais de base: Utopia our realideade?* ed. Alfonso Gregory (Petropolis, Brazil: Vozes, 1973), 144–45.

59. See Avery Dulles, "The Church as Communion," in *New Perspectives on Historical Theology: Essays in Memory of John Meyendorff*, ed. Bradley Nassif (Grand Rapids: Eerdmans, 1996), 133.

Eastern Orthodox Ecclesiology

In the Eastern Church, there are four ancient patriarchates, namely Constantinople, Alexandria, Antioch, and Jerusalem. The fifth contemporary patriarchate is that of Moscow, the Russian Orthodox Church, by far the largest Orthodox church. In the former Eastern Europe there are a number of other autocephalous churches: in Serbia, Romania, and Bulgaria, among others. The third concentration of Orthodox churches is composed of the remainder, namely those in the United States, Western Europe, Africa, and some Asian countries such as China, Japan, and Korea.[60] Among the patriarchates, primacy belongs to that of Constantinople. Its role, however, is not to be compared to that of the Vatican in the Roman Catholic Church, because it has no power to interfere in the affairs of each self-governing patriarchate and church. Currently in the world church, the nomenclature "Eastern" is therefore not a geographical designation but rather a way to identify the church vis-à-vis the "Western church," that is, Roman Catholics, Anglicans, and Protestants.

What holds together such a diverse group of churches is sacramental communion and love of living tradition. "Conciliarity" is the term used by Orthodox theologians to emphasize the significance of the early councils to the unity of the church, beginning from that of Jerusalem in the book of Acts to the seven early ecumenical councils.[61] Throughout history and currently, "Eastern Orthodox theology claims to have preserved the integrity of the Apostolic Tradition (as implied by the term *orthodoxia*, lit. 'correct belief' or 'correct glory') by a direct, unbroken connection to the Church of the Apostles."[62] Because "holy tradition [is] the source of the Orthodox faith,"[63] the theology of the church draws heavily from the early sources, the church fathers of the East.

The most foundational ecclesiological statement in the Eastern tradition is that the church is an image of the Trinity.[64] Just as each person is made according to the image of the Trinity, so the church as a whole is an icon of the Trinity, "reproducing on earth the mystery of unity in diversity."[65] Whereas Western ecclesiologies are predominantly built on christological categories, the Eastern doctrine of the church seeks for a balance between Christology and

60. A fine up-to-date guide is John Binns, *An Introduction to the Christian Orthodox Churches* (Cambridge: Cambridge University Press, 2002).
61. Paraskevè Tibbs, "Eastern Orthodox Theology," in *Global Dictionary of Theology*, ed. William Dyrness and Veli-Matti Kärkkäinen (Downers Grove, IL: InterVarsity, 2008), 244.
62. Ibid.
63. Chapter title in Kallistos Ware, *The Orthodox Church*, new rev. ed. (London: Penguin Books, 1993), 195 (chap. 16).
64. See, further, Vladimir Lossky, *The Mystical Theology of the Eastern Church* (New York: St. Vladimir's Seminary Press, 1997), 176–77.
65. Ware, *Orthodox Church*, 240.

pneumatology. Consequently, Eastern theologians speak about the church as the body of Christ and the fullness of the Holy Spirit.[66] John Zizioulas expresses this principle with the help of two concepts: the church is *in-stituted* by Christ and *con-stituted* by the Holy Spirit.[67] Eastern pneumatological ecclesiology thus ideally balances hierarchy and charisms: "But the Church is not only hierarchical, it is charismatic and Pentecostal."[68] In the church of later days, these charismatic ministries have been less in evidence, but they have never been wholly extinguished.[69]

At the heart of Eastern Orthodox church life and ecclesiology stands the Eucharist. The Eucharist is the sacrament of primacy. Therefore, the basic ecclesiological rule that goes back to the fathers says, wherever the Eucharist is, there is the church. Or, the church makes the Eucharist, and the Eucharist makes the church. Therefore, the divine liturgy with the celebration of the Eucharist is the center of Orthodox spirituality and church life.[70]

Protestant Ecclesiologies in the Twentieth Century

MAINLINE PROTESTANT THEOLOGIES OF THE CHURCH

A powerful reaction against classical liberalism, and particularly the program of Schleiermacher, was offered by the Reformed theologian Karl Barth. Along with beginning to launch the huge writing project of his multivolume *Church Dogmatics*, Barth was instrumental in the drafting of the significant antiestablishment Barmen Declaration; this statement called the church to a radical obedience to God and God alone vis-à-vis the growing political threat of the Nazi regime. The Barmen statement provided a serious warning against those churches that seemed to be succumbing to Caesar.[71]

Barth's doctrine of the church is conditioned by three theological loci: pneumatology, Christology, and the Word of God. But even though it is the Holy Spirit who calls the church, it is still a "phenomenon of world history,"[72] a human society. This is the gateway to the emphasis on the visible nature of the church. Barth rejects the idea that the church is invisible, labeling this view "ecclesiological docetism."[73]

66. Lossky, *Mystical Theology*, 157, 174.

67. John Zizioulas, *Being as Communion: Studies in Personhood and the Church* (Crestwood, NY: St. Vladimir's Seminary Press, 1985), 22.

68. Ware, *Orthodox Church*, 249.

69. Ibid., 249–50; see also Lossky, *Mystical Theology*, 190–92.

70. Ware, *Orthodox Church*, 13, 242, 275.

71. The Barmen Declaration is also included in the Constitution of the Presbyterian Church (U.S.A.). For the context and texts, see Arthur C. Cochrane, *The Church's Confession under Hitler* (Pittsburgh, PA: Pickwick, 1976).

72. Karl Barth, *Church Dogmatics*, ed. G. Bromiley and T. F. Torrance, 4 vols. (Edinburgh: T&T Clark, 1956–1975), IV/1, 652.

73. Ibid., 653.

Barth advocates a congregational church government rather than episcopal or presbyterial. He prefers terms such as "community" and "congregation";[74] "the church is when it takes place."[75] Naturally the question arises: Who are the true Christians, and how does one then recognize the true church? Barth opposes two mistaken ways common in the past, namely, the sacramentalism of the Roman Catholic Church and the "moralism" of Anabaptism. The first one ends up being a human action to limit the freedom of the Spirit, and the latter, a presumptuous human desire to be infallible in their judgment of who are true Christians.[76] Barth's alternative is to begin with the doctrine of election and define true Christians, and hence members of the true church, as "the men assembled in it who are thereto elected by the Lord."[77] Understandably, Barth is vehemently opposed to any alliance between the church and state.[78]

The book titled *The Church in the Power of the Spirit* (1977),[79] by another Reformed theologian, Jürgen Moltmann, has been hailed as one of the groundbreaking ecumenical treatises on the church in the twentieth century. The book follows a trinitarian plan: "The Church of Jesus Christ" (chap. 3), "The Church of the Kingdom of God" (chap. 4), and "The Church in the Presence of the Holy Spirit" and "The Church in the Power of the Holy Spirit" (chaps. 5 and 6, respectively). Echoing Barth, Moltmann affirms that the church is the church of Jesus Christ, subject to his lordship alone. As such it is bound together with the history and destiny of its Lord. The church is both the "church under the cross" and also the church of the "feast without end."[80]

Based on his idea of social Trinity and the example of Jesus's inclusive friendship, Moltmann argues for an "open" church: "Open and total friendship that goes out to meet the other is the spirit of the kingdom in which God comes to man and man to man."[81] The principle of the church's openness has several expanding layers: Israel, the world religions, and the economic, political, and cultural processes of the world are partners in history; these "partners," however, "are not the church and will never become the church."[82] In other words, the mission of the church is not to "spread the church but to spread the kingdom"; the church is not self-serving but rather serves the world and the kingdom.[83]

74. Ibid., 650.
75. Ibid., 652.
76. Ibid., 694, 696.
77. Ibid., 696.
78. Ibid., IV/2, 688.
79. With the subtitle *A Contribution to Messianic Ecclesiology* (London: SCM, 1977).
80. Moltmann, *Church in the Power of the Spirit*, 97, 114.
81. Ibid., 121.
82. Ibid., 134.
83. Ibid., 11.

For Moltmann, the church is also a "charismatic fellowship" of equal persons. There is no division between the office bearers and the people.[84] The church is where the Spirit's self-manifestation takes place in overflowing powers, *charismata*.[85]

What undoubtedly is one of the most significant presentations of the doctrine of the church in modern times can be found in the third volume of the Lutheran Wolfhart Pannenberg's *Systematic Theology*. In his massive discussion of ecclesiology, Pannenberg makes several significant moves. First, there is a pronounced pneumatological orientation to the doctrine of the church, based on the groundbreaking idea of the continuity of the Spirit's work in creation, sustenance of life, new birth, and the church. Second, unlike most systematic theologies that discuss the reception of salvation in the individual believer's life before the treatment of ecclesiological themes, Pannenberg places the soteriological discussion within his treatment of the doctrine of the church. The relationship between the individual believer and the church is mutual and perichoretic.[86] Third, the doctrine of election is joined to ecclesiology rather than to the first part of systematic theology, the doctrine of God and/or the human being, as is conventional.

In writing a contemporary ecclesiology, Pannenberg has aimed for the whole worldwide church rather than for any specific denomination, even his own (i.e., the Lutheran Church). To be more precise, he is not even satisfied to write to the church and Christians alone but to the rest of humanity as well, since in his view the church is an anticipation and a sign of the unity of all people under one God. He believes that "if Christians succeed in solving the problems of their own pluralism, they may be able to produce a model combining pluralism and the widest moral unity which will also be valid for political life."[87]

While joining with some Protestant criticisms of Vatican II's idea of the church as the "sacrament," Pannenberg materially affirms the idea by regarding the church in Christ as a sign of the coming unity of all people under one God: "As the body of Christ the church is the eschatological people of God gathered out of all peoples, and it is thus a sign of reconciliation for a future unity of a renewed humanity in the kingdom of God."[88] In keeping with his "universal" theological vision in which God and his coming rule is the overarching framework and goal, Pannenberg places not only the church but also

84. Ibid., 298.
85. Ibid., 294.
86. Wolfhart Pannenberg, *Systematic Theology*, trans. Geoffrey W. Bromiley (Grand Rapids: Eerdmans, 1998), 3:xv.
87. Wolfhart Pannenberg, "Christian Morality and Political Issues," in *Faith and Reality* (Philadelphia: Westminster, 1977), 38.
88. Ibid., 43.

society under the kingdom. In other words, he sets God's rulership over all human orders.[89]

ECCLESIOLOGIES OF FREE CHURCHES AND PENTECOSTAL MOVEMENTS

"Believers' Churches"

Many specialists are of the opinion that the Free Church congregational model might well be the major paradigm in the third millennium alongside the Catholic one.[90] Owing to the heritage of the Radical Reformation, Christian communities such as the Anabaptists and (later) Mennonites, Baptists, Congregationalists, Quakers, some Methodist and Holiness movements, and Pentecostals, as well as a growing number of independent movements, are usually included under the somewhat elusive concept of "free churches." Another self-designation used by many among these Christians is "believers' church."[91] Yet another term is sometimes used: the "gathered church" as over against the "given church" of the older traditions.[92]

The key defining factor, going back to Reformation times in Europe, is freedom from the state (thus *free* churches) as well as the practice of *believer's* baptism rather than infant baptism. The other key defining features are voluntary membership (thus *gathered*), participation of all in ministry, autonomy of the local church, and biblicism and love of Scripture, as well as stress on discipleship, so much so that often there is a policy of exclusion from membership should community standards be violated. Free Churches usually celebrate sacraments, but their theology is not sacramental. Ministry patterns can be flexible, and even where ordination is practiced, in most cases it does not hinder laypeople from participating in all ministries.[93] Evangelization and mission are standard hallmarks of Free Churches.

Pentecostal Churches

While nothing like a uniform definition of Pentecostalism exists, a helpful orientation to the myriad of movements known by that umbrella name is the terminology adopted by *The New International Dictionary of Pentecostal and Charismatic Movements*.[94] That typology lists, first, (classical) Pentecostal

89. Ibid., 3:49–57.
90. Miroslav Volf, *After Our Likeness: The Church as an Image of the Trinity* (Grand Rapids: Eerdmans, 1998), 12.
91. See, further, Franklin H. Littell, "The Concept of the Believers' Church," in *The Concept of the Believers' Church*, ed. James Leo Garrett (Scottdale, PA: Herald, 1969), 15–33.
92. George H. Williams, "The Believers' Church and the Given Church," in *The People of God: Essays on the Believers' Church*, ed. Paul Basden and David S. Dockery (Nashville: Broadman, 1991), 325–32.
93. For an up-to-date, well-informed discussion, see Robert Muthiah, "Believers Church Tradition," in *Global Dictionary of Theology*, 105–9.
94. Edited by S. Burgess, rev. and expanded ed. (Grand Rapids: Zondervan, 2002).

denominations such as Assemblies of God or Foursquare Gospel, owing their existence to the famous Azusa Revival in 1906; second, charismatic movements, Pentecostal-type spiritual movements within the established churches beginning in the 1960s (the largest of which is the Roman Catholic Charismatic Renewal); and third, neo-charismatic movements, some of the most notable of which are the Vineyard Fellowship in the U.S.A., African Initiated Churches, and the China House Church movement, as well as innumerable independent churches and groups all over the world. Since its inception, Pentecostal movements have spread dramatically across the globe.[95]

At the center of Pentecostalism stands charismatic, dynamic spirituality rather than a novel theological discovery. Theologically, the Holy Spirit is not the center of worship. Jesus Christ and God, in the power of the Spirit, are the center. Pentecostals believe that all church members, not only the ordained—or the educated—will be empowered by the Holy Spirit to exercise spiritual gifts, reach out to nonbelievers, and help those in need.

Most often, Pentecostals follow typical Free Church traditions in their understanding of the church. A typical way to describe the Pentecostal notion of the church is to call it a charismatic fellowship, the body of Christ. Understandably, Pentecostal ecclesiology is of an ad hoc nature that leaves much room for improvisation; it is often practical rather than systematic in nature, and is strongly restorationist; in other words, there is a desire to "go back" to the New Testament type of church life. Pentecostals exhibit all forms of church structures, from congregational to episcopal to all kinds of independent models. Since Pentecostals have been predominantly "practitioners" rather than "theologians," the theology of the church is still emerging.[96]

The Emerging Churches

With striking titles such as *ChurchNext* (2000) or *The Liquid Church* (2002),[97] we are witnessing the newest expression of the church, known under the flexible rubric of the "Emerging Church" or the "Fresh Expressions of the Church." In the American context, the baby boomer generation was served with the so-called seeker-friendly suburban-based churches that catered to all kinds of individual and family needs. More recently, we have heard of "Purpose

95. Up-to-date, accessible presentations can also be found in Cecil M. Robeck, "Charismatic Movements," and Allan H. Anderson, "Pentecostalism," in *Global Dictionary of Theology*, 145–54 and 641–48, respectively.

96. Some promising signs are the following: "Perspectives on Koinonia: Final Report of the Dialogue between Roman Catholics and Some Pentecostal Leaders (1985–1989)," in *Information Service* 75, no. 4 (1990): 179–91; Amos Yong, *The Spirit Poured Out on All Flesh: Pentecostalism and the Possibility of Global Theology* (Grand Rapids: Baker Academic, 2005), chap. 3; Chan Simon, "Mother Church: Toward a Pentecostal Ecclesiology," *PNEUMA: The Journal of the Society for Pentecostal Studies* 22 (Fall 2000): 177–208.

97. Eddie Gibbs, *ChurchNext* (Downers Grove, IL: InterVarsity, 2000); Pete Ward, *The Liquid Church* (Peabody, MA: Hendrickson, 2002).

Driven" churches. Most recently, these kinds of models, while still having an appeal with their own generation, are giving way to those of Gen-Xers and other postmodern generations.[98] One of the main reasons for the mushrooming of these new forms of Christian communities is the obvious decline of membership and activity in much of mainline Christianity in North America and particularly in Europe.[99]

The most thorough study—ethnographic as well as theological—on both sides of the Atlantic Ocean, *The Emerging Churches*, by Eddie Gibbs and Ryan Bolger, suggests that a clear-cut ecclesiology can hardly be found among these groups and movements. Nevertheless, while they function partly virtually and many of them meet in places other than sanctuaries—particularly in the UK where they often gather in pubs—definite characteristics and "practices" seem to be common to most:

> Emerging Churches (1) identity with the life of Jesus, (2) transform the secular realm, and (3) live highly communal lives. Because of these three activities, they (4) welcome the stranger, (5) serve with generosity, (6) participate as producers, (7) create as created beings, (8) lead as body, and (9) take part in spiritual activities.[100]

The church life and the emerging theological activity among these communities are an interesting mix of old and new. On the one hand, there is a harking back to some aspects of sacramentality and mysticism, and on the other hand, there is a desire to connect with the latest moves in postmodern culture and ways of thinking. The title *How (Not) to Speak of God* by Peter Rollins[101] of Belfast, Ireland, the founder of the *Ikon* community, provides a wonderful experience of the coming together of these two orientations.

The Ecumenical Movement: Striving for the Unity of the Church

Nearly everybody would agree that "ecumenicity was the great new fact in the history of the church."[102] A number of initiatives and developments prepared for the coming into existence of the contemporary ecumenical movement, with the establishment of the World Council of Churches in 1948 as the most

98. See George Ritzer, *The McDonaldization of Society: An Investigation into the Changing Character of Contemporary Social Life* (Thousand Oaks, CA: Pine Forge, 1996).

99. Peter Brierly, *The Tide Is Running Out* (London: Christian Research, 2000); George Gallup Jr. and D. Michael Lindsey, *Surveying the Religious Landscape* (Harrisburg, PA: Morehouse, 2000).

100. Eddie Gibbs and Ryan Bolger, *The Emerging Churches: Creating Christian Community in Postmodern Cultures* (Grand Rapids: Baker Academic, 2005), 45.

101. Peter Rollins, *How (Not) to Speak of God* (Brewster, MA: Paraclete Press, 2006).

102. Pelikan, *Christian Doctrine and Modern Culture*, 282.

visible sign. The Anglican Lambeth Quadrilateral in 1920 (originally issued in 1888) elevated Scripture, Creeds, the two sacraments of baptism and the Eucharist, and episcopacy as the basis of church unity.[103] In the formation of the Church of South India from Anglican, Methodist, Congregationalist, Presbyterian, and Reformed churches, the question of the episcopacy seemed to be a particularly problematic issue, but was adopted into that church's life.[104] The 1920 encyclical from the (Orthodox) Synod of Constantinople suggested a fellowship of churches similar to the League of Nations. On the part of the United States, the formation in 1898 of the Federal Council of the Churches of Christ in America—now the National Council of Churches, U.S.A.—meant a significant ecumenical step in the growing efforts toward unity.[105] Church formations—such as the United Church of Canada, made up of Methodists, Congregationalists, and Presbyterians in 1925, and the United Church of Christ (U.S.A.), composed of Congregational Christian Churches and the Evangelical and Reformed Church in 1957—gave further indication of the increasing desire for unity.

The most significant push toward concerted efforts for unity came from the Edinburgh Missionary Conference, chaired by John R. Mott in 1910, whose centennial was celebrated in June 2010 in Edinburgh. The completion of the missionary task seemed to necessitate the coming together of all Christian churches under one goal.[106] The International Missionary Council was formed in 1921 to coordinate Protestant missionary efforts. The Life and Work movement was established in 1925 under the leadership of Nathan Söderblom to tackle the issues of peace, ethics, and international relations. And in 1927 the first Faith and Order Conference was convened, led by Episcopalians, to discuss issues of doctrine and constitutions.[107]

The first two agencies came together in 1948 to help establish the World Council of Churches (WCC) in Amsterdam, and the third one joined in 1961. While Eastern Orthodox churches took part from the beginning, until the 1960s, the early work of the WCC was predominantly Protestant. The Roman Catholic Church is the only major confessional family outside the WCC, along with most Pentecostals and many other Free Churches.[108]

103. "The Chicago-Lambeth Quadrilateral," can be found at Anglicans Online, http://anglicansonline.org/basics/Chicago_Lambeth.html.

104. See, further, Pelikan, *Christian Doctrine and Modern Culture*, 284–86.

105. For history and current situation, see the National Council of Churches website, http://www.ncccusa.org/.

106. See, further, Paul E. Pierson, "Missionary Conferences, World," in *Global Dictionary of Theology*, 562–65. The Edinburgh 2010 website is at http://www.edinburgh2010.org/.

107. See, further, Risto Saarinen, "Ecumenism," in *Global Dictionary of Theology*, 263–69.

108. The most comprehensive and accessible resource on various facets of ecumenism and the ecumenical movement, including the WCC, is the *Dictionary of the Ecumenical Movement*, ed. Nicholas Lossky et al. (Geneva: WCC Publications, 1991). For key texts, see *The Ecumenical*

The WCC is not a church but rather a "fellowship of churches," currently about 350 churches from all continents. Its self-understanding was established in the 1961 New Delhi basis statement as

> a fellowship of churches which confess the Lord Jesus Christ as God and Saviour according to the scriptures, and therefore seek to fulfill together their common calling to the glory of the one God, Father, Son and Holy Spirit.[109]

Its purpose is

> not to build a global "super-church," nor to standardize styles of worship, but rather to deepen the fellowship of Christian churches and communities so they may see in one another authentic expressions of the "one holy, catholic and apostolic church." This becomes the basis for joining in a common confession of the apostolic faith, cooperating in mission and human service endeavours and, where possible, sharing in the sacraments. All these acts of fellowship bear testimony to the foundational declaration of the WCC that the Lord Jesus Christ is "God and Saviour according to the Scriptures."[110]

Specifically in the area of ecclesiology, Faith and Order and the WCC have both worked for decades in calling churches together in order to reflect on the nature, mission, and life of the church. *The Nature and Mission of the Church*,[111] a document constantly under revision, is a significant attempt to outline the main features of an ecumenical understanding of the church. The document gathers together and develops several key ecclesiological themes currently at the center of discussion, such as the trinitarian basis of the church, the church's missionary nature,[112] and the idea of the church as communion. The last theme was developed significantly at the Faith and Order 1993 Santiago de Compostela meeting under the title "Towards Koinonia in Faith, Life and Witness."[113] A large ecumenical vision is presented in *Church and World: The Unity of the Church and the Renewal of Human Community* (1990).[114] In 1982 Faith and Order launched the document titled *Baptism,*

Movement: An Anthology of Key Texts and Voices, ed. Michael Kinnamon and Brian E. Cope (Grand Rapids: Eerdmans/Geneva: WCC Publications, 1997).

109. "The Basis of the WCC," World Council of Churches, http://www.oikoumene.org/en/who-are-we/self-understanding-vision/basis.html.

110. "The WCC and the Ecumenical Movement," World Council of Churches, http://www.oikoumene.org/en/who-are-we/background.html.

111. Faith and Order Paper 198 (Geneva: WCC, 2005).

112. Significantly enough—and echoing a main development in current ecclesiology—the document's name was changed from its 1998 version *The Nature and Purpose of the Church* to its current form, highlighting the missionary nature of the church.

113. See *On the Way to Fuller Koinonia: Official Report of the Fifth World Conference on Faith and Order*, ed. Thomas F. Best and Günther Gassmann (Geneva: WCC, 1994).

114. Faith and Order Paper 151, 2nd rev. (Geneva: WCC, 1990).

Eucharist, and Ministry,[115] to be consulted in the following discussion on sacraments and ministry.

An important part of the ecumenical work happens constantly in the form of bilateral and multilateral dialogues between Christian churches. In most countries there is a national council of churches (such as the NCC, USA) which works in close cooperation with Faith and Order, facilitating ecumenical conversations, events, and projects at national, regional, and local levels. There are also a number of informal ecumenical contacts between leaders as well as laypeople at various levels, making a significant contribution to the search for genuine unity.

While there is no agreement about the form and shape of "visible unity," the ecumenical movement at large has adopted that as the main goal.[116] There are also a number of dividing issues with regard to ministry, sacraments, and, say, the issues of evangelism and proselytism, which call for patient, long-term consideration and mutual understanding.

Worship, Sacraments, and Ministry of the Church

Worship and Liturgy

The center of Eastern Orthodox church life is the celebration of the Eucharist in the Divine Liturgy. The Orthodox Church follows the Byzantine liturgical tradition going back to the ancient church, particularly to St. Chrysostom's Constantinopolitan liturgy.[117] The earthly worship is an icon of the everlasting Heavenly Liturgy; worship is thus "nothing else than 'heaven on earth.'"[118] The same is said of the liturgy produced by the Catholic tradition.[119]

Catholic liturgical renewal movements started in the latter part of the nineteenth century in many European countries, including France, Germany, Belgium, and Austria.[120] Then in the twentieth century it took root in America. On both continents, it was greatly shaped and nurtured by the Benedictine tradition. The encyclical *Mediator Dei*, issued by Pope Pius XII in 1947, was one of the significant precursors of the changes in liturgy at Vatican II with its call for a more active participation of the faithful. Vatican II enthusiastically acknowledged and reaffirmed the Liturgical movement's aspirations.

---

115. Faith and Order Paper 111 (Geneva: WCC, 1982).

116. For theologies of unity, see Saarinen, "Ecumenism," 266–68.

117. See Tibbs, "Eastern Orthodox Theology," 246.

118. Ware, *Orthodox Church*, 265. Appropriately, chap. 13 is titled "Orthodox Worship I: The Earthly Heaven."

119. *Sacrosanctum concilium* 1.8, at the Vatican website: http://www.vatican.va/archive /hist_councils/ii_vatican_council/documents/vat-ii_const_19631204_sacrosanctum -concilium _en.html.

120. Keith F. Pecklers, *The Unread Vision: The Liturgical Movement in the United States of America 1926–55* (Collegeville, MN: Liturgical Press, 1998), 1–24.

Sacrosanctum concilium (*The Constitution on the Sacred Liturgy*) set worship in perspective by claiming that "the liturgy is the summit toward which the activity of the Church is directed: it is also the fount from which all her power flows"[121] and encouraged full and conscious participation of all.[122] In order to facilitate active participation, the council established the use of the vernacular as the language for liturgy. Another significant change was the turning of the altar around so that the priest and people face each other.[123]

The Church of England was also influenced by the Liturgical movements:

> Though there have been many and notable exceptions, a good deal of evidence suggests that in the first three decades of the [twentieth] century much public worship was often sluggish, dull, individualist and sacerdotalist. . . . The striking changes in worship in the mainstream British churches since the 1930s are in the main attributable to the Liturgical Movement, though there are other antecedents, and more recently, the charismatic movement has played (some observers claim) an invigorating role.[124]

The "other antecedents" referred to in the text are influences from the Free churches.

Mainline Protestant churches have also revised and updated liturgies and liturgical texts during the twentieth century. In 1972 *The Worshipbook: Services and Hymns* was published as a joint project of the Presbyterian Churches in the United States. In 1978 the Lutheran Church in the United States published its revised *Lutheran Book of Worship*, offering more individual choices in liturgy and also an expanded variety of musical styles.

Free churches, generally speaking, do not follow liturgical order but rather give more space to spontaneity and participation of both ordained and lay people, and are often characterized by lively, dynamic music styles. The growing influence of Pentecostal/charismatic spiritualities is being felt not only among Free churches and independent churches but also among Roman Catholics and mainline Protestants. It is not uncommon at all nowadays for praise groups with guitars and other popular instruments to be part of liturgical services.

Sacraments

Water Baptism

The preferred term for sacraments in Eastern Orthodoxy is *mystery*, well attested in both biblical and patristic literature. While in contemporary Orthodox

---

121. *Sacrosanctum concilium* 1.10.
122. Ibid., 2.14.
123. Haight, *Christian Community*, 405–6.
124. Terence Thomas, *The British: Their Religious Beliefs and Practices, 1800–1986* (Oxford: Routledge, 1988), 122.

theology beginning from the seventeenth century the number of sacraments is usually seven, throughout history there has been no defined number set.[125] The Roman Catholic Church acknowledges seven sacraments as well: baptism, confirmation, Eucharist, penance, anointing the sick, ordination, and matrimony.[126] In addition to the seven traditional ones, some Pentecostals and other Free churches also practice foot washing.[127]

In the Roman Catholic and Orthodox traditions—and similarly in other churches with sacramental theologies, such as Anglican and Lutheran[128]—water baptism effects regeneration and unites the person with Christ and his church. The Orthodox Church has kept the sacraments of baptism and confirmation integrally linked; once baptized, the infant is anointed with oil and offered the first Eucharist.[129] In Roman Catholicism and Lutheranism, confirmation (which is not called a sacrament in Lutheranism) takes place several years after baptism.

In the Reformed tradition, baptism is understood in two ways: The Zwinglian branch considers it mainly as a sign of inclusion in the community of Christ but not as regenerative. The Calvinist majority oscillates between Lutheran and Zwinglian understandings in the sense that while it does not consider the rite regenerative in the sense the sacramental traditions do, it does consider it a "seal" of the covenant with God. As such it is done with a view to forthcoming faith.[130]

Free churches understand water baptism as an "ordinance," in other words, as an act ordained by Christ. Rather than sacramental, it is a public response of a believer. Rather than infant baptism as in Catholic, Orthodox, Anglican, and Lutheran churches, Free churches practice believer's ("adult") baptism by immersion.[131] While most Reformed traditions follow infant baptism customs, some are open to both practices. The Reformed Karl Barth's criticism of sacramental baptismal practice and advocacy of

125. See, further, John Meyendorff, *Byzantine Theology: Historical Trends and Doctrinal Trends* (New York: Fordham University Press, 1987), 191–92.

126. *Lumen Gentium* 2.11.

127. For a brief discussion of foot washing as a sacramental act, see Harold D. Hunter, "Ordinances," in *The New International Dictionary of Pentecostal and Charismatic Movements*, 948–49.

128. While these hold sacramental theologies—meaning that the sacrament effects regeneration—Lutheran tradition of course denies the Catholic principles of *ex opera operato* (which teaches that the rite is valid by virtue of "the work done").

129. Meyendorff, *Byzantine Theology*, 192–95.

130. See, e.g., Charles Hodge, *Systematic Theology* (1872; repr., Grand Rapids: Eerdmans, 1973), 3:582.

131. Faith and Order Paper 111 (Geneva: WCC, 1982), 3–7. For a careful, ecumenically sensitive Baptist view, see Stanley J. Grenz, *Theology for the Community of God* (Grand Rapids: Eerdmans, 1994), 529–31; for a similar Anabaptist treatment, see Thomas N. Finger, *A Contemporary Anabaptist Theology: Biblical, Historical, Constructive* (Downers Grove, IL: InterVarsity, 2004), 160–84.

believer's baptism has naturally received an enthusiastic response from many Free churches.[132]

While Christian churches are far from agreeing on many disputed issues with regard to the sacrament of water baptism, the 1982 WCC document *Baptism, Eucharist and Ministry* (BEM) makes significant contributions. BEM describes baptism in many dimensions: as participation in Christ's death; conversion, pardoning, and cleansing; the gift of the Spirit; incorporation into the body of Christ; and sign of the kingdom.[133] While God's gift, baptism calls for faith and lifelong commitment.[134] Acknowledging that "baptism upon personal profession of faith is the most clearly attested pattern in the New Testament documents," BEM recommends both modes of baptism, infant and believer's—as long as it is an "unrepeatable" practice—as a way to mutual acknowledgment of baptism administered in the name of the Triune God.[135] While differences exist about how Spirit baptism and water baptism—or chrismation and baptism—relate to each other, all churches make a close connection between baptism in the Spirit and in water.[136]

EUCHARIST

Roman Catholic tradition employs the term "transubstantiation" for describing the process that takes place at the eucharistic consecration: the bread and wine undergo a "metaphysical" change into Christ's blood and body. Therefore, the Eucharist is a sacrifice.[137] Orthodox tradition believes in the real presence of Christ in the Eucharist, but it refrains from human conceptual attempts to describe it as Catholics or Lutherans have done.[138] Similarly to Catholics, the Orthodox regard the Eucharist primarily as a sacrifice, an offering back to God what God has given us, as the words of the liturgy say: "Your own from Your own we offer You, in all and for all."[139] Unlike in the Catholic Church, typically Holy Communion is received only a few times a year, with exceptions such as the Russian Church.

---

132. For a summary of discussion and sources, see Dale Moody, *Baptism: Foundation for Christian Unity* (Philadelphia: Westminster, 1967), 50–71.

133. "Baptism," in *Baptism, Eucharist and Ministry*, Faith and Order Paper 111, January 15, 1982, WCC, http://www.oikoumene.org/en/resources/documents/wcc-commissions/faith-and-order-commission/i-unity-the-church-and-its-mission/baptism-eucharist-and-ministry-faith-and-order-paper-no-111-the-lima-text.html, 3–7.

134. Ibid., 8–10.

135. Ibid., 11–16.

136. Ibid., 14.

137. *Catechism of the Catholic Church* (Washington, DC: United States Catholic Conference, 1994), sec. 1333, www.usccb.org/catechism/text/. For a concise contemporary discussion, see Brother Jeffrey Gros, FSC, "The Roman Catholic View," in *The Lord's Supper: Five Views*, ed. Gordon T. Smith (Downers Grove, IL: InterVarsity, 2007), 13–31.

138. Meyendorff, *Byzantine Theology*, 201–2.

139. Ware, *Orthodox Church*, 85.

The technical Lutheran term to describe Christ's presence is "consubstantiation" (Christ "under," "in," and "above," the elements).[140] The widest intrachurch variety with regard to the understanding of the Lord's Supper can be found in the Reformed tradition going back to the time of the Reformation.[141] While for Zwingli's anti-Catholic "memorial" or symbolic understanding the distinction between "sign" and "reality" is crucial, in Calvin's "representational" understanding such a distinction is not allowed. The elements "point beyond themselves to bring to heart and mind the reality of salvation."[142] In general, Free churches, such as Baptists and Pentecostals, have followed a "thin" theology of Christ's presence following some form of "memorial" understanding.[143]

Inspired by liturgical renewals stemming from the end of the nineteenth century, several theologians such as Karl Rahner, Hans Küng, and Edward Schillebeeckx have helped Catholic theology to come to a more proper formulation of the classic transubstantiation doctrine. In addition to reestablishing the integral link between the Word and sacraments, these theologians, through the notions of symbol, embodiment, and relationality have conceived of the presence of Christ and the effects of the sacrament in a way that is also more in keeping with the general move away from a substance ontology to a relational ontology.[144] Protestant theologians such as Pannenberg have joined in the use of terms such as "transsignification," which simply means a change in the "meaning" of an act such as when a paper is "changed" into a letter.[145]

As it does with baptism, *BEM* elaborates the many dimensions of the Eucharist:[146] thanksgiving to the Father, anamnesis or memorial of Christ, invocation of the Spirit, communion of the faithful, and meal of the kingdom. Because Christian life is deepened by the celebration of the Eucharist, it would be good to enjoy it every week.[147] Wisely, *BEM* does not engage the theological controversies such as how to define Christ's presence but rather concentrates on what Christians may be able to affirm together.

---

140. John R. Stephenson, "The Lutheran View," in *The Lord's Supper: Five Views*, 41–58; while this essay represents the Lutheran Missouri Synod viewpoint, it also gives an introduction to other Lutheran orientations.

141. An accurate, accessible discussion is Leanne Van Dyk, "The Reformed View," in *The Lord's Supper: Five Views*, 67–82.

142. Ibid., 70.

143. See Roger E. Olson, "The Baptist View," and Veli-Matti Kärkkäinen, "The Pentecostal View," in *The Lord's Supper: Five Views*, 91–108 and 117–35, respectively.

144. For helpful discussion, see Regis A. Duffy, "Sacraments in General," in *Systematic Theology: Roman Catholic Perspectives*, ed. Francis Schüssler Fiorenza and John P. Galvin, vol. 2 (Minneapolis: Fortress, 1991), esp. 201–5.

145. Pannenberg, *Systematic Theology*, 3:300–303.

146. "Eucharist," in *BEM*, 5–26.

147. Ibid., 30–31.

Orthodox, Roman Catholics, Lutheran Missouri Synod, and some other churches do not practice eucharistic hospitality, while many others do, such as (other) Lutheran, Methodist, Anglican, and most Free churches.

MINISTRY

Ministerial Patterns and Ordination

The "Orthodox Church is an hierarchical church,"[148] and its ministry structures are centered on the apostolic succession of bishops. Here there is similarity with the Roman Catholic Church, as explained in "The Church Is Hierarchical," chapter 3 of *Lumen Gentium*. Both of these churches have continued the ancient three-tiered form of ministry with bishop, priest, and deacons.[149] While Catholics require that priests and bishops be unmarried celibates, Eastern tradition allows marriage for priests if they marry before ordination; as a general rule, the episcopal office is reserved for unmarried (including widowers) and thus is often occupied by a monk.

As mentioned above, for the Roman Catholic Church an important part of the episcopal structure are the episcopal colleges, which need to be linked with the see of the bishop of Rome. In the Orthodox Church, they are called the councils of bishops. While the episcopal office is the highest teaching office in both churches, Eastern tradition puts a greater stress on the reception of faith by the whole community of the faithful.[150] Differently from other Protestant theologians, the Lutheran Pannenberg—while not willing to have non-Catholic churches be placed under the jurisdiction of the Vatican—is open to the pope-like universal spokesperson for the global Christian church as a sign of unity.[151]

Anglican and some Lutheran churches[152] continue the three-tiered ministry pattern with the episcopal office. There is also a growing number of Free churches all over the world, particularly Pentecostal, that call some ministers bishops. Most Protestant churches maintain a two-tiered ministry pattern with pastors (ministers of the Word and sacrament) and deacons. Whatever form of ministry any particular church opts for, for *BEM* the call for mutual recognition of ministers is of utmost ecumenical importance.[153]

Virtually all Christian churches practice some form of ordination to set apart some members for public office. Eastern Orthodox and Roman Catholics

148. Ware, *Orthodox Church*, 248.
149. For the Roman Catholic theology and offices of ministry, see *Lumen Gentium*, chap. 3, and *Christus Dominus* (Decree on the Pastoral Office of the Bishops in the Church) of Vatican II.
150. Ware, *Orthodox Church*, 251.
151. Pannenberg, *Systematic Theology*, 3:420–31.
152. While episcopacy is a rule in some Lutheran churches such as in all Scandinavian countries and in many African countries, there are also many Lutheran churches that do not have bishops; in the Evangelical Lutheran Church of America, episcopacy is a fairly new phenomenon.
153. "Ministry," in *BEM*, 51–55.

consider ordination a sacrament. For both churches, ordination cannot be re-voked; Roman Catholics express this with the ancient idea of an "undeletable mark" placed on the life of the ordained. A major difference between Roman Catholic and Protestant understandings of ordination is that according to *Lumen Gentium*[154] there is an "essential" difference between the ordained and laypersons. The person who occupies the office of priesthood through ordination has a particular power (*potestas*) that other baptized Christians do not have, even if someone who holds office in the church is not a Christian in some higher degree. Protestant theology of ordination does not allow such a distinction.

The Reformation doctrine of the priesthood of all believers has appealed to biblical passages such as 1 Pet. 2:9. According to Luther, some Christians are appointed by the congregation into an ordained ministry primarily for the sake of order.[155] A significant development among all churches from the Orthodox[156] to Roman Catholics (as the above discussion explains) to Protestants is the desire to empower laypersons into a more active participation in ministry.[157] In general Free churches and Pentecostal movements seem to have been most successful in putting this principle into practice.[158] This is also the call of *BEM*.[159] Having affirmed the importance of ordained ministry in the church, the document stresses the mutual conditioning of the ordained and the laity.[160] While the ordained ministers mediate Christ's authority, theirs is not an authoritarian but rather an upbuilding and encouraging way of acting;[161] a proper manner is one that is "personal, collegial and communal."[162]

Women in the Church and Ministry

The Presbyterian feminist theologian Letty M. Russell confesses that "I have always found it difficult to walk away from the church, but I have also found it difficult to walk with it. . . . The alienation is shared with many other women and men."[163] While few women theologians go to the extreme of urging women to withdraw (at least for the time being) from the male-dominated

---

154. *Lumen Gentium* 2.10.

155. See, further, Paul Althaus, *The Theology of Martin Luther*, trans. Robert C. Schultz (Philadelphia: Fortress, 1966), 294–332.

156. Ware, *Orthodox Church*, 249–50.

157. For ecumenical discussions, see Veli-Matti Kärkkäinen, "The Calling of the Whole People of God into Ministry: The Spirit, Church, and Laity," *Studia Theologia: Scandinavian Journal of Theology* 54, no. 2 (2000): 144–62.

158. See, further, Paul Beasley-Murray, "The Ministry of All and the Leadership of Some: A Baptist Perspective," in *Anyone for Ordination?* ed. Paul Beasley-Murray (Tunbridge Wells, UK: Monarch Publications, 1993), 157–74.

159. "Ministry," in *BEM*, 3, 5.

160. Ibid., 12.

161. Ibid., 15–16.

162. Ibid., 26.

163. Letty M. Russell, *Church in the Round: Feminist Interpretation of the Church* (Louisville: Westminster John Knox, 1993), 11.

churches,[164] a number of them are looking for a more inclusive, affirmative way of conceiving the Christian community and its ministry.

While the place of women in the church touches wider issues than just ministry and ordination, these two stand at the heart of contemporary discussions. Orthodox and Catholic churches—joined by a number of the most conservative Protestant churches such as Baptist and Lutheran—do not allow female ordination, whereas most Anglican and mainline Protestants do. *BEM* issues a passionate appeal for the churches to find a way to minister both for men and women; at the same time, the document leaves it open whether various church traditions will see it fit to ordain women.[165]

Knowing that our language—in this case the way God-talk is carried on in the church and Christian discourse—shapes our perception of reality, the Roman Catholic Elizabeth Johnson issues a call to expand and make more inclusive our way of speaking of God, employing female images and metaphors alongside the traditional ones.[166] Russell's *Church in the Round*, which utilizes the symbolism of the table to create new images of the church, employs the common cultural image of hospitality. So much in the home happens around the kitchen table, and some of the most precious memories go back to table fellowship. Furthermore, the feminist church attempts to reach to the margins and searches for liberation from all forms of dehumanization, be it sexual, racist, or any other forms of exploitation. This means that men can also be feminists if they are willing to advocate for women. The search for freedom and equality is continuing the ministry of Christ, who welcomed people of all ages and both sexes into God's reign.[167]

The feminist understanding considers ministry in the life of the church to be the recognition of gifting from God and thus open to both men and women.[168] Therefore, the core issue of ministry is not necessarily an insistence on the right of ordination for women but rather a revision of the whole concept of ordination. In patriarchal styles of leadership, authority is exercised by standing above in the place of power. Feminist styles of leadership would draw their model of behavior from a partnership paradigm that is oriented toward community formation. In feminist styles of leadership, authority is exercised by standing with others and seeking to share power and authority. Power is seen as something to be multiplied and shared rather than accumulated at the top. In this search for a new approach to leadership in the church, feminist ecclesiologists are again drawing from the example of Jesus, who literally turned the tables.[169]

164. This call is issued in Rosemary Radford Ruether, *Women-Church: Theology and Practice of Feminist Liturgical Communities* (San Francisco: Harper & Row, 1985).
165. "Ministry," in *BEM*, 18.
166. Elizabeth A. Johnson, *She Who Is: The Mystery of God in Feminist Theology* (New York: Crossroad, 1992), 127–41.
167. Russell, *Church in the Round*, 22–23.
168. Ibid., esp. 47–54.
169. Ibid., 54–63, 67–74.

Defining Ecclesiological Topics and Challenges

The Transformation of the Global Church

In the beginning of the third millennium, nothing less than a "Macro-reformation"[170] is taking place before our very eyes as Christianity is moving from the global North (Europe and North America) to the global South (Africa, Asia, Latin America): by 2050, only about one-fifth of the world's three billion Christians will be non-Hispanic whites. "If we want to visualize a 'typical' contemporary Christian, we should think of a woman living in a village in Nigeria or in a Brazilian *favela*."[171] At the same time, the composition of the church worldwide is changing dramatically: as of now, one half of all Christians are Roman Catholics, another quarter is composed of Pentecostal/charismatics (in three subgroups as outlined above), and the rest is composed of Eastern Orthodox Christians, by far the largest segment, and mainline Protestants, including Free churches.[172]

What are some of the ecclesiological implications of this dramatic shift? There are going to be two major poles of the Christian church in terms of size and influence, namely, Roman Catholic and Pentecostal/charismatic. They together comprise three-fourths of the membership. All this means that conservative and traditional mind-sets will be strengthened around the Christian church, even when theological liberalism reigns in Western academia and in the worldwide Christian communions led by leaders from the global North. The "Pentecostalization" of the Christian church, in terms of Pentecostal/charismatic spirituality and worship patterns infiltrating all churches, is yet another implication.

The Question of Ecclesiality

The rapid reconfiguration of the global church brings to the center of the ecclesiological and ecumenical conversations the question of what makes the church, church. In other words, what are the necessary and sufficient conditions for a community to be called "the church" in the theological sense? Two extreme poles in the discussion emerge: on the one hand, the Eastern Orthodox and Roman Catholic traditions, which do not consider other Christian communities

---

170. Justo L. González, *Mañana: Christian Theology from a Hispanic Perspective* (Nashville: Abingdon, 1990), 49.

171. Philip Jenkins, *The Next Christendom: The Coming of Global Christianity* (Oxford: Oxford University Press, 2001), 2. The book title is of course most unfortunate: there will never be another Christendom. Yet the basic argument of the book is not compromised by the uninformed choice of the title.

172. The basic statistical source is David B. Barrett, George T. Kurian, and Todd M. Johnson, *World Christian Encyclopedia*, 2nd ed. (New York: Oxford University Press, 2001); for global statistics, see esp. pp. 12–15, as well as the January edition of *International Bulletin of Missionary Research*.

as "churches" but rather Christian "communities,"[173] and, on the other hand, Free churches, whose requirements for the ecclesiality of the church are "minimalist." The Magisterial Reformation churches stand in between, as it were.

As far as the conditions of ecclesiality are concerned, the episcopal[174] and Free church traditions differ especially in three respects: (1) According to Catholic and Orthodox tradition, a bishop in apostolic succession is needed to ensure the presence of Christ, while in Free churches there is no episcopacy (and even if they do have ministers called "bishops," there is no claim for apostolic succession nor to the ecclesially constitutive role of that minister). (2) The reason why a legitimate bishop is needed in episcopal churches is that he guarantees the legitimacy of the celebration of the Eucharist, which is the church-constitutive event, whereas in Free churches Christ's presence is not mediated primarily sacramentally but rather "directly," in an unmediated way to the whole community. (3) According to the episcopal tradition, therefore, the church is constituted through the performance of an objective sacramental event, whereas in the Free church tradition what makes the church, church is the coming together of people who have made a "personal" response of faith (and usually received believer's baptism). This is not to say that a personal response of faith is unimportant to Catholics and Orthodox any more than to say that sacraments play no role in Free churches. Rather, it is to say that in episcopal churches it is not the personal faith that constitutes the church and that in Free churches the celebration of the sacrament of the Lord's Supper is a faith-strengthening rather than a church-forming activity.[175]

For Lutheran and Reformed theologies ecclesiality is conditioned—following the Lutheran Augsburg Confession, number 7—on the preaching of the pure gospel and the right administration of the sacraments. Bishops may belong to the ministry pattern, as in the Lutheran Church, but they are not church-constitutive.

Communion Ecclesiologies

The recent ecumenical document "Toward a Lutheran Understanding of Communion" offers one of the most succinct and inclusive definitions of communion, highlighting its multifaceted and multidimensional nature: "*Communio/koinonia* is often used to express the unity of the church across all time and space, the nature of life together in the local church, and the relationship between local churches in a regional and global context."[176] Similarly, *Lumen*

173. *Lumen Gentium* 15.

174. The term *episcopal* in its general theological sense means those churches that regard the bishop as a necessary condition of the ecclesiality of the church.

175. See, further, Volf, *After Our Likeness*, 133–35.

176. "Toward a Lutheran Understanding of Communion," #2, in *The Church as Communion*, ed. Heindrich Holze, Lutheran World Federation Documentation No. 42 (Geneva: Lutheran World Federation, 1997), 13.

Gentium presents a thick communion ecclesiology by speaking of God's desire "to make men holy and save them, not as individuals without any bond or link between them, but rather to make them into a people who might acknowledge him and serve him in holiness."[177] This means nothing less than that Christian salvation is communal, communitarian in nature—even though salvation is personally appropriated. No other contemporary theologian has advanced this line of argumentation more thoroughly than the Orthodox John Zizioulas in his celebrated *Being as Communion*.[178] His argumentation is simple and profound: from the fact that the God of the Bible exists as divine communion, Father, Son, and Spirit, we know that genuine personhood exists only in communion—thus the subtitle of the book, *Studies in Personhood and the Church*. Moreover, the proper mode of existence of the human *person* is communion with God and other human beings.[179] For Zizioulas, becoming Christian means nothing less than a move from "biological individuality" to an "ecclesial personhood."[180]

Communion theology has also been enthusiastically adopted by the ecumenical movement as a main paradigm. "*Koinonia* is the fundamental understanding of the Church emerging from the bilateral dialogues," summarizes a recent WCC document;[181] *koinonia* is also at the core of the Faith and Order document *The Nature and Mission of the Church*.[182]

The Church as Mission—Missional Ecclesiologies

Whereas until recently mission was a separate task or "department" of the church, there is an ecumenical consensus in contemporary theology that the church as such exists as mission; the church's nature is missionary. Vatican II's *Ad Gentes*, therefore, speaks of the "pilgrim Church . . . as missionary by her very nature."[183] Similarly, *The Nature and Mission of the Church* speaks of the mission of the church as deriving from the "reflection of the communion in the Triune God,"[184] meaning that "mission belongs to the very being of the Church."[185]

177. *Lumen Gentium* 2.9.
178. Zizioulas, *Being as Communion*, esp. 124–25.
179. Ibid., 15.
180. Ibid., 49.
181. Fifth Forum on International Bilateral Conversations: Report (Geneva: WCC, 1991), 46.
182. *The Nature and Mission of the Church: A Stage on the Way to a Common Statement*, Faith and Order Paper 198, December 15, 2005, WCC, http://www.oikoumene.org/en/resources/documents/wcc-commissions/faith-and-order-commission/i-unity-the-church-and-its-mission/the-nature-and-mission-of-the-church-a-stage-on-the-way-to-a-common-statement.html, esp. 57–66.
183. *Ad Gentes* 1.2.
184. *Nature and Mission*, 34.
185. Ibid., 35.

The late United Reformed Bishop Lesslie Newbigin, a long-term missionary to India, was instrumental—upon his return from the mission field to his homeland Great Britain—in launching the idea of the West as the "mission field" and thus the need for all churches everywhere to adopt a missional approach and existence.[186] As a result, an ecumenical network and research initiative by the name "Gospel and Our Culture" was launched;[187] soon it was followed by similar networks in the United States[188] and beyond.

In the American context, the 1998 book titled *Missional Church: A Vision for the Sending of the Church in North America* made an effort to bring together World Council of Churches discussions of *missio Dei* ("the mission of God") and Lesslie Newbigin's missionary insights to bear on North America.[189] This collection of essays by representatives of the Gospel and Our Culture Network urges the church to move away from a Christendom model that focuses on maintenance to a missional way of life based on outreach and expansion. Michael Frost and Alan Hirsch define the missional church as one that seeks to "discern God's specific missional vocation for the entire community and all of its members."[190]

Concluding Reflections

Along with the doctrine of the Trinity and pneumatology, ecclesiology has risen to the center of theological reflection at the international and ecumenical level. The need for a thick account of the meaning and nature of Christian community arises out of many factors, such as the loss of the sense of community in the hyperindividualistic culture of modernity and the process of globalization that has also brought about an unprecedented diversifying of the world church. One could also add that the traditional anchoring of the status of the church, either in divine revelation after modernity's eradication of the self-evident role of Scripture as authority, or in the sociocultural role in the society after the passing away of Christendom, has come under serious suspicion. On top of everything, there is also the urgent need for the Christian

186. The best way to get into these basic ideas is Lesslie Newbigin, *The Gospel in a Pluralist Society* (Grand Rapids: Eerdmans, 1989).

187. Introduction, activities, and resources can be found at http://www.gospel-culture.org .uk/index.htm.

188. See, e.g., The Gospel and Our Culture Network at http://www.gocn.org/.

189. *Missional Church: A Vision for the Sending of the Church in North America*, ed. Darrell Guder (Grand Rapids: Eerdmans, 1998).

190. Michael Frost and Alan Hirsch, *The Shaping of Things to Come: Innovation and Mission for the 21st-Century Church* (Peabody, MA: Hendrickson, 2003), 11–12. A helpful and up-to-date discussion of basics of the missional church concept can be found in Alan Roxhburg, "The Missional Church," *Theology Matters: A Publication for Presbyterians for Faith, Family and Ministry* 10, no. 4 (2004): 1–5; http://www.theologymatters.com/2004.cfm.

church in the beginning of the third millennium to reflect on her relation to other faith communities such as the Islamic *umma*.

Many new opportunities can also be found in the current situation, such as the rediscovery of the meaning of "personhood" in philosophy, psychology, and theology in terms of relationships, nurtured by a relational understanding of the Trinity. The rise to prominence of communion ecclesiology is to be seen as a result of these developments. Christian salvation and the vision of eschatological fulfillment are thus to be seen as genuinely communal in nature.

Consequently, we can speak of the renaissance of the doctrine of the church and ecclesiological reflection. Lessons and challenges from the developments in ecclesiology during the past 150–200 years will certainly continue to enrich such a theological renewal and undertaking.

For Further Reading

Basden, Paul, and David S. Dockery. *The People of God: Essays on the Believers' Church*. Nashville: Broadman, 1991.

Boff, Leonardo. *Ecclesiogenesis: The Base Communities Reinvent the Church*. Maryknoll, NY: Orbis, 1986.

Chan, Simon. "Mother Church: Toward a Pentecostal Ecclesiology." *PNEUMA: The Journal of the Society for Pentecostal Studies* 22 (Fall 2000): 177–208.

Gibbs, Eddie, and Ryan Bolger. *The Emerging Churches: Creating Christian Community in Postmodern Cultures*. Grand Rapids: Baker Academic, 2005.

Haight, Roger. *Christian Community in History*. Vol. 2, *Comparative Ecclesiology*. New York: Continuum, 2005.

Jenkins, Philip. *The Next Christendom: The Coming of Global Christianity*. Oxford: Oxford University Press, 2001.

Küng, Hans. *The Church*. New York: Image Books, 1976.

Moltmann, Jürgen. *The Church in the Power of the Spirit: Contribution to Messianic Ecclesiology*. Translated by Margaret Kohl. London: SCM, 1977.

Pannenberg, Wolfhart. *Systematic Theology*. Vol. 3. Translated by Geoffrey W. Bromiley. Grand Rapids: Eerdmans, 1998.

Rausch, Thomas P. *Towards a Truly Catholic Church: An Ecclesiology for the Third Millennium*. Collegeville, MN: Liturgical Press, 2005.

Russell, Letty M. *Church in the Round: Feminist Interpretation of the Church*. Louisville: Westminster John Knox, 1993.

Ware, Kallistos. *The Orthodox Church*. New rev. ed. London: Penguin Books, 1993.

15

• • •

ESCHATOLOGY

MICHAEL HORTON

For two millennia, Christians have confessed their confidence in Christ's bodily return to raise the dead, to judge, and to renew and reign over a restored cosmos forever. Despite this remarkable consensus, the sharpest differences among Christians concerning eschatology (*ta eschata*: "last things") arise over how to interpret biblical prophecies, especially the millennium. Although Rev. 20 represents the only explicit biblical reference to a thousand-year era, it has fueled considerable reflection, commentary, and speculation throughout church history. After providing some broader background, this essay surveys eschatological options over the last 150–200 years under four general themes: (1) background on millennial views, (2) the expectation of catastrophe or consummation, (3) Antichrist and the debated secret rapture, and (4) heaven and hell.

The History of the Future and the Future of History: Millennial Debates

Belief in a literal one-thousand-year reign of Christ is called *millenarianism*, from the Latin *mille* (thousand), which translates the Greek word for thousand, *chilia*.[1] In modern times, three schools of interpretation have been

---

1. Although millenarianism (or millennialism) is more familiar today, for most of church history this position was called *chiliasm* (following the Greek over the Latin).

identified and defended: premillennialism, postmillennialism, and amillennialism. *Premillennialists* hold that Christ will return before the millennium. *Postmillennialists* generally teach that Christ will return after a golden age of extraordinary blessing throughout the world through wide-scale conversion to the gospel. *Amillennialists* maintain that the "thousand years" referred to in Rev. 20 is symbolic and represents the present era of Christ's reign in grace, to be consummated at his return in glory.

Early Jewish and Christian Eschatologies

Given the significance of the later prophets, it is not surprising that Second Temple Judaism was charged with apocalyptic expectations for "the age to come." Denying the resurrection, the Sadducees (a minority, but powerful for their support of Caesar) were more oriented toward stabilizing the status quo. However, most (led by the Pharisees) expected a divine disruption of history. Through the nation's strict rededication to Torah, the Messiah would arrive, the dead would be raised, and the just would inherit a revived geopolitical theocracy.[2] Other groups, like the Essenes, abandoned the religiously compromised temple and leadership in Jerusalem altogether, establishing desert communities that were highly ascetic (including celibacy), in preparation for an imminent apocalypse. They interpreted prophecies in the light of current events in Jerusalem.

Ancient and Medieval Eschatologies

In the main, the ancient church seems to have held that the kingdom of God had been inaugurated with Christ's first advent, yet awaited its full consummation in the future: the position most closely associated today with amillennialism.[3] The first widespread millenarian movement was associated with the Montanists in the third century. With two young women, Prisca and Maximilla, Montanus led a popular movement that eventually included Tertullian among its number. The failure of its predictions, eccentric asceticism, and sharp opposition between the visible (fallen) and invisible (spiritual) church led to its ecclesiastical condemnation. Although the Montanist movement died out,

2. More than a century before Christ, the vision of a literal golden age at the end of history was anticipated in 1 Enoch. A similar eschatology may be found in the much later apocryphal text of 4 Ezra, although there the whole creation is destroyed—including the Messiah himself—after a four-hundred-year reign. Seven days later, the resurrection and judgment take place, ushering in the new heavens and earth.

3. Although Justin Martyr held something close to what we would call historical premillennialism, he acknowledged that this was not the most widely held view of his day. For one of the best treatments of patristic perspectives on eschatology, see Charles E. Hill, *Regnum Caelorum: Patterns of Millennial Thought in Early Christianity* (Grand Rapids: Eerdmans, 2001). For his treatment of Justin's views, see esp. 194–95.

its combination of millennial fervor, spiritual enthusiasm, and restorationist ecclesiology would be revived at various points throughout church history.

At the same time, with the transition from persecution to imperial favor under Constantine, the earlier type of amillennialism, which recognized the precariousness of the church's existence in this clash between the two ages, surrendered to a more triumphalistic version. "Our divinely favored emperor," said the church father Eusebius concerning Constantine, "receiving, as it were, a transcript of the divine sovereignty, directs, in imitation of God himself, the administration of this world's affairs." With divine mandate, therefore, the emperor "subdues and chastens the open adversaries of the truth in accordance with the usages of war."[4]

Augustine, who advocated a more nuanced version of ancient amillennialism in the fifth century, increasingly demurred from this triumphalism—especially in the wake of revived paganism after the fall of Rome. The bishop of Hippo came to emphasize the eschatological tension between "this age" and "the age to come."[5] His *City of God* distinguished clearly the "two cities" of this present age—each with its own commission, purpose, destiny, and means.

However, it was triumphalism that won out, with a dominant eschatological narrative of the gradual progress of the church as the realized kingdom of God: "Christendom" as a union of cult and culture. An allegorized interpretation of Israel's theocracy (including holy wars) guided this fusion. Much as in early Judaism, apocalyptic eschatologies (namely, imminent judgment and renewal from outside of the present system) erupted from time to time in the medieval era in sharp criticism of the reigning establishment. Thus, the Constantinian distortion of amillennialism in the direction of a fully realized kingdom of God fostered a conservative temperament, while millenarian movements encouraged radical criticism of the status quo, understanding Christ's kingdom as an apocalyptic and anti-institutional reality. The story of Christendom reminds us that the attempt to Christianize the secular is as easily described as the secularization of the church.

Among many apocalyptic movements in the Middle Ages, one is especially noteworthy for its long-term influence. Sicilian monk Joachim of Fiore (1132–1202) wrote a commentary on the book of Revelation that interpreted its apocalyptic imagery in literal and futuristic terms. Dividing history into three periods, Joachim advanced the thesis that the Age of the Father (from the time of Adam to the time of Christ: the order of the married) was the era of law; the Age of the Son (from Christ to Joachim's day: the order of the clergy) was

4. Eusebius, *Orat.* 1.6–2.5, quoted in Douglas Farrow, *Ascension and Ecclesia: On the Significance of the Ascension for Ecclesiology and Christian Cosmology* (Grand Rapids: Eerdmans, 2009), 115.
5. See Robert Markus, *Saeculum: History and Society in the Theology of St. Augustine* (Cambridge: Cambridge University Press, 1989). See also his more recent (and somewhat revised) work, *Christianity and the Secular* (Notre Dame, IN: University of Notre Dame Press, 2006).

the era of grace. The third state—the Age of the Spirit—began with Benedict's rule (the order of the monks) and Joachim expected it to dawn fully in 1260. Both the secular life of marriage, family, and civil society and the church with its visible ministry of Word and sacrament would be surpassed by the universal realization of the monastic ideal. Everyone will know God directly and immediately in that age, producing a complete spiritual unity of the human race.[6]

Many of Joachim's followers pushed his views even further, identifying Frederic II with the Antichrist; but even with the emperor's death in 1250, new predictions arose. His ideas influenced an entire age, especially the utopian aspirations of Renaissance figures. Among other notables, Christopher Columbus appealed to Joachim's eschatology, as did Roger Bacon, Nicholas of Cusa, Girolamo Savonarola, and Amerigo Vespucci, who lent his name to the suitably named "New World." It also inspired more radical movements, including the Brethren of the Free Spirit and Anabaptism. While most Anabaptists were pacifists, Thomas Müntzer and John of Leyden led violent revolutions in an effort to establish the kingdom of God. Taking over the German city of Münster, radical Anabaptists established a communist and polygamous regime.[7]

Reformation Eschatologies

Though not always consistent in their practice, the Protestant Reformers affirmed the distinction between two kingdoms: the kingdoms of this age, which are instituted by God for the preservation of justice, peace, and order, and the kingdom of Christ, which is visible at present through the ministry of preaching and sacrament.[8] The earthly realms are defended with the temporal sword, while the heavenly kingdom flourishes through the Word and Spirit.

Not always successful in practice, the Reformers nevertheless went a long way toward recovering the sense of the church's precariousness in this present age—its ambiguity as an "already"/"not yet" reality, simultaneously justified and sinful.[9] Both the fusion of the two kingdoms in Christendom and the

6. Bernard McGinn, *The Calabrian Abbot: Joachim of Fiore in the History of Western Thought* (New York: Harper & Row, 1985); Ann Williams, "Recent Scholarship on Joachim of Fiore and His Influence," in *Prophecy and Millennialism: Essays in Honor of Marjorie Reeves*, ed. Ann Williams (London: Longman, 1981); Norman Cohen, *The Pursuit of the Millennium: Revolutionary Messianism in Medieval and Reformation Europe and Its Bearings on Modern Totalitarian Movements* (New York: Pimlico, 1993); Ronald Knox, *Enthusiasm* (Oxford: Oxford University Press, 1950); Delno C. West and Sandra Zimdars-Swartz, *Joachim of Fiore: A Study in Spiritual Perception and History* (Bloomington, IN: Indiana University Press, 1983).

7. Eugene F. Rice Jr. and Anthony Grafton, *The Foundations of Early Modern Europe 1460–1559*, 2nd ed. (New York: Norton, 1994), 163–68, 178–83; Marjorie Reeves, *Joachim of Fiore and the Prophetic Future: A Medieval Study in Historical Thinking* (London: SPCK, 1976).

8. Luther's views on this point are well known, but Calvin urges the same distinction in the *Institutes* (see especially 2.15.3; 4.5.17; 4.20.1, 8).

9. Douglas Farrow especially points to Calvin's contribution in this respect in his excellent book *Ascension and Ecclesia*, 176–77.

apocalyptic fanaticism of the radicals represented attempts to transform this spiritual kingdom under the cross into a geopolitical kingdom of glory. The Reformers argued that both versions are driven by the same eschatological misunderstanding of Christ's disciples as they expected a recovery of the theocracy even when the messianic King had himself arrived.[10] It was precisely this misunderstanding that left Jesus's contemporaries (even his disciples) disillusioned when his triumphal entry into Jerusalem was followed by his crucifixion, they insisted.[11]

The myth of Christendom persisted, however, in both Roman Catholic and Protestant colonial expansion. Many Protestants interpreted the surprising British defeat of the Spanish Armada in 1588 as the destruction of the dragon and the beginning of the end of Antichrist's rule. Cromwell's Commonwealth was riot with millennial fanaticism, enlivened by appeals (such as John Milton's) to Joachim of Fiore's speculations of a Third Age of the Spirit.[12]

During the era of the American Revolution, many preachers—Anglican, Presbyterian, and Congregationalist—interpreted the prophecies in the book of Revelation as if they were being fulfilled directly in the contest with Romanism and infidelity. The new nation (*novus ordo seclorum*) would become the center of world missions as well as political, social, moral, and economic progress based on Christian principles. However much Joachim might have objected to the secularization of his eschatology in terms of the myth of human progress, Kant, Lessing, Hegel, and Marx invoked the abbot's apocalyptic vision of a future utopian age of intuitive revelation apart from any need of external authorities.

Catastrophe or Consummation?

Does the kingdom of God grow up within history, from an acorn to an oak tree? Or does it arrive like a violent wind, "from above," breaking up history and judging it? Answers to these questions continued to shape the imagination of Christendom and its rivals.

10. Calvin, *Institutes*, 4.5.17.

11. The Augsburg Confession (art. XVII) rejected chiliasm, identifying it with the Anabaptists "who now scatter Jewish opinions that, before the resurrection of the dead, the godly shall occupy the kingdom of the world, the wicked being everywhere suppressed." The Reformed concurred, as in the Second Helvetic Confession's rejection of "the Jewish dream of a millennium, or golden age on earth, before the last judgment." Calvin similarly dismissed millenarian views (4.25.5) and Archbishop Cranmer rejected such views as a "fable of Jewish dotage" (Anglican Articles, art. 41). Therefore, such references should not be interpreted as an anti-Semitic slur, but a comparison of chiliastic movements of their day to the misunderstanding of Jesus's contemporaries. See Philip Schaff, *History of the Christian Church* (Peabody, MA: Hendrickson, 2004), 2:381.

12. Marjorie Reeves, "Joachim of Fiore and the Images of the Apocalypse According to St. John," *Journal of the Warburg and Courtauld Institutes* 64 (2001): 281–95; cf. Michael Fixler, *John Milton and the Kingdoms of God* (Evanston, IL: Northwestern University Press, 1964).

Progress toward the Golden Age

With the rise especially of German idealism, eschatology became assimilated to history—of course, a particular history (namely, Western modernity).[13] In many respects, this development may be seen as a secularized (or rather, *more* secularized) version of the realized eschatology of Christendom. In the wake of Immanuel Kant (1724–1804), the kingdom of God was identified with a universal kingdom of morality guided by practical reason.

Especially with G. W. F. Hegel (1770–1831) and Friedrich Schleiermacher (1768–1834), this kingdom was understood in terms of the mystical and progressive unfolding of Spirit (*Geist*) in history and culture. Instead of a dramatic (apocalyptic) disruption of history from above, Schleiermacher associated the coming of the kingdom with "the Transcendental Power of Providence," which is always at work in every natural event.[14] Jesus Christ represents the unity of divinity and humanity, not in terms of a Chalcedonian Christology, but in his unique attainment to a perfect and complete "God-consciousness" that others may realize in varying degrees through association with him. In all of these ways, the original meaning of *eschata* as "last things" was emptied. Belief in the resurrection of Jesus Christ and all who are united to him was abandoned in favor of a progressive realization of God-consciousness in history.[15]

By the end of the nineteenth century, this identification of the kingdom with historical progress was a settled feature of liberal Protestantism, especially in the thought of Richard Rothe (1799–1867) and Albrecht Ritschl (1822–1889). According to the founder of the American social gospel movement, Walter Rauschenbusch (1861–1918), any adequate theology for the social gospel must "not only make room for the doctrine of the kingdom of God, but give it a central place and revise all other doctrines so that they will articulate organically with it."[16] We must avoid any emphasis on the future of the kingdom that would "paralyze or postpone redemptive action on our part."[17]

Ironically, it was not liberalism as much as evangelical revivalism that shaped the American version of this "Christendom" thesis (which persists, ironically, even in the apparently contradictory forms of dispensationalism, especially in defense of a "Christian America"). Although Ritschl's senior by thirty-two years, apparently with no direct dependence on Kant, American evangelist

13. Robin Barnes, "Images of Hope and Despair: Western Apocalypticism: ca. 1500–1800," in *The Encyclopedia of Apocalypticism*, vol. 2, *Apocalypticism in Western History and Culture*, ed. B. McGinn (New York: Continuum, 2000), 143–84.

14. Friedrich Schleiermacher, *The Christian Faith*, trans. H. R. Mackintosh and J. S. Stewart (Edinburgh: T&T Clark, 1928), §56.

15. Nathan D. Hieb, "The Precarious Status of Resurrection in Friedrich Schleiermacher's *Glaubenslehre*," *International Journal of Systematic Theology* 9, no. 4 (October 2007): 398–414.

16. Walter Rauschenbusch, *A Theology for the Social Gospel* (New York: Macmillan, 1918), 131.

17. Ibid., 143.

Charles Finney (1792–1875) shared the Pelagian theological assumptions of ripening modernity, wedded to a vaguely postmillennial vision of the church as a society of moral and social reformers.

There were also premillennial movements in nineteenth-century America, wedded to a restorationist ecclesiology (e.g., the Millerites, the Adventists, Jehovah's Witnesses, Latter-Day Saints, Campbellites, and other groups)—many arising in the region of Finney's frequent revivals, nicknamed the "Burned-Over District."[18] In many of these cases, the capital of Christ's universal kingdom would be established in the city or town of the movement's origin.

However, postmillennialism remained the default setting of mainstream American Protestantism. Julia Howe's "The Battle Hymn of the Republic" (1861) illustrates just how far American Protestants were willing to go in identifying a political cause—indeed, a war—with the last judgment. From John Winthrop's announcement of Puritan New England as "a shining city on a hill" to Woodrow Wilson's "war to end all wars," the church's progressive advance of world missions, schools, relief agencies, hospitals, and political reforms (i.e., liberal-democratic values) at home and abroad fueled the sense of American exceptionalism in God's plan for the world's future. Evangelical optimism toward the *belle époque* (or the "gay nineties," as it was known in the United States) is evident in the founding of *The Christian Century* in 1900, as a fusion of Finney's revivalistic legacy and the social gospel movement. Meanwhile, in Roman Catholic countries, the pope continued to require absolute obedience of all states and rulers. In fact, the First Amendment to the U.S. Constitution was identified as the "Americanist heresy" by the Vatican until the mid-twentieth century.[19]

However, a decisive blow, not only to secularized and liberal versions but to more conservative postmillennial views, was dealt by the First World War. Dreams of paradise turned to visions of Armageddon, and the Second World War seemed to justify this outlook.[20]

Crisis and Catastrophe

Although initially enamored with Charles Finney's social activism, evangelist D. L. Moody (1837–1899) eventually concluded that the world is a "wrecked

18. Whitney R. Cross, *The Burned-Over District: The Social and Intellectual History of Enthusiastic Religion in Western New York, 1800–1850* (New York: Harper Torchbooks, 1965).

19. The remarkable American Jesuit theologian John Courtney Murray was formative in developing a Roman Catholic social doctrine that was compatible with liberal democracy. See his *We Hold These Truths: Catholic Reflections on the American Proposition* (New York: Sheed & Ward, 1960). Although he met staunch opposition by the Vatican, his views made a strong impression at the Second Vatican Council, as is especially evident in the council's *Dignitatis Humanae*.

20. James Moorhead, "Apocalypticism in Mainstream Protestantism, 1800–Present," in *The Encyclopedia of Apocalypticism*, vol. 3, *Apocalypticism in the Modern Period and the Contemporary Age*, ed. Stephen J. Stein (New York: Continuum, 2000), 72–107.

vessel." "God has given me a lifeboat and said to me, 'Moody, save all you can.'"[21] Whereas revival was usually regarded as an instrument of Christianizing society through evangelism and social action, Moody now focused all of his energies on converting individuals: "soul-saving."

John Nelson Darby (1800–1882), an Anglo-Irish lawyer ordained in the (Anglican) Church of Ireland, became convinced that the prophecies of Isaiah, Daniel, and Revelation referred to a future kingdom that was utterly distinct from the church. In 1832 he formally severed his ties with the Church of Ireland and articulated his belief in a "secret rapture" of believers prior to the tribulation, and the return and millennial kingdom of Christ. A founding figure in the rise of the Plymouth Brethren, Darby is the father of *dispensational premillennialism*.

Distinguished from *historic premillennialism* by its belief in a stark separation of Israel and the church and a secret rapture of believers prior to a seven-year tribulation, dispensationalism also divided history into seven distinct periods. These are the dispensations of (1) innocence (pre-fall); (2) conscience (post-fall to Noah); (3) human government (Noah to Abraham); (4) promise (Abraham to Moses); (5) law (Moses to Christ); (6) grace (the church age); (7) kingdom (the millennial age).[22]

Like postmillennialists, dispensational premillennialists have interpreted biblical prophecy as referring to current events. However, for the former, this interpretation assumed a more gradual optimism toward the future, while it entailed for the latter a more pessimistic view of the imminent future as an apocalyptic conflagration. Both have had their opportunity to shape U.S. culture, including foreign policy.[23]

Classic dispensationalism teaches that the millennium will consist of a renewed theocracy with a rebuilt temple and sacrifices. According to Lewis Sperry Chafer and John Walvoord, there will be a revival of Israel's theocracy under the Messiah, including animal sacrifices in a rebuilt temple.[24] According to Charles Ryrie, "the Church is not fulfilling in any sense the promises

21. Wilbur M. Smith, ed., "The Second Coming of Christ," in *The Best of D. L. Moody* (Chicago: Moody, 1971), 193–95. Quoted in George Marsden, *Fundamentalism and American Culture* (New York: Oxford University Press, 1980), 38.

22. Dispensationalism spread rapidly, especially through a series of annotated reference Bibles from Cyrus I. Scofield to Charles Ryrie to John MacArthur Jr. and the founding of Bible colleges and seminaries, such as the Moody Bible Institute and Dallas Theological Seminary. It has been popularized by numerous Bible prophecy conferences, the most successful television and radio evangelists, and national bestsellers, from Hal Lindsey's *The Late Great Planet Earth* to the recent *Left Behind* series by Tim LaHaye and Jerry Jenkins.

23. Ernest Sandeen, *The Roots of Fundamentalism: British and American Millenarianism, 1800–1930* (Chicago: University of Chicago Press, 1970); cf. Paul Boyer, *When Time Shall Be No More* (Cambridge, MA: Harvard University Press, 1994).

24. Lewis Sperry Chafer and John Walvoord, *Major Bible Themes* (Grand Rapids: Zondervan, 1974), 357–58.

to Israel. . . . The Church age is not seen in God's program for Israel. It is an intercalation."[25] In fact, it may be said that the modern state of Israel and its geopolitical significance are the focus of prophetic interest among advocates of this school.

Just as *historic premillennialists* see a closer relationship between Israel and the church in the New Testament,[26] some amillennialists have argued that God still has a purpose for ethnic Israel, anticipating a wide-scale ingathering of Jews to Jesus Christ at the end of the age.[27] More recently, some dispensationalists, such as Craig Blaising and Darrell Bock, have formulated *progressive dispensationalism*, which moves away from the sharp distinction between Israel and the church and affirms that the kingdom of Christ is in some sense present although it will be fully realized in the millennium.[28]

If classic dispensationalism treats most biblical prophecies as still future, a small circle of evangelicals, called *full preterists*, argue that even Christ's second coming and final judgment have been fulfilled. However, *partial preterists* hold that the second coming of Christ to raise the dead and judge the world are still future.[29]

Broader Trends in Contemporary Eschatology

After centuries of assimilating the kingdom of Christ to the progress of secular culture, liberal Protestantism was shaken from within by the "consistent eschatology" of Albert Schweitzer (1875–1965). In sharp contrast to the idea of a gradual evolution of the kingdom of love, Schweitzer argued that Jesus expected an imminent kingdom arriving from above, bringing cataclysm and judgment. However, when this kingdom did not materialize, Jesus surrendered himself to death in the hope that it would somehow provoke the

25. Charles C. Ryrie, *The Basis of the Premillennial Faith* (New York: Loizeaux Bros., 1953), 136. "Intercalation" means the insertion of something out of the ordinary, like a day in a month for a leap year.

26. George Eldon Ladd's work remains the ablest statement of historic premillennialism. See his *The Blessed Hope* (Grand Rapids: Eerdmans, 1956) and his *Commentary on Revelation* (Grand Rapids: Eerdmans, 1987).

27. In defense of this view (also held by Geerhardus Vos and Herman Ridderbos), see John Murray, "The Last Things," in *Collected Writings of John Murray* (Edinburgh: Banner of Truth, 1982), 2:409.

28. Craig A. Blaising and Darrell L. Bock, *Progressive Dispensationalism* (Wheaton: Victor, 1993).

29. Full preterism is defended in the 1878 book by J. S. Russell, *Parousia: The New Testament Doctrine of Our Lord's Second Coming* (Grand Rapids: Baker, 1999). Partial preterism is defended in R. C. Sproul, *The Last Days according to Jesus* (Grand Rapids: Baker, 1998), and Kenneth Gentry Jr., "The Preterist View," in *Four Views of the Book of Revelation*, ed. Marvin Pate (Grand Rapids: Zondervan, 1998). An outstanding rebuttal of the full preterist view is found in Keith A. Mathison, ed., *When Shall These Things Be? A Reformed Response to Hyper-Preterism* (Phillipsburg, NJ: P&R, 2004).

Father to act on his behalf. After his death, Jesus's followers transformed his apocalyptic anticipation of an imminent dawn of the kingdom into a steady growth of the church.[30]

In reaction to both liberalism and Schweitzer's "consistent eschatology," a group emerged in the 1920s and 1930s, known early on as the dialectical circle (early Bultmann, Barth, Gogarten, and Brunner). The early tendency at least (most fully and lastingly represented by Bultmann) was to set history and eschatology in antithesis as virtually synonymous with a time-eternity dualism.[31]

After his disillusionment with his liberal Protestant mentors, Barth turned from history and the optimistic idea of moral progress to a radical emphasis on eschatology as its antithesis. A servant of neither stability nor revolt, God's revolution negates the state; it does not reform it. God's activity from above disrupts the pretentious "march of history" toward human utopias.[32] Jesus Christ is not the first among equals or a pioneer of social progress to be emulated; he is the event that brings an end to so-called history.[33] If the vertical arrow from heaven was absorbed into the horizontal arrow in liberal historicism, Barth's eschatology tends to isolate the history of the Christ-event (*Heilsgeschichte*) from wider history ("history so-called"). "Nothing which will be has not already taken place on Easter Day—included and anticipated in the person of the one man Jesus. . . . Strictly speaking there are no 'last things,' i.e. no abstract and autonomous last things apart from and alongside Him, the last One."[34] Amillennialist Herman Ridderbos judged the "eschatological" view of Bultmann and even Barth as "docetic." "It leaves no room for the kingdom in its real and beneficent presence."[35]

However, in the aftermath of the Second World War, there was a flowering of renewed interest in history especially centered at Heidelberg University (associated with the names of Cullmann, von Rad, Bornkamm, and von Campenhausen). This circle renewed interest in the history of Israel and its covenant theology after a century of anti-Jewish presuppositions in German biblical scholarship. A young member of this circle, Wolfhart Pannenberg, sought to relate eschatology to history in developing his theology of the

30. Albert Schweitzer, *The Quest of the Historical Jesus: A Critical Study of Its Progress from Reimarus to Wrede*, trans. William Montgomery (1906; repr., Minneapolis: Augsburg Fortress, 2001); Albert Schweitzer and Ulrich Neuenschwander, *The Kingdom of God and Primitive Christianity* (New York: Seabury, 1968).

31. Rudolf Bultmann, *History and Eschatology: The Presence of Eternity*, Gifford Lectures, 1954–1955 (New York: Harper, 1962).

32. Karl Barth, *Der Römerbrief*, ed. H. Stoevesandt (1919; repr., Zürich: Theologische Verlag, 1985), 505–7.

33. Karl Barth, *Paul's Epistle to the Romans*, ed. E. Hoskyns (Oxford: Oxford University Press, 1933), 38.

34. Karl Barth, *Church Dogmatics* II/2, 489–90.

35. Herman Ridderbos, *The Coming of the Kingdom*, trans. H. de Jongste, ed. Raymond O. Zorn (Philadelphia: P&R, 1962), 104.

kingdom.[36] Pannenberg's eschatology is future oriented. Only in the end is the meaning of the whole of history finally revealed. However, as the prolepsis of the end, Christ's resurrection is the fully realized aspect of eschatology that warrants the Christian hope.

Jürgen Moltmann's Theology of Hope

Jürgen Moltmann joined this broader Heidelberg trajectory, but with a more radical expectation of the power of Christ's future to transform the present. Indeed, eschatology is the principal theme of Moltmann's work.[37] Since he has shaped contemporary eschatological thinking more decisively than any living theologian, a fuller summary of Moltmann's views is appropriate.

Whereas Barth tended to see eschatology as a hope *beyond* (or above) history in an eternity-time dualism, Moltmann sees eschatology as the hope *within* history that propels us toward the future. Timothy Gorringe has pointed out, "In terms of cultural background, Barth's theology begins in apocalypse and ends with relative stability; Moltmann begins with relative stability and moves increasingly into the insecurity signified by the preoccupation of present-day culture with apocalypse."[38] Moltmann's *Theology of Hope* (1967) is especially directed against Barth's "epiphany of the eternal present," Gorringe notes.[39] Moltmann realizes that the resurrection for Barth is "no longer an eschatological happening. It is simply and solely the transcendent endorsement of the redemptive significance of the cross of Christ."[40] At the same time, dispensationalism is dangerously attached to a negative apocalypticism, anticipating the destruction of the world in a violent conflagration rather than in a kingdom of peace. Navigating between these, Moltmann insists, "Christian eschatology—eschatology, that is, which is messianic, healing and saving—is millenarian eschatology."[41] Moltmann is seeking a millennial reign of

36. Wolfhart Pannenberg, *Theology and the Kingdom of God* (Philadelphia: Westminster, 1969).

37. On Moltmann's more postmillennial than premillennial orientation, see Richard Bauckham, "The Millennium," in *God Will Be All in All: The Eschatology of Jürgen Moltmann*, ed. Richard Bauckham (Edinburgh: T&T Clark, 1999), 132–33.

38. Timothy Gorringe, "Eschatology and Political Radicalism," in Bauckham, *God Will Be All in All*, 92.

39. Ibid., 104. Similarly, Miroslav Volf observes, "Eschatology was the heartbeat of Barth's theology. But it was an eschatology that managed to posit itself, so to speak, only by denying itself. It was an 'eternalized' eschatology, which had much to do with the present (the transcendent 'eternal Moment' in the early Barth) or with the past (the 'hour' of Christ's coming in the later Barth), but little with the future—either the future of God or the future of God's world (CoG 15)" (Miroslav Volf, "After Moltmann," in Bauckham, *God Will Be All in All*, 233–34).

40. Jürgen Moltmann, *The Way of Jesus Christ* (Minneapolis: Fortress, 1993), 231.

41. Jürgen Moltmann, *The Coming of God: Christian Eschatology*, trans. Margaret Kohl (Minneapolis: Fortress, 1996), 202. For an interesting reflection on how he developed his early foci, see Moltmann, "Can Christian Eschatology Become Post-Modern? Response to M. Volf,"

Christ that need not go through the apocalyptic catastrophe of Armageddon. "Without millennial hope, the Christian ethic of resistance and the consistent discipleship of Christ lose their most powerful motivation."[42]

Joachim of Fiore returns throughout Moltmann's work. In fact, the dust jacket of his *History and the Triune God* (1992) reproduces Joachim's three-ages chart. In *The Trinity and the Kingdom*, he argues, "If we want to overcome the monotheistic interpretation of the lordship of God by the trinitarian understanding of the kingdom, then we must go back to Joachim of Fiore, and rediscover the truth of his trinitarian view of history. Joachim was counted as an 'Enthusiast' and an outsider." However, Moltmann challenges the verdict, ever since Aquinas, that Joachim "dissolved the doctrine of the Trinity in history." Like many before him, Moltmann finds the speculations of the Calabrian monk "revolutionary."[43] "Ever since the Phrygian prophecy and Montanism, this promise has continually awakened the expectation of a special period of revelation belonging to the Holy Spirit. . . . Joachim's great idea was to identify the seventh day of world history with the kingdom of the Spirit. The great 'sabbath' of history, before the end of the world, and the kingdom of the Spirit mean the same thing."[44]

Moltmann is quite aware of the way in which modernity (especially Lessing, Comte, and Marx) capitalized on Joachim's prophecies, even if they interpreted them in a secularized manner.[45] However, he believes that something like Joachim's trinitarian eschatology can challenge "the doctrine of the two kingdoms," although Moltmann revises Joachim's trinitarian scheme away from three sequential stages toward a more dialectical view.[46] What Moltmann especially wants to carry over from Joachim is the apocalyptic anticipation of the Spirit's imminent renewal of all things through the agency of the people of God.

---

in Bauckham, *God Will Be All in All*: "What next? is a typically modern question—generally an American one. So what comes 'after' the modern? We have it: the post-modern. What comes after the post-modern? We have it: the ultra-modern. Or are these merely further installments of modernity, which is always out to outstrip itself—a kind of post-ism? If we look at the ever-shorter 'shelf-life' of what is produced, and the speeding up of time, then the post- and ultra-modern are no more than modernity in new packaging" (259). Moltmann says that after writing *Theology of Hope*, he came as a visiting professor at Duke and found that it was being used to bolster American optimism. Thereafter, "I promised friends that if I were to come back I would only talk about 'the theology of the cross.' This is what I then did in 1972 with my book, *The Crucified God*, which appeared in English in 1974" (260). The Reformation attack on millenarianism as a "Jewish dream" caught his attention. "The Reformation critics no doubt grasped the fact: anyone who banishes the millennium from the Christian hope has no further interest in Israel and no positive relationship to the Jews" (262).

42. Moltmann, *Coming of God*, 201.
43. *The Trinity and the Kingdom* (Minneapolis: Fortress, 1993), 203.
44. Ibid., 203–9.
45. Ibid., 206.
46. Ibid., 209.

Moltmann's views have been criticized on a number of fronts. Mark C. Mattes complains that Moltmann's eschatology conceives of believers almost exclusively as actors rather than receivers, building the kingdom through our efforts rather than receiving it through the hearing of the gospel as pure promise.[47] This is not quietism, but the liberation of the church to fulfill the Great Commission and of believers to fulfill their worldly callings alongside unbelievers. By contrast, says Mattes, "Along with Engels and Bloch, who maintained that communism was indebted to [Thomas] Müntzer, Moltmann believes that the human is always an agent (*homo semper agens*), not a recipient." He continues,

> The paradoxes that help preserve faith, described by Luther (that one is simultaneously lord and servant, sinful and righteous, that God is hidden and revealed, and that Jesus Christ is human and divine), are flattened out into a "Christ transforming culture" perspective, effected, strangely enough, by means of a counterculture—"Christ against culture," to use the helpful typology of H. Richard Niebuhr (1894–1962). . . . Here, the gospel is given within the matrix of law.[48]

But this misses the important fact that "misplaced trust" is the root cause of ethical problems and can only be challenged by proclamation of the gospel.[49] In fact, Mattes goes so far as to call Moltmann a "post-tribulation premillennialist of the 'left.'"[50]

Richard Bauckham (praised by Moltmann as an accurate reader of his work) observes, "The pre-Constantinian church was by no means unanimously millenarian," as Moltmann claims, and amillennialists in this period certainly did not hold a triumphalist view of church or empire.[51] Like dispensationalists, Moltmann charges amillennialism with a "spiritualizing" tendency. However, if Augustine and his colleagues believed in the resurrection of the dead in a renewed heavens and earth, they can hardly be scolded for embracing amillennialism because of a "spiritualizing" tendency. Any "spiritualizing," Bauckham observes, is not due to amillennialism but to "the strong Platonic influence in the tradition."[52]

---

47. Mark C. Mattes, *The Role of Justification in Contemporary Thought* (Grand Rapids: Eerdmans, 2004), 89–90.

48. Ibid., 91.

49. Ibid., 92.

50. Ibid., 95.

51. Bauckham, "Millennium," 130. "The popular view that the martyrs ascend at death to be with Christ in his heavenly kingdom may have seemed incompatible with the expectation of an earthly kingdom and may have led to a non-millenarian reading of Revelation 20 already in the pre-Constantinian period, anticipating Augustine's exegesis of the reign of the martyrs as their present rule in heaven (*De Civ. Dei* 20.9)" (ibid.).

52. Ibid., 130–31.

Second, Bauckham thinks that Moltmann collapses premillennialism and postmillennialism into a single eschatology, erroneously identifying Joachim's thought as premillennial.[53] Third, Moltmann assumes that an amillennial perspective negates the renewal of the present creation in favor of a "hope for souls in the heaven of a world beyond this one."[54] However, Bauckham notes, amillennialists expect a total renewal of creation at Christ's return and not simply in a thousand-year reign.[55] Moltmann argues, "Before the millennium there is no rule of the saints," but only the church: "the brotherly and sisterly, charismatic, non-violent fellowship of those who wait for the coming of the Lord."[56] However, this argument is "in danger of suggesting that while it is premature for Christians to attempt to exercise absolutist and violent domination over the world now, they will exercise such domination in the coming millennium."[57] If this is so, Bauckham judges, the Anabaptist radicals were not wrong in principle but only in their timing.[58] Furthermore, "according to Revelation, it is not only in the millennium that the saints rule (20:4) but also in the New Jerusalem (22:5)." Why substitute a penultimate for an ultimate realization of the restoration of creation?[59] "According to Moltmann, only the millennium supplies a 'goal of history' (CoG 133–134, 137, 193, 197)."[60] However, is not this goal realized in an everlasting new creation even more than in a thousand-year reign?[61] In fact, Miroslav Volf argues that "understood as transition, the millennium is not only unnecessary but *detrimental*."[62]

Fourth, for those who deny a literal millennium in the future, Bauckham says that Moltmann insists the end of history can only be anticipated as "'an abrupt Big Bang,' to which he attaches the terms 'Hiroshima images' and 'catastrophe.'"[63] However, Bauckham replies, this is far from the view held by amillennialists, for whom God's act of new creation "redeems and renews and transfigures" rather than destroys creation in catastrophe. On the other hand, "even the world history that reaches its goal in Moltmann's millennium would end with 'an abrupt Big Bang,' if that were the appropriate way to

53. Ibid., 131–32. "This is not just terminologically confusing; it also deprives him of a distinction between two kinds of futurist millenarianism which is essential to an accurate reading of the Christian millenarian tradition and its relationship to the secular eschatologies of the modern period." See Moltmann, *The Coming of God*, 147, 153, 194.
54. Bauckham, "The Millennium," 135, citing Moltmann, *The Coming of God*, 147.
55. Bauckham, "The Millennium," 135–36.
56. Ibid., 136, citing Moltmann, *The Coming of God*, 184.
57. Bauckham, "The Millennium," 137.
58. Ibid., 138.
59. Ibid.
60. Ibid.
61. Ibid., 139.
62. Volf, "After Moltmann," 243.
63. Bauckham, "The Millennium," 140.

conceptualize the end."[64] Bauckham writes, quoting Moltmann, "'Only the new earth offers possibilities for the new embodiment of human beings' (CoG 104). Yet in Moltmann's millennium there are precisely human beings risen to new embodiment *without the new earth*. . . . Moltmann's millenarianism here has the problem which all millenarianism has: how to characterize the millennium in such a way as to make it intelligible as transitional rather than final."[65]

Moltmann's theology (including his eschatological views) has been formative in liberation theologies, especially in Latin America.[66] Besides the widely divergent views of Moltmann and American millenarianism, futuristic eschatologies of imminent hope or apocalypse are now exercising a powerful influence beyond the West, even beyond Christianity.[67]

Antichrist and the Secret Rapture

Given the enduring significance and influence (sometimes direct, sometimes indirect) of dispensational premillennialism on American evangelicals, its emphasis on the future advent of the Antichrist and a secret rapture should be mentioned in some detail. These ideas deeply shape many of their views of church, state, evangelism, and cultural engagement.

According to classic dispensationalists, the seventy weeks of Daniel's vision (Dan. 9) should be interpreted literally as 490 years, 483 of which are from the command to restore and rebuild Jerusalem (Dan. 9:25) to the appearance of the Messiah.[68] "The day of the Lord," write Lewis Sperry Chafer and John Walvoord, "refers to that lengthened period extending from the rapture of the church and the judgments following this event on the earth, to the end of His millennial reign (Isa. 2:10–22; Zech. 14)."[69] After the secret rapture, the primary role of evangelizing those who are alive during the tribulation

64. Ibid., 140–41.
65. Ibid., emphasis added. It should be noted that Moltmann himself makes even further problems for himself on this score when he says, "Theological tradition has always related the word consummatio to the created world: De consummatione mundi is the title given to the relevant article in seventeenth-century Lutheran and Reformed theology: the old heaven and the old earth are to become a new imperishable heaven and a new imperishable earth" (Moltmann, "Can Christian Eschatology Become Post-Modern?", 262). If this is so, then everything that he has said thus far in criticism of the tradition is at least in need of qualification to avoid obvious contradiction.
66. R. M. Levine, "Apocalyptic Movements in Latin America in the Nineteenth and Twentieth Centuries," in *Encyclopedia of Apocalypticism*, 3:140–78.
67. James F. Rinehart, *Revolution and the Millennium: China, Mexico, and Iran* (Westport, CT: Praeger, 1997).
68. Chafer and Walvoord, *Major Bible Themes*, 305–6. For an amillennial interpretation of Daniel's "weeks," see Kim Riddlebarger, *A Case for Amillennialism: Understanding the End Times* (Grand Rapids: Baker, 2003), 149–56.
69. Chafer and Walvoord, *Major Bible Themes*, 309.

will be given to Jewish converts. The tribulation itself will be led by a revived Roman Empire (the feet stage of Dan. 2 and the ten-horn stage of the fourth beast of 7:7).[70] After a seven-year period of peace, the Antichrist—a Middle Eastern dictator in league with Russia—will break his treaty with Israel. The great tribulation will last for forty-two months, "leading up to the second coming of Christ."[71]

According to Chafer and Walvoord, those who merge the rapture and the second coming "into one event" are guilty of "spiritualizing" prophecy.[72] Thus, the rapture is sharply distinguished from the second coming—and is, in fact, separated by the great tribulation. "In contrast with the Rapture, where there is no evidence that the world as a whole will see the glory of Christ, the second coming to the earth will be both visible and glorious."[73] After the total destruction of the cosmos, God will create a new heaven and earth.[74] There are seven resurrections in all.[75] "Beginning at this point in the prophetic program, approximately forty-two months before the second coming of Christ (cf. Rev. 12:6), Satan and the wicked angels are at long last excluded from heaven."[76]

In summary, then, classic dispensationalism anticipates a secret rapture, followed by the tribulation, the second coming, the judgment of the nations regarding their treatment of Israel ("the Great White Throne Judgment" of Rev. 20:11–15), followed by the destruction of heaven and earth, resurrection of the unrighteous, the judgment of believers' works ("the Bema Seat Judgment"), and finally the creation of new heavens and a new earth.[77]

The Antichrist

One of the most explicit references to the Antichrist or "man of lawlessness" is found in 2 Thess. 2:1–12. Various groups throughout the medieval period identified the Antichrist with a pope or with the papal office more generally. The Protestant Reformers generally shared this view.[78] However,

---

70. Ibid., 315.
71. Ibid., 321.
72. Ibid., 332. This recurring charge is rarely defended but simply assumed, even though evangelical amillennialists and postmillennialists do not dispute the historical character of these prophetic fulfillments.
73. Ibid., 333.
74. Ibid., 353: "In this discussion it will be assumed that prophecy should be interpreted in the same literal sense as any other theme of divine revelation." However, interpreting prophetic and apocalyptic literature—or, for that matter, parables and poetry—as if they were historical narrative results in violence to the actual intention of the text.
75. Ibid., 340–43.
76. Ibid., 362.
77. Ibid., 366–69.
78. John R. Stephenson, *Eschatology: Confessional Lutheran Dogmatics* (Ft. Wayne, IN: Luther Academy, 1993), 12:79. As Stephenson explains, "Luther lays his finger on the sacrilegious expression of the papal claims set forth in Boniface VIII's *Unam Sanctam* of 1302:

contemporary amillennialists have pointed out the exegetical difficulties with this reading.[79]

Many of the most popular representatives of dispensational premillennialism routinely ignore the cautions of others in their school against contributing to a legacy of failed speculations. Many evangelicals anticipate the imminent appearance of the Antichrist, often in the most elaborate detail. Associating the "man of sin" with various world leaders, the most recent candidate is identified by Hal Lindsey as current U.S. president Barack Obama.[80]

In an amillennial interpretation, the apostle Paul (writing most likely in the early 50s) may have been prophesying any number of future Caesars or perhaps the whole line of "antichrists" who establish their own parody of a messianic kingdom.[81] In any case, in 2 Thess. 2:7 Paul says that "the mystery of lawlessness is already at work." Amillennialists also point out from this passage that the revealing of "the man of lawlessness" occurs as a precursor to Christ's return and gathering of his saints—with no intervening periods of tribulation or a millennium mentioned. At the same time, the passage warns against the teaching of some "that the day of the Lord has come" (v. 2). It is a future event, with the Antichrist taking "his seat in the temple of God, proclaiming himself to be God" (v. 4). If we are to take this straightforward prophecy literally, it could not have been fulfilled after the destruction of the temple in 70 CE, nor is there any reference here (or elsewhere) to the Antichrist's taking his seat in a rebuilt temple.

Amillennialists point out that the desecration of the temple under Titus (who reigned from 79 to 81) seems to fit Paul's prophecy ideally.[82] Furthermore, they also refer to the epistles of John, where believers are warned, "Children, it is the last hour, and as you have heard that antichrist is coming, so now many antichrists have come. Therefore we know that it is the last hour" (1 John 2:18). This tribulation from within as well as without was evident already in the apostasy of some (v. 19). "This is the antichrist, he who denies the Father and the Son" (v. 22). Specifically, those who deny that "Jesus Christ has come in the flesh" are "not from God." "This is the spirit of the antichrist, which you heard was coming

---

'Furthermore, we declare, say, define, and proclaim to every human creature that they by necessity for salvation are entirely subject to the Roman Pontiff.'" Luther thundered, "This is a powerful demonstration that the pope is the real Antichrist who has raised himself over and set himself against Christ, for the pope will not permit Christians to be saved except by his own power, which amounts to nothing, since it is neither established nor commanded by God" (quoted in Stephenson, *Eschatology*, 80).

79. Riddlebarger, *Case for Amillennialism*, 22.

80. Hal Lindsey, reported by Amy Sullivan, "An Antichrist Obama in McCain Ad?" *Time*, August 8, 2009, http://www.time.com/time/politics/article/0,8599,1830590,00.html.

81. Kim Riddlebarger, *The Man of Sin* (Grand Rapids: Baker Books, 2006).

82. Amillennialists often refer to the vivid and tragic description of the brutal destruction of Jerusalem and its temple (with no stone left upon another) by Jewish historian Josephus, himself captured in the war. See Josephus, *The War of the Jews* 6.4.3.

and now is in the world already" (1 John 4:2–3). Just as the antichrist is spoken of
by Paul and John as "coming" and yet as "in the world already," amillennialists
argue that the tribulation is coming and is already present. In the upper room
Jesus prepared his disciples for imminent persecution (John 15–16).

The Secret Rapture

Belief in a secret rapture was unknown in the church until it was formulated by
John Nelson Darby in the nineteenth century. In the United States today, however,
it is perhaps the most popular, or at least familiar, interpretation of 1 Thess.
4:13–18. In this passage we are told that those who are alive when Jesus returns
will be "caught up" with those who have died in Christ, to join his descent.

> For the Lord himself will descend from heaven with a cry of command, with the
> voice of an archangel, and with the sound of the trumpet of God. And the dead
> in Christ will rise first. Then we who are alive, who are left, will be caught up
> together with them in the clouds to meet the Lord in the air, and so we will always
> be with the Lord. Therefore encourage one another with these words. (vv. 16–18)

According to dispensationalist teaching, this passage prophesies a secret rapture
(from the Greek verb "to catch up") of believers alive on the earth, followed by
a seven-year great tribulation. After the battle of Armageddon, Christ returns
with all of his saints to reign.[83]

Both amillennialists and postmillennialists take issue with dispensationalist
readings of this passage. In this passage, Paul comforts believers who mourn
the death of fellow saints by assuring them that those who have died are already
with the Lord and will return with him at "the coming of the Lord"—and
only one "coming" is mentioned here. Further, he says that we who are alive
at this coming will *not* precede those who have died, and his reference is not
to a secret rapture prior to the resurrection but to the latter itself: "And the
dead in Christ will rise first," followed by the resurrection of those who are
still alive, so that all of the elect may join Christ's retinue as he comes on
the clouds of the final judgment.[84] Far from being a secret event, this event is
described by Paul in the most public terms (compare with Matt. 24:30–31).

Heaven and Hell

In spite of the divergences we have surveyed so far, mainstream Christianity
has enjoyed a remarkable consensus concerning the reality of Christ's bodily
return to raise the dead, to judge, and to reign in everlasting righteousness.

83. John Walvoord, *The Rapture Question*, rev. ed. (Grand Rapids: Zondervan, 1979).
84. Riddlebarger, *Case for Amillennialism*, 130–48.

The idea of heaven as a place where souls are forever freed from their bodily carapace to enjoy a dreamlike existence is far from the biblical understanding. Some contemporary theologians, such as Rosemary Radford Ruether and John Hick, empty eschatology of its cosmic, earthy, and historical hope in the direction of Eastern religious ideas of reincarnation and the dissolution of personal identity.[85] In this way, "life after death"—the individual soul's survival beyond this life—replaces the Christian hope of the resurrection of the body and the life everlasting in a restored cosmos (Rom. 8:19–21).

According to biblical eschatology, heaven is a real place, not just a state of mind (Luke 24:51; John 14:2–4; Acts 1:11; 7:55–56). Furthermore, heaven and hell appear together, affirmed side by side, in the New Testament as well (2 Pet. 3:7–13; Rev. 21:1–9). How to understand these vivid biblical motifs has been a live conversation in modern theology.

Eternal Punishment

At the beginning of our Lord's ministry, John the Baptist pointed to the judgment entrusted to Jesus (Matt. 3:11–12). Jesus warns against the whole body being cast into hell (Matt. 5:30); in fact, no prophet or apostle spoke so vividly and repeatedly of the last judgment (Matt. 3:11–12; 5:30; 8:10–12; 13:40–42, 49–50; 22:13; 24:51; 25:30; Luke 16:19–31; Rev. 1:17–18; 6:8; 20:14–15). The term that Jesus often used, *Gehenna*, has its origins in the perpetually burning fire of the Ben Hinnom valley, where Israel imitated the pagan practices of its neighbors in child sacrifice (Jer. 19:5; 32:35). Among historic Christians, the existence of final punishment is affirmed, but with a variety of interpretations, especially in recent times.

APOKATASTASIS AND INCLUSIVISM

The concept of universal restoration (*apokatastasis*) was taught by the ancient Gnostics and also by the church father Origen, but was condemned at the Fifth Council of Constantinople in 553. Nevertheless, it has had its admirers throughout the ages, including John Scotus Erigena and some Anabaptist leaders (Hans Denck and Hans Hut), and it continues to inspire universalist speculations in our own day.[86] According to Origen's barely disguised Platonizing of Christian eschatology, all spiritual essences (including human souls) will

---

85. John Hick, *Death and Eternal Life* (New York: Harper & Row, 1976), esp. 399–424; Rosemary Radford Ruether, *Sexism and God-Talk* (Boston: Beacon, 1983).

86. Like Origen, some Roman Catholic theologians seek to revive *apokatastasis* by way of the dogma of purgatory, suggesting that after various levels of "suffering love," the souls of all will be finally educated in spiritual ascent. See, for example, Hans Urs von Balthasar's foreword and afterword in Valentin Tomberg's *Meditations on the Tarot: A Journey into Christian Hermeticism* (New York: Tarcher/Penguin, 2002), esp. 659. Evangelical theologian Clark Pinnock finds the concept of purgatory consistent with Arminian theology, while insisting on the possibility of some being finally annihilated in merciful love out of respect for their free will. See

be at last freed from the body and reunited with their origin, but only after passing through successive cycles of educative purgation through reincarnation in other worlds. Even Satan and his hosts will be at last reunited with God.

In recent decades, contemporary views concerning eternal punishment have been classified as (1) *pluralist* (all religions are paths to God), (2) *inclusivist* (salvation comes by Christ alone but not exclusively through explicit faith in Christ), and (3) *particularist* (also identified, usually by critics, as exclusivism or restrictivism, holding that salvation comes only through faith in Christ). Affirming a pluralist view, John Hick represents a wide agreement of liberal Protestants.[87] The conclusions of the Second Vatican Council on this matter are most appropriately identified as inclusivist.[88] Most evangelical positions today that reject particularism/exclusivism (salvation through explicit faith in Christ) embrace various forms of inclusivism rather than pluralism.

Generally speaking, inclusivism tends toward universalism without foreclosing the possibility that some may be lost. "Augustinian" inclusivists defend their position as an affirmation of God's sovereign grace, while others follow a more synergistic (Arminian) line of argumentation.

A representative of the first sort is Karl Barth. The logical consequence of his view concerning election is universal salvation. One may continue to object, to refuse to be defined by one's election and reconciliation in Christ, but that rejection is not finally decisive. "God does not permit [the human person] to execute this No of his, this contradiction and opposition."[89] Even God's No is overtaken by God's Yes; hence, Law must always be finally subsumed under Gospel.[90] "*This* No is really Yes. *This* judgment is grace. *This* condemnation is forgiveness. *This* death is life. *This* hell is heaven."[91] It might be suggested that for Barth human existence under the reign of sin, death, unbelief, and condemnation is finally like the existence of the prisoners in Plato's cave. It is not the truth of their reality, but a terrible dream from which they need to

---

John Walvoord, William Crockett, Zachary Hayes, and Clark Pinnock, *Four Views on Hell*, ed. William Crockett (Grand Rapids: Zondervan, 1996), 119–66.

87. John Hick, "The Pluralist View," in *Four Views on Salvation in a Pluralist World*, ed. Dennis L. Ockholm and Timothy R. Phillips (Grand Rapids: Zondervan, 1996), 27–59.

88. See paragraphs 836–43 of the *Catechism of the Catholic Church*, as well as the "Declaration on the Relationship of the Church to Non-Christian Religions," para. 2 in *The Documents of Vatican II*, ed. Walter M. Abbott, trans. and ed. Joseph Gallagher (New York: Herder & Herder, 1966), 662; Karl Rahner, *Theological Investigations* (New York: Crossroad, 1966), 1:131–32. Cf. Gavin D'Costa, who defends inclusivism over against Hick's pluralism as well as exclusivism, in *Theology and Religious Pluralism: The Challenge of Other Religions* (New York: Basil Blackwell, 1986).

89. Barth, *CD* IV/3.1, 3.

90. Ibid., II/2, 13: "The Yes cannot be heard unless the No is also heard. But the No is said for the sake of the Yes and not for its own sake. In substance, therefore, the first and last word is Yes and not No."

91. Karl Barth, *The Word of God and the Word of Man*, trans. Douglas Horton (New York: Harper & Bros., 1956, 1957), 120.

be awakened. "There is no one who does not participate in [Christ] in this turning to God. . . . There is no one who is not raised and exalted with him to true humanity."⁹² Nevertheless, according to Barth, we cannot say with certainty that every person will be saved because this would compromise the absolute freedom of God in grace. Barth insists, "The Church ought not to preach Apokatastasis."⁹³

Jürgen Moltmann follows a similar interpretation, although he seems less reticent to affirm universal salvation.⁹⁴ Like Barth, he bases his inclusivism on God's grace rather than on human goodness, but unlike Barth he makes suffering necessary to God's being and therefore compromises the very idea of grace as a free decision and act. In fact, Moltmann criticizes the notion of annihilation (see below) for making human free will ultimate rather than God's grace. Taking aim at a 1995 statement by the Church of England in defense of annihilation, Moltmann writes,

> The logic of hell is nothing other than the logic of human free will, in so far as this is identical with freedom of choice. . . . Does God's love preserve our free will, or does it free our enslaved will, which has become un-free through the power of sin? Does God love free men and women, or does he seek the men and women who have become lost? It is apparently not Augustine who is the Father of Anglo-Saxon Christianity; the Church Father who secretly presides over it is his opponent Pelagius. And it is Erasmus who is the saint of modern times, not Luther or Calvin. . . . The first conclusion, it seems to me, is that it is inhumane, for there are not many people who can enjoy their free will where their eternal fate in heaven or hell is concerned.⁹⁵

Accordingly, in this view, "God is merely the accessory who puts that will into effect."⁹⁶ By contrast, Moltmann insists, "The Christian doctrine of hell is to be found in the gospel of Christ's descent into hell, not in a modernization of hell into total non-being."⁹⁷ "The true universality of God's grace is not grounded in 'secular humanism'" but in "the theology of the cross."⁹⁸ Moltmann invokes Christoph Blumhardt: "Jesus can judge but not condemn."⁹⁹ "Judgment is not God's last word. . . . From this [new creation] no one is excepted. . . .

92. Karl Barth, CD IV/2, 271. A helpful discussion of Barth's view on this point is found in George Hunsinger, How to Read Karl Barth: The Shape of His Theology (New York: Oxford University Press, 1991), 128–35.
93. Barth, CD II/2, 417.
94. Jürgen Moltmann, "The Logic of Hell," in Bauckham, God Will Be All in All, 43–48.
95. Ibid., 44, reviewing The Mystery of Salvation: The Story of God's Gift, by the Doctrine Commission of the Church of England (London: Church House Publishing, 1995).
96. Ibid., 45.
97. Ibid., 46.
98. Ibid., 47.
99. Cited in ibid.

Transforming grace is God's punishment for sinners.[100] Therefore, as in Barth's view, wrath and grace, law and gospel, judgment and justification become virtually indistinguishable. Furthermore, human beings are not free to choose their own condemnation: "It is not the right to choose that defines the reality of human freedom. It is the doing of the good."[101]

Evangelical Arminians like Clark Pinnock and John Sanders share the presupposition that all of God's attributes are subservient to his love and that his purpose is to save every person. In fact, Pinnock recognizes that these theses function as presuppositions or "axioms" by which exegesis must be tested.[102] However, they argue that salvation is dependent on the free will of individuals and that saving revelation occurs apart from the gospel, even in and through other religions as "means of grace."[103] Therefore, where Barth and Moltmann ground inclusivism in a notion of God's universal electing grace in Christ, Pinnock's inclusivism is grounded in a notion of God's universal accessibility of grace for those who respond to it even apart from explicit faith in Christ. As Pinnock acknowledges, his version is especially indebted to the "anonymous Christian" concept of Karl Rahner and the Second Vatican Council.[104] Pinnock appeals to the examples of Melchizedek, Job, and Paul's quotation of pagan poets in Acts 17 to defend the idea that God reveals himself in a saving way outside of biblical revelation.[105]

ANNIHILATION

Some Christians have concluded that the exegetical evidence for the reality of hell is impossible to reconcile with universal salvation. The question addressed

100. Ibid; emphasis added.

101. Ibid.

102. Clark Pinnock, "Overcoming Misgivings about Evangelical Inclusivism," *Southern Baptist Journal of Theology* 2, no. 2 (Summer 1998): 33–34. He remarks that "the evidence for it [inclusivism] is less than one would like." Yet he adds, "But the vision of God's love there is so strong that the existing evidence seems sufficient to me" (35).

103. These theses are defended in the following works of Clark H. Pinnock: "An Inclusivist View," in Okholm and Phillips, *Four Views on Salvation*, 251–54; *A Wideness in God's Mercy: The Finality of Jesus Christ in a World of Religions* (Grand Rapids: Zondervan, 1992); "Acts 4:12—No Other Name under Heaven," in *Through No Fault of Their Own? The Fate of Those Who Have Never Heard*, ed. William Crockett and James Sigountos (Grand Rapids: Baker, 1991), 114. See also John Sanders, *No Other Name: An Investigation into the Destiny of the Unevangelized*, ed. Gabriel Fackre, Ronald H. Nash, and John Sanders (Grand Rapids: Eerdmans, 1992); Sanders, "Inclusivism," in *What about Those Who Have Never Heard? Three Views on the Destiny of the Unevangelized* (Downers Grove, IL: InterVarsity, 1995). See also Amos Yong, *Beyond the Impasse: Toward a Pneumatological Theology of Religions* (Grand Rapids: Baker, 2003); Stanley J. Grenz, "Toward an Evangelical Theology of Religions," *Journal of Ecumenical Studies* 31 (Winter-Spring 1995): 49–65. Within evangelical circles, a more Augustinian (and guarded) interpretation of inclusivism is argued by John Stackhouse, *What Does It Mean to Be Saved? Broadening Evangelical Horizons of Salvation* (Grand Rapids: Baker Academic, 2002), and by Terrence L. Tiessen, *Who Can Be Saved? Reassessing Salvation in Christ and World Religions* (Downers Grove, IL: InterVarsity, 2004).

104. Pinnock, "Overcoming Misgivings," 34.

105. Ibid., 35–36.

by annihilationism is not the scope of God's mercy, but the nature of hell. Annihilationists claim that the notion of eternal, conscious torment is based on the Greek doctrine of the immortality of the soul. Some annihilationists (such as Philip E. Hughes) could be considered exclusivists (i.e., salvation through explicit faith in Christ alone), while others (such as Clark Pinnock) are inclusivists. At the same time, they often interpret various passages as teaching that unbelievers are raised on the last day for destruction (the second death) rather than for everlasting, conscious torment. Because they are destroyed, Scripture can still speak in apocalyptic terms of "their smoke going up forever" and their being eternally annihilated. However, this need not entail everlasting conscious punishment.[106]

Historically, annihilationism has been held only among Adventists, Jehovah's Witnesses, and Christadelphians. More recently, however, it has gained ground especially in British evangelicalism, including (possibly) C. S. Lewis, as well as John Wenham, Phillip E. Hughes, and, more tentatively, John Stott.[107] Its most polemical advocates include Clark Pinnock and Edward Fudge.[108]

In its place, they argue for *conditional immortality*. At the final resurrection and judgment, the immortal God will grant immortality to believers and condemn unbelievers to destruction. Satan and the false prophet are said to suffer eternal consciousness in hell, but no one else (Rev. 14:9–11; 20:10). Jesus's description of the fire as "eternal" and "unquenchable" (Matt. 3:12; 18:8; 25:41; Luke 3:17) can be interpreted as annihilation. Positively, advocates of this view appeal to passages that speak of unbelievers perishing (John 3:16) and being destroyed (Matt. 10:28), and believe that the reference in Rev. 20 to the "second death" can only refer to this annihilation. Similarly, in Matt. 10:28, Jesus warns hearers to "fear him who can destroy both soul and body in hell."

TRADITIONAL VIEWS OF THE LAST JUDGMENT REVISITED

Advocates of traditional Christian views concerning the final state have mounted impressive exegetical and theological arguments.[109] First, it is impor-

---

106. One of the most extensive treatments of eternal punishment from this perspective is Edward W. Fudge, *The Fire That Consumes: A Biblical and Historical Study of the Doctrine of Final Punishment* (Fallbrook, CA: Providential, 1982). Various studies interact thoughtfully with Fudge's thesis, including Robert A. Peterson, *Hell on Trial: The Case for Eternal Punishment* (Phillipsburg, NJ: P&R, 1995). Cf. Edward W. Fudge and Robert A. Peterson, *Two Views on Hell: A Biblical and Theological Dialogue* (Downers Grove, IL: InterVarsity, 2000); Christopher W. Morgan and Robert A. Peterson, eds., *Hell under Fire: Modern Scholarship Reinvents Eternal Punishment* (Grand Rapids: Zondervan, 2004).

107. For John Stott's view, see David L. Edwards and John Stott, *Essentials: A Liberal-Evangelical Dialogue* (Downers Grove, IL: InterVarsity, 1988), 314–20.

108. Clark Pinnock, "The Conditional View," in Crockett, *Four Views on Hell*, 135–66; Edward Fudge, *The Fire That Consumes: A Biblical and Historical Study of Final Punishment* (Fallbrook, CA: Verdict, 1982).

109. In addition, the following resources are recommended: Ronald Nash, *Is Jesus the Only Savior?* (Grand Rapids: Zondervan, 1994); R. Douglas Geivett, "Is Jesus the Only Way?" in *Jesus under Fire: Modern Scholarship Reinvents the Historical Jesus*, ed. Michael J. Wilkins and J. P.

tant to distinguish different types of "universalism." While Origen's doctrine
may be characterized as Platonic and (though anachronistically), somewhat
Pelagian, the view of Barth and Moltmann might be better described as "Augustinian universalism."[110] In fact, the latter view is hyper-Augustinian (indeed,
hyper-Calvinistic). At least for traditional Augustinians (exclusivists), there is
ordinarily no salvation apart from faith in Christ—not because of a Pelagian
triumph of the human will over against divine grace, but because of God's
freedom to show this mercy to whomever he will and to hold the nonelect
responsible for their rejection of the gospel.

According to Barth and his school, one practical outcome of this view is a
strongly objective doctrine of God's sovereign, electing, and irresistible grace.
Everyone is elect in Christ, the Elect One, and therefore there is no place for
questioning this fact. Everyone is already saved in Christ, at least *de jure*.[111] At
the same time, with his refusal to endorse universal salvation *de facto*, for fear
of restricting God's freedom, Barth argued for the first time in church history
that some of those who have been unconditionally elected may nevertheless
be finally condemned. This final question mark opens a gap between God's
mysterious hiddenness and his revelation in Christ beyond that cleavage that
concerned Barth in the traditional view.

Although Brunner objected as strongly as Barth to the traditional Augustinian doctrine of election, he recognized that according to the New Testament,
only the elect are "in Christ," and they are "those who believe."[112] Barth mistakes human responsibility for synergism.[113] Besides ignoring the conditions in
Scripture, Brunner suggests that Barth eliminates "the vital tension, based on
the dialectic of God's Holiness and Love, by means of a monistic *schema*."[114]
We do recognize in Jesus Christ the consistency of God's love and holiness,
Brunner affirms. "But outside of Jesus Christ, outside of faith, God's Holiness
is not the same as His Love, but *there* it is His wrath; *there* what God is 'in
Himself' is not the same as that which He is 'for us,' *there* it is the unfathom-

Moreland (Grand Rapids: Zondervan, 1995); and R. Douglas Geivett and W. Gary Phillips, "A
Particularist View: An Evidentialist Approach," in *Four Views on Salvation*; D. A. Carson, *The
Gagging of God: Christianity Confronts Pluralism* (Grand Rapids: Zondervan, 1996); Ajith
Fernando, *The Supremacy of Christ* (Wheaton: Crossway, 1995); Paul R. House and Gregory A.
Thornbury, eds., *Who Will Be Saved? Defending the Biblical Understanding of God, Salvation,
and Evangelism* (Wheaton: Crossway, 2000); Douglas Moo, "Romans 2: Saved Apart from the
Gospel?" in *Through No Fault of Their Own?* 137–45; Daniel Strange, *The Possibility of Sal-
vation among the Unevangelized: An Analysis of Inclusivism in Recent Evangelical Theology*
(Carlisle, UK: Paternoster, 2002).
    110. See Oliver D. Crisp, "Augustinian Universalism," *International Journal for Philosophy
of Religion* 53 (2003): 127–45.
    111. Barth, *CD* IV/3, 811.
    112. Emil Brunner, *Dogmatics*, vol. 1, *The Christian Doctrine of God*, trans. Olive Wyon
(Philadelphia: Westminster, 1946), 315.
    113. Ibid., 316.
    114. Ibid., 334, 336.

able, impenetrable mystery of the '*nuda majestas*'; *there* is no election, but rejection, judgment, condemnation. . . ."[115]

With respect to the inclusivist position, it should be noted that although revelation progresses from Old Testament shadows to New Testament reality, the object of faith is the same. However, the religions of the nations are regarded as idolatrous throughout this history. Ever since Justin Martyr, some Christians have claimed that the pagan philosophers prepared the way for Christ among the gentiles as Moses and the prophets prepared the Jews. But this is to confuse general revelation with special revelation and the law with the gospel. Furthermore, critics often point out the problems with interpreting Melchizedek and other examples as "noble pagans."[116]

At the same time, confessional Protestants have never argued that there is absolutely no salvation apart from explicit faith in Christ. Besides upholding the caveat concerning God's freedom to have mercy on whomever he chooses, Reformed churches teach that since the children of believers are comprehended with their parents in the covenant of grace, in the words of the Canons of Dort, "godly parents ought not to doubt the election and salvation of their children whom it pleases God to call out of this life in their infancy (Gen. 17:7; Acts 2:39; 1 Cor. 7:14)."[117] Similarly, the Westminster Confession inserts the important caveat to an ancient formula when it asserts that outside of the visible church "there is no *ordinary* possibility of salvation" (emphasis added).[118]

Finally, with respect to annihilationism, Jesus's teaching concerning the final separation of the saved and the lost seems to treat punishment and life as equally eternal: "And these will go away into eternal punishment, but the righteous into eternal life" (Matt. 25:46). Regardless of one's conclusion,

115. Ibid., 337. Brunner adds (in my concluded ellipsis), ". . .but no eternal decree."

116. Regarding the auspicious but enigmatic Melchizedek, see James L. Kugel, *Traditions of the Bible: A Guide to the Bible as It Was at the Start of the Common Era* (Cambridge: Harvard University Press, 1988), 276–78. Whatever his precise relationship to Abraham, Job's allusion to Ps. 8:4 (Job 7:17–18) and direct quotations of Ps. 107:40 in chapter 12 (vv. 21–24) place him squarely in God's covenant community. The examples often put forward by inclusivists are treated respectfully and carefully in *Faith Comes by Hearing: A Response to Inclusivism*, ed. Christopher W. Morgan and Robert A. Peterson (Downers Grove, IL: IVP Academic, 2008). However one interprets Paul's quotations from pagan poets in Athens (Acts 17), they serve his major point, namely, that however lenient God may have been in "the times of ignorance," the appearance of Christ in these last days leaves everyone without excuse (Acts 17:30–31). It is the universal-public character of Christ's decisive work and coming judgment that gives to the missionary enterprise the kind of urgency that is found throughout the book of Acts.

117. Canons of Dort, 1.17, in the *Psalter Hymnal: Doctrinal Standards and Liturgy of the Christian Reformed Church* (Grand Rapids: CRC Publications, 1976), 95. There is also the example of the death of David's week-old son. "I shall go to him," David said, "but he will not return to me" (2 Sam. 12:23).

118. The Westminster Confession of Faith, chap. 25, *Trinity Hymnal*, revised ed. (Atlanta: Great Commission Publications, 1990), 863.

leading proponents of the traditional view do not appeal to a Greek concept of immortality to ground their exegetical arguments.

Conclusion

That the issues treated in this chapter have generated millennia of debate is a tribute to the integral significance of eschatology in Scripture. It may well be that extreme versions of both postmillennialism and amillennialism are giving way at least in evangelical eschatologies to a more "middle ground" position occupied by historical premillennialists (including progressive dispensationalists) and amillennialists. However, the vitality of traditional dispensationalism is evident in the enormous success of popular evangelical end-times books and movies that often blur any distinction between exegesis and fiction.[119] Furthermore, an implicit postmillennialism seems to have been revived in recent years among evangelicals, especially through the influence of Brian McLaren, N. T. Wright, and Jim Wallis. Whatever position we take on these questions, Herman Ridderbos reminds us, "Affirming together the 'already' and 'not yet' aspects of the kingdom is one of the fundamental presuppositions for understanding the gospel."[120]

For Further Reading

General

Bauckham, Richard, ed. *God Will Be All in All: The Eschatology of Jürgen Moltmann*. Edinburgh: T&T Clark, 1999.

Boyer, Paul. *When Time Shall Be No More*. Cambridge: Harvard University Press, 1994.

Hill, Charles E. *Regnum Caelorum: Patterns of Millennial Thought in Early Christianity*. Grand Rapids: Eerdmans, 2001.

McGinn, Bernard. *The Calabrian Abbot: Joachim of Fiore in the History of Western Thought*. New York: Harper & Row, 1985.

Moltmann, Jürgen. *The Coming of God: Christian Eschatology*. Translated by Margaret Kohl. Minneapolis: Fortress, 1996.

Ridderbos, Herman. *The Coming of the Kingdom*. Translated by H. de Jongste. Edited by Raymond O. Zorn. Philadelphia: P&R, 1962.

---

119. Hal Lindsey's *The Late Great Planet Earth*, new ed. (Grand Rapids: Zondervan, 1998), was the bestselling book of the 1970s in the United States, and the *Left Behind* series by Tim LaHaye and Jerry Jenkins topped the best-seller lists throughout the 1990s.
120. Ridderbos, *Coming of the Kingdom*, 106.

Schweitzer, Albert. *The Quest of the Historical Jesus: A Critical Study of Its Progress from Reimarus to Wrede*. Translated by William Montgomery. Minneapolis: Augsburg Fortress, 2001.

Millennial Perspectives

AMILLENNIALISM

Beale, G. K. *The Book of Revelation: A Commentary on the Greek Text*. Grand Rapids: Eerdmans, 1998.

Johnson, Dennis. *Triumph of the Lamb: A Commentary on Revelation*. Phillipsburg, NJ: P&R, 2001.

Riddelbarger, Kim. *A Case for Amillennialism*. Grand Rapids: Baker, 2003.

Venema, Cornelis. *The Promise of the Future*. Edinburgh: Banner of Truth, 2000.

POSTMILLENNIALISM

Davis, John Jefferson. *The Victory of Christ's Kingdom: An Introduction to Postmillennialism*. Moscow, ID: Canon, 1996.

Mathison, Keith. *An Eschatology of Hope*. Phillipsburg, NJ: P&R, 1999.

HISTORIC PREMILLENNIALISM

Blomberg, Craig, and Sung Wook Chung, eds. *The Case for Historic Premillennialism: An Alternative to "Left Behind" Eschatology*. Grand Rapids: Baker Academic, 2009.

Ladd, George Eldon. *The Blessed Hope*. Grand Rapids: Eerdmans, 1956.

DISPENSATIONAL PREMILLENNIALISM

Blaising, Craig A., and Darrell L. Bock. *Progressive Dispensationalism*. Grand Rapids: Baker Academic, 2000.

Ryrie, Charles. *Dispensationalism*. Revised and expanded. Chicago: Moody, 2007.

LIST OF CONTRIBUTORS

Brian Brock (PhD, King's College, London) is a lecturer in moral and practical theology at the University of Aberdeen, Scotland. He is the author of *Christian Ethics in a Technological Age* and *Singing the Ethos of God*.

Stephen R. Holmes (PhD, King's College, London) is senior lecturer in systematic theology at the University of St. Andrews, Scotland. He is the author of several articles and books, including *Listening to the Past: The Place of Tradition in Theology*.

Michael Horton (PhD, University of Coventry and Wycliffe Hall, Oxford) is J. Gresham Machen Professor of Systematic Theology and Apologetics at Westminster Seminary California. He is the author or editor of more than fifteen books, including *Covenant and Eschatology* and *The Christian Faith*.

Kelly M. Kapic (PhD, King's College, London) is professor of theological studies at Covenant College in Lookout Mountain, Georgia. He is the author or editor of numerous articles and books, including *Communion with God: The Divine and the Human in John Owen's Theology* and *God So Loved He Gave: Entering the Movement of Divine Generosity*.

Veli-Matti Kärkkäinen (DrTheol, University of Helsinki) is professor of systematic theology at Fuller Theological Seminary in Pasadena, California. He serves on numerous editorial boards and is the author of several books, including *The Doctrine of God: A Global Introduction* and *Pneumatology: The Holy Spirit in Ecumenical, International, and Contextual Perspective*.

Richard Lints (PhD, University of Notre Dame) is Andrew Mutch Distinguished Professor of Theology at Gordon-Conwell Theological Seminary in South Hamilton, Massachusetts. He is an ordained minister in the Presbyterian

Church in America and the author or editor of several books, including *Renewing the Evangelical Mission* and *The Fabric of Theology*. He has taught at several other schools, including Yale Divinity School, the University of Notre Dame, and Westminster Theological Seminary.

Bruce L. McCormack (PhD, Princeton Theological Seminary; DrTheol h.c., Friedrich Schiller University) is Charles Hodge Professor of Systematic Theology at Princeton Theological Seminary in Princeton, New Jersey. He is a world-renowned Barth scholar and the author or editor of several volumes, including *Karl Barth's Critically Realistic Dialectical Theology* and *Engaging the Doctrine of God*.

Richard R. Osmer (PhD, Emory University) is Thomas W. Synnott Professor of Christian Education at Princeton Theological Seminary in Princeton, New Jersey. He is an ordained minister in the Presbyterian Church (USA) and the author of *The Teaching Ministry of Congregations* and *Practical Theology: An Introduction*.

Fred Sanders (PhD, Graduate Theological Union) is associate professor of theology in the Torrey Honors Institute at Biola University in La Mirada, California. He is the author of *Jesus in Trinitarian Perspective* and *The Image of the Immanent Trinity*.

Katherine Sonderegger (PhD, Brown University) is professor of theology at Virginia Theological Seminary in Alexandria, Virginia and an ordained deacon and priest in the Episcopal Church. She is the author of *That Jesus Christ Was Born a Jew: Karl Barth's "Doctrine of Israel"* and is currently working a systematic theology.

Daniel J. Treier (PhD, Trinity Evangelical Divinity School) is associate professor of theology at Wheaton College in Wheaton, Illinois. He is the author of *Introducing Theological Interpretation of Scripture* and *Ecclesiastes and Proverbs* in the Brazos Theological Commentary on the Bible and served as associate editor of the *Dictionary for Theological Interpretation of the Bible*.

Kevin J. Vanhoozer (PhD, University of Cambridge) is Blanchard Professor of Theology at Wheaton College in Wheaton, Illinois. He is the author, coauthor, or coeditor of dozens of books, including *Remythologizing Theology*, *The Drama of Doctrine*, the *Dictionary of Theological Interpretation of Scripture* (with Craig Bartholomew, Daniel J. Treier, and N. T. Wright), *Hermeneutics at the Crossroads* (with James K. A. Smith and Bruce Ellis Benson), and *The Cambridge Companion to Postmodern Theology*.

John Webster (PhD, University of Cambridge) is chair of systematic theology at the University of Aberdeen, Scotland. He is the cofounding editor of the *International Journal of Systematic Theology* and was elected a fellow of the Royal Society of Edinburgh in 2005. His many books include *Holy Scripture: A Dogmatic Sketch*, *Holiness*, and *Barth's Early Theology*.

Telford Work (PhD, Duke University) is associate professor of theology at Westmont College in Santa Barbara, California. He is the author of *Deuteronomy* in the Brazos Theological Commentary on the Bible and *Living and Active: Scripture in the Economy of Salvation*.

John Webster (PhD, University of Cambridge) is chair of systematic theology at the University of Aberdeen, Scotland. He is the founding editor of the *International Journal of Systematic Theology* and was elected a fellow of the Royal Society of Edinburgh in 2005. His many books include *Holy Scripture: A Dogmatic Sketch*, *Barth*, and *Barth's Moral Theology*.

Telford Work (PhD, Duke University) is associate professor of theology at Westmont College in Santa Barbara, California. He is the author of *Deuteronomy* in the Brazos Theological Commentary on the Bible and *Living and Active: Scripture in the Economy of Salvation*.

INDEX

Printed and bound by CPI Group (UK) Ltd, Croydon, CR0 4YY

09/06/2025

14685652-0001